Select Essays on Indian Economy

A SET OF TWO VOLUMES

1

Volume One

DR. C. RANGARAJAN is presently the Chairman of the Twelfth Finance Commission. Earlier, he was Governor of Andhra Pradesh for five years (1997-2003) and just before that he was Governor, Reserve Bank of India for five years (1992-1997). As Governor RBI, Dr. Rangarajan gave a major thrust to financial sector reforms. The institutional environment was altered to make monetary policy a more effective instrument of economic policy. The exchange rate regime underwent a fundamental change.

He was member of the Planning Commission during 1991-92. Prior to that he held the position of Deputy Governor, Reserve Bank of India, for almost a decade. During this period, he was instrumental in bringing about a number of changes in the credit and financial system, both in terms of induction of new instruments and new institutions.

Dr. Rangarajan has been a member of the Economic Advisory Council to the Prime Minister between 1985 and 1991. He was the Chairman of the National Statistical Commission which was set up to reform the Indian Statistical System.

He has taught at the Wharton School of Finance & Commerce, University of Pennsylvania and the Graduate School of Business Administration, New York University. In India, he has taught at Loyola College, Madras; University of Rajasthan, Jaipur; Indian Statistical Institute, New Delhi and for well over a decade and a half at the Indian Institute of Management, Ahmedabad.

He is the author or co-author of the following books : Short-term Investment Forecasting (1974); Principles of Macroeconomics (1979); Strategy for Industrial Development in the '80s (1981); Innovations in Banking (1982); Indian Economy : Essays on Money and Finance (1998); Perspectives on Indian Economy (2000); and Structural Reforms in Industry, Banking and Finance (2000).

Many of his analytical writings have been published in various national and international journals.

Among the several awards received by him are : Business Man of the Year 1997 (Madras Management Association); Honorary Fellow, Indian Institute of Management, Ahmedabad 1997; Award of Excellence in Finance (Bank of India) 1998; Finance Man of the Decade (Bombay Management Association) 1998; Financial Express Award for Economics 1998; Wharton-Indian Alumni Award for Outstanding Leadership (2002).

Dr. Rangarajan was awarded *Padma Vibhushan* by the President of India in January, 2002.

Set of Two Volumes

1

Volume One

Select Essays on Indian Economy

C. Rangarajan

Edited by

R. KANNAN

AF

Academic Foundation NEW DELHI

www.academicfoundation.com

First Published in 2004 by
ACADEMIC FOUNDATION
4772-73 / 23 Bharat Ram Road,
(23 Ansari Road), Darya Ganj,
New Delhi - 110 002. INDIA.

Phones : 23245001, 02, 03, 04.
Fax : +91-11-23245005.
e-mail : academic@vsnl.com
www : academicfoundation.com

Select Essays on Indian Economy
(a set of two volumes)
by C. Rangarajan
ISBN 81-7188-338-9

Laser-Typeset at AF's DTP Division.
Printed at Print Perfect, Mayapuri Industrial Area, New Delhi.

Dedicated to

Dr. Haripriya Rangarajan

My constant companion and support
during the past 37 years

CONTENTS

Volume 1 *(the present volume)*

Part II
Monetary System and Financial Sector

CONTENTS

Volume 2 (the companion volume)

Part III

Fiscal Sector

Part IV

External Sector

Preface

When it was first suggested to me that some of my articles published in the past could be brought together in a volume, I was hesitant. However, I was persuaded that these articles, some of which appeared more than two decades ago, had broken new ground and that it would still be useful to bring them together as a collection. Of the 24 essays in the two volumes, only four are from the Seventies. No article published earlier than that has been included. This collection also omits articles included in my other publications. This causes some interruption in the continuity of economic thinking and leaves certain gaps in the topics covered. Some of the key articles on monetary policy, financial sector and exchange rate management do not, therefore, find a place. Nevertheless, the range of subjects covered is wide.

The first section on Macroeconomic issues includes several articles connected with Industrial Policy and Industrial Growth. There is a lengthy essay on the interrelationship between agricultural growth and industrial performance. For the first time, an attempt had been made to bring out the links between the two sectors, both through the routes of supply and demand. Apart from some technical essays on the use of input-output tables, capital-output ratios and the mechanics of planning, there is one comprehensive review of the recent economic reforms.

The second section deals with issues relating to monetary and financial sectors. Apart from explaining in one article the analytical foundations of the Chakravarty Committee Report, an econometric model has been presented in another article to study the relative impact of money supply on output and prices. Such a model is necessary to gain a better understanding of the inflationary process.

A detailed essay on the role of monetary policy is also included, besides a paper on financial sector reforms.

The third section deals with fiscal policy issues from the broader perspective of macroeconomic management. The section includes an article on the dynamics of debt accumulation which is perhaps one of the earliest articles to be published in India in this area. A reasonably large sized econometric model is also presented in one of the articles to study the impact of government expenditures financed through alternative channels.

The last section includes articles on exchange rate management and on the evolution of the Balance of Payment scenario in our country. The Report of the High Level Committee on Balance of Payments, of which I was the Chairman, is also included. Apart from laying down the appropriate policies to be pursued, this Report is the only source which outlines the reasons for the shift of the exchange rate arrangement initially to LERMS and later to a market determined exchange rate system.

— C. RANGARAJAN

New Delhi

Acknowledgements

I am happy to acknowledge the help received from many in preparing the various articles in these volumes.

First and foremost, my thanks go to the co-authors of several articles. As co-authors, they have contributed in an equal measure in giving shape to these articles. In this context, I wish to thank Mr. M.S. Ahluwalia, Mrs. R.R. Arif, Mr. Anupam Basu, Mr. Narendra Jadhav, Mr. R. Kannan, Mr. M.S. Mohanty, Mr. K.S. Reddy, Mr. Raaj Kumar Sah, Mr. J.K. Satia, Mr. Anoop Singh and Mr. V. Sundararajan.

Second, my thanks are due to the Editors and Publishers in whose journals these articles originally appeared. I wish to thank the Director General, International Food Policy Research Institute, Washington, Editor and Publishers of Review of Economics and Statistics, the International Economic Association and Macmillan Press Limited, Editor of Economic Development and Cultural Change and University of Chicago Press and Editors of Artha Vijnana, Economic and Political Weekly, Indian Economic Journal, Money and Finance, and RBI Occasional Papers.

I also want to thank Mr. A. Samantaraya, Mrs. Astha Ahuja Ali and Mr. Surajit Das for correcting the proofs and ensuring the accuracy particularly of the tables and mathematical symbols.

Finally, I wish to thank Mr. K.U.B. Rao of Reserve Bank of India, who did the preliminary work in collecting the various articles and Mr. R. Kannan for editing these volumes along with an exhaustive Introduction.

— *C. Rangarajan*

Acknowledgements

[illegible]

Introduction

Contributions of Dr. C. Rangarajan are well known and well documented in a number of publications, both domestic and international. When we talk about contributions, one can think of the following:

a. New concepts, which will help the readers and the policy makers to understand the working of a particular phenomenon better;

b. Redefinition of the existing concepts which may be due to changing economic environment;

c. New measurement techniques for the existing concepts, in order to enhance the understanding of the working of those phenomena. For example, some concept may be defined by accountants in a particular way, whereas the economists may define the same concept in a different manner, to bring out clearly the economic implications;

d. A new variation to the relationship between economic variables, which will help the readers to understand the interlinkages better. This would also help the policy makers to plan their actions taking into account the inside lags and outside lags;

e. A new dimension to the policy formulation, based on item 'd'.

It is important to note that Dr. Rangarajan has made substantial contributions in each of the above areas. As of today, some volumes are already available bringing out his involvement in various policy formulations, which are in the form of lectures delivered by him from time to time.

My association with Dr. C. Rangarajan goes back to the time he became the Deputy Governor of the Reserve Bank of India. His guidance and advice are the principal factors for my achievements. I had the opportunity to discuss with him many important economic issues and also assist him in addressing some of them. Both myself and many of my colleagues who worked closely with him used to feel strongly that his research/econometric contributions to various sectors of Indian economy are not available in one place. The present volume is an attempt to fill this gap and it will provide easy access to some of his path-breaking articles which are frequently referred to.

Usually one may think that his contributions are only in the field of monetary economics. It is not so. It covers agriculture, industry, planning, banking, fiscal, Balance of Payments, exchange rate policy and international monetary system as well. We have selected important contributions in each of these areas and presented them in this volume. We have excluded the articles published in the other volumes of his. For the convenience of readers, let me attempt to capture briefly the summary findings or principal messages of some of these papers.

The book is presented in two volumes, while volume I covers first two parts, *viz.*, 'agriculture, industry and the economy' and 'monetary system and financial sector', the second part covers fiscal and external sectors.

Agriculture, Industry and the Economy

The first study included in this volume entitled "Agricultural Growth and Industrial Performance in India" (1982), is perhaps one of the earliest studies to express fully the linkage between agriculture and industry. The importance of agriculture for industry lies not only in the raw materials supplied by agriculture but also in the demand for industrial output it generates. In fact, agriculture influences industry through three types of linkages – production, demand, and savings and investment. A macroeconomic model incorporating all these relationships is constructed in this study to examine the effects of agriculture on the economy. The model asks what the effect on industry would be, if agriculture grew at a certain rate. Historical data covering 12 years (1961-72) are used to estimate the quantitative relationships. Appropriate lag structures are also introduced. The simulation exercise indicates that a one per cent growth in agricultural output increases industrial production by about 0.5 per cent and national income by a little more than 0.7 per cent.

A crucial concern during the 1970s was the deceleration in the growth of industrial production. In his article "Industrial Growth: Another Look" (1982), Dr. Rangarajan has examined the factors contributing to the slow growth in industrial production. This analysis is very important as it shows that while in the early years of Plan formulation, the biggest constraint in the rate of growth was seen to be the low savings ratio, over the years the country has been able to raise the savings and investment ratios to very impressive levels. However, the rise in Incremental Capital-Output Ratio (ICOR) has nullified the output increase that would otherwise have come from the increase in the share of investment to income. While explaining the slow growth, he tried to find an answer through analysing the changes in the value of ICOR. Important findings of this study are:

- There should be an attempt to bring down the sectoral ICORs. In this respect, greater attention needs to be paid to the efficient utilisation of capital.
- The possibility of stepping up the investment rate much beyond 25 per cent may be difficult. With the savings and investment rate stabilising at that level, higher growth rate can occur only if we learn to lower the Incremental Capital-Output Ratio. The changes in the output mix need not run into the ideological conflicts which were witnessed at the time of the Second Five-Year Plan.
- In planning for investment, we should move towards a system of what can be described as sequential strategic sector planning — a system of planning in which the planners identify the constraining sectors in the economy and invest more in them so that the constraints are relaxed and output growth is activated. However, the point to be made at this juncture is that, unless we are able to identify outputs and sectors in which it is possible to lower the Incremental Capital-Output Ratio, we will continue to creep along a five to six per cent growth rate even in industry.

In his paper on "Industrial Growth in the 80s — Facts and Some Issues" (1990), Dr. Rangarajan focussed on the need for technology upgradation and modernisation. He also emphasised that certain priorities need to be set here so that the maximum impact can be derived by the economy. He writes: "Capital goods industries in particular must remain competitive in terms of quality and cost; otherwise this can have adverse implications for the user sectors. This is where industrial policy ties in with foreign trade policy. The transit from a protected environment to a more competitive situation is not always easy. Industrial units must learn to adjust their production pattern in response to the changing situation. Even as liberalisation of licensing facilitates entry, this can result in excess capacity in certain sectors. Financial institutions have, therefore, a role in realistically assessing the feasibility and prospects of new investment proposals. While facilitating entry, the policy framework should also permit exit where it becomes necessary so that chronic sickness can be avoided."

In his article on "Paradigm Shifts in Industrial Policy" (2002), Dr. Rangarajan discusses the performance of the industrial sector in the post-liberalisation period. While during the period 1992-93 to 1996-97, the annual growth rate in industrial production was 7.4 per cent, it averaged only 5.1 per cent in the next five years. He points out that while the sharp decline in industrial production occurred in 1997-98 according to the old index, it occurred only in 1998-99 under the new index. He discusses the new challenges faced by industry under the three heads – globalisation and competition, productivity growth and technology intensity. He has pleaded for drawing up road maps for different segments of industry to achieve productivity and efficiency levels comparable to the best in the world. He emphasises four critical factors in enhancing the level of investment, *viz.*, the need for continuation of economic policy to sustain expectations in the right direction and in this respect, consensus among decision makers and legislators; importance of good governance; need for introducing investment budget in the Government budget; and stability in the rates of taxation and tariff rates in enhancing the confidence of investors.

In his paper on "Conflict between Employment and Inflation" (1983), Dr. Rangarajan had examined the Indian data in relation to price changes and output changes in the industrial sector. The trade-off between wage changes and employment, known as Philips curve, is one of the celebrated themes of macroeconomics. In the long run, such a trade-off can exist only if expectations of price changes continually remain below the actual changes. The link between price changes and employment goes beyond the dynamics of the labour markets. The important findings of this study are: (i) employment and output are well correlated but the rate of growth of the former is lower than that of the latter. In general, it appears that periods marked by sharp increase in price level are associated with lower growth rates of output and years of low price changes with high growth rates in industrial output; (ii) a desegregated analysis of the output and price changes relating to various industry groups also indicated a negative association between price change and output change. The general conclusion is that contrary to the general belief industrial output has grown faster in periods of small price increases than in period of high price increases.

One of the most popular quantitative relationship in growth theory and development planning has been the capital-output ratio and more importantly its variant, the Incremental Capital-Output Ratio (ICOR). The relationship between investment and incremental output has been used in many growth models as a simplification of the conventional production function, assuming capital to be the binding constraint in the growth process. Dr. Rangarajan in his paper on Capital-Output Ratios in the Indian Economy of which I was the co-author (1992) analysed ICOR sector wise so as to bring out the sources of changes in the value of ICORs. The primary aim of this paper was to analyse the behaviour of ICORs and Average Capital-Output Ratios. Attention was also paid on methodological issues in measuring ICOR.

Between 1950s and 1960s, gross ICOR increased by about 35 per cent, of which changes in sectoral ICORs accounted for 58 per cent while the changes in sectoral composition accounted for the balance 42 per cent. Between 1960s and 1970s, 65 per cent was accounted for by changes in sectoral ICORs. But during 1980-88, gross ICOR declined considerably. Even during this phase, changes in sectoral ICORs accounted for a major proportion (78 per cent). The analysis shows that not only have the changes in sectoral ICORs influenced the changes in ICORs more as compared with changes due to sectoral composition, the share of this source was increasing in the four decades. Hence, any effort to reduce the ICOR for the economy as a whole should concentrate on reducing sectoral ICORs.

The impact of price rise of key inputs on other commodities is usually studied using the input-output table. In his paper (1981) on "Impact of Hike in Prices of Coal and Petroleum Products on the Other Sectors of the Economy", (of which R.K. Sah and K.S. Reddy were co-authors) a new methodology was suggested by which the impact of the increase in the price of one commodity on other can be calculated under a situation where the prices of specific commodities are not allowed to rise even though input prices go up. This was applied to a situation in India when coal and petroleum prices were increased without increasing the prices of railway services and electricity.

Dr. C. Rangarajan has been a pioneer in forecasting corporate investment. In 1970, he evolved a new technique to forecast corporate investment using the data available with the term lending institutions on the phasing of capital expenditures of projects sanctioned by them. These may be regarded as a kind of anticipatory data for forecasting. Although this study was restricted to the enterprises, which availed assistance from the term lending institutions, the technique produced a robust estimate. Since most of the companies went to the financial institutions for assistance, this estimate could be regarded as a reliable reflection of the behaviour of the entire corporate sector. It may be of interest to note that forecast of corporate investment using this methodology has been made continuously for the last thirty years. This methodology has provided an indication of not only expected aggregate capital expenditures but also sector wise and state wise expected expenditures. The paper included in this volume 'Corporate Investment in 1979 – A Forecast' is one example of the annual forecasts using the methodology developed.

In his paper on "Economic reforms: An Assessment", Dr. Rangarajan, after analysing the origins of the New Economic Policy, provides a detailed description of the recent reform measures and their impact. He writes, "The year 1991 is an important landmark in the post-Independent economic history of India. The country faced a severe economic crisis, triggered in part by a serious balance of payments situation. The crisis was converted into an opportunity to effect some fundamental changes in the content and approach to economic policy." The reform measures which initially covered the areas of industrial policy, foreign trade, foreign investment, fiscal system, monetary and exchange rate management and financial sector have now been extended to other areas, such as power and communications.

Some of the major points emphasised by him are recapitulated here :-

- The thrust of the new economic policy is towards creating a more competitive environment in the economy as a means to improving the productivity and efficiency of the system. This is to be achieved by removing the barriers to entry and the restrictions on growth of firms. While the industrial policy seeks to bring about a greater competitive environment domestically, the trade policy seeks to improve international competitiveness subject to the protection offered by tariffs which are coming down. The private sector is being given a larger space to operate in, as some of the areas earlier reserved exclusively for the public sector are also now allowed to the private sector.
- There has been some success in reducing fiscal deficit but not to the desired extent. Some are critical of the fact that whatever reduction that had been brought about was almost by reducing capital expenditure.
- Judged by the standard criteria of growth rates of national income and per capita income, external balance and inflation rate, the Indian economy has done well since liberalisation.
- Differences in growth rates among states have become more pronounced after liberalisation. However, many of these low growth states have not been actively involved in the liberalisation process. If the regional disparities have grown, it is at least in part a reflection of the quality of governance. It is interesting to note that the ranking of the states according to income growth rate differs considerably between Eighties and Nineties.

- Clearly, the lesson of Indian development experience is that monopolies whether of State or private sector do not lead to efficiency. The need to create, promote and sustain a competitive environment is absolutely essential. India is no longer a country producing goods and services for the domestic market alone. Indian firms are becoming and have to become global players. At the minimum they have to meet global competition. However, even as we do create conditions for more effective functioning of the enterprises, some of the concerns, such as emphasis on agriculture, fiscal consolidation and public sector reforms need special attention.
- Liberalisation programme to be successful must ensure that the benefits accrue to all sections of society and that it commands the acceptance of a wide constituency. Efficiency and equity should not be posed as opposing considerations. They must be weaved together to produce a coherent pattern of growth. There is no conflict between the process of liberalisation and the social obligations of the State. There is nothing inherent in the liberalisation process which should hinder the special responsibilities of the State in relation to the poor and underprivileged. In fact, a more efficient economy which should be the outcome of the process of liberalisation would enable the State to meet better its responsibilities in the socio-economic arena.

Monetary System and Financial Sector

For the first time since its establishment, the Reserve Bank of India set up in December 1982 a committee under the Chairmanship of Prof. Sukhamoy Chakravarty to undertake a comprehensive review of the working of the monetary system in our country. The mandate to the Committee was wide in as much as it covered almost every aspect of the monetary and financial system. The Committee submitted its Report in April 1985. It is well known that public discussions on monetary policy have considerably improved after the publication of this Report and this Report paved the way for many research work on monetary policy in India. Although Dr. Rangarajan was only one of the members of this Committee, it is known that he was the principal contributor to the deliberation and the drafting of the Report.

In his article on the Chakravarty Committee Report (1987), Dr. Rangarajan explains at length the analytical framework underlying its recommendations. There are five building blocs in the Report, *viz.*, the objectives of monetary policy, the relationship between price and money supply, the link between reserve money and money supply, the understanding between the RBI and the Government regarding net RBI credit to Government and the role for interest rate. The principal points made by him are as follows:

- The objectives of monetary policy are no different from the overall objectives of economic policy, whether it be economic growth, social justice, better distribution of income, maintenance of price stability or promotion of savings. However, price stability becomes a major concern of monetary policy, as this is the objective which can be handled most effectively by monetary instruments.
- Regarding the trade-off between growth and inflation, a higher growth rate can be achieved only at the cost of a fairly high inflation rate. Over a longer time period, growth cannot be however bought with the aid of higher price and there is no evidence to show that a higher growth rate is associated with higher inflation rate. In India the contrary is the case.
- In the Indian situation, supply shocks are very frequent and therefore, inflation cannot be treated purely as a monetary phenomenon. Nevertheless, there was enough evidence to show that all price increases in India over the last few decades could not be explained by a structuralists explanation. Money does count and in a significant way.
- The impact of money supply on the economy at a given point of time would depend on a variety of factors such as existence of excess capacity. It should not, however, be inferred that the impact of money on output and on prices is indeterminate. Money has an impact on both output and prices.
- Estimation of a demand function for money is a useful exercise to understand the inter-relationship among money, output and prices. In fact, if one were to deny the existence of reasonably stable demand function for money, it would amount to denying any role for monetary policy in inflation management.

- Notwithstanding the need for facilitating the growth process, it is important to regulate the growth in money supply over a period of time. A scheme of monetary targeting with feed-back would be most appropriate. This will require in the Indian context a co-ordination between fiscal and monetary authorities in steering the growth of money supply which is consistent with real growth and an acceptable order of increase in prices.
- 'Money also matters' is a position that must be distinguished from 'money does not matter' or 'money alone matters'. Too much of it can, through price increase, cause distortions in the economy just as too little can hinder the smooth functioning. The art of central banking lies in ensuring the appropriate balance.

In a period of frequent and sharp changes in reserve requirements, the stability of the multiplier cannot be studied without adjusting the monetary base. In his paper (1984) on "Reserve Money: Concepts and Policy Implications for India", (the co-author was Shri Anoop Singh) he illustrated the nature of the adjustment that should be made to the published data on reserve money to study this problem. The second objective of the paper was to use the new adjusted series to examine the lags in the impact of reserve money on various definitions of the money stock. For this purpose, quarterly data have been used for the period 1973/74–1981/82. His analysis suggested that the adjustments to reserve money resulted in a series that showed a systematic and well defined relationship between reserve money and money supply.

The role of money and monetary policy in the determination of real output and price level has been increasingly receiving attention since the Chakravarty Committee. The models differ in their approach and focus. In some models the emphasis is on production and supply while in others it is on demand factors. Dr. Rangarajan's paper on "Money, Output and Prices: A Macroeconometric Model" (of which R.R. Arif was co-author) (1990), is one of the pioneering works in India, with emphasis on the determination of money supply and its impact on both output and prices. The model is aggregate in nature. The main linkages in the model are as follows: the stock of money varies endogenously through the feedback from reserve money, which changes to accommodate fiscal deficits. The price level is determined by money supply and output. The government budget is affected by the price level and output. The latter is influenced, among other factors, by changes in real money supply acting as a proxy for real credit. The empirical results show that the price effects of an increase in money supply are stronger than the output effects. Since government revenue collections do not keep pace with government expenditures as nominal incomes rise, the resource gap widens during a period of continued price increases. The policy simulations show that while a substantial increase in government capital expenditures increases output, its impact on output and prices also depends on the extent of the resource gap met by borrowing from the Reserve Bank. As the proportion of the resource gap met by borrowing from the Reserve Bank increases, the trade-off between output and prices worsens sharply. Because the trade-off in terms of inflation is extremely high, sustained monetary expansion is not a viable policy tool.

Developments in monetary policy closely mirror the changes in overall economic policy. The decade of 1990s has seen far reaching changes in India's economic policy. In his K.R Narayanan oration (2001), ("Monetary Policy in a Developing Economy: The Indian Experience") he puts very succinctly, the Indian experience with respect to monetary policy as an instrument of economic management. In this oration, after narrating the developments, he raises a few issues of monetary policy, which are of much relevance, especially in the context of conducting monetary policy in a globalised environment. He, in particular, raises issues pertaining to the objectives of monetary policy, the role of interest rates, exchange rate policy, central bank autonomy etc. The concept of threshold level of inflation which was mooted by him earlier is also elaborated in this oration.

In developing economies like India, trade flows, both visible and invisible, dominate the balance of payments. That is why for the exchange rate regime in India, continuous monitoring of the real exchange rate with an appropriate base becomes important. It provides valuable information to the authorities on the behaviour of the current account to which it is intrinsically linked. A monetary policy geared to domestic price stability in this situation helps to avoid disruptive adjustments in the exchange rate. In that sense, monetary policy and exchange rate management become intertwined.

Increasingly, macroeconomic stability as an objective of central banking is closely linked to financial stability. It is easy to see how the two are inter-linked. Financial stability broadly implies the stability of the important institutions and markets forming part of the financial system. Financial stability requires that the key institutions in the financial system are stable, in that, there is a high degree of confidence about meeting contractual obligations without interruption or outside assistance. While the complementarities between the objectives of macrostability and financial stability are easily recognised, one question that needs to be addressed is whether there can be a conflict between the two objectives. It is not inconceivable to have situations in which the price stability objective might call for a restrictive policy, while the financial market conditions may demand a somewhat liberal policy to provide relief. Normally, price stability should provide an environment favourable to financial stability. If on occasions dealing directly with financial stability becomes necessary, it must be done as in the case of intervention in the foreign exchange markets.

In his inaugural address at the Bank Economists Conference, 1997, ("Financial Sector Reforms: The Second Phase") Dr. Rangarajan explained the challenges before the Indian banking system. Some of the issues are still relevant as they figure very prominently in the Second Generation Reforms. He explained the four building blocks which formed part of the banking sector reforms, *viz.*, (a) modifying the policy framework; (b) improving the financial soundness and credibility of banks; (c) creating a competitive environment; and (d) strengthening of the institutional framework. The first phase of financial sector reforms had laid the base for a sound and viable banking system even though we have to travel still some distance. Going by the experiences of commercial banks in other countries, he identified the following aspects to dominate the future course of banking development in India, *viz.*, greater specialisations by banks in different niches of the market such as retail, agriculture, export, small-scale and corporate sector; greater reliance on non-fund business such as advisory and consultancy services, guarantee and custodial services; greater overlap in product coverage between commercial banks and non-bank financial intermediaries; and greater financial disintermediation with large companies accessing securities debt domestically and from financial markets abroad.

Another area of importance outlined in this paper is asset-liability management. The most important element in this process is to build into the analysis, possible future behaviour of variables such as interest rates. Thus, asset-liability management is a process and it must be practiced on an on going manner. Managements must regularly forecast assumptions and develop contingencies to accommodate changes expected. Given these challenges, banks will need to chalk out a plan of action. In this context, two tasks appear important. One is technology upgradation and the other is organisational improvement.

Fiscal Sector

We often ask these questions with reference to fiscal sector, *viz.*, What is fiscal deficit? How is it measured? What is the relationship between fiscal deficit and other macro variables like interest rates and money supply? Does the financing of fiscal deficit has other macro implications? What is the relationship between fiscal deficit and debt? What should be done to ensure a sustainable level of debt? It is interesting to note that Dr. Rangarajan has addressed these issues at one time or other. For this volume, I have selected five papers, which led to considerable future research. Let me briefly mention the conclusions of these five papers.

Dr. Rangarajan's paper "Dynamics of Interaction between Government Deficit and Domestic Debt in India" (co-authored by Anupam Basu and Narendra Jadhav) which appeared in the RBI Occasional Papers in its September 1989 issue has made significant vibrations in the economic research world, because it is the first paper of this kind which has gone into the definitional issues of fiscal deficit, measurement problems, interaction with other macro variables and then suggested various conditions for sustainability of domestic debt in the Indian context. The important conclusions which emerged from this study are as follows:

- Available measures of government deficit and domestic debt are accounting figures rather than proper economic aggregates. They were replaced by analytically meaningful measures. Alternate government deficit estimates for 1970-71 and for the 1980s have been derived, which indicate that government deficit in India as a ratio of GDP has significantly widened during the 1980s.

- The gross fiscal deficit expanded from 3.5 per cent of GDP in 1970-71 to the average of seven per cent of GDP in the first half of the 1980s and further to the average of 9.3 per cent in the four year period ended in 1988-89. Contemporaneously, the gross primary deficit worsened from 3.5 per cent of GDP to as much as 7.6 per cent of GDP during same period.
- Starting from the inter-temporal budget constraint, analytical expressions in the form of difference equations were derived so as to establish the dynamic interlinkages between government deficits and different modes of financing them. This framework was used to conduct two thought experiments, *viz.*, (a) In "debt-financing scenario", the question addressed is: what would be the future time profile of debt-GDP ratio if the government deficit is allowed to evolve passively and domestic borrowings excluding those from the RBI are used for financing it while maintaining the other modes of financing at their current ratios to GDP? (b) In monetary-financing scenario, the question addressed is what would be the projected impact on inflation if the government deficit is allowed to evolve passively, financed by resorting to additional net RBI credit while holding the domestic "debt financing" and foreign financing at their base year ratios to GDP? The major conclusion is that while pure debt financing scenario leads to unacceptable levels of debt to GDP ratio, which is also reflected in high ratios of interest payments to revenue receipts, monetary financing leads to very high levels of inflation.

In the second paper under this section entitled "Fiscal Deficit, External Balance and Monetary Growth: A Study of Indian Economy", he along with M.S. Mohanty examined various macroeconomic impacts of fiscal deficit in India with special emphasis on the nature of relationship between deficit, external balance and monetary growth. The macro model covering the period 1971-72 to 1993-94 developed in the paper provided an integrated framework to study the various dimensions of fiscal deficit and is used to evaluate different policy options for maintaining sustainable internal and external balance in the Indian economy. The policy simulation results reveal that fiscal deficit in general results in widening of current account deficit in the balance of payment, although this outcome critically depends on how the deficit is financed. In the case of monetary financing scenario, the price and income effects reinforce each other, leading to a deterioration in the external balance in the short run as well as in the long run. Thus, in any effort to maintain a sustainable balance of payments situation, domestic economic policy aimed at maintaining absorption and prices at appropriate levels has an important role to play. The paper observed that resort to deficit financing to promote public investment and growth involves costs in terms of loss of control on inflation. Even when borrowing from the market finances the deficit, a prudent limit for such borrowing becomes essential. For example, the policy simulations to study the impact of 10 per cent increase in real public expenditure in non-agricultural sector finances and money creation shows that in the long run while output increases by 2.66 per cent, prices rise by 18.33 per cent.

In an article published in 1971, Dr. Rangarajan describes the operation of the government securities market as it then existed. During 1970s, the government securities market in India reflected the mixed character of the Indian economy. The two features of the Indian economy that had shaped the nature of the market were: (a) the direct and dominant role of the Government in the total investment outlays of the economy, and (b) Government ownership of the major financial institutions. The investment policy of these institutions became part of the allocation of resources between the public (Government) and private sectors. In this paper, he argued that if a genuine market was to be developed, a necessary condition was to make the interest offered on government securities competitive. An appropriate increase in the interest rate would have the effect of making the financial institutions hold government securities at the then prescribed level, even if the statutory restrictions were withdrawn. However, for a broad market to emerge, a wide spectrum of owners was required so that at any given time there would be a large number of buyers and sellers. He maintained that unless there is an active secondary market in India, the Reserve Bank of India could not effectively use the tool of open market operations.

The fifth paper included in this section deals with the linkage between government expenditure and money supply. In the textbook discussions of fiscal and monetary policies based on the standard Keynesian model, the stock of physical capital is assumed to be constant. This is a valid assumption if one were to deal only with very short run effects of various policies. But an analysis of dynamic effects is called for when one deals with the various dynamic extensions of the Keynesian model. In this paper Dr. Rangarajan (V. Sundararajan was co-author) introduced various modifications to standard Keynesian model, *viz.*, the government budget constraint which specifies that the total government expenditures equals tax revenue plus the changes in money supply plus the changes in bond supply; wealth is introduced as an additional independent variable both in the consumption function and in the demand function for money; the impact of changes in investment on capital stock. This model followed framework of Hicks-Keynes IS-LM analysis and discussed how the conclusions of IS-LM analysis and some of its extensions would be modified when some of the restrictive assumptions are removed. Thus, this analysis should be viewed as an exercise in short run dynamics, rather than as a long run analysis.

The major conclusions that emerge from this study are: (a) when government expenditures are financed by money creation, income expands continuously. The capital stock may increase or decrease while the former is likely to be the normal situation; (b) when the increased government expenditures are financed by bond creation the multiplier becomes finite and positive. There is no possibility of income multipliers becoming negative. The capital stock declines. Attention of the readers is drawn to the limitations of the model in a postscript added subsequently.

External Sector

Although many developing countries have realised the importance of income from exports in augmenting growth, there are very few country-specific econometric studies which have focused on the impact of export fluctuations on national income. The paper on "Impact of Export Fluctuations on Income: A Cross-Country Analysis" (co-author V. Sundararajan) addresses this issue. A major bone of contention has been whether developing countries experienced a greater degree of fluctuation in exports than developed countries and whether such fluctuations affected the growth rate of income. This paper not only suggested a robust methodology instead of the usual cross-country regressions in measuring the impact of export fluctuations on domestic income, but also brings out the differences in export-income multipliers between developed and developing countries. It was found that the long run multipliers relating to both income and investment were generally larger for developing countries than for developed countries. For each country studied, an increase in the instability to exports led to an increase in the instability in income. In the case of five countries, it led to a decline in growth rate.

In the article on "India's Balance of Payments: The Emerging Dimensions" Rangarajan traces the developments in India's balance of payments since 1970s. He examines the crisis of 1990-91 and narrates the manner in which the issue was handled. He suggests various policy measures which need to be kept in mind in future to avoid such a crisis. He was optimistic on the balance of payments front. He felt that with an export growth of 15 per cent per annum and import growth of 9 to 10 per cent per annum, the future scenario might turn out to be manageable. However, there could be slippages on both counts. Even when the current account deficit came down, the balance of payments would still need watching, as financing requirements would be large because of the repayments of old debts that would fall due. Referring to the discussions about convertibility of the Indian rupee, he adds that perhaps, this was a subject which would not have merited discussion a few years earlier. It is the unification of the exchange rate and more so the strength shown by the rupee which have brought to the fore the issue of convertibility. In fact, the question of convertibility does not arise when exchange rate is over-valued. Convertibility essentially means the ability of residents and non-residents to exchange domestic currency for foreign currency, without limit, whatever be the purpose of the transactions. The major risk is the possibility of capital flight. Another risk is the possibility of macroeconomic instability arising from movement of short term capital movements, very often described as 'hot money'. A free movement of funds will lead to integration of financial markets and, therefore, an efficient domestic financial system is a pre-requisite for the introduction of capital account convertibility.

Fixed exchange rate system collapsed in 1973 with no official agreement on what was to replace it, and the major currencies were set afloat in world currency markets. The countries forming the European Monetary Systems floated as a group against other major currencies and maintained a form of managed floating within adjustable margins against each other. The developing countries had not resorted to independent floating but had either pegged their currencies to one of their major currencies or, to a basket of currencies. In their article "The Exchange Rate System: Some Issues", (1984) Rangarajan and Ahluwalia argue that the functioning of the floating rate system was not as smooth as the proponents had expected. The authors raise certain critical questions regarding the concept of target zone. They argue that the target Real Effective Exchange Rates (REER) to be pursued by the major countries must be consistent with the patterns of current surpluses and deficits envisaged and that there must be confidence that intervention will be symmetrically followed by countries at either end of the target zone. They rightly emphasise the need for a high order of macroeconomic co-ordination, which has been lacking. An important issue arising out of the adoption of floating rates is what it does to the need for reserves. The two dominant characteristics associated with the floating rate system are its equilibrating and insulating properties. As a result of the operation of both these properties, it is argued that the demand for international reserves would go down and that countries could manage with a lower order of reserves than under fixed exchange rate system. This has not been the case in reality. In fact, a country may not have much more freedom in its monetary policy with floating exchange rate system than under fixed exchange rate system. The adoption of target zones would require monetary policy to be supplemented by intervention. This paper clearly mentions that developing countries have a deep interest in the efficient functioning of the international exchange rate system like industrialised countries and any modifications in this area which improves the functioning of the world economy and world trade would contain significant advantages to the developing countries. The conclusion of this paper is relevant even today, *viz.*, the international monetary system must remain 'international' and in this regard the goal that is sought to be achieved by both developed and developing countries must be one of the optimal global welfare.

In "Exchange Rate Adjustments: Causes and Consequences" (1991), Rangarajan explains the downward adjustments made in Rupees' exchange rate in 1991. He justifies the step as follows: "To restore the competitiveness of our exports and in general to bring about a reduction in the trade and current account deficits, it had become imperative to make a downward adjustment of the rupee. In determining the extent of adjustment, it is necessary to bear in mind four relevant factors: (1) differentials in the price levels between India and the major industrialised countries, (2) extent of real depreciation of the currencies of the countries competing with India, (3) the degree of correction required in our Balance of Payments and (4) market expectations. Taking all these factors into account, the depreciation of the rupee value by 18 to 19 per cent seems appropriate". He also stresses that the depreciation of the rupee is a necessary but not a sufficient condition for export growth and for an improvement in the Balance of Payments. A complementary set of policies needs to be put in place which will facilitate expansion of output particularly for exports and curb aggregate demand to keep prices under check.

The Government of India appointed in 1991 a High Level Committee on Balance of Payments under the chairmanship of Dr. C. Rangarajan, to study a wide gamut of issues relating to the capital account in the Balance of Payments. The terms of reference required the Committee (a) to make projections of the various elements in Balance of Payments over the next five years and estimate the financing gap taking into account the repayment obligations; (b) to study the appropriate mix of capital flows and to suggest measures to bring about the desired changes; (c) to examine and suggest ways of changing the existing structure of debt; (d) to examine the possibility of converting certain types of existing debt into equity, to suggest ways to enhance the flows of invisible earnings, including private remittances through the banking system; and (e) to examine the functioning of the existing exchange rate regime in the context of the move to Exim-Scrip and to consider the implications of a shift to convertibility on current transactions in the near future. The Report of the High Level Committee is reproduced in this volume, since the recommendations laid the framework for external sector management for the next several years. These recommendations have stood the test of time and have contributed to the strengthening of the external sector.

A major recommendation of the Committee related to the exchange rate policy. The Committee submitted an Interim Report in February, 1992 which outlined the Liberalised Exchange Rate Management System (LERMS). The LERMS was introduced with effect from March 1, 1992 as a first step towards the full convertibility of the rupee on current account. The new system attempted to combine the advantages of a relatively stable managed float and the balancing properties of a freely floating rate of exchange by creating a dual exchange rate system, one official and the other determined by the market. In its final report, the Committee recommended a unified market determined exchange rate system. In the light of the experience gained under LERMS, the Committee considered two options: change the proportion at the official rate as an intermediate step or to bring about a unified market without any intermediate step. The Committee noted that while the intermediate step would have the advantage of moderation in inflationary pressures, the disadvantages such as the implicit tax, albeit to a lesser extent, on exports and inward remittances, etc. would continue to exist. It, therefore, recommended that a decision be taken to unify the exchange rate, as an important step towards current account convertibility. The other recommendation of the Committee related to the level and composition of foreign currency reserves and policies towards gold, composition of commercial borrowings including short term debt, NRI deposits and foreign investment. All combined, these recommendations were designed to strengthen export competitiveness of this country, and the prudent and effective management of external sector.

— R. KANNAN*

* Appointed Actuary, SBI Life Insurance Company Ltd., Mumbai (on Deputation from the Reserve Bank of India).

Part I

Agriculture, Industry and the Economy

1

Agricultural Growth and Industrial Performance in India

I. INTRODUCTION

In an economy such as India's, where approximately half of the gross domestic product originates in agriculture and allied activities, it is generally assumed that the influence of agriculture on industry is strong. Before this assertion can be validated, however, the channels through which agricultural performance influences industrial growth must be clearly delineated. Only the examination of each of these links will show to what extent the performance of agriculture explains the behaviour of industry.

There are at least five separate channels of influence. First, because agriculture requires industrial inputs, such as fertiliser, growth in agriculture generates demand for such industrial products. Perhaps, as the technology of agricultural production changes, this link will become stronger.

Second, agriculture supplies the inputs needed by agriculture-based industries. This segment of the industrial structure accounted for 66 per cent of total industrial output in 1946, 47 per cent in 1960, and 34 per cent in 1970. Obviously, the availability of agricultural raw materials must have a significant influence on these industries.[1]

Third, agriculture influences the output of industrial consumption goods through demand. Industrial consumption goods include clothing, footwear, sugar, edible oils, and furniture. It is not often recognised that rural consumption of industrial consumption goods

International Food Policy Research Institute, (Research Report 33), October 1982.

is nearly two-and-a-half times that of urban consumption. However, it is necessary to distinguish between the output effect and the effect of the terms-of-trade between agricultural and industrial products on demand.

Given the income elasticities of demand for industrial consumption goods of the rural population, the effect of an increase in rural income resulting from a rise in agricultural production can be estimated. The changing pattern in the distribution of rural income and the elasticities of demand of the different classes will have to be taken into account to understand the effects in the long run. The effects of the terms-of-trade need to be analysed from both the rural and urban perspectives. An increase in the terms-of-trade in favour of agriculture (particularly food prices) will adversely affect the demand for non-food items in urban areas. The cross elasticity of demand is negative, especially among lower-income groups in urban areas where food consumption is a sizeable part of the total budget.

In rural areas, the effects of the terms-of-trade are not necessarily either solely positive or solely negative. The effects for lower income groups will be the same in rural areas as in urban areas because the bulk of the rural population in this income group also buys food. For rural upper-income groups, the negative effect on demand arising from the increase in the terms-of-trade in favour of food can be offset by the increase in the income resulting from the improvement in agricultural prices. Thus, the overall effect of the change in the terms-of-trade will be a combination of the effects for all population groups. The effect of an increase in food prices on the demand for non-food items by different expenditure groups in rural areas can be broken into two parts. First, there is the negative cross elasticity of demand. Second, there is the positive income effect, which will depend on the increase in total expenditure from a rise in prices and on the expenditure elasticity of demand for non-food items of that expenditure group. Thus, the effect of a one per cent rise in food prices will be Eif + an_i, where Eif is the cross elasticity of demand for good 'i' (non-food), 'a' is the percentage increase in total expenditure due to a one per cent increase in food prices, and 'n_i', is the expenditure elasticity for 'i' (non-food) of that group. The value of 'a' will be zero for low-income groups that do not sell any food; its value is likely to increase moving from lower- to higher-income groups. Strictly speaking, if the effects of foodgrain prices alone are considered, the value of 'a' will depend on the share of foodgrain output in the total output of each group. Also, because the income, relevant in this context, is monetary income, it will depend on the marketed surplus of each group. Thus, for higher-income groups in rural areas, the combined effect of the two parts can be positive.[2]

The fourth channel of influence is via government savings and public investment. A rise in agricultural production can result in increased government savings by increasing the amount of indirect taxes collected and by improving freight earnings for the railways. In addition, when crops are good, the Government spends less on programs such as drought relief. An increase in government savings may, in turn, be reflected in higher public investment, which may generate the demand for the output of basic and capital goods industries. The combined weight of the basic and capital goods industries in total industrial production is 53 per cent. One explanation for the decline in the growth rate of the industrial sector since 1965 is the fall in public investment; therefore, the link between public investment and agricultural performance, however indirect it may be, should be explored.

Fifth, fluctuations in agricultural production may affect private corporate investment decisions through the impact of the terms of trade on profitability. A low and stable price for wage goods (particularly food) may lead to increased profitability for industrial goods, which may be conducive to increased private corporate investment. On the other hand, an increase in the terms-of-trade in favour of agriculture may promote rural household savings and investment.

Whereas some of the channels emphasise the link between agriculture and industry on the supply side, others stress the link on the demand side. In subsequent chapters, each of these links is examined separately to see how strong each influence has been in India during the past 20 years. A model is constructed, which incorporates all these relationships, so that one can study the overall impact of agriculture's performance on the economy. First, however, a look at industrial growth and agricultural performance during the period 1955-75 will highlight some of the trends.

II. SALIENT FEATURES OF INDUSTRIAL AND AGRICULTURAL GROWTH

There are two distinct periods in the history of industry in India during the 20 years beginning in 1955. In the first decade industrial production increased at an average annual rate of 7.1 per cent, but in the second decade, 1965-75, the growth rate fell sharply to 3.9 per cent. Undoubtedly, the industrial structure of India is far more diversified now than it was in 1950. But the sluggishness of industrial production persisted for more than a decade and by 1975 had spread to all branches of industry.

Table 1 provides data on the rate of growth of industrial and agricultural production since 1951. Data on the growth rates of different sectors, such as basic goods, capital goods, and consumer goods, are also provided. Table 2 shows year-to-year rates of growth in the components of industrial and agricultural production from 1961 to 1975. The highest industrial growth rate was achieved during the period 1961-65. On average, industrial production grew by nine per cent per year. The sharpest increase was in the capital goods industries, which grew at an annual rate of 19.7 per cent. This is partly accounted for by the low base those industries started from. During this period, the rate of growth of the consumer goods industries was five per cent, which was the highest growth rate achieved by this segment of industrial output in any five-year period.

The period 1966-70 witnessed a dramatic decline in production. The growth rate fell to 3.7 per cent. Although all segments of industrial production suffered during this period, the worst hit were the capital goods industries, which declined on an average of 1.4 per cent a year. The growth rate of the consumer goods industries declined only slightly. The growth rate of the agriculture based industries decreased from 3.9 per cent in the previous period to 1.6 per cent during this period.

During 1971-75, the growth rate of industry was 3.6 per cent — almost the same as in the previous period. However, the rates of growth of the different segments were strikingly different. The consumer goods industries suffered most during this period. Their growth rate fell to 1.6 per cent. The capital goods industries improved their performance, and there was little change in the growth rate of agriculture-based industries. Thus, whereas the decline in industrial output during 1966-70 was primarily due to the setback in capital goods industries, during 1970-75 it was due to the decline in consumer goods industries.

Table 1

Growth Rates in the Output of Different Sectors of Industry and Agriculture, 1951-76

(per cent)

Sector	*1951-55*	*1956-60*	*1961-65*	*1966-70*	*1971-76*
Industry					
General index	6.68	5.70	9.0	3.7	3.6
Use-based classification					
Basic goods industries	30.90[a]	4.71[a]	10.5	6.2	5.3
Capital goods industries	—	—	19.7	-1.4	5.4
Intermediate goods industries	5.79	9.83	7.19	3.99	1.84
Consumer goods industries	3.43	2.88	5.0	4.0	1.6
Input-based classification					
Agriculture-based industries	—	—	3.9	1.6	1.3
Metal-based industries	—	—	16.49	3.89	4.78
Chemical-based industries	—	—	8.25	9.51	2.90
Sectoral indicators					
Transport	—	—	12.87	1.60	4.09
Electrical & allied activities	—	—	13.68	12.23	5.08
Agriculture					
All crops	4.3	4.3	-1.0	6.8	2.7
Foodgrains	5.3	3.9	-2.0	8.9	2.0
Non-foodgrains	2.6	5.1	0.9	3.5	2.4

Sources: The figures for industry from 1951 to 1961 are from V. V. N. Somyajulu, "Structural Changes and Growth in Indian Industries 1946-1970," *Asian Economic Review* 16 (December 1974): 131-184; the figures for industry after 1961 are from Reserve Bank of India, *Report on Currency and Finance*, various volumes (Bombay: Reserve Bank of India, various years). All figures for agriculture are from India, Ministry of Agriculture and Irrigation, Directorate of Economics and Statistics, *Estimates of Area and Production of Principal Crops in India*, various issues (Delhi: Controller of Publications, various years).

a: These figures are for the investment goods industries, which are the basic and capital goods industries.

Table 2 shows that, except during 1960-65 when rates of growth were uniformly high, the year-to-year changes have been quite uneven. During 1966-70, the highest rate of growth for industry as a whole was 7.5 per cent and the lowest was -0.4 per cent. During 1971-75 the highest and lowest growth rates achieved were 5.7 per cent and 1.6 per cent respectively. Nor did the different segments of industry grow at the same pace in all years. For example, during 1971-75 the highest growth rates in the basic, capital, and consumer goods industries were reached in 1975, 1973, and 1972 respectively. The disparate behaviour of output in different segments of industry points to the need for examining the factors affecting industry in each of the periods.

Against this background of industrial performance, it may be worthwhile to see whether developments in agriculture paralleled those in industry. Computing the growth rate for agriculture, where output changes have been quite sharp from year to year, is a hazardous exercise, particularly if the time period chosen is as short as five years. The inclusion or exclusion of a single year can alter the growth rate substantially. Based on longer time series, however, the general view now held is that there has been no significant decline in the rate of growth of agricultural output in recent years. A decline, if there is one, is perceptible only in non-foodgrains.

From the data on agricultural performance and industrial production, it is possible to see that certain movements are similar. Industrial production rose at an average annual rate of 6.2 per cent between 1950 and 1960. This period was also marked by the rapid growth of agricultural output, particularly of foodgrains. Between 1950/51 and 1955/56, foodgrain production rose at an average annual rate of 5.3 per cent. During the next five years, the rate of growth was 3.9 per cent per year. Although industrial production proceeded at an even pace, more or less, foodgrain output fell in four out of five years.

The drought years of 1965 and 1966 had a dramatic effect on industrial production. Industrial output, which had been growing steadily at about nine per cent per year in the previous five years, stopped growing in 1966 and 1967 (Table 2). The revival of industrial growth seen in the next three years was again associated with better performance in agriculture. More recently, the fall in the

Table 2

Annual Rates of Growth in Industrial and Agricultural Production, 1961-75

(per cent)

Year	*All Industries*	*Basic Goods*	*Capital Goods*	*Consumer Goods*	*Agriculture-Based Industries*	*All Crops*	*Food*	*Non-food*
1961	9.2	12.7	18.0	6.6	5.2	0.0	0.8	-0.2
1962	9.7	13.3	29.6	1.3	2.8	-0.15	-3.1	1.8
1963	8.3	14.2	11.1	2.2	2.6	2.4	0.6	2.6
1964	8.6	3.8	17.7	7.4	6.6	10.6	10.8	11.7
1965	9.2	8.6	22.0	7.5	2.4	-16.7	-19.0	-11.4
1961-65 **Average**	**9.0**	**10.5**	**19.7**	**5.0**	**3.9**	**-1.0**	**- 2.0**	**0.9**
1966	-0.4	5.2	-13.9	2.9	-0.9	0.0	2.6	-3.2
1967	-0.4	2.1	-2.3	-4.3	-4.4	21.5	28.0	11.5
1968	6.8	10.2	3.4	4.9	3.5	-1.5	-1.0	-2.1
1969	7.5	8.9	1.7	10.1	5.5	6.7	6.7	6.4
1970	5.1	4.6	4.9	6.4	4.5	7.2	8.9	5.1
1966-70 **Average**	**3.7**	**6.2**	**-1.4**	**4.0**	**1.6**	**6.8**	**8.9**	**3.5**
1971	4.2	4.6	5.5	3.2	0.5	0.0	-1.3	2.0
1972	5.7	8.0	0.9	4.7	5.6	-8.0	-8.2	-7.8
1973	1.6	-3.1	15.8	0.5	-0.1	9.9	7.8	14.4
1974	2.0	3.9	4.3	2.2	-1.0	-3.2	-5.4	1.1
1975	4.7	13.3	0.5	-1.5	-1.6	15.2	22.0	2.5
1971-75 **Average**	**3.6**	**5.3**	**5.4**	**1.6**	**1.3**	**2.7**	**2.9**	**2.4**

Sources: Calculations from data in India, *Economic Survey*, various issues (Delhi: Controller of Publications, various years); Reserve Bank of India, *Report on Currency and Finance*, various volumes (Bombay: Reserve Bank of India, various years); R. N. Lal *Capital Formation and Its Financing in India* (Columbia, Mo.: South Asia Books, 1977); Vidya Pitre, "A Study of Trends in India's Imports: 1960-61 to 1974-75," *Economic and Political Weekly*, May 9, 1981, pp. 851-862; and Isher J. Ahluwalia, *Behaviour of Prices and Output in India* (Madras: The Macmillan Company of India, 1979).

Notes: The growth rates of industrial production and their components up to 1970 were computed from the series with index 1960 equals 100 and thereafter from the index 1970 equals 100. The growth rates of agricultural output and their components were computed from the series with the triennium ending 1961/62 as a base.

output of the consumer goods industries in 1973 and 1975 was associated with a fall in agricultural output in 1972 and 1974. But during the period 1961-65, when industrial growth was rapid, agricultural growth was erratic. Agricultural output rose only in 1963/64 and 1964/65. Whereas the foodgrain terms-of-trade rose during this period, their increase was moderated by annual imports of foodgrains of about five million metric tons.

Thus, although there appears to be a rough parallel between industrial growth and agricultural performance, one should not, even in theory, expect industrial production to be a simple reflection of agricultural performance. Industrial growth is fuelled by many factors that are not directly influenced by agriculture.[3] On the other hand, raw data may hide some of the influences of agriculture on industrial performance because of the lags involved. Also, if there are several links between agriculture and industry, it is quite possible that whereas some may lead to an increase in industrial production, others may decrease. As already pointed out, the effects of agricultural output on the demand for industrial consumption goods and on the terms of trade for different groups of people are different. In some situations, governmental policy may partly offset the effects. A sharp rise in agricultural prices resulting from a decline in agricultural output may be offset by imports. It is therefore necessary to study the influences separately and then to combine them to find the total effect for a given period.

III. LINKS BETWEEN AGRICULTURE AND INDUSTRY

The channels of influence discussed earlier can be grouped into three types of linkages – production linkages, demand linkages, and savings and investment linkages. The purpose of this chapter is to examine separately the nature and significance of each of these linkages in order to construct a macro model.[4]

Production Linkages

Agriculture and industry are linked to each other through the input-output relationship. The output of agriculture provides inputs for many industries, such as sugar, cotton textiles, jute textiles, and tobacco. The proportion of the value of agricultural inputs to the total value of output in these industries varies from 20 per cent in matches to 95 per cent in *gur* and *khandsari,* which are both forms of brown sugar. Agriculture also absorbs the outputs of other sectors as inputs required in the production process. The major industrial outputs coming under this category are fertilisers and electricity. With an input-output table, it is possible to compute a number of measures that illustrate this type of linkage.[5]

At India's present stage of development, it is only natural that the production linkages are not strong. (The Asian Development Bank's Second Asian Agricultural Survey also found that the intersectoral linkages were weak in several other Asian countries.[6]) According to a table of intersectoral transactions for 1968/69,[7] the total value of the output of agriculture and allied activities (including animal husbandry, forestry, and fishing) was Rs. 19,702 crores.[8] The total value of inputs used in agriculture was Rs. 4,840 crores. Of this, Rs. 3,571 crores was the value of inputs coming from agriculture and allied activities. Thus only inputs worth Rs. 1,269 crores came from the industrial and service sectors. This was only 6.4 per cent of the value of total agricultural output. The flow of the output of agriculture and allied activities to other sectors constituted only a small share of the total value of their output. Output worth Rs. 2,489 crores went to non-agricultural sectors as inputs. This was approximately 13 per cent of the total output of agriculture and allied activities.

Dividing the economy into three sectors, agriculture, manufacturing, and services, and taking into account direct and indirect requirements, one can see that an increase of Re. 1.00 in the final demand for agricultural goods results in an increase in the output of manufactured goods of Re. 0.09 and of services of Re. 0.02, whereas an increase of Re. 1.00 in the final demand for manufactured goods results in an increase in the output of agricultural goods of Re. 0.26.[9] In fact, a rupee increase in manufactured goods has a greater effect on agricultural output than on services. These data also show that the dependence of industry on agriculture is greater than that of agriculture on industry.

The dependence of agriculture on industry for inputs hinges on the technology used in agriculture. Similarly, the dependence of industry on agriculture for inputs hinges on the growth of processing industries, which in turn depends on the amount of income and perhaps export demand. In the short run there is no mechanism for strengthening these linkages, but in the long run structural changes in the production pattern of the economy are important.

Demand Linkages

The factors influencing the demand for industrial consumption goods – both rural and urban in origin – need to be understood clearly. As mentioned earlier, rural demand will be influenced by output changes in agriculture and by the terms-of-trade. If the terms-of-trade improve in favour of agriculture, those who buy agricultural commodities will benefit. It is well known that the bulk of industrial consumption goods in rural areas is bought by upper-income groups.[10] Because they often are also the sellers of agricultural commodities, an improvement in the terms-of-trade in favour of agriculture may increase the demand for industrial consumption goods.[11] To test this hypothesis, an equation is estimated relating non-food expenditures (in constant prices) of the rural sector to the index of agricultural output (AQI) and the terms-of-trade (TT), which is defined as the ratio of the price of agricultural commodities to the price of manufactured finished products.[12] The independent variables are each lagged by one period. The data used to estimate the equation covers the period 1960/61-1970/71.[13]

The estimated equation for rural non-food expenditures is:

Rural non-food expenditures =

$$-757.287 + \underset{(7.7)}{42.026\ AQI_{t-1}} + \underset{(7.08)}{22.526\ TT_{t-1}}$$

$$\bar{R}^2 = 0.95$$

The equation shows that the effects of both agricultural output and the terms-of-trade are positive. The numbers in parentheses are t-values. Both coefficients are statistically significant. The positive coefficient for the terms-of-trade is not only the result of the "pure" price effect, but also of the effect on monetary income brought about by a rise in agricultural prices relative to prices of manufactured goods.[14] The AQI is substituted for by the index of marketed surplus (MKS) as an independent variable.[15]

The revised equation is:

Rural non-food expenditures =

$$432.584 + \underset{(4.04)}{36.564\ MKS_{t-l}} + \underset{(2.47)}{15.806\ TT_{t-l}}$$

$\bar{R}^2 = 0.87$

Both independent variables are significant in this equation also.

In estimating the demand for urban non-food expenditures, income originating in the non-agricultural sector (Y_{NA}) and the foodgrain terms-of-trade (FGTT), which are defined as the ratio of the price of food to the price of manufactured finished products, are included as independent variables. Thus,

Urban non-food expenditures =

$$1{,}114.43 + \underset{(3.18)}{0.234\ Y_{NAt-l}} - \underset{(1.24)}{5.275\ FGTT_{t-l}}$$

$\bar{R}^2 = 0.58$

As is to be expected, the coefficient of income is positive and the coefficient of foodgrain terms-of-trade is negative, though the latter variable is not statistically significant.

The major item included in non-food expenditures is cloth consumption. The equation for rural demand for cloth is:

Rural cloth consumption =

$$491.516 + \underset{(1.78)}{3.473\ AQI_{t-l}} + \underset{(7.2)}{8.190\ TT_{t-l}}$$

$\bar{R}^2 = 0.90$

The equation for urban demand for cloth is:

Urban cloth consumption =

$$-68.084 + \underset{(5.42)}{0.037\ Y_{NAt-l}} - \underset{(0.84)}{0.341\ FGTT_{t-l}}$$

$\bar{R}^2 = 0.86$

Income or the proxy for income in both equations has a positive coefficient, whereas the terms-of-trade have a positive coefficient only for rural consumption. The foodgrain terms-of-trade have a negative (though not statistically significant) coefficient for urban consumption.

Savings and Investment Linkages

Agricultural performance may affect the economy by influencing savings and investment. The effects on Government and on households should be analyzed separately. The savings of Government will be influenced by agricultural output, industrial output, and the terms-of-trade. Rises and falls in output have immediate effects on government revenues and eventually affect government expenditures. For instance, a severe decline in agricultural output may force the Government to undertake relief measures, thereby increasing government expenditures. The terms-of-trade, particularly for foodgrains, also affect government expenditures through their effect on allowances payable to government employees.[16] As a rule, one expects agricultural and industrial output to influence government savings positively and the foodgrain terms-of-trade to influence them negatively. Both influences may work with a lag.

The household sector includes individuals and all non-corporate forms of business. Household savings are largely influenced by income. The effect of the terms-of-trade on household savings is analogous to their effect on the demand for industrial consumption goods. Rural savings are influenced positively whereas urban savings are influenced negatively. A survey conducted by the National Council of Applied Economic Research (NCAER) shows that in 1967/68, net rural and urban savings were Rs. 1,296 crores and Rs. 708 crores respectively.[17] Thus rural savings were 1.83 times higher than urban savings. If this is the pattern of household savings, the total effect of the terms-of-trade on household savings and, therefore, investment can be positive.

The effect on the corporate sector can be traced directly to investment. Output, both agricultural and non-agricultural, will influence corporate investment positively through the effect on the demand for industrial goods. An increase in agricultural prices relative to industrial prices will have a negative influence. There are two reasons for this. First, a relative increase in non-foodgrain prices adversely affects the profitability of agriculture-based industries by increasing the costs of production. Second, a relative increase in foodgrain prices may push up the wage costs, thus reducing profitability.

During the period 1961-65, the average of the index of the net barter terms-of-trade between agriculture and industry was 104.6. During the period 1966-70, the average of the index was 123.48. For 1,259 medium and large public limited companies surveyed by the Reserve Bank of India during 1961-65, the average profits were 10.3 per cent of total capital employed. During 1966-70 this percentage, for 1,420 medium and large public limited companies, fell to 9.4. Industries not dependent on agricultural inputs are adversely affected only by an increase in foodgrain prices. Agriculture-based industries are affected not only by the prices of foodgrains but also by the prices of non-foodgrain agricultural products. Profits as a percentage of the total capital employed fell more conspicuously in agriculture-based industries than in others.[18]

The estimated equations relating to household and government savings and corporate investment are presented below. Savings are measured in constant prices. Current price figures are deflated by the implicit investment cost index of the Central Statistical Organisation. The data used cover the period 1952/53-1972/73. For the household sector, two independent variables are used — the index of national income in constant prices (NYI) and terms-of-trade (TT). The same independent variables are used to explain corporate investment. For government savings, in addition to national income, the foodgrain terms-of-trade are used as an independent variable.[19]

Therefore, household savings =

$$-2{,}910.25 + \underset{(7.2)}{27.07\ NYI_{t-1}} + \underset{(2.2)}{17.32\ TT_{t-1}}$$

$\bar{R}^2 = 0.93$

Government savings =

$$-122.667 + \underset{(10.91)}{10.3\ NYI_{t-1}} - \underset{(2.81)}{4.25\ FGTT_{t-1}}$$

$\bar{R}^2 = 0.88$

and Corporate investment =

$$-451.66 + \underset{(6.68)}{8.86\ NYI_{t-1}} - \underset{(3.51)}{9.78\ TT_{t-1}}$$

$\bar{R}^2 = 0.74$

Income has a positive effect on the savings of both households and Government. The terms-of-trade have a negative effect on investment in the corporate sector and on government savings, whereas, they have a positive influence on household savings.

IV. THE MACROECONOMIC MODEL

In constructing a model to study the effects of agricultural performance on industrial growth, the three types of linkages mentioned above are kept in mind. Because the primary aim of the study is to determine the influence of agriculture on industry, agricultural output and its components, foodgrains and non-foodgrains, are treated as exogenous variables.[20]

In this model, national income is determined by agricultural and industrial output. Because agricultural output is treated as exogenous, the most important variable to be determined within the system is industrial output. The features of this model that distinguish it from others are the decomposition of total industrial output into consumption goods and basic and capital goods and the separate determination of the output of each segment. The output of consumption goods is directly determined by certain income factors, and the terms-of-trade between agriculture and industry are also determined endogenously. The output of basic and capital goods is derived from the influence of agricultural output and the terms-of-trade on investment by different sectors of the economy.

The Equation System

The equations used in the model are presented in Table 3. Equation (1) states that the index of national income is determined by the indexes of agricultural output and industrial output. This is treated as a stochastic equation, and not as an identity, because the third component in national income — income originating from the service sector — is determined by the output of the other two sectors.[21]

Table 3

Equation System of the Model

Equation Number	*Equation*
1	$NYI_t = a_0 + a_1 AQI_t + a_2 IQI_t + U_{1t}$
2	$ICI_t = b_0 + b_1 IQI_{t-1} + b_2 AQI_{t-1} + b_3 FGTT_{t-1} + U_{2t}$
3	$FGTT_t = c_0 + c_1 IQI_{t-1} + c_2 NAFG_t + c_3 ICI_t + U_{3t}$
4	$NFGTT_t = d_0 + d_1 ICl_t + d_2 NFI_{t-1} + d_3 DMRMI_t + U_{4t}$
5	$TT_t = e_1 FGTT_t + e_2 NFGTT_t$
6	$GCFHH_t = g_0 + g_1 NYI_{t-1} + g_2 TT_{t-1} + U_{6t}$
7	$GCFPC_t = h_0 + h_1 NYI_{t-1} + h_2 TT_{t-1} + U_{7t}$
8	$DSAVPU_t = k_0 + k_1 NYI_{t-1} + k_2 FGTT_{t-1} + U_{8t}$
9	$GCFPU_t = I_0 + I_t DSAVPU_t + I_2 DKIF_t + I_3 T + U_{9t}$
10	$GCF_t = GCFPC_t + GCFHH_t + GCFPU_t$
11	$IBKI_t = m_0 + m_1 GCF_t + m_2 MKI_t + U_{11t}$
12	$IQI_t = n_0 + n_1 ICI_t + n_2 IBKI_t + U_{12t}$

Note: The variables are defined in Appendix 1.

Equations (2), (3), and (4) determine respectively, the output of industrial consumption goods, the ratio of food prices to the prices of manufactured consumption goods, and the ratio of non-food prices to the prices of manufactured consumption goods. These three equations have been derived using certain assumptions about the behaviour of these markets. According to equation (2), output of industrial consumption goods in the current period is determined by demand, which is dependent on agricultural output, industrial output, and the ratio of food prices to those of manufactured consumption goods, all of the previous year.[22] Equation (3) is derived from the relationship between prices of manufactured consumption goods and the output of consumption goods, on the one hand, and between food price and the availability of food and demand for food, on the other. As the supply curve of industrial consumption goods slopes upward, the price of industrial consumption goods will rise as output determined by demand increases. In the foodgrain market, supply is fixed exogenously. The price of foodgrains is, therefore, determined by demand factors and supply. Demand factors influence the price of foodgrains positively and supply negatively.[23]

Thus the ratio of food prices to the price of manufactured consumption goods is dependent on three variables: the industrial output of the previous year, the net availability of foodgrains in the current year, and the output of consumption goods in the current year. The industrial output of the previous year affects the ratio positively because it pushes up the price of food through increased demand for food. The net availability of foodgrains (which includes the domestic output of the previous year and imports of the current year) has a negative effect, as the price of food falls with increased availability. The output of consumption goods has a positive influence on the price of manufactured consumption goods and therefore, a negative effect on the ratio of foodgrain price to the price of manufactured consumption goods.

Similarly, in equation (4), the ratio of the price of non-food grains to the price of manufactured consumption goods is negatively influenced by the availability of non-foodgrain output and the import of raw materials. The output of industrial consumption goods will affect both the numerator, which is the price of non-foodgrain output, and the denominator, which is the price of manufactured consumption goods. The sign of the coefficient of this particular variable depends on the relative effect of the output of manufactured consumption goods on the price of non-food agricultural output and the price of manufactured goods. Equation (2), together with equation (3), implies that the price of industrial consumption goods in the current period is adjusted to the amount of output determined by demand. However, in the next period the current-period price influences demand for industrial consumption goods. Thus, it becomes clear that the output of manufactured consumption goods over time is not determined by demand factors alone.

Equation (5) is simply an identity that treats the terms-of-trade between agriculture and industry as a weighted average of the ratio of food prices to the price of manufactured consumption goods and the ratio of non-food price to the price of manufactured consumption goods. The weights depend on the output of foodgrains and non-food grains, which in the model are treated as exogenous. In fact, equation (5) could have been avoided altogether and the two terms-of-trade variables could have been introduced separately where appropriate. But in estimating some of the equations, the introduction of two separate variables raises problems of multicollinearity.

Equation (6) relates the gross fixed capital formation of the household sector to the national income and terms-of-trade between agriculture and Industry, both of the previous period. Note that the gross fixed capital formation of the household sector also includes investment on farms. Therefore, as argued in Chapter 3, the terms-of-trade variable is expected to have a positive influence. Equation (7) makes gross capital formation of the private corporate sector dependent on national income and the terms-of-trade of the previous year. The terms-of-trade variable is expected to exercise a negative influence on profitability and therefore on investment by the corporate sector.

Equation (8) determines the savings of the public sector. The national income of the previous period and the foodgrain terms of trade of the previous period are used as explanatory variables. The former variable is expected to have a positive effect and the latter a negative effect, as has already been explained. Equation (9) relates the gross capital formation of the public sector to the savings of the public sector, capital inflows from abroad and a time trend, which is added to express the planners' intention to continue increasing public investment.

Equation (10) is an identity, stating that total gross capital formation is equivalent to the sum of the gross capital formation by the household, corporate, and government sectors. In equation (11), output of basic and capital goods is related to gross capital formation and to imports of capital goods. The former has a positive influence and the latter, a negative influence.

In equation (12), total output of industrial production is made a function of the output of industrial consumption goods and the output of capital goods. Like equation (1), equation (12) is treated as a stochastic equation and not as an identity, because output of intermediate goods is taken to be determined indirectly by the output of industrial consumption goods and of basic and capital goods.

This model does not incorporate the output effect of investment. Nor is money introduced in the model because behaviour is linked to relative price ratios. Figure 1 is a diagrammatic representation of how the model works. Total agricultural output — foodgrain output, non-foodgrain output, capital inflows, imports of foodgrains, raw materials, and capital goods — is treated as exogenous. The terms-of-trade, the output of industrial consumption goods, the output of basic and capital goods, the output of industrial production, the gross fixed capital formation of the various sectors, and national income are endogenously determined.

The Estimated Equations

The model uses observations for the period 1961-72. This period was chosen because uniform data are available for the entire period. Although the number of observations is limited, the period represents years of industrial growth as well as decline. After 1972 there was a change in the weights attached to basic and capital goods and consumption goods, making it extremely difficult to construct a series for later years with the earlier weights. Furthermore, consistent data for the components of gross fixed capital formation are not available. The precise definition of the variables used in the model are given in Appendix 1.

All the equations are estimated using ordinary least squares (see Table 4). Because the model is recursive, this procedure is admissible. In addition, the correlations between the residuals have been examined to make sure this procedure is legitimate.[24] In order to test the degree of independence among contemporary disturbances, the correlation matrix of errors was estimated. At the one per cent level of significance, none of the errors are correlated with one another. At the five per cent level, there are four correlations out of a total of 45 that are significant. When the equations concerned are re-estimated using two-stage least squares, the resulting equations are not very different from the estimates obtained with ordinary least squares.

The coefficients in the various equations are in agreement with expectations. Output of industrial consumption goods is positively influenced by the industrial output and the agricultural output of the previous year. These two variables represent the effects of income. Both are statistically significant. The foodgrain terms-of-trade of the previous year have a negative impact. An alternative formulation of the same equation used marketable surplus as an independent variable instead of total agricultural output. This, however, did not explain any more than the equation used.[25]

Figure 1

Structure of the Model

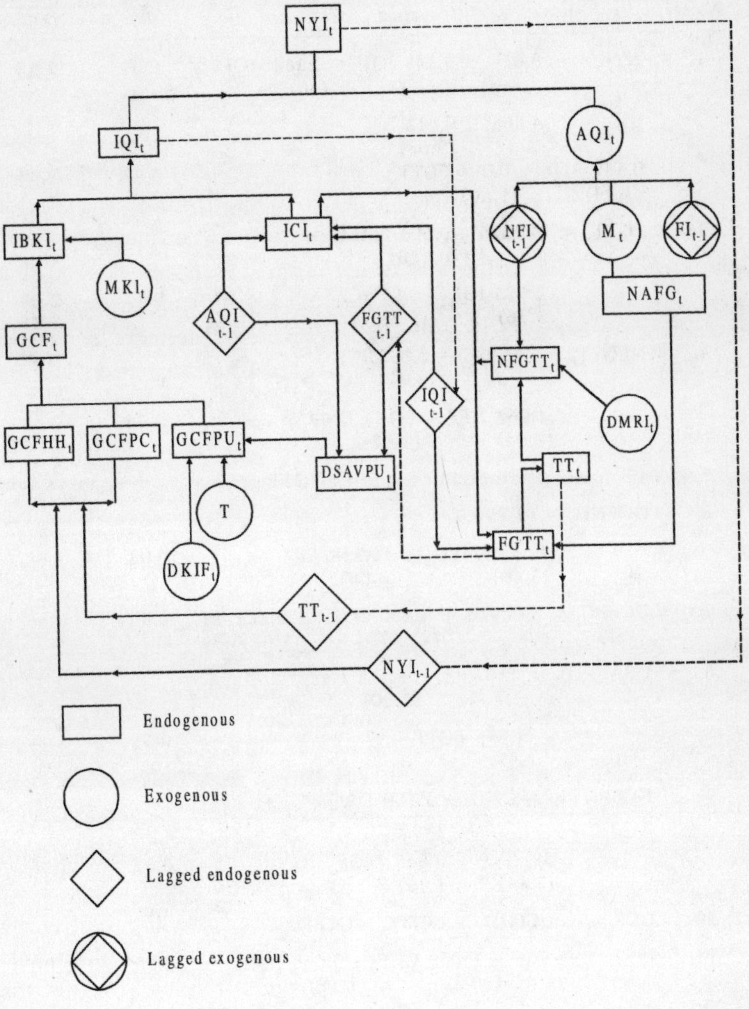

Note: The segmented lines connect the present and past values of the same variables.

Table 4
Estimated Equations

Equation Number	*Equation*	$\bar{R}^2$	*D.W.*
1	$NYI_t = 9.664 + 0.343\ IQI_t + 0.542\ AQI_t$	0.99	2.38
	(21.9) (30.72)		
2	$ICI_t = 4.868 + 0.612\ IQI_{t-1} +$		
	(9.68)		
	$0.447\ AQI_{t-1} - 0.094\ FGTT_{t-1}$	0.97	1.94
	(3.94) (1.60)		
3.	$FGTT_t = 140.274 - 0.503\ NAFG_t +$		
	(0.426)		
	$2.113\ IQI_{t-1} - 2.07\ ICI_t$	0.71	2.00
	(3.36) (1.78)		
4.	$NFGTT_t = 132.996 + 0.893\ ICI_t -$		
	(3.47)		
	$1.062\ NFI_{t-1} - 0.167\ DMRMI$	0.56	0.88
	(1.94) (1.02)		
5.	$TT_t = 0.446\ FGTT_t + 0.554\ NFGTT_t$		
6.	$GCFHH_t = -2{,}196.0 +$		
	$11.679\ NYI_{t-1} + 18.518\ TT_{t-1}$	0.93	2.90
	(3.40) (6.06)		
7.	$GCFPC_t = 535.116 + 4.430\ NYI_{t-1} - 5.261\ TT$	0.40	2.35
	(2.33) (3.07)		
8.	$DSAVPU_t = 134.483 + 6.113\ NYI_{t-1} -$		
	(3.90)		
	$1.896\ FGTT_{t-1}$	0.55	1.19
	(1.77)		
9.	$GCFPU_t = 245.277 + 1.180\ DSAVPU_t +$		
	(2.06)		
	$39.75\ T + 0.665\ DKIF_t$	0.57	1.38
	(2.44) (1.86)		
10.	$GCF_t = GCFHH_t + GCFPC_t + GCFPU_t$		
11.	$IBKI_t = -1.708 + 0.060\ GCF_t - 0.048\ MKI_t$	0.98	2.00
	(10.22) (1.18)		
12.	$IQI_t = 10.189 + 0.508\ IBKI_t + 0.379\ ICI_t$	0.99	1.17
	(12.23) (4.72)		

Note: The variables are defined in Appendix 1. The number in parentheses are t-statistics. The equation numbers refer to the equations in Table 3.

In determining the foodgrain terms-of-trade, industrial output of the previous year has a positive effect and the availability of foodgrains has a negative one. The output of industrial consumption goods has a negative sign, as is to be expected, because it must influence positively the denominator of the ratio. The non-foodgrain terms-of-trade are positively influenced by the output of industrial consumption goods. This variable affects both the numerator and the denominator of the ratio. The net effect is positive. The availability of non-foodgrains and the importation of raw materials have negative influences.

The terms-of-trade positively affect fixed investment by households and negatively affect fixed investment by the corporate sector.[26]

Income has a positive influence on fixed investment by the household and corporate sectors. Public savings are positively influenced by the national income of the previous year and negatively influenced by the foodgrains terms-of-trade of the previous year. Public sector fixed investment is positively influenced by public savings, capital inflows and the time trend. Output of basic and capital goods is positively influenced by gross fixed capital formation, which is the sum of gross fixed capital formation in the household, corporate and public sectors. Imports of capital goods have a negative impact on output of basic and capital goods.

The explanatory power of most of the equations judged by the value of $\bar{R}^2$ is satisfactory. The D.W. statistic is inconclusive in only four equations. For the rest of the equations, the hypothesis of autocorrelation can be rejected. The performance of the model is tested in simulation I by simulating it for the sample period, using the estimated equations and incorporating the given values of the exogenous variables. The actual and simulated values for all the simulations are given in Appendix 2, Tables 9 to 14, and charts depicting the behaviour of the actual and simulated series are provided in Appendix 3, Figures 2 to 7.

Simulations of the Model

The two series correspond closely for most of the variables. To compare the performance of the simulated series with the actual series in relation to the endogenous variables, the mean absolute error and the mean absolute percentage error are calculated.[27]

Absolute Error	Mean Absolute Percentage Error	Mean Variable
NYI	1.18	0.954
IQI	3.73	2.47
IBKI	6.68	3.93
ICI	2.63	2.12

Note: Both are found to be small.

It is, however, more instructive to look at the rates of growth. Table 5 gives the growth rate of some of the variables. The actual growth rate of national income was about 3.3 per cent and the simulated growth rate was 3.1 per cent. The actual growth rate of industrial production was five per cent, whereas the simulation I rate was 4.6 per cent.

Table 5

Actual and Simulated Growth Rates of Selected Variables, 1961-72

Variable	*Actual*	*Simulation I*	*Simulation IV*	*Simulation V*
NYI	3.27	3.101	3.122	3.811
IQI	5.00	4.579	4.625	5.079
IBKI	6.02	5.389	5.404	5.803
ICI	4.15	4.016	4.155	4.772

Sources: Calculations from data in India, *Economic Survey*, various issues (Delhi: Controller of Publications, various years); Reserve Bank of India, *Report on Currency and Finance*, various volumes (Bombay: Reserve Bank of India, various years); R.N.Lal, *Capital Formation and Its Financing in India* (Columbia, Mo.: South Asia Books, 1977); Vidya Pitre, "A Study of Trends in India's Imports: 1960-61 to 1974-75," *Economic and Political Weekly*, May 9, 1981, pp. 851-862; and Isher J. Ahluwalia, *Behaviour of Prices and Output in India* (Madras: The Macmillan Company of India, 1979)

Notes: The figures in this table are the growth rates of time series that have been computed using semi-log equations. NYI stands for the index of national income: it is in 1960/61 prices. IQI stands for the index of industrial production; 1960 equals 100. IBKI stands for the index of the output of the consumer goods industries; 1960 equals 100. Simulation I is the basic model described in the text. Simulations IV and V use that model, but simulation IV assumes a steady increase in agricultural output and simulation V raises the growth rate of agriculture by one per cent.

The year-to-year rates of growth in national income and different components of industrial production for the actual and simulated series are also computed (see Table 6). The declines in national income in 1965 and 1972 are captured in the simulated series. However, the crucial test of the model is in relation to industrial production. The sharp decline in the rate of growth in industrial production in 1966 is captured by the simulation. In 1967, industrial production showed a small negative growth rate whereas the simulation shows a slight positive change.

For basic and capital goods, however, there are large differences between the two series in the year-to-year growth rates.

Table 6

Actual and Simulated Annual Growth Rates in National Income and Industrial Production, 1962-72

	National Income		Industrial Production		Outcome of the Consumer Goods Industries		Outcome of the Basic and Capital Goods Industries	
Year	Actual	Simulation I	Actual	Simulation I	Actual	Simulation I	Actual	Simulation I
1962	1.9	2.0	9.7	7.6	1.3	9.7	18.9	7.5
1963	5.6	3.6	8.3	5.8	2.2	3.1	13.1	8.1
1964	7.5	7.6	8.6	5.4	7.4	3.8	9.9	2.3
1965	-5.1	-5.0	9.2	9.3	7.5	7.4	12.1	11.5
1966	0.9	0.3	-0.4	0.6	2.9	-0.05	-2.6	0.9
1967	8.2	11.1	-0.4	2.6	-4.3	-1.9	0.2	5.3
1968	2.9	2.2	6.8	7.1	4.9	8.7	7.8	7.0
1969	6.3	3.7	7.5	1.1	10.1	5.8	6.5	-1.2
1970	5.9	6.6	5.1	7.0	6.4	2.6	4.7	10.1
1971	1.1	1.9	0.9	4.9	3.2	7.9	3.4	3.9
1972	-1.3	-2.9	7.1	2.2	4.7	3.8	8.4	1.9

Sources: Calculations from data in India, *Economic Survey*, various issues (Delhi: Controller of Publications, various years); Reserve Bank of India, *Report on Currency and Finance*, various volumes (Bombay: Reserve Bank of India, various years); R.N.Lal, *Capital formation and Its Financing in India* (Columbia, Mo.:South Asia Books, 1977); Vidya Pitre. "A Study of Trends in India's Imports: 1960-61 to 1974-75," *Economic and Political Weekly*, May 9, 1981, pp. 851-862; and Isher J. Ahluwalia, *Behaviour of Prices and Output in India* (Madras: The Macmillan Company of India, 1979).

Simulation I, the basic simulation of the model, assumes that the disturbance term attached to each equation takes on the expected value, which is zero. Such simulations are deterministic. On the other hand, stochastic simulation takes into account the presence of the stochastic element in each behavioural equation. In this type of simulation, a random value from a normal distribution with mean zero and variance equal to the estimated variance of the disturbance is added to each equation.[28] The model is also simulated stochastically for the sample period. Each stochastic simulation experiment is replicated 60 times to obtain the mean values of the variables. Table 7 shows that the mean values obtained through stochastic simulation are in close agreement with the deterministic solution. The mean absolute percentage error between the two series is almost negligible. In the subsequent simulations, which study the effects of certain variables on the total system, only the deterministic simulation is used. In all, five simulations are included. Table 8 compares the simulated trends in national income.

Effects of a One-Time Increase in Agricultural Output

To study the effect of an increase in agricultural output in one year, the index of agricultural output — both foodgrain and non-foodgrain output — is raised by one per cent in 1963, and to study its effect over a period of time, a second simulation is attempted. In 1963, the year in which agricultural output is increased by one per cent, national income is 0.51 of one per cent higher under Simulation II than under Simulation I. In the following year, income is 0.16 of one per cent higher (see Table 8). The total effect spread over a number of years will increase income by 0.76 per cent. Because income originating in agriculture during this period constituted only 50 per cent of the national income, the rest of the increase in income must have been contributed by the effect of agriculture on the rest of the economy.

Table 7

Deterministic and Stochastic Simulations, 1961-72

Year	NYI		IQI		IBKI		ICI	
	Deterministic Simulation	*Mean Stochastic Simulation*	*Deterministic Simulation*	*Mean Stochastic Simulation*	*Deterministic Simulation*	*Mean Stochastic Simulation*	*Deterministic Simulation*	*Mean Stochastic Simulation*
1961	105.09	105.02	115.45	115.15	130.99	131.74	102.15	100.88
1962	107.22	106.66	124.20	122.99	140.87	138.99	112.02	111.32
1963	111.03	110.97	131.35	131.14	152.33	151.43	115.51	115.41
1964	119.47	118.76	138.42	136.89	162.97	159.80	119.89	120.41
1965	113.49	112.76	151.31	149.20	181.74	178.24	128.77	127.65
1966	113.84	113.13	152.19	150.53	183.50	180.92	128.71	126.80
1967	126.42	126.25	156.16	155.76	193.19	192.80	126.19	125.52
1968	129.24	128.79	167.22	165.77	206.74	203.37	137.22	137.41
1969	134.02	134.30	168.98	169.62	204.28	205.60	145.16	144.41
1970	142.93	142.83	180.89	180.44	224.88	223.27	148.97	149.66
1971	145.72	145.51	189.83	189.38	233.65	223.02	160.82	159.94
1972	141.49	141.71	194.09	194.69	237.92	239.53	166.24	165.60
Mean Absolute Error	0.356	0.356	0.917	0.917	1.810	1.810	0.786	0.786
Mean Absolute Percentage Error	0.294	0.294	0.606	0.606	0.997	0.997	0.608	0.608

Sources: Calculations based on data in India, *Economic Survey*, various issues (Delhi: Controller of Publications, various years); and Reserve Bank of India, *Report on Currency and Finance*, various volumes (Bombay: Reserve Bank of India, various years).

Note: NYI stands for the index of national income; it is in 1960/61 prices. IQI stands for the index of industrial production; 1961/62 equals 100. IBKI stands for the index of the output of the basic and capital goods industries; 1960 equals 100. ICI stands for the index of the output of the consumer goods industries; 1960 equals 100.

Table 8

Simulated Trends in National Income, 1961-72

Year	*Simulation I*	*Simulation II*	*Simulation III*	*Simulation IV*	*Simulation V*
1961	105.089	105.089	105.089	102.23	105.65
1962	107.224	107.224	107.224	105.97	108.52
1963	111.032	111.595	111.058	109.96	113.13
1964	119.472	119.660	119.483	113.70	123.01
1965	113.488	113.497	113.498	117.96	117.33
1966	113.842	113.883	113.849	123.94	118.39
1967	126.423	126.444	126.428	127.59	132.52
1968	129.241	129.258	129.245	130.24	136.47
1969	134.019	134.030	134.022	132.99	142.61
1970	142.927	142.936	142.929	137.12	153.29
1971	145.724	145.731	145.725	140.45	157.43
1972	141.492	141.497	141.493	143.60	153.66

Sources: Calculations from data in India, *Economic Survey*, various issues (Delhi: Controller of Publications, various years); Reserve Bank of India, *Report on Currency and Finance*, various volumes (Bombay: Reserve Bank of India, various years); R.N.Lal, *Capital Formation and Its Financing in India* (Columbia, Mo.: South Asia Books, 1977); Vidya Pitre, "A Study of trends in India's Imports: 1960-61 to 1974-75," *Economic and Political Weekly*, May 9, 1981, pp. 851-862; and Isher J.Ahluwalia, *Behaviour of Prices and Output in India* (Madras: The Macmillan Company of India, 1979).

Notes: Simulation I is the basic model described in the text. The other four simulations add different assumptions to that model. Simulation II adds a one per cent increase in foodgrain and non-foodgrain output in 1963. Simulation III raises the foodgrain terms of trade in 1962 by one. Simulations IV assumes a steady increase in agricultural output. Simulation V raises the growth rate of agriculture by one per cent.

Effects of Foodgrain Terms-of-Trade

As stated before, the foodgrain terms-of-trade affect industrial production through the demand for industrial consumption goods and for basic and capital goods. The effect on consumption goods is direct. The effect on basic and capital goods is reflected through the impact on savings and investment. To assess the total effect on the system, these two effects must be combined.

The foodgrain terms-of-trade are treated as an endogenous variable in this system. Their effect on the system can be studied by raising the constant term in the foodgrain terms-of-trade equation by one and then tracing its effect on the total system. Thus, the model is simulated by increasing the constant term by one for the year 1962. This is Simulation III. Then the differences in national income that arise as a consequence are studied (see Table 8). The predicted values for five selected variables are given in Appendix 2, Table 12.

Increasing the foodgrain terms-of-trade by one in 1962 causes the index of national income to rise by 0.023 in 1963. In the second year the index of income goes up by 0.009, in the third year by 0.008, in the fourth year by 0.006 and in the fifth year by 0.004. The negative effect of a rise in the foodgrain terms-of-trade on consumption goods is almost compensated for by the positive effect, such a rise has on savings and investment and, therefore, on the production of basic and capital goods. Simulation results show that the net effect of a rise or fall in the foodgrain terms-of-trade on the economy is negligible. It must be noted, however, that the construction of the model ignores the effects of changes in the foodgrains terms-of-trade on production. If, in fact, production increases as a result of a rise in the foodgrain terms-of-trade, the positive effect may increase.[29]

Effects of a Steady Increase in Agriculture

To study the impact of a steady increase in agricultural output on the economy during this period, the actual values of agricultural output are replaced in Simulation IV by the values obtained by fitting a trend line. (Table 5 shows the growth rates of four select variables under this simulation.) The predicted values for five select variables are given in Appendix 2, Table 13. With a steady increase in agricultural output, national income increases by 3.12 per cent a year, compared with 3.10 per cent in Simulation I (see Table 5). Because no changes have been made in the annual imports of foodgrains, the steady increase moderates the fluctuations in the foodgrain terms-of-trade. For example, the foodgrain terms-of-trade according to Simulation I were 155.61 in 1966 and 162.49 in 1967. But with a steady increase in output and the same amount of imports, the foodgrain terms-of-trade for these two years were 133.99 and 143.23. The foodgrain terms-of-trade in Simulation IV are higher than in Simulation I in the later years because output is lower in those years according to the trend.

Effects of an Increase in the Agricultural Growth Rate

What would have been the effect on the economy if the growth rate in agriculture had been one per cent higher? According to the data for agricultural output, the annual rate of growth during the period studied was 2.35 per cent. The model is simulated using a growth rate in agriculture of 3.35 per cent. After obtaining trend values for the new growth rate, deviations from the trend are superimposed in the same proportions as in the historical period. This new set of data is used for agricultural output and then the model is simulated (Simulation V). (The growth rates for four select variables from this simulation are found in Table 5.) The effect on national income is shown in Table 8 and Appendix 2, Table 14 and contains the predicted values for five variables. The growth rate of national income in this simulation is 3.81 per cent, compared with 3.10 per cent in Simulation I. The growth rate of industrial production increases from 4.58 per cent to 5.08 per cent. The effect on industrial consumption goods is greater than that on basic and capital goods. One can conclude from this, as well as from Simulation II, that a one per cent increase in agricultural output has the effect of increasing the national income by a little more than 0.7 per cent. These results show that agriculture can act to some extent as a stimulus to industrial development.

V. CONCLUSION

The primary focus of this study is on determining the effects of agricultural performance on industrial growth. Agriculture influences industry in many ways. It provides the raw materials needed by agriculture-based industries. It generates direct demand for the output of consumption goods industries. It creates indirect demand for the output of basic and capital goods industries through its effect on the savings and investment of the different sectors.

In this report, a model is constructed to evaluate these interacting effects. Appropriate lag structures are also introduced. The model does not explicitly incorporate the demand for foodgrains that arises as a result of industrial growth. However, a part of this effect is captured through the foodgrain terms-of-trade. Thus, the model does not directly answer the question of what rate of growth in agriculture corresponds to a given rate of growth in industry. It poses the question the other way around. It asks what the impact on industry would be if agriculture grew at a certain rate. Data covering 12 years are used to estimate the quantitative relationships. It must be noted at the outset that the quantitative effects revealed by the data depend on the strategies of development that were actually adopted.

The main conclusion that emerges from this analysis is that agriculture exercises a reasonably strong influence on the growth of industry. The simulations show that a one per cent growth rate in agriculture can by itself generate a rate of growth of 0.5 per cent in industry. This is a strong influence considering that industrial growth is not totally dependent on what happens in agriculture. However, because the ability to raise the agricultural growth rate is limited, industry cannot rely on agriculture alone to stimulate growth.

The effects of agriculture's performance are felt by the consumption goods industries and by the basic and capital goods industries. The effect on demand for industrial consumption goods is direct. The effect on the output of basic and capital goods occurs through savings and investment. The savings and investment of the different sectors are affected by the size of agricultural output as well as by the terms-of-trade between agriculture and industry. The effects on the output of the capital and basic goods industries are less strong than the effects on the output of consumption goods industries.

Although agricultural output and the terms-of-trade, both influence industrial output, this study shows that the net effect of a rise in the foodgrain terms-of-trade on the economy is negligible. The negative effect on the output of consumer goods industries is cancelled out by the positive effect on the output of the basic and capital industries.

The importance of agriculture for industry lies not only in the raw materials supplied by agriculture but also in the demand for industrial output it generates. The quantitative estimates of the linkages show that the impulses generated by agriculture can have an important influence on the rest of the economy.

APPENDIX 1

DEFINITIONS OF VARIABLES

AQI	:	Index of agriculture production; its base period is the triennium ending in 1961/62.
DKIF	:	Capital inflows; in 1960/61 prices.
DMRMI	:	Index of inedible crude material imports, except fuel; 1960/61 prices.
DSAVPU	:	Savings of the public sector; in Rs.10 million.
FGTT	:	Index of the terms-of-trade of foodgrains; P_f / P_m
GCF	:	Gross fixed capital formation; the sum of GCFHH, GCFPC and GCFPU.
GCFHH	:	Gross fixed capital formation of households; in Rs 10 million, 1960/61 prices
GCFPC	:	Gross fixed capital formation of the private corporate sector; in Rs.10 million, 1960/61 prices.
GCFPU	:	Gross fixed capital formation of the public sector; in Rs.10 million, 1960/61 prices.
IBKI	:	Index of the output of the basic and capital goods industries; 1960 equals 100.
ICI	:	Index of the output of the consumer goods industries, 1960 equals 100.
IQI	:	Index of industrial production; 1960 equals 100.
MKI	:	Imports of capital goods (Rs.10 million) deflated by the unit value index of capital goods imports.
NAFG	:	Net availability of foodgrains; imports of one year plus domestic production of the year before.
NFGTT	:	Index of the terms-of-trade for non-foodgrains; P_{nf} / P_m.
NFI	:	Index of non-foodgrain production; its base period is the triennium ending in 1961/62.
NYI	:	Index of national income; in 1960/61 prices.
P_f	:	Price index of foodgrains; 1961/62 equals 100.
P_m	:	Price index of finished manufactured goods; 1961/62 equals 100.
P_{nf}	:	Price index of non-foodgrains; 1961/62 equals 100.
TT	:	Index of the terms-of-trade; the ratio of the price of agricultural commodities to the price of manufactured finished products.

APPENDIX 2

SIMULATION TABLES

Table 9

Actual Values of Six Endogenous Variables, 1961-72

Year	*NYI*	*IQI*	*IBKI*	*ICI*	*FGTT*	*TT*
1961	103.51	109.2	114.4	106.6	100.00	100.00
1962	105.50	119.8	136.1	108.0	101.94	99.32
1963	111.37	129.7	154.0	110.4	109.52	103.24
1964	119.77	140.8	169.3	118.6	135.20	121.20
1965	113.72	153.8	189.8	127.5	132.75	122.16
1966	114.73	153.2	184.8	131.3	147.58	134.35
1967	124.12	152.6	185.1	125.7	179.53	148.20
1968	127.70	163.0	199.6	131.9	152.27	135.90
1969	135.84	175.3	212.6	145.3	147.57	139.14
1970	143.98	184.3	222.6	154.1	138.93	135.14
1971	145.50	186.1	230.8	159.7	134.37	124.75
1972	143.62	199.4	250.1	167.2	147.62	130.98

Sources: Calculations from data in India, *Economic Survey*, various issues (Delhi: Controller of Publications, various years); Reserve Bank of India, *Report on Currency and Finance*, various volumes (Bombay: Reserve Bank of India, various years); R.N.Lal, *Capital formation and Its Financing in India* (Columbia, Mo.: South Asia Books, 1977); Vidya Pitre, "A Study of trends in India's Imports: 1960-61 to 1974-75," *Economic and Political Weekly*, May 9, 1981, pp. 851-862; and Isher J.Ahluwalia, *Behaviour of Prices and Output in India* (Madras: The Macmillan Company of India, 1979).

Notes: NYI stands for the index of national income; it is in 1960/61 prices. IQI stands for the index of industrial production; 1960 equals 100. IBKI stands for the index of the output of the basic and capital goods industries; 1960 equals 100. ICI stands for the index of the output of the consumer goods industries; 1960 equals 100. FGTT stands for the index of the terms-of-trade for foodgrains, defined as the ratio of the price index of foodgrains (1961/62 equals 100) to the price index of manufactured goods (1961/62 equals 100). TT stands for the index of the terms-of-trade, defined as the ratio of the price of agricultural commodities to the price of manufactured finished products.

Table 10

Predicted Values of Six Endogenous Variables, Simulation 1, 1961-72

Year	*NYI*	*IQI*	*IBKI*	*ICI*	*FGTT*	*TT*
1961	105.09	115.45	130.99	102.15	101.24	100.53
1962	107.22	124.20	140.87	112.00	113.22	110.83
1963	111.03	131.35	152.33	115.51	125.04	113.94
1964	119.47	138.42	162.97	119.89	129.41	119.84
1965	113.49	151.31	181.74	128.77	122.65	114.11
1966	113.84	152.19	183.50	128.71	155.61	134.95
1967	126.42	156.16	193.19	126.19	162.49	140.81
1968	129.24	167.22	206.74	137.22	141.45	128.77
1969	134.02	168.98	204.28	145.16	148.92	136.27
1970	142.93	180.89	224.88	148.97	142.76	129.42
1971	145.72	189.83	233.65	160.82	140.89	130.67
1972	141.49	194.09	237.98	166.24	147.57	137.76

Sources: Calculations from data in India, *Economic Survey*, various issues (Delhi: Controller of Publications, various years); Reserve Bank of India, *Report on Currency and Finance*, various volumes (Bombay: Reserve Bank of India, various years); R.N.Lal, *Capital formation and Its Financing in India* (Columbia, Mo.: South Asia Books, 1977); Vidya Pitre, "A Study of trends in India's Imports: 1960-61 to 1974-75," *Economic and Political Weekly*, May 9, 1981, pp. 851-862; and Isher J.Ahluwalia, *Behaviour of Prices and Output in India* (Madras: The Macmillan Company of India, 1979).

Notes: NYI stands for the index of national income; it is in 1960/61 prices. IQI stands for the index of industrial production; 1960 equals 100. IBKI stands for the index of the output of the basic and capital goods industries; 1960 equals 100. ICI stands for the index of the output of the consumer goods industries; 1960 equals 100. FGTT stands for the index of the terms-of-trade for foodgrains, defined as the ratio of the price index of foodgrains (1961/62 equals 100) to the price index of manufactured goods (1961/62 equals 100). TT stands for the index of the terms-of-trade, defined as the ratio of the price of agricultural commodities to the price of manufactured finished products.

Simulation I is the basic model described in the text.

Table 11

Predicted Values of Six Endogenous Variables, Simulation II, 1961-72

Year	*NYI*	*IQI*	*IBKI*	*ICI*	*FGTT*	*TT*
1961	105.09	115.45	130.99	102.15	101.24	100.53
1962	107.22	124.20	140.87	112.00	113.22	110.83
1963	111.59	131.35	152.33	115.51	124.69	113.79
1964	119.60	138.97	163.68	120.39	128.38	118.98
1965	113.49	151.34	181.46	129.20	122.91	114.44
1966	113.88	152.31	183.74	128.69	155.68	134.98
1967	126.44	156.22	193.27	126.25	162.60	140.89
1968	129.26	167.28	206.81	137.25	141.52	128.82
1969	134.03	169.01	204.33	145.18	148.97	136.28
1970	142.94	180.91	224.91	148.99	142.80	129.45
1971	145.73	189.85	233.68	160.83	140.92	130.69
1972	141.50	194.09	237.99	166.25	147.59	137.77

Sources: Calculations from data in India, *Economic Survey*, various issues (Delhi: Controller of Publications, various years); Reserve Bank of India, *Report on Currency and Finance*, various volumes (Bombay: Reserve Bank of India, various years); R.N.Lal, *Capital formation and Its Financing in India* (Columbia, Mo.: South Asia Books, 1977); Vidya Pitre, "A Study of trends in India's Imports: 1960-61 to 1974-75," *Economic and Political Weekly*, May 9, 1981, pp. 851-862; and Isher J. Ahluwalia, *Behaviour of Prices and Output in India* (Madras: The Macmillan Company of India, 1979).

Notes: NYI stands for the index of national income; it is in 1960/61 prices. IQI stands for the index of industrial production; 1960 equals 100. IBKI stands for the index of the output of the basic and capital goods industries; 1960 equals 100. ICI stands for the index of the output of the consumer goods industries; 1960 equals 100. FGTT stands for the index of the terms-of-trade for foodgrains, defined as the ratio of the price index of foodgrains (1961/62 equals 100) to the price index of manufactured goods (1961/62 equals 100). TT stands for the index of the terms-of-trade, defined as the ratio of the price of agricultural commodities to the price of manufactured finished products.

Simulation II adds a one per cent increase in foodgrain and non-foodgrain output in 1963 to the basic model described in the text.

Table 12

Predicted Values of Six Endogenous Variables, Simulation III, 1961-72

Year	*NYI*	*IQI*	*IBKI*	*ICI*	*FGTT*	*TT*
1961	105.09	115.45	130.99	102.15	101.24	100.53
1962	107.22	124.20	140.87	112.00	114.22	111.27
1963	111.06	131.43	152.55	115.42	125.24	113.98
1964	119.48	138.45	163.01	119.92	129.51	119.89
1965	113.50	151.34	181.79	128.78	122.69	114.13
1966	113.88	152.21	183.53	128.72	155.64	134.97
1967	126.43	156.17	193.22	126.19	162.52	140.83
1968	129.25	167.23	206.75	137.23	141.46	128.78
1969	134.02	168.99	204.29	145.16	148.93	136.25
1970	142.93	180.89	224.88	148.98	142.77	129.43
1971	145.73	189.84	233.65	160.82	140.91	130.68
1972	141.49	194.09	237.98	166.24	147.58	137.76

Sources: Calculations from data in India, *Economic Survey*, various issues (Delhi: Controller of Publications, various years); Reserve Bank of India, *Report on Currency and Finance*, various volumes (Bombay: Reserve Bank of India, various years); R.N.Lal, *Capital formation and Its Financing in India* (Columbia, Mo.: South Asia Books, 1977); Vidya Pitre, "A Study of trends in India's Imports: 1960-61 to 1974-75," *Economic and Political Weekly*, May 9, 1981, pp. 851-862; and Isher J. Ahluwalia, *Behaviour of Prices and Output in India* (Madras: The Macmillan Company of India, 1979).

Notes: NYI stands for the index of national income; it is in 1960/61 prices. IQI stands for the index of industrial production; 1960 equals 100. IBKI stands for the index of the output of the basic and capital goods industries; 1960 equals 100. ICI stands for the index of the output of the consumer goods industries; 1960 equals 100. FGTT stands for the index of the terms-of-trade for foodgrains, defined as the ratio of the price index of foodgrains (1961/62 equals 100) to the price index of manufactured goods (1961/62 equals 100). TT stands for the index of the terms-of-trade, defined as the ratio of the price of agricultural commodities to the price of manufactured finished products.

Simulation III is the basic model described in the text with the foodgrain terms-of-trade raised by one in 1962.

Table 13

Predicted Values of Six Endogenous Variables, Simulation IV, 1961-72

Year	*NYI*	*IQI*	*IBKI*	*ICI*	*FGTT*	*TT*
1961	102.23	114.34	130.99	99.22	110.23	103.88
1962	105.97	121.56	138.33	108.43	120.42	111.86
1963	109.96	129.41	150.43	112.93	124.92	112.32
1964	113.70	136.44	160.20	118.38	128.37	118.92
1965	117.96	144.90	173.08	123.46	131.11	121.96
1966	123.94	158.26	194.87	129.49	133.99	123.23
1967	127.59	164.75	200.89	138.54	143.23	132.74
1968	130.24	168.22	204.54	142.82	148.48	134.98
1969	132.99	171.90	209.67	145.65	149.78	134.69
1970	137.12	179.48	222.08	149.00	149.46	133.37
1971	140.45	184.61	227.77	154.94	152.91	136.48
1972	143.60	189.13	233.60	159.04	155.31	141.18

Sources: Calculations from data in India, *Economic Survey*, various issues (Delhi: Controller of Publications, various years); Reserve Bank of India, *Report on Currency and Finance*, various volumes (Bombay: Reserve Bank of India, various years); R.N.Lal, *Capital formation and Its Financing in India* (Columbia, Mo.: South Asia Books, 1977); Vidya Pitre, "A Study of trends in India's Imports: 1960-61 to 1974-75," *Economic and Political Weekly*, May 9, 1981, pp. 851-862; and Isher J. Ahluwalia, *Behaviour of Prices and Output in India* (Madras: The Macmillan Company of India, 1979).

Notes: NYI stands for the index of national income; it is in 1960/61 prices. IQI stands for the index of industrial production; 1960 equals 100. IBKI stands for the index of the output of the basic and capital goods industries; 1960 equals 100. ICI stands for the index of the output of the consumer goods industries; 1960 equals 100. FGTT stands for the index of the terms-of-trade for foodgrains, defined as the ratio of the price index of foodgrains (1961/62 equals 100) to the price index of manufactured goods (1961/62 equals 100). TT stands for the index of the terms-of-trade, defined as the ratio of the price of agricultural commodities to the price of manufactured finished products.

Simulation IV is the basic model described in the text with a trend line added that shows agricultural output increasing steadily.

Table 14

Predicted Values of Six Endogenous Variables, Simulation V, 1961-72

Year	*NYI*	*IQI*	*IBKI*	*ICI*	*FGTT*	*TT*
1961	105.65	115.45	130.99	102.15	100.96	100.34
1962	108.52	124.73	141.56	112.49	111.64	109.78
1963	113.13	132.48	153.52	116.90	122.21	114.72
1964	123.01	141.32	166.91	122.26	126.04	117.59
1965	117.33	154.73	185.35	132.95	120.75	112.47
1966	118.39	156.08	187.83	133.18	151.53	132.12
1967	132.52	160.58	197.85	131.60	157.24	137.41
1968	136.47	173.18	213.26	144.19	131.75	123.00
1969	142.61	175.79	211.11	153.99	139.02	130.62
1970	153.29	189.28	233.75	159.23	130.64	122.40
1971	157.43	199.91	244.21	173.27	125.88	122.32
1972	153.66	205.51	249.73	180.62	135.48	130.66

Sources: Calculations from data in India, *Economic Survey*, various issues (Delhi: Controller of Publications, various years); Reserve Bank of India, *Report on Currency and Finance*, various volumes (Bombay: Reserve Bank of India, various years); R.N.Lal, *Capital formation and Its Financing in India* (Columbia, Mo.: South Asia Books, 1977); Vidya Pitre, "A Study of Trends in India's Imports: 1960-61 to 1974-75," *Economic and Political Weekly*, May 9, 1981, pp. 851-862; and Isher J. Ahluwalia, *Behaviour of Prices and Output in India* (Madras: The Macmillan Company of India, 1979).

Notes: NYI stands for the index of national income; it is in 1960/61 prices. IQI stands for the index of industrial production; 1960 equals 100. IBKI stands for the index of the output of the basic and capital goods industries; 1960 equals 100. ICI stands for the index of the output of the consumer goods industries; 1960 equals 100. FGTT stands for the index of the terms-of-trade for foodgrains, defined as the ratio of the price index of foodgrains (1961/62 equals 100) to the price index of manufactured goods (1961/62 equals 100). TT stands for the index of the terms-of-trade, defined as the ratio of the price of agricultural commodities to the price of manufactured finished products.

Simulation V is the basic model described in the text with the growth rate of agriculture increased by one per cent.

APPENDIX 3

FIGURES COMPARING ACTUAL AND SIMULATED VALUES

Figure 2

Index of National Income, Actual and Simulated, 1961-72

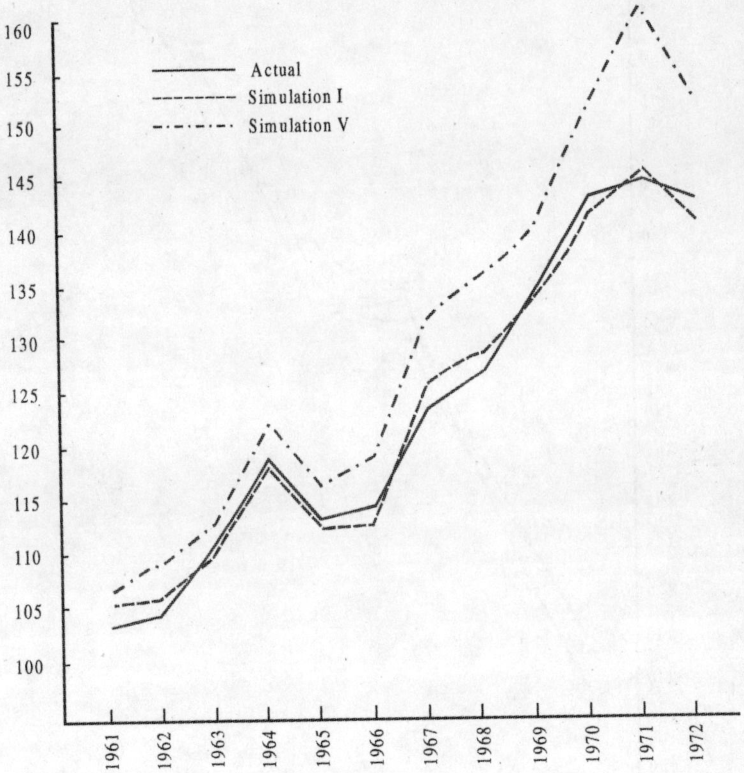

Source: India, *Economic Survey*, various issues (Delhi: Controller of Publications, various years.)

Note: Simulation I is the basic model described in the text. Simulation V uses the model but increases the growth rate of agriculture by one per cent.

Figure 3

Index of Industrial Production, Actual and Simulated, 1961-72

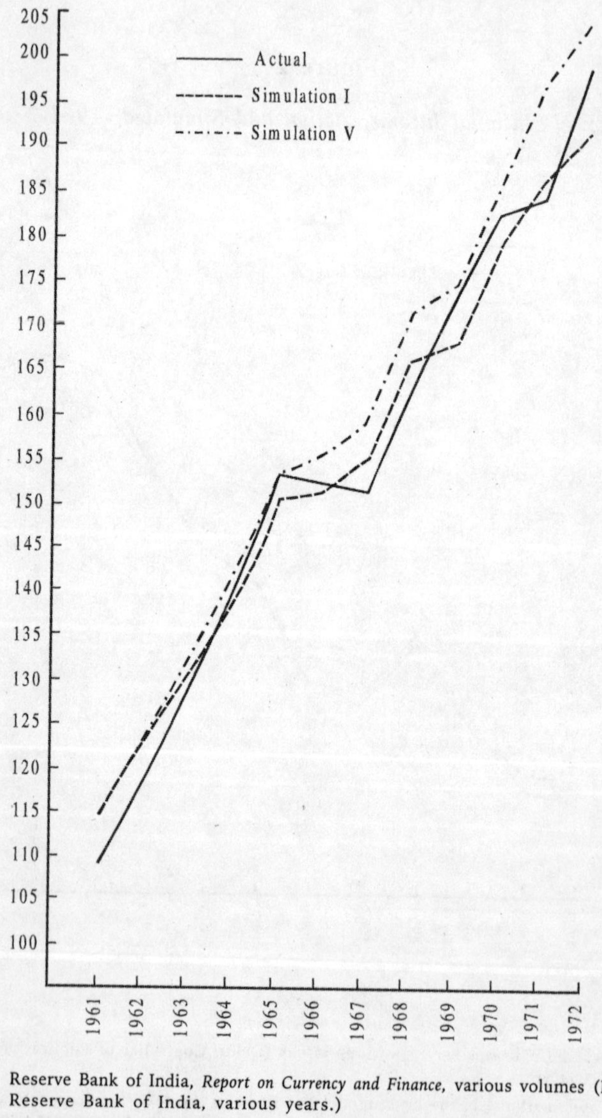

Source: Reserve Bank of India, *Report on Currency and Finance*, various volumes (Bombay: Reserve Bank of India, various years.)

Note: Simulation I is the basic model described in the text. Simulation V uses the model but increases the growth rate of agriculture by one per cent.

Figure 4

Index of the Output of the Consumer Goods Industries, Actual and Simulated, 1961-72

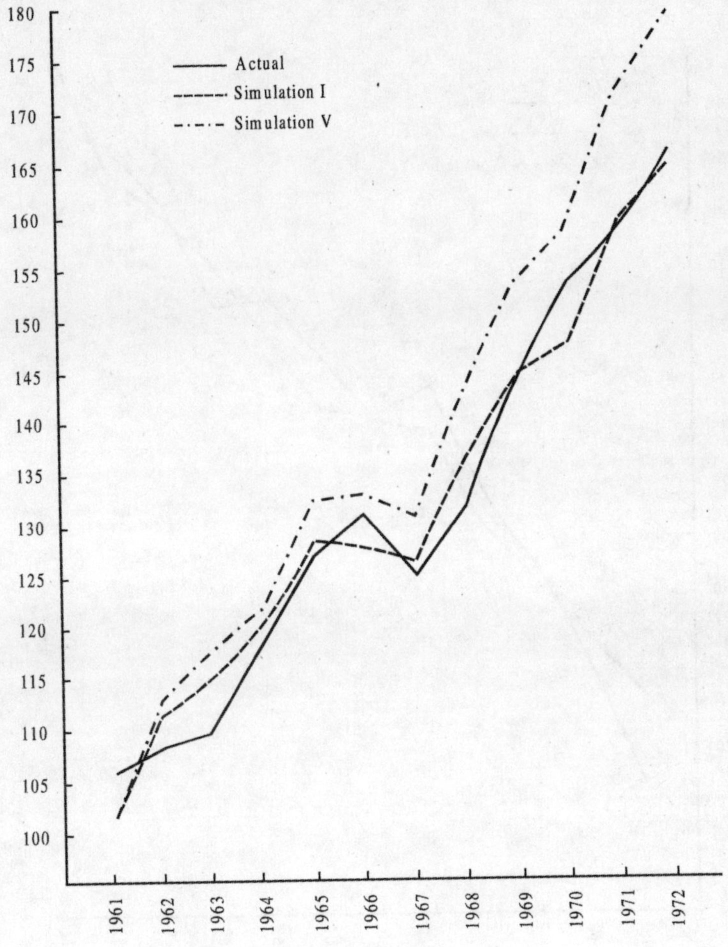

Source: Reserve Bank of India, *Report on Currency and Finance*, various volumes (Bombay: Reserve Bank of India, various years.)

Note: Simulation I is the basic model described in the text. Simulation V uses the model but increases the growth rate of agriculture by one per cent.

Figure 5

Index of the Output of the Basic and Capital Goods Industries, Actual and Simulated, 1961-72

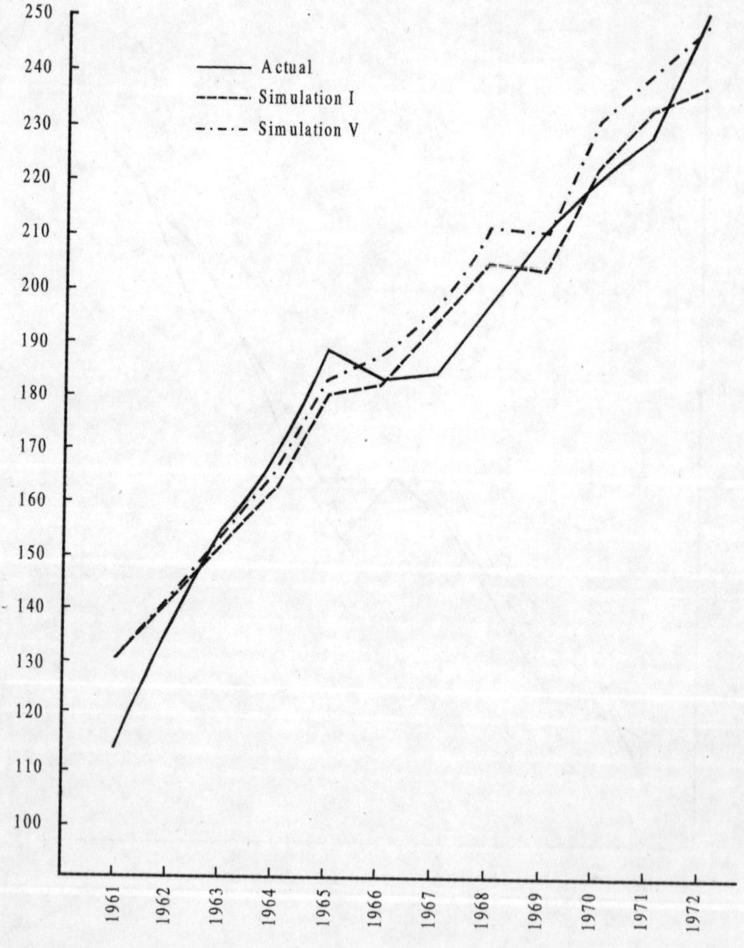

Source: Reserve Bank of India, *Report on Currency and Finance,* various volumes (Bombay: Reserve Bank of India, various years.)

Note: Simulation I is the basic model described in the text. Simulation V uses the model but increases the growth rate of agriculture by one per cent.

Figure 6

Foodgrain Terms-of-Trade, Actual and Simulated, 1961-72

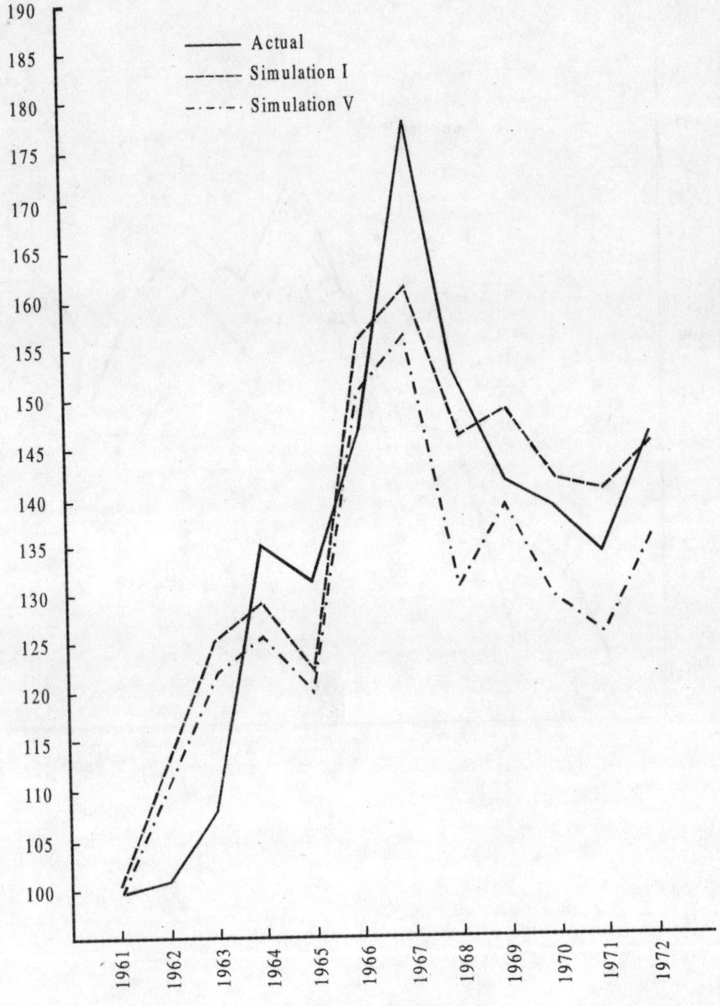

Source: India, *Economic Survey*, various issues (Delhi: Controller of Publications, various years.)

Note: Simulation I is the basic model described in the text. Simulation V uses the model but increases the growth rate of agriculture by one per cent.

Figure 7

Terms-of-Trade, Actual and Simulated, 1961-72

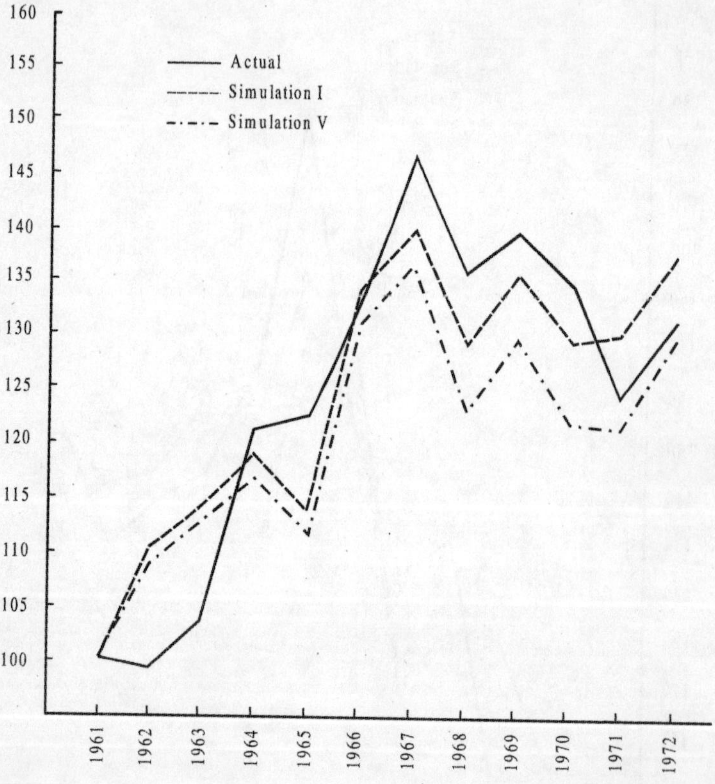

Source: India, *Economic Survey*, various issues (Delhi: Controller of Publications, various years.)

Note: Simulation I is the basic model described in the text. Simulation V uses the model but increases the growth rate of agriculture by one per cent.

Bibliography

Ahluwalia, Isher J., *Behaviour of Prices and Output in India*. Madras: The Macmillan Company of India, 1979.

Asian Development Bank, *Rural Asia: Challenge and Opportunity*. New York: Praeger Publishers, 1978.

Chakravarty, S., "On the Question of Home Market and Prospects for Indian Growth." *Economic and Political Weekly*. Annual Number, August 1979, pp. 1229-1242.

Fisher, Franklin M., "Dynamic Structure and Estimation in Models." *In The Brookings Quarterly Econometric Model of the United States*, pp. 589-635. Edited by J. S. Duesenberry, E. Kirk, G. Fromm, and L.R. Klein. Chicago: Rand McNally, 1965.

India, *Economic Survey* various issues, Delhi: Controller of Publications, various years.

India, Ministry of Agriculture and Irrigation, Directorate of Economics and Statistics. *Estimates of Area and Production of Principal Crops in India*, various issues, Delhi: Controller of Publications, various years.

Lal, R. N., *Capital Formation and Its Financing in India*. Columbia, Mo.: South Asia Books, 1977.

Lele, Uma and Mellor, John W., "Technological Change, Distributive Bias and Labour Transfer in a Two Sector Economy," *Oxford Economic Papers* 33 (November 1981): pp. 426-441.

Mellor, John W., "Food Price Policy and Income Distribution in Low-Income Countries." *Economic Development and Cultural Change* 27 (October 1978): pp. 1-26.

———. *The New Economics of Growth., A Strategy for India and the Developing World*. ithaca, N.Y.: Cornell University Press, 1976.

Mitra, Ashok, *Terms of Trade and Class Relations. An Essay in Political Economy* London: Frank Cass, 1977.

Nadkarni, M.V., "Marketable Surplus and Market Dependence: A Millet Region of Maharashtra." *Economic and Political Weekly*, March 29, 1980, pp. A13-A24.

Narain, Dharm, *Distribution of the Marketed Surplus of Agricultural Produce by Size-Level of Holdings in India*: 1950-51. Bombay: Asia Publishing House, 1961.

National Council of Applied Economic Research, *All India Household Survey of income, Savings, and Consumer Expenditure*, New Delhi: NCAER, 1972.

Nayyar, D., "Industrial Development in India: Some Reflections on Growth and Stagnation." *Economic and Political Weekly* Special Number, August 1978, pp. 1265-1278.

Patnaik, P., "Disproportionality Crisis and Cyclical Growth." *Economic and Political Weekly*, Annual Number, February 1972, pp. 329-336.

Pitre, Vidya, "A Study of Trends in India's Imports: 1960-61 to 1974-75." *Economic and Political Weekly*, May 9, 1981, pp. 851-862.

Radhakrishna, R., "Demand Functions and Their Development Implications in a Dual Economy, India." *The Developing Economies* 16 (June 1978): pp. 199-210.

Raj, K. N., "Growth and Stagnation in India's Industrial Development." *Economic and Political Weekly* Annual Number, February 1976, pp. 223-236.

Rangarajan, C. "Strategic Issues in Industrial Development." *The Economic Scene*, January 1980, pp. 7-14.

Reserve Bank of India, *Report on Currency and Finance*, various volumes, Bombay: Reserve Bank of India, various years.

———. "Inter-Industry Transactions in the Indian Economy", *Reserve Bank of India Bulletin*, November 1978, pp. 892-935.

Roy, S., "Demand for Industrial Consumer Goods in India – A Study of Linkages." Ph,D. thesis, Indian Institute of Management, Ahmedabad.

Rudra, A. *Relative Rates of Growth – Agriculture and Industry*. Bombay: University of Bombay, 1967.

Somyajulu, V.V.N. "Structural Changes and Growth in Indian Industries 1946-1970.": *Asian Economic Review* 16 (December 1974): pp. 131-184.

Sowey, Eric R. "Stochastic Simulation of Macro Econometric Models: Methodology and Interpretation." *In Econometric Studies of Macro and Monetary Relations*, pp. 195-227. Edited by Alan A. Powell and Ross A. Williams, New York: Elsevier-North Holland, 1973.

Srinivasan, T.N. and Narayan, N.S.S. "Economic Performance in Stimulating Agricultural Production in a Developing Economy." *Economic and Political Weekly*, Annual Number, February 1977, pp. 225-240.

Thamarajakshi, R., "Role of Price Incentives in Stimulating Agricultural Production in a Developing Economy". *In Food Enough or Starvation for Millions*, pp. 325-479. Edited by Douglas Ensminger, Columbia, MO.: University of Missouri, 1976.

Vaidyanathan, A., "Constraints on Growth and Policy Options," *Economic and Political Weekly*, September 17,1977, pp. 1643-1650.

* The author wishes to thank John Mellor, Dharm Narain, G.M. Desai, K. Krishnamurthi, Afzal Ali, B.M. Desai, and C. G. Ranade for many useful discussions on points raised in the paper. They are, however, in no way responsible for any errors that may remain in the paper. The author is also grateful to Nguyen Khai and Veena Padia for the excellent computational assistance they provided in Washington and Ahmedabad.

Notes

1. These two direct links between agricultural production and industrial production will be weakened if the industrial inputs required by agriculture are imported or if the agricultural inputs used in industry are exported, instead of being processed domestically.

2. For a discussion of this type of effect and some empirical estimates see: R. Radhakrishna, "Demand Functions and Their Development Implications in a Dual Economy, India," *The Developing Economies* 16 (June 1978): pp. 199-210.

3. The deceleration in industrial growth since 1966 has been the subject of many studies. For example, see: P. Patnaik, "Disproportionality Crisis and Cyclical Growth," *Economic and Political Weekly*, Annual Number, February 1972, pp. 329-336; K.N. Raj, "Growth and Stagnation in India's Industrial Development," *Economic and Political Weekly*, Annual Number, February 1976. pp. 223-236; T.N. Srinivasan and N.S.S. Narayan, "Economic Performance since the Third Plan and its Implications for Policy," *Economic and Political Weekly*, Annual Number, February 1977, pp. 225-240; A. Vaidyanathan, "Constraints on Growth and Policy Options," *Economic and Political Weekly*, September 17, 1977, pp. 1643-1650; D. Nayyar, "Industrial Development in India: Some Reflections on Growth and stagnation," *Economic and Political Weekly* Special Number, August 1978, pp. 1265 -1278; S. Chakravarty, "On the Question of Home Market and Prospects for Indian Growth," *Economic and Political Weekly* Annual Number, August 1979, pp. 1229-1242; C. Rangarajan, "Strategic Issues in Industrial Development," *The Economic Scene*, January 1980, pp. 7-14.

4. For a pioneering study of the links between agriculture and industry, see A. Rudra, *Relative Rates of Growth – Agriculture and Industry* (Bombay: University of Bombay, 1967).

5. Several ratios for understanding the agriculture-industry linkages are suggested in Asian Development Bank: *Rural Asia Challenge and Opportunity* (New York: Praeger Publishers, 1978), pp. 102-126 and pp. 362-383.

6. Ibid.

7. Figures are taken from Reserve Bank of India, "Inter-industry Transactions in the Indian Economy," *Reserve Bank of India Bulletin*, November 1978, pp. 892-935.

8. In 1972, U.S. $ 1.00 was equal to Re. 0.13. A crore equals 10 million.

9. The A matrix of input coefficients that was obtained was as follows:

0.1812	0.1242	0.0199
0.0415	0.3887	0.1678
0.0112	0.0968	0.0949

The $(1 - A)^{-1}$ matrix was:

1.2357	0.2630	0.0760
0.0907	1.7046	0.3181
0.0250	0.1857	1.1399

10. National Sample Survey statistics show that the top 10 per cent of the rural population accounts for 38 per cent of the rural consumption of industrial goods. It has remained more or less at this level for several rounds. For details see S. Roy, "Demand for Industrial Consumer Goods in India- A Study of Linkages" (Ph.D. thesis, Indian Institute of Management).

11. Many studies have shown that the bulk of the marketable surplus is concentrated in the hands of large landholders. See Dharm Narain, *Distribution of the Marketed Surplus of Agricultural Produce by Size-Level of holdings in India*: 1950-51 (Bombay: Asia Publishing House, 1961). A recent micro study on Maharashtra shows that, for wheat, land holdings of more than 10 acres accounted for 60 per cent of the total marketed surplus. Taking all foodgrains into account, these holdings accounted for 80 per cent of the marketed surplus. See M.V. Nadkarni, "Marketable Surplus and Market Dependence: A Millet Region of Maharashtra," *Economic and Political Weekly*, March 29, 1980, pp. AI4-A16.

12. Rural non-food expenditures were computed by applying the ratio of rural non-food expenditures to total non-food expenditures as revealed by the national income statistics on total non-food consumption expenditures. Food expenditures included those on cereals, milk and milk products, edible oils, meat, eggs, fish, sugar, salt, and other foods. Expenditures on these items as well as rent and taxes were deducted from total consumption expenditures to obtain non-food consumption expenditures.

13. Two years for which NSS data were not available were omitted.

14. The pure-price effect of an increase in food prices on the demand for non-food items has been found to be negative. See Radhakrishna, "Demand Functions and Their Implications," pp. 199-210; John W. Mellor, "Food Price Policy and Income Distribution in Low-Income Countries," *Economic Development and Cultural Change* 27 (October 1978): pp. 1-26.

    One way of separating the pure-price effect from the kind of income effect referred to here is to introduce the index multiplied by terms-of-trade – not the index of agricultural output – as an independent variable to indicate the buying power of agriculture. If, along with this variable, the price of food grains is introduced, the two effects can be separated.

15. Data on the index of marketed surplus were taken from R. Thamarajakshi's article "Role of Price Incentives in Stimulating Agricultural Production in a Developing Economy," *in Food Enough or Starvation for millions*, ed. Douglas Ensminger (Columbia, Mo.: University of Missouri, 1976), pp. 325-479.

16. Government savings as a percentage of tax revenue fell from 18 per cent in 1965/66 to 12 per cent in 1966/67 and to nine per cent in 1967/68.

17. National Council of Applied Economic Research, *All India Household Survey of Income, Savings, and Consumer Expenditure* (New Delhi: NCAER, 1972), p. 81.

18. For an analysis of this problem, see Ashok Mitra, Terms of Trade and Class Relations. An Essay in *Political Economy* (London: Frank Cass, 1977), pp. 147-158. Also see John W. Mellor, *The New Economics of Growth. A Strategy for India and the Developing World* (Ithaca, N. Y.: Cornell University Press, 1976), pp. 138-141.

19. The total terms-of-trade variable and the foodgrain terms-of-trade variable used in these equations are taken from Thamarajakshi, "Role of Price Incentives." She defines the total terms-of-trade as the net barter terms-of-trade of all products traded between agriculture and non-agriculture. The foodgrain terms-of-trade are defined as the ratio of the price of foodgrains to the price of non-agricultural products purchased by agriculture.

20. It is possible to make agricultural output an endogenous variable by making it a function of past investment and the terms-of-trade between agriculture and industry, which are determined within the system, and certain other exogenous variables, such as weather. For one such attempt see Isher J, Ahluwalia, *Behaviour of prices and Output in India* (Madras: The Macmillan Company of India, 1979). However, because this paper stresses the effects of agriculture on industry, agricultural output is treated as an exogenous variable in the model.

21. Consider the following identity:

$$NYI = a_1\ AQI + a_2\ IQI + a_3\ SI,$$

where NYI, AQI, and IQI have the same meaning as before and SI is the index of income originating from the service sector. Suppose that:

$$SI = b_0 + b_1\ AQI + b_2\ IQI + U.$$

Then, if the latter is substituted for the former, then:

$$NYI = a_3\ b_0 + (a_1 + a_3\ b_1)\ AQI + (a_2 + a_3\ b_2)\ IQI + a_3 U.$$

22. Chapter 3 differentiates between rural and urban non-food consumption expenditures, showing why the ratio of agricultural prices to the prices of manufactured goods has different effects in rural and urban areas. Logically, that dichotomy should have been used in the macro model also. Unfortunately, there are not enough data available to build a separate series showing consumption of industrial consumption goods in rural and urban areas. Therefore, only one equation is used. The inclusion of the foodgrain terms-of-trade of the previous year in equation (2) also needs some explanation. What this equation implies is that demand of industrial consumption goods in the current year is determined by the effective income of the previous year. This income is decomposed into two parts–output and relative price.

23. The market for foodgrains may be specified:

$F^d = a - bp_f + c\ IQI$ (demand for food),

$F^s = \bar{s}_f$ (supply of foodgrains), and

$F^d = F^s$ (equilibrium condition),

where F is the quantity of foodgrains, p_f is the price of foodgrains, and IQI is the index of industrial production. In the demand equation, the appropriate income variable is taken as the index of industrial production. It follows from this that

$$p_f\ a/b - 1/b\ F + c/b\ IQI.$$

24. In a recursive system, ordinary least squares can be used to estimate the equations, provided the error terms of the equations are independent. The Proximity Theorem of World somewhat modifies the rigor of these conditions. As Franklin M. Fisher put it, "If all terms above the diagonal in A are nearly zero; if cross equation covariance between contemporary disturbances is small and if there is little serial correlation, ordinary least squares will not do too badly. "(Franklin M. Fisher: "Dynamic Structure and Estimation in Models," in *The Brookings Quarterly Econometric Model of the United States*, ed. J.S. Duesenberry, E. Kirk, Go Fromm, and L. R. Klein [Chicago: Rand McNally, 1965], p. 598).

25. If marketable surplus is used as an independent variable, one can relate it at the next stage to total agricultural output and income distribution. It may then be possible to study the impact of income distribution on the entire system. The link between marketable surplus and the terms-of-trade and the relative share of labour is discussed in Uma Lele and John W. Mellor, "Technological Change, Distributive Bias and Labour Transfer in a Two Sector Economy," *Oxford Economic Papers* 33 (November 1981): pp 426-441.

26. The explanatory power of the equation relating to gross fixed capital formation in the private corporate sector is not good. However, when the time period is extended to begin in 1952/53, the same equation offers a significantly better explanation, as can be seen in Chapter 3.

27. The variables are defined in Appendix 1.

28. For an examination of the role and purpose of stochastic simulation see Eric R. Sowey, "Stochastic Simulation of Macro Econometric Models: Methodology and Interpretation" in *Econometric Studies of Macro and Monetary Relations*., ed. Alan A. Powell and Ross A. Williams (New York: Elsevier- North Holland, 1973), pp. 195-227.

29. The possible effects on agricultural output of a rise in the terms-of-trade in favour of agriculture under conditions of stagnant and changing technologies is discussed in John W. Mellor, "Food Price Policy," pp. 1-26. Ashok Mitra is, however, quite emphatic in his conclusion. He writes, "It is not possible to argue that, in India, the output of most of the principal crops has responded positively to the shift in terms-of-trade in favour of agriculture." See Ashok Mitra, *Terms of Trade and Class Relations*., p. 121.

2

Industrial Growth

Another Look

An aspect of the Indian economy that has been causing concern in recent years is the deceleration in the rate of growth of industrial production. It is to this question that this paper is addressed. In many ways, India's industrial performance since Independence has been impressive. Notwithstanding the difficulties faced in the measurement of industrial output over a long span of time — an issue to which we shall come later — there is enough evidence to indicate that aggregate industrial output has increased fivefold over a 30-year period, giving a compound rate of growth of six per cent per annum.

The performance looks even more impressive if it is judged by the criterion of the range and sophistication of the output manufactured. The output of capital goods industries, which consists primarily of machinery, had a weight of less than five per cent in the index of industrial production in 1956; its weight has increased to almost 16 per cent in 1970. The output of basic and capital goods industries, taken together, now account for 50 per cent of the total value added in industrial production. This striking change in the composition of industrial output is also reflected in India's exports. Engineering goods had a negligible share in India's total exports in 1950. They now have a share of almost 11 per cent.

While India's performance in the industrial sector is certainly impressive since Independence, compared to the rate of growth of two per cent per annum experienced by the country in the previous 50 years, there are some disturbing trends in the rate of growth of industrial production which call for serious attention. A feature of

Economic and Political Weekly, Vol. XVII, Nos. 14, 15 and 16, Annual Number 1982.

industrial performance which has been the subject of many writings and discussions in recent years has been the fact that while industrial production increased at an average rate of 7.8 per cent in the decade following 1955, the rate of growth fell to 3.7 per cent in the next decade 1965-75. Even if we include the more recent years, when performance has been slightly better, the rate of growth comes to only 4.3 per cent. The data on industrial production, available for 15 years since 1965, indicate that of the 15 years, there are two years in which the growth rate was negative and four years in which the annual rate of growth was less than two per cent.

Violent fluctuations in agricultural output are understandable in a country which is highly dependent on the bounties or otherwise of nature. But sharp fluctuations in industrial output have raised the question whether there is something endemic in the economic system which has been responsible for this or whether it is simply a coincidence of circumstances.

Before taking up the various hypotheses that have been offered to explain the phenomenon of deceleration, let us briefly highlight some of the features of industrial performance that deserve attention in this context. As mentioned earlier, there are difficulties in computing any index over a long time-span. The weights keep changing, and that makes comparison between one time period and another very difficult. We can construct an index based on common, unchanging, weights but that does not present, a true picture of the situation. Also, the index of industrial production underestimates the level of output because the index is based largely on the data derived from the registered manufacturing organisations. The output in the unregistered sector in manufacturing does not get fully reflected in the index. We, therefore, constructed a different series taking the data on value added in manufacturing, both in the registered and unregistered sectors, and compared it with the index of manufacturing which is a sub-set of the index of industrial production. Over a 15-year period, it is found that the annual rates of growth according to the two series are in agreement in most years (Table 1). There are, however, some exceptions — such as 1966 — when the data on value added in manufacturing shows a positive growth rate where as the index of manufacturing shows a decline in growth rate.

Table 1

Rates of Growth in Manufacturing

Year	*Index of Value Added in Manufacturing*[1]	*Index of Manufacturing in Industrial Production*[2]
	1960 = 100	1960 = 100
1961-62	9.5	8.4
1962-63	6.1	9.1
1963-64	7.8	9.4
1964-65	7.9	8.9
1965-66	1.3	2.6
1966-67	1.9	1.2
1967-68	3.1	-0.1
	1970 = 100	1970 = 100
1971-72	2.7	6.2
1972-73	4.2	3.9
1973-74	4.8	2.1
1974-75	2.4	1.2
1975-76	2.4	3.8
1976-77	9.5	10.9

Note: 1. Data on value added from manufacturing in registered and unregistered sectors, in rupees at constant prices, are available (See National Accounts Statistics, October 1975 and February, 1980). These have been added to obtain value added for the entire manufacturing sector.

2. Data on industrial production available on the monthly basis have been used to construct the index for fiscal years.

The growth rates for 1968-69, 1969-70 and 1970-71 have not been calculated since monthwise data on industrial production are not readily available.

When one looks at the index of industrial production, it is seen that the best period was between 1961 and 1965. In this period the annual average rate of growth was nearly nine per cent (Table 2). There was not even a single year in this period when the growth rate was less than eight per cent. The sharpest increase was in the capital goods industries, where the average annual rate of growth was nearly 20 per cent. The basic goods industries rose by 10.5 per cent during this period and the output of consumer goods industries rose by five per cent. The sharp downturn occurred between 1966 and 1970, when the average growth rate fell to 3.7 per cent. And the most noticeable decline was in the capital goods industries

Table 2

Year-to-Year Rates of Growth in Industrial Production

Year	All Industries	Basic Goods Industries	Capital Goods Industries	Consumer Goods Industries
1961	9.2	12.7	18.0	6.6
1962	9.7	13.3	29.6	1.3
1963	8.3	14.2	11.1	2.2
1964	8.6	3.8	17.7	7.4
1965	9.2	8.6	22.0	7.5
Average	**9.0**	**10.5**	**19.7**	**5.0**
1966	-0.4	5.2	-13.9	2.9
1967	-0.4	2.1	-2.3	-4.3
1968	6.8	10.2	3.4	4.9
1969	7.6	8.9	1.7	10.2
1970	5.1	4.6	4.9	6.4
Average	**3.7**	**6.2**	**-1.4**	**4.0**
1971	4.2	4.6	5.5	3.2
1972	5.7	8.0	0.9	4.7
1973	1.6	-3.1	15.8	-0.5
1974	2.0	3.9	4.3	2.2
1975	4.7	13.3	0.5	-1.5
Average	**3.6**	**5.3**	**5.4**	**1.6**
1976	9.9	14.3	10.5	10.2
1977	5.2	5.1	5.5	6.4
1978	6.9	4.8	2.7	10.0
1979	1.3	2.3	2.7	-2.2
1980	0.8	-1.0	4.6	0.4
Average	**4.8**	**5.1**	**5.2**	**4.9**

where, over the five-year period, the average rate of growth turned out to be negative. The rate of growth of consumer goods industries, at four per cent per annum was only a small decline from the previous period. During 1971-75, the growth rate of industrial production was 3.6 per cent per annum — which was no different from the growth rate achieved in the previous five year period. During this period, while the basic goods industries and capital goods industries maintained a rate of growth of five per cent, the rate of growth in consumer goods industries fell to 1.6 per cent per annum. Thus, while the period 1966-70 was marked by a sharp decline in capital goods industries, the subsequent five-year period was marked by a steep fall in the output of consumer goods industries. During 1976-1980, the average rate of growth rose to 4.8 per cent. This was more or less the rate of growth experienced by all segments of industries. Thus, while undoubtedly the rate of growth of industrial production since 1966 has been much lower than what was experienced in the previous period, in trying to provide an explanation for this, it is important to note that the impact on different segments has been different in the different time periods.

The explanations that have been offered cover a wide spectrum. At one end, there are those who locate the cause for deceleration in the periodic shocks that the economy had received in the form of war in 1965 and 1971, the oil crisis in 1973, and the droughts in 1965 and 1966. According to them, it is these shocks which prevented the economy from gaining momentum and achieving a higher rate of industrial growth.

But at the other end, there is the explanation offered by economists influenced largely by the Marxian analysis. These assert that the crisis in industrial growth is rooted in the path of development that India has adopted and that there is no way out unless the fundamental property relations and structure of income distribution are altered. It may be convenient to deal with the various hypotheses and explanations suggested, by grouping them into two broad categories — *viz.*, those that stress the supply constraints on growth and those that stress the demand constraints. We shall therefore proceed first to state the various hypotheses, test them with the help of empirical data available, and finally formulate our own position on the issue.

The explanation emphasising supply constraints basically argues that the growth rate of industrial production has been hampered primarily by the non-availability of critical inputs such as power, imported raw materials and agricultural raw materials. The agro-based industries had a weight of approximately 60 per cent in the total industrial production in 1950. It has declined sharply over the years, but its weight is still 33 per cent. It is, therefore, not improbable that fluctuations in agricultural output, in so far as, they affected the supply of raw materials required by the agro-based industries, might have had an impact on industrial production. Needless to say, availability of power is another critical factor. Disturbed industrial relations can also be regarded as a constraint operating on the supply side. Those who think that the supply constraint has been the most important impediment — this includes, in the main, economists who speak for the Government — do not necessarily argue that the same bottleneck has been faced from year to year.[1] The constraints that operate on the supply side might change from year to year. Their main contention is that, but for these constraints some of which are man-made and some acts of God, the growth rate would have been higher.

In the early phase of the development of the country, the question of demand constraint was never raised. However, in recent years, fears have been expressed that the real constraint on industrial growth in India may be operating from the demand side. If this is so, it has serious consequences for the future growth of industrial production. The concept of demand constraint, however, does not lead to a single explanation. The factors leading to demand restriction are seen to be different for basic and capital goods industries and for consumer goods industries.

In relation to capital goods industries, it has been argued that, by 1965, the possibilities of import substitution had been exhausted, and that further growth in the output of capital goods industries could therefore come only from an increase in demand which perhaps was not forthcoming. Import substitution, in the early phase, implies only the substitution of the foreign source of supply by domestic source of supply. Consequently, while the growth of capital goods industries upto 1965 had been helped by a strategy of import substitution which did not require a fresh increase in demand, in the subsequent period, growth of these industries has been hampered by the lack of generation of additional demand.[2]

Another stream of thought, bearing on the demand constraint in relation to capital goods industries, is that a high level of demand for these industries can be maintained only if investment is growing at a reasonably high rate. It is pointed out, therefore, that the sharp decline in public investment, noticed after 1966, was mainly responsible for the decline in the growth of capital goods industries.[3] Another strand of thinking intertwined with this is that private investment in India moves more or less in unison with public investment and that public investment stimulates private investment. Thus this theory postulates a complementary relationship between the two sectors rather than the usual approach which says that public investment 'crowds out' private investment. If this proposition is true, a decline in public investment will result in a decline in private investment as well, and the two, together will have a serious impact on the output of goods industries.

Turning to the demand constraint operating on the output of consumer goods, a major link is sought to be established between the demand for consumption goods and the performance of the agricultural sector. This hypothesis centres on the nature of the inter-relationship between industry and agriculture.[4] As mentioned previously, agriculture influences industry on the supply side, through the availability of raw-materials needed for industries. But another important influence is via the demand route. If, under the category of industrial consumption goods, we include such output as clothing, footwear, sugar and edible oils, then rural consumption of these commodities is nearly two-and-a-half times that of urban consumption. It should not be surprising, then, if fluctuations in agricultural output have had a considerable impact, may be with some lag, on the demand for industrial consumption goods. If agricultural output increases and agricultural income grows as a result, the demand for these goods rises. On the other hand, poor agricultural performance will affect adversely, the demand for industrial consumption goods.

These effects are plain enough to see, but there is another route through which demand can be influenced — and, that is through the terms-of-trade between agriculture and industry. By terms-of-trade, we mean the ratio of agricultural price to the price of manufactured goods. One will have to trace the impact of a change in terms-of-trade on three different classes of people — the urban group, the rural poor, and the rural upper-class. A rise in food price in relation to manufactures affects adversely, the demand for non-food items in urban areas. The cross-elasticity of demand is negative, and this is all the more so in lower income groups in urban areas where food consumption is a sizeable part of the budget. In the case of the lower income groups in rural areas, the impact is likely to be the same as that in urban areas, since this segment of rural population also buys food. In the case of upper income groups in rural areas which have a marketable surplus, the negative effect on demand, resulting from the rise in terms-of-trade in favour of agriculture can be offset by the increase in income arising from the improvement in agricultural prices. Thus the overall effect on the demand for industrial consumption goods because of the rise in terms-of-trade will depend upon the combined effect on all the three groups we mentioned.

Agricultural performance can also affect the demand for capital goods by affecting the level of savings and investment of the household, Government, and corporate sectors. Savings and investment of rural households may be helped by a rise in the terms-of-trade in favour of agriculture. On the other hand, a rise in agricultural prices relative to manufactures may have a negative influence on the corporate sector. First, a relative increase in non-food prices, by increasing the cost of production, may affect adversely the profitability of agro-based industries. Second, a relative increase in foodgrains prices may push up the wage cost and thereby reduce the profitability. The savings of the government sector will be influenced both by agricultural output and the terms-of-trade. The rise and fall in agricultural output has an impact on government revenue and expenditures. A severe decline in agricultural output may force the Government to undertake several relief measures, thereby forcing it to increase expenditures. A rise in foodgrains price will affect government expenditure through the impact it has on the compensation payable to the government employees. Thus, there are several channels through which the impact of agricultural performance will be felt on industry. The argument of some has been that there has been a fall in the rate of growth in agricultural output since 1966 and that, it is this which has been responsible for the slow-down in the rate of growth of industrial production.

Let us conclude the list of hypotheses by including one more which traces the demand constraint on industrial consumption goods to the unequal income distribution[5] and leads to the conclusion that the base of the market for industrial consumer goods in India is not only narrow, but is shrinking. The argument quite simply is that the market for industrial consumption goods is concentrated in the top 10 per cent of the population, and that as this income group gets saturated with consumption, there will be no further expansion in demand. Once the demand for consumption goods begins to fall, in the subsequent stages the demand for machinery and capital goods will also fall, and a crisis will then automatically develop. A continued growth in the demand for industrial consumption goods is possible only if the market widens. This can be accomplished, according to this hypothesis, only by a drastic redistribution of income. This group of analysts sees in the improvement in the terms-of-trade in favour of agriculture the rising power of kulaks and the pauperisation of the urban proletariat and the rural poor.

We have just outlined the basic premises of the various hypotheses suggested and we shall now try to show how far these various theories stand the test of empirical verification. It must be noted that, not all these theories are mutually exclusive. Nevertheless, each of the hypotheses certainly seems to say that the factor emphasised by it is the key factor responsible for the deceleration in industrial growth.

Taking the supply constraint hypothesis first: It is easy to identify several years following 1966 when output was held back because of the non-availability of critical inputs. It is worth noting in this context that electricity generation, which had maintained an average annual rate of growth of 14 per cent during the 1960-65, declined to an average 6.3 per cent in 1970-75 (Table 3). In fact, looking at the performance of industry in the current year and the two previous years, it is quite obvious that, what has helped industrial production achieve a rate of growth of 10 per cent in the current year, has been the removal of infrastructure constraints. Thus, a year-by-year analysis of the factors inhibiting growth clearly indicates that, since 1966, one can easily identify six or seven years where the cause of deceleration can be traced to supply bottlenecks. These bottlenecks have arisen, in most years, not so much from inadequate investment as from an inefficient use of existing investment. Nevertheless, it must be noted that supply availability is only a necessary but not a sufficient condition for industrial growth.

Table 3

Year-to-Year Rates of Growth in Select Variables

(per cent)

Year	All Crops	Foodgrains	Non-Foodgrains	Electricity Generated
1961-62	0.0	0.8	-0.2	18.3
1962-63	-0.2	-3.1	1.8	14.0
1963-64	2.4	0.6	2.6	17.4
1964-65	10.6	10.8	11.7	10.1
1965-66	-16.7	-19.0	-11.4	11.6
1966-67	0.0	2.6	-3.2	10.3
1967-68	21.5	28.0	11.5	13.2
1968-69	-1.5	-1.0	-2.1	15.1
1969-70	6.7	6.7	6.4	9.6
1970-71	7.2	8.9	5.1	7.4
1971-72	0.0	-1.0	2.0	9.1
1972-73	-8.0	-8.2	-7.8	5.9
1973-74	9.9	7.8	14.4	3.3
1974-75	-3.2	-5.4	1.1	5.2
1975-76	15.2	22.0	2.5	13.0
1976-77	-7.0	-9.0	-2.6	11.5
1977-78	14.4	15.5	12.6	3.4
1978-79	3.5	4.3	1.4	12.2
1979-80	-15.5	-18.2	-9.4	2.1

Talking of demand constraint on the output of capital goods, the import substitution hypothesis does sound plausible as an explanation of the earlier growth and the later deceleration. But it really overstates the case. With the virtual ban of certain kinds of output, there is no doubt that some of the industries must have been helped a great deal by such a policy. But there is no evidence to indicate that the policy came to so sudden an end in 1965-66, as to cause a sharp fall in the production of capital goods. The index of machinery imports, with the base 1960-61 = 100, rose from 103 in 1961-62 to 143 in 1965-66; between 1966-67 and 1970-71, it declined from 101 to 74 (Table 4). Thus, in the latter period, imports declined at a sharp rate, whereas in the former period, machinery imports actually increased. The share of imported machinery to investment in machinery declined from 38.6

per cent in 1961-62 to 27.8 per cent in 1965-66. But it continued to fall during the next five years from 29 per cent to 16.8 per cent. Thus, it is difficult to sustain the proposition that it is the exhaustion of the possibilities of import substitution that brought about the collapse in the growth of capital goods industries between 1966 and 1970. A commodity wise analysis does not show any negative correlation between the rate of growth in imports and the rate of growth in production. Thus this hypothesis has a very limited role in explaining the behaviour of even one segment of industrial production — *viz.*, the output of capital goods industries.

Table 4

Index of Imports

(1960-61=100)

Year	*Machinery*
1961-62	103
1962-63	114
1963-64	125
1964-65	132
1965-66	143
1966-67	101
1967-68	95
1968-69	88
1969-70	73
1970-71	74
1971-72	96
1972-73	140
1973-74	87
1974-75	76

Source: Vidya Pitre, 'A Study of Trends in India's Imports, 1960-61 to 1974-75', *Economic and Political Weekly*, May 9, 1981.

The link between industrial performance and agricultural growth is crucial in an economy such as ours, where income originating in agriculture still contributes 45 per cent of the national income and where agriculture is still subject to severe exogenous shocks from time to time. Many studies in the past have shown that the link between agriculture and industry, based on the input and output relationship, has not been strong in India. This is the conclusion that the Second Asian Agricultural Survey also reached. For example, in 1968-69, the total value of the output of agriculture and allied activities was Rs. 19,720 crore. The total value of inputs used by them was Rs. 4,840 crores. However, of this, Rs. 3,571 crores was the value of inputs coming from agriculture and allied activities themselves. Thus inputs worth Rs. 1,269 crore alone came from industry and services sectors. This constituted no more than 6.4 per cent of the value of the total agricultural output. Again, the flow of agriculture and allied activities to other sectors constituted only a small proportion of the total value of their output. Only output worth Rs. 2,489 crore went to non-agricultural sectors as inputs. This is approximately 13 per cent of the total output of agriculture and allied activities. Dividing the economy into three sectors — agriculture, manufacturing and services and by taking into account the direct and indirect requirements, it is found that the rupee increase in the final demand of agriculture results in an increase in the output of manufacture by rupee 0.09 and of services by rupee 0.02, whereas a one rupee increase in the final demand of manufacture results in an increase in the output of agriculture by rupee 0.26. These data indicate that the dependence of industry on agriculture is greater than that of agriculture on industry. Dependence of agriculture on industry for inputs varies with the level of technology used in agriculture. Similarly, the dependence of industry on agriculture for inputs, varies with the growth of various processing industries.

At the present moment, the link through the input-output relation does not appear to be very strong. This, however, is only a partial picture. Even a cursory glance of the data relating to rates of growth in industry and agriculture will show the kind of impact agriculture has had on industry. During 1961-65, agricultural output fell in 1961 and 1962, and the output of consumer goods industry fell in the following years 1962 and 1963. Moreover, the sharp decline in agricultural output in 1965-66 and 1966-67 is reflected in the slower growth rate in consumer goods industries in 1966 and 1967. Even in the more recent period, the decline in agricultural output in 1972-73 and 1974-75 is reflected in the fall in the output of consumer goods industries in 1973 and 1975. Thus, with a lag of one year, agriculture seems to affect directly the output of consumer goods industry with some exceptions (see Tables 2 and 3). The fall in agricultural output in 1969 did not result in a decline in the output of consumer goods industries in 1969. However, to isolate the various types of influences, there is need to construct a broader framework of analysis.

Table 5

Imports of Machinery and Fixed Capital Formation

(Rs. in crores at current prices)

Year	*Gross Domestic Fixed Capital Formation in Machinery & Equipment*	*Imports of Machinery and Transport Equipment*	*(2) as Percentage of (1)*
	(1)	(2)	(3)
1961-62	952	368	38.6
1962-63	1116	387	34.7
1963-64	1378	437	31.7
1964-65	1623	478	29.5
1965-66	1772	492	27.8
1966-67	1887	536	28.4
1967-68	1976	503	25.4
1968-69	2040	516	25.3
1969-70	2221	395	17.8
1970-71	2346	328	14.0
1971-72	2810	376	13.4
1972-73	3352	432	12.9
1973-74	4099	557	13.6
1974-75	5171	696	13.5
1975-76	6031	935	15.5
1976-77	6810	1048	15.4
1977-78	7419	1110	14.9

Source: Column 1, CSO, National Accounts Statistics.
Column 2, RBI, Report on Currency and Finance.

We had mentioned earlier, the various channels of influence having a bearing on the demand for industrial production. Both agricultural output and terms-of-trade, influence the demand for industrial consumption goods — the former positively, and the latter negatively on some groups and positively on others. Both these again influence savings and investment of the household, Government, and corporate sectors — and thereby influence the demand for the output of basic and capital goods industries. In order to understand the total effect, a macro model was constructed, where all these relationships were explicitly postulated and estimated.[6] In the model, agricultural output was treated as exogenous, since the purpose was to study the impact of agriculture. The terms-of-trade were determined within the system and so, too, the output of the different segments of industrial production. Data tend to confirm the *a priori* hypotheses stated earlier. Agricultural output has a positive impact on the demand for industrial consumption goods. On the other hand, the total effect of foodgrains terms-of-trade, after taking into account both the rural and urban impact, is found to be negative. But the elasticity is negligible. Agricultural output and terms of trade have a positive impact on household savings and investment. This means that a rise in agricultural prices in relation to manufacturing, prices, promotes rural savings. This should not come as a surprise, because a survey conducted by the National Council of Applied Economic Research in 1967-68 showed that rural household savings were 1.83 times urban savings.[7] The terms of trade elasticity with respect to household investment was 1.5. A rise in agricultural prices in relation to manufacturing prices, operating through cost and profitability, has an adverse effect on corporate investment. And the elasticity works out to -1.5. The rise in the foodgrains terms-of-trade has a significantly negative impact on government savings. A rise in agricultural output has a positive influence both on government savings and corporate investment.

The negative impact of a rise in the foodgrains terms-of-trade on urban non-food expenditures is also evident from an analysis of the National Sample Survey data. A disaggregated analysis in relation to cloth consumption also brings out this fact. But in relation to both expenditures, the rural response is positive to changes in terms of trade. Taking the model as a whole, it is seen that the positive and negative effects of a rise in terms-of-trade tend to cancel out. What then is the total effect of agricultural performance on industrial growth? We simulated the model to find out what the rate of industrial production would have been, had the agricultural growth rate been one per cent higher than what was historically experienced. The conclusion that emerges is that an increase in the agricultural growth rate by one per cent will have an effect of slightly less than one per cent on national income. This implies that a one per cent rate of growth in agriculture results in the industrial output rising by close to one per cent. This must be deemed to be a sizeable impact, even though magnitude might be less than what some agricultural fundamentalists may believe it to be. A one-shot increase or decrease in agriculture has its reverberations on the economy for the next three to four years.

There is considerable difference of opinion among agricultural economists, as to whether there has been any decline in the trend rate of growth in agricultural production. Various kinds of trend equations have been estimated in support of either position. Without entering into this argument, our study shows that fluctuations in agriculture output can have a significant impact on industrial performance. However, it would be wrong to conclude that the behaviour of industrial production since 1966 can be explained purely in terms of agricultural performance. The dynamics of industrial growth is more complex. But it is apparent that, unless agriculture grows at a steady and reasonable rate, industrial growth will itself run into problems.

Those who argue that income distribution is the root cause of deceleration adduce that the demand base for industrial goods is very narrow in terms of population coverage. For example, in 1964-65, using National Sample Survey data, it has been estimated that in the rural sector the richest 10 per cent of the population was responsible for 32.2 per cent of the total consumption of industrial goods, whereas the poorest 50 per cent accounted for only 22 per cent of the total. The consumption inequalities were even more pronounced in the urban sector where the top 10 per cent purchased 39.3 per cent of the industrial goods and the bottom five deciles absorbed just 20 per cent of the total. While these data show that the market for industrial consumption goods is concentrated in the upper income segments of the population, it still does not prove that the markets are narrowing or shrinking.

To support the hypothesis of a shrinking market, two sets of data are provided. The National Sample Survey provides data on different types of consumption expenditure for different expenditure classes. Using these data, the percentage of per capita consumption expenditure, spent on industrial consumption goods is computed for

Table 6

Growth of Production and Imports in Some Select Industry Groups

	Production			*Imports*			*Production*			*Imports*		
	1961	*1965*	*Average Annual Growth Rate*	*1961*	*1965*	*Average Annual Growth Rate*	*1966*	*1970*	*Average Annual Growth Rate*	*1966*	*1970*	*Average Annual Growth Rate*
Non-electrical Machinery	121.1	238.8	19.1	121.0	157.0	9.6	295.5	369.5	9.4	120.4	71.0	-14.28
Electrical Machinery	110.0	204.4	15.4	108.0	184.0	13.2	225.1	362.7	12.2	131.0	162.0	14.4
Transport Equipment	116.7	204.3	15.7	81.0	96.0	2.72	156.0	132.0	-7.9	42.0	31.0	-13.9
Manufacturing of Metals	112.4	205.6	16.2	79.0	71.0	1.6	208.4	219.0	6.3	48.0	24.0	-11.7

different deciles of population in the rural and urban areas. Such a computation, according to one estimate, shows, that while the lowest six deciles spent around two-fifths of their consumption expenditures on industrial goods in 1952-53, 12 years later, the ratio was around three-tenths.[8] A similar trend is noted for urban India. Second, once again using the NSS data, the share of each decile in the total market of industrial goods is computed and such an analysis shows that, in the aggregate consumption of industrial goods in rural areas, the lower six deciles were consuming proportionately less of the total consumption in 1964-65 than in 1952-53. Thus the conclusions drawn are: (i) the ratio of expenditure on industrial consumption goods to total expenditure of consumption goods is falling, and (ii) the lower deciles of population are slowly withdrawing from the market for industrial goods. The two, together, portend a dangerous trend for industrial growth.

Even though there is some evidence to show that there has been a decline in the percentage of consumer expenditure spent on industrial consumption goods, the trend does not appear to be strong, especially if we extend the data beyond 1964-65. We replicated the study by extending the analysis up to 1973-74, i.e., the 28th round of NSS.[9] The analysis shows a small decline in the percentage of expenditure on industrial consumption goods. But, strangely enough, this decline occurs not only in the lower deciles of the population but also in the top decile of the population. The basic reason adduced for the decline in the percentage of per capita expenditure on industrial goods is that, as food prices rise, they pre-empt the income in favour of food, leaving less available for other expenditures. One would have expected that the expenditure on consumption goods by the upper deciles would have increased since the rise in the terms-of-trade in favour of agriculture ought to have benefited at least the upper-income group. In fact, even the per capita rural expenditure on industrial consumption goods shows a decline for the upper income groups as well. It is well known that NSS data for the top-income groups is quite suspect. Moreover, our analysis of the percentage of the total market in each fractile class shows that, as far as the urban areas are concerned, the share of middle deciles has clearly gone up. However, in the rural areas no distinct trend was noticeable.

The decline in the percentage of per capita consumption expenditure on industrial consumption goods does not lead to the conclusion that the market in any absolute sense is narrowing. Even if the percentage were decreasing, the total market can expand so long as this decline is offset by a rising population. In absolute amount, even for the bottom deciles, there is no decline in the consumption of industrial goods. The poorest decile of population in the rural areas consumed Rs. 77.7 crore of industrial goods in 1960-61. The same section consumed Rs.98.1 crore in 1973-74. (Table 7A and 7B). In fact, the crisis in the system can develop only if a stage is reached where the withdrawal of the lower deciles of the population is not compensated by the increase in the upper decile. This can happen only if the top 10 per cent of the population reaches a saturation point with respect to consumption of industrial goods. It is hard to accept this argument, since the per capita consumption expenditure of the top five per cent of the rural population in 1973-74 was still less than Rs. 75 per month at 1964-65 prices. Undoubtedly, a different distribution of income would have resulted in a demand package which is different from the current package of industrial consumption goods. However, at the present level of per capita income of the top decile, it is difficult to sustain the proposition, that the distribution of income as such, has set a limit on industrial growth.

It is also worth noting, in this context, that one of the basic premises of this approach – *viz.*, that terms-of-trade had improved in terms of agriculture continually – is also not confirmed by the data. The behaviour of terms-of-trade has not always been in one direction in this period. Agricultural terms-of-trade worsened in the early 1950s, improved till early 70s, and perhaps has declined thereafter. However, this excursion into the data of NSS does indicate one thing: and that is, that organised industry at the present moment is catering to only a very limited segment of the population. This is partly reflected in the higher rate of growth of durable consumption goods. The creation of a mass market will imply that organised industry will have to produce products that can go to satisfy at least the middle deciles of the population.

Table 7A

Market Size for Industrial Consumption Goods (Rural)

(Rs. in millions at 1964-65 prices)

Fractile Class (Percentage)	ROUNDS										
	16	17	18	19	20	21	22	23	24	25	28
0-5	325.16	366.99	390.37	368.39	388.85	336.07	336.07	323.67	333.14	356.20	424.28
5-10	452.68	522.43	483.97	447.67	455.65	421.32	395.81	423.06	458.07	460.21	557.39
10-20	1131.70	1157.77	1164.27	1113.93	1097.38	1032.61	1005.72	1075.49	1150.38	1164.82	1369.90
20-30	1460.53	1472.34	1483.87	1463.49	1446.04	1178.73	1249.68	1284.47	1369.00	1398.92	1674.94
30-40	1750.93	1821.86	1835.43	1822.37	1722.84	1432.01	1503.60	1508.75	1639.60	1742.02	1841.32
40-50	1990.08	2105.84	2063.72	2227.86	2009.18	1782.71	1847.13	1840.06	1983.24	2147.63	2456.95
50-60	2630.66	2481.57	2401.59	2507.51	2371.88	2099.31	1986.54	2288.61	2316.38	2563.64	2606.68
60-70	3096.16	3045.16	2972.31	3057.48	2915.94	2352.60	2648.72	2747.35	3164.86	3177.25	3538.45
70-80	4150.98	4342.75	3702.83	3793.89	3545.89	3268.31	3116.73	3287.64	3732.64	3770.06	4114.16
80-90	6012.95	5915.57	4967.55	4996.38	4576.73	4047.63	4361.43	4470.17	4997.14	4986.88	6322.62
90-95	4516.12	4198.57	3362.68	3688.59	3502.06	3165.24	2959.90	3631.70	3789.50	3598.45	4506.25
95-100	9916.24	9830.16	10049.237	8657.23	8652.67	6651.87	5451.78	9264.01	8953.22	8343.53	10082.92

Note: The term 'Industrial Consumption Goods' is taken to include the following categories of the NSS data : (1) clothing (2) footwear (3) fuel and light (4) durables, (5) miscellaneous goods and services.

Source: Siddhartha Roy, "Demand for Industrial Consumer Goods in India: A Study of Linkages" (A thesis submitted to Indian Institute of Management, Ahmedabad, under the Fellow Programme).

Table 7B

Market Size Industrial Consumption Goods (Urban)

(Rs. in millions at 1964-65 prices)

Fractile Class (Percentage)	ROUNDS 16	17	18	19	20	21	22	23	24	25	28
0-5	98.43	105.49	100.224	186.48	101.62	81.26	90.17	97.90	111.384	110.40	147.43
5-10	148.62	136.66	145.82	141.80	135.66	105.85	128.42	138.74	158.22	156.23	188.07
10-20	364.66	388.41	381.85	339.91	321.61	257.68	323.52	336.78	407.84	391.23	473.98
20-30	496.84	484.31	468.05	436.15	409.61	295.10	409.85	436.36	506.08	520.35	555.27
30-40	588.71	626.25	595.33	531.37	468.28	345.35	474.34	523.63	606.61	626.23	684.79
40-50	691.83	756.68	759.70	665.49	566.75	451.20	560.69	640.00	822.23	755.35	799.15
50-60	854.00	909.17	939.10	828.28	652.65	539.95	707.14	763.08	928.77	1047.16	1000.37
60-70	1059.31	1183.45	1111.48	1013.60	819.22	622.27	921.36	968.95	1198.38	1236.97	1092.62
70-80	1440.84	1496.10	1409.15	1356.59	1073.79	835.04	1178.21	1280.00	1659.91	1679.85	1532.16
80-90	2114.86	2091.67	2272.08	1970.89	1588.16	1124.80	1779.34	2244.47	3312.47	3596.00	2135.65
90-95	2313.13	1557.96	1698.80	1839.84	1459.83	825.42	1367.29	1633.56	2004.91	1845.77	1500.47
95-100	2382.97	3610.306	3413.13	2916.41	2088.91	1408.67	2325.27	2303.77	3036.50	2798.03	3872.42

Note: The term 'Industrial Consumption Goods' is taken to include the following categories of the NSS data : (1) clothing (2) footwear (3) fuel and light (4) durables (5) miscellaneous goods and service.

Source: Siddhartha Roy, "Demand for Industrial Consumer Goods in India: A Study of Linkages" (A thesis submitted to Indian Institute of Management. Ahmedabad, under the Fellow Programme).

The hypothesis that decline in public investment is the cause of the deceleration of economic growth, found much acceptance in the early 1970s. The gross fixed capital formulation in the public sector reached a peak in 1965-66, and thereafter it started to decline in real terms till 1972-73. Thus, between 1950-51 and 1965-66, public fixed capital formation grew at 12.2 per cent and private fixed capital formation at 4.2 per cent per annum (Table 8). The overall compound rate of growth for fixed capital formation was 7.4 per cent. This rate fell to 3.3 per cent during the six years following 1965-66. Public investment started declining in absolute amount, and reached again the level achieved in 1965-66 only in 1972-73. The gross fixed capital formation by the public sector stood at Rs. 293 crores in 1950-51, and the private sector investment in that year was nearly three times at Rs. 847 crores (Table 9A). Because of the more rapid growth in investment in public sector, by 1964-65 public investment was approximately equal to private investment.

Then began the sharp decline in public investment. The increase in public investment prior to 1965-66 was made possible both by a rise in public savings and by a substantial inflow of real resources from abroad (Table 10). The decline in public investment was triggered by the severe droughts of 1965 and 1966, and was further compounded by the fall in capital inflows from abroad. As mentioned previously, some people postulate a complementary relationship between public investment and private investment. Public investment affects private investment in two ways. Both of them in the current period compete for the savings that are available; and so, the more one has, the less will be available to the other. On the other hand, public investment of the previous periods can stimulate private investment in the current period, because of the growth in the demand generated by public sector investment and expenditure. To the extent that public sector investment is in infrastructure facilities, it can also lead to a lowering of the cost of producing private sector output. Thus, in trying to understand the relationship between the two sectors, one has to take into account both the 'crowding out' effect and the 'stimulation effect' and find out which, in the long run, will be more dominant. It may be noted that, during 1966-1972, when public investment was declining, private investment surged forward. In 1972-73, once again, private sector investment was higher than public investment. However,

Table 8

Rates of Growth in Gross Fixed Investment

	1950-51 (at 60-61 prices)	*1965-66 (at 60-61 prices)*	*Compound Rate of Growth (in %)*	*1965-66 (at 60-61 prices)*	*1971-72 (at 60-61 prices)*	*Compound Rate of Growth (in %)*	*1970-71 (at 70-71 prices)*	*1977-78 (at 70-71 prices)*	*Compound Growth Rate (in %)*
Gross Fixed Investment									
Total	1140	3333	7.4	3333	4059	3.3	6305	9412	5.9
Public	293	1649	12.2	1649	1603	-0.47	2394	4078	8.0
Private	847	1684	4.7	1684	2456	6.5	3911	5311	4.5
Corporate	97	324	8.4	324	459	5.97	545	7811	5.3

when one compares private corporate investment with public sector investment, one sees a much closer positive relationship between the two (Table 9 A and Chart).

Table 9A

Gross Fixed Capital Formation

(Rs. in crores at 1960-61 prices)

Year	*Public Sector*	*Private Sector*	*Total*	*Private Corporate Sector*
1950-51	293	847	1140	97
1951-52	356	741	1097	103
1952-53	374	617	991	112
1953-54	421	695	1040	65
1954-55	504	779	1185	129
1955-56	668	804	1472	115
1956-57	714	1058	1772	196
1957-58	716	968	1684	291
1958-59	810	827	1637	217
1959-60	1018	749	1767	192
1960-61	1055	1101	2156	326
1961-62	1061	1254	2315	492
1962-63	1214	1265	2479	376
1963-64	1390	1411	2801	565
1964-65	1570	1586	3156	509
1965-66	1649	1684	3333	324
1966-67	1492	1854	3346	329
1967-68	1400	2136	3536	373
1968-69	1417	2174	3591	353
1969-70	1400	2638	3758	347
1970-71	1448	2316	3764	415
1971-72	1603	2456	4059	459
1972-73	1987	2346	4333	561

Source: See, R.N. Lal, "Capital Formation and Its Financing in India", pp. 107, 116.

Chart

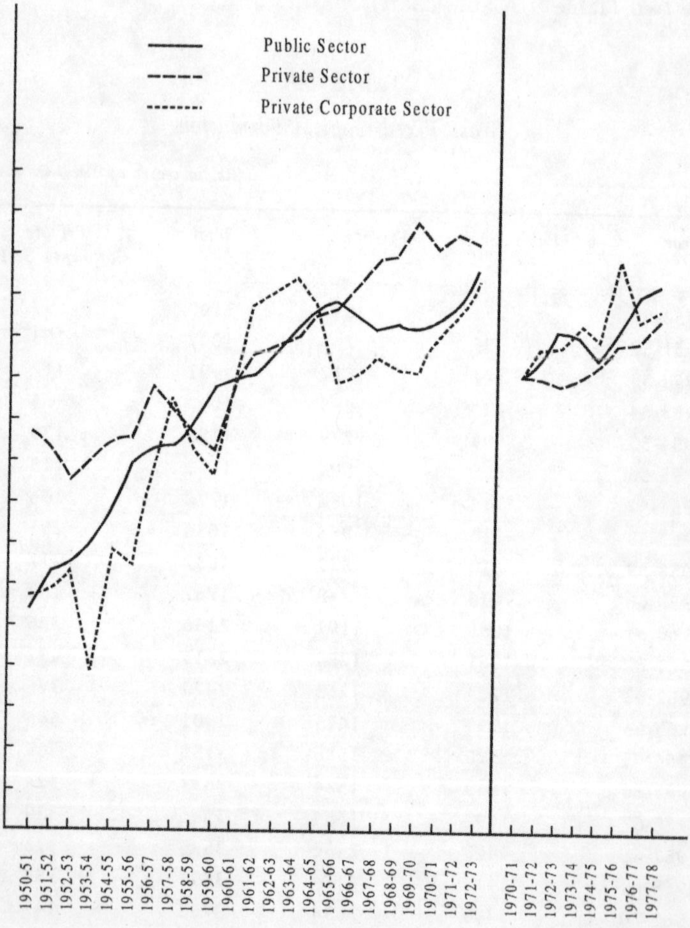

There are a number of ways of testing the relationship between public investment and private investment.[10] One simple way of trying to understand the relationship is to regress the private sector investment or corporate investment on public sector investment of the previous period and on savings less public investment of the current period. Estimated equations in this respect show that, in the case of private investment, the positive and negative effects almost cancel out each other; whereas in the case of private corporate investment the positive effect seems to dominate the negative.[11] The investment stagnation hypothesis, which may seem to provide an explanation of the phenomenon that occurred between 1966 and 1972, fails to carry conviction when we go beyond that period. In fact, public investment started moving up from 1971-72, and during the next six year period, public investment grew at eight per cent per annum and private investment continued to grow at the trend rate of growth of 4.5 per cent per annum (Table 9 B). The crucial question that arises, then, is why has industrial production not picked up even after a growth rate of six per cent per annum is maintained in gross fixed capital formation. Whatever the factors that might have operated in the past in holding down the industrial growth rate, the critical question to ask now is why has not the industrial growth rate picked up even after a substantial rise in investment?

Table 9B

Gross Fixed Capital Formation

Year	*Public Sector*	*Private Sector*	*Total*	*Private Corporate Sector*
1970-71	2394	3911	6305	545
1971-72	2648	4038	6686	634
1972-73	3166	3893	7059	655
1973-74	3134	3926	7060	758
1974-75	2678	4245	6923	671
1975-76	3161	4571	7732	1093
1976-77	3927	4842	8759	745
1977-78	4078	5334	9412	781

Source: Central Statistical Organisation, *National Accounts Statistics*, February, 1980. Figures in current prices for all the series have been deflated by a common Index.

Before we attempt to answer this question, let us summarise where we stand in relation to the past. The problem with any of the explanations offered is that the proponents of each theory tend to believe that there is just one explanation that will account for the entire sequence of events that happened over the 30-year period. While it is important to isolate the critical from the accidental, it is also not wise to search for a single explanation. The period 1960-65 was marked by a high growth rate in industrial production because public investment was rising at a very sharp rate, aided partly by the sizeable inflow of real resources from abroad. The demand constraint in relation to capital goods industries was not operating at least in part because of the policy of import substitution. Although agricultural production was not behaving well during this period, foodgrains prices still ruled low because of the import of concessional foodgrains.

Table 10

Capital Inflows and Public Savings

(Rs. in crores at 1970-71 prices)

Year	*Gross Fixed Capital Formation in Public Sector*	*Net Capital Inflows*	*Public Savings (Gross)*
1952	374	-40.2	171.4
1953	421	-15.9	155.2
1954	504	28.4	186.3
1955	668	63.7	210.7
1956	714	416.6	268.1
1957	716	526.8	271.7
1958	810	400.0	242.8
1959	1018	241.6	199.8
1960	1055	481.0	425.0
1961	1061	332.4	389.2
1962	1214	412.2	530.2
1963	1390	392.7	632.9
1964	1570	515.1	701.0
1965	1649	482.7	652.0
1966	1492	663.7	480.4
1967	1400	571.3	455.0
1968	1417	276.9	571.0
1969	1400	152.9	655.0
1970	1448	233.2	742.0
1971	1603	272.7	718.0
1972	1982	157.8	705.0

Source: Current prices data: RN Lal, *op. cit* p 107 and 207.
Data in current prices have been deflated by CSO's investment deflator.

The output of consumer goods industries, except in two years, maintained a fairly high rate of growth. The decline in industrial growth during 1966-70, could be traced mainly to the droughts of 1966 and 1967, and the subsequent inability to raise public investment. The period 1971-75, when public investment once again picked up, the basic and capital goods industries showed a moderate rise. But the consumer goods industries suffered severely, as the general price level rose to unbelievably new height. The period 1976-80 was marked by a moderate rise in industrial production, and more or less all segments of industrial production maintained the same rate of growth. However, this period on the whole was plagued by various kinds of infrastructural constraints, which prevented it from achieving the full benefits of the investment increase.

In the early years of plan formulation in this country, the biggest constraint in the way of economic growth was seen to be in the low savings ratio which was considered inevitable in the low income countries. Over the years, through a variety of techniques and efforts, the country has been able to raise the savings and investment ratio. Gross capital formation, as a percentage of gross domestic product at current market prices, rose from 10 per cent in 1950-51 to 21.8 per cent in 1979-80. The savings rate achieved by India is comparable to the rate achieved in middle-income and even some high-income industrialized countries. The investment stagnation hypothesis does not seem right, when one looks at the investment-income ratio. Inspite of the substantial jump in the investment-income ratio, gross fixed capital formation has been growing only at 5.9 per cent in recent years as compared with 7.9 per cent in the period 1950-51 to 1965-66. Since income growth rate is lower, total investment is not rising at a faster rate as compared with the previous period, inspite of stepping up the ratio of investment to income.

Infact, what lies at the root of all this is the rising Incremental Capital-Output Ratio (ICOR). The rise in Incremental Capital-Output Ratio has nullified the output increase that could otherwise have come from the increase in the share of investment to income. The capital-output ratios actually experienced in the economy had turned out to be much higher than those anticipated in the plan documents. The calculation of the capital-output ratio is beset with many statistical problems. A comparison over time raises more issues. Changing relative prices can affect the ratio. One can also get different results, depending on whether the ratio measured is one of net investment to increase in the net domestic product or gross investment to increase in Gross Domestic Product. The latter will always give a higher ratio. According to the Sixth Plan document, the incremental gross capital-output ratio had risen from 3.2 in the First Plan to 5.7 in the Fourth Plan. Leaving aside other factors, such as changing lag pattern and weather-induced fluctuations in output, changes in the aggregate Incremental Capital-Output Ratios over time are influenced by two factors: one, change in the Incremental Capital-Output Ratio of the different sectors; and two, change in the output mix. The rise in Incremental Capital-Output Ratio due to change in the output mix can be policy-induced, as happened between the First and the Second Plans. The sectoral capital-output ratios presented in the Sixth Plan document are again revealing (Table 11). In almost every sector, even the planned ICOR is very high. In sectors such as electricity and transport and communication, the ratios are as high as 34.3 and 11.1, respectively. If past experience is any guide, the realised Incremental Capital-Output Ratios may turn out to be larger than those implied in the Plan. We have shown in Table 12 the actual ICOR for the various sectors using the data for the period 1970-71 to 1977-78.

The rise in Incremental Capital-Output Ratio calls for a systematic analysis of the factors that have contributed to this rise. We witnessed, some years ago, the co-existence of non-availability of power and underutilisation of capacity in the power sector. While it is always possible for underutilisation to occur, because of the absence of complementary investment, a significant degree of underutilisation of capacity essentially shows an inefficient use of the available capital. It can very well be argued that an improvement in capacity utilisation can only lead to a one-shot increase in output. That is true. But if the additional investment that is being added every year is more effectively utilised than is being done now, it should be possible to extract a higher growth rate from the economy. International comparisons of ICORs have problems.

Table 11

Sectoral Incremental Capital-Output Ratios in Sixth Plan

(Rs. in crores at 1979-80 prices)

	Investment (at market prices)	*Incremental GDP (at factor cost)*	*ICOR*
Agriculture	33468	7049 (25.2)	4.74
Mining & manufacturing	52090	7540 (26.9)	6.91
Construction	1760	1389 (4.9)	1.26
Electricity & gas	23554	686 (2.5)	34.33
Transport, communications, storage & trade*	26255	6733 (24.0)	3.90
Other Sectors	21583	4602 (16.4)	4.69
Total	158710	27999 (100.0)	5.67
Total at market price		37994	4.20

Note: Figures in brackets refer to percentage to total. Since sectoral domestic product at market price is not available, investment at market prices has been divided by gross domestic product at factor cost. This will overstate the ICOR. In the next Table also, the same procedure has been adopted.

*: For Transport communication alone the ICOR is 11.10.

Table 12

Sectoral Incremental Capital-Output Ratios During 1970-71 to 1977-78

(Rs. in crores at 1960-61 prices)

	Investment (at market price)	*Incremental GDP (at factor cost)*	*ICOR*
Agriculture	11414	2913	3.92
Mining & manufacturing	18009	2078	8.67
Construction	1070	594	1.80
Electricity, gas & water supply	5307	244	21.75
Transport & communication	11854	2167	5.47
Other sectors	13545	2018	6.71
Total	61199	10014	6.11

Source: Central Statistical Organisation, National Accounts Statistics, February 1980.

It is nevertheless true that India has one of the highest Incremental Capital-Output Ratios among the developing economies. The ICOR for rapidly developing economies such as Korea is as low as 2.0. In fact, the mean for 22 industrialised countries was 4.9. The Indian ratio is close to this figure. It should also be noted that industrially advanced countries are content to grow at two to three per cent, which is not the case for a country such as ours. Two things are required. First, there should be an attempt to bring down the sectoral ICORs. In this respect, greater attention needs to be paid to the efficient utilisation of capital. Second, investment choices should also be governed by the level of ICOR. Some serious thinking is called for whether investment in some of the projects, such as petro-chemical complexes or even steel plants, at certain locations are justified. The composition of investment from this angle needs a close look. Industrial growth in future is not going to be free from the problems that may arise from fluctuations in agricultural output or rising terms of trade in favour of agriculture or from infrastructure bottlenecks now and then. But, having learnt to raise our investment rate to a level comparable to that in any industrialised country, we ought to turn our attention more closely to improving the productivity of capital and thereby decreasing the capital-output ratio.

The possibility of stepping up the investment rate much beyond 25 per cent must be ruled out. With the savings and investment rate stabilising at that level, higher growth rate can occur only if we learn to lower the incremental capital-output ratio. The changes in the output mix need not run into the ideological conflicts which were witnessed at the time of the Second Five-Year Plan.

The question is not whether more capital goods or more consumer goods should be produced. The question really is, which commodity can be produced at a lower capital-output ratio. Increased investment in electricity, which has a high Incremental Capital-Output Ratio does not necessarily mean that the overall ratio should increase. If, for example, lack of power has been responsible for underutilisation of capacity elsewhere, the increased output flowing from electricity should generate increased output in the other sectors and to that extent, the aggregate ICOR will be lowered. In planning for investment, we should really move towards a system of what can be described as 'sequential strategic sector planning' – a system of planning in which the planners identify the constraining sectors in the economy and invest more in them, so that the constraints are relaxed and output growth is activated. However, the point to be made at this juncture is that, unless we are able to identify outputs and sectors in which it is possible to lower the Incremental Capital-Output Ratio, we will continue to creep along a five to six per cent growth rate even in industry.

This paper has not touched upon an issue that has been put forward vehemently by the industrialists in recent months. Many of them see in the regulatory measures, the stumbling block to faster industrial growth. Also, they find the present taxation policy, not providing the corporate sector, with adequate funds for growth. Corporate sector investment constitutes only 10 per cent of the total investment. Nevertheless, its importance and role cannot be underestimated. In a planned economy, controls cannot be dispensed with. It should be possible, however, to work out a compromise between the compulsions of social purpose and the incentives needed for private action. Much of the controversy in this regard is centered around the allocation of total savings between the corporate and the public sector.

Given the need to lower the incremental capital-output ratio, it is necessary to understand which sector is more productive for what output. While the allocation among sectors is important, the focus of this paper is on some of the fundamental factors bearing on industrial growth, such as inter-sectoral linkages, income distribution, and efficient utilisation of capital. The economy no longer operates under a low savings constraint. The constraints of yesteryears have disappeared but in the place have come newer challenges.

An 8 to 10 per cent growth rate in industrial production is absolutely essential if the economy is to achieve an overall growth rate of five per cent. And this will come only if we can extract more out of the capital that we have so far invested and the capital that we will continue to invest. Therein lies the key to future industrial growth and this is the lesson that recent industrial experience teaches us.

* This is a slightly modified version of the Reserve Bank of India Endowment Lecture, delivered at the Indian Institute of Management, Ahmedabad, on December 1, 1981. The author is thankful to Veena Padia for her help in collecting and analysing the data.

Notes

1. See for example, the reasons given for the decline in the industrial production in 1979-80 and the subsequent rise in the next two years in the *Economic Survey* of these years.
2. Among other things, this point is stressed by D. Nayyar, (1978), p 1277. For a refutation of this hypotheses, see A. V. Desai, (1981), p 387.
3. T. N. Srinivasan, and N. S. S. Narayana, (1977).
4. The various links between agriculture and industry have been spelt out in A. Vaidyanathan, (1977), p 1644. Also see K.N. Raj, (1976), pp 228-231.
5. D. Nayyar, (1978) and R. Sau, (1974)
6. C. Rangarajan, (1980).
7. I. Z. Bhatty and M. T. R. Sarma, (1977), p 283.
8. R. Sau, (1974), p 1281
9. S. Roy, (1981).
10. For a full-fledged model, see V. Sundararajan, and S. Thakur, (1980).
11. In order to find out the relationship between the private investment and public investment, we estimated the following equations using the data for the period 1952-53 to 1972-73.

Private Corporate Investment =

$$206.350 + \underset{(2.70)}{0.227\ PUI_{t-1}} - \underset{(0.665)}{2.586\ TT_{t-1}} + \underset{(0.337)}{0.233\ (S\text{-}PUI)_t} + \underset{(1.26)}{0.313\ \Delta\ YNA_t}$$

$\bar{R}^2 = 0.671$

Private Investment =

$$-1182.66 + \underset{(3.07)}{0.432\ PUI_{t-1}} + \underset{(2.07)}{13.488\ TT_{t-1}} + \underset{(4.32)}{0.499\ (S\text{-}PUI)_t} + \underset{(0.14)}{0.341\ \Delta YNA_t}$$

Where,

PUI = Public Investment in real terms.

TT = Terms of trade between agriculture manufactures.

S = Savings in real term come in real terms.

YNA = Non Agricultural Income in real terms. t values are given in brackets.

References

Bhatty, I. Z. and Sarma, M. T. R., [1977]: 'Saving Behaviour in India and Implications for Policy' in Wadhva, C. D. (ed): "Some Problems of India's Economic Policy" Second Edition, pp 276-289.

Desai, A. V., [1981]: 'Factors Underlying the Slow Growth of Indian Industry', *Economic and Political Weekly*, Volume XVI (10-12), pp 381-392.

Nayyar, D., [1978]: 'Industrial Development in India: Some Reflections on Growth and Stagnation', *Economic and Political Weekly* XII (31-33), pp 1265-1278.

Raj, K. N., [1976]: 'Growth and Stagnation in Indian Industrial Development', *Economic and Political Weekly*, Volume XI (5-7), pp 225-223 & Rangarajan. C [1980]: "Agricultural Growth and Industrial Performance in India — A Study of Interdependence" (mimeo).

Roy, S., [1981]: "Demand for Industrial Consumer Goods in India: A Study of Linkages" (A thesis done under the guidance of the author and submitted to Indian Institute of Management, Ahmedabad, under the Fellow Programme).

Sau. R., [1974]: 'Some Aspects of Intersectoral Resource Flows', *Economic and Political Weekly*, Volume VIII (31-33), pp 1277-1284.

Srinivasan, T. N. and Narayana, N. S. S., [1977]: 'Economic Performance Since the Third Plan and Its Implications for Policy', *Economic and Political Weekly*, Volume XII (6-8), pp 225-239.

Sundararajan, V. and Thakur, S., [1980]: 'Public Investment, Crowding Out and Growth: A Dynamic Model Applied to India and Korea', IMF Staff Papers, Volume 27(4), pp 814-855.

Vaidyanathan, A., [1977]: 'Constraints on Growth and Policy Options', *Economic and Political Weekly*, Volume XII (38), pp 1643-1650.

3

Industrial Growth in the 80s

Facts and Some Issues

There is no doubt that in the Eighties, industrial production has shown a strong increase. The index of industrial production with the base 1980-81=100 has shown a compound annual rate of growth between 1980-81 and 1988-89 of 7.7 per cent. During this period, while mining grew at an annual rate of nine per cent and electricity at 8.9 per cent, manufacturing grew at 7.3 per cent (Table 1). In the more recent period between 1984-85 and 1988-89, the overall Index of Industrial Production grew at an annual rate of 8.5 per cent and the manufacturing sector at nine per cent, though there has been a marked deceleration in the rate of growth in the current year. The performance in the Eighties stands in striking contrast to the performance in the Seventies when the overall industrial production grew only 4.2 per cent. Even in the period 1974-79, the growth rate was only 6.2 per cent. Data derived from the Annual Survey of Industries on gross value added by registered and unregistered manufacturing sectors also confirm that the manufacturing sectors achieved a distinctively higher growth rate during the Eighties is compared with the earlier periods.

The infrastructure industries comprising electricity, coal, saleable steel, crude petroleum, petroleum refinery products and cement, accounting for roughly 29 per cent of the total weight of the industrial production, recorded a compound annual growth rate of 8.6 per cent (Table 2). This has in fact facilitated industrial expansion. This overall growth should not, however, cloud certain regional imbalances particularly with respect to electricity. Much of the improvement in the performance of the infrastructure

---

Fourth Annual Convocation address at the Indian Institute of Management, Lucknow, April 6, 1990 (RBI Bulletin, May, 1990).

industries, has been due to improved operational efficiency than to significant additions to investments. A break-up of industrial production at two-digit level shows that during the period 1980-81 to 1988-89, manufacture of electric machinery which includes electronics showed an annual growth rate of 17 per cent followed by manufacture of chemical and chemical products which grew at 11.2 per cent per annum (Table 3). The use-based classification of Index of Industrial Production throws more light on the pattern of industrial growth. During the period 1980-81 to 1988-89, basic goods comprising coal, steel and electricity grew at an annual rate of 8.3 per cent, capital goods industries at 9.5 per cent and intermediate goods industries at 6.5 per cent (Table 4). It is interesting to note that during a period of liberalised imports of capital goods, capital goods industries have shown a strong increase. They grew at 9.5 per cent per annum during the entire period of 1980-81 to 1988-89 and at 12.9 per cent during the period 1984-85 to 1988-89. The consumer goods industries, as a whole, rose by 6.5 per cent per annum but within consumer goods sector; while consumer durables rose by 15.5 per cent per annum, non-durable goods increased by 5.0 per cent per annum.

Table 1

Compound Annual Growth Rates: Indices of Industrial Production

(per cent)

Period	*Manufacturing*	*Mining & Quarrying*	*Electricity*	*General*
1	2	3	4	5
1970-80 (1970=100)	3.9	3.8	7.0	4.2
1980-81–1988-89 1980-81=100)	7.3	9.0	8.9	7.7
1984-85–1988-89 1980-81=100)	9.0	5.5	9.0	8.5

Table 2

Trends in the Performance of Infrastructure Industries @

Year	*Composite Index of Infrastructure Industries*	*Percentage Variation over the previous year*
1	2	3
1980-81	100.0	—
1981-82	115.5	+15.5
1982-83	124.5	+ 7.8
1983-84	132.5	+ 6.4
1984-85	145.0	+ 9.4
1985-86	156.7	+ 8.1
1986-87	168.4	+ 7.5
1987-88	178.6	+ 6.0
1988-89	193.1	+ 8.1
1989-90 (April-January)	201.0	+ 6.5
1988-89 (April-January)	188.8	+ 8.0

Note: Compound growth rate in infrastructure industries between 1980-81 to 1988-89 is 8.6 per cent per annum.

@ : Includes Electricity, Coal, Saleable Steel, Petroleum Crude, Petroleum Refinery Products and Cement. These six industries account for a weight of 28.77 per cent in IIP.

Table 3

Index of Industrial Production: (Base 1980-81=100)
(Annual Growth Rates)

(per cent)

Industry	Annual Growth Rates								Compound Growth between 1980-81 to 1988-89
	1981-82	1982-83	1983-84	1984-85	1985-86	1986-87	1987-88	1988-89	
1	2	3	4	5	6	7	8	9	10
Manufacture of Food Products	13.5	14.1	-6.5	-0.9	4.7	6.0	4.4	6.8	5.1
Manufacture of Beverages, Tobacco and Tobacco Products	4.3	3.4	-3.1	6.9	0.4	-12.1	-13.8	8.5	-1.0
Manufacture of Cotton Textiles	-0.3	-10.3	12.1	1.9	8.0	1.9	-1.2	-3.5	0.9
Manufacture of Jute, Hemp & Mesta Textiles	-4.3	-2.9	-15.8	27.1	-2.2	4.0	-10.0	12.3	0.3
Manufacture of Textile Products (including wearing apparel)	-3.3	-0.4	-4.4	3.8	18.0	-22.8	5.3	46.3	3.7
Manufacture of Wood & Wood Products	53.2	-0.1	9.5	29.2	3.1	10.3	-34.3	6.2	7.0
Manufacture of Paper & Paper Products	8.2	-2.5	3.6	20.6	12.6	9.9	1.9	3.0	7.0

(Contd...)

(...Contd...)

1	2	3	4	5	6	7	8	9	10
Manufacture of Leather, Fur & Leather Products etc.	28.1	-21.8	16.2	20.1	21.1	5.0	4.4	-4.4	7.4
Manufacture of Rubber, Plastic, Petroleum and Coal Products	19.1	-0.1	14.4	8.2	3.9	-2.2	3.7	8.5	6.7
Manufacture of Chemical and Chemical Products	16.9	3.7	8.1	9.0	8.1	13.7	14.5	16.1	11.2
Manufacture of Non-metalic Mineral Products	6.7	-2.8	18.1	13.0	13.7	1.9	-1.4	16.8	8.0
Basic Metal & Alloy Products		4.2	-8.7	12.8	9.0	8.4	6.9	6.9	4.7
Manufacture of Metal Products & Parts	-5.4	-5.0	-2.0	19.2	9.2	8.5	4.2	3.0	3.7
Manufacture of Machinery/Machine Tools except Electric Machinery	11.1	0.8	6.8	6.7	2.0	8.1	-1.8	15.2	6.1
Manufacture of Electric Machinery	3.9	11.5	23.5	4.0	34.8	27.0	31.6	4.6	17.0
Manufacture of Transport Equipment	8.1	3.0	10.9	6.6	3.2	6.7	4.8	13.1	7.0
Other Manufacturing Industries	49.2	3.9	-32.5	17.4	24.3	54.2	15.6	11.1	14.8
Total Manufacturing	**7.9**	**1.4**	**5.7**	**8.0**	**9.7**	**9.3**	**7.9**	**8.9**	**7.3**
Mining	17.7	12.4	11.7	8.8	4.2	6.2	3.8	7.9	9.0
Electricity	10.2	5.7	7.6	12.0	8.5	10.3	7.6	9.6	8.9
General	9.3	3.2	6.7	8.6	9.2	8.7	7.7	8.8	7.7

Source: Central Statistical Organization.

Table 4

Annual Compound Growth Rates of Index of Industrial Production
Use-Based Classification

(per cent)

	Basic Goods	Capital Goods	Intermediate Goods	Consumer Goods	Consumer Durables	Consumer Non-Durables	General Index
1	2	3	4	5	6	7	8
1970-80 (1970=100)	5.1	5.3	3.5	3.1	5.0	2.9	4.2
1980-81–1988-89 (1980-81=100)	8.3	9.5	6.5	6.5	15.5	5.0	7.7
1984-85–1988-89 (1980-81=100)	7.9	12.9	7.0	8.0	16.8	3.3	8.5

Given the weights of these various groups, it is possible to derive how much each of these groups has contributed to the overall growth. For the period 1980-81 to 1988-89, the overall growth in industrial production, as already mentioned was 7.7 per cent. Of this growth, 47 per cent was contributed by basic goods, 21 per cent by capital goods, 16 per cent by intermediate goods, seven per cent by consumer durable goods and nine per cent by non-durable consumption goods (Table 5). Quite clearly, basic and capital goods have contributed mainly to the overall growth. Consumer durable goods, which have a weight of only 2.55 per cent in the index, contributed as much as seven per cent to the overall growth. On the other hand, consumer non-durable goods, which have a weight of 21 per cent in the total index, contributed only nine per cent. The contribution of durable consumption goods to the overall growth at seven per cent, was higher than the contribution during the Fifth Plan period at 4.3 per cent (Table 6).

While during the past four decades, India has been able to build a diversified industrial structure, the policies pursued have also resulted in a high cost economy. The 1980s saw several policy initiatives aimed at improving the competitiveness of Indian industry and also in bringing about greater modernisation and cost efficiency. This meant adoption of several measures to facilitate capacity creation and output expansion and to remove procedural impediments. Measures to facilitate capacity creation have taken the form of delicensing a number of industries and increasing the threshold level for licensing substantially subject to certain locational prescriptions. Minimum capacity levels have been prescribed for selected industries with a view to preventing fragmentation of capacity at uneconomic levels. Under this policy, existing manufacturing units are automatically allowed to expand their capacities up to the prescribed minimum economic levels, while new units are sanctioned only for the minimum capacity levels. The facility of broad banding — which enables manufacturing enterprises to adjust their product mix in line with changing market conditions and facilitate better capacity utilisation — has been allowed in respect of a number of industries.

Table 5

Contribution of the use-based groups to the Annual Average Growth Rate in General Index

(Base: 1980-81=100)

Item	*Weight*	*Seventh Plan Period (1984-85-1988-89) (four years)*		*1980-81-1988-89 (eight years)*	
		Contribution	Contribution Weighted Sectoral Growth	Contribution	Contribution Weighted Sectoral Growth
1	2	3	4	5	6
1. Basic Goods	39.42	37.59	3.21	46.87	3.37
2. Capital Goods	16.43	26.11	2.18	21.12	1.60
3. Intermediate Goods	20.51	15.46	1.32	15.73	1.25
4. Consumer Goods	23.65	20.85	1.77	16.28	1.49
Of which:					
a) Durable Goods	2.55	7.16	0.62	6.65	0.51
b) Non-durables	21.10	13.69	1.15	9.63	0.98
Total	**100.00**	**100.00**	**8.50***	**100.00**	**7.71***

*: Obtained as the average of annual growth rate for the period.

Table 6

Contribution of the Use-Based Groups to the Annual Average Growth Rate

(Base 1970=100)

Item	*Weight*	*Fifth Plan Period (1974-75 to 1978-79)*	
		Contribution	Contribution Weighted Sectoral Growth
1	2	3	4
1. Basic Goods	32.28	48.07	3.00
2. Capital Goods	15.25	13.46	0.84
3. Intermediate Goods	20.95	13.78	0.86
4. Consumer Goods	31.52	24.69	1.54
Of which:			
a) Durable Goods	3.41	4.25	0.26
b) Non-durables	28.11	20.44	1.28
Total	**100.00**	**100.0**	**6.24**

Industrial growth is very much linked to foreign trade policy. A policy of permitting imports, only if domestic production does not fulfil the domestic demand irrespective of cost and price factors, can only result in inefficiency in the production process. Therefore, an attempt has been made to liberalize the import of capital goods and other intermediates so that Indian industry is not isolated completely from external competition. Obviously, care has to be taken to ensure that domestic capital goods industries — which are inherently efficient and which are in the process of modernisation — are not placed at a disadvantage. It is necessary to identify clearly products in which the country has a comparative advantage – if not today but in the immediate future. However, the incentive structure aimed at protecting these industries, which have dynamic comparative advantage, should be phased out over a period of time. The changes in the industrial licensing policy made in recent years have been in the right direction. In fact, licensing should be limited only to areas where the desired changes in output cannot be brought about through price and fiscal instruments. By and large, output composition should be influenced through such changes in income distribution, as can be brought about and through fiscal incentives and disincentives.

There is evidence to show that there has been some improvement in productivity in Indian industry. The Incremental Capital-Output Ratio, which is one measure of the efficiency of the production system, has shown some decrease thus implying improvement in productivity. Gross Incremental Capital-Output Ratio at 1980-81 prices was 3.80 for the decade of the Fifties, 5.33 for the decade of Sixties, 6.12 in the decade of Seventies and during the period 1980-81 to 1987-88, this works out to 4.22. For the manufacturing sector alone, the incremental capital-output ratio was 3.16 during the Fifties, 5.75 during the Sixties and 6.41 during the Seventies. For the period 1980-81 to 1986-87, this appears to have declined to 4.87. Several studies have shown that as measured by Domestic Resource Cost there are several segments of the Indian industry which are efficient by international standards. These studies also show that while in the production of some of the basic products like steel India may be uncompetitive, it is competitive at the downstream level.

In relation to industrial growth, two important questions have been raised. The first issue is whether the high rate of growth in industrial production seen in the last decade and more particularly in the last five years is sustainable, given the pattern of industrial output. The second issue relates to the employment potential of the present pattern of industrial growth.

It has been pointed out that the strong growth of durable consumption goods implies that the production structure is responding to demand from a restricted income group and therefore, future growth may be inhibited as demand from this group tapers off. Quite clearly, durable consumption goods have grown faster than any other sector of industrial production. Their weight in the total index is however, small. Therefore, the contribution of durable consumption goods to the overall growth during the Eighties has been only seven per cent. The picture is unlikely to change very much even if one takes account of the fact that some part of the output of basic and intermediate goods industries must have gone as inputs to the consumer durable goods industries. It is, therefore, difficult to sustain the argument that the faster growth achieved in the recent past is accounted for only by the growth in durable consumption goods industries. As mentioned before, there has been a substantial growth in the basic and capital goods industries as well.

In this context it is pertinent to note that output composition of consumption goods industries cannot be exogenously determined. The output composition is determined by the level and distribution of income and in that sense, the consumption vector is endogenous. When the production of durable consumption goods assumes a larger weight in the total Index of Industrial Production, industrial growth may begin to show noticeable year to year swings, as the demand for durable consumption goods can get bunched. The high rate of growth of durable consumption goods industries in the recent period reflects the rapid growth in the organised sector incomes. The revisions in the wage structures of government employees and others and the bulk payment of arrears must have had a direct impact on the consumption of durable goods. Given the distribution of income and the propensity to save, any direct curtailment of production of certain goods may not work because this can result in clandestine production or increased smuggling. The need to curtail ostentatious consumption in a poor country like ours cannot be over emphasised. The need gets further strengthened when these goods are import intensive. While fiscal measures can help to curb ostentatious consumption, an appropriate incomes policy, which covers the salaries and wages of the organised sector, is essential if the output composition is to be changed.

There is also another aspect to the widening of the demand base. At the present moment even some of the essential consumption goods are being produced at unit costs which place these commodities outside the consumption basket of lower income groups. The distinction between 'luxury' goods and 'non-luxury' goods becomes thin, when the unit costs of certain commodities are brought down substantially. Even now the consumption basket of the lower income groups may include commodities which would, in an earlier period, have been classified as 'luxury goods'. The route to widening the demand base also lies via improving efficiency and reducing the unit cost.

The second area of concern relates to the sluggishness in the growth of employment. Acceleration of growth in the Eighties has not been matched by a corresponding acceleration in employment.

The employment elasticity with respect to aggregate output appears to be declining. Changes in the occupational structure in favour of manufacturing and other non-agricultural activities are an essential part of the development process. It is in this context, the trend towards the decline in employment elasticities in manufacturing has been disturbing. Employment generating capacity of output growth in general has been tending to decline. Total employment in the organised private sector industry was 72.27 lakhs at the end of March 1980. It reached the peak of 75.52 lakhs at the end of March 1983 and thereafter it has consistently remained below that level, with the latest data for March 1988, placing it at 73.91 lakhs. Within the private organised sector, the fall in employment in manufacturing has been much more conspicuous. It attained the peak of 46.61 lakhs at the end of March 1982 and fell to 43.99 lakhs at the end of March 1988, thus showing an absolute fall of 5.6 per cent over a period of six years. Employment in the public sector has, however, been steadily rising in the Eighties.

The strategy for employment growth has to be carefully worked out so that the growth of employment opportunities goes hand in hand with technical and economic efficiency. Otherwise, growth itself cannot be sustained. In any programme of increasing the employment potential, agriculture still has to play a major role, though the labour absorptive capacity of agriculture has also started showing a declining trend, particularly in States which ushered in the Green Revolution.

In a labour abundant economy, choice of technology has necessarily to be biased in favour of labour. However, in a wide area of manufacturing activity involving the production of basic and capital goods, which involve the use of high technology, opportunities for shifting factor proportions in favour of labour may not be available. The production of these goods by their very nature is capital intensive. It is against this background that there has been a renewed emphasis on the development of small-scale industries, both traditional and modern. The advantages claimed in favour of the development of small-scale industrial units are two fold: (i) It leads to a decentralised production structure resulting thereby, in a wider geographical coverage; and (ii) Since these units are less capital intensive, there will be greater absorption of labour. The first proposition has validity and in a vast country like ours, a wider geographical coverage is an objective in itself. However, in relation to the second proposition, there are differences of opinion. In the case of modern small-scale industries, it is not clearly established that they are less capital-intensive than large-scale units. It cannot, therefore, be automatically assumed that promotion of these units will lead to larger employment. In the case of traditional industries, small-scale units are the rule and they are labour-intensive. However, two separate issues arise in the case of traditional industries. First, they are not always able to generate adequate surpluses and this can come in the way of sustained growth. Second, products using highly labour intensive techniques — particularly in the area of consumption goods — may not necessarily meet the taste requirements of consumers. All this is not to deny the possibilities of labour intensive techniques producing goods which are acceptable to the consumers and generating adequate surpluses. We need to identify these products and provide them with adequate support including an efficient marketing mechanism. Strangely, some of these products can be those which meet the needs of upper-income groups or meeting the demand of external markets. Protection of the output of certain small-scale industries which employ large labour and which may not meet the normal criteria of economic efficiency may still be resorted to provided the products so protected are limited. However, if in general, factor proportions are to respond to relative factor prices, greater attention needs to be paid to the determination of the prices of capital and labour. While fiscal incentives that favour capital intensity must in general be avoided, rigidities in the labour market must also be reduced if employment in the organised industrial sector is to expand. The policy framework must, therefore, be such as to promote efficient labour intensive techniques.

Indian industry needs technology upgradation and modernisation. Obviously, certain priorities need to be set here so that the maximum impact can be derived by the economy. Capital goods industries in particular must remain competitive in terms of quality and cost; otherwise this can have adverse implications for the user sectors. This is where industrial policy ties in with foreign trade policy. The transition from a protected environment to a more competitive situation is not always easy. Industrial units must learn to adjust their production pattern in response to the changing situation. Even as liberalisation of licensing facilitates entry, this can result in excess capacity in certain sectors. Financial institutions have, therefore, a role in realistically assessing the feasibility and prospects of new investment proposals. While facilitating entry, the policy framework should also permit exit, where it becomes necessary, so that chronic sickness can be avoided.

4

Paradigm Shifts in Industrial Policy

Introduction

All developed countries have gone through a process of transformation, which meant a shift from agriculture to industry. Between 1870 and 1930, the proportion of active population employed in agriculture had declined from 54 per cent to 23 per cent in the US, from 85 per cent to 51 per cent in Japan, and from 42 per cent to 25 per cent in France. Given this historical development world over, it is not surprising that growth was identified with industrialisation in the developing economies. The Indian planners, however, went a step further and talked of industrialisation with an emphasis on heavy industries. The Second Five-Year Plan (1956-61) gave expression to it, when it said that the Plan "accords high priority to industrialisation and especially to the development of basic and heavy industries". It was no doubt recognised that for the process of industrialisation to start, there has to be a transfer of resources from agriculture. The Second Five-Year Plan recognised this clearly when it said "development involves a transfer of part of the working force from agriculture to secondary and tertiary activities, but this, in turn, presupposes an increase in productivity in agriculture itself, if the food and raw material requirements of a developing economy are to be met" (Government of India: 1956). However, in actual fact, the realisation that inadequate agricultural growth and insufficient availability of wage goods, including foodgrains, could act as a restraint on industrial growth, came only later. The industry-agriculture relationship was mainly seen in terms of agriculture,

* An earlier version was delivered as the Fifth Nagaraj Memorial Lecture by the author at Hyderabad on November 5, 2002.

Money and Finance, Oct., 2002. pp 39-53.

making available the required raw materials. Once again, the recognition of the importance of agricultural growth and rural incomes as a source of demand for industrial goods, thereby fuelling industrial growth, came later.

Pre-Reform Industrialisation Paradigm

The process of industrialisation in India in the first four decades was governed by two considerations – import substitution and industrial licensing. Import substitution constituted a major plank of India's foreign trade policy and, therefore, of industrialisation. Planners, more or less chose to ignore the option of foreign trade as an engine of India's economic growth. This was primarily due to the then widely prevalent view that exports could not be a significant factor in economic growth of developing economies – a perspective that came to be termed "export pessimism" in the literature. A further impetus to the inward orientation was provided by the existence of a vast domestic market. In retrospect, it is clear that the policy makers not only underestimated the export possibilities but also the import intensity of the import substitution process itself. As a consequence, India's share of total world exports declined from 1.91 per cent in 1950 to a mere 0.53 per cent in 1992.

The inward looking industrialisation process did result in high rates of industrial growth between 1956 and 1966, as may be observed from Table 1. However, several weaknesses of such a process of industrialisation soon became evident, as inefficiencies crept into the system and the economy turned into an increasingly 'high-cost' one. Over a period of time, this led to a 'technological lag' and also resulted in poor export performance.

Foreign trade policy issues became the focus of intensive discussion in the early 1980s. It came to be realised that a scheme of import licensing, under which imports were permitted only to the extent that domestic production fell short of domestic demand, irrespective of difference in cost and prices would lead to inefficiency. The view gained ground that a more liberal policy of imports of capital goods and technology would enable India to reap the benefits of international division of labour.[1] The attempt, therefore, was to move away from import substitution *per se* towards efficient import substitution, so that considerations relating to cost and efficiency were incorporated in the overall policy framework. It also became increasingly clear that production for export could not be isolated from production for the home market.

Table 1

Annual Growth Rate in the Index of Industrial Production

(per cent)

Period	General Index	Basic Industries	Capital Goods	Intermediate Goods	Consumer Goods
1951 to 1955	6.7	30.9*	-	5.8	3.4
1956 to 1960	5.7	4.7*	-	9.8	2.9
1961 to 1965	9.0	10.5	19.7	7.2	5.0
1966 to 1970	3.7	6.2	-1.4	4.0	4.0
1971 to 1975	3.6	5.3	5.4	1.8	1.6
1976 to 1980	4.8	5.1	5.2	-	4.9
1981-82 to 1985-86	7.3	8.4	7.1	6.3	6.7
1986-87 to 1990-91	8.4	7.4	15.8	5.5	6.6
1991-92 to 1995-96	6.1	6.5	6.0	6.1	6.0
1996-97 to 2000-01$	5.7	4.2	7.7	7.1	5.5
1992-93 to 1996-97	7.4	6.8	8.9	8.5	6.6
1997-98 to 2001-02 $	5.1	4.1	4.7	5.8	5.5

Notes: * Figures represent investment goods industries, which are the basic and capital goods industries.

$ Refers to Base Year 1993-94=100 and all other periods since 1981-82 refers to Base Year 1980-81=100.

Sources: Rangarajan, C. (1982 and 1994), *Handbook of Statistics on Indian Economy, 2001*, Reserve Bank of India and the *Annual Report*, Reserve Bank of India 2001-02.

Another important element in the process of industrialisation was a system of industrial licensing under which a licence was required before setting up any large unit. This practice had roots in the belief that resources could be best allocated only by a planning authority and that licensing was the best way to manage limited resources. While the industrial licensing system underwent some changes in terms of threshold levels and types of products, it formed an essential part of government policy until the end of the 1980s.

New Economic Policy

The year 1991 is an important landmark in the economic history of post-Independent India. The country went through a severe economic crisis, triggered by a serious balance of payments situation. The crisis was converted into an opportunity to introduce some fundamental changes in the content and approach to economic policy. The response to the crisis was to put in place a set of policies aimed at stabilisation and structural reform. While the stabilisation policies were aimed at correcting the weaknesses that had developed on the fiscal and the balance of payments fronts, the structural reforms sought to remove the rigidities that had entered into the various segments of the Indian economy. The structural reforms introduced in the early 1990s broadly covered the areas of industrial licensing, foreign trade, foreign investment, exchange rate management and the financial sector. From the point of view of industrialisation, changes in the areas of licensing, foreign trade and investment had important implications. Even before the onset of reforms, the problems associated with industrial licensing were well recognised. The approach document of the Eighth Plan (1991-1996), submitted in May 1990 had remarked: "A return to the regime of direct, indiscriminate and detailed controls in industry is clearly out of question. Past experience has shown that such control system is not effective in achieving the desired objective. Also, the system is widely abused and leads to corruption, delays and inefficiency" (Government of India: 1990). One early step that was undertaken as part of the structural reform process was to dispense with licensing. Changes in foreign trade policy focussed on reducing the tariff rates and dismantling quantitative controls over imports. The tariff rates have been brought down in stages. Some caution in this regard had become necessary to enable the Indian industries, set up behind high protective tariff walls to adjust to the changed situation. The policy towards foreign investment underwent a significant change with foreign investors given the freedom to own majority shareholding over a wide spectrum of industries.

Without going into details, the common thread running through the various policy measures introduced since 1991 has been the improvement of the efficiency of the system. The thrust of the New Economic Policy has been towards creating a more competitive environment in the economy as a means to improving the productivity and efficiency of the system. This was to be achieved by removing the barriers to entry and the restrictions on the growth of firms. While the Industrial Policy of 1992 sought to bring about a greater competitive environment domestically, the counterpart Trade Policy, set out in the same year, sought to improve international competitiveness, subject to the degree of protection offered by the tariffs. The private sector was to be given a larger space to operate in as much as some of the areas, reserved exclusively earlier for the public sector, were now to be opened to the private sector. In these areas, the public sector would have to compete with the private sector, even though the public sector might continue to play the dominant role in the foreseeable future. What was sought to be achieved was the improvement in the functioning of the various entities, whether they were in the private or in the public sector.

Trends in Industrial Production

Before focussing on the challenges before industrialisation in the liberalised regime, let us take a brief look at the pattern and rate of growth of industrialisation in our country in the last five decades. Table 1 provides the basic data on the growth rate. In the 1950s, the average annual rate of growth of industrial production was 6.2 per cent. In the 1960s, while the first half had a very high growth rate, the second half showed a sharp decline. This deceleration in growth rate continued through the 1970s. Thus, over the fifteen-year period 1966-80, the rate of industrial growth was at a modest annual rate of four per cent. The growth rate picked up substantially in the decade of the 1980s, when the average annual growth rate was 7.8 per cent. There was a collapse of the industrial growth rate in 1991-92 and a small growth in 1992-93 (Tables 2, 3 and 4). Since 1992-93, the average annual growth rate till the end of that decade was six per cent. While the period 1992-93 to 1996-97, had an annual growth rate of 7.4 per cent, in the subsequent period the growth rate came down and the average for the next five years is only 5.1 per cent[2] (Table 1).

Table 2

Annual Growth Rates of Index of Industrial Production — Use-based Classification

Year	*General*	*Basic Goods*	*Capital Goods*	*Intermediate Goods*	*Consumer Goods*	*Consumer Durables*	*Consumer Non-durables*
Base: 1980-81=100							
Weight	100.00	39.42	16.43	20.51	23.65	2.55	21.10
1981-82	9.3	10.9	6.7	3.7	13.8	10.9	14.1
1982-83	3.2	7.0	3.7	1.0	-1.6	9.1	-2.8
1983-84	6.7	6.0	11.7	9.8	1.6	16.1	-0.4
1984-85	8.6	11.1	3.0	9.7	7.2	27.3	5.1
1985-86	8.7	6.8	10.6	7.5	12.5	18.7	11.5
1986-87	9.2	9.3	18.2	4.1	6.1	13.7	3.6
1987-88	7.3	5.5	15.9	2.7	9.8	7.6	10.3
1988-89	8.7	9.9	7.1	11.7	3.9	22.3	0.1
1989-90	8.6	5.4	21.9	4.3	6.5	2.4	7.5
1990-91	8.2	6.9	16.0	4.7	6.8	10.7	5.8
1991-92	0.6	6.5	-8.5	-2.1	1.0	-10.9	4.0
1992-93	2.3	2.6	-0.1	5.4	1.8	-0.7	2.4
1993-94	6.0	9.4	-4.1	11.7	4.0	16.1	1.4
1994-95	9.4	5.6	24.8	3.7	8.7	10.2	8.3
1995-96	12.1	8.3	17.9	11.8	14.3	36.1	8.8
1996-97	7.1	8.2	5.9	9.8	4.1	5.4	3.1
1997-98	4.2	7.0	-4.0	6.9	4.6	9.9	2.9
Base: 1993-94=100							
Weight	100.00	35.57	9.26	26.51	28.66	5.36	23.30
1994-95	9.1	9.6	9.2	5.3	12.1	16.2	11.2
1995-96	13.1	10.8	5.4	19.3	12.8	25.8	9.8
1996-97	6.1	3.0	11.4	8.1	6.2	4.6	6.6
1997-98	6.6	6.8	5.8	8.0	5.5	7.8	4.9
1998-99	4.1	1.7	12.6	6.1	2.2	5.6	1.1
1999-00	6.7	5.5	6.9	8.8	5.7	14.1	3.2
2000-01	5.1	3.9	1.7	4.5	8.0	14.6	5.8
2001-02	2.8	2.7	-3.4	1.6	6.0	11.5	4.1

Sources: *Handbook of Statistics on Indian Economy, 2001*, Reserve Bank of India and *Annual Report 2001-02*, Reserve Bank of India, 2001-02.

Table 3

Annual Growth Rates of Index of Industrial Production & Its Components

Year	*Mining & Quarrying*	*Manufacturing*	*Electricity*	*General*
		Base: 1980-81=100		
Weight	11.46	77.11	11.43	100.00
1981-82	17.7	8.0	10.2	9.3
1982-83	12.4	1.3	5.7	3.2
1983-84	11.8	5.7	7.6	6.7
1984-85	8.8	8.0	12.0	8.6
1985-86	4.1	9.7	8.5	8.7
1986-87	6.2	9.4	10.3	9.2
1987-88	3.7	7.9	7.6	7.3
1988-89	7.9	8.7	9.5	8.7
1989-90	6.3	8.6	10.9	8.6
1990-91	4.5	8.9	7.8	8.2
1991-92	0.6	-0.8	8.5	0.6
1992-93	0.6	2.2	5.0	2.3
1993-94	3.5	6.1	7.5	6.0
1994-95	7.5	9.8	8.5	9.4
1995-96	7.4	13.6	8.1	12.1
1996-97	0.4	8.6	3.9	7.1
1997-98	4.9	3.6	6.9	4.2
		Base: 1980-81=100		
Weight	10.47	79.36	10.17	100.00
1994-95	9.8	9.1	8.5	9.1
1995-96	9.8	14.1	8.1	13.1
1996-97	-2.0	7.3	4.0	6.1
1997-98	7.0	6.6	6.6	6.6
1998-99	-0.8	4.4	6.4	4.1
1999-00	1.0	7.1	7.3	6.7
2000-01	3.7	5.4	4.0	5.1
2001-02	1.3	2.9	3.1	2.8

Sources: Same as in Table 2.

Table 4

Industrial Growth Rates – Index of Industrial Production & National Accounts

Year	Index of Industrial Production		National Accounts*
	1980-81=100	1993-94=100	1993-94=100
1981-82	9.3	—	8.8
1982-83	3.2	—	7.3
1983-84	6.7	—	8.8
1984-85	8.6	—	6.4
1985-86	8.7	—	4.6
1986-87	9.2	—	8.1
1987-88	7.3	—	6.9
1988-89	8.7	—	9.8
1989-90	8.6	—	11.2
1990-91	8.2	—	6.8
1991-92	0.6	—	-1.2
1992-93	2.3	—	4.1
1993-94	6.0	—	6.4
1994-95	9.4	9.1	11.3
1995-96	12.1	13.1	12.9
1996-97	7.1	6.1	8.2
1997-98	4.2	6.6	3.0
1998-99	—	4.1	2.8
1999-00	—	6.7	4.2
2000-01	—	4.9	6.2
2001-02	—	2.8	2.9

Note: * Refers to value added in industry, that is, mining & quarrying, manufacturing and electricity, gas & water supply.

Sources: Same as Table 2.

The composition of India's industrial output has also undergone considerable change (Table 5). The share of basic and capital goods combined had reached a peak of 55.8 per cent of total output in 1980-81. It has since then come down. In the Index of Industrial Production with the base 1993-94, their share has come down to 44.8 per cent. The composition of output has greater significance in a closed economy than in an open economy. In a closed economy, the output of basic and capital goods has a link with investment. However, this need not necessarily be so in an open economy in which output composition reflects more the comparative advantage.

Table 5

Weights of Major Industrial Groups in IIP

Groups	*1956= 100*	*1960= 100*	*1970= 100*	*1980-81= 100*	*1993-94= 100*
Basic Goods	22.13	25.11	32.28	39.42	35.57
Capital Goods	4.71	11.76	15.74	16.43	9.26
Intermediate Goods	24.59	25.88	20.95	20.51	26.51
Consumer Goods	48.37	37.25	31.03	23.65	28.66
Consumer Durables	—	5.68	2.92	2.55	5.36
Consumer Non-durables	—	31.57	28.11	21.10	23.30

Sources: *Report on Currency and Finance*, Reserve Bank of India, various issues, and the *Handbook of Statistics on Indian Economy*, 2001, Reserve Bank of India.

While analysing the growth in industrial production, one must also look at the performance of the service sector. The growth rate of the service sector has shown a steady increase over the last five decades. The annual growth rate of the service sector was 6.7 per cent in the 1980s and 7.5 per cent in 1990s (Tables 6 and 7). In fact, it was only in 1990s, that the growth rate of the service sector has exceeded that of the industrial sector.

Another aspect of the industrialisation process in the post-liberalisation period has been the steady flow of Foreign Direct Investment (FDI). In 1991, the level of FDI flows into the country was $ 97 million. Through the 1990s it increased from year to year and reached a peak of $ 3,557 million in 1997-98. After some set back during the next three years, it has again started increasing. In 2001-02, the FDI inflows increased to $ 3,904 million, an increase of 67 per cent over the previous year. In 2002-03, upto the end of October, FDI inflows were at $ 1,984 million, marginally lower than that for the same period last year.

Table 6

Annual Growth Rates of Components of Gross Domestic Product
At factor cost and constant (1993-94) prices

(per cent)

Year	*Gross Domestic Product arising in*			*Total Gross*
	Agriculture & Allied	*Industry*	*Services*	*Domestic Product*
1971-72	-1.9	3.6	3.1	1.0
1972-73	-5.0	4.2	2.9	-0.3
1973-74	7.2	3.9	1.8	4.6
1974-75	-1.5	3.3	3.4	1.2
1975-76	12.9	4.2	7.8	9.0
1976-77	-5.8	8.4	5.3	1.2
1977-78	10.0	5.7	5.7	7.5
1978-79	2.3	11.2	5.4	5.5
1979-80	-12.8	-2.4	1.1	-5.2
1980-81	12.9	2.0	5.7	7.2
1981-82	5.3	8.8	5.4	6.0
1982-83	-0.7	7.3	4.8	3.1
1983-84	9.6	8.8	5.5	7.7
1984-85	1.5	6.4	6.0	4.3
1985-86	0.7	4.6	7.7	4.5
1986-87	-0.6	8.1	6.8	4.3
1987-88	-1.3	6.9	6.4	3.8
1988-89	15.5	9.8	7.2	10.5
1989-90	1.5	11.2	8.6	6.7
1990-91	4.1	6.8	6.1	5.6
1991-92	-1.5	-1.2	4.5	1.3
1992-93	5.8	4.1	5.1	5.1
1993-94	4.1	6.4	6.9	5.9
1994-95	5.0	11.3	6.9	7.3
1995-96	-0.9	12.9	10.0	7.3
1996-97	9.6	8.2	6.7	7.8
1997-98	-2.4	3.0	9.8	4.8
1998-99	7.1	2.8	8.0	6.6
1999-00	1.3	4.2	9.4	6.1
2000-01	-0.2	6.2	5.0	4.0
2001-02	5.7	2.9	6.2	5.4

Sources: Same as Table 2.

Table 7

Growth Rates of Components of Gross Domestic Product–Annual Averages

At factor cost and constant (1993-94) prices

(per cent)

Period	*Agriculture & Allied*	*Industry*	*Services*	*Gross Domestic Product*
1991-92 to 1995-96	2.5	6.7	6.7	5.4
1996-97 to 2000-01	3.1	4.9	7.8	5.9
1992-93 to 1996-97	4.7	8.6	7.1	6.7
1997-98 to 2001-02	2.3	3.8	7.7	5.4

Notes: Averages of annual rates of growth.

Sources: Same as Table 2.

Thus, in the post-liberalisation period, the total inflow of FDI has amounted to $ 23,710 million as at the end of October 2002. The total of portfolio inflows aggregate $ 23,022 million, over the same period, of which $ 9,019 million came in as proceeds of issuance of Global Depository Receipts (GDR) and American Depository Receipts (ADR) by Indian companies. The total inflow through the Foreign Institutional Investors (FII) during this period aggregates $ 12,792 million. Though the purchase of shares by FIIs may not add to investment directly, there is the possibility that those from whom the shares were bought, might have utilised these funds for investment.

New Challenges

Globalisation and Competition

Changes in the foreign trade and foreign investment policies have altered the environment in which Indian industries have to operate. The path of transition is, no doubt, difficult. A greater integration of the Indian economy with the rest of the world is unavoidable. We must recognise that there are many countries, which are knocking at the doors of the World Trade Organisation (WTO) to enter. It is important that Indian industry be forward looking and get organised to compete with the rest of the world at levels of tariff, comparable to those of other developing countries. Obviously, the Indian

Government should be alert to ensure that Indian industries are not the victims of unfair trade practices. The safeguards available in the WTO agreement must be fully utilised to protect the interests of Indian industries. India must take a proactive stand in the next round of trade negotiations and articulate its own demands. These would focus on what it wants from the global trading system, such as prohibition of unilateral trade action, establishing symmetry between the movement of capital and natural persons and zero tariffs in industrialised countries on labour intensive exports of developing countries.

Indian industry has a right to demand that the macroeconomic policy environment should be conducive to rapid economic growth. The configuration of policy decisions in the recent period has been attempting to do that. It is, however, time for Indian industrial units to recognise that the challenges of the new century demand greater action at the enterprise level. They have to learn to swim in the tempestuous waters of competition and away from the sheltered waters of the swimming pools. India is no longer a country producing goods and services for the domestic market alone. Indian firms are becoming and have to become global players. At the minimum, they must be able to meet global competition. The search for identifying new competitive advantages must begin earnestly. India's ascendancy in Information Technology (IT) is only partly by design. However, it must be said to the credit of policy makers, that once the potential in this area was discovered, the policy environment became strongly industry friendly.

How do India and Indian firms maintain a competitive edge? Analysing India's comparative advantage in engineering *vis-à-vis* China, a leading Indian industrialist[3] has commented, that in products that involved flexible manufacturing with a high level of product and industrial engineering, multivendor co-ordination and continuous improvement, the Chinese fared badly. They have been reported to excel at manufacturing processes that involve both relatively fewer steps, and doing so on a large scale. The commentator adds that what India lacks in mass manufacturing capacities can be made up by her capabilities in design innovations and by moving up the value chain. It is worth pondering over this comment. Experts from the various industries must judge the validity of this statement. However, this is just one illustration. Over a wide spectrum of activities, India's advantage, actual and that which can be realised in a short span of time, must be drawn up. Of course, in a number of cases, it will require building plants on a global scale. But, this need not necessarily be so in all cases. In fact the advent of IT is modifying the industrial structure. The revolution in telecommunications and IT is simultaneously creating a huge single market economy, while making the parts smaller and more powerful. In today's environment, the primary focus has to be on the strategy and quality of microeconomic business management and the goal must be to achieve higher levels of efficiency and productivity. A new productivity culture must emerge and with it, an organisational structure and incentive system that promote productivity. In this context, it is worth noting the turnaround in productivity, which the USA has achieved during the last decade.

Productivity Growth

Higher productivity in the industrial sector helps to achieve faster economic growth. A recent study on sources of output growth in developing countries found that about 60-70 per cent of per capita growth is explained by capital accumulation, about 10-20 per cent by human capital and the remaining is explained by improvement in Total Factor Productivity (IMF, 2000). Industrial growth in India, like many developing countries has seldom witnessed rapid productivity growth. Technically, productivity growth is usually measured in terms of Total Factor Productivity (TFP) growth. TFP is nothing but the ratio of output to a combination of all inputs used.

Several research studies have gone into the issue of productivity growth in Indian industry in the 1980s and in the post-liberalisation period. Unfortunately, there is no unanimity with regard to the conclusions. Results differ based on the methodology and data used. While several studies earlier found a substantial growth in productivity in the 1980s, some recent studies throw doubt on these conclusions. In the post-liberalisation period, one would *a priori* expect an improvement in productivity growth. However, one difficulty in analysing productivity performance in the post-liberalisation period is the lack of adequate observations. Even the few limited studies do not go beyond 1998. One detailed study of selected manufacturing industries finds a substantial improvement in the productivity growth (Trivedi *et al,* 2000). The same study finds an improvement of productivity in manufacturing in general. Similarly, a study which makes use of data on 487 firms come to the conclusion that, there is credible evidence of improvement in productivity in the post-reform period (Kathuria, 2002). On the contrary, another study, examining the productivity of the selected manufacturing groups, facing significant tariff reduction using data on 2300 firms, does not find evidence of acceleration of productivity growth in the post-reform period (Balakrishnan *et al*, 2000). A more recent study found evidence of a positive growth in TFP in Indian manufacturing sector in the post-reform period. The TFP growth is estimated at 3.4 per cent per annum for the period 1991-92 to 1997-98. However, this was a shade lower than the TFP growth of 3.8 per cent per annum during the 1980s (Ahluwalia *et al*, 2002)

Technology Intensity

Technology is the lifeblood of industry. Future progress will be propelled by technology, as it has been so in the past. The Indian manufacturing sector must be fully in tune with the latest development in technology. It is in this context that one must note with concern, the declining trend in the ratio of Research and Development (R&D) expenditures. The proportion of national resources spent on R&D by India has fallen steadily from a peak of 0.98 per cent in 1988 to 0.66 per cent in 1997. The bulk of R&D expenditure in India is accounted for by the public funded R&D institutions with industry spending only 28 per cent of national R&D expenditure. The decline in the proportion in national R&D expenditure may be due to the budgetary squeeze. However, even the rate of growth of R&D expenditure by industry has declined in the 1990s. A recent study analysing the trend in the R&D expenditure as a proportion of turnover of 4209 companies shows that the proportion of R&D expenditure has gone down from 0.868 per cent in the pre-reform period to 0.835 per cent in the post-reform period (Kumar and Aggarwal, 2000). The bulk of the decline is on account of local firms. The R&D intensity of these firms declined from 0.90 per cent to 0.831 per cent. Normally, it is expected that outward orientation will result in greater in-house R&D. Even adaptation of imported technology will require R&D efforts. It is necessary that industry associations make an in-depth analysis of R&D expenditures.

Road Map for Indian Industry

What we need today is a road map for the Indian industry. It must delineate the path, different industries must take to achieve productivity and efficiency levels, comparable to the best in the world. Of course, we must have our priorities. We must know where we have a distinct comparative advantage as in the case of IT (or biotechnology – BT). We must also know where the pay-off is highest in terms of employment. Agro-processing industries need a more focussed attention in this regard. In effect, what we require is a strategic plan for the growth of industries. The plan should address in relation to each major industry issues relating to technology upgradation, size and structure of firms and export potential. While industry-specific policies may be indicated, the focus must be on how to improve the functioning of individual enterprises to reach international standards. Where we cannot achieve such standards, we must be willing and honest enough to say so. However, the goal must be, how, through a combination of technology modernisation and changes in organisational structure which promote productivity, Indian industry can compete effectively in the world market. The 'old economy' dominates the Indian industry. We should not let the old economy to become 'older'. Cement, steel and textiles will not vanish. We must rejuvenate and revitalise the old economy with the new economy tools. All said and done, IT is an intermediate product. The task of preparing such plans or vision documents can be performed by any number of organisations. Even the Planning Commission, which has a responsibility to chalk out medium-term strategy, can undertake this task. Perhaps, industry associations, with the help of industry leaders and experts should prepare these documents. The purpose of these documents should not be to set targets. They ought to be qualitative in character. Mere identification of growth prospects is not enough. These documents should go deeper and pinpoint requisite actions at the enterprise level. It must kindle the spirit of entrepreneurship combined with excellence. As an eminent critic put it, the world cannot marginalise India; but India can marginalise herself (Bergsten, 1999). We must guard ourselves against this danger.

The recent slowdown in industrial production has caused much concern. After a strong growth between 1993-94 and 1996-97, there has been a steady decline in the growth rate. It is only the strong growth in the service sector that has helped to offset this trend and keep the overall growth rate at a reasonable level. Usually the employment elasticity of the service sector is high. However, the type of employment generated depends on the nature of services that grow.

For example, the strong growth in IT[4] can generate demand only for the relatively higher skilled.

One must have some understanding of the causes of the decelerating trend in industrial production in the last four years, if measures to counter the trend are to be taken. The slowdown in 1997-98 and 1998-99 can, to some extent be explained by the substantial building up of capacities in the previous three years. In fact, the investment: GDP rate reached its peak value of 26.53 per cent in 1995-96. However, the continued weakness needs additional explanation.

The familiar argument of imports being a cause of deceleration of domestic production is not substantiated because the import growth rate was weak. In fact, there is a positive correlation between growth rate in imports and industrial production (Tables 8 and 9). External demand has an important impact in an increasingly open economy. The deceleration in world trade growth since 2001 must have had some effect on domestic industrial production. Another factor that may have contributed to the deceleration of industrial production, is the deceleration in agricultural growth rate. The growth rate in agriculture between 1992-93 and 1996-97 was 4.7 per cent while between 1997-98 and 2001-02 it was 2.3 per cent. The period since 1996-97 is marked by a decline in investment rate (Table 10). While public investment declined from its peak value of 8.7 per cent in 1993-94 to 7.1 per cent in 2000-01, private corporate investment declined from its peak value of 9.6 per cent in 1995-96 to 5.9 per cent in 2000-01. In raising the growth rate of the economy, we need to focus on investment. While investment demand is part of aggregate demand, it is not so much the stimulation of overall demand as that of investment *per se* which is crucial for ensuring and sustaining faster growth.

In enhancing the level of investment, I would like to emphasise four critical factors:

- First, all investment decisions are based on future prospects. Continuation of economic policy thus becomes the key to sustaining expectations in the right direction. There has to be a consensus on the core elements of economic policy among decision-makers, legislators and political leaders.
- Second, if the 'feel good' factor is to be restored as a stimulant of 'animal spirits', good governance has an important role to play. Investors need to be assured of dynamism and efficiency in overall governance.

Table 8

Year-on-year Rates of Growth of Imports
In terms of its value in US dollars

(per cent)

Commodity	*1990-91*	*1991-92*	*1992-93*	*1993-94*	*1994-95*	*1995-96*	*1996-97*	*1997-98*	*1998-99*	*1999-2000*	*2000-01*	*2001-02*
Iron & Steel	-12.9	-32.2	-2.5	2.1	46.4	24.3	-5.2	3.7	-25.2	-10.5	-18.2	6.9
Non-Ferrous Metals	-13.9	-44.5	15.9	21.4	49.8	25.9	22.3	-16.8	-35.1	-8.5	-2.4	21.0
Capital Goods	**10.4**	**-27.5**	**7.1**	**37.8**	**22.4**	**35.2**	**-4.0**	**-1.3**	**2.7**	**-10.9**	**-0.3**	**4.2**
Manufactures of Metals	16.4	-22.6	11.8	22.3	15.6	34.9	13.7	2.8	16.9	6.6	-3.7	4.4
Machine Tools	37.2	-34.3	-3.9	-6.9	38.2	74.1	41.2	-19.6	-17.8	-24.6	-16.2	-11.9
Machinery except Electrical & Electronic	8.8	-30.6	13.4	13.9	44.9	43.9	-7.1	-0.6	-15.9	-9.8	-1.3	9.4
Electrical Machinery except Electronic	-12.8	-33.6	31.3	-75.3	23.2	53.7	-15.8	16.3	11.3	4.0	9.9	23.3
Electronic Goods					34.6	42.7	-18.7	46.6	6.5	25.8	25.3	13.6
Computer Goods					142.2	177.1	-30.1	101.5	-4.4	21.2	-13.2	-
Transport Equipment	4.6	-60.1	24.4	175.1	-12.3	-0.8	34.3	-29.2	-24.1	42.4	-38.4	-12.4
Project Goods	36.5	3.2	-13.1	27.0	14.2	29.0	-11.4	-17.9	54.5	-63.3	-24.2	-24.5
Non-Oil Imports	3.1	-22.2	12.3	11.2	29.5	28.3	-0.2	14.5	8.0	3.0	-5.9	6.3
Total Imports	**13.4**	**-19.4**	**12.7**	**6.5**	**22.9**	**28.0**	**6.7**	**6.0**	**2.2**	**17.2**	**1.7**	**1.1**

Sources: Same as Table 2.

Table 9

Rate of Growth of Imports of Investment Related Products
Averages of Annual Rates

(per cent)

Commodity	*1993-94 to 1996-97*	*1997-98 to 2001-02*
Iron and steel	16.9	-8.7
Non-Ferrous metals	29.9	-8.3
Capital Goods	**22.9**	**-1.1**
Manufactures of metals	21.6	5.4
Machine tools	36.6	-18.0
Machinery except electrical & electronic	23.9	-3.7
Electrical machinery except electronic	-3.6	12.9
Electronic goods	19.5	23.6
Computer goods	96.4	26.3
Transport equipment	49.1	-12.3
Project goods	14.7	-15.1
Non-Oil imports	17.2	5.2
Total Imports	**16.0**	**5.6**

Sources: Same as Table 2.

- Third, for generating a general mood of optimism, it may be useful for the Government to bring together in one place in the budget, the investment that will be made by the various Departments and Ministries. A consolidation of this can be called 'investment budget'. The present classification in the budget of 'capital' and 'revenue' expenditures does not correspond to the economist's concept of investment.
- Fourth, one important factor contributing to the confidence of investors is stability in the rates of taxation and tariff rates. Unexpected downward revisions in tariffs make a lot of difference to profit calculations. While reduction in tariff rates to bring them in tune with levels prevailing in other developing economies is an important element of the reform process, there is need to inject stability in the rates. When the next change is made, it must be made clear that rates would remain at that level for at least a period of three to four years. Stability in tariff rate can have a significant favourable impact on investment decisions. A similar logic applies to stability in the rates of taxation.

Table 10

Annual Growth Rates of Domestic Investment and of its Components
At current prices

(per cent)

Year	Total*	Gross Capital Formation: Household	Gross Capital Formation: Private Corporate	Gross Capital Formation: Public
1970-71	15.8	7.1	2.3	6.4
1971-72	16.9	7.5	2.5	7.0
1972-73	16.2	6.5	2.5	7.2
1973-74	16.7	6.7	2.5	7.5
1974-75	18.3	7.4	3.5	7.4
1975-76	19.0	7.0	2.6	9.4
1976-77	19.1	7.8	1.5	9.8
1977-78	18.7	8.4	2.3	8.0
1978-79	20.7	9.4	2.1	9.2
1979-80	21.4	8.8	2.5	10.0
1980-81	18.7	7.8	2.4	8.4
1981-82	22.4	6.9	5.4	10.1
1982-83	21.7	5.6	5.4	10.7
1983-84	19.7	6.8	3.2	9.7
1984-85	21.6	7.0	4.2	10.4
1985-86	23.7	7.6	5.2	10.8
1986-87	23.2	7.0	5.0	11.2
1987-88	22.1	9.1	3.5	9.5
1988-89	23.7	10.3	3.9	9.5
1989-90	23.7	10.1	4.0	9.5
1990-91	24.1	10.6	4.1	9.3
1991-92	21.9	7.4	5.7	8.8
1992-93	23.8	8.8	6.5	8.6
1993-94	21.3	7.4	5.6	8.2
1994-95	23.4	7.8	6.9	8.7
1995-96	26.5	9.3	9.6	7.7
1996-97	21.8	6.7	8.0	7.0
1997-98	22.6	8.0	8.0	6.6
1998-99	21.4	8.4	6.4	6.6
1999-00	23.3	9.6	6.5	7.1
2000-01	22.9	9.9	5.9	7.1
Averages over periods				
1971-72 to 1975-76	17.6	7.0	2.8	7.8
1976-77 to 1980-81	19.7	8.4	2.2	9.1
1981-82 to 1985-86	21.9	6.9	4.7	10.4
1986-87 to 1990-91	23.5	9.7	4.1	9.7
1991-92 to 1995-96	23.7	8.2	7.1	8.3
1996-97 to 2000-01	22.4	8.7	6.8	6.9
1992-93 to 1996-97	23.2	7.9	7.6	7.6
1993-94 to 1997-98	23.1	7.8	7.8	7.5

Note: * unadjusted for errors & omissions.

Source: As in Table 2.

National Accounts Statistics, 2002.

Notes

1. For instance, the *Report of the Committee on Trade Policies* (Government of India: 1984) stated that it was difficult to determine the optimum of openness of the economy added that "import liberalisation would be useful insofar as it would reduce monopoly profits, eliminate obsolete technologies and place an outside limit on import-competing activities where the domestic resource costs are too high."
2. It may be noted that the sharp decline in industrial production occurred in 1997-98 according to the earlier index of industrial production (Table 4). This is also corroborated by the National Accounts Statistics (Table 4). However, according to the new index of industrial production (Base 1993-94=100), the break happened only in 1998-99 (Table 4).
3. Gopal Srinivasan of TVS in an interview had made the remark that the Chinese threat was overstated (Srinivasan; 2001).
4. Including what is coming to be described in a generic fashion as Business Process Outsourcing (BPO) – encompassing software development, back offices, call centres, true design and process development.

References

Ahluwalia, I.J., Shubham Chaudhuri and Saumitra Chaudhuri, (2002): "Trade Liberalization, Productivity and Export Performance: A Study of the Indian Manufacturing Sector in the 1990s", *mimeo*.

Agarwal, R.N., (2001): "Technical Efficiency and Productivity Growth in the Central Public Sector Enterprises in India during 1990s", *Discussion Paper Series* No. 28/2001, Institute of Economic Growth, New Delhi.

Balakrishnan, Pulapre, K. Pushpangadan and M. Suresh Babu, (2000): "Trade Liberalisation and Productivity Growth in Manufacturing: Evidence from Firm-Level Panel data", *Economic and Political Weekly*, October 7, 2000, pp. 3679-3682.

Bergesten, C. Fred, (1999): "India and the Global Trading System", Fourteenth EXIM Bank Commencement Day Annual Lecture at Mumbai on March 10, 1999.

Government of India, (1956): *The Second Five Year Plan (1956-61)*, Planning Commission, New Delhi.

———. (1984): Report of the Committee on Trade Policies (Chairman: Abid Hussain), Ministry of Commerce.

———. (1990): *Approach Paper: The Eighth Five Year Plan (1991-96)*, Planning Commission, New Delhi.

———. (2002): *National Accounts Statistics 2002*, Central Statistical Organisation, Ministry of Statistics & Programme Implementation, New Delhi.

International Monetary Fund, (2000): *World Economic Outlook – Asset Prices and the Business Cycle*, May 2000, Washington, D.C.

Kathuria, Vinish, (2002): "Liberalisation, FDI and Productivity Spillovers: An Analysis of Indian Manufacturing Firms", *Working Paper Series* No. E/220/2002, Institute of Economic Growth, New Delhi.

Kumar, Nagesh and A. Aggarwal, (2000): "Liberalization, Outward Orientation and Inhouse R&D Activity of Multinational and Local Firms: A Quantitative Exploration for Indian Manufacturing", *Discussion Paper Series* No. 18/2000, Institute of Economic Growth, New Delhi.

Kuznets, Simon, (1966): *Modern Economic Growth: Rate, Structure and Spread*, Oxford and IBH Publishing Co., New Delhi.

Maizels, Alfred, (1970): *Growth and Trade*, NIESR Students' Edition 1, Cambridge University Press, London.

Mitra, Arup, (1999): "Total Factor Productivity Growth and Technical Efficiency in Indian Industrics", *Economic and Political Weekly*, Vol.XXXIV, No. 31, July 31, pp. M98-M105.

Neogi, C. and Ghosh B., (1998): "Impact of Liberalisation on Performance of Indian Industries: A Firm Level Study", *Economic and Political Weekly*, Vol. XXXIII, No. 9, February 28, pp. M16-M24.

Pradhan, G. and Barik K., (1999): "Total Factor Productivity Growth in Developing Economies: A Study of Selected Industries in India", *Economic and Political Weekly*, Vol. XXXIV, No. 31, July 31, pp. M92-M97.

Rangarajan, C., (1982): "Agricultural Growth and Industrial Performance in India", *Research Report* No. 33, International Food Policy Research Institute, Washington, D.C.

———. (1994): "Industrial Growth: Another Look", in Deepak Nayyar (1994) (ed.): *Industrial Growth and Stagnation: The Debate in India*, OUP.

———. (2002): "Globalisation and its Impact", *ICRA Bulletin – Money and Finance*, 2(8), January-March, pp. 36-54.

Srinivasan, Gopal, (2001): A comment made in *Businessworld*, Vol. 20, Issue: 37, 16-22 January.

Trivedi, Pushpa, Anand Prakash and David Sinate, (2000): "Productivity in Major Manufacturing Industries in India: 1973-74 to 1997-98", *RBI-DRG Study* No. 20, Reserve Bank of India, Mumbai.

5

Conflict between Employment and Inflation

Theory and Facts

The Problem

Is there a trade-off between inflation and employment? Can policy makers generate more employment through a deliberate policy of inflation? These questions have been debated at length since the introduction of the celebrated Philips Curve[1] which empirically showed a negative relationship between the rate of change in money wages and unemployment rate. The study of Philips which related to England has been reproduced for many countries. Apart from the empirical studies, there has been a growing volume of literature on the theoretical basis for such a trade-off.[2] Professor Tobin once described the Philips curve as 'an empirical finding in search of a theory'.[3] While there are some, who regard it as a case of 'measurement without theory'. If, in fact, there is a trade-off between the rate of change in money wages (or price level) and employment, a policy directed towards ensuring a rise in price level can be justified on the grounds of generating additional employment.

Theoretical Developments: Wage Rate Change and Unemployment

In the discussions on the Philips curve, two main issues have emerged. The first relates to conditions under which such a trade-off can exist. The second asks whether such a trade-off is temporary or permanent. The original explanation for a negative relationship between rate of change in wages and unemployment rate ran in terms of excess demand for labour relative to its supply. Lipsey[4]

Indian Institute of Management, Ahmedabad, 1983.

gave an elaboration of the microfoundations of the Philips curve. He derived the curve from the behaviour of the labour market. Lipsey's analysis of the labour market behaviour is based on two propositions: (i) The supply and demand for labour determine the equilibrium wage level; and (ii) the rate of change of the wage level in disequilibrium, is positively related to the extent of the disequilibrium as measured by the excess demand for labour. The greater the proportionate disequilibrium, the more rapidly will wages change. Since excess demand for labour is not directly observable, it has to be related to something that is directly observable and quantifiable. This was taken to be the percentage of labour force unemployed. The unemployment rate, however, is inversely related to excess demand as a proportion of the labour force. Thus a negative relationship emerges between rate of change in money wage and unemployment rate.

The major weakness of this explanation is that while the Philips curve deals with the change in the money wage rate, the supply and demand analysis of the labour market deals with the determination of the real wage rate. Obviously, the two concepts are interchangeable only under conditions of price stability. It has, therefore, been argued that to understand the Philips curve relationship, one has to introduce into the model the expected rate of price change. In fact in recent empirical studies of the rate of change in money wages in the developed countries, the researchers have found it necessary to include the rate of change in the price level as an independent variable besides the unemployment rate.[5]

Wage settlements are made at discreet intervals and at the time of each settlement it is the expected price level that plays a role in determining the real wages. Thus the Philips curve will shift and for every expected rate of price inflation, there will be a different curve. Even if it were possible to lower the unemployment rate by increasing the wage rate this advantage could be wiped out if the Philips curve were to shift to the right. The unemployment rate would then fall back to the original level. Whether or not it falls back to the original level depends upon the extent to which the curve shifts outward. When the expected rate of inflation becomes almost equal to the actual rate, the shift in the curve may be perfect and the original unemployment rate may return. Hence the argument that wage-rate changes unaccompanied by rising labour productivity may have only a temporary effect in reducing the unemployment rate. It must be noted that even in the context of the labour-market behaviour, the Philips curve relationship is only an explanation of a phenomenon in disequilibrium. The existence of such a disequilibrium in the developed economies is sought to be explained in terms of costs of search and information.

Price Level Change and Unemployment

The original Philips curve was transformed into a relationship between the rate of change in price level and unemployment by Samuelson and Solow[6] while engaged in replicating the Philips study for the United States. In their study, this transformation had only a limited meaning. They equated the rate of change in price level to that of the rate of change in money wage less the rate of change in labour productivity. However, later writers have used a wage-cost mark-up equation to relate the change in price level to the change in money wage. In fact it was thought that the Philips curve supplied the missing equation in the Keynesian system. The IS-LM curves yield the real output and, from the production function relating output and employment, it is possible to derive the level of employment given the real output. By calculating the unemployment rate and by using the Philips curve, the rate of change in the wage rate can be obtained. Using a wage-cost mark-up equation, the rate of change in the price level can in turn be obtained. Relating the change in the price level to the unemployment rate goes beyond the labour market dynamics.

Why should an increase in the price level generate additional employment? Suppose the economy is operating at a certain level of unemployment. If the authorities wish to reduce the unemployment rate by increasing the rate of monetary growth, what can happen? It is possible that producers may respond to the initial expansion in aggregate demand by increasing output. It is also possible that the prices of products will increase. However, since wage settlements are made at discreet intervals, as mentioned earlier, real wages may go down. This can increase the profitability of the firms and may make them increase their output and thereby employment. But as employees realise the loss in their real wages and begin to press for higher nominal wages in order to keep the real wages at the original level, the initial advantage gained by the firms will disappear. Thus the temporary trade-off between inflation and unemployment arises, as Friedman pointed out in his presidential address, 'not from inflation *per se* but from unanticipated inflation'. However, even Friedman found from his historical studies that the initial effects of a higher and unanticipated rate of inflation may last for two to five years. Thus to retain the benefit of an unanticipated inflation, the price level must keep rising.

Does the original Philips curve or its modified version help us in any way, in identifying whether a particular inflation is 'demand pull' or 'cost push'. Some have argued that while movement along the curve indicates 'demand pull', a shift of the curve indicates 'cost push'. But, a shift of the curve occurs not only because of 'union power' but also as a result of expectations. In the latter case, the 'cost push' is not separated neatly from 'demand pull'. As Lipsey once remarked, the Philips curve left inflation theory where it found it. Indian data for example reveal that real wages of workers have not increased over the period 1961-75 implying thereby, that the shifts in the curve must have been primarily to adjust money wages to price increases.

Inflation and the Growth Rate

Discussions in underdeveloped countries have been centred more on the relationship between the change in the price level and the growth rate in the economy, than on the unemployment rate. In the developing economies the amount of labour flowing through the 'market' is only a part of the labour supply, particularly in relation to sectors like agriculture. Thus attention has been focused more directly on the relationship between inflation and the growth rate of national income. Thus the question that is raised is whether there is a positive relationship between the rate of change in price level and the rate of growth of the economy. In linking the two, one is not looking solely at the functioning of the labour market. The link between inflation and the growth rate of income is the result of the dynamic interaction of a number of important relations. One can, however, raise at the outset, the question whether there is any historical evidence which throws light on the association between inflation and economic growth. All available historical studies indicate that there is no convincing evidence of any clear association, positive or negative, between the rate of inflation and the rate of economic growth. In Table 1 we have provided the data for the rates of growth in national income and in price level for a variety of countries during the period 1969-76. It is interesting to see that high inflation rates are found in countries with either high or low growth rates in national income. Similarly, there are countries with a low inflation rate and with a low growth rate. The absence of any neat relationship between rate of change in price level and rate of change in national income can be attributed to the fact that the economic and financial structure can be adapted to changing conditions. There are countries which have learnt to live with inflation by suitably modifying their financial structure. Countries which are not capable of modifying their financial structure in the face of inflation, suffer a great deal more. We shall refer to the historical experience of India in this context in the next section.

In discussing the relationship between change in price level and economic growth, one has to make a distinction between two different positions. One stand is that in the process of growth, a certain degree of increase in price level is inevitable. In this kind of analysis, the change in the price level is not given a causal role. It is treated as a consequence of growth. The opposite position is that inflation itself can be used as an instrument for generating economic growth. The implications of the first position for policy is that the policy-makers should not aim at absolute price stability, but should be content to allow the increase in price level inherent in the process of growth. It is the second position that calls for a clearer scrutiny.

The arguments that are usually put forward in favour of inflation are well known.[8] It is deemed to assist in the task of mobilising resources for development. The level of investment is sought to be raised by expanding bank credit. If the Government wants to secure additional resources, it can obtain them by issuing currency or by borrowing from the central bank and commercial banks. In this process, as the price level increases, it brings about a reduction in real terms of the purchasing power in the hands of others. It is this reduction in the purchasing power which results in the transfer of resources into the hands of the Government, thereby becoming available for investment. Hence the description that inflation is a

Table 1

Rates of Growth in Real National Income and Inflation (1969-76)

Countries	*High Inflation Rate (7% and above)*	*High Growth Rate (5% and above)*
Brazil	21.4	17.2
Colombia	16.2	6.3
Peru	13.5	5.0
Jamaica	12.3	7.0
Japan	10.1	6.9
Philippines	12.9	6.6
China	9.8	6.2
Mexico	8.8	5.9
France	8.0	5.5
Iran	7.5	16.3
Countries	*High Inflation Rate*	*Low Growth Rate (less than 5%)*
Chile	205.7	0.2
Pakistan	12.9	2.2
UK	11.7	1.0
India	**9.7**	**2.5**
Trinidad & Toboga	10.2	2.9
Italy	10.1	3.4
Australia	8.9	4.4
New Zealand	8.9	4.3
South Africa	8.1	4.3
Zambia	7.5	3.5
Belgium	7.1	4.4
Argentina	52.9	4.5
	Low Inflation Rate (less than 8%)	*High Growth Rate*
Libya	5.9	10.6
Iraq	5.9	8.2
Thailand	6.6	6.7
	Low Inflation Rate	*Low Growth Rate*
Cyprus	6.1	-0.2
Canada	6.5	4.5
USA	6.3	2.6
Switzerland	5.8	2.5
Germany	5.1	3.5

form of 'forced savings'. In this sense the transfer is basically from the holders of money balances to the creators of money balances. Whether or not there is a net addition to the savings of the economy will depend upon how the gainers from inflation — the Government in this case — utilise these resources. If all of this is saved, then the objective of raising resources for investment will be achieved. It has not always been the case that those who gain by inflation are less prone to consumption than those who lose by it. However, the rationale for inflation as a means of mobilising resources rests on the proposition that the marginal propensity of the gainers to save is greater than the marginal propensity of the losers to save. The net increase in savings also depends upon the reactions of the losers from inflation. The argument put forward so far rests on the assumption that the losers will react to the increase in the price level by reducing consumption. If, however, they react to the increase in price level by cutting their savings, then the total effect on the economy may be a net reduction in savings, so long as the marginal propensity to consume of the gainers is greater than zero. In the same way as the Government, the business community can also acquire more resources for investment through resorting to bank loans.

Even this brief description of the mechanism, by which inflation can promote savings, points to the fact that it is possible to transfer the resources only if the labour force acquiesces in a reduction of consumption and allows a shift in the share of total output going to investment. However, if other sections of the society are able to compete effectively and prevent their share of the cake being reduced, the impact of inflation can only be at best a one-shot increase in investment. The permanent effect, if any, will come from the income flow generated by the increase in investment. Any attempt continually to raise investment by this method will require a rate of change in price level which is always kept higher than any that wage-earners and others anticipate and can build into their wage bargains. But sooner or later, expectations are likely to coincide with the actual and the rise in price level will no longer accomplish any transfer of resources. It can also happen that even when it accomplishes the task of transferring resources, there may be other costs of inflation. The redistributive distortions, which may be treated as the cost of inflation, may sometimes outweigh the benefits of mobilisation and at that point also, inflation ceases to be a 'useful' instrument.

If inflation can result in a transfer of real resources only to a limited extent and that too only temporarily, the question can be asked as to how high growth rates are associated with high inflation rates in some countries. The answer is that it is not inflation which is doing the trick. Ultimately, the growth rate in real output is dependent upon such fundamental factors as resource endowments, technical and managerial capabilities and improvements in organisation. In the long run every economy gets adjusted to whatever rate of monetary growth it experiences. In many of the economies, where the inflation rate is high, attention is focussed on institutional arrangements such as indexation in order to avoid the harmful effects of inflation.

There is, however, one sense in which thc rclationship between price level changes and output changes becomes important. When an economy gets used to a certain rate of growth in credit, an attempt to put a sudden brake on it gives such a jolt to the economy that it results in a fall in production. The process of money creation is also a process of credit creation. The rate of growth in money supply can be restrained only by restricting the credit flowing either to the private sector or to the government sector. If, with a view to avoiding the distortion effects of inflation, an attempt is made to control the rate of growth in money supply, the sectors of the economy used to a larger volume credit may find it difficult to adjust to the lower levels of credit. This cannot but result in some shortfall in production. That is why, whenever the central bank wants to introduce a restrictive monetary and credit policy, there is a hue and cry from the business sector that this will affect production. This is not a totally imaginary fear even though the purpose of the restrictive credit policy is to force the credit using sectors to manage their business more efficiently with less credit. It is difficult to quantify how great this negative impact is and how long it will last.

Empirical Relationships in India: Changes in Price Level, Output and Employment

What does the historical experience of India reveal regarding the relationship between price level change and growth rates in output and employment? Table 2 provides the data on employment in the organized sector. It gives data separately for the public sector and private sector. It also gives separate data on employment in the manufacturing sector which includes establishments in both private and public sectors. Table 3 provides data on industrial production and on manufactures separately. In Table 4, data on price level are provided. In this paper, we have considered only employment in the organised sector defined as establishments which employ ten or more. For the kind of relationship that we are seeking, employment in the unorganised sector is not immediately relevant.

Table 2

Employment in the Organised Sector

	No. of Persons Employed ('000s)			*Annual Rates of Growth of Employment*			*Employment in Manufacturing Sector ('000s)*	*Annual Rate of Growth %*
	Public Sector	*Private Sector*	*Total*	*Public Sector %*	*Private Sector %*	*Total %*		
1960-1	7.050	5.040	12.090	—	—	—	3.389	—
1961-2	7.417	5.160	12.577	5.2	2.4	4.1	3.471	2.42
1962-3	7.953	5.450	13.403	7.1	5.8	6.5	3.779	8.87
1963-4	8.454	5.780	14.234	6.3	2.6	4.8	4.001	5.87
1964-5	8.957	6.040	15.997	6.0	8.1	6.8	4.245	6.10
1965-6	9.378	6.810	16.188	4.7	1.0	3.2	4.578	6.67
1966-7	9.634	6.680	16.314	2.7	-1.9	0.8	4.445	-1.83
1967-8	9.802	6.520	16.322	1.7	-2.4	0.1	4.441	-0.09
1968-9	10.095	6.530	16.625	2.3	1.2	1.8	4.527	1.94
1969-70	10.374	6.700	17.074	2.8	2.6	2.7	4.680	3.38
1970-1	10.731	6.760	17.491	3.4	0.9	2.4	4.761	1.73
1971-2	11.305	6.770	18.075	4.4	0.2	2.8	4.867	2.23
1972-3	11.975	6.849	18.824	5.9	1.2	4.1	5.066	4.09
1973-4	12.487	6.792	19.279	4.3	-0.8	2.4	5.206	2.76
1974-5	12.868	6.804	19.672	3.1	0.1	2.1	5.128	-1.5
1975-6	13.363	6.845	20.208	3.8	0.6	2.7	5.271	2.79
1976-7	13.849	6.867	20.716	3.6	0.3	2.5	5.379	2.05
Compound Growth Rate	4.3%	1.95%	3.4%	—	—	—	3.0%	—

Source: Reserve Bank of India Bulletin, February 1975 and October 1978.

Table 3

Industrial and Manufacturing Production

	Index of Industrial Production	*Annual Growth Rate in Industrial Production*	*Index of Manufacturing*	*Annual Growth Rate in Manufacturing Index*
1960	100.0	—	100.0	—
1961	110.6	10.6	109.2	9.2
1962	120.6	8.95	119.6	9.5
1963	130.6	8.38	129.1	7.9
1964	142.4	9.03	141.2	9.4
1965	151.5	6.39	154.0	9.1
1966	151.9	0.26	151.7	-1.5
1967	152.6	0.46	149.6	-1.4
1968	163.0	6.82	158.7	6.1
1969	175.3	7.55	170.6	7.5
1970	184.3	5.13	178.9	4.9
1971	192.0	4.2	178.9	0.0
1972	203.1	5.7	191.4	6.9
1973	206.4	1.6	193.4	1.04
1974	210.7	2.0	202.2	4.6
1975	220.6	4.7	207.7	2.7
1976	242.2	9.8	—	—
1977	254.9	5.2	—	—
Compound Growth Rate	**5.7%**	—	**5.0%**	—

As is to be expected, there is a close correlation between employment and output. In the log form the correlation coefficient between the Index of Industrial Production and that for employment in the private sector was 0.72 while that with total employment was 0.90. However, as is well known by now, production has grown at a faster rate than employment. During the period 1960-77 the compound rate of growth in the Index of Industrial Production was 5.7 per cent while that of employment in the private sector was 1.97 per cent. The index of manufactures rose by five per cent during this period while employment in the manufacturing sector increased by three per cent. From a double log relationship, it is seen that the elasticity of employment in relation to output in manufacturing sector is around 0.45 of one per cent. However, employment fluctuates less severely than output.

Table 4

Price Level Changes

	Index of Wholesale Prices	*Annual Growth in Wholesale Price Index*	*Index of Manufacturing Prices*	*Annual Growth Rate in Manufacturing Prices*
1961-2	100.0	—	100.0	—
1962-3	103.8	3.8	102.4	2.4
1963-4	110.2	6.2	104.8	2.3
1964-5	122.3	10.9	107.5	2.6
1965-6	131.6	7.6	115.3	7.3
1966-7	149.9	13.9	125.5	8.8
1967-8	167.3	11.6	130.9	4.3
1968-9	165.4	-1.2	132.7	1.4
1969-70	171.6	3.7	140.9	6.2
1970-1	181.1	5.5	151.7	7.7
1971-2	191.2	5.6	164.4	8.4
1972-3	210.4	10.0	180.5	9.8
1973-4	252.9	20.1	202.9	12.4
1974-5	316.7	25.2	247.4	21.9
1975-6	313.3	-1.1	262.6	6.1
1976-7	319.8	2.0	260.5	-0.8

In general, low rates of change in price level are associated with high rates of growth in industrial production. During the period studied, there were seven years in which the rate of growth in industrial production was six per cent and above. Of these, in four years the price increase was less than four per cent. Only in one year of high growth rate, was the price rise more than eight per cent. Of the eight years in which the growth rate was less than six per cent, in five the price increase was more than eight per cent. In 1973-74, when prices rose by about 20 per cent, industrial production grew by only two per cent. Thus, while there are exceptions, the general drift of the observations indicates a negative correlation between price level change and output change. The correlation coefficient between the percentage change in price level and percentage change in industrial production is -0.56. The correlation coefficient between the percentage change in price level and percentage change in private employment is positive but very low at 0.11. The correlation coefficient between price change and output change in relation to manufactures is -0.28.

We have also examined the relationship between price level change and output changes in several groups of industries over the period 1962-73. If the Philips relationship is held true, there should be a positive association between changes in real output and changes in prices. It must be admitted that when we study the relationship between the changes in price level and changes in output over a period of time, the observations for the various years are a combination of the shifts in the demand and supply curves. However, an examination of the data at a disaggregated level would still reveal whether an industry tends to grow when prices rise. In Table 5, columns 1 and 2 show the average annual percentage change in output and in prices for ten industry groups. In column 3 we have computed the correlation coefficient between the percentage change in output and percentage change in price level for the period 1962-73 for each of the industry groups. We have shown in column 4 the correlation between the relative change in output, defined as the rate of change in output of that industry less the rate of change in the total industrial production and the relative change in the prices, defined as the percentage change in the price level of that industry less the rate of change in the wholesale price index. It is interesting to observe from column 3 that in most of the industry groups the correlation turns out negative, that is the rate of change in price level and the rate of change in output are inversely related. This corresponds to the general picture that emerged regarding the relationship between the change in price level and the change in the Index of Industrial Production. However, column 4 shows that only in the case of five industries is the correlation between the relative change in output and relative change in price negative. These are industries in which price changes measured as deviation from the general price level were negatively associated with output changes measured as deviation from the general production index.

Table 5

Average Annual Rates of Change in Output and Prices by Industry Groups, 1962-73

Industry	*Rate of Growth*		*Correlation between*	
	Output %	*Prices* %	*Change in Output and Change in Prices*	*Relative Change in Output and Relative Change in Prices*
	1	2	3	4
Food Manufacturing	3.28	9.78	-0.495	0.278
Manufacture of Textiles	0.87	5.58	-0.459	-0.432
Manufacture of Paper and Paper Products	7.23	3.39	0.038	-0.089
Manufacture of Leather except Footwear	-3.25	0.78	0.361	0.090
Manufacture of Rubber Products	7.02	4.24	-0.089	0.517
Manufacture of Chemical Products	8.59	3.89	-0.107	0.093
Basic Metal Industries	5.43	7.13	-0.524	-0.082
Non-electrical Machinery	12.56	6.08	-0.263	-0.173
Electrical Machinery	11.96	5.12	-0.279	0.631
Manufacture of Transport Equipment	2.93	3.8	-0.555	-0.386

In a study of United States[9], Houthakker found in fact a stronger negative correlation between price changes and output changes by industry groups. On the basis of the correlation between relative change in output and relative change in prices, he was able to reach to the conclusion that inflation had been most rapid in industries that grew slowly. Our data also reveal that even at the disaggregated level, there is a negative association between price changes and output changes. It is difficult to explain this phenomenon except in terms of shifts in the supply and demand curves. A negative association can only mean that shifts in supply curves outweigh shifts in demand curves.

Both the aggregated and the disaggregated data tend to lead to one general proposition – that the growth rate in industrial production is much better in a situation of low inflation rates than high inflation rates. The question of causes and effects is difficult to unscramble. A year in which there is a shortage of output, prices can go up. Thus causation can run in either direction. However, the general belief that rising prices are good for industrial production is not supported by the data collected by us.

Price Level and Savings

One of the favourable effects expected of inflation is its impact on savings. As elaborated earlier, the favourable effect depends on whether there is a redistribution of income in favour of groups which have a higher marginal propensity to save. However, inflation can also undermine the basic motivation to save and thereby lower the propensity to save for everyone. To some extent, the impact of price changes, on the propensity to save, also depends on the form in which the savings are held. Price changes make the holding of fixed income financial assets unattractive. If a larger proportion of savings is held in the form of physical assets, it may promote savings. It has also been argued that higher prices usually arise from cheap money policies which may also have the effect of lowering the interest rates and this can discourage savings. Thus, a large number of factors which pull in opposite directions are in operation.

The analysis of the data of domestic savings in India does not reveal any close relationship to change in price level. Broadly speaking, the ratio of net domestic saving to Net National Product rose during the period 1955-66. Thereafter, there was a sharp decline and it was only in 1968 that the level attained in 1966-67 was achieved. From the data published by the CSO, there was no appreciable change in the savings ratio in 1973/74, when prices rose by 20 per cent. We have analysed the savings pattern separately for the household sector, the corporate sector and the government sector. Using the data for the period 1961-74, we estimated separate saving functions for the household sector, for the corporate sector and for the government sector. Only in the case of the household sector does one get a reasonably satisfactory relationship. But, even here the role of change in price level is not significant. We give below the estimated equations:

$$HHS = -1537.41 + \underset{(7.27)}{0.19009}\ PDY - \underset{(0.5308)}{5.0787} \left[\frac{\Delta P}{P}\right]_{t-1}$$

$$\bar{R}^2 = 0.798$$

$$HHS = -1501.59 + \underset{(6.64)}{0.18613}\ PDY - \underset{(0.0854)}{0.89699} \left[\overline{\frac{\Delta P}{P}}\right]_{t-1}$$

$$\bar{R}^2 = 0.793$$

Where HHS = Savings of the household sector in crores of rupees.

PDY = Personal disposable income in crores of rupees.

$\frac{\Delta P}{P}$ = Rate of change in price level.

$\overline{\frac{\Delta P}{P}}$ = Two - year average of rate of change in price level.

We have estimated other equations with various modifications of the price variable. In none of these equations was the price level significant. We are not reporting the function estimated for government savings, since it has not been possible at a reasonably satisfactory relationship. We give below the function estimated for the corporate sector using the data available from the RBI sample of large and medium-sized public limited companies.

$$\frac{\text{Profit retained}}{\text{Profit after tax}} = \underset{(7.85)}{0.338} + \underset{(2.59)}{0.01122} \left[\frac{\Delta P}{P}\right]$$

$$\bar{R}^2 = 0.251$$

The fit of the above equation is not good. It shows, however, that the retention ratio, in the case of companies, is positively influenced by the change in the price level. Our examination of the savings data– both in its aggregate and in its components — does not reveal any relationship between savings and the rate of change in the price level. They are not related strongly, either positively or negatively. In the absence of detailed savings and income data for different income groups, it is difficult to establish the direction of contribution of the different factors.

Conclusions

The Philips curve, at its best, is an explanation of the trade-off between wage changes and employment in a disequilibrium situation. In the long run, such a trade-off can exist only if expectations of price changes continually remain below the actual changes. The link between price changes and employment goes beyond the dynamics of the labour markets. The same is true when one thinks of the relationship between price change and the growth rate of the economy. Price changes can ensure a transfer of real resources only if the marginal propensity of the gainers to save from inflation is greater than the propensity of the losers to save from inflation. In the long run such a transfer can occur only if the losers from inflation are not able to restore their share of the cake. However, in the short run, for a variety of reasons, there can be a trade-off.

We have examined the industrial data in relation to price changes and output changes in the industrial sector. Employment and output are well correlated but the rate of growth of the former is lower than that of the latter. In general, it appears that periods marked by sharp increase in price level are associated with lower growth rates of output and years of low price changes with high growth rates in industrial output. A disaggregated analysis of the output and price changes relating to various industry groups also indicates a negative association between price change and output change. There can be several explanations for this phenomenon. Causation can run in either direction. However, the general conclusion is that contrary to the general belief, industrial output has grown faster in periods of small price increases than in periods of high price increases. There is also no evidence to show that price changes have had any effect upon savings.[10]

Notes

1. Philips, A. W., "The relation between unemployment and the rate of change of money wage rates in the United Kingdom, 1861, p. 195, *Economica, New Series* 25 (November, 1958).
2. See for example, Bergstrom, A.R. Catt, A.J.C. Peston, M.H. and Silverstone, B.D.J., *Stability and Inflation,* a volume of essays to honour the memory of A.W.H. Philips (Wiley, London, 1978).
3. Tobin, J., "Inflation and Unemployment", *American Economic Review* (March, 1962).
4. Lipsey, R.G., "The relation between unemployment and the rate of change of money wage rates in the United Kingdom, 1952-57", A further analysis *Economica New Series* 27 (February, 1960).
5. See Brechling Frank, "The trade-off between inflation and Unemployment" *The Journal of Political Economy* (July/August, 1968). The estimated equation for the US was:

$$W_t = 0.026 - \underset{(0.0013)}{0.051U_t} + \underset{(0.0013)}{0.0027\, U_{t-1}} + \underset{(0.093)}{0.386\, P_t} - \underset{(0.002)}{0.008\, D_2} - \underset{(0.002)}{0.013\, D_3} - \underset{(0.002)}{0.002\, D_4}$$

$$\bar{R}^2 = 0.63$$

In this equation W_t is the quarterly proportionate change in straight time earnings in US manufacturing; P_t is the quarterly proportionate change in the consumer price index; U is the unemployment percentage and the Ds are dummy variables for the second, third and fourth quarters. The period covered is 1948, first quarter, to 1965, fourth quarter.

6. Sameulson, P. A., and Solow, R.M. "Analytical Aspects of Anti-inflation Policy", *American Economic Review* (May, 1960).
7. Friedman, Milton, "The role of Monetary Policy", *American Economic Review* (March, 1968).
8. See Bernstein, E.M. and Patel, I.G, "Inflation to Economic Development", IMF, *Staff Papers*, Vol. II, 1951-52 and Johnson, H.G. "Is Inflation the inevitable price of rapid development or a retarding factor in Economic Growth", in *Essays in Monetary Economics* (Allen & Unwin, London, 1967).
9. Houthakker, H.S., "Growth and Inflation: Analysis by Industry", *Brookings Papers on Economic Activity*, (Prokings Institution, Washington DC, 1979).
10. There have been number of studies to find out the impact of price level on savings. In a study of five Asian countries, Williamson found that price played no role in the case of Korea, Taiwan and India. See Williamson, J.G., "Personal Savings in Developing Nations", *Economic Record* (June, 1968).

6

Capital-Output Ratios in the Indian Economy

(1950-51 to 1989-90)

Introduction

One of the most popular quantitative relationships in growth theory and development planning has been the capital-output ratio and more importantly, its variant, the Incremental Capital-Output Ratio (ICOR). The relationship between investment and incremental output has been used in many growth models as a simplification of the conventional production function, assuming capital to be binding constraint in the growth process. ICOR is often used (i) to estimate the requirements of capital formation to achieve a particular rate of growth, (ii) to derive the growth rate, once the resource position is known, (iii) to evaluate the performance of an economy and compare it with that of other countries and (iv) to guage the efficiency of an economy at two different points of time. The primary aim of this paper is to analyse the behaviour of ICORs and Average Capital-Output Ratios (ACORs)[1] during the last four decades. Section I discusses methodological and statistical problems encountered in computing the ICORs. In Section II, trends in ICORs and ACORs are presented. An analysis of sources of changes in ICORs is presented in Section III.

SECTION I

Incremental Capital-Output Ratio refers to the amount of capital required to produce one additional unit of output. This is basically a physical concept. Normally, this is measured by dividing the sum

---

Co-author: **R. Kannan.**
The Indian Economic Journal, Vol.42, July-September 1994.

of investment made in a given period by the incremental output during that period. The calculation of capital-output ratios, both incremental and average is beset with many methodological and statistical problems. These are dealt with below.

Methodological Issues

Capital as the Only Factor of Production

In working out the ICOR, one is considering the relationship between capital and output, thereby ignoring the effects of other factors of production. In this context, it is interesting to find out the extent of bias that enters when the effect of factors of production, other than capital are excluded. The bias can be quantified with the aid of a production function of Cobb Douglas type.

$$Y = A.L^{\beta}.K^{\alpha} \qquad \ldots(1)$$

Where

Y = Output

L = Labour and

K = Capital

From this function, we can deduce the following relationship:

$$\frac{\delta Y}{\delta K} = \alpha \frac{Y}{K} + \beta \frac{Y}{L} . \frac{\delta L}{\delta K} \qquad \ldots(2)$$

If capital is assumed to be the only factor, function (1) becomes:

$$Y = AK^{\alpha} \qquad \ldots(3)$$

The two production functions can give identical incremental capital-output relationship only if:

$$\beta \frac{Y}{L} . \frac{\delta L}{\delta K} = 0 \qquad \ldots(4)$$

And this is possible only at least one of the following is true:

$$\beta = 0, \quad \frac{Y}{L} = 0, \quad \frac{\delta L}{\delta K} = 0$$

If Y/L is to be zero then output (Y) is zero. If β is to be zero, the production function reduces to $Y=AK^{\alpha}$ with capital as the only factor.

Hence, neither Y/L nor β can be assumed to be zero so long as labour is recognized as an additional factor of production. $\delta L/\delta K=0$, implies that labour-capital ratio is at the optimum, so that the incremental labour-capital ratio is zero. This can be true only in rare situations. For all these reasons, the simple method of calculating incremental capital-output ratio perhaps understates the due ratio.

Lags in Relationship

In the estimation of ICOR, changes in output at time 't' is related to changes in capital stock of the same period, thereby assuming no gestation lag between investment and the consequent output. During a period of rising investment, ignoring gestation lag introduces an upward bias in the calculation of ICOR, as the absolute amount of investment at time 't' is higher than the investment at time t-L, where L is gestation lag. The approach paper to the Sixth Plan[2] has this comment to make on gestation lag.

"Logically, in computing the ICORs, the lag between investment and incremental output must be taken into reckoning. But on account of inadequate information on the time phasing of projects and the instability of the observed time phasing, the ICORs in the table have been computed by dividing total investment in a period by the incremental in value added during the same period. This procedure can be shown to be valid under certain rigorous assumptions. Even though these need not hold good exactly, as an approximation, the procedure used appears to be more satisfactory than any other that could have been used".

As shown in Appendix I, ignoring the lags will not result in any change in the ratio only when the growth rate of output (g) is considerably higher than the growth rate of investment (r), so that the ratio (r/g) approaches zero. This is, however, unlikely to be so. Hence, calculation of ICOR without gestation lag will normally overstate the ICOR.

Statistical Issues

Selection of Base Year

As capital-output ratio is a real measure and not a monetary one, both investment and incremental output must be measured at constant prices. However, it needs to be noted that calculations, even at constant prices, will not give unique values. The numerical values of capital-output ratios could change depending upon the base year selected. If investment prices are rising faster than output prices, the ICOR calculated for a period based on a more recent base year will be smaller than the one based on an earlier base year. This can be illustrated with the data relating to the period 1965-66 to 1969-70. The ICOR for this period works out to 4.13 at 1970-71 prices as against 4.62 at 1960-61 prices.

Compatibility

In the estimation of ICOR, the numerator (investment) is always measured at market prices, whereas the denominator (incremental output) can be at factor cost or market prices. Care has to be taken to ensure that both numerator and denominator are measured at market prices. Otherwise, this would render an upward bias in the estimated ICORs. This may not pose any difficulty while working out ICOR for an economy as a whole, but at the sectoral level this poses some data problems.

Maximum Information Content

In general, ICOR for a period is calculated by dividing the sum of investments made in each year by the incremental output between the base year and the terminal year. If one of these years happens to be an abnormal year, this will affect considerably the value of ICOR. Further, output has a tendency to vary substantially from year to year, particularly when agricultural output happens to be a significant proportion of total output as in India. A method that takes into account each year's output would be a better alternative. One way is to work out ICOR for each year during the period and take average of ICORs to arrive at ICOR for the period. But if incremental GDP turns out to be negative in any one year, the ICOR will be negative, which is not acceptable. To avoid this problem, GDP for each year can be estimated using a semi-log equation.

$$\text{Log } Y = a + bt$$

The incremental GDP derived from the estimates can be used in the calculation of ICOR for each year. This method has been followed in this study. The ICOR for a given period — say five or ten years —

is calculated by computing the geometric mean of the individual year ICORs. Geometric mean is better suited than arithmetic mean, as ICOR is a relative measure.[3] Yet another method of computing 'period ICORs' will be to regress output on capital stock such that the regression co-efficient yields the ICOR. However, this method requires a reliable series of capital stock estimates.

SECTION II

Capital-output ratios could be measured either in gross or net terms. The analytical point of using the ratio on a net basis is that it should include only that investment which expands capacity as distinct from investment which replaces capacity. The rationale is to maintain capacity intact and not capital intact. However, in view of the arbitrariness present in the estimation of depreciation allowances, gross ratios are preferred to that of net ratios. Furthermore, investment can be measured either including inventories or excluding them. We have presented in Tables 1 and 2, the estimated ICORs, both on gross and net basis and with/without inventories, for different plan periods.

Aggregate ICORs

During the first three Five-Year Plans, the ICOR exhibited a clear increasing trend, as it increased from 3.37 in the First Plan to 4.28 in the Second Plan and further to 5.29 in the Third Plan. However, it increased only marginally to 5.38 during Annual Plans and declined marginally to 5.28 during the Fourth Plan. During the Fifth Plan it rose to a peak of 6.21. However, it came down steadily to 4.23 between 1980-85 and further to 3.82 between 1985-90. If the data are analysed decade wise, the ICOR increased from 3.80 during the 1950s to 5.33 during the 1960s and further to 6.12 in the 1970s. But it declined considerably to 4.00 in the 1980s (Table 1).

Table 1

Gross ICOR

Year	With inventories			Without inventories		
	A	B	C	A	B	C
1950-51 to 1955-56	3.37	3.21	3.13	3.22	3.02	2.90
1956-57 to 1960-61	4.28	4.10	3.93	3.79	3.63	3.51
1961-62 to 1965-66	5.29	4.98	4.60	4.74	4.37	4.02
1966-67 to 1968-69	5.38	5.45	5.58	4.92	4.91	5.03
1969-70 to 1973-74	5.28	4.86	4.60	4.57	4.16	4.04
1974-75 to 1978-79	6.21	5.86	5.48	5.08	4.84	4.52
1980-81 to 1984-85	4.23	4.14	4.04	3.54	3.46	3.42
1985-86 to 1989-90	3.82	3.50	3.25	3.13	2.89	2.71
1950s	3.80	3.71	3.57	3.54	3.42	3.24
1960s	5.33	5.02	4.80	4.82	4.49	4.28
1970s	6.12	5.52	5.14	5.07	4.63	4.38
1980s	4.00	3.76	3.65	3.27	3.11	2.94

Note: A : No Lag.
B : One year lag between investment and output.
C : Two Years lag between investment and output.

The trends in ICOR noted in this study are in broad conformity with those of other recent studies.[4]

Net ICOR increased from 2.76 in 1950s to 3.17 in 1960s and further to 4.20 in 1970s but declined to 2.48 in 1980s (Table 2). In the four decades, the percentage increase in gross ICOR in 1960s over that of 1950s is more pronounced (40 per cent) than the increase in the 1970s (15 per cent). But in the case of net ICOR, the percentage increase in 1970s is more pronounced (32 per cent) than the increase in 1960s (15 per cent). However, the decline in ICORs in 1980s is almost same, both in gross and net ICORs. This indicates strongly that the pattern of depreciation was not uniform during the first three decades.

Incorporation of gestation lags in the calculation of ICORs does reduce the absolute level of ICORs. More the gestation lag, more the decline in the absolute value of ICORs. With one year lag between investment and output, gross ICOR, as compared with ICOR without lag declined by two per cent in 1950s, by six per cent in 1960s, by 10 per cent in 1970s and by six per cent in 1980s. With two years lag, gross ICOR declined by six per cent in 1950s, by 10 per cent in 1960s, by 16 per cent in 1970s and by nine per cent in 1980s.

Table 2

Net ACOR/ICOR

Period	ACOR*	ICOR					
		With inventories			Without inventories		
		A	B	C	A	B	C
1	2	3	4	5	6	7	8
1950-51 to 1955-56	0.87	2.26	2.19	2.11	2.12	1.98	1.85
1956-57 to 1960-61	1.23	3.17	3.15	2.93	2.64	2.61	2.53
1961-62 to 1965-66	1.55	3.29	3.11	2.86	2.76	2.53	2.30
1966-67 to 1968-69	1.81	3.08	3.18	3.22	2.66	2.77	2.87
1969-70 to 1973-74	2.01	3.46	3.37	3.30	2.70	2.64	2.61
1974-75 to 1978-79	2.32	4.27	4.03	3.82	3.18	2.86	2.63
1980-81 to 1984-85	2.69	2.90	2.76	2.66	1.99	1.87	1.78
1985-86 to 1989-90	2.61	2.34	2.10	1.93	1.58	1.42	1.33
1950s	0.99	2.76	2.62	2.58	2.40	2.36	2.27
1960s	1.64	3.17	3.08	2.91	2.71	2.58	2.47
1970s	2.22	4.20	4.02	3.69	3.00	2.91	2.80
1980s	2.65	2.48	2.37	2.27	1.67	1.60	1.54

Note: A : No Lag.
B : One year lag between investment and output.
C : Two years lag between investment and output.
* : With inventories and no lag.

Sectoral ICORs

In this paper sectoral ICORs have been computed, taking care to value both sectoral investment and output at market prices. Ratios have been calculated with and without gestation lags. The gestation lag for different sectors, as worked out by Gupta *et al* (1981)[5] have been used. Sector-wise ICORs for the period 1950-51 to 1987-88, are reported in Table 3.[6]

Table 3

Incremental Capital-Output Ratios (Gross)

Sector	1950-51 to 1959-60		1960-61 to 1969-70		1970-71 to 1979-80		1980-81 to 1987-88	
	1	2	1	2	1	2	1	2
1. Agriculture	2.090	2.084	4.964	4.624	5.807	5.466	4.231	4.053
2. Forestry	1.484	0.707	0.444	0.497	—	—	—	—
3. Fishing	2.965	2.672	3.323	2.995	4.929	4.586	2.412	2.038
4. Mining & Quarrying	2.841	2.674	5.122	3.032	10.206	5.675	10.188	5.815
5. Manufacturing	4.157	3.159	6.719	5.754	7.561	6.416	5.152	4.679
6. Electricity, Gas & Water supply	16.357	6.032	18.253	9.734	18.953	13.546	17.139	10.330
7. Construction	1.102	0.877	1.455	1.184	2.993	2.496	4.313	3.813
8. Trade, Hotels & Restaurant	1.633	1.540	1.172	1.168	2.945	2.383	4.676	3.139
9. Transport, Storage & Communication	12.216	8.960	15.727	15.073	9.209	8.191	6.726	5.249
10. Banking & Insurance	0.483	0.417	0.955	0.852	0.511	0.456	0.771	0.477
11. Real Estate, Ownership of Dwelling & Business Services	16.996	16.012	14.723	14.186	12.245	11.218	10.455	10.162
12. Public Admn. & Defence	9.313	8.515	6.225	6.363	7.673	7.301	5.004	4.771
13. Other Services	2.359	2.203	2.245	2.231	2.492	2.311	1.740	1.641

Note: 1. Sectoral GDP at market prices and without gestation lag.
2. Sectoral GDP at market prices and with gestation lag.

Considering the ratios without lags, it is seen that they range from 0.83 to 16.996, 0.44 to 18.252, 0.511 to 18.953 and 0.771 to 17.139 in the 1950s, 60s, 70s and 80s respectively. Except for 1960s, banking and insurance sector assumed lowest ICOR while electricity sector assumed highest ICOR for all decades, except for 1950s.

Analysing the trend in gross ICORs, sector-wise, during the three decades (1950-80), it is seen that in the 1960s, except for the sectors trade, real estate and public administration, all other sectors witnessed considerable increase in gross ICORs. The increase is maximum in agriculture (122 per cent) followed by banking and insurance (104 per cent), manufacturing (82 per cent), transport (68 per cent) and electricity (61 per cent). In the 1970s, increase in gross ICOR is more pronounced for sectors: construction (111 per cent), trade (104 per cent), mining and quarrying (87 per cent) and electricity (34 per cent). In the case of agriculture and manufacturing, the increase in gross ICOR is much less compared with the increase in the 1960s. An important feature in the trend value of ICORs during 1980-88 is the decline in the gross ICORs in many sectors, as against the increasing trend observed during the 1960s, and 1970s. While agriculture, fisheries, manufacturing, electricity, transport, real estate, public administration and others exhibited a lower ICOR for 1980-88 as compared with 1970-80, the sectors construction, trade, banking and insurance showed an increase in ICOR for this period. Gross ICOR in fisheries declined markedly by 56 per cent, as against about 25 per cent decrease in agriculture and manufacturing.

The ICORs calculated with lag and without lag indicate considerable differences, especially for the sector electricity, gas and water supply and transport, storage and communication. Furthermore, the differences are high in the earlier decades than in the later ones. This is to be expected as the gestation lags are long in these sectors. The sectoral ICORs tend to be overestimated because of the 'cross effects of sectoral investment' which occurs as a result of input-output relationship among sectors. These cross effects lead to an increased output in sectors other than the one in which investment is made. While this is accounted for in aggregate ICOR, it is not captured by the sectoral ratio.

Average Capital-Output Ratio

CSO (1989) has published the capital stock estimates, as on March 31, 1981, for different sectors and for the total economy, on a net basis. By considering the net capital formation of different sectors for other years. One can compute the capital stock estimates for the periods both prior to 1980-81 and after 1980-81[7]. Using the estimated net output, average capital-output ratio was estimated for each year. For decade-wise, geometric mean of ACORs was worked out (Table 2).

ACOR for the 1960s at 1.64, exhibited an increase of 66 per cent over that of 0.99 for the 1950s. During the 1980s, while net ICOR declined to 2.48 from 4.2 in the previous decade, ACOR increased from 2.22 to 2.65. The ACOR has increased at a declining rate because of the sharp decline in ICOR.

Between the '50s and '70s, ACORs of all sectors, except real estate, exhibited an increasing trend. During 1980-88, fishing, transport, real estate and public administration had lower ACORs as compared with that of 1970s. All the remaining sectors showed an increasing ACOR for this period (Table 4).

Table 4

Average Capital-Output Ratios (Net)

Sector	*1950-51 to 1959-60*		*1960-61 to 1969-70*		*1970-71 to 1979-80*		*1980-81 to 1987-88*	
	1	*2*	*1*	*2*	*1*	*2*	*1*	*2*
Agriculture	1.2877	1.2594	1.2966	1.2684	1.3858	1.336	1.618	1.543
Forestry	0.089	0.076	0.174	0.162	0.185	0.172	0.327	0.255
Fishing	0.459	0.368	0.845	0.570	0.631	0.609	0.625	0.599
Mining & Quarrying	–	–	0.871	0.288	2.412	1.690	5.196	3.166
Manufacturing	–	–	1.081	0.683	2.491	2.112	3.272	2.816
Electricity, Gas & Water Supply	7.563	5.410	14.138	5.685	20.710	14.428	26.693	17.441
Construction	0.040	0.037	0.1545	0.1134	0.322	0.277	0.679	0.569
Trade, Hotels & Restaurants	–	–	0.053	0.039	0.552	0.478	1.437	1.245
Transport, Storage	5.912	5.316	9.532	7.633	8.687	7.995	6.583	6.102
Banking & Insurance	0.285	0.239	0.347	0.316	0.338	0.307	0.350	0.310
Real Estate	19.519	19.337	16.639	16.243	14.023	13.924	12.166	11.836
Public Admn. & Defence	4.288	4.100	6.289	6.190	5.899	5.823	5.326	5.247
Other Services	0.492	0.480	0.796	0.765	0.879	0.867	0.911	0.874

SECTION III

Sources of Variation

With a view to identify the sources of variation in ICORs, the overall changes in gross ICORs have been decomposed into two components *viz.*, explaining changes in gross ICORs into (i) changes due to sectoral ICORs and (ii) changes due to sectoral weights in total output, and (iii) interaction coefficient between (i) and (ii), is as follows[8]:

$$C_1 - C_0 = \sum_{i=1}^{n} C_{1i}.W_{1i} - \sum_{i=1}^{n} C_{0i}.W_{0i} \quad ...(1)$$

$$= \sum_{i=1}^{n} (C_{1i} - C_{0i})\, W_{0i} + \sum_{i=1}^{n} (W_{1i} - W_{0i})\, C_{0i}$$

$$+ \sum_{i=1}^{n} (C_{1i} - C_{0i})(W_{1i} - W_{0i}) \quad ...(2)$$

$$= A + B + C$$

Where,

C_1 = Gross ICOR at time 1

C_0 = Gross ICOR at time 0

C_{1i} = Gross ICOR of sector i at time 1

W_{1i} = Share of sector i in total incremental output (= ΔGDP) at time 1

W_{0i} = Share of sector i in total incremental output at time 0.

A : Share due to changes in sectoral ICORs.

B : Share due to changes in sectoral weights

C : Interaction coefficient between A and B.

In working out sectoral weights the ratio of incremental sectoral output to that of incremental total output is to be considered, as incremental output is the denominator in ICOR. But the above-mentioned decomposition method suffers from the difficulty of finding an economically acceptable meaning of the interaction coefficient. Hence, we modified identity (2) as follows:

$$C_1 - C_0 = \Sigma (C_{1i} - C_{0i})\, \overline{W}_i + \Sigma (W_{1i} - W_{0i})\, \overline{C}_i \quad ...(3)$$

Where,

$$\overline{W}_i = \frac{1}{2}\left(W_{1i} + W_{0i}\right)$$

$$\overline{C}_i = \frac{1}{2}\left(C_{1i} + C_{0i}\right)$$

Table 5 gives sources of variation in ICORs, by applying the above methodology.

Table 5

Sources of Variation in Gross ICOR

	Period	*Percentage change due to*	
		Sectoral Composition	*Sectoral ICOR*
	1	2	3
1.	1950s and 1960s	42	58
2.	1960s and 1970s	35	65
3.	1970s and 1980-88	22	78

Between 1950s and 1960s, gross ICOR increased by about 35 per cent, of which changes in sectoral ICORs accounted for 58 per cent while the changes in sectoral composition accounted for the balance 42 per cent. Between 1970s and 1960s, 65 per cent of the increase in gross ICOR was explained by changes in sectoral ICORs and the balance 35 per cent by changes in sectoral weights. But during 1980-88, gross ICOR declined considerably. Even during this phase, changes in sectoral ICORs accounted for a major proportion (78 per cent)[10].

Thus we observed that not only have the changes in sectoral ICORs influenced the changes in ICORs more as compared with changes due to sectoral composition, the share of this source was increasing in the last four decades. Hence, any effort to reduce the ICOR for the economy as a whole should concentrate on reducing sectoral ICORs.

The behaviour of ICOR provides an approximate indicator of the capital efficiency of the system. Though there has been a welcome reduction in ICOR in the recent period, given the large time and the consequent cost over runs experienced by many of the projects, there is considerable scope for improving the ICOR. In seeking to achieve a higher growth rate in the economy, while all efforts should be made to raise the domestic savings rate – particularly of the public sector, equal attention needs to be paid to a more efficient utilization of the capital assets. A further improvement is both necessary and possible.

Notes

1. The ACOR indicates the relationship between the existing stock of capital and the resultant flow of current output. The ICOR, on the other hand, expresses the relationship between the amount of increase in output resulting from an increase in the stock of capital.
2. Planning Commission (1978): Sixth Five-Year Plan – An approach paper, page 48.
3. An alternative method of estimating ICOR has been suggested by Hashim. He writes, "The simplest and the most useful way of deriving ICOR is to express it as the ratio between the rate of investment and the growth rate in GDP for the corresponding period. Since at macro level one of the uses of ICOR is to get an idea of the size of investment required for the next plan period, this definition of ICOR comes more handy for this purpose also". This method implicitly assumes equality between marginal and average saving ratios, which is not always true and hence this method was not used by us.
4. One must recognize the methodological differences in the computation of ICORs, between this study and that of Krishnamoorthy and Sharma (K&S) and World Bank (WB), even though the broad trends emanating from these ratios are similar. While Raj and K&S have used a three year moving average of output to smoothen weather induced fluctuation, K&S assumed one year lag in estimating ICORs and no lag is assumed by Raj. WB obtained ICORs by dividing average real investment as a share of real gross value added at factor cost in each period by the corresponding rate of growth by real gross value added at factor cost. Hashim also adopted the same methodology. In the following table, we compare our results with that of others.

A. Gross ICOR

	With inventories		*Without inventories*	
Period	*Ours*	*Raj**	*Ours*	*Raj*
1	2	3	4	5
1950s	3.80	3.80	3.54	3.50
1960s	5.33	4.54	4.82	4.28
1970s	6.12	6.27	5.07	5.55
1980s	4.00	-	3.27	-

*: Raj K.N.: Some observations on Economic Growth in India over the period 1952-53 to 1982-83; *Economic & Political Weekly*, October 13, 1984, p.1803.

B. Gross ICOR**

Plan	Ours	K&S***
First	3.21	3.24
Second	4.10	4.45
Third	4.98	4.71
Fourth	4.86	6.62
Fifth	5.86	4.73
Sixth	4.14	4.04
Seventh	3.50	-

** : with one year lag between output and investment.

*** : Krishnamoorthy, K and Sharma, P.D.(1989): Capital-Output Ratios and Efficiency in India (mimeo).

C. Gross ICOR

	Period	Ours*	Hashim**
	1	2	3
1.	1951-52 - 1955-56	3.37	2.56
2.	1956-57 - 1960-61	4.28	3.58
3.	1961-62 - 1965-66	5.29	4.53
4.	1966-67 - 1970-71	4.81	2.99
5.	1971-72 - 1975-76	5.81	5.26
6.	1976-77 - 1980-81	6.56	7.56
7.	1981-82 - 1985-86	3.91	4.14
8.	1985-86 - 1989-90	3.82	3.76

* : Geometric mean of ICOR of each year for the period given under col.(1).

** : Hashim, S.R. (1990): "Forty Years of Indian Economy: Structure and Dimensions of Growth" (mimeo).

D.

Isher J. Ahluwalia, (1985) in her book "Industrial Growth in India: Stagnation since the Mid-Sixties", has estimated gross ACOR for the manufacturing sector. She observed that Gross ACOR increased from 2.34 during 1959-66 to 3.71 during 1966-80. Our calculations, which are on net basis, indicated a rise from 1.346 to 2.397 during these periods.

5. Gupta *et al,* (1981) derived the effective gestation lag for different sectors using the distributed lag model. Hence, ICOR for year 't' is $K_{t-L}/\Delta 0_t$, where ΔK_{t-L} and $\Delta 0_t$ are investment at time t-L and incremental output in year 't' respectively. Gestation lag for different sectors is given in Appendix II.

6. As the forestry sector indicated a negative growth rate in its output, ICOR could not be calculated for this sector.

7. However, for the sectors, mining and quarrying, manufacturing and trade, the net capital stock figures thus computed turned out to be negative in 1950s and hence ACOR could not be calculated for these sectors.
8. Dholakia, B.H., (1983) and Isher J.Ahluwalia, (1985) adopted this method for decomposition.
9. Gunnar Mydral, (1968): 'Asian Drama' – An inquiry into the poverty of nations – p. 1977.
10. Dholakia, (1983) has also come out with a similar observation that "the changes in sectoral capital-output ratios have been the primary source of variation in the aggregate capital-output ratio in the Indian economy observed during the last three decades and especially after the mid-sixties."

    Dholkia, B.H., (1983): "Behaviour of capital output ratios in Indian Economy", Chapter 6.

    Isher J. Ahluwalia, (1985) also observed similar feature for the manufacturing sector, p. 144.

Appendix I

Let us assume that investment and output are growing at an annual rate of 'r' per cent and 'g' per cent respectively.

Investment at time 't'

$I_t = I_0\,(1+r)^t$ ...(1)

Where,

I_0 = Initial investment.

As high powers of 'r' (i.e., r^2 and above) have very little impact on I_t (1) can be written as:

$I_t = I_0\,(1+rt)$ ...(2)

Output at time 't'

$Y_t = Y_0\,(1+g)^t$ ...(3)

On similar argument as above, (3) can be written as:

$Y_t = Y_0\,(1+gt)$ ...(4)

Incremental output at time 't'

$\Delta Y_t = Y_0\,(1+gt) - Y_0\,[1+g(t\text{-}1)] = Y_0 g$

$$\text{ICOR (without lag)} = \frac{I_0\,(1+rt)}{Y_0 g} \quad \text{...(5)}$$

Assuming a lag of 'L' years,

$$\text{ICOR (with lag)} \quad \frac{I_0\,(1+r)^{t-L}}{Y_0 g} = \frac{I_0[1+(t-L)r]}{Y_0 g} \quad \text{...(6)}$$

Error in ignoring lag (5-6)

$$\frac{I_0\,(1+rt)}{Y_0 g} - \frac{I_0[1+(t-L)r]}{Y_0 g} = \frac{I_0.L}{Y_0}\;\frac{r}{g} \quad \text{...(7)}$$

Hence, error is zero when at least one of the factors in RHS of (7) is zero. As I_0 and L cannot be zero, error is minimized when the ratio (r/g) approaches zero.

Appendix II

Sector-wise Period of Lag between Investment and Flow of Output

	Sector	*Period of Lag (Years)*
1.	Agriculture	1
2.	Forestry	4
3.	Fishing	2
4.	Mining	4
5.	Manufacturing	3
6.	Construction	3
7.	Electricity	6
8.	Transport	3
9.	Trade	2
10.	Banking	2
11.	Real Estate	2
12.	Public Administration	1
13.	Other Sectors	1

7

Impact of Hike in Prices of Coal & Petroleum Products on Other Sectors of the Economy

An Application of Input-Output Technique

When the price of a commodity increases, it has an impact on the prices of other commodities through the inter-industry dynamics. Earlier studies in this field have attempted to trace, for example, the effect of an increase in indirect taxes on certain commodities on the prices of the non-taxed commodities through the use of input-output table. The underlying assumption of all these studies is that the price of a commodity increases when prices of the inputs that go into the production of a commodity increase. In this paper we have attempted to present a methodology by which the impact of the increase in the price of one commodity on others can be calculated under a situation where the prices of specific commodities are not allowed to rise, even though input prices go up.

Methodology of Investigation

It is well known that Leontief input-output table can be converted into a set of price equations[1]. The prices of the various sectors in the base year can be broken down into various components as follows:

$$1 = \sum_{i=1}^{n} A_{ij} + V_{ij} \qquad \ldots(1)$$

Where,

A_{ij} = Re. of commodity 'i' required per Re. of commodity 'j'.

V_j = Re. of value added per Re. of commodity 'j'.

Co-authors: **Raaj Kumar Sah** and **K.S. Reddy.**
Artha Vijanana, Vol.23(2), 1981.

n = number of sectors in the economy, each identifiable by a commodity.

$A = (A_{ij})\ i = (l, n) \quad j = (l, n)$

$V' = [V_1, V_n]$

$L' = [l, 1]$ a(n × 1) vector of unity elements, then equation (1) can be rewritten in the matrix form as:

$L = A'L + V$

$L = (1 - A')^{-1}\ V$ ...(2)

If T_j = increase in the taxation on the jth commodity, expressed as a ratio of pre-taxation price and

$T' = [T_1, T_n]$

If F_j = final price of commodity 'j'

And $F = [F_l, F_n]$ then

$$F = \sum_{i=1}^{n} A_{ij}\ F_i + V_j + T_j \quad ...(3)$$

$F = (1 - A')^{-1}\ (V + T)$

If P_j = final price increases in commodity 'j' and

$P' = [P_1, P_n]$ then, given that all initial prices are unity in our exercise

$P = F - L = (1 - A')^{-1}\ T$ ...(4)

[from equation (2)]

Equations (1) and (2) imply that the price per unit of commodity is equal to the total outlays incurred in the production process. The total outlays include payments for self inputs and values added of the sector. Equation (4) has been the standard approach used by the earlier writers[2] to arrive at the impact of change in taxation or change in wage rate on the prices of the various commodities. The modification introduced here is that the final price increase in one or more commodities can be damped at a particular level (as a policy measure) and under such a situation, the final price impact of taxation and similar decisions directly affecting the price can be traced.

If the final price increase in commodity 'm' is clamped at 'Km' then equation (3) can be modified as:

$$F_j = \sum_{\substack{i=1 \\ i \neq m}}^{n} A_{ij} F_i + A_{mj} K_m + V_j + T_j \qquad \text{...(5a)}$$

for $j = 1, n; j \neq m$

$$F_j = K_m \quad \text{For } j = m \qquad \text{...(5b)}$$

An (n-l) × (n-l) matrix B can be defined such that all the elements of matrix A included except m[th] row and m[th] column elements. So also a vector C_R can be defined such that

$$C_m = \overline{(B_{m1} K_m, - - -, B_{mn-1} K_m)}$$

Then equation (5a) can be expressed.

$$F = BF + C_m + V + T$$

$$F = (1-B')^{-1} (C_m + V + T)$$

Hence,

$$P = (1-B')^{-1} (C_m + V + T) - L \qquad \text{...(6)}$$

If there are more than one sectors for which the final prices are clamped at a particular level, matrix B contains all the elements of matrix A except the elements of the rows and columns which correspond to these sectors and additional vectors similar to C_R can be defined.

In the model developed above, it has been assumed that the entire increase in the prices is passed on to the consumer except in the sectors for which the prices are controlled as a policy. This might not be true in all cases because of the price and the existence of excess capacity. The model also assumes that the prices of self inputs undergo a change, implying an absence of vertical integration which is not far from reality, as a class, in the Indian situation. A third assumption is that the value added in absolute terms does not change and hence it declines as a percentage of the final price. And finally the assumption of constant input-output coefficients, inspite of a price change might be valid only if there are no radical shifts in the relative prices of commodities.

Application of Model

An application of the situation described in the model presented above is found in the increase in the prices of coal and petroleum products announced in July, August and September, 1979. The increase in the prices of coal and petroleum products amounted to 45.4 per cent and 17.72 per cent respectively.[3] When the prices of these commodities were increased, as a matter of policy, the prices of railway services and electricity were not increased. By using the methodology indicated earlier, we have computed the impact of the increase in prices of petroleum products and coal on various commodities under four different assumptions: (a) when the prices of coal and petroleum products were increased with no restriction imposed on the increase in the price of any commodity; (b) situation (a) modified to take into account the restriction that the railway price alone will not be increased; (c) situation (b) modified to take into account the restriction that the electricity price will also not be increased and (d) situation (c) modified to take into account that the price of coal will not go up, beyond the initial increase of 45.4 per cent. The computed increase in the prices of various commodities under four different assumptions is given in Table 1.[4] In this table we have shown only those sectors, prices of which would increase by more than one per cent.[5]

It may be noted that the price of coal and petroleum products in situations (a), (b) and (c) have increased by a little more than the initial increase of 45.4 per cent and 18.7 per cent respectively. In situation (d) the price of coal has increased by only 45.4 per cent because we have not allowed its price to go up beyond its initial increase. The petroleum products, however, have been allowed to increase to 17.92 per cent because the prices of some of the products under this category are not controlled directly by the Government.

When no restriction is imposed on the increase in the price of any sector, the most affected sector is miscellaneous coal and miscellaneous petroleum products. Next in the order of impact are cement and electricity where the price increase would be close to two per cent. In the absence of any direct restriction, the price of railway services would have increased by 0.94 per cent. The restriction that the railway price should remain the same, inspite of the increase in the prices of coal and petroleum products, would benefit the sector,

'Miscellaneous coal and miscellaneous petroleum products' most, followed by cement, fertilizer, iron and steel and paper and paper products. This must have occurred due to the fact that transport is an important element in the cost of production of these commodities. With the additional restriction that even the price of electricity should not increase, the industry that gains most is fertilizers.

Table 1

Impact of Price Increase in Coal and Petroleum Products

Items	*Price Increase with no Restriction Imposed on any Sector*	*Price Increase with Railway Price Unchanged*	*Price Increase with Railway and Electricity Price Unchanged*	*Price Increase with Railway and Electricity Unchanged and Coal Price Fixed at an increase of 45.4%*
1. Coal	46.172	46.165	46.111	45.400
2. Petroleum Products	17.917	17.914	17.885	17.885
3. Miscellaneous Coal & Miscellaneous Petroleum Products	6.006	5.882	5.843	5.757
4. Cement	2.130	2.054	2.029	2.004
5. Electricity	1.816**	1.788	0.000	0.000
6. Iron & Steel	1.423	1.363	1.305	1.288
7. Fertilizer	1.221	1.158	0.986	0.975
8. Paper & Paper Products	1.138	1.095	0.961	0.960
9. Other Transport Service	1.132	1.131	1.128	1.128
10. Man-made Fabrics	1.037	0.990	0.926	0.917
11. Railway Services*	0.941**	0.000	0.000	0.000

* : For comparison purpose we have included railways, though its price increase is less than one per cent.

** : Electricity: The increase in the price of coal causes increase in the price of electricity by 1.633 per cent. The increase in the price of petroleum products causes increase in the price of electricity by 0.183 per cent.

Railways: The increase in the price of coal causes an increase in the price of railways by 0.814 per cent. The increase in the price of petroleum products causes the price of railways to increase by 0.127 per cent.

With the restrictions on the prices of coal, railway services and electricity, the industry most affected by the price increases announced is 'miscellaneous coal and miscellaneous petroleum products'. Its price goes up by approximately 5.8 per cent. Next in the order of impact is the cement industry, the price of which would have to go up by two per cent in order to compensate for the increase in the price of inputs. Taking into account the impact of all commodities and weighing them properly, we find that the wholesale price index would go up by 1.3 per cent approximately.[6]

Conclusion

Under the assumption that the price of a commodity will increase to the full extent of the increase in the price of inputs that go into its production, the inter-industry table can be used to study the effects of the increase in the price of any one commodity on the prices of all other commodities. It is, however, possible that either because of Government controls or because of demand factors, the prices of some of the commodities may not increase in spite of the increase in the price of inputs. Under these conditions, it becomes necessary to evolve a new computational procedure to estimate the impact on the prices of various commodities. This paper has outlined such a procedure and has applied it to a recent situation in India, when coal and petroleum prices were increased without increasing the prices of railway services and electricity.

* Authors are thankful to Professor R. Radhakrishna and an unknown referee for their comments on an earlier draft of this paper. However, we take full responsibility for any errors.

Notes

1. Leontief W., *Input-Output Economics*, New York University Press, 1966, pp. 142-145.
2. Radhakrishnan P.N. and Rangarajan C., "Price Effects of Commodity Taxation," *Economic and Political Weekly*, November 11, 1967, pp. 1981-1985.
3. The percentage increase in the coal price has been computed on the basis of following information : The price of Coal India Ltd., was increased from Rs. 64.71 to Rs. 101.18 per tonne of coal. The price of Singareni Collieries was increased from Rs. 68.70 to Rs. 99.20 per tonne of coal. Simultaneously the Government of India removed the excise duties imposed on coal prior to the increase of coal price. The excise duty imposed on non-cooking coal was Rs. 5 per tonne and on cooking coal was Rs. 7 per tonne. The percentage increase in the price of coal has been computed using appropriate weights.

The increase in the petroleum products was calculated on the basis of following information:

	Name of the Product	*Increase*
i.)	Kerosene and High Speed Diesel Oil	10 paise per litre
ii.)	Light Diesel Oil	32 paise per litre
iii.)	Fuel Oil	32 paise per litre
iv.)	Motor Spirit	35 paise per litre
v.)	Aviation Fuel	74 paise per litre
vi.)	All Other Products	25 per cent

After obtaining the base year prices, using appropriate weights, the percentage increase in petroleum products was obtained.

4. To calculate increase in prices, we have used the 66 × 66 inter industry matrix given in the Planning Commission document. "A Technical Note on the Approach to the Fifth Plan of India (1974-79)", April 1973. The technical coefficient refer to 1973-74 at 1971-72 prices.
5. Detailed sectorwise impact can be obtained from the authors, if so desired.
6. This is under the situation when the prices of coal, railway services and electricity are not increased. We have assumed that the prices of commodities like cement which are price controlled would also go up because of the increase in the prices.

8

Corporate Investment in 1979

A Forecast

Forecasting Technique

The methodology applied in this paper to forecast corporate investment relies on the data available with the term-lending institutions on the phasing of capital expenditures of projects sanctioned by them. These may be regarded as a kind of anticipatory data for forecasting. The details of the technique followed have been explained in my earlier writings.[1]

It has been observed that most projects in the corporate sector approach one or the other of all-India term lending institutions for obtaining the necessary financial assistance. The companies provide the lending institutions with data not only on the total cost of the project but also the capital expenditures (project as well as normal) to be incurred in the various years. This information forms part of the cash flow statements attached to the proposals. By aggregating the information on the phasing of capital expenditures of proposals sanctioned in all the previous years, it should be possible to forecast capital expenditures for any year. The scope of the study is strictly restricted to the enterprises which have taken assistance from the term lending institutions. Thus, obviously the estimates arrived at do not cover the entire corporate sector. Nevertheless, since most of the companies come to the financial institutions for assistance, this estimate can be regarded as a reliable reflection of the behaviour of the entire corporate sector. What is relevant from the point of the corporate sector as a whole is the trend revealed in the rate of change rather than the absolute figures.

Economic and Political Weekly, March 10, 1979.

The estimates that are derived, approximate more closely to the gross fixed asset formation than to net fixed asset formation. In the case of new companies there is no difference between gross and net fixed assets. But with respect to old companies, the cash flow statements, provided to the financial institutions relate to the entire company. Therefore, as mentioned previously, we take down not only the capital expenditures on projects but also the normal capital expenditures which are shown in the cash flow statements. In the last few years we have taken extra care to collect data on both types of capital expenditures. But we have faced some difficulties in this regard. There are some companies which have not provided data on normal capital expenditures. In the case of certain types of loans, such as those for balancing equipment, detailed data are not usually provided.

A limitation of this method of forecasting is that, part of the expenditures to be incurred in any year comes out of projects sanctioned in that very year itself and we have no information on this. The proportion of such expenditures has varied from year to year. In 1973, 1974 and 1976, the ratio was around 30 per cent. There was a sharp jump in the ratio to 45 per cent in 1977, which may perhaps be accounted for by the introduction of new schemes such as soft loan schemes and technical development fund schemes. Expenditures on projects coming under such schemes may not have much lag. This ratio has dropped to 28 per cent in 1978. Thus, a part of the capital expenditures to be incurred in a year will largely depend upon the factors that operate within that year and these cannot be forecast by our model. While the pending applications with the term lending institutions can give some clue, they do not provide a satisfactory indicator. However, this method at least indicates the minimum investment that will be made. Also, it indicates the expenditures that will have to be forthcoming out of the investment decisions of the forecast year in order to show a rise.

The other limitations of this model of forecasting have been pointed out by the author in his earlier writings. The validity of the estimates depends upon how closely companies adhere to the expenditure pattern outlined in the initial project proposal. Cost over-run of projects by itself is not a limitation. So long as companies seek assistance from the term lending institutions for financing the cost over-run, they would get incorporated in our estimates. In the case of such projects, necessary adjustments are also made in the phasing of capital expenditures in the light of the new information. Obviously companies which finance the over-run, out of their resources, will not be captured in our estimates. However, the crux of the problem is how closely even under normal circumstances, companies stick to their original phasing of capital expenditures. We made an analysis of 44 projects, comparing the original and the actual phasing of capital expenditures. It is difficult to draw any generalisations from this study. The one factor that emerges is that in the case of expenditures to be incurred in the year of sanction, planned expenditures are always higher than the actuals. It appears that normally projects provide for about 20 per cent of the cost of the projects to be incurred in the year of sanction. But the actuals are much closer to 10 per cent. There is some evidence to believe that the original and the actual phasing of capital expenditures are much closer for existing companies than for new companies. To some extent differences are also accounted for by the nature of the industries. Actual expenditures will perhaps be close to the planned ones in the case of loans granted under such schemes as soft loan schemes and technical development funds. The composition of the projects in terms of old and new companies, types of industries and types of loans vary from year to year. There is no general formula by which one can modify the original phasing of capital expenditures. We have to be content with making changes in the original phasing of capital expenditures as and when new information is made available to the financing institutions. However, some judgement will have to be exercised in relation to planned expenditures to be incurred in the year of sanction.

Forecasts of corporate investment using this model have been made in the past several years. However, one is naturally tempted to ask, how far these forecasts compare with actuals. It is rather unfortunate that we do not have a series on corporate fixed investment which is reliable and acceptable to all. At present, estimates are provided by the CSO, The Economic Times, and to some extent, by the Reserve Bank of India. An analysis of these estimates indicates that they differ from one another not only in absolute amount but also in terms of relative changes for several years. Though all the estimating agencies use the method of blowing up the figure obtained from a sample survey of companies, differences seem to arise because of lack of reliable data on the total paid up capital of all companies industrywise.[2] For 1972-73, 1973-74 and 1974-75, the Economic Times estimates of gross fixed assets formation of the corporate sector show a rise of 42.4 per cent, 6.5 per cent and 32.8 per cent, respectively. The corresponding rates of growth according to the CSO estimates which include co-operatives also are 31.4 per cent, 7.3 per cent and 16.4 per cent, respectively. Our final estimates showed a rise of 45.3 per cent, 14.7 per cent and 28.5 per cent, respectively. The substantial increases in gross fixed investment at least in nominal terms witnessed in 1972-73 and 1974-75 were captured by our forecast. For 1975-76, our forecast showed a fall whereas all other estimates showed a rise. Data since 1976-77 from RBI and CSO are yet to come.

Picture for 1978

Table 1 provides the data on the phasing of capital expenditures of projects sanctioned by the three major term lending institutions — IDBI, ICICI and IFCI.[3] Read horizontally, each row shows the expenditures to be incurred in the various years by companies whose projects were approved in a particular year. These include normal as well as project capital expenditures in the case of old companies and project expenditures in the case of new companies. Read vertically, each element indicates expenditures to be incurred in a year out of projects sanctioned in a previous year. The total of each vertical column indicates the expenditures to be incurred in a particular year out of projects sanctioned in all the years.

From Table 1 it can be noticed that the capital expenditures in 1978 will be Rs. 1,014 crores as against Rs. 955 crores estimated at this point for 1977. This would imply a growth rate of six per cent. It may, however, be noted that the estimates for 1977 as of now is Rs. 1,011 crores. This includes Rs. 56 crores spent in 1977 on projects sanctioned in 1978. The estimates for 1978 would also go up by a more or less similar amount when the projects sanctioned in 1979 are known. Therefore, one can conclude that corporate investment in 1978 rose by six per cent over the level reached in 1977. This also confirms the forecast made last year of a rise between five per cent and eight per cent.

Table 1

Phasing of Capital Expenditures on Projects Sanctioned by Lending Institutions

(Rs. in lakhs)

Year of Sanction	*1966*	*1967*	*1968*	*1969*	*1970*	*1971*	*1972*	*1973*	*1974*	*1975*	*1976*	*1977*	*1978*	*1979*	*1980*	*1981*
1960	72	39	44													
1961	217	76	41	21												
1962	269	238	134	52	26											
1963	1738	165	112	80	63	53	40	30								
1964	3498	1447	354	295	153	79	47	28	12	2						
1965	10147	7227	1897	754	449	203	184	135	21							
1966	5994	7393	6202	5930	2397	1127	623	397	359	151						
1967	201	4651	12160	9407	4377	2041	424	308	190	138	23	3	12			
1968		232	4276	9170	6655	4219	2768	1711	178	110	53	5				
1969			74	8914	14168	7859	6213	2172	445	164	54	12				
1970			279	74	4545	7817	6704	2193	647	403	176	332	315			
1971				63	766	7600	10990	9062	4487	854	396	260	260	238		
1972						762	15288	17531	11778	4036	977	357	283	229		
1973							2652	15622	26183	11053	5167	4046	1003	836		
1974						95	361	3889	19832	20413	14411	2193	1245			
1975								17	4016	11423	23122	21535	11854	5200	879	4076
1976										4248	19462	23084	13015	1652	701	
1977											6364	43703	45549	23537	8040	
1978											326	5638	27944	43002	32150	16957
Total	**22131**	**21468**	**25574**	**33759**	**34048**	**31844**	**46294**	**53095**	**68148**	**52995**	**70531**	**101168**	**101480**	**74694**	**41770**	**21033**

All the capital expenditures indicated are in current prices. The cost estimates of projects sanctioned in any year would be at the price level of that year. Thus, while aggregating the estimates of projects sanctioned in the previous years, there is need to reduce all the figures to a common price level. We have deflated all the elements in the columns by the combined price index of electrical machinery, non-electrical machinery and transport equipment with 1960-61 as 100. It is seen that the total capital expenditures for 1975, 1976 and 1977 would be Rs. 244 crores, Rs. 292 crores and Rs. 403 crores, respectively. The total capital expenditures for 1978 in real terms will also show a rise of six per cent over the level achieved in 1977.

The estimates provided are based on projects approved by the all-India institutions. There are cases where the financing of projects even in the corporate sector is done by state-level term lending institutions. However, we have found it difficult to collect at this point, detailed data on such projects. Also, there are other facilities such as the bill rediscounting scheme of IDBI, which also finance capital expenditures. The total amount disbursed by IDBI during 1977-78 under the scheme of rediscounting of bills came to Rs. 100 crores.

Pattern of Capital Expenditure in 1978

Table 2 provides an industrywise break-up of the capital expenditures incurred in 1978. 'Chemicals' and 'pharmaceuticals' (including fertilisers and pesticides) have topped the list with 19 per cent of the total capital expenditures. 'Paper' ranks second with 14 per cent of the total capital expenditures. 'Textiles' and 'cement' account for a slightly larger proportion of the total expenditures in 1978 than in 1977.

Table 3 indicates an industrywise analysis of the projects sanctioned in 1978. It shows where the new projects are being set up. The total number of projects approved in 1978 was 271 as compared with 302 during 1977. In the previous year, there was a sharp rise in the number of relatively small loans granted. During 1978 there were 78 soft loans and about 30 TDF projects. The total cost of projects sanctioned in 1978 came to Rs. 1,100 crores which is more or less equal to the total cost of projects sanctioned in 1977. In the previous year, 18 joint sector projects including a giant fertiliser project accounted for 33 per cent of the total cost of the projects. But during 1978 the joint sector projects contributed only seven per cent of the total cost. The total cost of the projects coming under the soft loan scheme was Rs. 183 crores.

Table 2

Industrywise Capital Expenditure for 1977 and 1978 and Expected Capital Expenditure for 1979

(Rs. in lakhs)

S.No.	*Industry*	*1977*	*1978*	*1979*
(1)	Chemicals & Pharmaceuticals	19774 (20.38)	18959 (18.77)	13382 (19.62)
(2)	Electrical	4381 (4.52)	9364 (9.27)	12630 (18.52)
(3)	Engineering	6648 (6.85)	3325 (3.29)	1676 (2.46)
(4)	Jute	287 (0.30)	1396 (1.38)	1424 (2.09)
(5)	Minerals & Metals	16704 (17.22)	12214 (12.09)	9567 (14.03)
(6)	Paper	9741 (10.04)	14489 (14.34)	4861 (7.13)
(7)	Textiles	11682 (12.04)	13358 (13.22)	12110 (17.76)
(8)	Transport	9552 (9.85)	6780 (6.71)	1818 (2.67)
(9)	Cement	4330 (4.46)	8073 (7.99)	5156 (7.56)
(10)	Miscellaneous	13910 (14.34)	13067 (12.93)	5567 (8.16)
	Total	**97009**	**101025**	**68191**

Note: Figures in brackets are percentages of total.

There is also a marked difference in the composition of industries assisted during the current year as compared with previous year. The two major industrial sectors in which new projects were being initiated in 1977 were fertilisers and pulp and paper. During 1978 electricity generation is the major sector accounting for 28 per cent of the total cost of the projects initiated. Next comes metal and metal products with 22 per cent; textiles account for 19 per cent and cement eight per cent.

Table 3

Industrywise Total Capital Cost and Phasing of Capital Expenditure on Projects Sanctioned by IDBI and ICICI During 1978

(Rs. in crores)

Industry	Total Project Cost	Years					Number of Projects	Completion Expected in			
		1977	1978	1979	1980	1981 and Onwards		Same Year	Next Year	Year After	Four or More Years
Automobile & Cycles	12.45 (1.13)	—	1.83	5.70	4.47	0.45	6	2	2	1	1
Cement	88.04 (8.00)	2.90	11.68	16.63	29.78	27.05	6	1	2	2	1
Chemicals & Petrochemicals (except Fertilisers & Pesticides)	70.25 (6.38)	5.68	17.45	37.11	10.01	—	27	11	12	4	—
Electrical Equipment	25.17 (2.29)	0.56	7.77	10.30	6.52	0.02	20	3	12	4	1
Electricity, Gas & Steam	303.40 (27.56)	—	28.63	75.70	118.61	80.46	3	—	—	1	2
Fertilisers & Pesticides	17.74 (1.61)	1.26	2.00	4.98	2.00	7.50	6	—	4	1	1
Food Products (other than Sugar)	3.06 (0.28)	—	1.59	—	0.47	1.00	3	2	—	—	1

(Contd...)

(...Contd...) (Rs. in crores)

Industry	Total Project Cost	Years					Number of Projects	Completion Expected in			
		1977	1978	1979	1980	1981 and Onwards		Same Year	Next Year	Year After	Four or More Years
Glass, Pottery, etc	25.21 (2.29)	3.10	5.78	12.00	4.33		5	—	2	3	—
Machinery Manufacture (other than Electrical)	24.14 (2.19)	2.13	10.58	8.51	1.73	1.19	27	4	19	2	2
Metals & Metal Products	242.54 (22.03)	2.08	51.14	71.67	56.50	61.15	43	12	22	4	5
Printing & Publishing	2.20 (0.20)	—	2.10	0.10			3	2	1	—	—
Pulp, Paper & Paper Products	31.50 (2.86)	1.53	11.26	16.91	1.77	0.03	13	2	7	3	1
Rubber Products	13.42 (1.22)	—	1.19	10.62	1.61	—	5	1	3	1	—
Shipping	—	—	—	—	—	—	—	—	—	—	—
Sugar	25.82 (2.35)	10.22	5.66	9.48	0.41	0.05	10	1	7	2	
Textiles	206.59 (18.77)	8.33	60.37	97.92	37.71	2.26	81	14	38	26	3
Wood, Cork & Hardboard	—	—	—	—	—	—	—	—	—	—	—
Miscellaneous	9.31 (0.84)	0.88	5.28	2.30	0.70	0.15	13	3	7	2	1
Total	**1100.84**	**38.67**	**224.31**	**379.93**	**276.62**	**181.31**	**271**	**58**	**138**	**56**	**19**

Note: Figures in brackets are percentages of total.

There were seven projects sanctioned during 1978 with a capital cost of more than Rs. 20 crores each. These seven projects include projects in electricity generation, steel expansion and cement production. These projects accounted for 55 per cent of the total cost of the projects.

Forecast for 1979

As of now, based on the projects sanctioned until the end of 1978, the capital expenditures in 1979 will be Rs. 747 crores. Thus, there is a gap of Rs. 268 crores to be filled in to come up to the level of 1978. Since normally the capital expenditures to be incurred in a year out of the projects sanctioned in that year itself does not exceed Rs. 250 crores, it is unlikely that the corporate investment in 1979 will exceed the level reached in 1978. Of course, there is an exception when in 1977 there was a very substantial amount of capital expenditures incurred in that year flowing out of projects sanctioned in that year. But this is an exception rather than the rule. Therefore, based on past general behaviour, it is hard to expect more than Rs. 270 crores of capital expenditures in 1979 out of the projects to be sanctioned in that year. Therefore, our conclusion is that corporate investment in 1979 will stay at the level reached in 1978.

* The author wishes to thank the authorities of the Industrial Development Bank of India, the Industrial Credit and Investment Corporation of India and the Industrial Finance Corporation of India for the co-operation extended to this study. The author also wishes to thank Ranjana Pendharkar for the valuable assistance rendered by her in collecting and analysing the data. The author is grateful to the Director and the Research Committee of the Indian Institute of Management, Ahmedabad for providing financial assistance for the project.

Notes

1. Samuel Paul and C. Rangarajan, "Short Term Investment Forecasting". Macmillan, 1974.

   C.Rangarajan, "Forecasting Capital Expenditures in the Corporate Sector", *Economic and Political Weekly*, December 19, 1970. "Investment in Private Corporate Sector in 1972: A Forecast", *Economic and Political Weekly*, February 26, 1972. "Capital Expenditures in Corporate Sector: Forecast for 1974", *Economic and Political Weekly*, August 31, 1974. "Capital Expenditure by Corporate Sector: A Forecast for 1975", *The Economic Times*, February 26, 1975. "*Corporate Investment in 1976*: A Forecast", *Economic and Political Weekly*, February 28, 1976, "Corporate Investment in 1977: A Forecast", *Economic and Political Weekly*, April 2, 1977. "Private Corporate Investment in 1978: A Forecast", *Economic and Political Weekly*, March 11, 1978.

2. For a discussion on this, see C. Rangarajan and Kirit Patel, "On Constructing a New Series on Corporate Fixed Investment", Paper presented at the Annual Conference of the Association for Research in National Income and Wealth, January, 1979.
3. For 1977, we have not been able to collect all data from all the term lending institutions. The data on projects sanctioned exclusively by IFCI remain to be collected. Since this is usually a small figure, this should not affect the conclusions drawn.

9

On the Goals and Mechanics of Replanning

There has been a renewed discussion on the mechanics of planning in this country. The focus of these discussions has been how to make plans responsive to changing conditions and needs. Currently, the planning authorities carry out only a mid-term appraisal once a plan has been formulated and becomes operative. The concept of a rolling plan, which has been recently mooted, would demand formulating a five-year plan at the beginning of each year, taking into account the performance of the economy in the previous year. In this paper, we argue that in most circumstances the task of replanning could be limited to readjusting the targets set for a given plan in the light of changing conditions and circumstances. As the paper will show, the task of readjusting targets is neither simplistic nor mechanical. Under this alternative approach, a fresh five-year plan need not be prepared every year.

It is recognised on all hands that there should be continuous planning. Flexibility is needed to take into account the changing economic conditions as well as the performance of the plan in the immediate past. A rolling plan, which involves the formulation of a fresh five-year plan at the beginning of each year, could embrace a wide set of circumstances. It need not work within the framework postulated in a given five-year plan. It would have the freedom to change the objectives, alter the priorities, and thus involve the planning authorities in a great deal of virtually fresh assessments. Such a task undoubtedly enables the planners greater flexibility, since they are not bound by the limits set by any five-year plan.

Co-author: **J.K. Satia.**
Economic and Political Weekly, Vol.XIII, Nos. 6 & 7, Annual Number, February 1978.

However, such an elaborate replanning at such frequent intervals might immerse the Planning Commission in details of planning without giving it sufficient time to make an assessment of the performance of a plan.

Therefore, granting the need for replanning, a fruitful approach would be to make a mid-term assessment of the plan more than a mere performance appraisal exercise. In an earlier paper in 1976,[1] the authors had suggested that the monitoring and evaluation of plan performance should not only recognise shortfalls in the targets, but also readjust the targets. But such a readjustment has to be worked out in view of the need for consistency in the plan and its original objectives.

Circumstances Demanding Replanning

It has been stated, again and again, that the need for replanning arises because conditions have changed. We list below some of the circumstances which would call for replanning.

1. When the plan for a five-year period is being formulated, the base year income and output of the various sectors are not known. The planners make a tentative estimate of these variables and build the plan on the basis of those estimates. When the base year actuals are known, they may sometimes deviate very much from the original estimates, calling for a substantial revision of the targets set under the plan. Everyone is familiar with what happened to the Fifth Five-Year Plan. Because of severe shortfalls in the achievements of targets set for the Fourth Plan, the base-year estimates incorporated in the Draft Fifth Plan document had to undergo revision which, in turn called for a substantial modification of the targets set in the Draft Plan document. Thus, a change in the initial conditions will itself necessitate replanning.
2. The attainment of targets set for some sectors in the terminal year of the plan might become impossible for a variety of reasons. In these circumstances, it may become necessary to alter the targets set for the other sectors because consistency can not be maintained otherwise. This is perhaps a major reason for replanning. Our past planning experience has shown

that failure to achieve targets has been almost endemic. Thus, monitoring in the Planning Commission should result not only in taking steps to correct the factors responsible for failing to achieve targets but also in readjusting targets for all sectors, if the original targets for certain sectors are unachievable. There may also be situations where unplanned surpluses may be generated in certain sectors calling for modification of the original targets.

Table 1

Effect of Shortfall in Electricity – Final Demand Objective

(Rs. in crores)

	Original	*New Level Without Restriction*	*New Level with Restriction*
Employment	21.590	21.533 (-0.057)	21.199 (-0.391)
National Income	47098	46932 (-160.0)	45434 (-1664)
Investment	6824	6804 (-19.7)	6128 (-695.3)
Consumption	40274	40128 (-140.3)	39306 (-968.7)

Table 2

Effect of Shortfall in Electricity – Employment Objective

(Rs. in crores)

	Original	*New Level Without Restriction*	*New Level with Restriction*
Employment	21.590	21.593 (+0.003)	21.416 (-0.174)
National Income	47098	47027 (-71)	45487 (-2611)
Investment	6824	6855 (+31)	5762 (-1062)
Consumption	40274	40172 (-102)	39725 (-1549)

Table 3

Shortfalls with Higher Weights on Investment: Final Demand Objective

(Rs. in crores)

	Original	*Electricity Output Cut by 10 per cent - Unrestricted*	*Restricted to 80 per cent*
Investment	6824	6811 (-13)	6250 (-574)
Consumption	40274	40130 (-144)	39137 (-1137)
National Income	47098	46941 (-157)	45387 (-1711)

3. A plan may have a number of objectives. It may seek to achieve a particular rate of growth not only in income but also in employment. Thus, implicitly or explicitly, there may be a trade-off between these objectives. The planners may have opted for a specific combination of rates of growth in output and employment. If it happens that, in the first two years, there develops a hiatus between the rates in output and employment, the planners might want to correct this tendency and emphasize more on the rate of growth in one variable than in the other in the subsequent years. The following example may make the position clear. The planners might have opted for combination of a rate of growth, five per cent in income and four per cent in employment. If it happens that in the first two years, the income growth rate has been maintained, but the employment growth rate has been only half of what was contemplated, in the next three years the planners might want to put greater emphasis on employment than on income. The need for replanning, therefore, arises for working out a new trade-off between employment and income without drastically altering the targets originally set.

4. The necessity to replan may be imposed on the planners by external circumstances. A striking example of such a situation was the abnormal increase in the prices of petroleum products that the world witnessed in the early '70s. It can also arise from external situations such as foreign aggression.

Replanning may also be called for when objectives of the planners change. But that falls under a different category. Undoubtedly, a fresh plan will have to be prepared if there is to be a change in the basic objectives. However, such changes cannot occur from year to year. A five-year interval is perhaps a reasonable period of time in which to keep the objectives unchanged. Nevertheless, as indicated earlier, even within the framework of a given set of objectives, replanning would be called for if some of these conditions change. However, replanning along the lines suggested in this paper is appropriate only if the expected shortfalls or surpluses in targets are small. Far-reaching changes in the circumstances, such as foreign aggression, will call for more or less total abandonment of the original plan and formulation of a new plan.

Recognition of Need for Replanning

In our planning process, the annual plan provides a degree of flexibility to take care of the changing circumstances. The mid-term appraisal provides opportunity to the planners to assess the performance of the plan in the first two years of the plan period. However, this evaluation focuses only on questions like why certain shortfalls have occurred, what the bottlenecks were, and what attempts should be made to resolve these difficulties. The Fourth Plan Mid-Term Appraisal states:

> Our detailed assessment of the first half of the plan that is now behind us is helpful in bringing out our achievements as well as in locating the sectors, projects and programmes to which further attention needs to be paid urgently to rectify the shortfalls that are emerging... We are engaged in detailed exercises for identifying the measures necessary to increase output in public and private sectors industries. On the basis of these enquiries, necessary steps will need to be implemented in a time-bound manner (p iii).

However, such corrective action may not always lead to achievement of the original plan targets. The Mid-Term Appraisal further states:

> Substantial shortfall in the plan adjusted target for net value-added in mining and manufacturing seems unavoidable. Since, in 1971-72 the actual rate in the two sub-sectors is likely to be much below the required rate, even taking into account the envisaged vigorous efforts to ease the various constraints on industrial growth, substantial shortfalls in the adjusted Fourth Plan targets is unavoidable (p iv).

Appendix I

Final Demand under Various Conditions

(Rs. in crores)

Sector	Original	Final Demand Unrestricted	Objective Restricted to 80 per cent	Employment Unrestricted	Objective Restricted to 80 per cent
Agriculture & Allied Sectors	19073	19072	19033	19087	19471
Mining	226	223	180	239	282
Other Food & Agro-based Sectors	3749	3748	3682	3742	3258
Textiles	3425	3423	3317	3424	3094
Wood Products	240	239	192	243	192
Paper & Paper Products	244	238	195	247	195
Leather & Rubber Products	273	270	218	271	218
Chemicals	570	566	456	571	456
Petroleum Products	235	233	188	240	188
Cement & Cement Products	163	159	130	164	130
Basic Metals & Metal Products	875	872	701	880	700
Non-electrical Machinery	1240	1238	1107	1240	992
Electrical Machinery & Equipment	669	667	556	673	535
Transport Equipment	728	720	611	757	582
Miscellaneous Products	543	537	434	545	434
Electricity	175	86	140	0	140
Construction	4149	4152	4077	4150	3777
Railways	725	729	580	726	591
Other Transport	1003	1000	896	1013	1067
Other Services	8756	8756	8735	8825	9185
Total	**47098**	**46932**	**45434**	**47027**	**45487**

Appendix II

Gross Output and Employment under Various Conditions

(Electricity cut by 10 per cent, in crores)

Sector	Gross Output					Employment Levels				
		Final Demand Objective		Employment Objective			Final Demand Objective		Employment Objective	
	Original	Unres-tricted	Restricted to 80 per cent	Unres-tricted	Restricted to 80 per cent	Original	Unres-tricted	Restricted to 80 per cent	Unres-tricted	Restricted to 80 per cent
Agriculture & Allied Sectors	26565	26543	26367	26565	26565	15.386	15.373	15.271	15.386	15.386
Mining	1040	1016	890	1040	992	0.193	0.189	0.165	0.193	0.184
Other Food & Agro-Based Sectors	4226	4218	4140	4213	3683	0.130	0.129	0.128	0.130	0.113
Textiles	4190	4179	4034	4190	3771	0.221	0.220	0.213	0.221	0.199
Wood Products	386	381	330	386	322	0.030	0.030	0.026	0.031	0.026
Paper & Paper Products	540	523	457	540	449	0.029	0.028	0.025	0.029	0.024
Leather & Rubber Products	559	524	465	559	459	0.019	0.019	0.017	0.020	0.016
Chemicals	2580	2443	2250	2456	2221	0.097	0.047	0.043	0.043	0.043
Petroleum Products	449	440	382	449	391	0.024	0.024	0.021	0.024	0.021
Cement & Cement Products	1096	1083	1020	1096	970	0.072	0.072	0.068	0.072	0.064
Basic Metals & Metal Products	3316	3280	2898	3305	2777	0.107	0.106	0.094	0.108	0.090
Non Electrical Machinery	1466	1238	1311	1466	1181	0.060	0.054	0.054	0.060	0.048
Electrical Machinery & Equipments	1031	1022	889	1031	853	0.043	0.043	0.037	0.043	0.036
Transport Equipments	1128	1123	961	1128	926	0.051	0.051	0.044	0.052	0.043
Miscellaneous Products	666	651	538	666	538	0.041	0.040	0.033	0.041	0.033
Electricity	1004	904	904	904	904	0.067	0.061	0.061	0.068	0.068
Construction	4915	4915	4805	4915	4495	0.215	0.215	0.210	0.216	0.198
Railways	1269	1269	1084	1269	1081	0.161	0.161	0.137	0.161	0.137
Other Transport	1619	1605	1457	1619	1607	0.570	0.566	0.514	0.571	0.567
Other Services	13252	13190	12974	13252	13252	4.124	4.105	4.038	4.124	4.120
Total	—	—	—	—	—	**21.590**	**21.533**	**21.199**	**21.593**	**21.416**

Thus, while the shortfalls are recognised, not much attention is paid to the problem of readjusting the plan target themselves when serious shortfalls occur in some of the key sectors. Whatever adjustments are made in the targets are usually *ad hoc*. The shortfall in the output of one sector leads not only to less availability of that output for final demand but also affects the output of other sectors. The impact of such inter-sectoral imbalances may be felt in the production of both consumption goods and capital goods. Reallocation of targets also implies a reallocation of output of each sector. Here again, while the need for replanning to ensure consistency in the event of serious shortfalls is recognised, no systematic approach has been offered in how to perform this task.[2] We provide below, some possible approaches to this task and also indicate the choices that need to be made.

Methodology for Replanning

The circumstances leading to the need for replanning basically imply that there have been deviations from originally planned outputs in a few sectors. Some of these deviations can be corrected either by inventory adjustments or by manipulation of imports and exports. However, this may not be feasible in all circumstances. As remarked earlier, such deviations lead to inter-sectoral imbalances.

In such situations, two types of replanning measures are necessary. One is to initiate corrective measures in management to make up for the deficiency. The other is to readjust the targets themselves taking into account inter-sectoral imbalances. We address ourselves to the methodology of readjusting the plan targets when shortfalls or surpluses that occur in certain sectors cannot be corrected during the plan period.

Appendix III

Intermediate and Final Use of Electricity under Various Conditions

(Rs. in crores)

Sector	Final Demand Objective			Employment Objective		
	Original	Restricted to 80 per cent	Decline per cent	Original	Restricted to 80 per cent	Change per cent
Agriculture & Allied Sectors	217	217	0	217	222	+2
Mining	7	6	10	7	9	+25
Other Food & Agro-based Sectors	73	72	2	73	63	-13
Textiles	106	103	3	106	96	-9
Wood Products	3	2	22	3	2	-20
Paper & Paper Products	18	14	20	18	14	-20
Leather & Rubber Products	10	0	20	10	8	-20
Chemicals	35	20	20	35	28	-20
Petroleum Products	7	7	1	6	5	-20
Cement & Cement Products	9	7	22	9	7	-19
Basic Metals & Metal Products	44	35	20	44	35	-20
Non-electrical Machinery	48	42	11	47	38	-19
Electrical Machinery & Equipment	22	18	17	22	17	-20
Transport Equipment	24	20	16	24	19	-19
Miscellaneous Products	47	37	20	47	37	-20
Electricity	216	172	20	215	172	-20
Construction	95	93	2	95	86	-8
Railways	43	34	19	43	35	-18
Other Transport	30	27	10	30	32	+6
Other Services	55	54	0	55	57	+4

Appendix IV

Final Demands with Higher Weights on Investment

(Rs. in crores)

Sector	Original	Electricity Output by 10 per cent Unrestricted	Restricted to 80 per cent
Agriculture & Allied Sectors	19073	19071	19010
Mining	226	223	180
Other Food & Agro-based Sectors	374	3747	3642
Textiles	3425	3422	3276
Wood Products	240	239	192
Paper & Paper Products	244	237	195
Leather & Rubber Products	273	269	218
Chemicals	570	564	456
Petroleum Products	235	233	188
Cement & Cement Products	163	158	130
Basic Metals & Metal Products	875	875	738
Non-electrical machinery	1240	1240	1135
Electrical Machinery & Equipment	669	669	580
Transport Equipment	728	721	635
Miscellaneous Products	543	541	434
Electricity	175	159	140
Construction	4149	4152	4093
Railways	725	728	580
Other Transport	1003	1000	835
Other Services	8756	8756	8722
Total	—	**46941**	**45387**

In the Indian planning exercise, the endeavour has always been to construct a plan that is mutually consistent. Two types of consistencies are attempted. One is the consistency between investment and saving. The other is the consistency of inter-sectoral flows. The input-output table, incorporating the flows of goods from one sector to another, is used to determine what the output of the different sectors should be, given the final demand for consumption and investment. If all the targets are fulfilled, then this leads to the most efficient use of resources. But, if the targets are not achieved, serious imbalances may occur, leading to waste of resources.

When the output of some sectors fails to expand at the rate at which it was expected to expand in these sectors, a new final demand vector (F') needs to be estimated. The output vector of all the sectors which is consistent with the new final demand F' is given by $(I-A)^{-1}F'$, where A is the matrix of input-output co-efficients. The new output vector must satisfy the following set of conditions. The output of sector 'i' should not exceed the original planned output x_i for all sectors where there is no shortfall. In the case of other sectors, the output should not exceed the revised expected output. Let x' denote the vector of possible output. Then any feasible final demand vector F' must satisfy the following constraints:

$$(I - A)^{-1} F' \leq X'$$

Obviously, there will be many feasible values of the final demand vector F' that will satisfy the above constraints.[3] A question, therefore, remains as to which of the feasible demand vectors is preferable.

The choice of the feasible, final demand vector should be so made as to achieve the original objectives of the plan as closely as possible. However, there the plan may have had several objectives. A compromise may also have been made among these objectives. While replanning, a fresh trade-off may have to be made among the objectives. Several alternative formulations are possible, depending upon the criteria the new final demand vector should satisfy. We indicate some of these below.

(i) The original priorities, perhaps, can be preserved if we obtain a new set of final demand which minimally deviates from the original vector.[4]

If the deviation is measured as the square of the difference between the new and original final demand, then we can write the objective function as that of minimising the function.

$$\Sigma (F_i - F_i')^2.$$

This problem can be formulated as the following quadratic programme.

$$\text{Min } \Sigma (F_i - F_i')^2$$

$$\text{s.t. } (I - A)^{-1} F' \leq x' \qquad \ldots(1)$$

$$F' \geq 0 \quad (i = 1, 2, \ldots \ldots, n)$$

Such a criterion would be desirable for two reasons: (i) As mentioned earlier, the new vector of final demand will reflect with minimum alterations, priorities implicit in the original vector of final demand which have been arrived at to satisfy a variety of considerations, and (ii) since the implementation of the plan till that time period would have proceeded according to the original goals, deviating as little as possible from the original intentions would cause the least disruption.

It is open to the planners, however, to assign differing weights to the deviations for different sectors, if it is regarded that the fulfilment of certain targets at this point is considered more desirable. One such scheme will be to give higher weights to sectors whose output is primarily for investment. This would obviously reduce the deviations for these sectors, but would more adversely affect the final demand of other sectors.

(ii) If on the other hand, employment rather than income is considered to be the main objective, we should obtain the sector-wise employment which minimally deviates from the originally planned employment.[5] Once again, if the deviation is measured as the square of the difference between the new and original employment, then we can write the objective function as that of minimising the function $\Sigma(E_i - E_1')^2$, where E_i and E_1' respectively, represent the original and new employment levels in the ith sector. The employment level in any sector 'i' is assumed to be dependent upon the output X and proportional to it. Let W_i represent the employment per unit of output. Then $E = WX_i$. The new outputs in any sector I depend upon the chosen feasible final demand vectors F' and can be written as:

$$\Sigma_j T_{ij} F_j'$$

where T' is the co-efficient in the ith row and j^{th} column of the matrix $(I-A)^{-1}$. Therefore, E_i' is given by:

$$W_i \Sigma_j T_{ij} F_j'$$

This problem can, once again, be formulated as the following quadratic programme.

$$\text{Min } \Sigma W_i [X_i - \Sigma T_{ij} F_j']^2 \qquad ...(2)$$

$$\text{s.t. } (I - A)^{-1} \quad F' \leq X'$$

$$F_i' \geq 0, \quad (i = 1, 2, \ldots n)$$

(iii) Since there can be a trade-off between income and employment, these two objectives of minimal deviation from the original vector of final demand and from the original levels of sectorwise employment can be combined with desired weights to constitute a new objective. Once again, quadratic programming formulations would result.

Finally, one more difficulty needs to be resolved about the definition of the constraint set. If any of the objectives mentioned above is used, then it may so happen that the new final demand of some sectors will be considerably less than the original final demand. This may not be acceptable. Such a difficulty could be resolved by appending the following constraint which ensures that the new final demand of a sector is not permitted to fall below[6] a certain level of original final demand:

$$F_i' \geq K_i F_i$$

Where K_i is the predetermined constant.

Illustrative Exercise: Fall in Electricity

The example in this section shows the use of the technique as well as the insights that can be gained from the possible results. The data on final demand, gross domestic output and imports for the various sectors, and total co-efficients of input-output table for the year 1973-74 were used.[7] For ease of manipulation, the 66 sector input-output Table included in the "Technical Note" was aggregated to a 20 sector input-output table using the usual procedures of aggregation. We have ignored the implications of imports. We have combined the gross domestic output with imports and treated the total as the required output of each sector. Employment per unit of output for the various sectors has been computed from the data available from the various sources.[8]

The final demand and the gross output for 1973-74 are reproduced in Appendix I and Appendix II, respectively. These are the output levels to be attained by each of the sectors if the final demand is to be met. Interpreted in another way, the planner must ensure the fulfilment of these targets with respect to gross output if the final demand (i.e., the national income) has to be reached. Given these data, one could ask: how are the targets to be readjusted and what will be the impact on the economy, if there are shortfalls in the output of one or more sectors? We have analysed this problem when there is a shortfall of 10 per cent in the output of electricity.[9] The objective is to minimise the sum of the square of deviations either for final demand or employment. While we have illustrated the example of a shortfall, the same analysis holds good for understanding the implications of surpluses.[10]

Final Demand Objective

It is easy to see that, if it is decided to cut the allocation of electricity by 10 per cent to all the sectors as a result of a shortfall of 10 per cent in the output of electricity, this will have the most serious effect on the economy. Since all these sectors of the economy use electricity as an input, in the context of the linear production function implicit in all input-output tables, the output of all the sectors will decrease by 10 per cent. The national income in such a situation would decrease by 10 per cent. The output of electricity for 1973-74 was planned at Rs. 1,025 crores and the national income for 1973-74 was planned to be Rs. 47,098 crores. A reduction in the output of electricity, by approximately Rs. 100 crores, would result in the fall of national income by Rs. 4,700 crores, if the allocation of every sector is cut by 10 per cent. This would also be the result if the planner imposes the condition that the output of no sector shall decline by more than 10 per cent.

This, however, need not be the case if electricity can be substituted by other forms of energy. But, even if no substitution is possible, as is implicit in the input-output table, a more judicious re-allocation of electricity can result in a much smaller deviation of the final demands of all sectors. Appendix I and II give the sectorwise gross output and final demand, if we solve the mathematical programme given in Model 1 and 2. Table 1 summarises some of the important conclusions which emerge when the objective of the planners is to minimise the deviations in the final demand.

When no restriction is imposed regarding the extent of a fall in the final demand of any of the sectors, the final demand of electricity is cut by Rs. 89 crores. Almost all the shortfall in the output of electricity of Rs. 100 crores is borne by the electricity sector itself.

Thus the impact on the economy is minimised by cutting down the final consumption demand of electricity rather than the intermediate use of electricity. The national income in this case declines by Rs. 160 crores, with the fall felt mostly in consumption.

Perhaps, it may not be possible to absorb the total shortfall by reducing the consumption of electricity directly. Therefore, we solve the mathematical programming model with the additional restriction that the level of final demand in any sector is not allowed to fall below 80 per cent of the original levels. Obviously, then there is much less freedom to re-allocate targets. As a result, the adverse impact on the economy will be higher. Because of this restriction, the decline in the final demand of electricity is only about Rs. 35 crores. The fall in the national income is quite substantial and is about Rs. 1,600 crores. The reduction in the final demand occurs both in the sectors producing consumption goods and those producing investment goods.

Employment Objective

We also solved the problem using the employment objective. When no restrictions are placed on final demands, the resultant employment level is nearly the same as the original. There is only a marginal decline of Rs. 71 crores in the national income. It is even less than a decline of Rs. 160 crores in the national income when the final demand objective is used, because sectorwise deviations in final demand are not emphasized when the employment objective is used.

However, when the additional restriction is imposed, that the level of final demand in any sector is not allowed to fall below 80 per cent of the original levels, the results are of some interest. The fall of Rs. 1,611 crores in the national income is nearly equal to the fall when the final demand objective was used. However, the reduction in investment sectors is higher (Rs. 1,062 crores as opposed to Rs. 695 crores in final demand objective) and the reduction in the consumption sector is correspondingly lower when the employment objective is used. Also, as is to be expected, the fall in employment is less under the new objective than under the final demand objective. This reveals the nature of trade-off between the employment and income objectives.

Allocation of Electricity

When the vector of final demand changes, the flow of output of each sector to the different sectors will also be altered. Obviously, in a planning system, the required flows must be allocated such that the targets in relation to final demand can be met. Appendix III indicates the allocation of electricity to the various sectors under the old and the demand objective, when restrictions are imposed[11], indicates that there are nine sectors to which the electricity now allocated is around 80 per cent of what was allocated before. Thus, even though the reduction in the output of electricity is 10 per cent, the allocation to these sectors is cut by about 20 per cent. There are five sectors where the reduction in allocation is approximately 10 per cent. There is practically no cut in the allocation of electricity to the other sectors. When the employment objective is used, the allocation of electricity to all sectors, except four, declines — the four being agriculture, mining, other transport and other services, thus highlighting the importance of these sectors in generating employment.

'Slack' in Output

Appendix II indicates the 'slack' in output in the various sectors. The term 'slack' is defined here as the difference between the original output contemplated under the plan and the revised output necessary under the new conditions. This implies that if capacity has been created to provide the output originally contemplated this will result in excess capacity.[12] The original vector of final demand includes an investment component based on the requirement to increase the output in the various sectors to the planned levels. Thus, it is possible with the revised output levels to lower somewhat the investment requirements. However, the planners may disregard this if it is felt that the creation of capacity is based on longer term requirements and therefore, shortfalls experienced during short periods should not be allowed to affect the investment programme. Since our gross output includes imports, the 'slacks' also indicate the maximum extent to which imports can be cut in these sectors.

Alteration in Investment Programme

The revised vector of final demand in Table 1 and 2 shows a cut in the output of sectors which may be producing investment goods. Unlike in the case of 'slack' in the gross output of the various sectors where the planner has a choice to increase or not to increase capacity, a reduction in the final demand of sectors providing investment goods implies that the level of investment cannot be increased and has therefore to be less than what was contemplated earlier. We have already indicated in Tables 1 and 2 the fall in investment that would be necessitated in the various circumstances. The needed resource mobilisation would be smaller to the extent of the fall in investment.

Weights for Consumption and Investment Goods Sectors

As mentioned at the beginning, faced with the task of re-arranging the vector of final demand, consequent on the reduction in the output of certain sectors, the planner might want to attach different weights to different sectors. It is quite possible that the planner might regard the investment component of the final demand to be preserved more than the consumption of the final demand. Such a need can be taken care of giving a higher weight to the investment goods producing sectors.[13] We have modified the model by introducing the weight of two, for all the investment goods sectors and a weight of one, for other sectors in the objective function. The results that emerge are given in Appendix IV. Some of the major conclusions are given in Table 3.

As is to be expected, the fall in investment is less with higher weights for the investment goods sector. A similar situation in relation to employment objective does not arise.

Summary And Conclusion

As our planning experience has shown, there have been many years in which the output targets set for the various industries have fallen far short of the planned levels. Occasionally, surpluses too have existed. In these circumstances, the need for flexibility in planning has been recognised. In the recent discussions, the rolling plan concept has been proposed to provide for such flexibility.

In this paper, we have examined the conditions needing replanning. It is seen that, unless there is a change in the objectives, an alternative approach for replanning is available which strives to maintain the priorities implicit in the original plan.

The planners should strive not only to take measures which bring the actual output close to the planned levels but also to refix the targets set for the various sectors, taking into account the inter-sectoral consistency. In this paper, we have provided mathematical programming formulations which will help planners in resetting the targets in such contingencies. The new set of output targets to be fixed would vary, depending on whether the objective is to remain as close as possible to the original vector of final demand or to original levels of sectorwise employment. As our illustrative exercise shows that there is a trade-off between employment and income, which the planners must consciously choose.

* The authors gratefully acknowledge the computational assistance provided by V. Venkat Rao and Sudarshan Rao.

Notes

1. See, Rangarajan, C, and Satia, J. K, "Re-allocation of Plan Targets in the case of Shortfalls in Some sectors", *Vikalpa*, Volume 1, No 3, July 1976.
2. Gunnar Myrdall mentions the problem but does not specify an approach for replanning. See Gunnar Myrdall, "Asian Drama", Volume III, pp. 1937-1940.
3. The problem that arises when the output of a sector cannot expand beyond a particular level is touched upon by Chiou-Shuang Yan, "Introduction to Input-Output Economics" (Prentice-Hall, 1969). He suggests that the final demand of any sector be treated as a variable and the equations solved to determine the gross output of other sectors and the final demand of one sector. Apart from the arbitrariness in the selection of a sector whose final demand is to be treated as a variable, there is no guarantee that the final demand of that sector will be positive.
4. One possible objective is to maximise national income, i.e. to maximise F'_i. Then the following linear programme can be used to find the new demand vector.

   $$\text{Max } \Sigma_i F'_1$$

   Such that $$(I - A)^{-1} F' \leq X'$$

   $$F'_i \geq 0, \quad (i = 1, 2, \ldots n)$$

   Where n represents the number of sectors. Similar formulations are possible if growth rate is taken as an objective. The difficulty with these objectives, however, is that the original plan may not have aimed at the maximisation of either national income or growth rate. Indeed, value judgements keeping in view the overall long term goals would have been incorporated by the planners in formulating the original plan.
5. As in footnote 3, it is possible to form mathematical programmes with the objective of maximising employment. However, similar to arguments in (3) can be made against this objective also.

6. It is possible that such constraints may lead to infeasibility. Therefore, care would have to be exercised in selecting K_i.
7. These data were taken from the Technical Note on the Approach to the Fifth Plan of India (Government of India, Planning Commission).
8. Data on the manufacturing sector were obtained from the *Annual Survey of Industries*. Regarding employment in agriculture we have used the same proportion as according to the 1971 Census.
9. In an earlier paper referred in footnote 1, the effect of shortfall in steel was also investigated.
10. Our methodology attempts only to ensure consistency of inter-sectoral flows under new conditions. It becomes necessary as the next step to establish the consistency between saving and investment.
11. When there are no restrictions, there is not much change in allocation to other sectors, as the bulk of the cut is borne by electricity itself.
12. By providing for selective imports, it is possible to increase the domestic production of these sectors which develop excess capacity due to shortfalls in output and this increased production can be exported. Our model can be modified to take into account possible alterations in the export and import vectors.
13. The final demand of the following sectors is primarily for investment. Basic metals, and metal products, non-electrical machinery, electrical machinery and equipment, transport equipment, and miscellaneous products. Two-thirds of the final demand of construction sector is also for investment. These sectors are considered as investment goods producing sectors.

10

Economic Reforms

An Assessment

The year 1991 is an important landmark in the post-independent economic history of India. The country faced a severe economic crisis, triggered in part by a serious balance of payments situation. The crisis was converted into an opportunity to effect some fundamental changes in the content and approach to economic policy. It is now more than a decade since the reforms were introduced. It is time to take stock of the situation, assess the impact of the economic reforms and indicate the corrections we need to make.

Evolution of Development Policy

Reforms, in a sense, are a product of circumstances. Changing environment, domestic and international, as well as societal demands call for continuous adjustment of policies. At times, the changes that are required are radical. Economic reforms thus come in waves and in sequence. In our own country, the first wave of reform started with the launching of planning with an emphasis on industrialisation, more particularly of heavy industries. The second wave, the precise dating of which may be difficult, began when it was found that the growth rate was weak and the trickle down effect was not adequate and when the need to focus directly on poverty alleviation became evident. The third wave which began in late Eighties gathered momentum after 1991. The new reform measures seek to redefine the roles of State and market so as to improve the productivity and efficiency of the system and thereby accelerate growth and to enable the State to focus more intensively on certain socio-economic goals.

The first Dr. Babasaheb Ambedkar Oration delivered at the University of Mumbai in September, 2001.

The Indian economy, during the period 1947-90 acquired a great degree of internal strength and resilience in terms of promoting a large and diversified industrial base, both in the public and private sectors, bringing about a turn-around in the long-standing stagnation of agriculture, leading to achievement of near self-sufficiency in food, and creating a large reserve of skilled manpower. However, over time, several constraints became apparent in accelerating and sustaining growth rates to the levels comparable with some of the fast growing economies of the contemporary times.

First, a major constraint on growth stemmed from the eroding macroeconomic balances in the economy towards the end of the 1980s, caused by high levels of deficit in Government budgets, rising inflation rates and deteriorating external payments situation. Sustaining the growth momentum of the order seen in the 1980s seemed less likely in the environment of increasing macroeconomic instability. Second, despite some notable achievements in the real sector, such as a substantial improvement in the domestic saving and investment rates, the gap between the potential and actual rate of growth became evident and this was attributed to the lack of a proper incentive mechanism and desired public policy environment to stimulate capital accumulation and productivity growth in the economy. What made this gap appear glaring and provided the motivation for change was the fact that, it was around this time that a number of developing countries were undertaking structural reforms, and gaining competitive strengths in response to the changing world economic environment. Public policy reform was fast emerging as a prerequisite to achieve the potential growth. These developments also brought to focus, the limitations of economic controls and regulations for attaining high growth. Third, the erstwhile relatively closed structure of the Indian economy itself proved a barrier to maximizing the growth potential, particularly in an environment of shifting comparative advantages in some of the key sectors in favour of the developing economies.

The prospects for improving growth through the outward oriented trade policies acquired a great deal of importance in the context of changing world environment, highlighted by the growth of multilateralism, the reduction of protectionism and the dismantling of the stiff trade barriers. These developments enhanced the scope for promoting efficiency in domestic industry through trade competition and creating conditions for augmenting the domestic capital base through cross-border flow of savings.

In the 1950s and 1960s, the dominant view in the literature on development economics was that Government had an important role to play and that it should undertake activities that would compensate for "market failure". "Market failure" was perceived as the inability of markets to optimally allocate resources over time, that is, for investment because of the "myopic" nature of markets. The literature also emphasised the benefit of a co-ordinated and consistent set of investment decisions. It is this line of reasoning that led most developing countries including India to formulate economy wide plans. However, four decades of development experience have shown that there can be "government failure" as well. The regulatory State in many countries has resulted not only in economic losses due to misallocation of resources arising from faulty investment decisions but also from diversion of resources to rent-seeking activities because of the very regulations themselves. One of the reasons for the emergence of skepticism regarding the benefits of state intervention has been the growing perception that government failures on account of political factors and bureaucratization may, in many cases, exceed market failures. Given the importance of incentive-reward system in achieving consistent improvement in efficiency, it is felt that markets may provide better incentive frame-work in many activities. Closely related to these institutional factors is the belief that a competitive environment tends to create a better climate conducive to enhancing efficiency. In other words, while there can be some doubt as to the capacity of the competitive market structures to determine the ends, there is more confidence in competition as a means of achieving the desired ends. Thus, if there is a lesson to be drawn from the development record of the last four decades, it is that there can be both "government failure" and "market failure" and that the critical issue is not so much the presence or absence of State intervention, as the extent and quality of that intervention. The new economic policy builds on this experience.

There was enough evidence of the slowing of the growth rate of the economy and the deterioration of efficiency by the beginning of 1970s. However, these signals were not picked up to bring about changes in policy. While a policy of the liberalization of the Indian economy was initiated in the mid-1980s, the change was slow and lacked a comprehensive and self-sustaining character, which is an essential requirement of a successful reform strategy. The crisis in 1991, provided an immediate context for the realignment of the macroeconomic fundamentals, through a programme of economic stabilization and long-term structural reforms to accelerate the growth potential of the Indian economy. The structural reforms in the early stages covered the areas of industrial licensing, foreign trade, foreign investment, exchange rate management and the financial sector. Since then it has been extended to other areas.

Content of Reform

Details of the reform process are well known. They are, therefore, referred to briefly. India, since the days planning was introduced, had practised a system of industrial licensing under which a license was required before setting up any large unit. This practice had roots in the belief that resources could be best allocated by a planning authority and that licensing was the best way to manage limited resources. Over years, it became obvious that such a system was inefficient and led only to corruption and creation of rent. In fact, the Approach Document of the Eighth Plan submitted in May 1990 had also said: "A return to the regime of direct, indiscriminate and detailed controls in industry is clearly out of question. Past experience has shown that such a control system is not effective in achieving the desired objective. Also, the system is widely abused and leads to corruption, delays and inefficiency." One early step that was undertaken as part of the structural reform process was to do away with licensing. The elimination of barriers to entry and expansion was well received and had very little opposition.

Import substitution constituted a major plank of India's foreign trade policy. This was primarily due to the highly pessimistic view taken on the potential for export earnings. A further impetus to the inward orientation was provided by the existence of a vast domestic market. The inward looking industrialisation process did result in high rates of industrial growth between 1956 and 1966. However, as inefficiencies crept into the system, the economy turned into an increasingly high cost one. This also led to a 'technological lag' and resulted in poor export performance. As part of the structural reforms, a bold initiative was taken to reduce the tariff rates and dismantle quantitative controls over imports. The peak tariff rates which were as high as 200 per cent have been brought down to 35 per cent and the dispersion has also been reduced. The quantitative controls have also been phased out. The tariff rates were brought down in stages, as some caution in this regard had become necessary in order to enable the Indian industries which had been set up behind high protective tariff walls to adjust to the changed situation.

The policy towards foreign investment has undergone a sea change. Prior to 1991, the policy towards foreign investment was restrictive and at best, permissive. While it welcomed foreign investment, in most cases it was limited to 40 per cent. Majority ownership was an exception rather than the rule. This policy was given up and foreign investors were given the freedom to own majority share holding. A Foreign Investment Promotion Board (FIPB) was set up to be proactive with respect to foreign investment. While foreign individuals are not allowed to invest in Indian stock markets, recognised institutional investors are allowed to invest in the stock market. Portfolio investors have the freedom to sell the shares at any time and repatriate the funds. Thus a fundamental change in the approach to private capital flows occurred after 1991.

Along with the change in the policies in foreign trade and foreign investment, a significant change occurred with respect to exchange rate management. From a managed floating system under which the exchange rate was officially determined, the regime has passed through several phases to reach a market-based system under which the exchange rate is determined by forces of demand and supply. Current account transactions have been freed of exchange control regulations and controls over several transactions on capital account have been eased. While the central bank of the country intervenes in the foreign exchange market, it does so primarily to prevent volatility and instability.

The financial sector underwent a major change. The financial sector in India is dominated by the public sector. Most of the banks as well as the insurance institutions are State-owned. Broadly speaking, reforms in the financial sector are aimed at Indian banks conforming to international prudential standards and simultaneously imparting a greater element of competition in the financial system. The administered structure of interest rates has been dismantled with freedom given to banks to fix the rates of interest on deposits and loans. New private sector banks have been licensed. The regulation of the capital market also received considerable attention in order to provide greater protection to investors. The financial sector reforms have been reviewed more than once by a committee. The process of enlarging the scope for the private sector and imparting a greater element of competition is continuing and has since been extended to other areas such as tele-communication.

There is a common thread running through all the measures introduced since July 1991. The objective is simple and that is to improve the efficiency of the system. The regulatory mechanism involving multitudes of controls has fragmented capacity and reduced competition even in the private sector. The thrust of the new economic policy is towards creating a more competitive environment in the economy as a means to improving the productivity and efficiency of the system. This is to be achieved by removing the barriers to entry and the restrictions on growth of firms. While the industrial policy seeks to bring about a greater competitive environment domestically, the trade policy seeks to improve international competitiveness subject to the protection offered by tariffs which are coming down. The private sector is being given a larger space to operate in, as some of the areas earlier reserved exclusively for the public sector are also now allowed to the private sector. In these areas, the public sector will have to compete with the private sector, even though the public sector may continue to play the dominant role. What is sought to be achieved is an improvement in the functioning of the various entities, whether they are in the private or public sector by injecting an element of competition. There is, however, nothing in the New Economic Policy which takes away the role of the State or the public sector in the system. The New Economic Policy of India has not necessarily diminished the role of State; it has only redefined it, expanding it in some areas and reducing in some others. As it has been said, somewhat paradoxically 'more market' does not mean 'less Government', but only 'different Government'. However, if the public sector is truly to play its role, it needs to improve its efficiency and productivity and generate the necessary surpluses as were originally envisaged. It is only an efficient public enterprise system that can enable the Government to meet its social obligations. If one hears the word 'market' mentioned more often these days, it was only because 'market' was very nearly a dirty word in this country for well over four decades. What is needed is an optimal mix of 'market' and 'State'. It is necessary to create a matrix of activities and the kinds of intervention and determine for each activity, what form of intervention works best. Even in relation to government intervention, a view must be taken whether it should take the form of ownership or regulation. With limited resource availability, Government should reallocate resources more in areas where it has a comparative advantage over the market and vacate those where it has less of an advantage. Taken together, the reform measures in the various areas constitute a new chapter in India's economic policy. However, there are many areas where reforms have made little progress. A major concern has been with respect to loss making public sector units and how to deal with them. Public sector reforms in general have not received adequate attention. The process of privatisation has been slow, because of the lack of required consensus. Analysts and policy makers are talking today of second generation reforms. This implies the deepening of the reform process wherever it has been initiated earlier and bringing within its scope new areas.

Post-reform Performance

The performance of the Indian economy in the post-reform period has been extensively commented upon. Judged by the standard criteria of growth rates of national income and per capita income, external balance and inflation rate, the Indian economy has done well since liberalisation. Between 1981-82 and 1990-91, the growth rate of the economy was 5.6 per cent per annum. The year 1991-92 was an exceptionally bad year for reasons well known. Indeed, there is no justification to include that year as part of the post-reform period, particularly while judging the effectiveness of the reform process. On the contrary, there could be a justification to include 1991-92 as part of the pre-reform period. If we leave out 1991-92, between 1992-93 and 2000-01, the average annual growth rate comes to 6.3 per cent. Even if we include 1991-92 the annual growth rate in the Nineties will be 5.7 per cent. It is interesting to note that between 1992-93 and 1999-2000 there was only one year in which the growth rate was less than five per cent. The coefficient of the variation of growth rate in the Nineties is distinctly lower than in the Eighties. With a slowing down of the population growth rate, the per capita income growth rate in the Nineties has been 3.8 per cent. Between 1992-93 and 2000-01 the industrial growth rate was 6.6 per cent per annum and the growth rate in services was 7.9 per cent. The gross domestic savings rate of the economy on an average during the period 1992-93 to 1999-2000 has remained at 23.1 per cent of GDP. Inflation rate as measured by the Wholesale Price Index (WPI), though high in the early Nineties, started declining from 1995-96 and the average inflation rate has been around five per cent since then. The current account deficit after reaching the high of 3.1 of GDP in 1990-91 has been steadily declining during the Nineties and has been around one per cent of the GDP in the last few years. With the current account deficit remaining low and with continued capital inflows, it has been possible to add to the foreign exchange reserves. These reserves have increased from $ 5.8 billion in 1990-91 to $ 38.0 billion by March, 2000. They have subsequently increased by $ 6 billion. The macro economic indicators do show a distinct improvement in the performance as compared with the previous periods. However, even in relation to the growth rate, a disturbing trend is that there has been a distinct slowing since 1997-98. While the growth rate between 1992-93 and 1996-97 was 6.5 per cent, in the subsequent four years the growth rate has been 5.8 per cent. The growth rate in the current year is not likely to be higher than this average.

Concerns and Issues

The liberalisation process has come in for criticism from two opposite ends. First, there are those who feel that the process has been slow and not sufficiently comprehensive. These critics attribute the current slow down in the growth rate to this factor. On the other hand, there are critics who view the reform process as misconceived, ignoring the basic realities of our country. There are four aspects of these criticisms which deserve attention.

A major criticism of the liberalisation process is that the higher growth rate achieved has made no dent on poverty and unemployment. Based on the National Sample Survey (NSS) data on consumption expenditure, over years certain methodologies have been evolved to estimate the number of people below poverty line. Estimates of the percentage of the people below poverty line based on various National Sample Survey rounds show that the combined rural and urban poverty ratio came down from 44.48 per cent in 1983 to 38.86 per cent in 1987-88 and further to 35.07 per cent in 1993-94. However, based on the smaller annual samples, some analysts had come to the conclusion that there was a rise in the poverty ratio since 1993-94. This, if confirmed, would have been a disturbing trend. However, recently, results of the large sample survey data on consumer expenditure for 1999-2000 have been released. These results show a sharp decline in poverty ratio to 26.10 per cent. Certain technical questions have been raised about the comparability of the latest survey data with the earlier surveys. The use of two reference periods in the latest survey, according to some, has vitiated comparability. However, some independent studies done, using the data collected on consumption expenditure in the employment survey also show a decline in the poverty ratio after 1993-94, even though the decline is not as strong as indicated by the large sample survey on consumption expenditure. In the past, it has always been found that higher economic growth is accompanied by faster reduction in the poverty ratio. However, there has been a significant change in the sectoral pattern of growth in the Nineties. There has been a distinct slowing down in the growth rate in agriculture while the tertiary sector has grown strongly. The growth rate of agricultural production at 2.8 per cent in the Nineties had been much lower than 4.1 per cent in Eighties. While the trend of reduction in poverty ratio is reassuring, a further look at the pattern of growth has become essential, since agricultural and associated rural activities still constitute the major source of employment.

Employment figures indicate that between 1990-91 and 1997-98, overall employment grew only at an average rate of one per cent, with the employment in the organised and unorganised sectors growing at 0.6 per cent and 1.1 per cent respectively. Part of the explanation for this phenomenon lies in the imperfections in the labour market which induce preference for capital in relation to labour, contrary to the pattern of factor endowments in the country. The abundant supply of labour must become the source of expanded output. Where there is a transition from one industry to another, appropriate social safety nets and retraining facilities must be put in place.

One of the major planks of the liberalization policy has been to reduce the fiscal deficit. Of course, some people question the wisdom of focussing on fiscal deficit as an indicator of financial health. In seeking to defend higher fiscal deficits, the theory of Keynes is invoked. This is a case of applying a principle out of its context. Keynes was writing when a balanced budget was the order of the day, even at times of depression and he felt that, under those circumstances, a deficit was in order. But what we are discussing now is not whether there should be a fiscal deficit or not but what order of deficit is desirable. In this respect, the original Keynesian framework is inadequate because the model did not take into account the implications of alternative modes of financing Government expenditure. Borrowing from the market can have an impact on the interest rate, while financing through money creation has inflationary implications and at one step removed on nominal interest rate.

There has been some success in reducing fiscal deficit but not to the desired extent. Some are critical of the fact that whatever reduction that had been brought about was almost by reducing capital expenditures. Total expenditures as a proportion of GDP came down by three percentage points between 1990-91 and 1997-98. This was achieved by a reduction in capital expenditures as a proportion of GDP by 2.1 percentage points and revenue expenditures by 0.9 percentage points. The revenue to GDP ratio has remained more or less at the pre-reform level, despite significant tax reform measures introduced. Without doubt, the best way of reducing fiscal deficit is by reducing revenue deficit. But unfortunately, revenue expenditures have kept increasing. Wages, salaries and pensions have continued to rise. In many states, they account for almost the whole of state's own revenue receipts. Subsidies, after an initial decline have remained at the same level as percentage of GDP. At state level, implicit subsidies have increased enormously. The fiscal deficit can be contained at a reasonable level only by widening the tax base and raising the ratio of revenue to taxes and by limiting revenue expenditures.

Yet another area of concern of the critics is that enough attention is not being paid to social infrastructure areas. Literacy levels have risen in India. Nevertheless, they remain well below what is desirable. Basic health facilities have not reached every one. But the fault for this situation cannot be laid at the doors of liberalization. The distortions in priorities occurred much earlier. In fact, the very purpose of liberalization is to reduce the role of the State as an entrepreneur and direct investor and expand its role in areas such as social infrastructure, where State alone can play a dominant role. The need for expanded State intervention in areas of education, health and sanitation cannot be under estimated. It is necessary to generate the surplus to fulfil the socio-economic obligations. It is also to be noted that better education and health are a function of not only levels of expenditures but also the efficiency with which such expenditures are incurred. For example, according to the Human Development Report 1991, both Sri Lanka and India had a similar human expenditure ratio of 2.5 per cent of GDP. Human expenditure per capita in 1988 was $ 10 for Sri Lanka while it was $ 9 for India. However, in the ranking of Human Development Index, Sri Lanka occupied 75th rank, whereas India was lower, down at 123rd rank. Part of the reason for the difference in the ranking could be enhanced expenditure at a certain level over a longer period. The Human Development Report itself admits, "Even government expenditure cannot be considered in isolation. Its impact depends not just how much money is spent but on how and in what environment it was spent".

The fourth area of concern has been the growing disparities in income among states. Differences in growth rates among states have become more pronounced after liberalization. During the Eighties, the growth rate of State Domestic Product ranged from a low of 3.6 per cent per annum to a high of 6.6 per cent. In the Nineties, the variation has been from a low of 2.7 per cent per annum to a high of 9.6 per cent. Some of the highly populous states have registered very low growth rates in the post-liberalization period. Tax devolution formulas as well as Planning Commission allocations of grants and loans are heavily weighted in favour of population and the inverse of per capita income. Nevertheless, the populous states have grown weakly in the last seven year period and this has contributed to the increase in the overall poverty ratio also. Many of these states have not been actively involved in the liberalization process. If the regional disparities have grown, it is at least in part a reflection of the quality of governance. It is interesting to note that the ranking of the states according to income growth rate differs considerably between Eighties and Nineties. The rank correlation coefficient between the two periods is only 0.283. This implies that some states which have grown slowly in the earlier period, have had higher growth rates in latter period.

As one surveys the period since 1991-92, it is clear that the economy has shown distinct improvement in several areas. The broad philosophy of promoting a competitive environment must be pursued. At the same time, if the growth momentum is to be maintained, some areas need focussed attention. Mention was made earlier of the problems arising from the slow down in agriculture. A comprehensive agricultural policy encompassing a higher level of public investment, a shift from subsidies to investment in terms of public expenditure, consolidation of holdings, a proactive programme to foster exports, intensified agricultural research to raise yields and evolving a better cropping pattern needs to be thought of. Growth in agriculture has several implications for the economy. It leads to a reduction in poverty, a greater expansion in employment given the Indian situation and a more broad based growth.

Second, as mentioned earlier, fiscal consolidation is a necessary prerequisite for sustained growth. The finances of the state governments are particularly under greater pressure. The appropriate level of fiscal deficit has a relationship to the level of household savings and more particularly, to the savings in financial assets. Even as of now, very nearly the whole of the household savings in financial assets is appropriated by the public sector. There is validity in the argument that government expenditures should shift in favour of capital expenditures. Unfortunately, the trend has been in the opposite direction. Containing the growth rate of revenue expenditures has become essential. In a developing economy like India, where a significant proportion of people remains poor, subsidies are an essential component of government expenditures. However, they need to be targeted appropriately, so that they accrue only to the deserving. We must make an effort to evolve a consensus on how to deal with subsidies, user charges and reducing revenue expenditures. This is indeed the task of the political managers of the economy. With different parties in power in different states, it should be possible to achieve a significant degree of consensus on this issue of fiscal prudence.

Public sector still continues to dominate the economy in several important sectors. Even as attempts are being made to disinvest wherever feasible, there is no doubt that we must pay adequate attention to improving the functioning of public sector enterprises, where their presence is essential. In fact, in certain areas, disinvestment can only follow the strengthening of the enterprises. This is very much true in the case of electricity generation and distribution. Many committees and commissions have studied these problems. It is high time that a policy package is put together and implemented for bringing about a significant improvement in the efficiency of public sector enterprises.

Clearly, the lesson of Indian development experience is that monopolies — whether of State or private sector — do not lead to efficiency. The need to create, promote and sustain a competitive environment is absolutely essential. India is no longer a country, producing goods and services for the domestic market alone. Indian firms are becoming and have to become global players. At the minimum they have to meet global competition. However, even as we do create conditions for more effective functioning of the enterprises, some of the issues discussed earlier, such as emphasis on agriculture, fiscal consolidation and public sector reforms need special attention.

The recent slow down in the growth rate of the economy points to the importance of the role of investment and effective governance. These two factors are inter-related. The strong growth exceeding seven per cent per annum which was witnessed for three consecutive years beginning 1994-95 was fueled by heavy investment. Investment is the major driving force of growth. We should create an environment which is conducive to investment. All investment decisions are based on future prospects. Continuance of economic policy is basic to sustaining expectations in the right direction. Equally important is the confidence in the future course of the economy. It is in this context that governance becomes a key concern. Policies have to be right. But that is not enough. They must be pursued with vigour and conviction. They have to be implemented with single-minded devotion. This is one lesson that we have to learn from China.

In any economic system, State can play many roles. One can at least identify three important roles: (1) as a producer of goods and services, (2) as a regulator of the system, and (3) as a supplier of "public goods" or "social goods" like primary education and health. The decreasing role of State as a producer of goods and services and the increasing role of market in such areas simultaneously enhance the role of State as a "regulator" and "facilitator". The regulatory role comes into play in order to maintain competitive conditions in the market and to ensure that the basic rules of the game are followed by every one. This is indeed an important aspect of 'governance' and may warrant appropriate legislative changes.

Development has many dimensions. Economic growth is only one aspect. Nevertheless, accelerated economic growth is a necessary condition for achieving many other dimensions of development. Development must ensure equality of opportunities for all. However, equality of opportunities does not necessarily guarantee equalities in incomes. With some people being good at converting opportunities into income and others not being so, different individuals will end up with different levels of income. That is why it is necessary to assure every one a minimum level of living along with equality of opportunities. Every citizen must have his basic needs met. These basic needs include access to services such as education, health care and shelter. Without sacrificing these goals, the economy must remain efficient. It is only an efficient economy that can generate the surplus, necessary to meet the socio-economic goals. We need, therefore, to stress simultaneously on economic development in the conventional sense of accelerating growth rate and social development in the sense of securing for every one the basic needs. The two have a mutually interacting beneficial impact and the two must be pursued together. Any strategy of development which ignores any one of the two legs will be unsustainable. Efficiency and equity should not be posed as opposing considerations. They must be weaved together to produce a coherent pattern of growth.

Table 1

Selected Macroeconomic Indicators of India, 1990-91 to 1999-2000

Item	1990-91	1991-92	1992-93	1993-94	1994-95	1995-96	1996-97	1997-98	1998-99	1999-2000	Average 1990-2000	Average 1992-2000
GDPFC (1993-94=100) (Growth Rate)	5.3	1.5	4.5	6.0	7.0	7.3	7.5	5.0	6.8	6.4	5.7	6.3
Rate of GDCF at Constant Prices (%)	25.9	21.7	22.3	22.3	26.0	26.8	24.5	25.0	23.0	23.3	24.1	24.2
Gross Domestic Saving Rate at Current Prices (%)	24.3	22.9	22	22.7	24.8	25.1	23.2	23.5	22.0	22.3	23.3	23.2
Industrial Production (Growth Rate)	8.2	0.6	2.3	6.0	8.9	13.1	6.1	6.6	3.8	8.1	6.4	6.9
Agricultural Production (Growth Rate)	3.8	-2.0	4.2	3.8	5.0	-2.7	9.3	-6.1	7.8	-0.7	2.2	2.6
Food Grains Production (Growth Rate)	3.3	-4.2	4.7	4.1	3.9	-6.3	10.1	-3.2	5.8	2.6	2.1	2.7
WPI (1993-94=100) (Rate of increase)	10.3	13.7	10.1	8.4	12.5	8.1	4.6	4.4	5.9	3.3	8.1	7.2
CPI (Industrial Workers) (Rate of increase)	11.6	13.5	9.6	7.5	10.1	10.2	9.4	6.8	13.1	3.4	9.5	8.8
Exports (US $ million) (Growth Rate)	9.2	-1.5	3.8	20	18.4	20.8	5.3	4.6	-5.1	13.2	8.9	10.1
Imports (US $ million) (Growth Rate)	13.5	19.4	12.7	6.5	22.9	28.0	6.7	6.0	2.2	11.4	12.9	12.1
Foreign Exchange Reserves (US $ million)	5834	9220	9832	19254	25186	21687	26423	29367	32490	38036	—	—
Current A/C Deficit (as % of GDP)	-3.1	-0.3	-1.7	-0.4	-1.0	-1.7	-1.2	-1.4	-1.0	-0.9	-1.3	-1.2
US $ Exchange Rate	17.9	24.5	30.7	31.4	31.4	33.5	35.5	37.2	42.1	43.3	—	—

Source: Handbook of Statistics on Indian Economy, 2000, Reserve Bank of India, Mumbai.

Part II

Monetary System and Financial Sector

11

The Analytical Framework of the Chakravarty Committee Report on the Monetary System

For the first time since its establishment, the Reserve Bank of India set up in December, 1982, a committee under the Chairmanship of Prof. Sukhamoy Chakravarty to undertake a comprehensive review of the working of the monetary system in our country. I was privileged to be a member of the Committee and took an active part in the writing of the report. The mandate to the Committee was wide in as much as it covered almost every aspect of the monetary and financial system. The Committee submitted its report in April, 1985. In the light of the various comments made on the report during the last two years, it may be useful to take a look at the totality of the recommendations and more particularly at the analytical framework underlying its recommendations.

There are five major building blocks in the report. The first building block relates to the objectives of monetary policy. Monetary policy is an arm of economic policy. Therefore, in that sense, the objectives of monetary policy are no different from the overall objectives of economic policy, whether it be economic growth, social justice, better distribution of income, maintenance of price stability or promotion of savings. All these are the objectives of economic planning in our country and therefore of economic policy and monetary policy. However, the effectiveness of different instruments of economic policy in pursuing different objectives is not always the same. It is in this context that price stability becomes a major concern of monetary policy, as monetary policy instruments are more effective in relation to this objective than other policy instruments.

Reserve Bank of India Bulletin, September, 1987.

An important issue that arises in this context is whether there is a trade-off between economic growth and inflation. In the short run perhaps there is such a trade-off. But that trade-off is at a heavy cost. A higher growth rate can be achieved only at the cost of a fairly high inflation rate. Under those circumstances it is important to find out whether such a trade-off is acceptable. Over a longer time period, growth cannot be however bought with the aid of higher price and there is no evidence to show that a higher growth rate is associated with higher inflation rate. In India, the contrary is the case.[1] It is price stability which provides the appropriate environment in which growth can occur and social justice can also be attained. In a society in which a significantly large proportion of the population is in the unorganised sector, price rise goes against social justice. This precisely is the reason which prompted the Committee to accord price stability an important place among the objectives of monetary policy. Price stability in this context is not to be interpreted in the absolute sense of no increase in prices; such an absolute price stability is not feasible in a large and complex economy, undergoing a structural transformation. Imbalances to some extent are inevitable. Against the background of historical experience, the Committee suggested that an average annual increase in the Wholesale Price Index of no more than four per cent should be the objective.

This leads to the second building block which examined the relationship between price stability and money supply. There has been a perennial controversy between the structuralists and non-structuralists on the sources of inflation. In the Indian situation, as the report points out, supply shocks are very frequent and therefore, inflation cannot be treated purely as a monetary phenomenon. Nevertheless, there is enough evidence to show that all price increases in India over the last few decades cannot simply be explained by a structuralist explanation. Money does count and in a significant way.

What exactly then is the relationship between money, output and prices? This is the core of monetary economics. Ever since the days of the Quantity Theory of Money, economists have been discussing this issue. The Quantity Theory of Money, in its extreme form, argued that money has no impact on output and therefore, an increase in money supply results in a proportionate increase in the price level. The Keynesian analysis, on the other hand, on the assumption of stickiness in prices, argues that an increase in money supply will lead to a fall in the rate of interest, both nominal and real, stimulating investment which through a multiplier process would lead to an increase in income. Perhaps, the real world lies somewhere between these two extremes. The impact of money supply on the economy at a given point of time would depend on a variety of factors such as existence of excess capacity.

It should not, however, be inferred that the impact of money on output and on prices is indeterminate. Money has an impact on both output and prices and the analytical framework presented in the report goes into some detail on this. The process of money creation is a process of credit creation. Money comes into existence because credit is given either to the Government or to the private sector or to the foreign sector. Since credit facilitates the production process, it has a favourable impact on output. But at the same time the increased money supply raises demand with an upward pressure on prices. The output effect and the price effect must be taken together to judge the overall impact on the economy.

In the final analysis, estimation of a demand function for money is a useful exercise to understand the inter-relationship among money, output and prices. In fact, if one were to deny the existence of reasonably stable demand function for money, then it would tantamount to denying any role at all for monetary policy in inflation management. Almost all econometric models constructed for India do have a demand function for money as part of the system and these functions are found to be statistically satisfactory. In some models the demand for money equation is converted into a price equation with prices being dependent on nominal money supply and real income. And these equations have proved to be reasonable predictors of the behaviour of price over a period of time. Econometrically speaking, even equations with a high degree of significance ($\bar{R}^2$ of 0.98) do not predict well, percentage changes in prices on a year-to-year basis. The relationship, however, holds good reasonably well over a period of time. Averages of price changes over a period of, say, five years, are predicted with reasonable accuracy and this should be sufficient as a guide to policy. Seeking to find a direct year-to-year correspondence between changes in money supply and real income, on the one hand, and the price level on the other, is a simplistic approach to the problem and absence of such correspondence does not disprove the existence of an essential link between money supply, income and prices. Given the various instruments of credit control available to the monetary authority, a demand function for money, which has a reasonable degree of stability, is indeed, a useful guide since these instruments can be used effectively if the actual price behaviour deviates from the expected.

In relation to the demand function for money, two technical issues are normally raised. One relates to causality. The question that is often raised is whether causation runs from money to prices or from prices to money. The causality tests have proved to be inconclusive, partly because of the role played by expectations in determining prices. Notwithstanding the causality tests, it is quite clear that no econometrically tested model of inflationary process has found it possible to do without 'money' as a statistically significant variable. Even if money supply 'accommodates' to changes in prices, there must be a limit to this accommodation if the spiralling effect is to be avoided.

Another issue in this context relates to the appropriate monetary aggregate to be used in the demand function for money or in the price equation. Should it be narrow money or broad money or some weighted average of the various components? The weighted average concept does run into serious problems. If money is defined both as a medium of exchange and a store of value, how does one define 'moneyness'? Ultimately the choice of the aggregate must depend upon which explains better the price changes in conjunction with other variables. The concept of broad money has this advantage in that in balance sheet terms, it has a direct link to the expansion in credit.

The third building block relates to the link between reserve money and money supply. This relationship cannot be properly understood by looking at the raw figures. Raising or lowering of the Cash Reserve Ratio (CRR) affects the multiplier. Therefore, in order to understand the underlying relationship, it is necessary to take into account the impact of changes in the Cash Reserve Ratio. Several studies have shown that there is a reasonable degree of association between reserve money adjusted for changes in reserve requirements and money supply in India.[2]

It has been argued that the money multiplier depends not only on the Cash Reserve Ratio and the ratio of currency to deposits but also on the demand for credit. Addition to reserve money leads only to an increase in the credit creating capacity of the commercial banks. The actual expansion would depend upon the demand for credit which would in turn be related to the behaviour of the real sector. While this position is theoretically valid, it is to be noted that in the Indian context with an administered structure of interest rates with varying rates of interest for different activities, demand for credit is not a binding constraint. The rates of interest charged on some activities are well below the market rates and demand for credit at those rates of interest are highly elastic. In fact, the Indian commercial banks do not voluntarily hold any excess reserves and whatever excess reserves they may be holding are involuntary, due to inadequate facilities for quick transmission of funds from far flung branches.

The main proposition of the report is that money supply needs to be regulated if price stability is to be one of the objectives of the monetary policy and if money supply is to be regulated, there has to be an understanding between the Government and the Reserve Bank on the extent of the credit that the latter can give to the former. This can be conceived of the fourth building block. It is quite evident from the past data that a major factor contributing to reserve money has been the Reserve Bank credit to Government. Therefore, monetary regulations in the Indian context can be achieved only through co-operation between the Government and the Reserve Bank. In order to achieve the overall objectives of planned economic development in an environment of reasonable price stability, the report has recommended the adoption of a flexible system of monetary targeting. Apart from defining the target in terms of range, the target range itself is to be modified as events unfold during a year. The committee has unambiguously stated that a constant money supply growth rate is not feasible in the Indian context where supply shocks are frequent and where significant structural changes are sought to be achieved to facilitate the growth process. This, however, does not take away the need for regulating the overall growth in money supply over a period of time and a scheme of monetary targeting with feedback would ensure the necessary co-ordination between fiscal and monetary authorities in steering the growth of money supply consistent with real growth and an acceptable order of increase in prices.

The report envisages a role for interest rate policy which is supportive of the regulations of money supply. This is the fifth building block of the report. No doubt, the important interest rates are all administered and the report does not make a significant departure from this position. Nonetheless, as the principal participants in the money and capital markets happen to be in the government sector, certain guidelines in regard to the determination of interest rates have been presented in the report. The report clearly recognises that borrowings by Government should be at a slightly lower rate as compared to other organised sectors. However, interest rates even for Government need to be positive in real terms. Assuming a rate of growth of the economy of the order of four to five per cent, which can be taken as a ceiling on the pure rate of interest for the economy as a whole, the maximum real interest rate on long-term government borrowings has been suggested at three per cent per annum. Together with Treasury bills for which only a marginally positive real interest rate has been recommended, the average interest rate on the entire spectrum of government borrowings from the market is likely to be even lower than three per cent. The real interest rate suggested for government borrowings is, therefore, not really high.

Even when interest rates do not play the allocative role, there is a need to see that the interest rate structure of the organised financial system is in reasonable correspondence with 'market determined' rates. Bank depositors must be paid reasonable rates if the general public are to be induced to place deposits with banks. When real rates on deposits become negative, there is a tendency for funds to move from the organised to the unorganised sectors. The lending rates of banks must have a reasonable margin over cost of raising funds if banks are to function as viable economic units, even though an element of cross subsidisation may be built into the interest rate structure. Since banks invest 37.5 per cent of their demand and time liabilities in Government and other approved securities, rates on Government and government guaranteed bonds must also bear a reasonable relationship to the cost of raising funds by banks. A realistic interest rate structure has an important role to perform in attracting savings in the form of financial assets to the desired extent. The report, therefore, lays great stress on the role of interest rate policy. A feature of the proposals contained in the report in regard to interest rates which has attracted much attention is the reference to expected inflation rate in determining the level of interest rates on government securities and other instruments. Had there been no captive market for government securities, buyers would have naturally exercised their judgement in regard to the attractiveness of the nominal returns by taking into account the expected inflation rate over the concerned period. In the absence of such a signal, a process of trial and error is inevitable.

Apart from cost of credit, the report has given considerable emphasis on two other aspects of credit. It has stressed the importance of effective utilisation of credit so that with a given order of increase in money and credit, efforts are directed towards maximising output. To the success of this task, the efforts aimed at increasing the productivity of bank credit have no doubt much to contribute. It is, therefore, necessary to effect a change in the credit delivery system and in the credit mechanism in order to be able to achieve effective utilisation of credit.

Money as a medium of exchange and as a store of value, plays an important role in an economy. It lubricates the economy and as the saying goes, keeps the wheels of agriculture, industry and commerce going. Money is a facilitating device. Ultimately the growth of an economy depends on such fundamental factors as mobilisation of real resources, level of technology and efficiency in management. Increase in money supply must match the increased demand arising from higher real income which itself can be stimulated partly by increase in money. 'Money also matters' is a position that must be distinguished from 'money does not matter' or 'money alone matters'. Too much of it can, through price increase, cause distortions in the economy just as too little can hinder the smooth functioning. The art of central banking lies in ensuring the appropriate balance.

Notes

1. For an elaboration of this see, Rangarajan, C., 'Conflict between Employment and Inflation: Theory and Facts', in Austin Robinson, et al. (ed.) *Employment Policy in a Developing Country: A Case Study of India*, Vol. I, pp. 114-130.
2. Rangarajan, C. and Anoop Singh, "Reserve Money: Concepts and Policy Implications for India", *Reserve Bank of India Occasional Papers*, June, 1984.

12

Reserve Money: Concepts and Policy Implications for India

Introduction

This paper is concerned with specifying the relationship between reserve money and alternative measures of the money stock. In the traditional monetary base/money multiplier framework, the basic relationship may be expressed as:

$$M = m.H$$

where 'M' is a measure of the stock money, 'H' denotes the monetary base, and 'm' is the money multiplier. The discretionary ability of the monetary authority to influence the supply of money is usually reflected in variations in the monetary base. Changes in the multiplier, on the other hand, usually reflect the behaviour of the commercial banks, in particular their demand for excess or borrowed reserves; and that of the public, in particular their demand for currency and their preference between time and demand deposits. Shifts in such behaviour impart complexity to the relationship between reserve money and money supply. However, such shifts have been observed to occur slowly over a period of time.

In this monetary base/multiplier framework, changes in reserve requirements can be captured either in the multiplier, or in the monetary base. The former procedure is the commonest, and has the additional advantage that the data on the monetary base need no consequential adjustment following changes in the reserve requirement ratio. In this method, the money multiplier tends to rise when the reserve requirement ratio is reduced, indicating the greater multiple expansion of bank liabilities facilitated by the reduced

---

Co-author: **Anoop Singh.**
RBI Occasional Papers, Vol.5, No.1, June 1984.

ratio. Alternatively, the impact of changes in the reserve requirement ratio can be reflected in the monetary base by applying an appropriate adjustment. The rationale for making such an adjustment to the monetary base is to capture in it, as completely as possible, elements of the monetary authority's discretionary action, including therefore changes in reserve requirements. Use of a reserve money series adjusted in this manner, results in a multiplier that would be relatively more stable than obtained otherwise. In this framework, an increase in the reserve requirement ratio would reduce the adjusted monetary base, consequent to the additional impounding of deposits achieved by the measure.

The objective of this paper is two-fold: first, to illustrate the nature of the adjustment that is considered most appropriate to make to the published data for India on reserve money. Application of this methodology results in an adjusted series on reserve money, incorporating the effects of Cash Reserve Ratio (CRR) changes. The CRR instrument has been used actively in India since 1973/74. A new adjusted series on reserve money has been constructed for the period since 1973/74. The second objective of the paper is to use the new adjusted series to examine the lags in the impact of reserve money on various definitions of the money stock. For this purpose, quarterly data have been used for the period 1973/74 to 1981/82.

Our analysis suggests that the adjustments to reserve money result in a series that shows a systematic and well defined relationship to the alternative concepts of the money stock.

Adjusted Reserve Money

The Relevance of the Adjustment

The importance of the monetary base derives from its use as a set of assets that constrain the money supply. It is an aggregate that can be measured quickly and accurately by the monetary authority. As an instrument of monetary control, its usefulness depends on the extent to which the monetary authority can determine its expansion and, on the extent to which it bears a systematic relationship with the money stock. The objective of this section is to define the variable most appropriately. Subsequently, its relationship with alternative measures of the money stock is explored.

In its unadjusted form, the impact of changes in cash reserve requirements is captured in the multiplier. However, as discussed above, the impact of reserve money as an instrument of control can be understood easier, if the effects of reserve requirement changes are included in the computation of the base. During periods when the legal cash reserve requirement is changed, the growth rate of a monetary base that incorporates the resultant impact would diverge, compared with a series unadjusted for such changes. For example, if the reserve requirement is raised, the adjusted monetary base can be expected to grow more slowly compared with its unadjusted counterpart, provided the increased cash reserve requirement is complied with by the system.[1]

The concept of the adjusted monetary base has been applied progressively more frequently in the last decade. Its widest application has been to United States data. The Federal Reserve Bank of St. Louis has published such a series since August 1968 and, in the course of successive articles, has defined and refined the methodology of the Reserve Adjustment Magnitude.[2] Since March 1979, the Board of Governors of the Federal Reserve System have also published a monetary base series incorporating the effects of reserve requirement changes. Both definitions of the adjusted series are similar, differing only in relatively unimportant ways.

In the Indian case, Gupta (1979) has explained the nature of the adjustment, and stressed that the monetary authority can control the adjusted base more effectively through changing reserve requirements. In this manner, the adjusted monetary base can be regarded as being closer to a policy variable in money supply analysis. The same procedure is seen as resulting in the money multiplier being largely an independently determined variable as far as the monetary authority is concerned.

However, not all studies of the subject agree that use of the reserve base adjusted for reserve requirement changes improves the framework for monetary control. Sharpe (1980), concludes that the adjusted concept proves inappropriate as the relevant independent variable in an analysis of money supply influences for Australia. Sharpe's study finds significantly different lag structures for the reserve base variable and the reserve requirement variable in his money supply relationships.

The Methodology of the Adjustment

The methodology of the adjustment factor is designed to keep the money multiplier invariant to changes in the cash reserve requirement. In this method, the difference between the current period CRR and that of a base period is applied to the net Demand and Time Liabilities (DTL) of the current period. The resultant adjustment factor is a measure of the reserves liberated or absorbed by the change in the reserve requirements compared with the base period. This may be expressed as:

$$\text{Adjustment} = (r_t - r_0)\ \text{DTL} \qquad ...(1)$$

where r_0 is initial or benchmark CRR;

r_t is the current period CRR; and

DTL comprises the set of bank liabilities (demand and time) relevant to computation of the CRR. In this case, DTL data relate to the penultimate Friday of the month.

This does not complete the computation of the adjustment factor. Considerations has to be given to at least two additional influences. First, where incremental reserve requirements are applicable, these need to be incorporated into the adjustment factor to the extent that they did not prevail at the base date. Second, the adjustment factor as derived above assumes compliance with the reserve requirements; to the extent that shortfalls result in some periods they need also to be reflected in the adjustment factor.

Inclusion of the Incremental Reserve requirements (IR) results in the following:

$$\text{Adjustment} = (r_t - r_0)\ \text{DTL} + \text{IR} \qquad ...(2)$$

The adjustment factor thus derived is then subtracted from the unadjusted series of reserve money, to yield what shall here be called the adjusted (1) series.

Finally, any net defaults of commercial banks with respect to the average and incremental reserve requirements need to be incorporated. Shortfalls in the compliance with the reserve requirements, release bank reserves in the same manner that an increase in the monetary base would boost bank reserves. Shortfalls are included in the adjustment factor by subtracting the absolute amount of CRR defaults, measured on a net basis for all commercial banks:

$$\text{Adjustment} = (r_t - r_0)\ \text{DTL} + \text{IR} - \text{DF} \qquad \ldots(3)$$

where DF is the net CRR default for all commercial banks. Use of this more comprehensive adjustment factor yields what shall here be called the adjusted (2) series of the monetary base. Both adjusted series have been reconstructed on an end-month basis since April 1973 and are presented in Appendix Table 2.[3] This table also includes a series on adjusted bank reserves obtained by subtracting currency in circulation from the respective adjusted reserve money series. Comparisons between the unadjusted and adjusted series are afforded by Tables 1 and 2.

Table 1

Quarterly Average Growth Rates – Reserve Money, Bank Reserves, and Money

(per cent)

	Reserve Money					*Bank Reserves*		*Aggregate Deposits*
	Un-adjusted	*Adjusted 1*	*Adjusted 2*	M_1	M_3	*Adjusted 1*	*Adjusted 2*	
1973/74								
I	12.9	9.6	9.6	7.9	7.2	10.5	10.5	5.8
II	1.0	-1.2	-1.2	-0.1	2.8	13.0	13.0	5.9
III	3.7	1.5	1.6	1.4	3.4	-7.8	-6.4	3.9
IV	4.9	5.0	5.7	5.8	3.8	-9.6	-2.8	3.2
1974/75								
I	5.1	6.3	8.1	7.3	5.6	-0.9	20.2	10.8
II	-5.0	-3.4	-5.7	-1.0	1.0	21.7	-8.1	4.6
III	1.0	-0.5	-0.5	-3.2	1.4	7.2	7.2	2.8
IV	1.9	3.1	3.1	3.6	2.9	7.8	7.8	3.1
1975/76								
I	5.6	5.6	5.6	5.0	5.0	1.4	1.4	4.4
II	-3.5	-3.6	-3.6	-1.2	2.1	0.1	0.1	5.2
III	0.8	0.7	0.7	-0.4	2.7	-1.8	-1.8	3.5
IV	2.1	2.1	2.1	3.3	2.7	5.3	5.3	4.3
1976/77								
I	9.2	9.2	9.2	7.2	7.0	17.2	17.2	6.4
II	0.2	0.1	0.1	0.8	4.2	4.8	4.8	6.2
III	4.6	0.8	1.6	3.6	5.7	-17.6	-10.8	6.7
IV	5.7	4.9	5.5	4.4	3.7	4.0	9.4	3.2

(Contd...)

(...Contd...)

	Reserve Money					*Bank Reserves*		*Aggregate Deposits*
	Un-adjusted	*Adjus-ted 1*	*Adjus-ted 2*	M_1	M_3	*Adjus-ted 1*	*Adjus-ted 2*	
1977/78								
I	8.4	6.8	5.3	6.8	6.7	2.3	-10.2	6.5
II	-0.7	-2.2	-2.2	-1.7	2.6	9.9	9.9	5.1
III	6.0	5.3	5.4	4.4	4.8	16.6	17.6	5.1
IV	2.6	1.3	1.2	4.1	4.2	-5.3	-6.1	5.0
1978/79								
I	10.6	10.1	10.1	7.6	6.3	20.3	20.3	5.4
II	-1.5	-3.0	-3.0	-1.0	2.8	-21.7	-21.7	4.2
III	6.0	4.8	5.0	7.2	5.9	14.7	16.2	6.3
IV	8.7	7.1	7.0	7.0	5.4	11.8	10.4	5.0
1979/80								
I	8.7	8.8	8.8	6.3	5.6	16.9	16.9	4.8
II	1.0	-0.5	-0.5	1.7	4.1	-11.0	-11.0	5.3
III	4.4	4.1	4.1	1.0	3.1	40.4	40.4	4.3
IV	3.8	3.5	3.5	5.3	4.1	-14.2	-14.2	3.3
1980-81								
I	5.0	4.3	11.8	4.7	4.5	-3.0	-3.0	4.2
II	-2.7	-4.3	-10.7	-2.9	1.7	-8.9	-8.9	3.6
III	7.3	7.8	7.8	6.4	5.0	25.4	25.4	4.8
IV	4.8	5.4	5.6	6.8	5.2	5.7	6.8	5.1
1981/82								
I	5.3	6.1	5.9	5.9	5.4	7.0	5.9	5.3
II	0.4	-2.2	-2.2	-1.3	2.5	4.9	4.9	4.3
III	1.0	-0.2	7.2	3.4	3.3	-14.9	-6.5	3.7
IV	1.9	0.7	-3.0	1.4	1.8	-14.9	6.6	1.6

Source: Appendix Table 2.

Tables 1 and 2 present quarterly and six-monthly average growth rates for the various reserve money and money supply series. In some periods, the adjusted series on reserve money differ quite significantly from their unadjusted counterpart. During periods when the CRR was raised, the growth rate of the adjusted (1) series is revealed to be significantly less than the growth rate yielded by unadjusted reserve money. Similarly, when the CRR was lowered (1974/75), the adjusted series, appropriately, grew more rapidly, particularly when account is taken of the defaults. In summary, the adjustment factors introduced alter not only the magnitude of change in reserve money, but also the direction of change.

Table 2

Six-Monthly Average Growth Rates – Reserve Money, Bank Reserves, and Money

(per cent)

	Reserve Money			M_1	M_3	Bank Reserves		Aggregate Deposits
	Un-adjusted	*Adjus-ted 1*	*Adjus-ted 2*			*Adjus-ted 1*	*Adjus-ted 2*	
1973/74								
1	-	12.7	12.7	-	-	16.7	16.7	-
2	6.8	3.4	3.8	4.3	6.7	-7.0	-2.1	5.2
1974/75								
1	4.9	7.1	7.9	9.8	8.1	4.3	13.8	11.5
2	-2.6	-0.7	-2.0	-1.9	3.4	22.3	6.6	6.8
1975/76								
1	4.7	5.2	5.2	6.3	0.6	5.3	5.3	8.7
2	0.1	-0.1	-0.1	0.6	5.6	0.8	0.8	8.4
1976/77								
1	10.4	10.4	10.4	9.4	11.1	23.2	23.2	12.1
2	7.7	3.3	4.4	6.3	9.9	-14.0	-4.5	11.6
1977/78								
1	11.0	8.1	7.0	8.2	10.1	9.5	-1.4	10.9
2	7.0	4.8	4.9	5.6	8.4	18.8	19.3	10.4
1978/79								
1	11.2	9.2	9.1	9.2	10.0	4.3	3.8	10.3
2	9.7	6.9	7.0	10.4	10.2	6.7	7.4	11.2
1979/80								
1	13.8	12.3	12.2	10.9	10.6	16.6	15.9	10.2
2	6.9	5.6	5.6	4.6	7.3	22.8	22.8	8.7
1980/81								
1	5.5	3.9	7.7	5.9	7.5	-14.4	-14.4	7.8
2	8.4	8.3	4.5	8.4	8.6	22.9	23.6	8.6
1981/82								
1	8.0	7.7	7.6	8.7	9.5	12.7	12.0	11.0
2	2.2	-1.0	4.5	3.2	5.4	-19.4	-1.2	6.7

Source: Appendix Table 2.

Further comparison between the alternative series is yielded by Chart 1 to 3 which contrast the unadjusted monetary base with the adjusted base inclusive of CRR defaults. The adjusted monetary base is demonstrated to grow more slowly, particularly after 1976/77 when successive increases were made in the CRR (Chart 1). The resultant, multiplied for narrow money is revealed to be considerably more stable than that base on the normally published series on the monetary base (Chart 2). In addition to the stability, the declining trend evident in the multiplier obtained from the unadjusted base is now absent. This highlights the alternative procedures for incorporating the impact of CRR changes in the reserve money multiplier framework of analysis. *Ceteris paribus,* more stringent cash reserve requirements depress the multiplier, based on unadjusted data on the monetary base. Incorporation of the impact of CRR changes in the computation of an adjusted reserve money series demonstrates more clearly the impact of those changes.

Chart 3 compares the quarterly and six monthly growth rates yielded by the two series on reserve money. In 1974/75, when the CRR was lowered, the adjusted series grew more rapidly, a result that is different in direction as well as degree from the unadjusted series. After 1976/77, the growth rates of the adjusted series are significantly below those yielded by the unadjusted series, and demonstrate more clearly the trends indicated by Chart 1.

Monetary Control Through the Monetary Base

The importance of the monetary base as a control aggregate to influence variations in the money stock, and in aggregate GNP, has varied, depending on the institutional environment. In some countries, the monetary base has been used directly as the monetary target in the implementation of monetary policy, in place of intermediate targets such as alternative measures of the money stock. In most other cases, the monetary base has been considered, along with measures of money market conditions, as an appropriate policy guide through which to control the money stock. The latter approach leaves open the consequent issue of the transmission mechanism linking the main intermediate monetary aggregate with the changes in aggregate income and activity. Clearly, however, such transmission mechanisms are implicitly assumed in most exercises involving monetary aggregate targeting.

The rationale for using the monetary base as a control aggregate usually derives from the consideration that most monetary authority actions influence, and even determine, the monetary base. Incorpo-

Chart 1

Monetary Base 1973-74 to 1981-82
(Quarterly Averages)

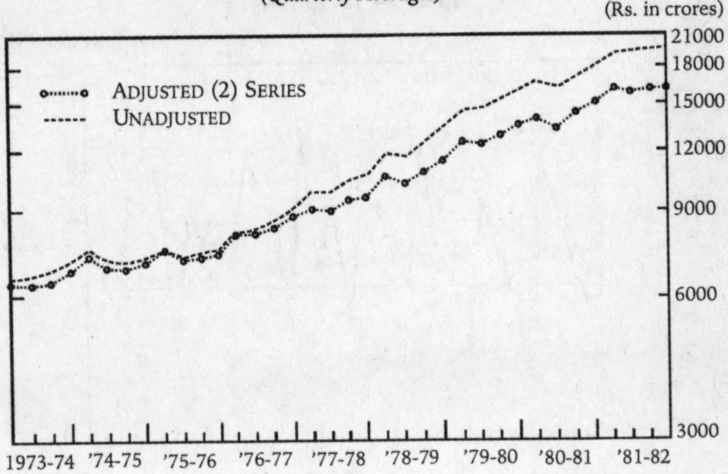

Chart 2

Alternative Measures of the Narrow Money Multiplier
1973-74 to 1981-82
(Based on Quarterly Averages)

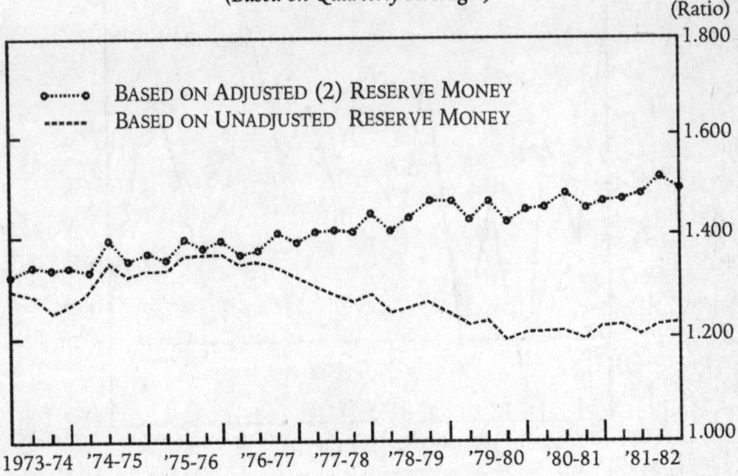

Source: Based on Appendix Table 2.

Chart 3

Growth Rates of Alternative Measures of the Monetary Base 1973-74 to 1981-82

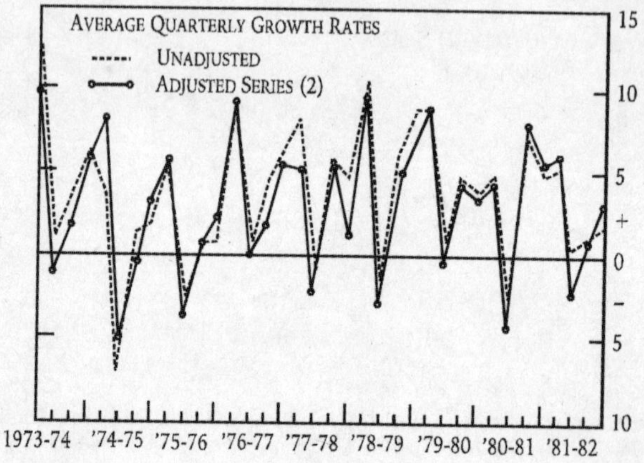

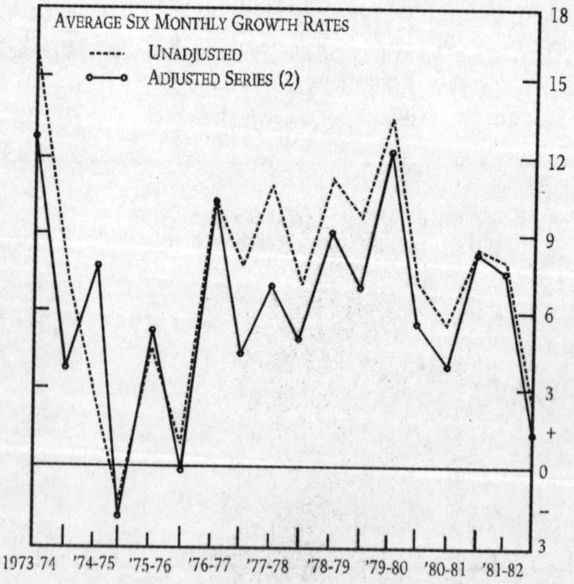

Source: Based on Appendix Table 1 and 2.

ration of the impact of cash reserve requirement changes in the computation of an adjusted monetary base is intended to consolidate further the effects of such actions into a summary aggregate. In countries with developed money market and debt management activities, the major sources of change in the monetary base are the frequent open market operations of the monetary authority. In these countries, such open market transactions are usually the key instrument to offset changes in other sources of reserve money expansion; these transactions have the potential of placing greater control over the monetary base with the monetary authority.

In countries with limited open market operations, greater attention needs to be addressed to the other factors influencing the monetary base. The importance of the monetary base, as the set of assets constraining the money supply, remains. In these countries, data on changes in the monetary base are also often available more quickly than other monetary aggregates. However, because of the relatively more important role played by sources of reserve money change not under the direct control of the monetary authority, the use of data on the monetary base requires greater care. In the very short run, there may be erratic movements over which the monetary authority has relatively little control. In these circumstances, a somewhat longer time span of control and analysis may be more appropriate. Systematic relationships may be implicity in the quarterly or six monthly averages that are not yielded readily by weekly or monthly data, because the latter exhibit greater statistical noise. These considerations apply equally, although in different degrees, to monetary authorities in developed and less developed monetary systems; the difference may be reduced to the choice of the appropriate time span for controlling or targeting monetary base developments. It is our judgement that measures for a week or even a month may be of too short a period for inference on underlying trends; data spanning three month periods may constitute the minimum time perspective for systematic analysis.[4]

The object of this section is to develop the quantitative relationship between the monetary base and alternative measures of the money stock in India. This does not necessarily imply that other indicators of money market conditions, such as total or net borrowed bank reserves, are unimportant. Certainly, bank reserves may be the more appropriate guide to changes in aggregate deposits. However, in India, excess reserves have generally been small. In these circumstances, it may be more appropriate to focus on the monetary base rather than on alternate measures of bank reserves. Certainly, developments in the currency to deposits ratio can significantly alter the relationship between the monetary base and money supply. However, even here, it is important to distinguish between those variations in the currency to deposits ratio that are expected and those that are unexpected.[5]

Our enquiry into the quantitative relationship between the monetary base and money stock is intended to yield conclusions on the usefulness of the monetary base as a control aggregate. As a monetary base, we use the total reserves instead of unborrowed reserves as is the practice in some countries. Borrowings are excluded in some of these countries as these are deemed to be temporary in nature. In India, with bulk of the borrowings taking the form of refinance entitlements for food procurement credit and export credit, there is no case for netting reserves for borrowings. Consistent with the arguments presented in Section II above, the wider definition of the monetary base is used for the analysis. The reserve money/multiplier identity may be expressed in its simple aggregative form as:

$$M = mH \qquad \ldots(1)$$

where 'M' is the money stock;

'm' is the multiplier consistent with the choice of the money stock measure;

and

'H' is the monetary base defined as the adjusted (2) series.

The multiplier is determined principally by factors outside the control of the monetary authority (e.g., by households), and if it is prone to erratic fluctuations, errors may result in the control of the money supply through changes in the monetary base. However, in most countries, changes in reserve money constitute the main factor, determining changes in money supply. The timing of the impact of reserve money changes differs, depending on the institutional environment. The effect of a change in reserve money on a measure of money supply is not necessarily contemporaneous, but may be distributed over a period of time. The quantitative work undertaken here attempts to determine the most dominant lag structure. The various econometric exercises proved to be unexpectedly robust in their results, in the sense that broadly similar or consistent conclusions were yielded from the alternative specifications.

In specifying a simple model based on the identity expressed in (1), the lagged effect of the monetary base needs to be carefully formulated. In particular, the impact of previous period reserve money developments needs to be assessed. This may be incorporated by analyzing alternative equations with different specifications for the termination of the lagged effect. In our case the dominant effects originated from current period and, to a lesser extent, previous period developments in the monetary base. These may be expressed in linear form as:

$$M_t = A_o + A_1H_t + A_2H_{t-1} + A_3t \qquad \ldots(2)$$

and $$M_t = A_o + A_1H_t + A_3t \qquad \ldots(3)$$

In these equations, the variable t has also been included to incorporate the possibility of a time trend in the money multiplier. These equations were estimated using quarterly data for the period 1974/75 I to 1981/82 IV. The statistical results are summarized in Table 3 for alternative concepts of the money stock. The results suggest a high order of statistical significance, with the time trend also being statistically significant. Decomposition of the current period reserve money effect into current and previous quarter variables results in the total effect remaining about the same. This applies to each of the two measures of the money stock and to the aggregate deposits equations. The statistical properties of the equations are good.

The results for equations, where aggregate deposits was the dependent variable, were less encouraging in their statistical properties, although a significant statistical association was obtained with reserve money as defined for our purposes. Where lagged bank reserves was specified as the independent variable, there was greater evidence of autocorrelation.

Table 3

Estimate of Money – Reserve Money Equation: Original Specification

(per cent)

Sample Period: 1974/75 I – 1981/82 IV

$M_t = A_0 + A_1H_t + A_3t$

$M_t = A_0 + A_1H_t + A_2H_{t-1} + A_3t$

Aggregate	A_0	A_1	A_2	A_3	D.W.	$\bar{R}^2$
M_1	-972.06	1.47	-	27.09	1.98	0.99
	(-6.27)	(45.08)		(2.58)		
M_1	-902.75	1.13	0.33	34.18	1.91	0.99
	(-3.78)	(16.3)	(4.93)	(2.06)		
M_3	-7,144.60	3.40	-	309.02	1.87	0.99
	(-8.69)	(19.53)		(5.47)		
M_3	-12,829.03	1.05	0.38	1,406.13	2.25	0.99
	(-6.45)	(9.95)	(3.38)	(12.83)		

Note: 't' ratios in parentheses. Corrected for the Cochrane-Orcutt procedure.

A more stringent test of the robustness of the above equations is afforded by specifying them in terms of first differences.[6] This yields equations of the type:

$$\Delta M_t = B_0 + B_1 \Delta H_t \qquad ...(4)$$

$$\text{and } \Delta M_t = B_0 + B_1 \Delta H_t + B_2 \Delta H_{t-1} \qquad ...(5)$$

Specification of the equations in first difference form implies that the money stock and reserve money variables are measured in terms of their growth. Estimation of these equations for the similar period yields the results present in Table 4. Again, the associations specified in the equations are statistically significant. The growth in M_1 appears to be relatively more closely influenced by the growth in reserve money, compared with the results for broad money. Acceptable results for the growth in aggregate deposits were again not obtained. While the results for M_3 are slightly less satisfactory than for M_1 the coefficients of the lagged variables remain significant, even at the one per cent level.

Table 4

Estimate of Money – Reserve Money Equation: Specification Based on First Differences

(per cent)

$\Delta M_t = B_0 + B_1 \Delta H_t$

$\Delta M_t = B_0 + B_1 \Delta H_t + B_2 \Delta H_{t-1}$

Aggregate	B_0	B_1	B_2	*D.W.*	$\bar{R}^2$
M_1	94.31 (2.58)	1.24 (13.78)	-	2.17	0.83
M_1	56.62 (1.17)	1.09 (12.36)	0.29 (3.23)	2.09	0.82
M_3	1,185.16 (5.29)	0.78 (8.40)	-	2.50	0.63
M_3	1,011.58 (5.47)	0.98 (8.14)	0.31 (2.40)	2.67	0.68

Note: 't' ratios in parentheses. Adjusted for the Cochrane-Orcutt procedure.

Finally, the association between the monetary aggregates and the monetary base may be specified within a framework of partial adjustment. In this framework, the actual change in money stock is specified to be some proportion (λ) of the difference between the equilibrium and previous period level of the monetary aggregate. This may be expressed in log-linear terms as:

$$\log M_t = \lambda(\log M^*_t - \log M_{t-1}) \qquad ...(6)$$

where 'λ' is the coefficient of adjustment specified to be $0 \leq \lambda \leq 1$ and 'M^*_t' is the equilibrium money stock.

Combining the equation with an equilibrium condition for M^*_t and M^*_t results in an equation of the following type:

$$\log M^*_t = C_0 + C_1 \log H_t + C_2 \log M_{t-1} \qquad ...(7)$$

The results of this equation, estimated for M_1 and M_3, are reported in Table 5. Again, the equations appear to be fairly well specified; the respective coefficients of determination are very high and the coefficients are all significant at the one per cent level. While the Durbin-Watson statistic has been reported in the Table, this test for serial correlation is not strictly valid in the presence of lagged dependent variables. However, computation of the alternative Durbin 'h' statistic indicates the absence of serial correlation, most clearly for the M_1 equation, strengthening the acceptability of the results. The long run impact of reserve money on M_1 and M_3 respectively, is indicated by the value of C_3, these tend to confirm the results obtained from the regressions presented in Table 3.[7]

Table 5

Estimate of Money Reserve Equation: Specifications Based on Lagged Adjustment

(per cent)

Sample Period: 1974/75 I - 1981/82 IV

$\log M_t = C_0 + C_1 \log H_t + C_2 \log M_{t-1}$

Aggregate	C_0	C_1	C_2	λ	C_3	*D.W.*	$\bar{R}^2$
M_1	0.16 (-4.62)	0.85 (13.14)	0.22 (3.58)	0.782	1.09	1.95	0.99
M_3	-0.11 (1.17)	0.42 (9.55)	0.66 (17.00)	0.340	1.22	2.75	0.99

Note: 't' ratios in parentheses. Adjusted for the Cochrane-Orcutt procedure.

Finally, the equations in Table 5 may be tested further to establish their forecasting ability in dynamic simulations. Within-sample dynamic simulations were conducted for the two equations and the results are reported in Table 6.

Table 6

Dynamic Simulations of M_1 and M_3 Equations Based on Partial Adjustment, 1974-75/1981-82

(per cent)

Aggregate	*Mean Absolute Error*	*Root Mean Square Error*
M_1	0.11	0.15
M_3	0.48	0.70

The simulations of the two equations perform markedly well. Chart 4 sketches the actual and expected values for M_1 and M_3 obtained from these dynamic simulations. These results strengthen

Chart 4

Dynamic Simulations of M_1 and M_3 Based on Lagged Adjustment 1974-75 I – 1981-82 IV

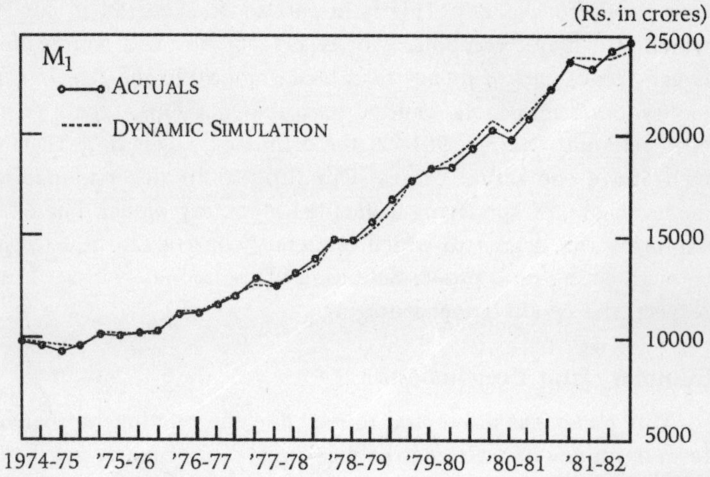

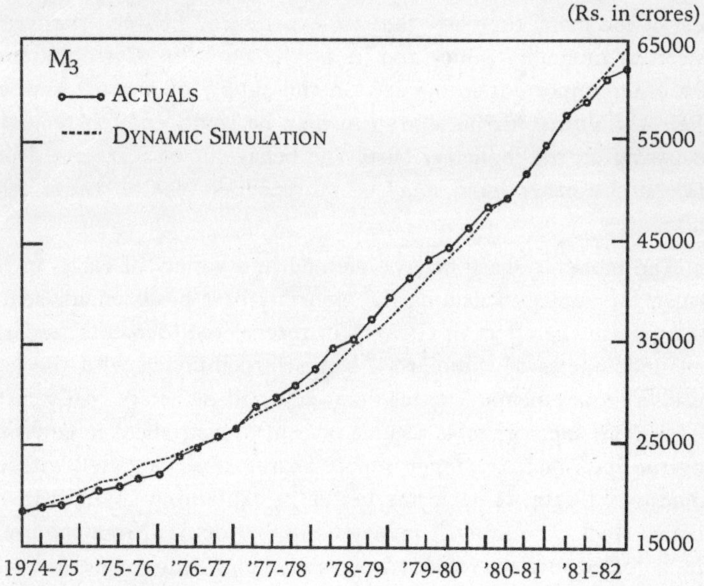

Source : Based on results reported in Table 5.

confidence in the equations; in particular, the total impact of reserve money on the respective monetary aggregates is similar to the results obtained by earlier equations. Based on the statistical properties of the equations, it is seen that there is a closed impact of the monetary base on narrow money. This is in part to be expected as currency which is a major component of reserve money and constitutes a larger part of narrow money than broad money. In the case of broad money, other influences, omitted from the equations, appear to have been relevant. During 1981-82, the estimated values have remained well above the actual values. Our interest in this paper is not, however, one of specifying a detailed monetary model, but one of exploring the degree to which monetary control can be exercised through acting on a proper definition of the monetary base. In this respect, the results are encouraging.

Summary and Conclusions

This paper has attempted to examine the relationship between reserve money and alternative measures of the money stock. The lagged response of the money stock to changes in reserve money is one of the many time lags that are experienced between the formulation of monetary policy and its implementation. Certainly, there are other important influences on the supply of money; however, their variability in the short run may be small enough to justify focussing on the monetary base. The behaviour of aggregate deposits, on the other hand, may be more dependent on these other influences.

The monetary base may be defined in a variety of ways. In this paper, the published data on the monetary base has been adjusted to incorporate the effect of changes in reserve requirements, and also net deficiencies of commercial banks in complying with the legal reserve requirements. The resultant adjusted monetary base appears to be more appropriate as a guide or control instrument in determining the intermediate money supply aggregates. Compared with the unadjusted data, it performs better in explaining changes in the money stock. The implicit money multiplier derived from the use of the adjusted monetary base displays greater stability compared with that based on the unadjusted series.

Use of the adjusted series enables more systematic quantitative relationships to be estimated between the monetary base and M_1 and M_3. Our results demonstrate that the lag in the impact of reserve money on both measures of money supply is very short. This is particularly so for M_1. In the case of both M_1 and M_3, the current quarter impact is the most dominant. The equations are well estimated with acceptable statistical properties. It is also suggested that quarterly data are the most appropriate for measuring this response. Use of monthly data does not yield useful systematic relationships, a reflection of the statistical noise present in data of such short duration. A preliminary review suggests that the relationships are even stronger when six monthly data are used. However, more work is necessary for establishing similarly strong relationships with aggregate deposits. The results indicate that in general, changes in reserve money are useful and important guides to the behaviour of money supply.

APPENDIX

Table 1

Changes in Cash Reserve Requirements 1973-74/1981-82

Effective Date	*Change*
May 31, 1973	The Cash Reserve Ratio (CRR) was raised from 3 per cent to 5 per cent of net Demand and Time Liabilities (DTL) of banks.
Sept. 8, 1973	The CRR was raised from 5 per cent to 7 per cent.
Sept. 22, 1973	The CRR was raised from 7 per cent to 8 per cent.
June 29, 1974	The CRR was reduced from 8 per cent to 5 per cent.
Dec. 4, 1974	The CRR was reduced from 5 per cent to 4.5 per cent.
Dec. 28, 1974	The CRR was reduced from 4.5 per cent to 4 per cent.
Sept. 4, 1976	The ratio was raised from 4 per cent to 5 per cent.
Nov. 13, 1976	The ratio was again raised to 6 per cent.
Jan. 14, 1977	An incremental cash reserve requirement was introduced, which provided that 10 per cent of incremental DTL be also maintained as cash reserves from this date.
Oct. 30, 1980	Banks were exempted from the further application of the incremental cash reserve requirement.
July 31, 1981	CRR raised from 6 per cent to 6.5 per cent.
Aug. 21, 1981	CRR raised from 6.5 per cent to 7 per cent.
Nov. 27, 1981	CRR raised from 7 per cent to 7.25 per cent.
Dec. 25, 1981	CRR again raised from 7.25 per cent to 7.50 per cent.
Jan. 29, 1982	CRR raised to 7.75 per cent.
April 9, 1982	CRR reduced from 7.75 per cent to 7.25 per cent. In respect of the non-resident account schemes, the CRR applicable was reduced to the statutory minimum, 3 per cent.
June 11, 1982	CRR reduced from 7.25 per cent to 7.0 per cent.

APPENDIX

Table 2

Reserve Money and Bank Reserves – Adjusted for CRR Changes, 1973-82

(Rs. in crores)

	Reserve Money			*Bank Reserves*	
	Unadjusted	*Adjusted 1*	*Adjusted 2*	*Adjusted 1*	*Adjusted 2*
1973/74					
April (last Friday)	6,313	6,313	6,313	573	573
May	6,503	5,312	6,312	444	444
June	6,743	6,546	6,546	717	717
I (average)	6,519	6,390	6,390	578	578
July	6,641	6,438	6,438	668	668
August	6,462	6,255	6,255	683	683
September	6,662	6,244	6,244	609	609
II (average)	6,588	6,312	6,312	653	653
October	6,842	6,422	6,422	619	619
November	6,842	6,416	6,416	628	628
December	6,803	6,377	6,502	560	585
III (average)	6,829	6,405	6,413	602	611
January	7,055	6,620	6,620	599	599
February	7,180	6,746	6,786	567	607
March	7,260	6,820	6,929	467	576
IV (average)	7,165	6,729	6,778	544	594
Annual average	**6,775**	**6,459**	**6,473**	**631**	**646**
1974/75					
April (last Friday)	7,417	6,970	7,113	394	537
May	7,592	7,138	7,336	469	667
June	7,584	7,353	7,538	754	939
I (average)	7,531	7,154	7,329	539	714
July	7,363	7,124	7,124	700	700
August	7,096	6,857	6,857	649	649
September	6,994	6,754	6,754	619	619
II (average)	7,151	6,912	6,912	656	656
October	7,101	6,857	6,857	708	708
November	7,094	6,848	6,848	667	667
December	7,044	6,921	6,921	734	734
III (average)	7,080	6,875	6,875	703	703
January	7,013	6,887	6,887	648	648
February	7,242	7,114	7,114	791	791
March	7,387	7,259	7,259	834	834
IV (average)	7,214	7,087	7,087	758	758
Annual average	**7,244**	**7,007**	**7,051**	**664**	**708**

(Contd...)

(...Contd...)

	Reserve Money			Bank Reserves	
	Unadjusted	Adjusted 1	Adjusted 2	Adjusted 1	Adjusted 2
1975/76					
April (last Friday)	7,518	7,388	7,388	753	753
May	7,665	7,533	7,533	750	750
June	7,666	7,532	7,532	805	805
I (average)	7,616	7,484	7,484	769	769
July	7,475	7,337	7,337	801	801
August	7,351	7,212	7,212	779	779
September	7,229	7,089	7,089	729	729
II (average)	7,352	7,213	7,213	770	770
October	7,445	7,303	7,303	777	777
November	7,362	7,219	7,219	714	714
December	7,425	7,280	7,280	777	777
III (average)	7,411	7,267	7,267	756	756
January	7,423	7,278	7,278	788	788
February	7,544	7,398	7,398	774	774
March	7,732	7,584	7,584	826	826
IV (average)	7,566	7,420	7,420	796	796
Annual average	**7,486**	**7,346**	**7,346**	**773**	**773**
1976/77					
April (last Friday)	8,110	7,957	7,957	931	931
May	8,325	8,169	8,169	952	952
June	8,352	8,194	8,194	913	913
I (average)	8,262	8,107	8,107	933	933
July	8,235	8,071	8,071	949	949
August	8,211	8,045	8,045	936	936
September	8,386	8,218	8,218	1,050	1,050
II (average)	8,277	8,111	8,111	978	978
October	8,609	8,268	8,275	906	913
November	8,701	8,121	8,148	779	806
December	8,676	8,141	8,305	733	897
III (average)	8,662	8,177	8,243	806	872
January	8,872	8,328	8,461	772	905
February	9,042	8,477	8,569	776	868
March	9,544	8,938	9,061	965	1,088
IV (average)	9,153	8,581	8,697	838	954
Annual average	**8,588**	**8,244**	**8,290**	**889**	**934**

(Contd...)

(...Contd...)

	Reserve Money			*Bank Reserves*	
	Unadjusted	*Adjusted 1*	*Adjusted 2*	*Adjusted 1*	*Adjusted 2*
1977/78					
April (last Friday)	9,779	9,064	9,064	797	797
May	9,992	9,225	9,225	924	924
June	10,001	9,200	9,200	849	849
I (average)	9,924	9,163	9,163	857	857
July	9,710	8,848	8,848	806	806
August	9,994	9,097	9,077	1,064	1,064
September	9,867	8,934	8,934	955	955
II (average)	9,857	8,960	8,960	942	942
October	10,212	9,243	9,243	1,131	1,131
November	10,614	9,606	9,606	1,185	1,185
December	10,508	9,457	9,489	977	1,009
III (average)	10,445	9,435	9,446	1,098	1,108
January	10,700	9,565	9,565	1,200	1,200
February	10,523	9,362	9,362	872	872
March	10,941	9,750	9,750	1,049	1,049
IV (average)	10,721	9,559	9,559	1,040	1,040
Annual average	**10,237**	**9,279**	**9,282**	**984**	**987**
1978/79					
April (last Friday)	11,643	10,330	10,330	1,233	1,233
May	11,687	10,375	10,375	979	979
June	12,237	10,877	10,877	1,542	1,542
I (average)	11,856	10,527	10,527	1,251	1,251
July	11,521	10,109	10,109	742	742
August	11,792	10,317	10,317	1,140	1,140
September	11,712	10,203	10,203	1,054	1,054
II (average)	11,675	10,210	10,210	979	979
October	12,131	10,555	10,555	1,054	1,054
November	12,310	10,654	10,654	1,049	1,049
December	12,671	10,910	10,956	1,266	1,312
III (average)	12,371	10,706	10,722	1,123	1,138
January	13,185	11,206	11,206	1,133	1,133
February	13,431	11,488	11,488	1,328	1,328
March	13,716	11,722	11,722	1,307	1,307
IV (average)	13,444	11,472	11,472	1,256	1,256
Annual average	**12,336**	**10,729**	**10,733**	**1,152**	**1,156**

(Contd...)

(...Contd...)

	Reserve Money			Bank Reserves	
	Unadjusted	Adjusted 1	Adjusted 2	Adjusted 1	Adjusted 2
1979/80					
April (last Friday)	14,257	12,192	12,192	1,430	1,430
May	14,723	12,589	12,589	1,439	1,439
June	14,863	12,673	12,673	1,534	1,534
I (average)	14,614	12,485	12,485	1,468	1,468
July	14,923	12,719	12,719	1,392	1,392
August	14,871	12,499	12,499	1,103	1,103
September	14,479	12,057	12,057	1,422	1,422
II (average)	14,758	12,425	12,425	1,306	1,306
October	15,593	13,151	13,151	1,958	1,958
November	15,315	12,836	12,836	1,827	1,827
December	15,323	12,815	12,815	1,713	1,713
III (average)	15,410	12,934	12,934	1,833	1,833
January	15,774	13,188	13,188	1,711	1,711
February	15,730	13,106	13,106	1,250	1,250
March	16,465	13,857	13,857	1,759	1,759
IV (average)	15,990	13,384	13,384	1,573	1,573
Annual average	**15,193**	**12,807**	**12,807**	**1,545**	**1,545**
1980/81					
April (last Friday)	16,763	13,969	13,969	1,504	1,504
May	17,062	14,247	14,247	1,689	1,689
June	16,528	13,677	13,677	1,385	1,385
I (average)	16,784	13,964	14,964	1,526	1,526
July	16,499	13,587	13,587	1,421	1,421
August	16,355	13,382	13,382	1,435	1,435
September	16,144	13,141	13,141	1,315	1,315
II (average)	16,333	13,370	13,370	1,390	1,390
October	17,328	13,230	14,230	1,863	1,863
November	17,576	14,467	14,467	1,690	1,690
December	17,655	14,523	14,523	1,676	1,676
III (average)	17,520	14,407	14,407	1,743	1,743
January	17,593	14,427	14,427	1,478	1,478
February	18,055	14,881	14,881	1,657	1,657
March	19,441	16,264	16,324	2,392	2,452
IV (average)	18,363	15,191	15,211	1,842	1,862
Annual average	**17,250**	**14,233**	**14,238**	**1,625**	**1,630**

(Contd...)

(...Contd...)

	Reserve Money			*Bank Reserves*	
	Unadjusted	*Adjusted 1*	*Adjusted 2*	*Adjusted 1*	*Adjusted 2*
1981/82					
April (last Friday)	19,018	15,814	15,814	1,693	1,693
May	19,303	16,072	16,072	1,861	1,861
June	19,712	16,459	16,459	2,360	2,360
I (average)	19,344	16,115	16,115	1,971	1,971
July	20,271	16,765	16,765	2,498	2,498
August	18,965	15,233	15,233	1,801	1,801
September	19,046	15,289	15,289	1,903	1,903
II (average)	19,427	15,762	15,762	2,067	2,067
October	19,906	16,130	16,257	2,024	2,151
November	19,462	15,556	15,658	1,688	1,780
December	19,507	15,493	15,788	1,568	1,863
III (average)	19,625	15,730	16,901	1,760	1,932
January	19,763	15,600	16,111	1,524	2,035
February	19,766	21,680	15,614	1,288	2,095
March	20,446	16,290	16,659	1,679	2,048
IV (average)	19,992	15,835	16,397	1,497	2,059
Annual average	**19,597**	**15,860**	**16,044**	**1,824**	**2,007**

ANNEXURE

Sources and Description of the Data

1. Monetary Data

The data on narrow money (M_1) used for the exercises in this paper differ from the published series. The adjustments that have been made to the published data are intended to ensure greater comparability over time. These adjustments are discussed in the study on Monetary Policy in India contained in the supplement to the RBI Occasional Papers Vol. 3, No. 1 (June 1982). Briefly, savings deposits data after March 1978 were reclassified to reflect the recommendations of the Second Working Group on monetary concepts. Use of the methodology evolved by the Group resulted in about 85 per cent of savings deposits being classified with time deposits; the remainder were treated as being akin to demand deposits. The published data, prior to March 1978, continue to reflect the previous methodology which had resulted in quite the opposite proposition of savings deposits being classified with demand and time deposits. Consistency was sought to be assured by applying to the data prior to March 1978, the assumption that 85 per cent of savings deposits be reclassified as time deposits. Application of the new methodology to three sample periods in the 1960s and 1970s confirmed the appropriateness of extending the assumption, that 85 per cent of savings deposits are more in the nature of time deposits, to the previous period data.

M_1 and M_3 data are both presented in the June 1982 RBI study.

2. Data on CRR Deficiencies

In computing the adjustment factor to reserve money, discussed in the text of the paper, one component was the calculation on net bank defaults in relation to the CRR requirement. The data for net bank defaults are presented in the supplement to the June 1982 issue of the RBI Occasional Papers.

Notes

1. Appendix Table 1 lists the CRR changes.
2. From the vast literature published in the *Federal Reserve Bank Quarterly Review*, the following contain the principal developments of the concept and methodology: Anderson and Jordan (1968), Burger (1975), Balbach and Burger (1976), Burger and Rasche (1977), Anderson and Karnosky (1977), Gilbert (1980), and Balbach (1981).
3. Under the present regulations, banks are to maintain the required cash reserves as an average of daily balances over a week. Hence the level of balances maintained on a particular day such as Friday does not correspond closely to the level of deposits. However, in the absence of consolidated data on daily balances, we have used the average of the last Friday figures of each month. In

fact the fit between reserves and money supply would have considerably improved, had we used the average daily balances.

4. Balbach (1981) suggests that in any event, month-to-month fluctuations in money growth have little impact on economic activity. Over longer periods, controllability of money supply is better assured, as multiplier values display greater stability.
5. Further discussion on this issue is contained in Johanne and Rasche (1981).
6. Often, when regressions are estimated with levels acceptable $\bar{R}^2$ are obtained. However, low values for the Durbin-Watson statistic may still be indicative of misspecification. In these cases, the $\bar{R}^2$ values derived from the regressions estimated in first differences may be a better guide of the association between the variables.
7. While the mean lag in the case of M_1 suggest virtually instaneous adjustment, the results in the case of M_3 are indicative of a longer period for the adjustment to be complete. The latter result needs to be interpreted with caution, particularly because there is some evidence of autocorrelation here.

References

Anderson, Leonall C. and Jordan, Jerry L., "The Monetary Base Explanation and Analytical Use", *Federal Reserve Bank of St. Louis Review* (August 1968).

Anderson, Leonall C. and Karnosky, Deniss, "Some Considerations in the Use of Monetary Aggregates for the Implementation of Monetary Policy", *Federal Reserve Bank of St. Louis Review* (September 1977).

Balbach, Anatol B., "How Controllable is Money Growth", *Federal Reserve Bank of St. Louis Review* (April 1981).

Balbach, Anatol B. and Burger, Albert E., "Derivation of the Monetary Base", *Federal Reserve Bank of St. Louis Review* (November 1976).

Burger, Albert E., "The Relationship Between Monetary base and Money: How Close?" *Federal Reserve Bank of St. Louis Review* (October 1975).

Burger, Albert E., "Alternative Measures of the Monetary Base", *Federal Reserve Bank of St. Louis Review* (June 1979).

Burger, Albert E. and Rasche, Robert H., "Revision of the Monetary Base", *Federal Reserve Bank of St. Louis Review* (July 1973).

Garvy, George, "Reserve Requirements Abroad", *Federal Reserve Bank of New York Monthly Review* (October 1973).

Gilbert, R. Anton, "Revision of the St. Louis Federal Reserve's Adjusted Monetary Base", *Federal Reserve Bank of St. Louis Review* (December 1980).

Gupta, Suraj B., *Monetary Planning for India* (Oxford University Press: Delhi, 1979).

Johannes, James M., and Rasche, Robert H., "Can the Reserves Approach to Monetary Control Really Work", *Journal of Money, Credit, and Banking* (August 1981).

Kaminow, Ira, "Required Reserve Ratios, Policy Instruments and Money Stock Control", *Journal of Monetary Economics* (October 1977).

Khatkhate, Deena R. and Villaneuva, Delano P,, "A Behavioural Theory of the Money Multiplier in the United States: An Empirical Test", *IMF Staff Papers* (March 1972).

Singh Anoop, Shetty S.L., and Venkatachalam T.R., "Monetary Policy in India: Issues and Evidence", supplement to the *Reserve Bank of India Occasional Papers*, Vol.3, No.1 (June 1982).

13

Money, Output and Prices

A Macroeconometric Model

I. INTRODUCTION

The role of money and monetary policy in the determination of real output and price level is increasingly receiving attention. Empirical research on the factors influencing economic growth includes several attempts to develop econometric models of the Indian economy. Beginning with simple models, empirical research has made considerable progress in the study of the structure and functioning of various sectors of the economy. In recent years, a greater emphasis on policy issues is also observed. The models differ in their approach and focus. In some models the emphasis is on production and supply while in others it is on demand factors. Some studies pay special attention to the government sector; some recent attempts focus on the interrelationship among money, output and prices and the identification of the sources of growth and inflation. Some of the recent studies in this area are indicated in the list of references at the end of the paper.

This paper outlines the framework of a model of the Indian economy that emphasises the determination of money supply and its impact on both output and prices. The model is aggregative in nature. Nevertheless, it helps to understand the broad interrelations among money, output and prices and should be useful for policy analysis and short-term forecasting. The main linkages in the model are as follows. The stock of money varies endogenously through the feedback from reserve money, which changes to accommodate fiscal

---

Co-author: **R.R. Arif.**
Economic and Political Weekly, April 21, 1990.

deficits. The price level is determined by money supply and output. The government budget is affected by the price level and output. The latter is influenced, among other factors, by changes in real money supply acting as a proxy for real credit.

Having constructed a prototype model, the policy implications of an increase in real capital expenditure of the Government on the three major macroeconomic variables – real output, money supply and prices – is sought to be captured through simulation exercises. In the next section, the macroeconomic trends over the period 1961-62 to 1984-85 are discussed. The analytical framework of the model in Section III describes the interrelations among the fiscal, monetary and the real sectors. The estimates of the structural parameters of the model are presented in Section IV. The complete model, along with its simultaneous solution and the tests of validation are examined in Section V. The results of some policy simulation exercises are presented in Section VI.

II. MACROECONOMIC TRENDS: 1961-62 TO 1984-85

National income at constant prices increased at a trend rate of 3.7 per cent per annum during 1961-62 to 1984-85. The rate of increase has been marginally higher since the Seventies. The annual trend rate of growth during 1975-76 to 1984-85 was 4.02 per cent compared to 3.63 per cent during 1961-62 to 1970-71.

Broad money increased at a trend rate of 14.8 per cent per annum during 1961-62 to 1984-85. It rose at 11.4 per cent per annum during the first decade and 18.4 per cent during the last 10 years. Reserve Bank credit to Government was by far the most important source of reserve money expansion and hence of monetary expansion. Changes in foreign exchange assets have also been important in some years since the mid-seventies.

There has been a notable rise in the rate of saving over the period. The gross saving rate increased from around 15 per cent in the Sixties to around 22 per cent in the Seventies, and stayed around 21 per cent in the early Eighties. Additions to real capital stock in the economy increased at the rate of five per cent per annum during the period 1961-62 to 1984-85. Public sector investment accounted for 43 to 44 per cent of the aggregate investment during this period. In the early Eighties, it formed about 52 per cent of the total investment.

Current expenditure of the Government increased faster than capital expenditure over the period. As total expenditure has increased at a rate higher than the rate of growth in current revenues the resource gap of the Government has also been widening. As a proportion of NNP, the resource gap was around 10 per cent in the Sixties and Seventies. This proportion has risen by two to four per cent in the Eighties. More than half the resource gap is financed by domestic non-market borrowings. Reserve Bank credit to Government as a proportion of the resource gap has increased from around eight per cent in the Sixties to 20 per cent in the early Eighties.

The inflation rate, as measured by the Wholesale Price Index was 84 per cent per annum on a trend basis during the period 1961-62 to 1984-85. There were erratic year-to-year fluctuations in the annual rate of inflation ranging from a fall in 1968-69 to an increase of the order of 20 per cent and above in same years. The average annual trend rate of inflation was around seven per cent both during 1961-62 to 1970-71 and during 1975-76 to 1984-85.

These salient features of the growth of the economy provide the background for the specification of the structural equations that describe the behaviour of major macroeconomic variables and the factors influencing them. The specifications were chosen to bring out the inter-relations among the various sectors of the economy and to identify the crucial factors that need to be considered in policy formulation.

III. FRAMEWORK OF THE MODEL

Among economists, there is no unanimity on how changes in money supply ultimately affect the real economy. The classical view that a change in money supply results in changes in the price level and the Keynesian theory that the full impact is seen only on output under conditions of less than full employment represent two polarised approaches between which the real system probably lies. In a realistic model, the mechanism linking the quantity of money with money income must be able to differentiate between its impact on output and on prices.[1] Accordingly, this paper outlines the framework of an aggregative model of the Indian economy in which the impact of a change in the quantity of money, both on the price level and on output is sought to be captured.

The model focuses mainly on the determination of money supply and its links with fiscal operations and on the impact of money stock on output generation. While RBI credit to finance public sector investment leads to monetary expansion, the investment itself will sooner or later lead to higher output. The fiscal stimulus to growth operates through capital expenditures adding to real capital stock which as a factor of production, directly affects the level of output. Another feature of the model is the attempt to link credit and output by introducing real money or credit as an additional variable in the production function, besides capital stock. Both variables are expected to affect output with a lag of one year.

Together with money supply and output, price behaviour is the third important economic indicator endogenous to the model. The forces interacting within the economy cause changes in the behaviour of prices. In our model an increase in credit is reflected by monetary expansion. The inflationary impact of monetary expansion will be neutralised only to the extent of the higher output that credit expansion would have helped to generate. The transmission mechanism of the monetary and output impulses works simultaneously to determine the price level with partial adjustments over time. The extent of inflation will depend upon the various elasticities quantifying the relationships among money, output and prices. To capture their interactions, the entire process is built into a dynamic simultaneous system.

Government Operations

Current expenditure (consumption expenditure and others) of the Government in real terms (GCER) is determined according to a partial adjustment process related to real income. Real capital expenditures of the Government are autonomous or policy-determined. Government's nominal revenue (GR) is related to nominal income according to a partial adjustment mechanism.

Nominal capital receipts (GCR) of the Government are categorised as borrowings from banks (ΔGBBS), borrowings from other financial institutions (GBNB), non-market borrowings (GNMB) and borrowings from abroad (GEB). Government's domestic borrowings from banks (ΔGBBS) are reflected by the banks' net investment in government securities. These investments are determined by the banks' deposit resources and the Statutory Liquidity Ratio (SLR). The holding of government securities by other financial institutions (GBNB) and borrowings from abroad (GEB) are two components of government's capital receipts that are not behaviourally estimated in this study. Non-market borrowings comprise small savings, provident funds, special borrowings from RBI against compulsory deposits and other capital receipts. As these constitute part of the savings of households, this component of government borrowings may be related to national income. The total domestic borrowing of Government include the holding of dated securities by the RBI. This component, however, is not treated as government's capital receipts. It is included in the net RBI credit to Government.

That portion of the resource gap uncovered by capital receipts is the fiscal deficit of the Government (RBCG). The budgetary deficit as defined in the budget documents does not reflect the full extent of RBI credit to Government since it excludes the RBI's absorption of dated government securities. Therefore, the budgetary deficit, adjusted for the net absorption of dated securities by the Reserve Bank, constitutes the fiscal deficit.

A detailed specification of the government's budgetary operations thus provides a link between the fiscal sector and the monetary sector through the endogenous determination of the resource gap and therefore of Reserve Bank credit to Government (RBCG) which is a major source of reserve money. Deposits of the banking system are determined as a linear function of aggregate money stock. Two alternatives to determine the supply of money were examined. In the first version, money stock is estimated from a linear function $M_3 = a + b\ RM$. Alternatively, money supply can be obtained from the identity $M_3 \equiv m\ RM$ where m is the multiplier. Under both alternatives, reserve money is endogenously determined within the system as:

$$RM \equiv RBCG + RBCC + RBFA + GCL - RMNL$$

where RBCG is the net RBI credit to Government and RBCC the RBI credit to the commercial sector which includes refinance provided to commercial banks, NABARD and other financial institutions. RBFA denotes the net foreign exchange assets of the RBI, GCL – the government's currency liabilities and RNML – the net non-monetary liabilities of the RBI.

In this model, Reserve Bank credit to Government is the only endogenous component of reserve money. It represents the fiscal deficit of the Government which is the residual emerging from government expenditures, net of revenues and their borrowing programmes. The fiscal aggregates, in turn, are influenced by income, prices, etc. Inflation-induced larger budgetary deficits lead to an increase in RBI credit to Government and hence money supply, which in turn, puts further pressure on prices. The model thus tries to capture the two-way causation between prices and money supply through the fiscal sector.

Demand for Money and Price Determination

The monetary variable (M_3) includes currency with the public, aggregate deposits of the public and other deposits with the RBI. The demand for real money is specified as a function of real income (YR) and the nominal rate of interest on fixed deposits (iT). The demand for money function can be formulated as:

$$M_3/P = f\{YR, iT, (M_3/P)_{-1}\}$$

where 'P' is the Wholesale Price Index. It is assumed that at any point of time the actual money stock partially adjusts to the long-run desired level. The rate of interest is institutionally determined by the monetary authority. The sign of the coefficient of 'iT' would depend upon the interest elasticities of demand for real narrow money and of demand for real time deposits. During the period under study, a comparatively static spectrum of interest rates was prevalent in India. Changes in the rates, when they occurred, were stepwise. Expectedly, in our empirical work it turned out to be a weak explanatory variable and was therefore omitted. This, however, does not imply that the rate of interest as a variable can be ignored in policy formulation.

The money demand function can well be written as a price equation.

$$P = f(YR, M_3, P_{-1})$$

Ceteris paribus, an increase in real output results in a fall in the price level while an increase in money stock will lead to a rise in the price level.

Supply of Output

In this model, a single aggregative production function for the whole economy is considered, though it could be legitimately argued that a disaggregated analysis of output by major sectors is more meaningful to determine the supply of real output. The log linear specification simply states that the supply of output (NNP at 1970-71 prices) is determined by real capital stock and real money, both acting with a lag.

The inclusion of real money balances in the production function needs some elaboration. The rationale rests on the increased 'economic efficiency' of the monetary economy compared with the barter economy. It has been argued that an increase in the absorption of real money balances results in a more efficient organisation of the production and market system and as a result, labour and capital are retired from the function of exchange and are available for use in the production process itself. This implies that real balances have a marginal productivity which is positive and which decreases as the intensity of their use increases. Changes in the stock of money are deemed to affect real output, contrary to the classical dichotomy which implies neutrality of money. In industrially advanced economies, several studies have been done to test the importance of real balances as input in the production function[2]. While some empirical studies have found real balances a valid factor of production, others have not confirmed their importance. Nevertheless, in view of the importance of real credit in the Indian economy, it was decided to introduce real money as a variable in the production function.

Capital stock, which is a significant variable in the production function, is decomposed according to sector of origin – public, private corporate and private non-corporate. Real capital stock in the public sector is augmented by real capital expenditures of the Government. Capital stock in the private corporate sector is assumed to be influenced by real output in the economy (lagged one year) and government's capital expenditures. The capital stock in the private non-corporate sector consists of investment in business, agriculture and real estate by the household sector. This is assumed to be exogenous.

IV. ESTIMATES OF STRUCTURAL PARAMETERS

The structural equations of the model are estimated from annual data for the period 1961-62 to 1984-85. The choice of the period was mainly governed by the availability of data on a consistent basis. The basic data are taken from *National Accounts Statistics* (1970-71 series) of the CSO and Reports on Currency and Finance of the Reserve Bank of India. The variables and their notations are listed in Appendix 1.

The model has both linear and log-linear equations. The behavioural equations are estimated by the method of Ordinary Least Squares (OLS). Despite its limitations, the OLS technique is widely used to estimate structural parameters, particularly when the number of variables covered is large and the size of the sample observations is small.

Several alternative formulations were estimated for each function. Ultimately equations were chosen on the basis of economic and statistical criteria like appropriateness of the sign according to *a priori* theory, coefficient of determination adjusted for degrees of freedom (R^2), Durbin-Watson statistics (DW and H), standard errors (SEE) and t-tests. In addition, the ability of the equations in explaining the turning points was also considered. The empirical results are discussed below.

Government Operations

The major constituents of government operations that form a part of the budget are studied here. These fiscal variables which are combined aggregates of the Central and state governments, have direct and indirect links with other sectors in the model, particularly with money supply, output and prices. The constituents considered for the analysis are government's current expenditure (GCE), current revenue (GR), capital expenditure (GKE) and capital receipts (GCR). Current expenditure and revenue are sought to be explained by behavioural equations. Real capital expenditure is exogenous and is later used as a policy variable. Capital receipts of the Government consist of domestic market borrowings, domestic non-market borrowings and borrowings from abroad. The movements in the first two components are sought to be explained endogenously. Borrowings from commercial banks are related to aggregate deposits. Borrowings from abroad is assumed to be exogenous to the system.

Current Expenditure and Revenues

Current expenditures of Government include consumption expenditure, interest payments and subsidies. It is specified that desired real current expenditures (GCER) are a function of real economic activity and that actual current expenditures adjust to the desired level with a lag. Net National Product (NPP) at factor cost is taken as the indicator of economic activity. The function is estimated in real terms as:

$$\text{Ln GCER} = -4.524 + \underset{(2.366)}{0.956}\ \text{Ln YR} + \underset{(3.860)}{0.380}\ \text{Ln GCER}_{-1}$$

$\bar{R}^2 = 0.970 \quad DW = 1.899$

The estimated income elasticity is 0.96 in the short run and 1.54 in the long run. Aggregate income shows a significant positive impact on current expenditures.

As revenues are targeted in nominal terms, the variable chosen is at current prices, explained as a function of national income, also at current prices. Since lags are likely in the collection of revenues, a partial adjustment framework is specified.

$$\text{Ln GR} = -1.069 + \underset{(3.031)}{0.430}\ (\text{YR*P}) + \underset{(4.977)}{0.619}\ \text{Ln GR}_{-1}$$

$\bar{R}^2 = 0.998 \quad DW = 1.304$

The long-run elasticity with respect to nominal income in this relationship is 1.13. The government revenue function in real terms (GRR) was also estimated so that a comparison could be made with the government current expenditure equation estimated in real terms.

$$\text{Ln GRR} = -4.136 + \underset{(4.522)}{0.964}\ \text{Ln YR} + \underset{(2.293)}{0.327}\ \text{Ln GRR}_{-1}$$

$\bar{R}^2 = 0.974 \quad DW = 1.928$

The long-run elasticity with respect to real income in this relationship is 1.43. The empirical evidence shows that both in the short run and in the long run there is a positive correspondence between income and revenue on the one hand and between income and current expenditures on the other. When measured in real terms the long-run elasticity with respect to income is higher in the case of expenditure than in the case of revenue.

It is also seen that the gap between total expenditure (comprising current as well as capital expenditures) and revenue in nominal terms is (RG) positively related to nominal income.

$$\text{Ln RG} = -3.599 + \underset{(30.196)}{1.122}\ \text{LnY}$$

$$\bar{R}^2 = 0.975 \qquad DW = 0.607$$

This implies a widening resource gap as nominal income increases.[3]

Capital Account

The real expenditure on capital account by the public sector (GKER) is policy determined. Total public expenditure is derived as the sum GKER.P + GCER.P. The difference between total expenditures and current revenues represents the fiscal resource gap (RG) to be financed by domestic and external borrowings. That portion of the resource gap uncovered by the government's total borrowings (GCR) is financed through RBI credit to Government. Leaving external borrowings as exogenous, domestic borrowings are estimated within the model as follows:

For its domestic borrowings, Government relies on three main sources.

(i) Investments in Government securities by banks (GBBS);

(ii) Investments in Government securities by financial institutions such as LIC, UTI, etc (GBNB); and

(iii) Other non-market funds (GNMB) comprising small savings, provident fund, other deposits and reserves, special borrowings from RBI accounts, compulsory deposits and miscellaneous capital receipts.

The holdings of government securities by banks is determined by their aggregate deposits and the Statutory Liquidity Ratio. A dummy variable was included to take into account the unusual increase in the banks' investments in government securities in 1977-78.

$$GBBS = -4618.810 + 0.231D + 19584.150\ SLRG + 157.850\ DYB$$
$$(65.569) \qquad (3.528) \qquad (0.424)$$

$\bar{R}^2 = 0.996 \qquad DW = 1.495$

As the Statutory Liquidity Ratio moved within a very narrow range during this period, its exclusion would not affect the relationship in flow form. Hence change in the banks' holding of government securities is directly related to change in aggregate deposits.

$$\Delta GBBS = 164.219 + 0.293\Delta D$$
$$(8.066)$$

$\bar{R}^2 = 0.744 \qquad DW = 2.089$

Borrowings from other financial institutions are determined by growth in their aggregate resources. As the regressions to explain this variable (GBNB) did not yield satisfactory results, it is not estimated by a behavioural equation. In the simulation exercises, the ratio of these borrowings to the resource gap as observed in the historical situation was used.

The third component of government's domestic borrowings (GNMB) is a composite variable. National income (Y) at current prices is the major determinant of this variable. A dummy variable (DYNM) was included to capture the unusual variation in the series observed in some years. The following equation estimates government's non-market borrowings:

$$GNMB = -881.683 + 0.076Y - 930.873\ DYNM.$$
$$(18.219) \qquad (1.645)$$

$\bar{R}^2 = 0.939 \qquad DW = 0.744$

The marginal coefficient of the impact of an increase in income on small savings, provident fund, etc, is estimated to be 0.076. Even though the overall fit is good, since the year-to-year errors are high, this equation was also dropped in the policy simulations, to be replaced by the actual ratio of non-market borrowings to the resource gap during each year of the sample period.

Money Supply

Monetary base (RM) is determined through the identity connecting reserve money to its sources. In this model, all components of reserve money except Reserve Bank credit to Government (RBCG) are treated as exogenous. Reserve Bank credit to Government is endogenously determined by the behaviour of the fiscal deficit.

The supply of money (M_3) is related to reserve money (RM).

$$M_3 = -4390.722 + 3.249\ RM$$
$$(87.520)$$
$$\bar{R}^2 = 0.997 \qquad DW = 2.203$$

The explanatory power of the equation is good. The estimated values of M_3 are close to the actual values for the sample period except for one or two years. The marginal reserve money multiplier is estimated to be 3.2.

The money multiplier, as it is called, is affected by a behavioural characteristic which is the ratio of currency to deposits and a policy variable, the Cash Reserve Ratio. It has been argued that the money multiplier depends not only on the Cash Reserve Ratio and the ratio of currency to deposits but also on the demand for credit. Addition to reserve money leads only to an increase in the credit creating capacity of the commercial banks. The actual expansion would depend upon the demand for credit which would in turn be related to the behaviour of the real sector. While this position is theoretically valid, it is to be noted that in the Indian context, with an administered structure of interest rates with varying rates of interest for different activities, demand for credit is not a binding constraint. The rates of interest charged on some activities are well below the market rates and demand for credit at those rates of interest is highly elastic. In fact, the Indian commercial banks do not voluntarily hold any excess reserves and whatever excess reserves they may be holding are involuntary, due to inadequate facilities for quick transmission of funds from far flung branches.

For a proper estimation of the relationship between money supply and reserve money, at the minimum it is necessary to adjust the series on reserve money for changes in the Cash Reserve Ratio. In fact, such an adjusted series are found to give a better explanation of changes in money stock particularly when quarterly data are used[4]. However, since we are dealing with annual time series, adjustments have not been made for changes in Cash Reserve Ratio. But in the simulation of the model, money supply is endogenously derived as $M_{3t} = m_t.RM_t$ where 'm_t', the actual multiplier observed from year to year, is treated as an exogenous variable in the system. The monetary base itself is determined as a sum of its components.

Incremental bank deposits are estimated as a linear function of changes in money stock,

$$\Delta D = -33.63 + 0.791\ \Delta M_3$$
$$(0.473)\quad (66.960)$$

$\bar{R}^2 = 0.995 \qquad DW = 2.020$

CONCEPTUAL DIAGRAM OF THE MODEL

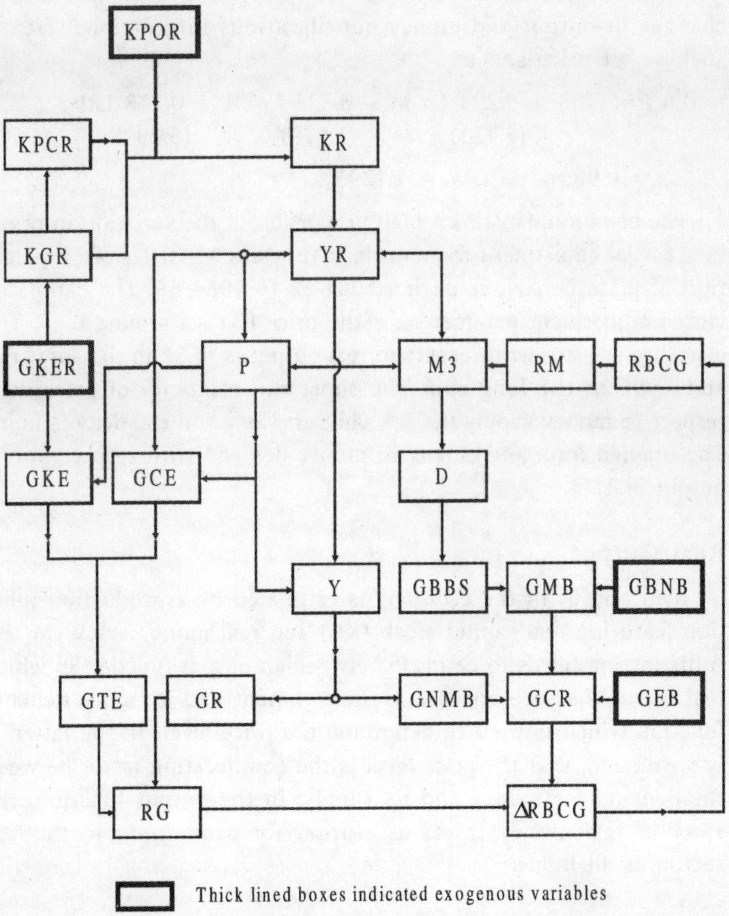

Demand for Money and Price Level

The money demand function rewritten as a price equation p = f (YR, M_3, P_{-1}) was estimated in several forms. The general price level is represented by the average of the monthly index of wholesale prices.

The price level responds positively to monetary expansion and falls with higher real output. The lagged price variable serves as a proxy for price expectations besides incorporating the lagged effect of output and money supply on the current year's price. A dummy variable was introduced to take into account the unusually high inflation observed in 1973-74 and 1974-75, as a result not only of changes in output and money but of various international factors such as oil price shocks.

$$\begin{aligned} \text{Ln } P = 2.768 &+ 0.294 \text{ Ln } M_3 - 0.525 \text{ LnYR} + 0.718 \text{ LnP}_{-1} \\ &\quad\;\; (7.711) \qquad\qquad (1.879) \qquad\quad (6.299) \end{aligned}$$

$$\bar{R}^2 = 0.995 \qquad DW = 2.129$$

The equation explains a high proportion of the variation in prices in a partial adjustment framework. It provides a satisfactory explanation of price behaviour during 1961-62 to 1984-85. The estimated lagged adjustment parameter for the price level is around 0.28. The elasticity of price with respect to real output is -0.52 in the short run and -1.96 in the long run. The short run elasticity of price with respect to money supply is 0.29 while the long-run elasticity is unity. The implied income elasticity of money demand with respect to real output is 1.74.

Real Output

Real output in the economy is estimated by a production function featuring real capital stock (KR) and real money stock (M_3/P). A distinction needs to be made between an output function in which real money balance appears as an argument and a money demand function which is used to determine the price level. In the latter, it is postulated, that the price level is the equilibrating factor between the demand for money and its supply. In the output function, the stock of real money enters as a proxy for bank credit to the real sector, as an input.

$$\text{Ln YR} = 4.938 + \underset{(5.931)}{0.294 \text{ Ln KR}_{-1}} + \underset{(3.781)}{0.234 \text{ Ln } (M_3/P)_{-1}}$$

$\bar{R}^2 = 0.972 \qquad DW = 1.498$

The equation specifies that output responds to the explanatory variables with a lag. The elasticity of output is found to be 0.29 with respect to real capital stock and 0.23 with respect to real money balances. Disaggregated production functions might have been able to better capture the impact of real money on output.

Capital Stock

Capital stock in the economy is disaggregated into three sectors, *viz.*, public sector (KGR), private corporate sector (KPCR) and private non-corporate sector (KPOR). Investment in the public sector is related to the real capital expenditure of Government. The function estimates additions to capital stock as

$$\text{KGR} = -925.020 + \underset{(15.357)}{1.088 \text{ GKER}} + \underset{(0.174)}{3.428 \text{ DYKG}}$$

$\bar{R}^2 = 0.929 \qquad DW = 1.65$

The role of the public sector is that of a catalyst for development. Hence, the impact of public sector's capital expenditure which consists primarily of investment in infrastructure is conducive to a climate of greater economic activity – including real investment in the private corporate sector. Thus, capital stock in the private corporate sector is explained in terms of the previous year's output and by investment activity in the public sector.

$$\text{Ln KPCR} = 0.442 + \underset{(2.451)}{0.444 \text{ Ln KGR}} + \underset{(0.792)}{0.071 \text{ Ln YR}_{-1}} + \underset{(2.030)}{0.377 \text{ Ln KPCR}_{-1}}$$

$\bar{R}^2 = 0.998 \qquad DW = 1.286$

The explanatory power of the equation is good but the coefficient of lagged output is statistically insignificant. The elasticity with respect to previous year's output is 0.07 in the short run and 0.11 in the long run. The elasticity of private sector capital stock with respect to the capital stock of the public sector is estimated as 0.44 in the short run and 0.71 in the long run.

There are different views on the question whether public investment in India crowds out investment in the private sector. The impact of public sector in this model is to be viewed as the impact of investment in critical areas. By strengthening infrastructure, it acts as a stimulus to the private sector.

Modelling investment behaviour in the non-corporate (unorganised or households) sector, which consists of both households and non-corporate bodies including agriculture, is a difficult task. Accordingly, investment in this sector is treated as exogenous.

Stability of Structural Coefficients

The behavioural equations of the model are OLS estimates with annual data for 24 years. Earlier regressions obtained with slightly different sets of data were useful to examine the sensitivity of the parameters to small shifts in the data. On the whole, the structural coefficients of the model are stable, except in the case of four behavioural functions in the fiscal sector. In particular, the equations relating to public sector borrowings (GBBS and GNMB) did not perform well according to this test.

V. THE MODEL AND ITS PERFORMANCE

The analysis in the preceding section shows that the individual behavioural equations satisfy most criteria of goodness of fit. The signs of the estimated parameters are in accordance with a prior theoretical expectations. Now we examine the model as a complete entity.

Simultaneous Solution

In this model of the Indian economy covering the period 1961-62 to 1984-85, there are 20 relationships specified in terms of 10 behavioural functions and 10 identities. The latter were necessary to complete the structure of the system. The predetermined set comprises 15 exogenous and 10 lagged endogenous variables. The model with all the estimated equations and identities is given in Table 1.

To evaluate the performance of the model as a whole, both static and dynamic solutions were obtained. The actual and estimated values of the endogenous variables were then compared and the Root Mean Squared Percentage Errors (RMSPE) and the Mean Absolute Percentage Errors (MAPE) were computed. For a static solution, the

Table 1

Complete Model Structure

	Equation	$\bar{R}^2$	DW	SEE	Mean
1.	$\text{Ln YR} = \underset{(24.241)}{4.93795} + \underset{(3.781)}{0.23395}\ \text{LnM3}_{-1} - \underset{(3.781)}{0.23395}\ \text{LnP}_{-1} + \underset{(5.931)}{0.29408}\ \text{LnKR}_{-1}$	0.972	1.50	0.04	10.52
2.	$\text{Ln GCER} = \underset{(3.570)}{-4.54153} + \underset{(3.860)}{0.95552}\ \text{LnYR} + \underset{(2.366)}{0.38028}\ \text{LnGCER}_{-1}$	0.970	1.90	0.07	8.86
3.	$\text{GCE} = \text{GCER} * \text{P}$	—	—	—	—
4.	$\text{GKE} = \overline{\text{GKER}} * \text{P}$	—	—	—	—
5.	$\text{GTE} = \text{GKE} + \text{GCE}$	—	—	—	—
6.	$\text{Ln GR} = \underset{(2.511)}{-1.06916} + \underset{(4.977)}{0.61906}\ \text{LnGR}_{-1} + \underset{(3.031)}{0.43029}\ \text{Ln (YR.*P)}$	0.998	1.30 1.58*	0.04	9.92
7.	$\Delta\text{GBBS} = \underset{(0.955)}{-164.21902} + \underset{(8.067)}{0.29269}\ \Delta\text{D}$	0.744	2.09	990.43	804.39
8.	$\text{GMB} = \Delta\text{GBBS} + \overline{\text{GBNB}}$	—	—	—	—
9.	$\text{GNMB} = \underset{(2.587)}{-881.68394} + \underset{(18.219)}{0.07624}\text{Y} - \underset{(1.645)}{930.87338}\ \overline{\text{DYNM}}$	0.939	0.74	911.66	3877.61
10.	$\text{GCR} = \overline{\text{GMB}} + \overline{\text{GNMB}} + \overline{\text{GEB}}$	—	—	—	—

(Contd...)

(...Contd...)

	$\bar{R}^2$	DW	SEE	Mean
11. $\Delta RBCG = GTE - GR - GCR$	—	—	—	—
12. $RM = RBCG + \overline{RBCC} + \overline{RBFA} + \overline{GCL} + \overline{RNML}$	—	—	—	—
13. $M3 = \overline{m}_t \; RM$	—	—	—	—
14. $\Delta D = -33.62973 + 0.79082 \; \Delta M3$ (0.473) (66.960)	0.995	2.02	242.46	3309.39
15. $LnP = 2.76749 + 0.29404 \; LnM3 - 0.52519 \; LnYR + 0.71829 \; LnP_{-1} + 0.05676 \; Ln \; \overline{DYP}$ (1.105) (7.711) (1.879) (6.299) (4.345)	0.995	2.13 -0.65*	0.04	0.32
16. $NID = 0.15279 + 0.84366 \; P$ (8.001) (80.037)	0.997	1.23	0.04	1.50
17. $Y = YR * NID$	—	—	—	—
18. $\Delta KGR = -925.02019 + 1.08759 \; \overline{GKER} + 3.42818 \; \overline{DYKG}$ (2.736) (15.357) (0.174)	0.929	1.65	351.16	3549.70
19. $Ln \; KPCR = 0.44172 + 0.44351 \; LnKGR + 0.07057 \; LnYR_{-1} + 0.37710 \; LnKPCR_{-1}$ (0.777) (2.451) (0.792) (2.030)	0.998	1.28 3.02*	0.02	9.46
20. $KR = KGR + KPCR + \overline{KPOR}$	—	—	—	—

Notes : Exogenous variables are indicated by bars.
Figures in brackets are t-statistics.
*: Durbin's h-statistic.

actual lagged values of the endogenous variables are used in the set of predetermined variables to solve for the values of the current endogenous variables. Therefore, each year's solution is independent of the previous year's estimation. The static simulation provides a single period, short-run simultaneous solution of the model without any carry over effects of errors from the previous years' estimates. The dynamic solution, on the other hand, is a more stringent method of evaluation. Here, the current year's solution vector of endogenous variables is linked to the estimated values of the earlier years. It thus provides a dynamic solution path of the endogenous variables over the entire period of simulation. It is to be noted that in dynamic solutions, errors get compounded over time. A large error in the estimation of any endogenous variable in any year gets transmitted throughout the system and affects the magnitude of errors in all the subsequent years.

Evaluation

Graphs 1 to 4 present actual observations in their model estimates. Most of the turning points are caught by the simulated paths of the macroeconomic aggregates. The residuals indicate that the simultaneous solution is not free from bias. For some variable, the size of the errors in the dynamic solution is substantially larger than in the static solution as seen from the MAPE and RMSPE statistics (Appendix 2). This is the result of the cumulative nature of the residuals over the dynamic simulation time path, to which reference was made earlier.

The RMSPEs in ten dynamic predictions are less than four per cent in the case of variables (e.g., output and capital stock) in the real sector. The errors vary from five to six per cent for prices, government expenditure and revenues. In the case of the different components of government's domestic borrowings, the errors are higher; and these are transmitted to the estimates of RBI credit to Government (RBCG), reserve money (RM) and hence money supply (M_3). The dynamic simulation errors in the monetary sector are of the order of 10 per cent.

On the whole, the model performs well. During the simulation period (1975-76 to 1984-85) average annual monetary expansion was 18.39 per cent, output growth was 4.02 per cent and inflation

Graph 1

Real Output (YR)

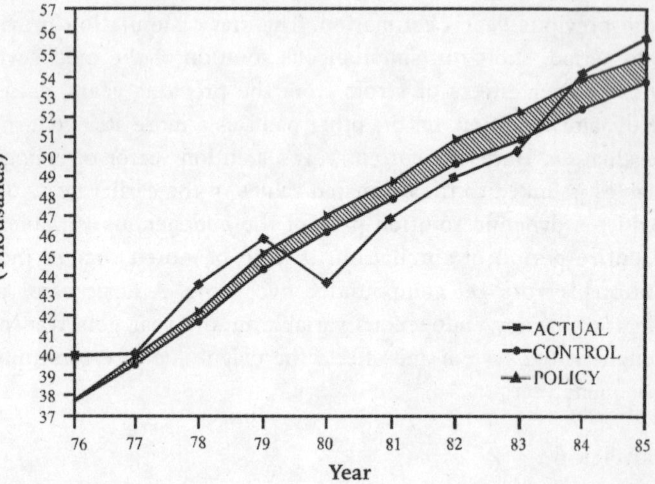

Graph 2

Money Supply (M3)

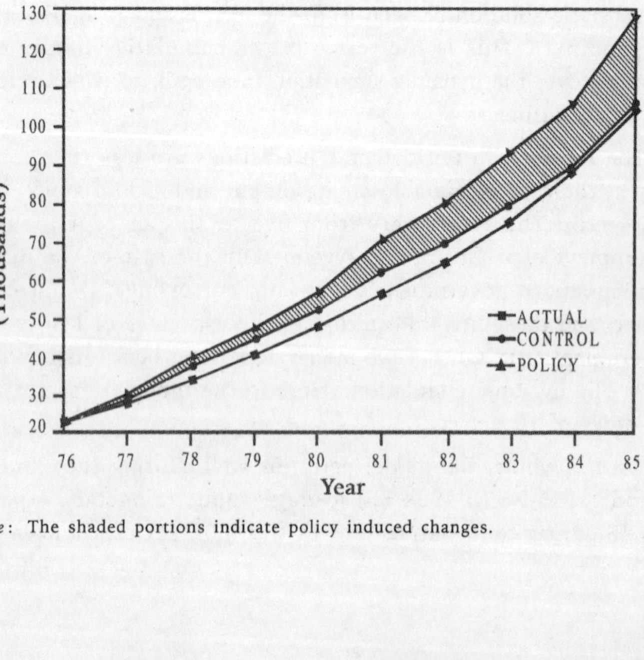

Note: The shaded portions indicate policy induced changes.

Graph 3

Price Level (P)

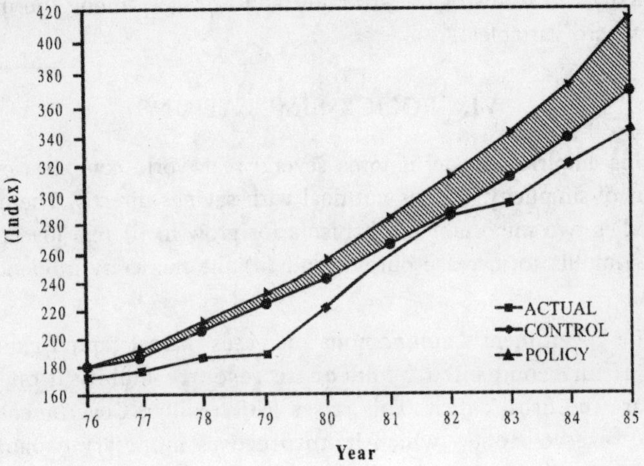

Graph 4

Resource Gap (RG)

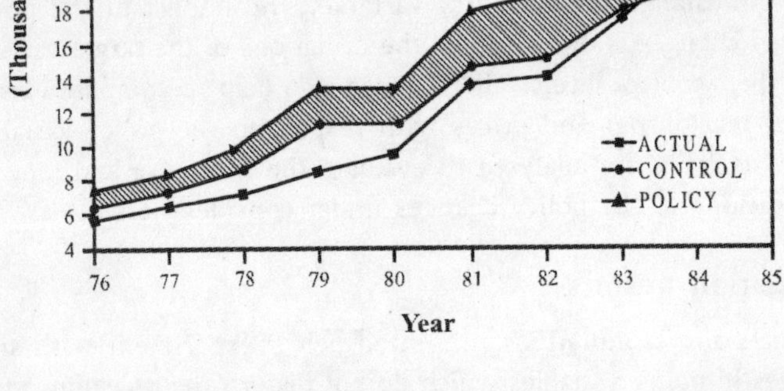

Note: The shaded portions indicate policy induced changes.

was 7.90 per cent. The dynamic solution of the model for this period estimated the three corresponding growth rates as 18.40 per cent, 4.17 per cent and 8.28 per cent, indicating a close correspondence to the actuals in terms of the structure and linkages among the important macro variables.

VI. POLICY SIMULATIONS

This empirical model ignores several real world complications in favour of simplicity. It does not deal with savings directly. The model embodies two important mechanisms for growth: (i) real investment as a stimulus to increase output; and (ii) the monetary influence on output.

The government's autonomous increases in real capital expenditure, if unaccompanied by adequate resource mobilisation, will increase the fiscal deficit. This raises RBI credit to Government and hence reserve money, which in turn causes monetary expansion. Simultaneously, the real sector experiences a policy-induced growth in output. Higher output would also increase government revenues. The inflationary impact of an increase in money supply consequent upon a rise in government's real capital expenditure is counteracted to the extent output increases.

In the dynamic solution, the lags in the model begin to operate the dual effects of monetary expansion- *viz.*, output growth (eq. 1) and price increase (eq. 16) triggered by the exogenous policy shock, interact within the partial adjustment framework built into the various equations in the system. Considerable importance attaches to the ultimate changes (gains or losses) in the target variables as a result of a unit change in the policy variable. The impact of the policy-induced changes is measured by the deviations of the target variables from their control levels. The changes also help to compute elasticities of real output and prices with respect to the policy variables. These statistics are analysed to evaluate the short run and long run implications of the policy changes under consideration.

Simulation Results

The policy simulations presented below experiment with small changes in policy variables which do not disturb the prevailing structure. To begin with, the base run is obtained with all the exogenous variables at their original levels. In this environment, the model is allowed to work through its dynamic time path for 10 years beginning 1975-76 to provide estimates of the endogenous variables (control solution). In order to examine the effect of any policy (say, higher public capital expenditure), it is necessary to raise the policy variable above its original control level and to simulate its impact on the economy, keeping all other exogenous conditions unaltered. Having altered only the exogenous policy variable under *ceteris paribus* conditions, the model is once again allowed to run through the same temporal path to yield a new set of estimates (policy solution) of the endogenous variables. The difference between the Control and the Policy solution is attributed to the policy under investigation.

Three types of simulation techniques were attempted. Under the first two techniques, all the variables in the control solution take their historic values over the sample period. The policy simulation in the first case is a single exogenous shock administered once in the base year. The effects of this shock are then allowed to work through the system for 10 years. The second alternative is a 10 per cent increase in the policy variable above its historic level each year – that is, a repeated shock during each year of the simulation period. The third alternative consists of a base run wherein every exogenous variable is maintained at its mean level throughout the period. In the policy run the exogenous shock is a sustained increase of 10 per cent above the mean level of the selected policy variable.

All the three simulation techniques yielded similar results. The simulations discussed in the analysis that follows are of the second kind-dynamic runs over the historic time path, with the policy variable raised 10 per cent over its historic value every year from 1975-76 to 1984-85.

Increased Government Capital Expenditure

Real capital expenditure of the Government (GKER) is an exogenous variable in the model. By varying this policy variable, its impact on the economy was studied. A sustained shock of 10 per cent above its level during the sample period was administered to the model. All other exogenous variables were maintained at the control level.

The effect of higher real capital expenditure on real output depends on the responsiveness of output to higher capital stock, credit availability and also on the relative speed with which prices escalate. The pressure on prices is linked to the monetary expansion caused by deficit financing which becomes necessary to finance a part of the higher level of capital expenditure. When prices rise, the level of nominal capital expenditure also rises to maintain the policy determined level of real government investments. As total nominal expenditures of Government increase faster than revenues, the resource gap widens, requiring further borrowing from the Reserve Bank.

Three target variables, *viz*, real output, money and prices which are of prime importance, have been chosen to assess the impact of policy changes. One of the intermediate variables to be monitored is the incremental resource gap. Besides the direct impact of the increase in the capital expenditure on output, the target variables will also be influenced by the extent to which the resource gap widens and how this resource gap is financed. In this simulation experiment, two components of government borrowings, *viz.*, borrowings from other financial institutions (GBNB) and non-market borrowing (GNMB) were assumed to maintain the historical shares relative to the resource gap. Commercial banks' credit to Government increases endogenously with deposit expansion. The uncovered deficit is met by RBI credit to Government which results in higher monetary expansion. Graphs 1 to 4 show the dynamic paths of selected target variables during 10 years. Important multipliers estimated from the policy simulations are given in Table 2.

The immediate impact of this policy is an increase in monetary expansion by 1.92 per cent and a half a per cent increase in prices, both over the base level. There is no initial impact on output since both credit and capital stock act with a lag of one year. Within two years, money supply expands by 3.98 per cent and real output increases marginally by 0.32 per cent. The net effect on prices is an increase of 1.28 per cent. When the policy is allowed to work through the system for 10 years, the long-term changes in the target variables are monetary expansion of 14.68 per cent, output higher by 1.66 per cent and inflation higher by 7.01 per cent. The annual average elasticities of money, output and prices with respect to GKER are 1.47, 0.17 and 0.70 respectively. The results indicate that in the short run approximately 23.4 per cent of the resource gap is met by net RBI credit to Government. In the long run the resource gap which is 23.2 per cent larger than the control level is met to the extent of 22.3 per cent by net RBI credit to Government.

Table 2

Effects of Sustained 10 per cent Increase in GKER

Target Variable	*Annual Average Percentage Increases*		
	Impact	*Short Run*	*Long Run*
Real output (YR)	—	0.32	1.66
Money supply (M_3)	1.92	3.98	14.68
Price level (P)	0.57	1.28	7.01
Resource gap (RG)	13.80	14.76	23.18
Real capital stock (KR)	0.39	0.64	2.09

We ran several alternative simulations, varying the proportion in which the resource gap will be met by RBI credit to Government. For example, if the assumption that non-market borrowings of the Government meets a fixed proportion of the resource gap is relaxed, and if they are allowed to increase in relation to income according to equation 6, the resource gap increases over the base level by 20.4 per cent in the short run and by 56.1 per cent in the long run. In such a situation, 48.9 per cent of the resource gap is met by net RBI credit to Government in the short run and 32.8 per cent in the long run. As a consequence, while real output increases by 3.8 per cent, money supply increases by 51.2 per cent and the price level by about 24 per cent. The implication is that if a larger proportion of the resource gap of the Government is met by borrowing from the Reserve Bank, the trade-off between output and prices considerably worsens.

Sustained Increase in Money Supply

One of the aims of this model was to investigate the simultaneous influence of money supply on real output and prices. To measure the influence of monetary expansion in isolation, the model was simulated with the monetary and fiscal sectors exogenised (control solution). Then money supply – now a policy variable – was raised by 10 per cent above its historic level during 1975-76 to 1984-85. The resultant changes in real output and prices as percentage deviations from base level were measured in a dynamic framework (Table 3).

Table 3

Effects of Sustained 10 per cent Increase in M_3

Target Variable	*Annual Average Percentage Increases*		
	Impact	*Short Run*	*Long Run*
Real output	—	0.81	0.69
Price level	2.64	3.49	7.04
Real capital stock	—	—	0.01

As in the previous case, the immediate impact of monetary expansion is an increase in prices. A positive effect on real output is noticed in two years. The average annual increases over a decade are: real income higher by 0.69 per cent and a price rise of 7.04 per cent.

The model shows that prices are highly sensitive to monetary shocks. Because the trade-off in terms of inflation is extremely high, sustained monetary expansion is not a viable policy tool. As a consequence of the strong inflationary spiral, the impact of the policy on real output gets weakened in the long run. Other studies on developing countries have also reached a similar conclusion.[5] The size of the increase in NNP observed in the initial two years begins to decline gradually, so that the overall increase, averaged over the ten year sample period, is lower than in the short run.

This paper presents an econometric model of the Indian economy which emphasises the interrelationships among money, output and prices. The link between the monetary and the fiscal sectors has been explicitly modelled with the stock of money varying endogenously with fiscal deficits. The empirical results show that the price effects of an increase in money supply are stronger than the output effects. Since government revenue collections do not keep pace with government expenditures as nominal incomes rise, the resource gap widens during a period of continued price increases. The policy simulations show that while a substantial increase in government capital expenditures increases output, its impact on output and prices also depends on the extent of the resource gap met by borrowing from the Reserve Bank. As the proportion of the resource gap met by borrowing from the Reserve Bank increases, the trade-off between output and prices worsens sharply.

Appendix 1

A: Endogenous Variables

Sr. No	*Symbol*	*Description*
1	YR	Real * National Income (NNP at factor cost)
2	GCER	Government's Real Current Account Expenditure (Centre + states)
3	GCE	Current Account Expenditure of Government
4	GKE	Capital Expenditure of the Government (nominal)
5	GTE	Total Expenditure of the Government
6	GR	Current Account Revenues of the Government
7	GBBS	Borrowings of Government from Banks (stock)
8	GMB	Market Borrowings of Government
9	GNMB	Non-market Borrowings of Government
10	GCR	Capital Receipts of Government
11	RBCG	RBI Credit to Government (last Friday of March)
12	RM	Reserve Money
13	M3	Money Stock (last Friday of March)
14	D	Aggregate Deposits with Banks
15	NID	Price Deflator for National Income
16	P	Wholesale Price Index of All Commodities
17	KR	Gross Real* Capital Stock: Aggregate
18	KPCR	Gross Real* Capital Stock: Private Corporate Sector
19	KGR	Gross Real* Capital Stock: Public Sector
20	Y	National Income at Current Prices

* Base 1970-71

(Contd...)

(...Contd...)

B: Exogenous Variables

Sr. No	*Symbol*	*Description*
1.	GEB	External Borrowings of the Government
2.	RBCC	Reserve Bank Credit to Commercial and Co-operative Banks, Commercial Sector and NABARD (last Friday)
3.	RBFA	Reserve Bank's Foreign Exchange Assets (last Friday)
4.	GCL	Government's Current Liabilities to the Public
5.	RNML	Reserve Bank's Net Non-monetary Liabilities
6.	KPOR	Gross Capital Stock in the Unorganised Private Sector (at 1970-71 prices)
7.	DRBS	Change in Reserve Bank's Absorption of Dated Securities (last Friday)
8.	GKER	Capital Expenditures of the Government
9.	SLRG	Statutory Liquidity Ratio: Holding of Government Securities by Banks (the ratio is adjusted to omit investment in other approved securities)
10.	GBNB	Borrowings of Government from Financial Institutions other than Banks
11.	m	Money Multiplier
12.	DYB	Dummy Variable for Banks' Investment in Government Securities (1977-78)
13.	DYNM	Dummy Variable for Non-Market Government Borrowings (1967-68, 1974-75 and 1979-80)
14.	DYKG	Dummy Variable for Capital Stock in Public Sector (1962-63, 1965-66, 1968-69,1974-75 and 1979-80)
15.	DYP	Dummy Variable for High Inflation (1973-74 and 1974-75)

Appendix 2

*Estimation Errors**

Endogenous Variable	*Mean Absolute Percentage Error (MAPE)*		*Root Mean Square Percentage Error (RMSPE)*	
	Static	*Dynamic*	*Static*	*Dynamic*
Output				
YR	3.287	3.289	3.979	3.736
Y	1.586	6.141	2.263	7.531
Government Operations				
GTE	2.356	6.136	2.878	7.628
GR	1.709	5.762	2.316	6.154
GCR	6.526	13.333	8.930	16.307
Monetary Sectors				
RBCG	3.223	7.662	4.037	9.005
RM	2.566	6.064	3.079	6.869
M3	2.566	6.064	3.079	6.869
D	2.299	5.013	2.618	5.952
Prices				
P	4.421	7.418	4.984	8.972
NID	3.965	7.273	4.523	7.984
Capital Stock				
KR	0.268	0.665	0.336	0.813
KGR	0.449	1.356	0.596	1.481
KPCR	1.224	1.819	1.390	2.099

* Simultaneous solution for the period 1975-76 to 1984-85.

* The authors are grateful to K. Krishnamurti and Anupam Basu for their detailed comments on several aspects of this study. Special thanks are due to Y. S. R. Sarma for his initial contributions to the structuring of the model.

Notes

1. In this context, it is interesting to note Friedman's comment: "The general subject of division of changes in money income between price and quantity badly needs more investigation. None of our leading economists has much to say about it." Milton Friedman, *The Optimum Quantity of Money (Macmillan,* 1969), p 279.
2. Peter. S. Sephton, 'Money in the Production Function Revisited', *Applied Economics*, July 1988, pp 853-860.
3. For a similar conclusion see K. Krishnamurty, 'Inflation and Growth: A Model for India' in Krishnamurty and Pandit, *Macro Econometric Modelling of the Indian Economy*, (Hindustan Publishing Corporation, 1985) pp 39-42.
4. C. Rangarajan and Anoop Singh, 'Reserve Money: Concepts and Policy Implications for India', *Reserve Bank of India Occasional papers*, June 1984.
5. See Gerard. F. Adams and Vial Joaquin, 'Comparisons of Macro Econometric Models of Developing Economies', *Regional Seminar on Interlinked Country Model System*, New Delhi, February 27-March 1, 1989.

References

Agarwal, R, (1970): *An Econometric Model of India*, 1948-61.

Ahluwalia, I. J., (1979): 'Behaviour of Prices and Output in India: A Macroeconomic Aggregates', *RBI Occasional Papers*.

Arif, R. R., (1985): 'Differential Effects of Exogenous Factors on Macro Economic Aggregates', *RBI Occasional Papers*.

Bhattacharya, B. B., (1985): *Public Expenditure, Inflation and Growth: A Macro-Economic Analysis for India*, Oxford University Press, New Delhi.

Chakrabarty, T. K., (1987): 'Macro Econometric Model of the Indian Economy' *RBI Occasional Papers*.

Desai, M. J., (1974): 'Macro Econometric Models of India: A Survey' *Sankhya*, Series B.

Gupta, G. S., (1972): 'A Monetary Policy Model for India' *Sankhya*, Series B.

Jadhav, Narendra and Singh, Balwant, (1990): 'Fiscal Monetary Dynamic Nexus in India: An Econometric Model', *Economic and Political Weekly*.

Kannan, R., (1988): 'An Econometric Model of India's Balance of Payments', RBI, mimeo.

Krishna, Krishnamurty, Pandit and Sharma, (1989): 'Macro Econometric Modelling in India: A Selective Review of Recent Research' Seminar on Inter-linked Country Model System, New Delhi.

Krishnamurty, K and Pandit, V., (1985): *Macro Econometric Modelling of the Indian Economy: Studies on Inflation and Growth*, Hindustan Publishing Corporation.

Madhur, S., Nayak, P. and Roy, P., (1982): 'The Budget, 'Money and Credit', *Economic and Political Weekly*.

Pandit, V., (1984): 'Macro-Economic Adjustments in a Developing Economy: A Medium-Term Model of Output and Prices in India', (mimeo).

Pani, P. K., (1984): 'An Econometric Model of Indian Economy, with Special Reference to Output, Demand and Prices', *RBI Occasional Papers*.

Rangarajan, C., (1982): 'Agricultural Growth and Industrial Performance of India', Research Report 33, International Food Policy Research Institute.

Rao, D. C, Venkatachalam, T. R and Vasudevan, A., (1981): 'A Short-Term Model to Forecast Monetary Aggregates', *RBI Occasional Papers.*

Sarma, Y. S. R., (1982) 'Government Deficit, Money Supply and Inflation in India', *RBI Occasional Papers.*

Srivastava, D. K., (1981) 'Policy Simulations with a Macro Economic Model of the Indian Economy' *Journal of Policy Modelling.*

Sundararajan, V. and Subhash Thakur, (1980) 'Public Investment, Crowding-Out and Growth: A Dynamic Model Applied to India and Korea, *IMF Staff Papers.*

14

Monetary Policy in a Developing Economy

The Indian Experience

Developments in Monetary Policy

Developments in monetary policy closely mirror the changes in overall economic policy. The decade of 1990s has seen far reaching changes in India's economic policy. The content and approach to economic policy underwent a sea change. The country has become a more open economy. The roles of State and market are getting redefined. There is a common thread running through the various measures introduced since 1991 and that is to improve the productivity and efficiency of the system. This is sought to be achieved by imparting a greater element of competition in the system. It is in this context that monetary policy in India acquired a new role. Financial sector reforms, which were an integral part of the economic reforms programme, created a new institutional environment in which monetary policy had to operate.

In industrially advanced countries, after decades of eclipse, monetary policy re-emerged as a potent instrument of economic policy, in the fight against inflation in the 1980s. Issues relating to the conduct of monetary policy came to the forefront of policy debates in the 1980s. The relative importance of growth and price stability as the objective of monetary policy as well as the appropriate intermediate target of monetary policy became the focus of attention. Over the years, a consensus has emerged among the industrially advanced countries that the dominant objective of monetary policy should be price stability. Differences, however, exist among central banks even

---

K. R. Narayanan oration, November 19, 2001, Australia South Asia Research Centre (ASARC), The Australia National University.

in these countries as regards the appropriate intermediate target. While some central banks consider monetary aggregates and, therefore, monetary targeting as operationally meaningful, some others focus on the interest rate. There is also the more recent practice to ignore intermediate targets and focus on the final goal such as inflation targeting.

A similar trend regarding monetary policy is discernible in developing economies as well. Much of the early literature on development economics focused on real factors such as savings, investment and technology as mainsprings of growth. Very little attention was paid to the financial system as a contributory factor to economic growth, even though attention was paid to develop financial institutions which provide short term and long term credit. In fact, many writers felt that inflation was endemic in the process of economic growth and it was accordingly treated more as a consequence of structural imbalance than as a monetary phenomenon. However, with the accumulated evidence, it became clear that any process of economic growth in which monetary expansion was disregarded, led to inflationary pressures with a consequent impact on economic growth. Accordingly, the importance of price stability and, therefore, the need to use monetary policy for that purpose also assumed importance in developing economies. Nonetheless, the debate on the extent to which price stability should be deemed to be the overriding objective of monetary policy in such economies continues.

The Reserve Bank of India was set up in 1935. Like all central banks in developing countries, the Reserve Bank has been playing a developmental and a regulatory role. In its developmental role, the Reserve Bank focused attention on deepening and widening the financial system. It played a major part in building up appropriate financial institutions to promote savings and investment. In the realm of agricultural credit, term finance to industries and credit to export, the apex institutions that are now operating were essentially spun off from the Reserve Bank.

Strengthening and establishing new institutions to meet the country's requirements is a continuing process. The promotional role had taken the Reserve Bank into the area of credit allocation as well. Pre-emption of credit for certain sectors and that too at concessional rates of interest became part of the overall policy. Commercial banks over time had been required to provide a certain percentage of their total credit to certain sectors, which were regarded as 'priority sector'.

An active role by the Reserve Bank of India in terms of regulating the growth in money and credit became evident only after 1950s. During the 1950s, the average annual increase in the wholesale price was only 1.8 per cent. However, during the 1960s, the average annual increase was 6.2 per cent and in the 1970s, it was around 10.3 per cent. In the early years of planning, there was considerable discussion on the role of deficit financing in fostering economic growth. The First Plan said: "Judicious credit creation somewhat in anticipation of the increase in production and availability of genuine savings has also a part to play". Thus, deficit financing, which in the Indian context meant Reserve Bank credit to the Government, was assigned a place in the financing of the plan, though its quantum was to be limited to the extent it was non-inflationary. Monetary growth, particularly in the 1950s, was extremely moderate. However, as each successive plan came under a resource crunch, there was an increasing dependence on market borrowing and deficit financing. These became pronounced in the 1970s and thereafter. The single most important factor influencing the conduct of monetary policy after 1970 had been the phenomenal increase in reserve money contributed primarily by the Reserve Bank credit to the Government.

To summarise, the system as it existed at the end of 1970s was characterised by the following features. The Reserve Bank of India, as the central monetary authority prescribed all the interest rates on deposits and lending. The commercial banks were required to allocate a certain percentage of credit to what were designated as 'priority sector'. Credit to parties above a stipulated amount required prior authorisation from the central bank. After the nationalisation of major commercial banks in 1969, nearly 85 per cent of the total bank assets came under public sector. Apart from small private banks, foreign banks were allowed to operate with limited branches.

The increase in the scale of borrowing by the Government resulted in (a) the steady rise in Statutory Liquidity Ratio requiring banks to invest higher and higher proportion of their deposits in government securities which carried less than 'market rates' and (b) the Reserve Bank of India becoming a residual subscriber to securities and Treasury bills leading to monetisation of the deficit. The

Reserve Bank had, therefore, to address itself to the difficult task of neutralising to the extent possible, the expansionary impact of deficits. The increasing liquidity of the banking sector resulting from rising levels of reserve money had to be continually mopped up. The instrument of open market operations was not available for this task since the interest rates on government securities were well below 'market rates'. The task of absorbing excess liquidity in the system had to be undertaken mainly through increasing the Cash Reserve Ratio. In fact, in mid 1991, the cash reserve requirement was 25 per cent on incremental deposits. In addition, the Statutory Liquidity Ratio was 38.5 per cent. Thus, nearly 63.5 per cent of incremental deposits was pre-empted in one form or another.

In 1983, the Reserve Bank of India appointed a committee under the chairmanship of the distinguished economist Prof. Sukhamoy Chakravarty to review the working of the Indian Monetary System. I was a member of the Committee. The Committee's report covered a wide range. One of its major recommendations was to regulate money supply consistent with the expected growth rate in real income and a tolerable level of inflation. Recognising the fact that government borrowing from the Reserve Bank had been a major factor contributing to the increase in reserve money and therefore, money supply, the Committee wanted an agreement between the Central Government and the Reserve Bank on the level of monetary expansion and the extent of monetisation of the fiscal deficit. Without such coordination, the Committee felt that Reserve Bank's efforts to contain monetary expansion within the limits set by expected increase in output could become impossible. While this recommendation of the Committee was accepted in principle, it could take a concrete shape only in the Nineties.

In the wake of the economic crisis in 1991, triggered by a difficult balance of payments situation, the Government introduced far-reaching changes in India's economic policy. Monetary policy was used effectively to overcome the balance of payments crisis and promptly restore stability. An extremely tight monetary policy was put in place to reap the full benefits of the devaluation of the rupee that was announced. However, it did not stop with that. Financial sector reforms became an integral part of the new reform programme. Reform of the banking sector and capital market was intended to help and accelerate the growth of the real sector. Banking sector reforms covered a wide gamut. The most important of the reforms was the prescription of prudential norms including Capital-Adequacy Ratio. In addition, certain key changes were made with respect to monetary policy environment, which gave to commercial banks greater autonomy in relation to the management of their liabilities and assets. First and foremost, the administered structure of interest rates was dismantled step by step. Banks in India today enjoy the complete freedom to prescribe the deposit rates and interest rates on loans except in the case of very small loans and export credit. Second, the Government began borrowing at market rates of interest. The auction system was introduced both in relation to Treasury Bills and dated securities. Third, with the economic reforms emphasising a reduction in fiscal deficit, pre-emptions in the form of Cash Reserve Ratio and Statutory Liquidity Ratio were steadily brought down. Fourth, while the allocation of credit for the priority sector credit continued, the extent of cross subsidisation in terms of interest rates was considerably brought down because of the reform of the interest rate structure.

Monetary policy in the 1990s in India had to deal with several issues, some of which traditional but some totally new in the context of the increasingly open economy in which the country had to operate. In the first few years, monetary policy had to contend with the consequences of devaluation and the need to quickly restore price stability to obtain the full benefits of devaluation. While the fiscal deficit was being brought down, the question of monetisation of the deficit continued to remain an issue and a solution had to be found. This eventually led to a new agreement between Government and RBI on financing deficit. The system of ad-hoc Treasury bills, under which Government of India could replenish its cash balances by issuing Treasury bills in favour of the Reserve Bank and which had the effect of monetising deficit, was phased out. It was replaced by a system of Ways and Means advances, which had a fixed ceiling. The Reserve Bank of India continued to subscribe to the dated securities at its discretion. During 1993 and 1994, for the first time monetary policy had to deal with the monetary impact of capital inflows with the foreign exchange reserves increasing sharply from $ 9.2 billion in March 1992 to $ 25.1 billion in March 1995. In 1995-96, the change in perception with reference to exchange rate after a prolonged period of nominal exchange rate stability *vis-à-vis* the US dollar brought into play the use of monetary policy to stabilise the rupee — an entirely new experience for the central bank. Similar situations arose later on also at the time of the East Asian crisis. Monetary policy had begun to operate within a changed institutional framework, brought about by the financial sector reforms. It is this change in the institutional framework that gave a new dimension to monetary policy. New transmission channels opened up. Indirect monetary controls gradually assumed importance. With the progressive dismantling of the administered interest rate structure and the evolution of a regime of market determined interest rate on government securities, open market operations including 'repo' and 'reverse repo' operations emerged for the first time as an instrument of monetary control. Bank rate acquired a new role in the changed context. The Nineties paved the way for the emergence of monetary policy as an independent instrument of economic policy.

Monetary policy in the 1990s had also to be conducted in the context of the financial sector reforms. The need to reduce non-performing assets and to conform to the new prudential norms put the banking industry under great strain. While introducing banking sector reforms, care had to be taken to ensure that there was no compromise with the basic objectives of monetary policy.

In the post-reform period, the Indian economy has done well. Since 1992-93, the average annual growth rate of the economy in real terms has been 6.3 per cent. The average inflation rate, as measured by the Wholesale Price Index in the 1990s, has been 7.2 per cent. However, the significant fact to note is that the average inflation rate since 1996-97 has been less than five per cent. Broad money grew at an average annual rate of 17 per cent per annum. The exchange rate of the rupee in terms of US dollar has declined by 24 per cent since July 1997. This decline is smaller than what other countries in this region have experienced. The current account deficit has averaged since 1992-93 at one per cent of the GDP. The foreign exchange reserves in the country have risen from about $ 5 billion to $ 43 billion as of a recent date. These broad macroeconomic indicators show a substantial improvement in the Indian economy, even though several concerns such as slow reduction in poverty ratio and slow growth rate in agriculture persist.

Issues of Concern

Let me now focus on some of the issues which came to be debated extensively during 1990s. These issues are not specific to India or developing economies. They have been debated in the context of the developed countries also. Nevertheless, these issues which I want to highlight, have a special significance for developing countries like India.

Objective

The first question that needs to be addressed relates to the objective or objectives of monetary policy. A recurring question is whether monetary policy should be concerned with all the goals of economic policy. The issue of 'objective' has become important because of the need to provide a clear guidance to monetary policy makers. Indeed, this aspect has assumed added significance in the context of the increasing stress on the autonomy of central banks. Autonomy goes with accountability and accountability in turn requires a clear enunciation of the goals.

Since the inception of development planning, the broad objectives of India's economic policy have been to achieve a faster rate of growth, ensure reasonable degree of price stability and promote distributive justice. Working of monetary policy in India over the past several decades would reveal that monetary policy has emphasised these broad objectives of our economic policy. In one of my earlier articles, I had said, "In a broad sense the objectives of monetary policy can be no different from the over all objectives of economic policy. The broad objectives of monetary policy in India have been: (1) to maintain a reasonable degree of price stability and (2) to help accelerate the rate of economic growth. The emphasis, as between the two objectives, has changed from year to year, depending upon the conditions prevailing in that year and in the previous year."

The question of a dominant objective arises essentially because of the multiplicity of objectives and the inherent conflict among such objectives. Jan Tinbergen had argued decades ago that there should be as many instruments as there are objectives, if all objectives are to be fulfilled. Faced with multiple objectives that are equally relevant and desirable, there is always the problem of assigning to each instrument the most appropriate objective. This 'assignment rule' favours monetary policy as the most appropriate instrument to achieve the objective of price stability. It is this line of reasoning which has led to the single objective approach.

The crucial question that is being debated in India as elsewhere is whether the pursuit of the objective of price stability by monetary authorities undermines the ability of the economy to attain and sustain high growth. A considerable part of the relevant research effort has been devoted to the trade-off between economic growth and price stability. Empirical evidence on the relationship between growth and inflation in a cross-country framework is somewhat inconclusive because such studies include countries with an inflation rate as low as one to two per cent to those with inflation rates going beyond 200 to 300 per cent. These studies, however, clearly establish that growth rates become increasingly negative at higher rates of inflation.

The case of price stability as the objective of monetary policy rests on the assumption that volatility in prices creates uncertainty in decision-making. Rising prices adversely affect savings while they make speculative investments more attractive. The most important contribution of the financial system to an economy is its ability to augment savings and allocate resources more efficiently. A regime of rising prices vitiates the atmosphere for promotion of savings and allocation of investment. Apart from all these, there is a social dimension particularly in developing countries. Inflation adversely affects those who have no hedges against it and that includes all the poorer sections of the community. The fiscal consolidation also becomes easier in an environment of reasonable degree of price stability. In a period of rising prices, the gap between revenues and expenditures widens. Expenditures tend to grow at a faster rate than revenues because many components of expenditures such as employees' compensation are closely linked to variations in prices.

The question that recurs very often in the minds of the policy makers is whether in the short run, there is a trade-off between inflation and growth which can be exploited. In the industrial countries, a solution is sought through the adoption of Taylor's rule which prescribes that the signal interest rate be fixed taking into account the deviations of inflation rate from the target and actual output from its potential. In this rule, the coefficient of inflation deviation term is fixed at a level higher than unity. While the rule is intuitively appealing, there are serious problems in determining the value of the coefficients. In this context, the critical question to raise is: At what level of inflation, do adverse consequences begin to set in? It is this inflation threshold, which will provide some guidance to the policy makers. Below and around this threshold level of inflation, there is greater manoeuvrability for the policy makers to take into account other considerations. Interestingly, the Chakravarty Committee regarded the acceptable rise in prices as four per cent. This, according to the Committee, will reflect changes in relative prices necessary to attract resources to growth sectors. I have myself indicated that in the Indian context, inflation rate in the range of five to six per cent may be acceptable. There is some amount of judgment involved in this, as econometric models are not in a position to capture all the costs of inflation. This approach provides some guidance as to when policy has to become tight or to be loosened. It is also necessary for the policy makers to note that this order of inflation is higher than what the industrial countries are aiming at. This will have some implications for the exchange rate of the currency. While the open economy helps to overcome domestic supply shocks, it also imposes the burden to keep the inflation rate in alignment with other countries.

Intermediate Target

The second issue relates to the intermediate target. In India, since the mid-Eighties the, target chosen has been broad money. The Chakravarty Committee recommended a system of flexible monetary targeting. It is true that central banks in several countries in the industrial world have abandoned intermediate targets and have focussed on the final target such as inflation control. While this has the advantage of specifying the ultimate objective in clear and precise terms, it must be admitted that there is some uncertainty regarding the route through which this will be achieved. One of the reasons for the abandonment of intermediate targets in these countries has been the breakdown of the relationship between monetary aggregates and the inflation rate. The demand function for money has been found to be unstable. However, in India, studies show that the money demand function is a stable function of select variables and it can be used to reasonably predict inflation. Several statistical functions of the demand for money estimated by using the equilibrium and disequilibrium analysis provide overwhelming evidence on the long run stability of the money demand function. Perhaps, some of the factors that have contributed to the instability of the demand function for money in the industrially advanced countries such as financial innovations and large movements of funds across the border are yet to have the same impact in India. In the demand function for money in India, income emerges as the most dominant variable. Such a function enables the authorities to estimate the appropriate growth in money supply, given the expected increase in real output and the acceptable level in price increase. With the freeing of the interest rate structure, interest rate may also emerge as an appropriate intermediate variable in the coming years. In fact, with the inflation rate coming down and remaining in a narrow range, it will be possible to focus on interest rate along with overall monetary aggregates. However, as of now, money supply seems to be an appropriate target. Such a target is relatively well understood by the public and provides unambiguously, the stance of monetary policy.

The literature on monetary economics talks of four distinct monetary transmission channels. They are: (1) Quantum Channel, especially relating to money supply and credit, (2) Interest Rate Channel, (3) The Exchange Rate Channel, and (4) The Asset Prices Channel. While the emphasis in India so far has been on the quantum channel, with the development of financial markets and closer integration of such markets, the interest rate channel will assume importance. It must be noted that at the equilibrium, both quantity and price are determined. Changes in interest rates cannot be ordained. The appropriate quantitative changes in money will have to be brought about even though the signal for change may be given by the price variable like interest rate.

Level of Interest Rate

Another question of importance that has arisen relates to the appropriate level of interest rate. The nominal interest rate comprises of three elements: (i) the real rate of interest, (ii) inflation expectations and (iii) a discount factor for uncertainties. The effectiveness of monetary policy to bring down the nominal interest rate will depend on the impact that this policy will have on inflation expectations and on the perception of uncertainty in the economy. A monetary policy that is geared to maintain reasonable price stability, if it is successful, can help to bring down the interest rate in sympathy with the downward drift in inflation. Inflationary expectations can be broken, if the monetary authority enjoys high credibility. However, this leaves the real rate of interest to be determined. The real interest rate is not an observed variable. The real interest rate is influenced by several long-term factors such as saving and investment balance in the economy and the rate of return on capital. Theory tells us that on an economy-wide basis, this rate should not exceed the real rate of growth. In fast growing economies, the real rate of interest will be higher. In South Korea, during the years of very rapid economic growth, the real rate of interest was around six to seven per cent in several years. The real rate of interest is thus related to the rate of growth of the economy. In the early 1990s in India, the real rate of interest was low because the inflation rate was in the range of eight to ten per cent. However, with the break in the inflation rate beginning 1996-97, the real rate of interest has gone up. As mentioned earlier, the inflation rate on an average has remained at less than five per cent since 1996-97. However, it must be kept in mind that the real rate of interest will have to be relatively higher in developing economies which seek to maintain a high savings rate and which aim at growing at more than six to seven per cent per annum. This is typically the situation in India. A situation of high real rate of interest accompanied by high growth rate must be distinguished from other situations when real rates of interest may remain high. In this context, it is worth noting that the high level of nominal interest rate in developing economies may also be due to high intermediation costs. Improved efficiency can reduce the spread between the deposit rate and lending rate and bring the lending rate in closer alignment with fundamental factors.

Exchange Rate Management

The role of monetary authority in exchange rate management came into focus in the 1990s. Since 1975, the exchange rate of the rupee was determined with reference to the daily exchange rate movements of a selected number of currencies of the countries which were India's major trading partners.

The Reserve Bank of India was required to maintain the exchange rate within a band on either side of a base 'basket' value. This allowed the achievement of a medium-term Real Effective Exchange Rate (REER) objective through changes in the NEER. Such a regime could be maintained only with the support of extensive exchange controls and import controls. The reform measures introduced in 1991 included significant changes in the foreign trade regime and exchange rate management. The devaluation of the rupee in mid-1991 was followed by a system of dual exchange rate system in March 1992. A year later, the dual system was abolished and the country moved towards a unified market determined exchange rate system. The monetary authority does not intervene in the market process of rate determination as long as orderly conditions prevail in the exchange market and the exchange rate reflects macroeconomic fundamentals.

The approach to exchange rate by the monetary authorities in the developed world generally has been to let the market determine the rate. However, there have been several exceptions. There have been occasions when central banks in these countries have intervened, some times in a concerted way, when exchange markets became volatile. The Indian experience with market determined exchange rate system is that there have been several occasions when the RBI had to intervene strongly to prevent volatility. This happened in 1995 and 1996 and later in 1997 and 1998 at the time of the East Asian crisis. The impact of the East Asian crisis on the Indian market was minimal. This was partly due to the reason that while India subscribed to current account convertibility under Clause VIII of the IMF agreement, the capital account liberalisation was undertaken cautiously. Besides, India's current account deficit during this period was low. In fact, in 1991, a High Level Committee on Balance of Payments had made specific recommendations regarding the level of current account deficit, the size and composition of capital flows, the management of external debt including short term debt and the quantum of foreign exchange reserves. Implementation of these recommendations stood India in good stead at the time of the East Asian crisis.

In narrow underdeveloped markets like in India, there is a tendency for the herd instinct, which amplifies the fluctuations. This can cause volatile and destabilising movements in the exchange rate which may go beyond any correction, required by the fundamentals. Even in developed markets there is a tendency for the market to "overshoot", when a critical mass in terms of the perception of overvaluation in the exchange rate is reached. With narrow markets, the danger is greater. On such occasions, the monetary authority has to step in to ensure orderly market conditions. The monetary authority must, however, recognise that integration of markets is inevitable and therefore, action must be spread across the markets to achieve results.

In developing economies like India, trade flows both visible and invisible, dominate the balance of payments. That is why for the exchange rate regime in India, continuous monitoring of the real exchange rate with an appropriate base becomes important. It provides valuable information to the authorities on the behaviour of the current account to which it is intrinsically linked. A monetary policy geared to domestic price stability in this situation helps to avoid disruptive adjustments in the exchange rate. In that sense, monetary policy and exchange rate management become intertwined.

Financial Stability

Increasingly, macroeconomic stability as an objective of central banking is closely linked to financial stability. It is easy to see how the two are interlinked. Financial stability broadly implies the stability of the important institutions and markets forming part of the financial system. Financial stability requires that the key institutions in the financial system are stable, in that, there is a high degree of confidence about meeting contractual obligations without interruption or outside assistance. While the complementarity between the objectives of macro stability and financial stability are easily recognised, the one question that needs to be addressed is whether there can be a conflict between the two objectives. It is not inconceivable to have situations in which the price stability objective might call for a restrictive policy, while the financial market conditions may demand a somewhat liberal policy to provide relief. The Reserve Bank of India was extremely conscious of this dilemma. Banking sector reforms were in full swing in the 1990s, which necessarily put the banking system under strain. While facilitating the smooth transition, RBI took care that there was no dilution of the basic objectives of monetary policy. However, viewed as part of overall economic stability, financial stability need not run at cross-purpose with other dimensions of macroeconomic stability. Normally, price stability should provide an environment favourable to financial stability. If on occasions dealing directly with financial stability becomes necessary, it must be done as in the case of intervention in the foreign exchange markets. Actions to maintain financial stability in those circumstances may be in the long run interest of economic stability.

Autonomy of Central Banks

Autonomy of central banks has become an article of faith in the industrial countries. It has been written into the constitution setting up the European Central Bank. The literature on this subject is growing. There is a general consensus to give instrument independence to central banks among countries that have decided that the single objective of monetary policy is inflation control. Autonomy implies discretion to central banks to decide on the timing and nature of monetary policy intervention. It also calls for transparency in relation to both objectives and strategies. The increased use of explicit targets by central banks is part of the broader move to build credibility through transparency. It is quite true that in India, monetary policy has been very much conditioned by the stance of fiscal policy. The system of the scheme of *ad hoc* Treasury bills facilitated monetisation of the fiscal deficit without limit and without prior approval. The 1990s saw the phasing out of the system and the introduction of the scheme of Ways and Means Advance. This was a major step towards the achievement of greater discretion. The Fiscal Responsibility Bill, that is now before the Indian Parliament, takes this to its logical conclusion. When enacted, this would be a great step forward not only in fiscal but monetary management.

Two associated comments may be made in this context. First, an autonomous central bank does not mean lack of coordination with the Government. Nor does it imply lack of harmony. In fact, harmony in the sense in which it is used in classical symphonic music will be achieved. In a symphony, different artistes play different notes simultaneously but in effect create a blend that produces the best of music. However, the stances of monetary policy and fiscal policy cannot run at cross-purposes. For example, a lax fiscal policy accompanied by a tight monetary policy can lead to a sharp increase in interest rate. On the other hand, an accommodative monetary policy in a period of lax fiscal policy can lead to explosive increase in prices. While monetary and fiscal coordination is desirable, it is important at the same time that the monetary authority which has its own specific agenda, must have the institutional autonomy and should not be burdened with functions which may come in conflict with its own special objective. It is in this context that the Reserve Bank of India and Government of India are examining the issue whether the management of public debt can be delinked from RBI. Second, the emergence of an autonomous central bank does not mean that the 'state of bliss' has arrived. It only enables the central bank to pursue a consistent monetary policy over a long time. Then the onus of responsibility for the conduct of monetary policy will rest on the shoulders of the Reserve Bank, where it should logically rest. In an open economy, the task of the central bank will be rendered more difficult if it does not have the autonomy and discretion to make changes quickly in response to external shocks.

There was a time when it was said that central banking was neither a science nor an art but a craft. This is at best a half-truth. Central banking has never been a case of applying well-known remedies to well known problems. 'Rules *versus* discretion' has been a subject of long-standing debate in monetary policy. Rigid rules such as those implicit in gold standard will give to central banks no room for manoeuvrability. On the other hand, total discretion with respect to objectives and instruments will make monetary policy indeterminate. That is why the new phrase 'constrained discretion'. This will require the central banks to be transparent and explicit with respect to objectives and strategies, while leaving the freedom to them to choose the timing and nature of their actions. This is the type of autonomy towards which every central bank should move.

15

Financial Sector Reforms

The Second Phase

As we begin discussing about what should constitute the second phase of reforms, it is perhaps appropriate to take a brief look at what the impact of the first phase of reforms has been and what issues have been thrown up by the reform measures.

Financial sector reforms were initiated as a part of the overall structural reforms aimed at improving the productivity and efficiency of the economy. The financial sector reforms recognise the fact that the Indian banking system had, over the years, grown and that the geographical and functional coverage of the banking system has been truly impressive. However, questions have been raised from time to time on the viability of the banking institutions. Concerns have also been expressed about the deterioration in the quality of services provided by banks. It is with a view to finding solutions to these problems that financial sector reforms were initiated. The broad objective of the reforms has thus been to create a banking system that is both viable and efficient.

As I had mentioned at the time of the last meeting of the Bank Economists' Conference, there are four building blocks which have formed part of the banking sector reforms. These are: (a) modifying the policy framework; (b) improving the financial soundness and credibility of banks; (c) creating a competitive environment; and (d) strengthening of the institutional framework. Let me briefly emphasise the components of these various building blocks and also deal with some questions that have been raised in this context.

Inaugural Address, Bank Economists' Conference, 1997.

Policy Framework

The improvements in the policy framework are aimed at removing and reducing the external constraints bearing on the profitability and functioning of commercial banks. In effect, an attempt has been made to bring down very substantially, the pre-emptions in the form of reserve requirements and to give greater freedom to banks in the determinations of interest rates. The reductions in the reserve requirements have indeed been very substantial. This has had the effect of both expanding the lendable resources of banks as well as to improve the profitability. Between November 1995 and January 1997, the Cash Reserve Ratio had been five percentage points. Such a reduction has not happened in the past. The deregulation of the interest rate structure has given a high degree of freedom to banks in determining the deposit rate and the lending rates. Obviously this has put greater responsibility on the banks, and banks have to manage this freedom judiciously.

Financial Soundness and Health

In trying to improve the financial health and credibility of banks, a major step that has been undertaken has been to introduce internationally accepted prudential norms relating to income recognition, asset classification provisioning and capital adequacy. While world over it is recognised that strict prudential norms are extremely important in ensuring the soundness and solvency of commercial banks, sometimes questions are raised in this country as to the relevance of the prudential norms, and more particularly, with those relating to capital adequacy. The origin of the prescription of capital adequacy norms goes back to the Basle Committee Report on International Convergence of Capital Measurement and Capital Standards published in July 1988. In the early Eighties, increased competition internationally led to a concern over deteriorating capital levels in international banks and the erosion of reasonable risk/return relationship for banking business. Consequently, national authorities in many countries began to press their banks to improve their capital ratios. Furthermore, by 1982, market developments, particularly, the growth of new off-balance sheet instruments and techniques, were requiring banks and regulators to address a range of risks other than those traditionally arising from the banks' loan portfolio. All these factors came together to produce a growing realisation among central banks and regulatory authorities that some greater standardisation and enhancing of capital measures and standards were highly desirable in the interest of the system. The framework suggested a minimum of eight per cent capital to risk-weighted assets ratio which includes both on and off balance-sheet items.

The aim of this system is to relate capital to the risk of the portfolio of assets held by a bank. Further, at least four per cent risk-weighted assets was to be in the form of pure capital that is equity capital and free reserves. In looking at the pressure and influences on banking, it is difficult to overestimate the importance of the capital ratios now imposed on banks.

However, the prescription of Basle capital ratio of eight per cent has also drawn certain adverse comments. The prescription of a eight per cent ratio seems to follow a 'one size fits all' formula. In fact, the desired capital ratio should be an appropriate way of controlling and reflecting the riskiness of banks' portfolios. Also, the uniform application of a 100 per cent weighting to non-bank private sector corporates does not recognise the different quality of borrowers as reflected in their ratings. Further, the treatment of collateral was overly restrictive, as no credit is given for collateral which is not in the form of cash or government securities. Another argument heard particularly in India is that there is no need for this solvency based measure for government-owned banks. The basis for this argument is that when Government is the owner, it will meet all the obligations and there is no possibility of a public sector bank failing.

It is true that the eight per cent norm cannot be operated like a 'one size fits all' formula. This reflects only the minimum and it is for each regulatory authority to prescribe capital ratios for individual banks. The merit of the eight per cent prescription is that it is superior to a regime, when there was no such prescription and to countries introducing these norms in the initial phase the objective has to be to attain this minimum and then make the prescription bank specific. The concerns over the broad weighting categorisations and the lack of allowance for differences in quality between borrowers are being met by countries setting individual target ratios above eight per cent bank-wise where the regulatory perception is that the bank's portfolio carries a higher element of risk. Countries are at liberty to follow a detailed risk weighting model but this could distort comparisons among banks across countries. The risk weighting categorisation was only a broad brush formula so as not to make it too complicated. The argument that government banks do not have to follow prescribed Capital Adequacy Ratios as public are indifferent to the level of capitalisation in public sector banks, does not recognise the fact that banks are commercial entities and not departments of Government. Capital is a cushion against losses. Just because banks are owned by Government does not mean that the intrinsic commercial element is to be ignored. Banks deal in money and not in goods and this could lead to their being highly leveraged. More important, these norms prevent bank's balance-sheet ballooning rapidly during booms with inevitable adverse consequences.

Capital gives owners and managers powerful incentives to run the bank safely and soundly. The banks' capital ratios are now seen by the investment community and rating agencies as a sign of strength while at the same time providing flexibility for future business growth. If government banks are exempted from complying with Capital Adequacy Ratios, they will be at a disadvantage as compared to other banks, particularly in their foreign exchange and international operations, as it is not possible for the foreign banks and rating agencies to assess their solvency. The approach of wholesale and institutional clients is also to assess the counterparty risk (in this case the risk on the bank) and Capital Adequacy Ratio is an important financial indicator. If government banks which have disclosed large losses have not been affected in any manner and the public continue to have confidence in them, it is because these banks are under restructuring and steps are being taken for turning them around with capital adequacy norms having been already prescribed. Besides serving as a cushion against losses, bank capital promotes better corporate governance. There is also the question of level playing field when private banks are also operating in the country. If Capital Adequacy Ratios were to be abandoned, it will be very hard to put anything else in its place which can prevent anarchy in competition and unstable monetary developments. The eight per cent ratio is seen as a floor, and banking systems in some countries have ratios that are considerably higher.

One criticism of capital adequacy requirements is that banks prefer investments in risk free securities. In several countries where capital adequacy norms were introduced, initially there was some degree of down-sizing of assets. Nevertheless, in the Indian context, the introduction of the capital adequacy requirements has not been the prime reason for higher investments in government securities. For example, in 1994-95 and 1995-96, non-food credit expanded by 29.8 per cent and 22.6 per cent, respectively, despite the fact that these were the years when the pressure was greatly on to maintain capital adequacy requirement. The reasons for a larger investment in government securities in subsequent years must be traced to other reasons. Nevertheless, this ratio does emphasise the need for banks to have a balanced portfolio between risk-free assets and risk-assets.

Creating a Competitive Environment

The two major steps taken in this regard are - (a) allowing the nationalised banks, access to capital markets and thereby reduce share of the Government in the total equity. It has, however, been decided that the Government will hold at least 51 per cent of total equity; (b) within the current provisions of the Banking Regulations Act, new banks in the private sector are being allowed to be set up.

Some question the impact of partial privatisation in bringing about any change in the functioning of commercial banks. Having public as a part of the ownership of the banks indeed makes banks more conscious of the need to run the institutions efficiently and earn more profit. Access to the capital markets and listing of shares on the stock exchange themselves entail obligations on such banks in terms of publishing half-yearly results, etc. Presence of elected directors does make a difference to the functioning of the board. Banks under such circumstances become accountable to diverse categories of shareholders and become more responsive in that process.

Institutional Strengthening

A distinct feature of the Indian financial sector reform process has been the strengthening of the institutional framework relating to banking. This has taken the form of: (1) re-capitalisation; (2) strengthening the supervisory process; and (3) creating new institutions, such as Ombudsman and Debt Recovery Tribunals.

In this context, I must refer to the strengthening of the supervisory system, including the role of the external auditors. The RBI supervisory strategy comprises now both off-site surveillance and on-site inspections. A detailed off-site surveillance system based on prudential supervisory reporting framework on a quarterly basis covering capital adequacy, asset quality loan concentration, operational result and connected lending has been made operational. In regard to on-site inspection, the focus is now on the evaluation of the total operations and performance of the banks under the CAMELS system, i.e., Capital adequacy, Asset quality, Management, Earnings, Liquidity and internal control systems. Apart from evaluating asset quality and compliance with prudential norms, focus is now on the effective functioning of the board, management, earning capacity of banks as also efficacy of internal audit and control systems and risk management systems besides, regulatory compliance. The new approach to annual financial inspection has been adopted from the cycle of inspection commencing July 1997. An efficient result oriented on-site inspection system requires an efficient follow-up mechanism without which the very objective of inspection will be vitiated. The entire cycle of inspection and follow-up action is now completed within a maximum period of 12 months. Monitorable action plan for rectification of irregularities/deficiencies noticed during the inspection within a time-frame is drawn up and the progress in implementation pursued with the bank. Thus, the present supervisory system makes a substantial improvement over the earlier system in terms of frequency, coverage and focus as also the tools employed.

The role of the external auditors has been enhanced and enlarged. In the auditing of a bank, the auditors' primary duty is to express an opinion on the financial statement, such as the balance sheet and the profit and loss account. Besides the audit report on the financial statements, auditors of banks are also required to submit what has come to be known as Long Form Audit Report. Auditors are not required to verify compliance with SLR computation and prudential norms and also report serious irregularities to RBI. Further, auditors of nationalised banks should certify whether the transactions of banks are within the powers of the banks, and whether the returns received are adequate for the purpose of audit. The RBI has taken a number of measures to improve the transparency and disclosure in the published accounts of banks. From 1996-97, banks are required to disclose under 'Provisions and Contingencies' in the Profit and Loss Account, details of provision for bad and doubtful debts, provision for diminution in the value of investments, provision for tax separately, instead of showing it as conglomerate item. Banks are also required to disclose the Capital Adequacy Ratio, as well as percentage of net NPA to net advances. The above information will also have to be audited.

Impact of Financial Sector Reforms

One has begun to see the impact of the financial sector reforms, both on the financial results as well as in the services provided. Operating profits for 1996-97 have gone up from Rs. 7568 crore to Rs. 8898 crore in 1995-96 and net profit from a loss of Rs. 371 crore to a net profit of Rs. 3095 crore. All banks, except two, have met the minimum capital adequacy ratio. Sixteen public sector banks have capital adequacy ratios over 10 per cent and five between 9-10 per cent.

Reduction in NPAs has acquired more focussed attention. The level of NPAs is no doubt high but the percentages show a decreasing trend. The percentages vary sharply among banks. Percentage of gross NPAs has come down from 23 per cent in 1992-93 to 17.8 per cent in 1996-97. The percentage of net NPAs to net advances was 9.18 per cent. For purposes of international comparisons, it is this figure that should be taken into account. The priority sector advances accounted for 47 per cent of the total NPAs and non-priority sector for the balance.

New Challenges

The first phase of financial sector reforms has laid the base for a sound and viable banking system even though we have to travel still some distance. What is the emerging horizon? What are the new challenges and new opportunities? Going by the experiences of commercial banks in other countries, the following trends, as I have indicated elsewhere, may dominate the future course of banking development in India:

- greater specialisations by banks in different niches of the market such as retail, agriculture, export, small-scale and corporate sector;

- greater reliance on non-fund business such as advisory and consultancy services, guarantee and custodial services;
- greater overlap in product coverage between commercial banks and non-bank financial intermediaries; and
- greater financial disintermediation with large companies accessing securities debt domestically and from financial markets abroad.

All of these will require the banks to prepare a corporate plan over the next five years taking into account their own strengths and the markets in which they are looking to operate. Banks should not expect customers to walk in. They should seek customers. That will be the important change in the new scenario.

The Imperatives

In the environment of tomorrow, banks will have to learn to operate in a more deregulated interest rate environment and a diversified competitive market place. Both these will require banks to manage risk better.

Interest Rates

Interest rate regime in India has undergone a rapid transformation in the last five years or more. The structure of interest rates, which was extremely complex, has now been rationalised to fixing only three - as far as banking system is concerned. Besides a maximum deposit rate for one year maturity, the prescriptions include a lending rate for loans upto Rs. 25,000, another lending rate for loans between Rs. 25,000 and Rs. 2,00,000. The money market rates have been completely freed, as have the rates at which corporate entities can borrow from the capital market. Perhaps, the most striking transformation has been in the government securities market where the Central Government borrows both in terms of dated securities and Treasury bills through the auction system.

Banks need to equip themselves to operate in such a deregulated interest rate environment. This will imply that they should be able to fix the rates on deposits and loans depending on the overall liquidity conditions and demand factors. Obviously, in such situations, certain market leaders always emerge. Banks, over the last five years, have evolved a set of criteria for determining the rate charged on the individual borrowers. They have also understood recently that this does not give them unlimited freedom to fix the rate. Pressures of competition and the intensity of demand will determine what the appropriate level is. These lessons will have to be modified and improved upon as interest rate structure becomes more flexible. The deregulation of interest rates will also lead to innovations of various types and corporates and others have already started experimenting with floating rate issues.

With abundant liquidity, the interest rates have clearly shown a downward decline. This is reflected in Treasury bills of all maturities and dated securities. The CP rate as well as PLR have come down substantially. The lending rates are at the lowest level since 1988.

The management of the investment portfolio of the commercial banks will also require greater attention, since the prices of the securities will be affected with changes in interest rates. Therefore, the maturity pattern of the investment portfolio, and the distribution according to instruments are matters which must receive the attention of technical experts in the banks. It is quite conceivable to have a situation in which the investment portfolio will consist not only of Government and quasi-government paper, but also other instruments including securitised loans. All this will demand a proper attention on existing and expected levels of interest rates.

Diversified Market Structure

Banks will begin to function increasingly under competitive pressures. These may emanate from within the banking system as well as from non-banking institutions. A greater overlap in product coverage between commercial banks and non-bank intermediaries will occur. Thus, both on the liability and asset sides, banks will face increasing competition. Banks should be willing to offer products to savers which are competitive in terms of both price and service. On the lending side, apart from the competition from other intermediaries, corporates seeking funds directly from the market will also have an impact on the asset distribution of banks. This is already happening in our country. Apart from the very large funds that corporates have been able to raise from the domestic capital market, with the lower interest abroad, big Indian corporates have also begun to raise funds from the international markets. Some of the corporates have used the funds so raised to retire high cost domestic commercial bank credit. This type of disintermediation is not uncommon. Banks will have to take note of these developments. Lending is an important function of commercial banks and will remain the most profitable form of utilising funds. They cannot let an important asset of theirs to go down. Competition will compel banks to keep the interest spread to the minimum and in this context, banks can earn enough for themselves only by reducing the proportion of non-performing assets.

Banks will also have to pay attention to market segmentation, and greater specialisation in different niches of the market. It is important to note that bigness is not synonymous with success. Small and medium sized banks can also effectively compete if appropriate niche strategies are adopted.

Asset-Liability Management

In the context of these changes, risk management is emerging as an important area which needs a great deal of attention. Originally banks concentrated on asset management, treating themselves purely as deposit takers. Funds supply was regarded as a factor beyond their control. Asset management was governed by the basic principle that liquidity and profitability are opposing considerations. Risks and return were two inversely related variables which influenced the composition of assets. Effort was to distribute the assets in such a way that for a given level of liquidity the return was of the maximum. This approach is being substituted by a more comprehensive approach of asset-liability management which has been described as a continuous process of planning, organising and controlling asset and liability volumes maturities, rate and yields. The objective is to avoid the mis-match of asset-liability characteristics and liability is no longer treated as given. The liability structure can also be modified in tune with the asset structure that is desired. Banking is much more of a risky business today than it was a decade ago. The kinds of risks and the frequency of occurrence of such risks have increased dramatically. Both liability and assets are subject to interest rate risks. The asset quality of loans can be influenced by factors which go beyond the control of the lenders. It is in this context that provisioning for loan losses and need for adequate capital become important. In terms of asset-liability management, portfolio managers look at the variable and fixed components both under assets and liabilities. Asset-liability management is not a static concept. The most important element in the process of asset-liability management is to build into the analysis of possible future, behaviour of variables such as interest rates. Thus, asset-liability management is a process and it must be practised in an ongoing manner. Managements must regularly forecast assumptions and develop contingencies to accommodate changes expected.

Given these challenges, banks will need to chalk out a plan of action. In this context, two tasks appear important. One is technology upgradation and the other is organisational improvement.

Technology Upgradation

The impact of technology on banking has been spectacular in the industrially advanced countries. Against the background of growing volume of transactions and the need to meet customer needs expeditiously, technology upgradation has become indispensable. To strengthen internal control to improve accuracy of records and to facilitate provision of new products and services, banks will have to rely increasingly on computer based technologies. Apart from improving the functioning of banks at various levels, technology has a key role to play in developing a payments system network through which funds can be transmitted quickly and efficiently. I hope the VSAT Satellite based network will come into operation soon. Much groundwork has already been done by the RBI and banks.

Organisational Improvement

The second phase of reforms will also have to focus on the organisational effectiveness of banks for which the initiatives will have to come from banks themselves. I find many banks have already taken the initiative to seek the advice of in-house as well as external experts to look into these issues. The areas which need improvement are known. In-depth corporate planning combined with organisational restructuring are a necessary prerequisite to achieve desired results in terms of productivity and profitability. A properly designed management system that improves productivity and drives the behaviour of employees in delivering quality service must be clearly spelt out. There must be a vision and mission to which employees can relate. To achieve all these goals, public sector banks need to be given greater autonomy with respect to recruitment and promotion of personnel and in general, management of staff and in determining the organisational structure. Greater accountability has to go with greater autonomy. RBI and Government are actively looking into these issues.

Select Essays on Indian Economy

A SET OF TWO VOLUMES

2

Volume Two

DR. C. RANGARAJAN is presently the Chairman of the Twelfth Finance Commission. Earlier, he was Governor of Andhra Pradesh for five years (1997-2003) and just before that he was Governor, Reserve Bank of India for five years (1992-1997). As Governor RBI, Dr. Rangarajan gave a major thrust to financial sector reforms. The institutional environment was altered to make monetary policy a more effective instrument of economic policy. The exchange rate regime underwent a fundamental change.

He was member of the Planning Commission during 1991-92. Prior to that he held the position of Deputy Governor, Reserve Bank of India, for almost a decade. During this period, he was instrumental in bringing about a number of changes in the credit and financial system, both in terms of induction of new instruments and new institutions.

Dr. Rangarajan has been a member of the Economic Advisory Council to the Prime Minister between 1985 and 1991. He was the Chairman of the National Statistical Commission which was set up to reform the Indian Statistical System.

He has taught at the Wharton School of Finance & Commerce, University of Pennsylvania and the Graduate School of Business Administration, New York University. In India, he has taught at Loyola College, Madras; University of Rajasthan, Jaipur; Indian Statistical Institute, New Delhi and for well over a decade and a half at the Indian Institute of Management, Ahmedabad.

He is the author or co-author of the following books : Short-term Investment Forecasting (1974); Principles of Macro-economics (1979); Strategy for Industrial Development in the '80s (1981); Innovations in Banking (1982); Indian Economy: Essays on Money and Finance (1998); Perspectives on Indian Economy (2000); and Structural Reforms in Industry, Banking and Finance (2000).

Many of his analytical writings have been published in various national and international journals.

Among the several awards received by him are: Business Man of the Year 1997 (Madras Management Association); Honorary Fellow, Indian Institute of Management, Ahmedabad 1997; Award of Excellence in Finance (Bank of India) 1998; Finance Man of the Decade (Bombay Management Association) 1998; Financial Express Award for Economics 1998; Wharton-Indian Alumni Award for Outstanding Leadership (2002).

Dr. Rangarajan was awarded *Padma Vibhushan* by the President of India in January, 2002.

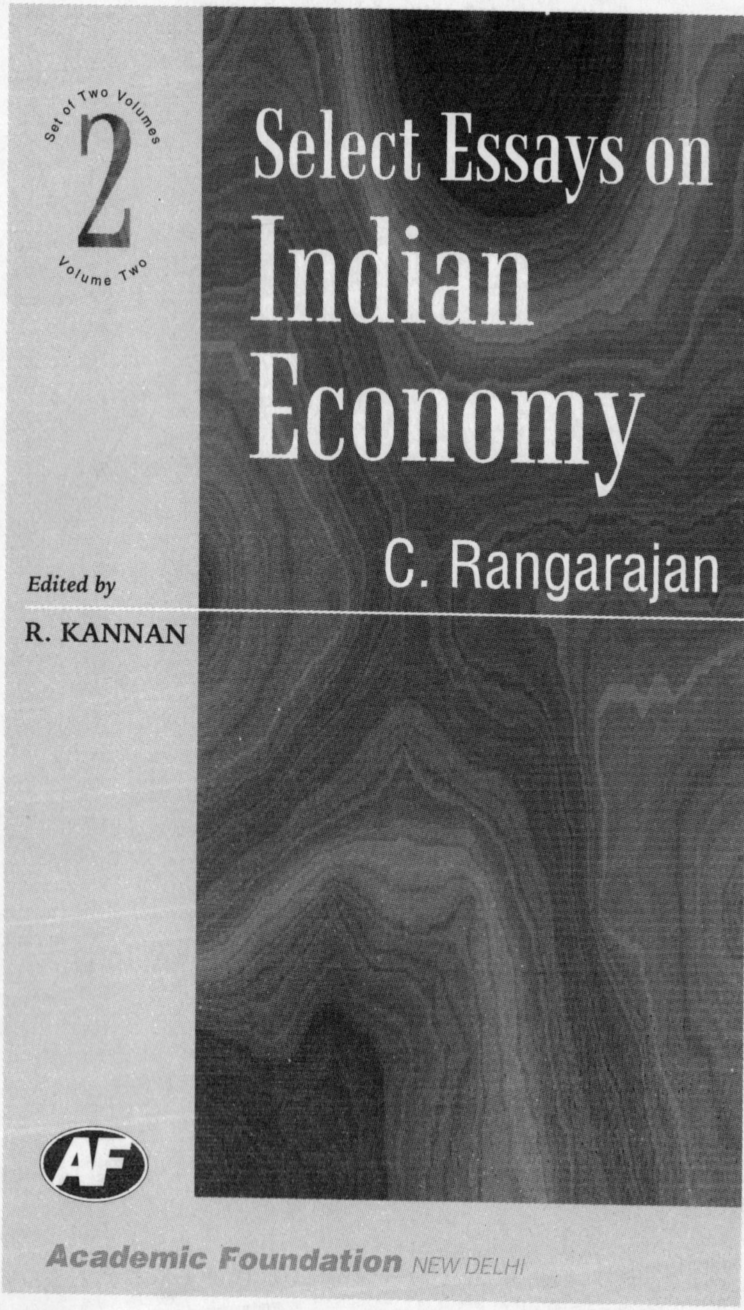
Set of Two Volumes
2
Volume Two
Select Essays on
Indian
Economy
C. Rangarajan
Edited by
R. KANNAN
AF
Academic Foundation NEW DELHI

First Published in 2004 by
ACADEMIC FOUNDATION
4772-73 / 23 Bharat Ram Road,
(23 Ansari Road), Darya Ganj,
New Delhi - 110 002. INDIA.

Phones : 23245001, 02, 03, 04.
Fax : +91-11-23245005.
e-mail : academic@vsnl.com
www : academicfoundation.com

Select Essays on Indian Economy
(a set of two volumes)
by C. Rangarajan
ISBN 81-7188-338-9

Laser-Typeset at AF's DTP Division.
Printed at Print Perfect, Mayapuri Industrial Area, New Delhi.

Dedicated to

Dr. Haripriya Rangarajan

My constant companion and support
during the past 37 years

CONTENTS

Volume 2 *(the present volume)*

Part III

Fiscal Sector

Part IV

External Sector

CONTENTS

Volume 1 (the companion volume)

Part II

Monetary System and Financial Sector

Part III

Fiscal Sector

1

Dynamics of Interaction between Government Deficit and Domestic Debt in India

Introduction

Several significant changes have taken place in the dimension as well as the financing pattern of government deficits in India since the early 1980s. Government deficit as a ratio of GDP has increased markedly and the bulk of the deficit is being financed by government's domestic borrowings. Heavy reliance on domestic borrowings has naturally led to a sharp increase in domestic debt of the Government held within as well as outside the RBI. As a result, concerns are being voiced about the prudence of large government deficits and sustainability of the growing domestic debt of the Government.

Implications of widening government deficits have received considerable attention among economists in leading industrial countries[1]. In the Indian context, however, these issues have not been adequately and rigorously investigated. Seshan (1987) was probably the first study to draw pointed attention to the possibility of domestic debt in India reaching unacceptably high level in the none too distant future. Subsequently, the report of the Comptroller General of India (1988) also warned against the alarming growth in domestic debt.

These prognoses are being seriously questioned on methodological grounds. For example, Rakshit (1989), finds that "the major part of the ongoing debate (on the problem of domestic debt is) somewhat heavy going" and that he "could not make much sense of the

---

Co-authors: **Anupam Basu and Narendra Jadhav.**
Reserve Bank of India Occasional Papers, Vol.10, No.3, September, 1989.

analytical constructs behind the discussions."[2] Rakshit's skepticism regarding the available predictions is understandable since they are based on simple trend analyses.

As a matter of fact, this subject calls for a comprehensive and much deeper analysis. First of all, the database has to be reconstructed. Available measures of government deficit and domestic debt are accounting measures rather than proper economic aggregates. These need to be replaced by analytically meaningful measures. Secondly, in the Indian context, widening government deficits have been financed primarily by resorting to net RBI credit to Government and by accumulating domestic debt outside the RBI, which have different macroeconomic implications and therefore, should be treated separately. Finally, the methodological basis of the currently available studies also needs to be made more rigorous. Rather than using the simple trend analysis, a sound analytical framework must be developed, so that the dynamic nexus between government deficits and different modes of financing them can be systematically explored. The present study makes an effort in these directions.

The main text of the study is organised as follows: Section I presents dimensions of fiscal imbalances in India. Alternate estimates of government deficit in India corresponding to different analytical measures suggested in the fiscal literature are presented. The issue of appropriate measurement of domestic debt in the Indian context is also discussed. Trends in these aggregates are examined with a view to providing an assessment of the emerging fiscal situation. Section II provides a brief survey of literature relating to perceived macroeconomic implications of domestic debt accumulation. Section III deals with the "debt-financing scenario"[3], wherein the focus is on the domestic debt held outside the RBI. An analytical framework is developed for projecting the debt-GDP ratio and is applied to the Indian data so as to make appropriate quantitative assessment. Section IV is then devoted to the "monetary financing scenario" wherein the focus is on the net RBI credit to Government. This section presents a suitable analytical framework for capturing quantitative implications of resorting to the RBI financing of government deficits and applies it to the Indian data. Finally, Section V presents conclusions.

At the very outset, some caveats and clarifications are in order. Among other things, it is assumed throughout the study that the authorities maintain a constant real GDP growth; also, while developing the debt-financing scenario, inflation rate is assumed to remain unchanged, as though, these were independent of fiscal policy actions. In reality, growing debt-GDP ratio and concomitant debt-service burden may stifle the economic growth and aggravate inflation. These feedback effects are ignored in the debt-financing scenario and attention is focussed only on the first round effects in order to keep the analysis uncluttered. Actual outcomes, therefore, are likely to be worse than those predicted in that scenario. On the other hand, in the "monetary-financing scenario", feedback effects on inflation have been duly incorporated.

Throughout the study, attention is focussed on the Central Government. Accordingly, measurement of government deficits, and the different means of financing them, as well as the measurement of domestic debt is with reference to the Central Government only.

I. DIMENSIONS OF FISCAL IMBALANCES IN INDIA

Fiscal imbalance in any economy is measured, typically, by the government deficit. Conceptually, government deficit is simply the difference between aggregate disbursements and aggregate receipts. In practice, however, different measures of government deficit are possible depending upon what items are deemed to comprise aggregate disbursements and aggregate receipts.

Government Deficits: Taxonomy of Concepts and Measures

Measurement of government deficit has received considerable attention in public finance literature, with a resurgence of interest in the subject in recent years. A wide spectrum of different concepts of government deficit have been developed. World Development Report (1988) published by the World Bank has emphasised that the "correct" way to measure the government deficit depends on the purpose of analysis. In the present context, therefore, it is necessary to choose the concept which can fully capture the impact of fiscal operations on the indebtedness of the Government.

In order to clarify the precise differences among different concepts of government deficit, it may be useful to begin with a simple analytical classification of the Central Government transactions in India. Exhibit 1 presents a fiscal balance sheet based on terminology used in the Indian budget documents.

Exhibit 1

Fiscal Balance Sheet

Receipts		*Disbursements*	
A. Revenue Receipts		**A. Revenue Expenditure**	
1. Tax Receipts	(R1)	1. Interest Expenditure	(E1)
2. Non-tax Receipts		2. Non-interest Expenditure	(E2)
a) Interest Earning	(R2)		
b) Non-interest Earnings	(R3)		
B. Financing Items		**B. Capital Disbursements**	
1. Grants	(R4)	1. Capital Expenditure	(E3)
2. Borrowings		2. Net Domestic Lendings	(E4)
i) Foreign Borrowings	(R5)		
ii) Domestic Borrowings			
a) Other than 91-day TBs*	(R6)		
b) 91-day TBs	(R7)		
iii) Change in Cash Balance	(R8)		
Aggregate Receipts (R) = (R1 + R2 + R3) + (R4) + (R5 + R6 + R7 + R8)		Aggregate Disbursements (E) = (E1 + E2 + E3 + E4)	

Note: *: Represent both "internal debt" liabilities like current market loans, special securities issued to the RBI, 182-day Treasury bills, as well as "other liabilities" like small savings, provident funds etc.

Like any other balance sheet, by definition, the fiscal balance sheet must always be in balance. In other words, the total resource-gap arising out of government transaction, i.e., the difference between aggregate disbursements (revenue expenditure, capital expenditure and net domestic lendings) and revenue receipts, must necessarily be

matched by the sum total of all financing items. The financing items include grants, foreign borrowings, domestic borrowings (net RBI credit to Government, current market loans, and other liabilities such as small savings, provident funds etc.) and change in cash balances.

Traditional Budget Deficit

In the Indian budgetary practice, traditionally, while the aggregate disbursements cover revenue expenditure, capital expenditure and net domestic lendings, receipts are not confined to revenue receipts alone. Grants, foreign borrowings and domestic borrowings (excluding 91-day Treasury bills) are also included in aggregate receipts.

In terms of the fiscal balance sheet presented in Exhibit 1, thus, the traditional deficit[4]

= (revenue expenditure + capital expenditure + net domestic lendings)

– (revenue receipts + grants + foreign borrowings + domestic borrowings excluding 91-day TBs)

= (E1 + E2 + E3 + E4) - [(R1 + R2 + R3) + (R4 + R5 + R6)]

= (R7 + R8)

In other words, the traditional budget deficit depicts only a part of the resource gap in current fiscal operations that is expected to be financed by (a) issuing 91-day Treasury bills and (b) running down on the government's cash balances with treasuries and the RBI.

This concept of government deficit is extremely narrow. Evidently, current fiscal operations lead to increases in several other liabilities of the Government. For example, besides foreign borrowings, there are internal debt liabilities like current market loans, special securities issued to the RBI and "other liabilities" such as small savings, provident funds etc. which in recent years have been absorbing significant fractions of resource gap in the government operations. In the budget documents, these are, however treated in the same way as revenue receipts are and, hence, the traditional budget deficit does not reflect the full magnitude of resource gap and relevant financing or borrowing requirements.

Monetary Concept of Government Deficit

Limitations of the traditional budget deficit were also emphasised by the Chakravarty Committee Report (1985). The report observed that the traditional measure of budget deficit does not reveal the full extent of the government's reliance on Reserve Bank credit. A part of new issues of government securities is taken up by the Reserve Bank when response from the public and financial institutions is inadequate. As a matter of fact, additions to Reserve Bank's holding of government securities contribute to an increase in the reserve money, much the same way as new issues of Treasury bills taken over by the Reserve Bank. The exclusion of additions to Reserve Bank's holding of government securities in the traditional measures of budget deficit, therefore, may severely understate the monetary impact of fiscal operations. Also, to the extent Treasury bills are held outside the Reserve Bank, the traditional budget deficit may overstate the monetary impact, the report, therefore, argued that "An unambiguous and economically meaningful measure of the monetary impact of fiscal operations is provided by the change in Reserve Bank credit to Government"[5].

The monetary concept of government deficit is somewhat broader than the traditional measure, but is suitable only for analysing the monetary impact of fiscal operations. In other words, the expanded coverage under the monetary concept of government deficit still falls considerably short of the coverage needed to capture the full impact of current fiscal stance on the overall indebtedness of the Government.

Fiscal Deficit

As noted before, the total resource gap or the overall financing requirement in government's fiscal operations is given by the excess of revenue expenditure, capital expenditure and net domestic lendings over revenue receipts. When grants are deducted from the overall financing requirement, the residual which represents the overall borrowing requirement may be called the gross fiscal deficit.

Thus, gross fiscal deficit

= (revenue expenditure + capital expenditure + net domestic lendings) – (revenue receipts + grants), which in terms of the fiscal balance sheet

= (R5 + R6 + R7 + R8)

Shortcomings of the traditional measure of budget deficit are evident when it is compared with gross fiscal deficit. While the gross fiscal deficit captures the entire shortfall in government's fiscal operations, that is expected to be covered by undertaking all borrowing operations (domestic and foreign) and/or running down on its cash holdings, the traditional measure is confined, besides the depletion of liquidity holdings, only to one particular form of domestic borrowings, i.e., 91-day Treasury bills, thus ignoring other domestic borrowings, i.e., such as current market loans, small savings, provident funds etc., as well as foreign borrowings.

In the context of developing countries, a sizeable part of Central government borrowings is on-lent to other sectors – state and local governments, public sector enterprises and the like. Such lendings are undertaken not to acquire a profitable financial asset but are actuated by motives of public policy – such as provision of resources where private capital may not be available. When net domestic lendings (lendings minus repayments) are deducted from the gross fiscal deficit, the residual may be called the net fiscal deficit.

Thus, net fiscal deficit

= gross fiscal deficit – net domestic lendings

= (revenue expenditure + capital expenditure)

- (revenue receipts + grants)

When the Central Government is the focal point of analysis, as is the case with the present study, the net fiscal deficit is, perhaps, more meaningful than the gross fiscal deficit[6].

Primary Deficit

One important limitation of the fiscal deficits is that they do not necessarily reflect the extent to which the current discretionary fiscal actions improve or worsen the government's net indebtedness. In particular, interest payments in the current period are obligatory, but reflect past budgets.

Corresponding to the two concepts of fiscal deficit, i.e., gross and net, two measures of primary deficits could be constructed. Thus,

Gross primary deficit[7]

= (gross fiscal deficit) – (interest payments – interest earnings)

= (revenue expenditure + capital expenditure + net domestic lendings) – (revenue receipts + grants) – (interest payments – interest earnings)

= (non-interest revenue expenditure + capital expenditure + net domestic lendings) – (non-interest revenue receipts + grants)

which, in terms of the fiscal balance sheet

= (E2 + E3 + E4) – (R1 + R3 + R4)

And, net primary deficit

= (non-interest revenue expenditure + capital expenditure) – (non-interest revenue receipts + grants)

= (E2 + E3) – (R1 + R3 + R4)

Primary deficit concepts, thus defined, indicate the precise extent to which current fiscal actions affect the indebtedness of the Central Government and is, therefore, most suitable for the present study. Accordingly, the analytical framework developed in subsequent sections is based on these measures.

Before proceeding further, it may be worthwhile to apply the measures discussed above to derive different government deficit estimates for India, to which we turn next.

Government Deficit in India: Alternate Estimates

Data series relating to various components of the fiscal balance sheet covering the period 1970-71 through 1990-91 are presented in the statistical statements (1 to 10) in the Data Appendix. Statistical derivation of different measures of government deficit is indicated in these statements. Evolution of the traditional deficit, gross primary deficit and gross fiscal deficit is also illustrated in Exhibits 2 and 3.

Exhibit 2

Alternate Deficit Measures

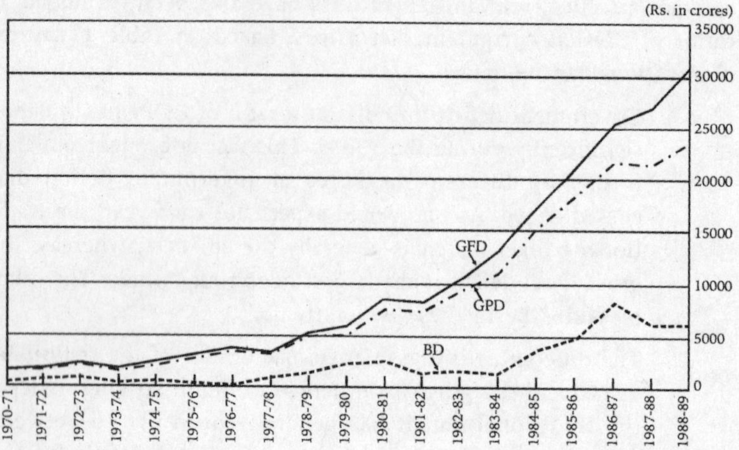

Exhibit 3

Alternate Deficit Measures As Ratios of GDP

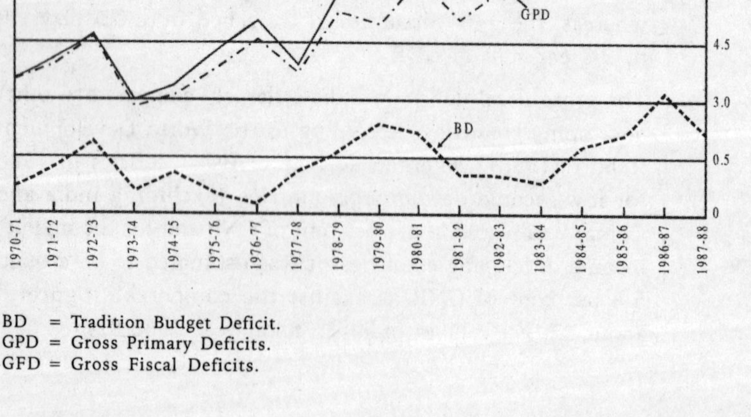

BD = Tradition Budget Deficit.
GPD = Gross Primary Deficits.
GFD = Gross Fiscal Deficits.

Table 1 presents a summary of different government deficit estimates in India for 1970-71 and for the 1980s. For any meaningful analysis, relevant absolute value must be normalised. Following the common practice, relevant magnitudes have also been expressed as ratios of GDP at current market prices. Based on Table 1, several observations can be made:

1. Government deficit in India (as a ratio of GDP) has widened significantly during the 1980s. This fact is brought out uniformly by different measures of government deficit discussed above. As one would expect, for each year, the traditional budget deficit is generally the smallest, whereas, the gross fiscal deficit is the largest one in magnitude. The other measures lie in these two extreme.

2. The differences in the relative magnitudes of the traditional deficit and the gross fiscal deficit are quite striking. Indeed, the traditional deficit has generally been placed between one-fifth and one-third of the gross fiscal deficit for the relevant year. It is evident, therefore, that the traditional budget deficit has been grossly understating the overall borrowing need arising out of the fiscal operations of the Government throughout the 1980s consistently.

3. Ignoring year to year variations, it can be seen that the traditional deficit expanded from 0.7 per cent of GDP in 1970-71 to the average of 1.3 per cent in the first half of the 1980s and to the average of 2.3 per cent in the next four years. During the comparable period, the gross primary deficit widened from 3.5 per cent to 6.1 per cent of GDP whereas, the gross fiscal deficit worsened from 3.5 per cent to 9.3 per cent of GDP.

4. The gross fiscal deficit in India is largely compared to other developing countries. According to the World Development Report (1988), weighted average of fiscal deficits in 1986 for low-income developing countries (excluding India and China) was placed at 5.1 per cent of GNP and for the middle-income developing countries, it was estimated to be around 5.8 per cent of GNP, as against the comparable figure of about 8.8 per cent in India (in fiscal year 1986-87).

Table 1

Estimates of Government Deficit in India

(Rs. in crores)

Year	*Traditional Deficit*	*Monetary Deficit*	*Gross Fiscal Deficit*	*Net Fiscal Deficit*	*Gross Primary Deficit*	*Net Primary Deficit*
1970-71	285 (0.7)	223 (0.6)	1,409 (3.5)	779 (2.0)	1,378 (3.5)	748 (1.9)
1980-81	2,578 (2.1)	3,551 (2.9)	8,514 (7.0)	5,325 (4.4)	7,613 (6.2)	4,424 (3.6)
1981-82	1,392 (1.0)	3,207 (2.2)	8,348 (5.8)	4,273 (3.0)	7,303 (5.1)	3,228 (2.3)
1982-83	1,657 (1.0)	3,368 (2.1)	10,470 (6.6)	5,817 (3.7)	9,314 (5.9)	4,661 (2.9)
1983-84	1,417 (0.8)	3,949 (2.1)	13,252 (7.1)	8,392 (4.5)	11,052 (5.9)	6,192 (3.3)
1984-85	3,745 (1.8)	6,055 (2.9)	17,390 (8.4)	10,946 (5.3)	15,303 (7.4)	8,859 (4.3)
1985-86	4,937 (2.1)	6,190 (2.6)	21,368 (9.1)	13,054 (5.6)	18,451 (7.9)	10,137 (4.3)
1986-87	8,261 (3.2)	7,090 (2.7)	25,656 (9.9)	16,350 (6.3)	21,759 (8.4)	12,453 (4.8)
1987-88	6,308 (2.1)	6,559 (2.2)	27,044 (9.2)	18,717 (6.4)	21,563 (7.3)	13,236 (4.5)
1988-89	6,242 (1.8)	6,503 (1.9)	30,846 (8.8)	20,777 (6.0)	23,558 (6.8)	13,489 (3.9)
1989-90 (RE)	12,663	14,300	36,274	23,998	27,229	14,953

(Figures in brackets indicate deficit as ratio of GDP at factor cost, current prices, 1989-90 GDP figure is CSO's quick estimate).

Source: Col. (1) : Statement 3, Col. (3); Col. (2) : RBI Reports on Currency & Finance, end-year data. Col. (3) : Statement 6, Col. (5). Col. (4) : Statement 7, Col. (5); Col. (5) : Statement 9, Col.(5); Col. (6) : Statement 10, Col. (5);

5. The overall borrowing requirement (as reflected in the gross fiscal deficit) can be readily decomposed into analytically meaningful components. In particular, the difference between fiscal and primary deficits gives the interest burden, whereas, the difference between gross and net primary (or fiscal) deficits gives the extent of net domestic lendings. During the four year period ended 1988-89, the gross borrowing requirement (as a ratio of GDP), on an

average, was 5.8 points percentage higher than in 1970-71. Of this increase, less than one-third was due to the enhanced interest burden and rest due to the increase in gross primary deficit. Of the increase in gross primary deficit, little over one-third was on account of rise in net domestic lendings and the balance due to higher net primary deficit.

6. As far as the sources of financing are concerned, net RBI credit to Government and domestic debt held outside the RBI, together, cover the bulk of the overall borrowing requirement. In fact, in 1970-71, less than 16 per cent of the overall borrowing need was financed by RBI credit which rose to about one-third on an average during the four year period ended 1988-89. Evidently, thus, proportionate reliance on the net RBI credit for financing government deficits appears to have remained high during the 1980s.

Measurement of Domestic Debt

In the Indian budgetary practice, there are two sets of liabilities which comprise domestic debt:

1. "Internal debt" which consists of current market loans, Treasury bill, special securities issued to RBI and the like, and,
2. "Other liabilities" which consist of small savings, Provident Funds etc. These liabilities are also classified as the debt because they involve servicing through interest payments and redemption.

The question of the appropriate measure of domestic debt boils down basically to the selection of relevant constituents under these two broad categories of domestic debt[8]:

1. In the category of "internal debt" there is an item entitled, "special floating and other loans" which comprises non-negotiable, non-interest bearing securities issued to international financial institutions like World Bank, IMF etc. These are merely accounting contra-entries and, therefore, ought to be excluded.
2. In the traditional method of compiling domestic debt statistics under the heading of the "other liabilities", an item entitled "reserve funds" which comprises depreciation and

reserve funds of railways. Posts and Department of Telecommunication etc. is included as an item of debt. These are, however, intra-governmental liabilities and should therefore be excluded.

3. In the same category, there is an item entitled "deposits" which is included as a debt item in the traditional method. This, however, is a grey area. This particular item comprises dozens of diverse items such as civil deposits, judicial deposits, deposits of local funds etc. Ideally, one ought to distinguish between "intra-governmental" and "non-intra governmental" deposits and only include the latter as a constituent of the domestic debt. Such information, however, is not available. *Prima facie*, however, almost all of them appear to be "intra-governmental" in nature, and may, therefore, be excluded.

With these adjustments, an analytical measure of the Gross Domestic Debt (GDD) can be derived. The corresponding net concept i.e., Net Domestic Debt (NDD) can then be obtained in a straightforward manner. For this purpose, debt obligations of others to the Central Government, such as Central Government's loans to the states, union territories and public enterprises, have to be netted out from the gross domestic debt.

Table 2 presents data on the gross and net domestic debt of the Central Government for some benchmark years using the revised method. As a memorandum item, gross domestic debt figures based on the traditional method are also presented. Here again, for meaningful comparison, absolute values have been normalised using GDP at current market prices. Based on Table 2, several observations can be made:

1. The domestic debt in India has increased very rapidly in the present decade. Since 1980-81, the Gross Domestic Debt (GDD) has increased nearly two-and-a-half times whereas the Net Domestic Debt (NDD) has increased as much as four times. It may be also noted that, for any given year, the method proposed here gives a smaller level of debt compared with the traditional method in view of the exclusions discussed above.

2. The Gross Domestic Debt to GDP ratio of 44.6 per cent for India in 1987-88 appears to be high in comparison with other developing countries. Indeed, it is broadly in line with the ratios recently estimated for selected industrial countries. Spaventa (1988), for example, has estimated that in 1986, four major industrial countries, *viz.*, Germany, France, U.K. and U.S.A. had their debt-GDP ratio in the range 36 per cent (for France) to 54 per cent (for U.K.).

Table 2

Evolution of Gross and Net Domestic Debt in India

(Rs. in crores)

	Gross Domestic Debt (GDD)				*Memo Item*
Year	*Net RBI Credit (Outstanding) to the Government*	*Domestic Debt held outside RBI*	*Gross Domestic Debt (GDD)*	*Net Domestic Debt (NDD)*	*Gross Domestic Debt by the Traditional Method*
(1)	*(2)*	*(3)*	*(4)*	*(5)*	*(6)*
1970-71	3,843	7,074	10,917	1,664	13,079
% of GDD	(35.2)	(64.8)	(100.0)		
% of GDP	(9.5)	(17.6)	(27.1)	(4.1)	(32.5)
1980-81	15,853	27,174	42,977	13,626	48,151
% of GDD	(36.9)	(63.1)	(100.0)		
% of GDP	(11.7)	(19.9)	(31.6)	(10.0)	(35.5)
1987-88	52,793	94,680	1,47,473	68,638	1,72,038
% of GDD	(35.8)	(64.2)	(100.0)		
% of GDP	(16.0)	(28.6)	(44.6)	(20.8)	(52.1)

3. As far as the distribution of Gross Domestic Debt holdings is concerned, about 36 per cent is held by the RBI, all others together accounting for the rest. Indeed, the RBI's share in the Gross Domestic Debt (GDD) has remained remarkably stable around 36 per cent since 1970-71, which suggests that net RBI credit to Government has grown in tandem with the enlargement of other domestic borrowings of the Government.

4. The net outstanding RBI credit to Government as a ratio of Net Domestic Debt (NDD) in 1987-88 was placed at about 77 per cent. Even when the traditional measure of domestic debt is used, the ratio works out to be around 57 per cent. These relatively large holdings of Net Domestic Debt by the RBI reflect the inadequate development of secondary markets for government securities in India.

II. MACROECONOMIC IMPLICATIONS OF DOMESTIC DEBT

Review of Literature

"The debate shows little signs of being resolved, although essentially the same arguments have been advanced for two centuries. For those who remain skeptical about the progress of economic science, the debt theory controversy provides ample corroboration".

— James Buchanan (1968)

Macroeconomic implications of domestic debt has been a subject of a long standing controversy in the fiscal literature. In fact, two distinct phases in the controversy are clearly discernible with the changing perceptions regarding the domestic debt. In the old tradition, domestic debts were created during wars or national emergencies and retired during peacetime. Correspondingly, theoretical discussions of domestic debt revolved around a narrow set of well-defined propositions. In the recent past, however, there is a break in this tradition, in that, many industrial countries have experienced a substantial "peacetime" accumulation of domestic debt. Accordingly, with the growing realisation that domestic debt accumulation is not necessarily transitory, theoretical treatments are increasingly becoming wider in their range.

Traditional Controversies

It may be worthwhile to review some propositions from the traditional debate which have contemporary relevance. At least two such propositions can be identified, one relates to the impact of domestic debt and other one concerns its incidence.

1. Way back in 1817, Ricardo enunciated a theorem which has been called the "Ricardian Equivalence Theorem". The theorem put

forth a proposition that domestic debt and a lump sum tax of equivalent amount exert identical effects on the individual.

This theorem, to an extent, has been misinterpreted, partly because the underlying assumptions are not given due consideration. The theorem was derived under the conditions of perfect certainty, perfect capital markets and on the assumption that individuals act 'as if' they will live forever. Within these restrictive premises, the contention of the theorem is simply that, for the individual each of the two alternatives (i.e., current taxation and domestic debt issue) impose a burden that in a present value sense is substantially the same. As clarified by Buchanan, "This Ricardian equivalence does not suggest, however, that the objective pattern of cost payments remains the same over the two alternatives. Taxation and debt issue remain different, not similar, financing institutions.... for the simple reason that taxes require a transfer of resource services from the individual to the fisc during the initial period, whereas debt issue postpones such transfer until later periods"[9].

Recently, Barrow and other Rational Expectation theorists have revived the Ricardian Equivalence Theorem. Their contention is that domestic debt does not have any adverse wealth effect on private savings. According to this school, when Government accumulates large domestic debt in relation to GDP, "rational" households anticipate higher taxes in the future. Because of this expectation, their "permanent" income is reduced. As a result, the impact of accumulated domestic debt falls on consumption rather than on savings, thereby avoiding the dampening effect on the saving rate.

2. Another widely discussed and recurring proposition in the traditional controversies is, "We owe it to ourselves". The essence of the argument here is that the interest payments arising out of domestic debt represent nothing more than transfers from taxpayers to bondholders and so long as both groups are members of the same polity, no macroeconomic cost is involved. On the basis of this proposition, domestic debt is often dismissed as of no macroeconomic consequence.

Fallacious nature of this proposition is increasingly being realised. As observed by Buchanan (1968), "This conception of national debt contains a fundamental flaw in its failure to translate opportunity cost or burden from aggregative components into

something that is meaningful to individual members"[10]. According to him, "The core of the fallacy lies in equating of the community as a unit, in some aggregated national accounting sense, with the individuals-in-the-community, in some political sense as participants, direct or indirect, in collective decision making"[11]. Accordingly, the belief that domestic debt is of no macroeconomic consequence is, therefore, illusory.

In the more recent literature, emphasis has shifted from issues such as whether or not the domestic debt matters towards those relating to "how" and "where" does it matter. This change of the focus is symptomatic of the recognition that the domestic debt does really matter. In fact, the fiscal literature, which was overwhelmingly oriented towards "micro" aspects, is now increasingly dealing with "macro" aspects related mostly to the accumulation of domestic debt. Some of these emerging strands are reviewed next.

Emerging Strands in Debt Literature

1. In the recent fiscal literature, considerable research effort is directed towards the so-called "sustainability" aspect of domestic debt. It must be emphasised, however, that the underlying notion actually relates to economic "stability" rather than "sustainability". This is evident from the fact that debt-financing of government deficits is deemed to be "sustainable" when the resultant debt-GDP ratio is converging to an asymptotic upper bound and is considered explosive otherwise.

It was Domar who pointed out, way back in 1944, that if the rate of interest is higher than the growth rate of the economy, any primary deficit will lead eventually to an explosive rise in the debt-GDP ratio. Recently, Bispham (1987) and Mason (1987) among others, have derived similar results more rigorously, based on intertemporal budget constraint. Basic algebra has been worked out and relevant stability conditions have been derived. Furthermore, formulae have been developed for quantifying the asymptotic upper bound when the debt-GDP ratio is non-explosive. This kind of analytical framework is very useful for deriving rigorous projections of the debt-GDP ratio for any economy.

2. Another important strand in recent fiscal literature relates to the impact of domestic debt on private savings. Boskin (1987) and Bagella (1987), for example, provide detailed analysis of the issue in the context of the US economy, where the saving rate has declined substantially in the recent years.

Of the four avenues by which national fiscal policies can affect private savings (i.e., the structure of taxation, redistribution from rich to poor, differential public and private propensities to consume and growth of domestic debt), Boskin finds that the growth of implicit and explicit domestic debt may be the major cause of the decline in the US saving rate.

3. Besides the potential impact of domestic debt on the overall saving rate, several specific issues are also being addressed. For example, in the Italian context, impact of domestic debt on financial markets has been explored by Pagano (1988), impact on households demand for monetary assets has been analysed by Bollino and Rossi (1988) and the relationship between debt accumulation and capital controls has been investigated by Giovannini (1988).

4. Implications of rising domestic debt for the conduct of macroeconomic policies has also been attempted. For example, issues relating to monetary and fiscal policy coordination with a high domestic debt have been discussed in the context of Italy by Tabellini (1988). Similarly, issues relevant for supply side policies in the context of the US economy have been examined by Paganetto (1987) and Eltis (1987).

Relevance for Developing Countries

It is evident from the review of fiscal literature presented above, that the available theoretical analyses as well as empirical applications have been designed specifically for dealing with debt accumulation in industrial economies. Corresponding literature in the context of developing countries is quite thin. In this regard, some broad observations may be made:

1. In developing countries like India, the rational expectation theoretic view is that domestic debt accumulation does not affect private savings, appears to have little practical relevance. The reasons

are not far to seek. As Rakshit has observed, "(i) individual economic units can hardly be as rational or have as much information as is presumed.... (ii) the distribution of tax burden is not closely linked with the pattern of holding of public debt...."[12]. It follows, therefore, that the possibility of households responding to debt accumulation by anticipating higher taxes in the future and, consequently, with the reduced "permanent" income, lowering consumption rather than savings, is farfetched in the context of developing economies.

2. In developing countries like India, the potential deleterious impact of "high" domestic debt is likely to emanate from interplay of a different set of factors. High debt-GDP ratio implies large interest payments, which in view of the constraints on raising direct taxes and the limited scope for lowering current outlays, may cause current budgetary savings and budgetary capital outlays to be squeezed. On the other hand, recourse to indirect taxes, especially those levied on intermediate inputs, would reduce the net value added in production to the extent that the incidence is not passed on to the consumers, thus adversely affecting productive efficiency. In sum, high debt-GDP ratio may result in lowering saving ratio and budgetary capital outlays and/or productive efficiency, thereby impeding economic growth.

In order to analyse diverse ramifications of the domestic debt accumulation, it is necessary, as the first step, to make rigorous forecasts of the debt-GDP ratio and the resultant interest burden, which is taken up in the next section.

III. DEBT-FINANCING SCENARIO

Analytical Framework

A convenient starting point for developing an analytical framework systematically linking government deficit with different modes of financing is provided by simple government budget constraint:

$$\text{Eq. (1)}\quad [(G(t)-T(t)] + iB(t-1) + i^{*}\,RG(t-1) = [(B(t)-B(t-1)] + [RG(t)-RG(t-1)]$$

Where,

G(t)	=	Government expenditure in period 't' (non-interest revenue expenditure plus capital expenditure).
T(t)	=	Government revenue receipts in period 't' (non-interest revenue receipts plus grants).
G(t)-T(t)	=	Primary deficit in period 't'.
B(t), B(t-1)	=	Gross domestic debt of the Government held outside the RBI ("debt-financing") for the periods 't' and 't-1', respectively.
RG(t), RG(t-1)	=	Net outstanding RBI credit to Government in period 't' and 't-1', respectively and
i	=	Average interest rate on domestic debt outside the RBI.
i*	=	Average interest rate on net outstanding RBI credit to Government.

The budget constraint given in Equation (1) simply states that the government deficit is wholly financed by "debt-financing" or by additional RBI credit to the Government. In other words, it is a closed economy government budget constraint in which, additionally, government's lending to other sectors is implicitly assumed to be zero. These simplifying assumptions are relaxed below.

The following additional notations may be introduced here for expositional convenience:

Y(t), Y(t-1) = GDP at current market prices in period 't' and ' 't-1' respectively.

p = Inflation rate.

n = Real GDP growth.

k = (n + p) = growth rate of nominal GDP.

As elaborated in Technical Appendix, with simple manipulations of the budget constraint, it can be shown that:

Eq. (2) $$\frac{B(t)}{Y(t)} = \left[\frac{G(t)-T(t)}{Y(t)}\right] - \left[\frac{RG(t)-RG(t-1)}{Y(t)}\right] + \left(\frac{i^*}{i+k}\right)\frac{RG(t-1)}{Y(t-1)} + \frac{1+i}{1+k}\left(\frac{B(t-1)}{Y(t-1)}\right)$$

The equation (2) is easy to interpret[13]. The first term on the right hand side of equation (2) suggests that the ratio of "debt financing"

to GDP tends to rise when the "primary deficit" increases in relation to GDP. The second term on the right hand side of equation (2) indicates that the ratio of "debt financing" to GDP tends to fall when change in outstanding net RBI credit to Government rises as a proportion of GDP. It is essential to note that the secular trend in the "debt-financing to GDP ratio will be affected directly by these first two terms, namely, the primary deficit as a ratio of GDP and the recourse to RBI financing as a ratio of GDP. The last terms in equation (2) are also important; even abstracting from the secular impact of the first two terms, it suggests the conditions under which the "debt-financing" to GDP ratio would grow at a declining rate and converge to a stationary value, as well as the condition under which the growth rate of the ratio would be rising continuously. For convergence, the so-called stability condition is that the nominal rate of interest (i) must be less than the growth of nominal GDP (k), that is, $i < k$: this same condition can be stated alternatively as $(i-p) < n$, that is, the real growth rate of GDP should be higher than the real interest rate. If this condition does not hold, equation (2) implies an explosive (or unbounded) growth of the ratio, even if the underlying trend components do not lead to a secular rise.

The exposition so far has not explicitly dealt with official foreign borrowing and net domestic lendings and effects of these operations on the government's budget constraint. To deal with these aspects as well as maintain the focus on the problems of domestic debt accumulation, a few simplifying assumptions are made as follows:

1. The official inflow of foreign resources denoted as [NF (t)-NF(t-1)] is exogenously determined and interest payments constitute a fraction (w) of the outstanding one-year lagged stock of official foreign debt [that is, equal to w.NF (t-1)].
2. The level of net domestic lendings denoted by (L(t)-L(t-1)) is a proportion (h) of the change in the domestic debt held outside the RBI. (B(t)-B(t-1)), i.e., a fixed proportion of domestic borrowings excluding RBI credit is always on-lent to the non-Central government sectors, and
3. The interest rate on the outstanding stock of loans advanced by the Government is fixed at (e).

With the above assumptions, the government budget constraint (eq. 1) can be reformulated as follows:

Eq. (3) $[G(t) - T(t)] + [iB(t-1) + i^* RG(t-1) + w\ NF(t-1)] + [L(t) - L(t-1) - eL(t-1)]$
$= [B(t) - B(t-1)] + [RG(t) - RG(t-1)] + [NF(t) - NF(t-1)]$

The above equation states that the net primary deficit interest payments on domestic and foreign debt and the government's net lending in excess of interest earnings on its previous lendings must be financed by enlarging the domestic "debt financing" or by additional money creation or else by resorting to foreign borrowings.

Using the notations in assumptions (i) above, the net external resource inflow is defined as follows:

Eq. (4) $F(t) = NF(t) - NF(t-1) - w\ NF(t-1)$

Using assumptions (ii) and (iii), it is seen that

Eq. (5) $L(t) - L(t-1) = h\ [B(t) - B(t-1)]$

Eq. (6) $L(t-1) = h\ B(t-1)$

Substituting eq. (4), (5), and (6) in eq. (3) and on rearrangement of terms, we get:

$$\text{Eq. (7)}\quad \frac{B(t)}{Y(t)} = \left(\frac{1}{1-h}\right)\left[\frac{G(t)}{Y(t)} - \frac{T(t)}{Y(t)} - \frac{[RG(t)-RG(t-1)]}{Y(t)} - \frac{F(t)}{Y(t)}\right] + \left[\frac{i^*}{(1-h)(1+k)}\right]\frac{RG(t-1)}{Y(t-1)} + \left[\frac{1+\left[\frac{i-eh}{i-h}\right]}{1+k}\right]\frac{B(t-1)}{Y(t-1)}$$

The eq. (7) has the same first order difference equation formulation as the earlier eq. (2)[14]. Moreover, if one assumes h = o, the coefficient of the lagged variable $\frac{B(t-1)}{Y(t-1)}$ in eq. (7) becomes $\frac{1+i}{1+k}$ which is the same as the coefficient of $\frac{B(t-1)}{Y(t-1)}$ in eq. (2).

The condition for stability of the domestic debt ratio in equation (7) is $\left[1+\frac{i-eh}{(1-h)}\right] < 1+k$

Which after some manipulation yields the stability condition [eh + (1-h). k]> i.

The weighted average of the interest rate on domestic lending (e) and the nominal GDP growth rate (k), using the ratio (h) of net lending to the net domestic borrowing as the weight, must exceed the interest rate on the government's domestic borrowing. If h=o, one has the already familiar condition k>i. Moreover, the condition has the interpretation that stability of the "debt financing" to GDP ratio can be achieved by appropriately raising the interest rate on domestic lending (e) and/or the nominal GDP growth rate (k) above the nominal cost of "debt financing" (i). It may be noted that artificially lowering the borrowing rate (i) is not a solution to the debt problem because at the limit it implies an unviable financial system. Depressing (i) would imply raising funds from captive financial institutions at a lower cost and an increasingly lower volume of directly mobilised household savings. In an inflationary environment, the captive financial institutions could not continue to operate profitably with lower interest earnings on government lending without raising their lending rates (or other service charges) to the non-government sectors and/or lowering deposit rates: one would then be either "crowding out" other borrowers or pushing savings out of the financial sectors into inflation hedges.

The equation (7) captures the dynamic relationship between primary deficit (as a ratio of GDP) and different modes of financing it. Accordingly, it forms the basis for projections under the assumed conditions.

The debt-financing scenario developed below addresses the following question: what would be the future time profile of "debt-financing" to GDP ratio, if the government deficit is allowed to evolve passively and domestic borrowings (other than those from the RBI) are used for financing it while the other modes of financing, such as, net RBI credit to Government and external financing are maintained at their current ratios of GDP?

In order to conduct this thought experiment, the basic dynamic relationship (eq. 7) needs to be suitably modified. As detailed in the Technical Appendix, the following form could be derived:

Eq. (8)
$$\frac{B(t)}{Y(t)} = \frac{1}{1-h}\left[\frac{G(t)}{Y(t)} - \frac{T(t)}{Y(t)} - \frac{F(t)}{Y(t)}\right]$$

$$-\left[\frac{k-i^*}{(1-h)(1+k)}\right]\frac{RG(t-1)}{Y(t-1)} + \left[\frac{1+\frac{i-eh}{i-h}}{1+k}\right]\frac{B(t-1)}{Y(t-1)}$$

which forms the basis for the "debt-financing" scenario.

Projections for Debt-GDP Ratio

In order to project the debt-GDP ratio under the "debt-financing" scenario, eq. (8) was used with the following numerical values assigned to selected parameters:

n = Real GDP growth = 5 per cent.

p = Inflation rate = 7 per cent.

i = Nominal interest rate on domestic debt held outside the RBI = 10.2 per cent.

i* = Nominal interest rate on domestic debt held by the RBI = 5.3 per cent.

e = Nominal interest rate on government's domestic lending = 7.4 per cent[15].

h = Fraction of domestic borrowings on-lent by the Government = 0.4.

The ratio of net outstanding RBI credit to Government to GDP and the ratio of net foreign inflow of official resources were held constant at their 1987-88 levels of 16 per cent and 0.87 per cent, respectively. On the other hand, expenditure–GDP ratio and receipts–GDP ratio were allowed to evolve endogenously.

Time profile for government expenditure[16] and receipts[17] and hence, the net primary deficit (all expressed as ratio to GDP) were derived using:

Eq. (9)
$$\frac{G(t)}{Y(t)} = \left[\frac{1+(u1)(n)+(v1)(p)}{1+n+p}\right]\frac{G(t-1)}{Y(t-1)} \text{ and}$$

Eq. (10) $$\frac{T(t)}{Y(t)} = \left[\frac{1+(u2)(n)+(v2)(p)}{1+n+p}\right]\frac{T(t-1)}{Y(t-1)}$$

where,

n = Assumed real GDP growth.

p = Assumed inflation rate.

u1 = Real income elasticity of nominal expenditure.

u2 = Real income elasticity of nominal receipts.

v1 = Price elasticity of nominal expenditure.

v2 = Price elasticity of nominal receipts.

Regression Equations

$$\log(G) = -8.2 + 2.395 \log(Y/P) + 0.647 \log(P)$$
$$(4.57) \quad (6.58) \qquad\qquad (3.47)$$

$\bar{R}^2 = 0.994$, DW = 2.21 SEE = 0.0259

(sample period 1970-71 to 1987-88)

$$\log(T) = -14.76 + 2.0730 \log(Y/P) + 0.5623 \log(P)$$
$$(3.04) \quad (5.01) \qquad\qquad (2.60)$$

$\bar{R}^2 = 0.99$, DW = 1.60, SEE = 0.0473

(Sample period 1975-76 to 1986-87)

(Figures in brackets indicate respective 't' values)

These regressions, which are satisfactory in their statistical properties, indicate that the real income elasticity of nominal government expenditure (u1) (i.e., 2.395) exceeds the corresponding elasticity of nominal revenue receipts (u2) (i.e., 2.073). Similarly, price elasticity of nominal expenditure (i.e., v1 = 0.647) exceeds the corresponding elasticity of nominal receipts (i.e., v2 = 0.562). These phenomena, widely observed in developing countries, confirm the hypothesis that the primary deficit tends to widen with a passive fiscal policy stance.

Having obtained the elasticity estimates, equations (9) and (10) were used for deriving projections of the net primary deficit as a ratio of GDP under the assumed real GDP growth and inflation rate. Given the time profile for the net primary deficit (as a ratio of GDP) and the assumptions regarding the other parameters, dynamic evolution of the debt-GDP ratio was derived as detailed in Table 3.

Table 3

Projections of Debt-GDP Ratio (1988-89 to 1999-2000)

Year	Ratios to Y(t)					
	G(t)	T(t)	F(t)	RG(t)	B(t)/Y(t)	Overall Debt-GDP Ratio
	(1)	(2)	(3)	(4)	(5)	(6)
1987-88*	17.10	12.60	0.87	16.00	28.60	44.60
1988-89	17.77	12.86	0.87	16.00	33.24	49.24
1989-90	18.47	13.12	0.87	16.00	38.53	54.53
1990-91	19.20	13.39	0.87	16.00	44.50	60.50
1991-92	19.96	13.66	0.87	16.00	51.18	67.18
1992-93	20.75	13.94	0.87	16.00	58.59	74.59
1993-94	21.57	14.22	0.87	16.00	66.78	82.78
1994-95	22.42	14.51	0.87	16.00	75.76	91.76
1995-96	23.30	14.81	0.87	16.00	85.55	101.55
1996-97	24.22	15.11	0.87	16.00	96.20	112.20
1997-98	25.17	15.42	0.87	16.00	107.74	123.74
1998-99	26.16	15.73	0.87	16.00	120.21	136.21
1999-2000	27.19	16.05	0.87	16.00	133.65	149.65

* : Actuals

Notes: 1. Col. (1) is based on the formula: $\left[\frac{1+(u_1)(n)+(v_1)(p)}{1+n+p}\right]\frac{G(t-1)}{Y(t-1)}$

2. Col. (2) is based on the formula: $\left[\frac{1+(u_2)(n)+(v_2)(p)}{1+n+p}\right].\frac{T(t-1)}{Y(t-1)}$

3. Col. (5) = 1.6666 [Col.(1)-Col.(2)-Col. (3)]

$$-0.0997\left[\frac{(RG(t))}{Y(t)}\right]+0.9827\left[\frac{B(t)}{Y(t)}\right]_{t-1}$$

4. Col. (6) = Col. (4) + Col. (5)

As indicated in Table 3, a passive fiscal stance is likely to result in enlargement of the net primary deficit to GDP ratio from 4.5 per cent in 1987-88 to as much as 11.1 per cent by the year 1999-2000. The corresponding gross primary deficit could easily be of the order of 19-20 per cent of GDP. Contemporaneously, the "debt-

financing" to GDP ratio would increase very rapidly from 28.6 per cent in 1987-88 to as much as 133.7 per cent and the overall debt-GDP ratio would shoot up from 44.6 per cent in 1987-88 and crossing the 100 per cent mark in 1995-96, would reach nearly 150 per cent by the turn of the century. Such a rapid escalation of debt-GDP ratio naturally raises the question of its sustainability.

Sustainability of Domestic Debt

In the recent fiscal literature, domestic debt accumulation is regarded 'sustainable' as long as the resultant debt-GDP ratio is converging to an asymptotic upper bound and is deemed to be explosive otherwise. This connotation of sustainability appears to be less meaningful for developing countries. In the context of developing countries, sustainability ought to be seen in terms of sustaining rapid economic growth. In this regard, the pre-emptive impact of mounting interest burden, emanating from rising debt-GDP ratio on the revenue receipts assumes crucial importance.

Gross interest burden of domestic debt can simply be defined as the ratio of Gross Domestic Interest Payments (GDIP) to government's revenue receipts (T). The level of Gross Domestic Interest payments, in turn can be derived as the product of interest rate and the stock of overall outstanding domestic debt at the end of the previous year. Thus,

$$\text{Gross Interest Burden (GIB)} = \frac{\text{Gross Domestic Interest Payments (GDIP)}}{\text{Government Receipts (T)}}$$

Which can be written as:

$$\text{GIB} = \frac{r\,D(t-1)}{T(t)}$$

$$= \frac{r\,D(t-1)}{(1+u_2 n+v_2 p)\,T(t-1)}$$

Where

D = Overall domestic debt.

r = Average interest rate on overall domestic debt.

u_2 = Real income elasticity of nominal receipts.

v_2 = Price elasticity of nominal receipts.

Thus,

$$= \frac{r}{1+u_2n+v_2p}\left[\frac{D(t-1)}{T(t-1)}\right]$$

$$\text{Eq. (11) GIB} = \left[\frac{r}{1+u_2n+v_2p}\right]\left[\frac{D(t-1)/Y(t-1)}{T(t-1)/Y(t-1)}\right]$$

Since the projections for debt-GDP ratio and receipts-GDP ratio have already been derived, eq. (11) can be readily used for obtaining corresponding projections of the Gross Interest Burden (GIB). It may be noted, however, that for policy purposes what is more relevant is the Net Interest Burden (NIB) rather than the gross burden, i.e., domestic interest receipts arising from the loans and advances of the Government should be netted out. A simple way to derive the Net Interest Burden (NIB) is to assume that the ratio of net to gross domestic interest payments remains unchanged at the base year level throughout the projection period. Relevant projections of gross and net interest burden for the period 1988-89 through 1999-2000 are presented in Table 4.

It is evident from Table 4 that the rapid increase in the debt-GDP ratio, corresponding Net Interest Burden (NIB) is also likely to go up substantially from about 11.4 per cent of receipts in 1987-88, to as much as 30.1 per cent of projected receipts by the turn of the century.

The enormity of this potential situation can be appreciated with a historical perspective. The net interest burden was actually negative until 1973-74. It was as low as one per cent of receipts in 1974-75 and increased to about 5.1 per cent of receipts in 1980-81. With the acceleration of domestic debt accumulation during the 1980s, it rose to about 12 per cent of receipts in 1987-88. And now, if the government receipts and expenditure are allowed to evolve passively, while relying on 'debt financing' of the resultant deficits, the net interest burden would shoot up to as much as 30 per cent of projected receipts by the year 1999-2000.

Table 4

Interest Burden of Domestic Debt

(Gross & Net)

Year	*Debt-GDP Ratio*	*T(t)/Y(t)*	*Gross Interest Burden GDIP/T NDIP/T*	*Net Interest Burden*
	1	2	3	4
1987-88*	44.60	12.60	26.16	11.43
1988-89	49.24	12.86	28.30	12.36
1989-90	54.53	13.12	30.71	[illegible]
1990-91	60.50	13.39	33.39	14.59
1991-92	67.18	13.66	36.34	15.88
1992-93	74.59	13.94	39.54	17.28
1993-94	82.78	14.22	43.02	18.80
1994-95	91.76	14.51	46.73	20.42
1995-96	101.55	14.81	50.67	22.14
1996-97	112.20	15.11	54.87	23.97
1997-98	123.74	15.42	59.30	25.91
1998-99	136.21	15.73	63.99	27.96
1999-2000	149.65	16.05	68.90	30.10

* Actuals

Notes:

1. Col. (1) = Col. (6) of Table 3.
2. Col. (2) = Col. (2) of Table 3.
3. Col. (3) = 0.0739 $\left[\frac{\text{Col}(1)}{\text{Col}(2)}\right] \times 100$.
4. Col. (4) = 0.4369 [Col. (3)].

Implications of such a large increase in the net interest burden are fairly obvious. In a developing economy like India, raising direct taxes is subject to serious socio-economic constraints. Alternatively, recourse to indirect taxes, especially those levied on intermediate inputs, is likely to hurt productive efficiency by reducing the net value added in production (to the extent that the incidence is not passed on to the consumers). On the other hand, on the expenditure side, current outlays tend to be sticky downwards. In such a fiscal environment, higher net interest burden may invariably lead to a squeeze on budgetary capital outlays, thereby stifling economic growth.

IV. MONETARY FINANCING SCENARIO

Section III has demonstrated what lies at the end of the rainbow, if the burgeoning government deficits is not arrested in time and "debt-financing" is used for financing the emerging deficit passively while maintaining the other modes of financing at their current ratios to GDP. Given the potential adverse implications of domestic debt accumulation, policy makers may be inclined to rely on some other way of financing the deficit rather than checking its expansion. In the Indian context, resorting to net RBI credit on a larger scale may, especially, be tempting.

This section accordingly develops a monetary financing scenario. The thought experiment here addresses the following question: if government deficit is allowed to evolve passively and is financed by resorting to additional net RBI credit, while maintaining the domestic "debt-financing" and foreign financing at their current ratios to GDP, what would be macroeconomic consequences for the economy?

Analytical Framework

As detailed in the Technical Appendix, the dynamic relationship between debt-GDP ratio and different modes of financing government deficit (i.e., eq. 7) can be suitably modified for deriving the monetary financing scenario. The relevant difference equation takes the form:

$$\text{Eq. (12)} \quad \left[\frac{RG(t)-RG(t-1)}{Y(t)}\right]$$

$$=\left[\frac{G(t)}{Y(t)}-\frac{T(t)}{Y(t)}-\frac{F(t)}{Y(t)}\right]+\left(\frac{i^*}{i+k}\right)\frac{RG(t-1)}{Y(t-1)}$$

$$+\left[\frac{h(k-e)-(k-i)}{1+k}\right]\frac{B(t-1)}{Y(t-1)}$$

This equation forms the basis of our monetary financing scenario.

In order to make eq. (12) operational, evolution of each of the terms on the right hand side must be traced. In this regard, several adjustments are needed:

1. The inflation rate must be allowed to adjust upwards in response to rising ratio of pure monetary financing to GDP. For this purpose, the following simple formulation is proposed:

Eq. (13) $\Delta P = \beta_o + \beta_1 (MFR)_{-1} + \beta_2 (\Delta P)_{-1}$

Where $MFR = \left[\frac{RG(t) - RG(t-1)}{Y(t)}\right]$

In this formulation, change in the price level (ΔP) in the current period is posited as a function of the lagged monetary financing ratio to GDP and the own lagged value[18].

Capturing the nexus between monetary financing and inflation, admittedly, requires a more elaborate model with due allowance made for appropriate real sector variables. The emphasis here, however, is on a thought experiment, which is adequately served by this simple specification.

2. When inflation rate is allowed to adjust upwards in response to rising monetary financing ratio, corresponding provision is also needed for revision of nominal interest rate on domestic debt. The indexation of interest rate on domestic debt held outside the RBI is assumed to take the following form:

Eq. (14) $i_t = p_t + 0.03$

On the other hand, interest rate on domestic debt held by the RBI is expected to take the form:

Eq. (15) $i^*_t = P_t - 0.02$

In other words, the nominal interest rate on domestic debt held outside the RBI is assumed to be maintained three percentage points above the inflation rate, whereas, the nominal interest rate on debt held by the RBI is assumed to remain two percentage points below the inflation. This corresponds roughly to the actual interest rate differentials in the base year.

Application to Indian Data

In order to apply the framework developed above to Indian data, the following numerical values were assigned to relevant parameters:

1. n = Real GDP growth rate = 5 per cent per annum[19].
2. h = Fraction of domestic borrowings on-lent by the Government = 0.5.
3. The domestic debt outside the RBI and foreign financing, both as ratios to GDP are maintained at their respective 1986-87 levels.

The relationship between price level and the monetary financing ratio, (i.e., eq. 13) was estimated using Indian data for the period 1970-71 to 1986-87 and the following regression equation was obtained:

$$\Delta P = \underset{(2.59)}{0.075} + \underset{(5.04)}{13.68}\,(MFR)_{-1} - \underset{(-2.81)}{0.7}\,(\Delta P)_{-1}$$

$$\bar{R}^2 = 0.71 \quad DW = 2.04$$

The price level was measured by the GDP (at factor cost) deflator and the net outstanding RBI credit to Government for the period 't' was measured as the average of the end-period values for periods 't-1' and 't'.

Based on the estimated relationships and the assumed values of relevant parameters, monetary financing scenario was derived recursively as follows:

The monetary financing ratio in the base year (1987-88), using the above mentioned regression equation, yields change in the price level and hence the inflation rate (P) in the next year. The inflation rate along with the assumed real GDP growth rate and the relevant estimated elasticities determine expenditure-GDP (G/Y) ratio and receipts-GDP (T/Y) ratio. The inflation rate also determines nominal interest rate (i) on debt held outside the RBI and nominal interest rate (i*) on debt held by the RBI. The values of (p), (i), and (i*) along with other parameters (h), (k) and (e) determine the coefficients for (RG/Y) and (B/Y) in the basic difference equation (eq. 12). Relevant substitutions then yield the pure monetary financing-GDP ratio in that year, which determines inflation rate in the next year and the whole process is repeated again.

Results of this scenario are presented in Table 5. As is evident from the Table, resorting to monetary financing is likely to set in motion a vicious circle of large deficit, higher monetary financing,

more inflation leading again to a larger deficit, and so on. Indeed, reliance on net RBI credit is likely to raise the monetary financing ratio from 2.4 per cent of GDP in the base year to 17.3 per cent of GDP and consequently, the inflation rate is likely to shoot up from under seven per cent in the base year to as much as 20 per cent within five years.

This order of acceleration of inflation emanating from monetary financing alone is very serious, given the most favourable conditions assumed. If the real GDP growth falters from the assumed five per cent rate, say due to supply side shocks such as adverse weather conditions etc., the inflation rate may easily flare up even beyond 20 per cent per annum in a matter of only five years.

SUMMARY AND CONCLUSIONS

1. Concerns are being voiced about the growing government deficits and the resultant rapid expansion of domestic debt in India and yet, relevant issues have not been adequately and rigorously investigated. The subject calls for a comprehensive and much deeper analysis than the treatments presently available. What is needed is a systematic analysis of the dynamic nexus between widening government deficits and different modes of financing them in the framework of inter-temporal budget constraint. This study makes an effort in that direction.

2. For a comprehensive analysis, first of all, the data base has to be reconstructed. Available measures of government deficit and domestic debt are accounting figures rather than proper economic aggregates. These need to be replaced by analytically meaningful measures.

Alternate government deficit estimates for 1970-71 and for the 1980s have been derived, which indicate that government deficit in India, as a ratio of GDP has significantly widened during the 1980s. The traditional budget deficit increased from 0.7 per cent of GDP in 1970-71 to the average of 1.3 per cent in the first half of the 1980s and to the average of 2.3 per cent in the next four years ending 1988-89. The traditional budget deficit, however, has been grossly underestimating the overall borrowing need arising out of the fiscal operations of the Government. Indeed, the traditional budget deficit

Table 5

Monetary Financing Scenario

Year	*p*	*ΔP*	*p*	$\frac{G(t)}{Y(t)}$	$\frac{T(t)}{Y(t)}$	*[Coefficient]* $\times\left[\frac{RG(t-1)}{y(t-1)}\right]$	*[Coefficient]* $\times\left[\frac{B(t-1)}{y(t-1)}\right]$	$\frac{\Delta RG}{Y}$ (=MFR)
	1	2	3	4	5	6	7	8
1986-87	3.62@	—	—	—	—	—	—	—
1987-88	3.9282@	0.308@	0.085@	0.171@	0.126@	—	—	0.024@
1988-89	4.1162	0.188	0.048	0.182	0.130	0.005	-0.001	0.047
1989-90	4.7022	0.586	0.142	0.193	0.129	0.021	0.010	0.086
1990-91	5.5432	0.841	0.179	0.204	0.126	0.034	0.014	0.117
1991-92	6.6302	1.087	0.196	0.215	0.123	0.047	0.016	0.146
1992-93	7.9422	1.312	0.198	0.227	0.120	0.059	0.016	0.173

@ denotes actuals.

has been roughly between one-fifth and one-third of relevant gross fiscal deficit, which correctly reflects the overall borrowing need. The gross fiscal deficit expanded from 3.5 per cent of GDP in 1970-71 to the average of seven per cent of GDP in the first half of the 1980s and further to the average of 9.3 per cent in the four year period ended in 1988-89. Contemporaneously, the gross primary deficit worsened from 3.5 per cent of GDP to as much as 7.6 per cent of GDP during same period.

An attempt has also been made to derive analytically more meaningful measures of domestic debt. The rapid increase in domestic debt in India is evident from the estimates obtained. According to the method proposed in the study, gross domestic debt expanded from 27.1 per cent of GDP in 1970-71 to 31.6 per cent of GDP in 1980-81 which rose further to as much as 44.6 per cent of GDP in 1987-88.

3. Starting from the inter-temporal budget constraint, analytical expressions in the form of difference equations were derived so as to establish the dynamic inter-linkages between government deficits and different modes of financing them. This framework was used to conduct two thought experiments:

(a) In "debt-financing scenario", the question addressed is: what would be the future time profile of debt-GDP ratio, if the government deficit is allowed to evolve passively and domestic borrowings, excluding those from the RBI are used for financing it while maintaining the other modes of financing at their current ratios to GDP?

(b) In monetary-financing scenario, the question addressed is: what would be the projected impact on inflation, if the government deficit is allowed to evolve passively, financed by resorting to additional net RBI credit while holding the domestic "debt financing" and foreign financing at their base year ratios to GDP?

4. Under the debt-financing scenario, the overall debt-GDP ratio is projected to increase very rapidly; rising from 44.6 per cent of GDP in 1987-88, the overall debt-GDP ratio would cross the 100 per cent mark in 1995-96, reaching as much as 150 per cent by the year 1999-2000.

With the rapid increase in the overall debt-GDP ratio, corresponding net interest burden (i.e., net domestic interest payments as ratio of projected receipts) would also rise substantially. The net interest burden was barely one per cent in 1974-75 and rose to about 12 per cent in 1987-88. With the projected acceleration of debt accumulation, it would shoot up to as much as 30 per cent of projected receipts by the turn of the century. Given the limited scope for raising receipts-GDP ratio and the tendency for current outlays to be sticky downwards, the higher net interest burden may invariably lead to a squeeze on budgetary capital outlays, thereby stifling economic growth.

5. Resorting to larger recourse to RBI financing is not a panacea of the problem either. The monetary financing scenario has demonstrated that such an attempt would lead to a vicious circle of large deficit, higher monetary financing, more inflation leading again to a larger deficit and so on. Indeed, the inflation rate, as measured by GDP deflator, which was under seven per cent in the base year could, by this factor alone, be pushed to unacceptably high level of about 20 per cent within a five year period. If the real GDP growth rate turns out to be less than five per cent per annum as assumed, say due to adverse weather conditions, the inflation rate may easily flare up even beyond 20 per cent per annum within a short span of time.

* Authors are grateful to the participants especially Dr. Raja Chelliah, Prof. Willem Buiter, Prof. Mihir Rakshit, Prof. A. Bagchi, Prof. B.B. Bhattacharya, Prof. S.P. Gupta and Ms. Ritu Anand for their comments and to Shri R.K. Patnaik, Shri R.K. Das and Smt. Yasmin Adenwala for assistance.

Notes

1. See for example, Giavazzi & Spaventa (Eds.) (1988) & Boskin, Flemming and Gorini (Eds.) (1987).
2. Rakshit (1989). p.1.
3. For the sake of brevity, domestic borrowings other than net RBI credit to Government is referred to as "debt-financing" in this study.
4. All government deficit measures have been so defined here as to have positive values, i.e., expenditure minus receipts rather than the other way round.
5. Chakravarty Committee Report (1985), p. 153.
6. The concept of fiscal deficit is widely used by the IMF. No distinction, however is made between gross and net deficit. In the IMF terminology, the fiscal deficit refers to gross fiscal deficit.
7. Coincides with the IMF's definition of primary deficit.

8. It may be noted that in this study, the term "domestic debt" is used rather than "public debt" or "internal liabilities" presently used in the literature. The term "public" is avoided because it may have a broader connotation covering the entire public sector whereas the focus here is only on the Central Government. The term "internal debt" is discarded because in the Indian budget documents, it refers only to a part of the debt, not covering small savings, etc. Finally, the term "internal liabilities" is not considered suitable because one rupee coins or notes also constitute an internal liabilities of the Government, but it does not qualify for being internal debt.
9. Buchanan (1968), p. 32.
10. Buchanan (1968), p.4.
11. Buchanan (1968), p.63.
12. Rakshit (1989), p.4.
13. Eq. (2) is a first order difference equation of the form $Y(t) - a\, Y(t-1) = f(t)$ which is linear with constant coefficients. For such equations, convergence to a stationary value requires $o < a < 1$. See R.G.D. Allen (1973), p. 185. This equation is essentially a discrete time version of a differential equation developed by Spanventa (1987).
14. Details of the derivation are in the technical appendix.
15. As quoted by Seshan (1987), Table 9.
16. G and T are defined as non-interest revenue expenditure plus capital expenditure and non-interest revenue receipts plus grants respectively, so that the difference equal the net primary deficit.
17. G and T are defined as non-interest revenue expenditure plus capital expenditure and non-interest revenue receipts plus grants respectively, so that the difference equal the net primary deficit.
18. Equivalently, the equation can also be interpreted as a relationship between price level (P) in the current period on the one hand and the lagged monetary financing to GDP ratio and the own lagged values for two periods on the other.
19. In terms of the sustainability condition derived in Section II, the assumption of five per cent real GDP growth and three per cent real interest rate on domestic debt held outside the RBI implies that explosive evolution of debt-GDP ratio is ruled out by construction. This has been done with a view to demonstrate the potential adverse impact of monetary financing even under a relatively favourable set of circumstances. The outcome could only be worse in less suitable environment.

References

Allen, R.G.D. (1973), Mathematical Economics, ELBS and Macmillan, Second Edition.

Bispham, J.A. (1987), "Rising Public Sector Indebtedness: Some More Unpleasant Arithmatic". *Private Savings and Public Debt*, edited by Boskin, Flemming and Gorini, Basil Blackwell, U.S.A.

Blanchard, O. J. (1984), "Current and Anticipated Deficits, Interest Rates and Economic Activity", *European Economic Review*, March.

Bollino, A. and Rossi N. (1988), Public Debt and Household's Demand for Monetary Assets in Italy: 1970-86 in *High Public Debt: The Italian Experience*, edited by Giavazzi and Spaventa, Cambridge University Press.

Boskin, M.J., Flemming, J.S. and Gorini, S. (1987) (Eds.), *Private Saving and Public Debt*, Basil Blackwell, U.S.A.

Buchanan, J.M., (1968), "Public Debt" in *International Encyclopedia of the Social Sciences*, The Macmillan Company and The Free Press.

Buiter, W.H., (1983), "A Guide to Public Sector Debt and Deficits", *Economic Policy*, 1. November.

Comptroller and Auditor General's Report (1988), (No.10): Government of India.

Dornbusch, R. (1978), "Inflation, Capital and Deficit Finance", *Journal of Money, Credit and Banking*, February.

Dornbusch, R. (1988), Discussion of "Introduction: Is there a Public Debt Problem in Italy", in *High Public Debt: The Italian Experience*, edited by Giavazzi and Spaventa, Cambridge University Press.

Dubashi, J. (1989), "Is India Going Bankrupt". A Publication of the Project for Economic Education, Bombay.

Eisner R. and Pieper, (1986), "Deficits, Monetary Policy and Real Economic Activity", *Public Debt and Macroeconomics*.

Giovannini, A. (1988), "Capital Controls and Public Finance: The Experience in Italy" in *High Public Debt: The Italian Experience*, edited by Giavazzi and spaventa, Cambridge University Press.

IMF (1986), : Manual of Government Finance Statistics.

Masson, P.R. (1985), "The Sustainability of Fiscal Deficits", IMF Staff Papers, Vol 32, No.4. December.

Pagano, M. (1988), "The Management of Public Debt and Financial Markets", in *High Public Debt: The Italian Experience*, edited by Giavazzi and Spaventa, Cambridge University Press.

Rakshit, M. (1989), "Internal Debt Trap: the Shadow and the Substance", Delivered as S.N. Sen Memorial Lecture, Calcutta.

Report of the Committee to Review the working of the Monetary System (1985): Reserve Bank of India, Bombay.

Seshan, A. (1987), "The Burden of Domestic Public Debt in India", *RBI Occasional Papers*, Vol. 8, No. I, June.

Spanventa, L (1987). "The Growth of Public Debt: Sustainability, Fiscal Rules, and Monetary Rules", *Staff Papers*, International Monetary Fund, Vol. 34, No. 2, June.

Tabellini, G. (1988), "Monetary and Fiscal Policy co-ordination with a High Public Debt" in *High Public Debt: The Italian Experience*, edited by Giavazzi and Spaventa, Cambridge University Press.

World Bank (1988), World Development Report.

TECHNICAL APPENDIX

The simple budget constraint is:

$$G(t) - T(t) + iB(t-1) + i^* RG(t-1) = [B(t) - B(t-1)] + [RG(t) - RG(t-1)]$$

$$\therefore \quad \frac{B(t)-B(t-1)}{Y(t)} = \frac{G(t)-T(t)+iB(t-1)+i^*RG(t-1)-[RG(t)-RG(t-1)]}{Y(t)}$$

Now, $\dfrac{B(t)}{Y(t)} - \dfrac{B(t-1)}{Y(t-1)} = \dfrac{B(t)}{Y(t)} - (1+k)\left[\dfrac{B(t-1)}{Y(t)}\right]$

Since $Y(t) = (1+k)\, Y(t-1)$

$$\Rightarrow \quad \frac{B(t)}{Y(t)} = \left[\frac{B(t)-B(t-1)}{Y(t)}\right] - k\left[\frac{B(t-1)}{Y(t)}\right] + \left[\frac{B(t-1)}{Y(t-1)}\right]$$

Combining the two results, we get,

$$= \frac{B(t)}{Y(t)} = \left[\frac{G(t)-T(t)}{Y(t)}\right] - \left[\frac{RG(t)-RG(t-1)}{Y(t)}\right] + \left[\frac{iB(t-1)}{Y(t)}\right] + \frac{i^*RG(t-1)}{Y(t)}$$

$$-k\,\frac{B(t-1)}{Y(t)} + \frac{B(t-1)}{Y(t-1)}$$

$$= \left[\frac{G(t)-T(t)}{Y(t)}\right] - \left[\frac{RG(t)-RG(t-1)}{Y(t)}\right] + \frac{i^*RG(t-1)}{Y(t)} + (i-k)\left[\frac{B(t-1)}{Y(t)}\right] + \frac{B(t-1)}{Y(t-1)}$$

Which using $Y(t) = (1+k)\, Y(t-1)$ simplifies to,

$$\text{(A.1)} \quad \frac{B(t)}{Y(t)} = \left[\frac{G(t)-T(t)}{Y(t)}\right] - \left[\frac{RG(t)-RG(t-1)}{Y(t)}\right] + \frac{i^*}{(1+k)} + \left[\frac{RG(t-1)}{Y(t-1)}\right] + \left(\frac{1+i}{1+k}\right)\frac{B(t-1)}{Y(t-1)}$$

Which is the equation (2) in the text.

In the general case, the intertemporal budget constraint is:

$$[G(t) - T(t)] + [iB(t-1) + i^* RG(t-1) + w\, NF(t-1)] + [L(t) - L(t-1) - eL(t-1)]$$

$$= [B(t) - B(t-1)] + [RG(t) - RG(t-1)] + [NF(t) - NF(t-1)]$$

In view of the assumptions, we have:

$$F(t) = NF(t) - NF(t-1) - w\, NF(t-1)$$

$$L(t) - L(t-1) = h\,[B(t) - B(t-1)]$$

$$L(t-1) = h\, B(t-1)$$

On substitution in the budget constraint, we get,

$$[G(t) - T(t)] + [iB(t\text{-}1) + i^{*} RG(t\text{-}1)] + h\,[B(t) - B(t\text{-}1)] - eh\,B(t\text{-}1)$$

$$= [B(t) - B(t\text{-}1)] + [RG(t) - RG(t\text{-}1)] + F(t)$$

$$\Rightarrow (l\text{-}h)\ [B(t) - B(t\text{-}1)]$$

$$[G(t) - T(t)] + [iB(t\text{-}1) + i^{*} RG(t\text{-}1)] - eh\,B(t\text{-}1)$$

$$- [RG(t) - RG(t\text{-}1)] - F(t)$$

$$\Rightarrow [B\ (t) - B(t\text{-}1)] = \left(\frac{1}{1-h}\right)[G(t) - T(t) - [RG(t) - RG(t\text{-}1)] - F(t)]$$

$$+\left[\frac{i^{*}}{1\text{-}h}\right] RG(t\text{-}1) + \left[\frac{i\text{-}eh}{1\text{-}h}\right] B(t\text{-}1)$$

$$\Rightarrow B(t) = \left(\frac{1}{1\text{-}h}\right)[G(t) - T(t) - [RG(t) - RG(t\text{-}1)] - F(t)]$$

$$+\left(\frac{i^{*}}{1\text{-}h}\right) RG(t\text{-}1) + \left[1 + \left(\frac{i\text{-}eh}{1\text{-}h}\right)\right] B(t\text{-}1)$$

$$\Rightarrow \frac{B(t)}{Y(t)} = \left(\frac{1}{1\text{-}h}\right)\left[\frac{G(t)}{Y(t)} - \frac{T(t)}{Y(t)} - \frac{RG(t)\text{-}RG(t\text{-}1)}{Y(t)} - \frac{F(t)}{Y(t)}\right]$$

$$+\left(\frac{i^{*}}{1\text{-}h}\right)\frac{RG(t\text{-}1)}{Y(t)} + \left[1 + \left(\frac{i\text{-}eh}{1\text{-}h}\right)\right]\frac{B(t\text{-}1)}{Y(t)}$$

Which, using $Y(t) = (1+k)\,Y(t\text{-}1)$ yields

$$\text{(A.2)} \quad \frac{B(t)}{Y(t)} = \left(\frac{1}{1\text{-}h}\right)\left[\frac{G(t)}{Y(t)} - \frac{T(t)}{Y(t)} - \frac{RG(t)\text{-}RG(t\text{-}1)}{Y(t)} - \frac{F(t)}{Y(t)}\right]$$

$$+\left[\frac{i^{*}}{(1\text{-}h)(1+k)}\right]\frac{RG(t\text{-}1)}{Y(t\text{-}1)} + \left[\frac{1 + \left(\frac{i\text{-}eh}{i\text{-}h}\right)}{1+k}\right]\frac{B(t\text{-}1)}{Y(t\text{-}1)}$$

Which is the basic difference equation [eq. (7)] in the text. If one assumes that there are no domestic lendings (i.e., $h = 0$) and no foreign financing, i.e., $F(t) = 0$, then eq. (A.2) reduces to eq. (A.1) as in the simple case.

(a) Difference Equation for "Debt-financing" Scenario

Collecting the terms involving net RBI credit, we have:

$$\left[\frac{i^*}{(1-h)(1+k)}\right]\frac{RG(t-1)}{Y(t-1)}-\left(\frac{1}{1-h}\right)\frac{RG(t)}{Y(t)}+\left(\frac{1}{1-h}\right)\frac{RG(t-1)}{Y(t)}$$

$$=\left[\frac{i^*}{(1-h)(1+k)}\right]\frac{RG(t-1)}{Y(t-1)}-\left[\frac{1}{1-h}\right]\frac{RG(t)}{Y(t)}+\left(\frac{1}{(1-h)(1+k)}\right)\frac{RG(t-1)}{Y(t)}$$

$$=\left[\frac{1+i^*}{(1-h)(1+k)}\right]\frac{RG(t-1)}{Y(t-1)}-\left[\frac{1}{(1-h)}\right]\frac{RG(t)}{Y(t)}$$

If the net RBI credit to government as a ratio of GDP is kept constant

$$\frac{RG(t)}{Y(t)}=\frac{RG(t-1)}{Y(t-1)}$$

Accordingly, the expression becomes,

$$=\left[\frac{1+i^*}{(1-h)(1+k)}\right]\frac{RG(t-1)}{Y(t-1)}-\left(\frac{1}{1-h}\right)\frac{RG(t-1)}{Y(t-1)}$$

$$=\left[\frac{i^*-k}{(1-h)(1+k)}\right]\frac{RG(t-1)}{Y(t-1)}$$

Which on substitution in (A.2) yields,

$$\text{(A.3)}\qquad \frac{B(t)}{Y(t)}=\left(\frac{1}{1-h}\right)-\left[\frac{G(t)}{Y(t)}-\frac{T(t)}{Y(t)}-\frac{F(t)}{Y(t)}\right]$$

$$-\left[\frac{k-i^*}{(1-h)(1+k)}\right]\frac{RG(t-1)}{Y(t-1)}+\left[\frac{1+\left(\frac{i-eh}{i-h}\right)}{1+k}\right]\frac{B(t-1)}{Y(t-1)}$$

which is the eq.(8) in the text, used for the "debt-financing" scenario.

(b) Difference Equation for Monetary Financing Scenario

The last term on the RHS of eq. (A.2) can simplified to:

$$\left(\frac{1}{1+k}\right)\frac{B(t-1)}{Y(t-1)}+\left[\frac{(i-eh)}{(1-h)(1+k)}\right]\frac{B(t-1)}{Y(t-1)}$$

$$=\left(1-\frac{k}{1+k}\right)\frac{B(t-1)}{Y(t-1)}+\left[\frac{(i-eh)}{(1-h)(1+k)}\right]\frac{B(t-1)}{Y(t-1)}$$

$$=\frac{B(t-1)}{Y(t-1)}-\left(\frac{k}{1+k}\right)\frac{B(t-1)}{Y(t-1)}+\left[\frac{(i-eh)}{(1-h)(1+k)}\right]\frac{B(t-1)}{Y(t-1)}$$

On substitution in eq. (A.2), we get,

$$\frac{B(t)}{Y(t)} = \frac{1}{(1-h)}\left[\frac{G(t)}{Y(t)} - \frac{T(t)}{Y(t)} - \frac{RG(t)-RG(t-1)}{Y(t)} - \frac{F(t)}{Y(t)}\right]$$

$$+\left[\frac{i^*}{(1-h)(1+k)}\right]\frac{RG(t-1)}{Y(t-1)} + \frac{B(t-1)}{Y(t-1)} - \left(\frac{k}{(1+k)}\right)\frac{B(t-1)}{Y(t-1)}$$

$$+\left[\frac{i-eh}{(1-h)(1+k)}\right]\frac{B(t-1)}{Y(t-1)}$$

If the "debt -financing" to GDP ratio is held at a constant level

$$\frac{B(t)}{Y(t)} - \frac{B(t-1)}{Y(t-1)} = 0$$

$$\Rightarrow \left(\frac{1}{1-h}\right)\left[\frac{G(t)}{Y(t)} - \frac{T(t)}{Y(t)} - \frac{RG(t)-RG(t-1)}{Y(t)} - \frac{F(t)}{Y(t)}\right]$$

$$+\left[\frac{i^*}{(1-h)(1+k)}\right]\frac{RG(t-1)}{Y(t-1)} + \left(\frac{(i-eh)}{(1-h)(1+k)} - \frac{k}{1+k}\right)\frac{B(t-1)}{Y(t-1)} = 0$$

Thus,

$$\text{(A.4)} \quad \left[\frac{RG(t)-RG(t-1)}{Y(t)}\right] = \left[\frac{G(t)}{Y(t)} - \frac{T(t)}{Y(t)} - \frac{F(t)}{Y(t)}\right] + \left(\frac{i^*}{1+k}\right)\frac{RG(t-1)}{Y(t-1)}$$

$$+\left[\frac{h(k-e)-(k-i)}{1+k}\right]\frac{B(t-1)}{Y(t-1)}$$

Which is eq. (12) in the text and forms the basis for the monetary financing scenario.

DATA APPENDIX

Statement 1

Budgetary Operations of the Government of India: Revenue Account (1970-71 to 1989-90)[1]

(Rs. in crores)

Year	*Revenue Receipts*[2]	*Revenue Expenditure*	*Balance on Revenue Account Surplus (+) Deficit (–)*
	(1)	(2)	(3) = (1) – (2)
1970-71	3,342	3,179	+ 163
1971-72	4,028	4,128	– 100
1972-73	4,578	4,593	– 15
1973-74	5,073	4,836	+ 237
1974-75	6,558	5,793	+ 765
1975-76	8,075	7,189	+ 886
1976-77	8,739	8,441	+ 298
1977-78	9,792	9,362	+ 430
1978-79	11,240	10,948	+ 292
1979-80	11,340	12,034	– 694
1980-81	12,829	14,544	– 1,715
1981-82	15,574	15,868	– 294
1982-83	18,091	19,346	– 1,255
1983-84	20,493	22,890	– 2,397
1984-85	24,384	27,881	– 3,497
1985-86	29,206	34,771	– 5,565
1986-87	34,768	42,544	– 7,776
1987-88	36,545	46,174	– 9,629
1988-89	42,991	54,106	– 11,115
1989-90 (RE)	51,341	64,690	– 13,349

Sources: (1) Articles on Finances of the Government of India PB Bulletin, various issues for the years 1970-71 to 1986-87.

(2) Government of India, Budget Documents for the years 1987-88 to 1990-91.

Note: 1. Data in respect of revenue receipts, revenue expenditure and balance on revenue account for the years 1970-71 to 1986-87 are as per old budgetary classification and, therefore, do not tally with the figures given in the recent budget documents.

2. Net of grants. 1989-90(RE) include transfer of Rs. 2,300 crores of OCC surplus from Public Account.

Statement 2

Budgetary Operations of the Government of India: Capital Account (1970-71 to 1989-90)

(Rs. in crores)

Year	*Capital Receipts**	*Capital Disbursement£*	*Balance on Capital Account Surplus (+) Deficit (–)*
	(1)	*(2)*	*(3)=(1) – (2)*
1970-71	2,524	2,972	– 448
1971-72	3,031	3,450	– 419
1972-73	2,974	3,829	– 855
1973-74	3,646	4,211	– 565
1974-75	3,297	4,782	– 1,485
1975-76	4,697	5,950	– 1,253
1976-77	5,607	6,036	– 429
1977-78	5,589	6,951	– 1,362
1978-79	6,938	8,736	– 1,798
1979-80	6,125	7,864	– 1,739
1980-81	9,432	10,295	– 863
1981-82	10,156	11,254	– 1,098
1982-83	13,286	13,688	– 402
1983-84	15,861	14,881	+ 980
1984-85	17,768	18,016	– 248
1985-86	16,763	16,135	+ 628
1986-87	18,529	19,014	– 485
1987-88	22,026	18,705	+ 3,321
1988-89	25,673	20,800	+ 4,873
1989-90(RE)	23,692	23,006	+ 686

Sources: (1) Articles on Finances of the Government of India, RBI Bulletin, various issues for 1970-71 to 1986-87.

(2) Government of India, Budget Documents for 1987-88 to 1990-91.

Note: * Includes foreign grants, foreign borrowings, domestic borrowings, excluding new 90-day TBs and recovery of loans and advances.

£ *As defined in the Budget Documents* which includes capital expenditure, loans and advances to states, union territories and public sector enterprises, and the discharge of internal and external debt. However, beginning from 1982-83, discharge of debt obligations are netted out both from receipts and expenditure side. Also the States' share of small savings are netted out from the year 1985-86 onwards.

Statement 3

Budgetary Operations of the Government of India: Traditional Deficit (1970-71 to 1989-90)

(Rs. in crores)

Year	*Balance on Revenue Account Surplus (+) Deficit (–)*	*Balance on Capital Account Surplus (+) Deficit (–)*	*Traditional Deficit[1] Surplus (+) Deficit (–)*
	(1)	*(2)*	*(3) = (1)+(2)*
1970-71	+ 163	– 448	– 285
1971-72	– 100	– 419	– 519
1972-73	– 15	– 855	– 870
1973-74	+ 237	– 565	– 328
1974-75	+ 765	– 1,485	– 720
1975-76	+ 886	– 1,253	– 367
1976-77	+ 298	– 429	– 131
1977-78	+ 430	– 1,362	– 932
1978-79	+ 292	– 1,798	– 1,506
1979-80	– 694	– 1,739	– 2,433
1980-81	– 1,715	– 863	– 2,578
1981-82	– 294	– 1,098	– 1,392
1982-83	– 1,255	– 402	– 1,657
1983-84	– 2,397	+ 980	– 1,417
1984-85	– 3,497	– 248	– 3,745
1985-86	– 5,565	+ 628	– 4,937
1986-87	– 7,776	– 485	– 8,261
1987-88	– 9,629	+ 3,321	– 6,308
1988-89	–11,115	+ 4,873	– 6,242
1989-90 (RE)	–13,349	+ 686	–12,663

Sources: Col. (1) from Statement 1. Col. (3).
Col. (2) from Statement 2. Col. (3).

Note: 1. Since the revenue receipts are net of grants, the estimates exceed the corresponding budget figures to that extent. For grants, see col. (4), Table 6.

Statement 4

Net Domestic Lending of the Government of India (1970-71 to 1989-90)

(Rs. in crores)

Year	Loans and Advances[$]	Recovery of Loans and Advances (gross)	Net Domestic Lendings
	(1)	(2)	(3)=(1)-(2)
1970-71	1,553	923	630
1971-72	1,807	1,297	510
1972-73	2,345	1,155	1,190
1973-74	2,432	1,471	961
1974-75	2,629	1,192	1,437
1975-76	3,151	1,486	1,665
1976-77	3,517	1,287	2,230
1977-78	4,155	2,288	1,867
1978-79	5,666	2,082	3,584
1979-80	4,720	1,461	3,259
1980-81	5,651	2,462	3,189
1981-82	6,248	2,173	4,075
1982-83	8,026[£]	3,373	4,653
1983-84	8,605[@]	3,745	4,860
1984-85	10,173	3,729	6,444
1985-86	12,179*	3,865	8,314
1986-87	13,431	4,125	9,306
1987-88	13,508	5,181	8,327
1988-89	15,129	5,053	10,076
1989-90(RE)	17,806	5,530	12,276

Sources: (1) Articles on Finances of the Government of India, RBI Bulletin, various issues for the years 1970-71 to 1986-87.

(2) Government of India, Budget Documents for the years 1987-88 to 1990-91.

Note: @ Excludes Rs. 400 crores of special loans to state governments to clear their overdrafts as on March 1983.

* Excludes Rs. 1.628 crores of Medium Term loans given to state governments to clear their overdrafts.

£ Excludes Rs. 1.743.4 crores of special loans to state governments to clear their deficits as on March 1983.

$ Including loans to Small Savings and short term Ways and Means advances.

Statement 5

Capital Disbursements of the Government of India (1970-71 to 1989-90)

(Rs. in crores)

Year	*Capital Expenditure*	*Net Domestic Lendings*	*Capital* Disbursements*
	(1)	(2)	(3) = (1) + (2)
1970-71	942	630	1,572
1971-72	1,117	510	1,627
1972-73	975	1,190	2,165
1973-74	1,009	961	1,970
1974-75	1,630	1,437	3,067
1975-76	2,250	1,665	3,915
1976-77	2,148	2,230	4,378
1977-78	2,243	1,867	4,110
1978-79	2,418	3,584	6,002
1979-80	2,439	3,259	5,698
1980-81	3,983	3,189	7,172
1981-82	4,299	4,075	8,374
1982-83	4,859	4,653	9,512
1983-84	6,276	4,860	11,136
1984-85	7,843	6,444	14,287
1985-86	7,973	8,314	16,287
1986-87	9,010	9,306	18,316
1987-88	9,580	8,327	17,907
1988-89	10,255	10,076	20,331
1989-90(RE)	11,562	12,276	23,838

Sources: Col. (1) = Capital disbursements (Col. [2]), Statement 2 minus (loans & advances and discharge of internal & external debt.)

Col. (2) = Col. (3), Statement 4.

Note: *: As defined in the fiscal balance sheet of the text, which represents the sum total of capital expenditure and net domestic lendings.

Statement 6

Gross Fiscal Deficit of the Government of India (1970-71 to 1989-90)

(*Rs. in crores*)

Year	*Revenue Expenditure*	*Capital Disbursements*	*Revenue Receipts*	*Grants*	*Net Fiscal Deficit*
	(1)	(2)	(3)	(4)	(5) = (1)+(2) −(3)−(4)
1970-71	3,179	1,572	3,342	—	1,409
1971-72	4,128	1,627	4,028	—	1,727
1972-73	4,593	2,165	4,578	—	2,180
1973-74	4,836	1,970	5,073	—	1,733
1974-75	5,793	3,067	6,558	—	2,302
1975-76	7,189	3,915	8,075	—	3,029
1976-77	8,441	4,378	8,739	195	3,885
1977-78	9,362	4,110	9,792	240	3,440
1978-79	10,948	6,002	11,240	223	5,487
1979-80	12,034	5,698	11,340	313	6,079
1980-81	14,544	7,172	12,829	373	8,514
1981-82	15,868	8,374	15,574	320	8,348
1982-83	19,346	9,512	18,091	297	10,470
1983-84	22,890	11,136	20,493	281	13,252
1984-85	27,881	14,287	24,384	394	17,390
1985-86	34,771	16,287	29,206	484	21,368
1986-87	42,544	18,316	34,768	436	25,656
1987-88	46,174	17,907	36,545	492	27,044
1988-89	54,106	20,331	42,991	600	30,846
1989-90(RE)	64,690	23,838	51,341	913	36,274

Sources: Col. (1) = Col. (2). Statement 1.
Col. (2) = Col. (3). Statement 5.
Col. (3) = Col. (1). Statement 1.
Col. (4) = From Budget Documents.

Note: *: As defined in the fiscal balance sheet of the text, which represents the sum total of capital expenditure and net domestic lendings.

Statement 7

Net Fiscal Deficit of the Government of India (1970-71 to 1989-90)

(Rs. in crores)

Year	*Revenue Expenditure*	*Capital Expenditure*	*Revenue Receipts*	*Grants*	*Net Fiscal Deficit*
	(1)	(2)	(3)	(4)	(5) = (1)+(2) −(3)−(4)
1970-71	3,179	942	3,342	—	779
1971-72	4,128	1,117	4,028	—	1,217
1972-73	4,593	975	4,578	—	990
1973-74	4,836	1,009	5,073	—	772
1974-75	5,793	1,630	6,558	—	865
1975-76	7,189	2,250	8,075	—	1,364
1976-77	8,441	2,148	8,739	195	1,655
1977-78	9,362	2,243	9,792	240	1,573
1978-79	10,948	2,418	11,240	223	1,903
1979-80	12,034	2,439	11,340	313	2,820
1980-81	14,544	3,983	12,829	373	5,325
1981-82	15,868	4,299	15,574	320	4,273
1982-83	19,346	4,859	18,091	297	5,817
1983-84	22,890	6,276	20,493	281	8,392
1984-85	27,881	7,843	24,384	394	10,946
1985-86	34,771	7,973	29,206	484	13,054
1986-87	42,544	9,010	34,768	436	16,350
1987-88	46,174	9,580	36,545	492	18,717
1988-89	54,106	10,255	42,991	600	20,770
1989-90(RE)	64,690	11,562	51,341	913	23,998

Sources: Col. (1) = Col. (2). Statement 1.
Col. (2) = Col. (1). Statement 5.
Col. (3) = Col. (1). Statement 1.
Col. (4) = From Budget Documents.

Statement 8

Net Interest Expenditure of the Government of India (1970-71 to 1989-90)

(Rs. in crores)

Year	*Interest Expenditure (Domestic)*	*Interest Expenditure (External)*	*Interest Receipts (Domestic)*	*Interest Receipts (External)*	*Net Interest Expenditure*
	(1)	(2)	(3)	(4)	(5) = (1)+(2) −(3)−(4)
1970-71	444	161	572	2	31
1971-72	503	167	597	2	71
1972-73	589	187	712	1	63
1973-74	690	192	735	1	146
1974-75	840	161	771	4	226
1975-76	1,038	190	930	3	295
1976-77	1,280	208	1,102	3	383
1977-78	1,437	209	1,428	12	206
1978-79	1,758	226	1,414	13	557
1979-80	2,057	235	1,351	9	932
1980-81	2,465	231	1,790	5	901
1981-82	3,002	258	2,209	6	1,045
1982-83	3,703	304	2,827	24	1,156
1983-84	4,513	356	2,644	25	2,200
1984-85	5,590	460	3,954	9	2,087
1985-86	6,965	538	4,579	7	2,917
1986-87	8,470	766	5,330	9	3,897
1987-88	10,202	1,034£	5,755	$	5,481
1988-89	13,002	1,259£	6,973	$	7,288
1989-90(RE)	16,227	1,483	8,665	$	9,045

Sources: Government of India, Budget documents.

Notes: £ Revised Estimates.

$ Figures in respect of interest receipts (External) are not available separately, but are included in domestic interest receipts.

Statement 9

Gross Primary Deficit of the Government of India (1970-71 to 1989-90)

(Rs. in crores)

Year	*Gross Fiscal Deficit*	*Net Interest Expenditure*	*Gross Primary Deficit*
	(1)	*(2)*	*(3)=(1)–(2)*
1970-71	1,409	31	1,378
1971-72	1,727	71	1,656
1972-73	2,180	63	2,117
1973-74	1,733	146	1,587
1974-75	2,302	226	2,076
1975-76	3,029	295	2,734
1976-77	3,885	383	3,502
1977-78	3,440	206	3,234
1978-79	5,487	557	4,930
1979-80	6,079	932	5,147
1980-81	8,514	901	7,613
1981-82	8,348	1,045	7,303
1982-83	10,470	1,156	9,314
1983-84	13,252	2,200	11,052
1984-85	17,390	2,087	15,303
1985-86	21,368	2,917	18,451
1986-87	25,656	3,897	21,759
1987-88	27,044	5,481	21,563
1988-89	30,846	7,288	23,558
1989-90 (RE)	36,274	9,045	27,229

Sources: Col. (1) : Statement 6, Col. (5).
Col. (2) : Statement 8, Col. (5).

Statement 10

Net Primary Deficit of the Government of India (1970-71 to 1989-90)

(Rs. in crores)

Year	*Net Fiscal Deficit*	*Net Interest Expenditure*	*Gross Primary Deficit*
	(1)	*(2)*	*(3)=(1)–(2)*
1970-71	779	31	748
1971-72	1,217	71	1,146
1972-73	990	63	927
1973-74	772	146	626
1974-75	865	226	639
1975-76	1,364	295	1,069
1976-77	1,655	383	1,272
1977-78	1,573	206	1,367
1978-79	1,903	557	1,346
1979-80	2,820	932	1,888
1980-81	5,325	901	4,424
1981-82	4,273	1,045	3,228
1982-83	5,817	1,156	4,661
1983-84	8,392	2,200	6,192
1984-85	10,946	2,087	8,859
1985-86	13,054	2,917	10,137
1986-87	16,350	3,897	12,453
1987-88	18,717	5,481	13,236
1988-89	20,770	7,288	13,482
1989-90 (RE)	23,998	9,045	14,953

Sources: Col. (1) : Statement 7, Col. (5).
Col. (2) : Statement 8, Col. (5).

2

Fiscal Deficit, External Balance and Monetary Growth

A Study of Indian Economy

Introduction

The external dimensions of the fiscal deficit have been a concern to the policy makers in developing countries. An endemic deficit in the external current account and a domestic saving-investment gap, or what may be referred to as the twin gap problem, are the typical outcome of development strategies that depend on budget deficits on a continuing basis to promote domestic capital formation and growth. While a moderate government deficit corresponding to a sustainable current account gap may be desirable in building up domestic capital formation, a persistently large fiscal gap, however, may turn the external payment situation unsustainable. Persistent high levels of current account deficit poses both a short term risk and a long term problem. To the extent that it generates an unfavourable market sentiment, the adverse effects on interest rate and exchange rate could turn the domestic policy unsustainable. The long term problems manifest through increased debt service payments, erosion in the long run investment prospects and a sustained loss of confidence in the economy. It is in this context that the measures to reduce domestic absorption and improve public saving constitute important policy ingredients of the adjustment towards creating a sustainable balance of payment environment.

The interrelationship between the fiscal deficit and external balance is evident from the following national income identity which

---

Co-author: **M.S. Mohanty**

Reserve Bank of India, Occasional Papers Vol.18, No.4, December 1997.

links domestic saving-investment gap to the current account gap in the balance of payments.

$$(X-M) = Y - (C+I+G) = (S_g - I_g) + (S_p - I_p) \qquad \text{... (1)}$$

The above identity states that the current account deficit (X-M) is the excess of domestic absorption, i.e., consumption (C), investment (I) and government expenditure (G) over income (Y); or stated differently, foreign saving equals the sum of the saving and investment gap of the public sector (S_g-I_g) and that of the private sector (S_p-I_p). It is obvious, therefore, that policies that reduce private savings and increase budget deficit lead to a deterioration in current account deficit. While equation (1) is an ex-post accounting identity and has to be satisfied for each period, the actual dynamics of the transmission of a fiscal deficit to the external current account needs to be worked out by identifying the routes through which domestic economic variables affect the external sector. The theoretical and empirical literature on transmission mechanism in the open economy context have made considerable progress over the years. Beginning with the basic Keynesian and absorption models, the empirical research in this area has proliferated in many directions, to account for the complex behavioural interactions between public and private sectors, as also among the various sectors within the economy, both in the static and intertemporal framework [see for example Polak (1957), Crips and Godley (1976) on Cambridge Economic Policy Group (CEPG) model, Khan and Knight (1981), Frenkel and Razin (1987), Haque *et al* (1990), Bartoli (1989) and Mansur (1989)]. The subject has also received a fair amount of attention in India in the context of the on-going stabilisation and structural adjustment programmes [Rakshit (1991), Mohanty and Joshi (1992), Sau (1992), Bhattacharya *et al* (1994), Rangarajan (1994), Rao and Singh (1995), Krishnamurty and Pandit (1997) and Mohanty (1997)].

This paper outlines an empirical model for the Indian economy to study the dynamic interrelationship between the internal and external balances in the economy. The model covering the period 1971-72 to 1993-94 provides an analytical framework for tracing the income and price routes of adjustment from fiscal deficit to current account deficit in the balance of payments. The main linkages in the model are as follows: fiscal deficits increase the aggregate demand level in the economy and may influence output (in the

absence of supply constraints), disposable income, consumption and investment, thus raising the import demand at each stage of transition. Given the availability of borrowed resources from non-monetary and external sources, a part of the deficit is financed by resorting to borrowing from the Reserve Bank. The stock of money, therefore, evolves endogenously through the feed-back from reserve money which varies with the changes in fiscal deficit. The money stock, along with output, determines the price level in the economy, which in turn determines the relative prices of imports and exports. To the extent that the nominal exchange rate deviates from its full purchasing parity level, given the domestic and world price levels, fiscal deficit financed by money creation leads to appreciation of real exchange rate, leading to a rise in imports and decline in the competitiveness of exports. The resulting current account deficit creates a financing need and increases the stock of external debt and interest payment, reinforcing the initial deterioration in the current account balance. A further source of transmission may stem from the changes in the financial balance of the private sector which is behaviourally linked to the government deficit. The prototype model is simulated to conduct certain counter-factual experiments on the policy implications of an increase in fiscal deficit.

The rest of the paper is organised as follows: Section I presents a discussion on the trends in government finances, monetary and real sectors and external balance. Section II outlines the analytical framework and the major features of the model. Section III presents the empirical estimates of structural parameters, while Section IV outlines the complete model and its simulation performance. The results of policy simulations are discussed in Section V, followed by concluding observations in Section VI.

I. TRENDS IN MAJOR ECONOMIC INDICATORS DURING 1970-71 TO 1993-94

The fiscal balance of the public sector during 1970s and 1980s showed a distinct deterioration. Total current revenue of the public sector, including the savings of departmental and non-departmental public enterprises, which increased from 14.4 per cent of GDP in 1970-71 to 22.8 per cent in 1990-91, came down to 22.2 per cent in 1993-94. At the same time, total public expenditure, which expanded

from 18.0 per cent of GDP to 31.6 per cent of GDP between 1970-71 and 1990-91, saw a little more than one percentage point decline to 30.2 per cent in 1993-94, following the expenditure adjustment measures initiated since 1991-92. Public sector fiscal deficit, defined as the excess of public sector expenditure on consumption, transfer payment and investment over the current revenue (as in the National Account Statistics) increased from 3.6 per cent of GDP in 1970-71 to 8.8 per cent in 1990-91, but fell to below eight per cent on an average in the next three years.[1] Alongside the increase in resource gap, the composition of government spending underwent a major change during this period. While government consumption increased from 8.8 per cent of GDP in 1970-71 to 11.2 per cent of GDP in 1993-94, that of transfer payments rose almost four times from 2.7 per cent to 10.4 per cent of GDP during this period. Gross investment of public sector, on the other hand, leap-froged from 6.5 per cent of GDP to 9.7 per cent of GDP in 1990-91 before declining steadily to 8.6 per cent in 1993-94 and its gross savings declined from 2.9 per cent of GDP in 1970-71 to 0.6 per cent in 1993-94.

In the monetary sector, the broad money stock (M3) grew by an annual average rate of 17.4 per cent during 1970-71 to 1993-94 which was essentially brought about by an annual average increase of 15.4 per cent in the outstanding Reserve Bank credit to the Government. The annual average inflation rate was placed at 8.8 per cent during this period with the highest inflation rate being recorded at 25.2 per cent in 1974-75 and the lowest being a negative of -1.1 per cent in 1975-76. During the period 1970-71 to 1993-94, real GDP at factor cost grew by an average rate of 4.3 per cent, marked by two years of negative growth in 1972-73 and 1979-80, and the highest growth of 10.6 per cent in 1988-89. Private sector economic behaviour, in terms of its consumption and investment pattern, revealed certain notable changes during this period. While real consumption of the private sector as a proportion of GDP at constant market prices declined from 75.4 per cent in 1970-71 to 61.6 per cent in 1993-94, its real investment increased from 10.6 per cent to 12.8 per cent during this period. The surplus saving of the private sector over its investment increased from an average of 3.8 per cent of GDP in 1970s to 4.6 per cent in 1980s and 6.8 per cent during 1990-91 to 1993-94, thus counteracting, to some extent, the deterioration in the saving-investment gap of the public sector, which

averaged 4.7 per cent in 1970s, 7.7 per cent in 1980s and 7.6 per cent during 1990-91 to 1993-94.

On the external side, nominal merchandise exports (in Rupees), according to the balance of payments data, grew by 17.5 per cent on an average during 1970-71 to 1990-91, which was outpaced by the growth of 18.6 per cent in merchandise imports. Thus, the trade deficit widened from one per cent of GDP in 1970-71 to 3.2 per cent in 1990-91. During the first three years following economic reforms, export and import growth averaged 29.1 per cent, and 16.9 per cent, respectively, and trade deficit declined to 1.3 per cent of GDP. A part of the deterioration in the trade balance during 1970s and 1980s was caused by the adverse movement of relative prices in the trade sector. On the export price front, the unit value index of export rose at an annual average rate of 9.7 per cent during 1970-71 to 1990-91. The nominal exchange rate of rupee, with respect to US $ during the same period, recorded an average rate of depreciation of 4.6 per cent, which was well below the domestic rate of inflation.

While the unit value index of imports registered an annual average increase of 11.6 per cent, much of this increase was concentrated on the price inelastic segment of imports. During the post-reform period, export prices recorded a sharp deceleration from 26.3 per cent in 1991-92 to 12.5 per cent in 1993-94, following the depreciation of the rupee by 36.4 per cent in 1991-92 and 25.2 per cent in 1992-93. The rate of depreciation fell to 2.3 per cent in 1993-94, with a large inflow of capital from abroad. There has been a steady fall in import prices growth in the post-reform period from 15.5 per cent in 1991-92 to -1.2 per cent in 1993-94. Taking into account the invisibles, transfers, investment income and other miscellaneous receipts, total current receipts in the balance of payments accounts recorded an average growth of 16.7 per cent as compared with the increase of 18.5 per cent in current payments during 1970-71 to 1990-91. During the post-reform period ending 1993-94, current receipts and current payments grew at an average rate of 30.2 per cent and 18.3 per cent, respectively, resulting in a considerable strengthening of the balance of payments. The current account balance during the period 1970-71 to 1993-94 remained in deficit throughout, with the exception of 1973-74, 1976-77 and 1977-78. In terms of ratio to GDP, current account deficit which averaged 1.1 per cent during 1970-71 to 1990-91 fell to 0.9 per cent during 1991-92 to 1993-94.

To summarise, the above trends in economic indicators underlined four major developments in the domestic sector which have had implications for the external sector. First, the persistent imbalance in the public sector saving-investment gap has been a primary source of the increase in the current account deficit in the balance of payments. The increase in private sector financial surplus only partly counteracted this deterioration. Second, the shift in the composition of government expenditure towards consumption and transfer payments led to a decline in public sector savings performance and choked the prospects for non-inflationary financing of public investment and growth. This was also a primary reason for increase in domestic absorption relative to output growth. Third, the high reliance on monetary financing to meet the public sector resource shortfalls led to an increase in domestic inflation, thereby, adversely affecting the relative prices in the external sector. This was mainly reflected on the increase in the supply price of exports. Fourth, the misalignment of exchange rate, especially during the first half of 1980s with the domestic inflation rate *versus* the inflation rates of our major trade partners resulted in loss of competitiveness of exports and built-in price bias towards imports. The situation was corrected in the post-reform period by effecting a major readjustment of the external value of the rupee and gradually moving over to a marked based exchange rate system.

Given the above backdrop of trends in major economic variables, the following section presents an analytical framework to study the various inter-linkages among the fiscal, monetary, real and external sector of the Indian economy.

II. FRAMEWORK OF THE MODEL

Theoretical literature discusses two major channels of transmission of fiscal impulses to the external sector, *viz.*, the income and the price routes of transmission. Fiscal deficits – whatever may be their intended purpose – almost immediately increase the aggregate absorption level in the economy relative to output. The output effect of deficit follows subsequently as government investment outlay raises the capital stock in the economy and as firms respond to domestic demand conditions by utilising the excess capacity already available with them. Therefore, while imports may

grow, as a consequence of the increase in absorption, the output effect will generate a chain of secondary impacts on demand for imports through disposable income, private consumption and investment. A further channel of transmission takes place through the relative price changes brought about by the financing side of deficit. When the fiscal deficit is entirely financed by issue of bonds to private sector, the monetary impact of such fiscal operation is limited to the central bank's discretionary policy to ease the pressure on interest rate. Bond financed deficits may, however, generate a wealth impact in the private sector financial portfolio and may increase the aggregate demand and price levels in the economy. Different schools of thought, however, stand divided on this issue. In the Keynesian framework, bond financed deficits are supposed to generate strong wealth impacts, which is contested by both neoclassical and Ricardian full foresight models [See for example a debate on this issue by Bernheim (1989) and Barro (1989)]. However, when the deficit is financed by borrowing from the central bank, the impact on prices is felt more quickly and directly. The inflationary outcome of deficit shifts the relative prices in favour of imports and away from domestic goods and exports resulting in an increase in net imports.

The model focuses mainly on the income and price channels of transmission and has the following major features. Determination of fiscal deficit and its financing constitutes the central feature of the model. The evolution of fiscal deficit is a process of determination of government revenues and expenditures, a large part of the latter being determined by policy considerations. The model follows a disaggregated approach to the determination of government revenue from taxes, property income and savings of departmental and non-departmental enterprises. While government consumption and interest payments are endogenously determined, transfer payments and public investments are assumed to be policy determined. Fiscal deficit is financed by increase in domestic credit, i.e., by borrowing from commercial banks and Reserve Bank, or borrowing from non-banking domestic sources or by way of net foreign borrowings. Among all the borrowing sources, some of which are endogenously determined in the model, Reserve Bank credit to the Government forms the vital link between the fiscal and monetary sector.

The relation between fiscal deficit, money and output forms the second important transmission channel in the model. An increase in fiscal deficit leads to monetary expansion, but to the extent that deficit is due to an increase in public investment, the long run impact on prices is expected to be lower than the case when deficit is incurred for current expenditure. Since the output function is augmented with a demand variable, the model recognises the short run expansionary impact of government expenditure on output[2]. Further, the model highlights the link between credit and output by introducing real money stock as an argument in the non-agricultural output function.

The interaction between fiscal deficit, private consumption and investment forms the third vital link in the model. A tax-cut or expenditure induced deficit increases the private disposable income, leading to higher consumption in the current period. The model assumes the short-sighted response of private sector to the government deficit, and therefore, rules out the tax discounting hypothesis central to the Ricardian Equivalence proposition. The empirical estimates of the private consumption function test for direct 'crowding out' impact of government consumption on private consumption. As is evident in the case of many developing countries, government consumption is found to be positively influencing private consumption in India, implying, perhaps, the complementary relation between the two.

Determination of investment level in the economy forms the fourth major aspect of the model. A single investment function for the entire economy may not accurately account for the behavioural characteristics of investment in different sectors. The model introduces disaggregation at a broad level, *viz.*, agriculture and non-agriculture, in order to capture the determinants of investment in these two sectors. Investment may come from private or public sector, the latter is largely a policy variable and hence, treated exogenous in the model. Private non-agricultural investment function is specified through the accelerator framework, augmented with a long run profit variable, interest rate and a variable representing credit availability conditions. Private agriculture investment, on the other hand, is dependent on the income originating from this sector and the government investment in agriculture. Gross investments in these two sectors, along with the depreciation requirement determine the level of capital stock, which in turn determines the output level in the economy.

The import demand is determined by an aggregate demand variable which is defined to include private absorption, government expenditure and exports. This constitutes the fifth important feature of the model. Export demand in the model is a function of export price relative to world price and the level of world income. Export price is expressed as an inverted export supply function which is postulated to depend on domestic cost and demand conditions. The endogenously determined levels of export and import of goods and services, together with net external interest payments and international transfers (net), generate the current account balance in the model. An important feature of the model is that the current account balance, apart from being determined endogenously, also influences the stock of external debt and interest payments with a self-generating feed-back effect.

The model, as it emerges, combines the features of both the absorption and monetary approach to external adjustment. By bringing out the nexus between money, output and prices, it places emphasis on the role of deficit and money in the real economy. The model is estimated using the data for the sample period 1971-72 to 1993-94. The sector-wise detailed feature of the model along with the empirical estimates of the parameters are discussed in the following section.

III. SPECIFICATION OF THE MODEL AND THE ESTIMATED PARAMETERS

Fiscal Operations

Given the objectives of the current exercise, government sector constitutes the most important subsector in the model. Consistent with the national income identity, linking fiscal deficit to the current account of balance of payments, the analysis here is based on the consolidated public sector, which in the Indian context comprises general government (Centre, states and union territories) and their departmental and non-departmental enterprises. It may be noted that the concept of fiscal deficit used in the budget documents mainly concerns with the measurement of borrowing requirement of the Government and may be ill-suited to study the aggregate demand impact of deficit (Blejer and Cheasty, 1991). The budgetary definition of gross fiscal deficit (revenue receipts minus total expenditure including net lending)

generally overstates the demand impact of deficit. A more meaningful analysis of government expenditure should be based on its economic classification into consumption, transfer payments, and investment, which can be combined with private sector absorption to study the domestic demand impact of fiscal deficit. Similarly, the revenue side of the budget also needs to be redefined to include the savings of the departmental and non-departmental enterprises of the Government. Therefore, some adjustment in the published data of fiscal deficit becomes essential to put them to economically more meaningful analysis. In view of this, data on the government sector for the study are drawn from the National Account Statistics which presents the economic and purpose-wise classification of government expenditure. In this paper, all nominal variables are denoted by higher case letters and real variables by lower case letters while change between two time points is indicated by the sign Δ.

Following budget constraint of the public sector provides the starting point of the analysis:

$$GXP - TR = \Delta BCG + \Delta RCG + \Delta FICG + DNB + EB + MISCR \quad ...(2)$$

where,

$$TR = DT + DIT + TM + NTX + SE \quad ...\ (2a)$$

$$GXP = CON + TRP + PCF \quad ...\ (2b)$$

Equation (2) shows that fiscal deficit, i.e., the excess of public sector expenditure (GXP) over current revenue (TR) is financed by increase in domestic credit to Government, i.e., by credit from commercial banks (BCG) and from Reserve Bank (RCG); borrowing from other sources, including financial institutions (FICG) and domestic non-banking institutions (DNB); external loans (EB) and miscellaneous capital receipts (MISCR). Total revenue of public sector comprises revenue from direct taxes (DT), domestic indirect taxes (DIT) and import taxes (TM) and non-tax revenue (NTX), consisting of income from property and entrepreneurship and miscellaneous current receipts of administrative departments and the gross savings (SE) of the departmental and non-departmental enterprises in the public sector. Expenditure in the public sector is incurred in the form of government consumption (CON), transfer payments (TRP) including interest payments (IP) and gross public capital formation (PCF).

Government Revenues

On the revenue side, tax and non-tax revenue functions are specified through a partial adjustment framework, with the assumption that at any point of time the actual tax revenue partially adjusts to the long run desired level. As revenues are targeted in nominal terms, both tax and non-tax revenue equations are estimated at their current price levels.

Revenue from direct taxes are posited to be a function of real income originating from non-agriculture sector (at factor cost) and domestic price level. Inflation is expected to increase tax revenue, since nominal tax collections should rise at least proportionally with prices. However, if lags in tax collection are long, revenue from direct taxes may not be elastic to inflation and real tax revenue may fall with inflation (Tanzi, 1977). On the other hand, nominal direct tax revenue is expected to rise more than proportionately, if tax brackets are not indexed to inflation. The net effect of inflation on tax revenue will, therefore, depend on the relative strengths of both the factors. The following equation provides the estimates of relative income and price elasticities of direct taxes in the partial adjustment framework:

$$\underset{}{\text{Ln DT}} = \underset{(-1.444)}{-2.171} + \underset{(1.042)}{0.316}\ \text{Ln ynar} + \underset{(2.549)}{0.305}\ \text{Ln P}$$

$$+ \underset{(4.749)}{0.660}\ \text{Ln DT}_{(-1)} + \underset{(5.602)}{0.154}\ \text{DDT} \qquad \ldots(3)$$

$\bar{R}^2 = 0.99, \quad h = 0.12, \quad SEE = 0.06, \quad Mean = 3.99$

Where 'ynar' is real GDP at factor cost originating from non-agricultural sector, 'P' is Wholesale Price Index and 'DDT' is a dummy. The figures in the brackets are the respective 't' values of the regression coefficients. The long run elasticity of direct tax revenue, with respect to real non-agricultural income works out to near unity during the period 1971-72 to 1993-94. The price elasticity of direct tax revenue is about 0.3 in the short run and 0.9 in the long run. The equation was estimated with a dummy to account for the significant changes in tax structure that has taken place since 1991-92 following the introduction of a comprehensive tax reform programme. As is expected, the dummy has a positive sign in the equation.

Indirect taxes are divided into two parts, domestic indirect taxes (DIT) and import taxes (TM). While the former is a function of real income and the price level, the latter is determined by the average import duty rate and the volume of import. The following two equations provide the estimates of domestic and trade taxes:

$$\underset{}{\text{Ln DIT}} = \underset{(-2.427)}{-2.496} + \underset{(2.073)}{0.347 \text{ Ln y}} + \underset{(2.974)}{0.369 \text{ Ln P}}$$

$$+ \underset{(6.469)}{0.682 \text{ Ln DIT}_{(-1)}} - \underset{(-4.08)}{0.065 \text{ DDIT}} \qquad \dots(4)$$

$\bar{R}^2 = 0.99$, $h = -1.33$, $SEE = 0.03$, $Mean = 5.27$

$$TM = MR \times (impt \times PIMP) \qquad \dots(5)$$

Where 'y' is real income at factor cost, 'DDIT' is a dummy, 'MR' is average import duty rate, 'impt' is real imports in rupees, and PIMP is price of import. The long run elasticity of domestic indirect tax revenue to real income is placed at 1.09. The price elasticity of domestic indirect tax revenue is estimated at 1.16, showing a more than proportional adjustment between inflation rate and the increase in indirect tax revenue. This should be expected, since most of the taxes on goods and services are levied at *ad valorem* rates, making the tax base elastic to inflation. The equation included a dummy to represent the significant changes introduced in the structure of union excise duties in the post-reform period, which had a short term negative effect on revenue. Import tax revenue was specified as an identity, linking the revenue to the average import duty rate, the volume of real imports and import prices.

On the non-tax revenue side, government property and entrepreneurial income together with miscellaneous current revenues are related to the level of economic activity, proxied by GDP at current market prices (YM). Gross savings of the departmental and non-departmental public enterprises which represent the net result of their commercial operations are assumed to be determined outside the system. It may be mentioned that the classification and definition of government property income has undergone frequent revisions due to, among others, the changing depreciation norms. In order to smooth out these breaks in data points, a shift dummy (DNTX) has been introduced in the non-tax revenue equation. The estimates of the parameters are as follows:

$$NTX = -1.435 + 0.016\ YM - 19.008\ DNTX \quad \text{...(6)}$$
$$\quad\quad (-0.679) \quad (26.449) \quad\quad (-4.109)$$

$\bar{R}^2 = 0.97$, DW = 1.44, SEE = 6.17, Mean = 40.72

Government Expenditure

Of the four major categories of expenditure considered in the model, *viz.*, consumption, interest payment, transfer payments and public investment, the latter two are treated exogenous in the system. Transfer payments consisting of subsidies and pension payments and other current transfers are influenced by a set of social and economic factors. They are frequently used as means to promote certain distributional objectives. In developing countries, public investment outlay subsumes several policy objectives and at times could be a residual item in the budget, given the revenue constraints and expenditure commitments in the current account of the budget. It could, however, be argued that in the case where deficit is monetised to a large extent, the financing constraints may not seem to be a binding constraint on the level of investment outlay in the budget.

Real consumption expenditure of the Government is related to economic activity which is proxied by the real GDP at market prices. Government consumption function is specified in real terms to underline the fact that Government desires to maintain a real level of consumption in each period. The estimated equation in the partial adjustment framework is as follows:

$$\text{Ln con} = -2.287 + 0.753\ \text{Ln ym} + 0.489\ \text{Ln con}_{(-1)} \quad \text{...(7)}$$
$$\quad\quad (-3.984) \quad (4.016) \quad\quad (3.642)$$

$\bar{R}^2 = 0.98$, h = 3.87, SEE = 0.05, Mean = 5.17

The short run and long run income elasticities of government consumption expenditure are placed at 0.71 and 1.47, respectively, during the sample period, which show the fast pace at which government real consumption responds to changes in economic activity. Total interest payment is divided into two parts, *viz.*, interest payment on internal debt and that on external debt. Gross internal and external interest payments are related to the respective outstanding debts at the beginning of the year and the average interest rates.

$$IPI = I_d \times IDBT_{(-1)} \quad \text{...(8)}$$

$$IPX^g = I_x^g \times XDBT^g_{(-1)} \quad \text{...(9)}$$

Where 'IPI' and 'IPX^g' are internal and external interest payments of the Government, respectively, 'I_d' and 'I_x^g' are average interest rates on internal and external debts, and 'IDBT' and '$XDBT^g$' are the outstanding internal and external government debt.

Total outstanding debt (TDBT) is defined as:

$$TDBT = TDBT_{(-1)} + \Delta TDBT \quad ...(10)$$

The change in outstanding debt (ΔTDBT) in any given year should ideally equal to the fiscal deficit in that year. However, since the published data on incremental debt do not accurately agree with the fiscal deficit (FD), the following functional form was used to estimate the incremental debt:

$$\underset{}{Ln\ \Delta\ TDBT} = \underset{(-0.603)}{-\ 0.175} + \underset{(18.649)}{1.077\ Ln\ FD} - \underset{(-4.169)}{1.549\ DDBT} \quad ...(11)$$

$$\bar{R}^2 = 0.97, \quad DW = 2.24, \quad SEE = 0.35, \quad Mean = 6.88$$

Outstanding external debt of the Government is determined by the flow of foreign borrowing (EB_g) during the year, together with the outstanding debt of the previous year, where EB_g is assumed as a fraction E of the change in total debt. The difference between the total debt and the external debt gives outstanding internal debt. The following identities explain the determination of two different components of government debt:

$$XDBT^g = XDBT^g_{(-1)} + EB^g + VLC \quad ...(12)$$

$$EB^g = E \times \Delta TDBT \quad ...(13)$$

$$IDBT = TDBT - XDBT^g \quad ...(14)$$

Government Borrowing

Financing of fiscal deficit takes place through following major ways:

1. Increase in commercial bank credit to Government (DBCG).
2. Increase in Financial Institutions' credit to Government (DFICG) mainly through their investment in government securities.
3. Borrowing from domestic non-banking sources, namely from households and others in the form of small savings, provident funds and special deposits.

4. Increase in other domestic miscellaneous capital receipts which represents net changes in deposit account, reserve funds, etc.
5. Borrowing from external sources (EB^g), and
6. Increase in net RBI credit to the Government, which essentially goes to meet the shortfall between the fiscal deficit and the borrowing from all other sources.

Commercial banks' credit to the Government is influenced by two major factors, growth in their aggregate deposits and the Statutory Liquidity Ratio. The following equation was considered for estimating the incremental commercial banks' credit to the Government:

$$\text{Ln } \Delta BCG = \underset{(-6.516)}{-3.307} + \underset{(13.924)}{1.331} \text{ Ln } \Delta DEP + \underset{(2.287)}{0.385} \Delta WSLR + \underset{(4.131)}{1.075} DBCG \quad \text{...(15)}$$

$\bar{R}^2 = 0.93$ DW = 2.09,   SEE = 0.35,   Mean = 3.06

The elasticity of incremental bank credit to the Government with respect to incremental deposits (ΔDEP) of commercial banks is estimated to be more than unity. Since the SLR requirements changed frequently even within a financial year, a weighted average rate was used to estimate the sensitivity of banks' investment in government paper to SLR changes. Here, the SLR variable represents the relevant ratio weighted by the number of days it remained in force during a year. The equation was estimated with a dummy (DBCG) to account for sharp variation in bank credit to Government in 1975-76 and 1977-78. Incremental deposits of commercial banks was linearly related to increase in M_3.

$$\Delta DEP = \underset{(-0.591)}{-1.118} + \underset{(111.228)}{0.814} \Delta M_3 + \underset{(1.689)}{8.226} DDEP \quad \text{...(16)}$$

$\bar{R}^2 = 0.99$,   DW = 2.12,   SEE = 9.32,   Mean = 252.57

Investment of Financial Institutions in government securities depends on the growth of their investible resources. Since the regression equation did not show satisfactory statistical relation between the two, this component of borrowing was assumed exogenous in the model. The following equation provided the estimates of domestic non-bank borrowing, which is related to the

nominal income (Y) and its own past values. Apart from the level of economic activity, a significant factor, explaining a large increase in the government borrowing through small savings and provident funds relates to the tax benefits offered to their investors. Studies have estimated that effective rate of return on some of the small savings instruments after taking into account the tax benefits was as high as 34 per cent in 1990-91 (Bagchi and Nayak, 1993). However, a satisfactory index of effective return on small savings on a time series basis is not available for evaluating the impact of this variable on government borrowing from the household sector.

$$\text{Ln DNB} = \underset{(-14.144)}{-7.151} + \underset{(20.438)}{1.449}\ \text{Ln Y} + \underset{(8.860)}{0.498}\ \text{Ln DDNB} \quad ...(17)$$

$\bar{R}^2 = 0.97$, DW = 0.53, SEE = 0.21, Mean = 3.66

The estimated income elasticity of small savings and provident fund receipts work out to 1.45, reflecting the combined influence of relatively faster growth of household savings in the 1970s and 1980s and the household's preference for these securities on account of their promise of high post-tax return.

The remaining component of government borrowing, i.e., miscellaneous capital receipt is treated exogenous in the model. This leaves the Reserve Bank credit to the Government which is obtained as a residual finance after exhausting the borrowings from all other sources. The following identity links the change in Reserve Bank credit to the Government to fiscal deficit and borrowing from other sources:

$$\Delta RCG = FD - \Delta BCG - \Delta FICG - DNB - EB^g - MISCR \quad ...(18)$$

Demand for Money and Price Determination

Price equation in the model takes the form of an inverted money demand function. In general form, the demand for real money balances could be postulated to take the following functional specification.

$$\text{Ln (M/P)} = \propto_0 + \propto_1 \text{Ln y} - \propto_2 i - \propto_3 \pi^e \quad ... (19)$$

Where the real money balance is expressed as a function of the real income (y), interest rate (i) and the inflation expectation (π^e). The signs of the coefficients in the equation are consistent with the theoretical expectation regarding the impact of various economic forces on demand for real money balances. The model includes two opportunity cost variables; namely, interest rate (i) and inflation rate

(π) representing the cost of holding money against other financial assets and goods, respectively. Inverting this function, we get an expression for price as:

$$\text{Ln } P = -\alpha_0 - \alpha_1 \text{ Ln } y + \alpha_2 i + \alpha_3 \pi^e + \text{Ln } M \quad ...(19a)$$

According to the above specification, price situation is essentially influenced by the monetary conditions, growth of real income and the peoples' desire to adjust their real money balances in response to changes in interest rate and inflation. Inflation rate in the model should be truely represented by its expected value. Since the price equation is specified in a partial adjustment framework, it is expected that the lagged price level would capture some of the effects of the expected inflation. The empirical version of the price equation is as follows:

$$\text{Ln } P = \underset{(2.185)}{2.407} - \underset{(-1.877)}{0.387} \text{ Ln } y + \underset{(3.524)}{0.253} \text{ Ln } M_3 + \underset{(7.797)}{0.738} \text{ Ln } P_{(-1)}$$

$$+ \underset{(2.185)}{0.073} \text{ DP1} + \underset{(5.892)}{0.153} \text{ DP2} \quad ...(20)$$

$\bar{R}^2 = 0.99$, $h = -0.93$, $SEE = 0.03$, Mean $= 4.74$

The general price level (P) refers to the index of wholesale prices. The lagged price variable in the model incorporates the lagged effect of output and money supply on the current year's price level. Interest rate had to be dropped from the model due to its weak statistical significance. The equation includes two dummies: 'DP1' represents the dummy for high inflation rates in 1973-74 and 1974-75 following the first oil shock and 'DP2' as the dummy for 1980-81 to account for the lag impact of second oil shock. The short run elasticity of price with respect to real income works out to -0.39 and that to 'M_3' to 0.25. As should be expected in the case of an inverted money demand function, long run elasticity of price to money supply works out to near unity (0.97). The corresponding long run elasticity to real income is placed at 1.48. The implicit income elasticity of money demand is placed at 1.53 for the sample period 1971-72 to 1993-94.

Interest Rate

Interest rate constitutes an important transmission channel of macroeconomic adjustment process, depending on how free and open is the financial market of an economy. In the case of developing

countries, with relatively regulated and close financial market, this transmission belt is expected to be weak, particularly in relation to the portfolio behaviour of the households which constitutes a major channel of adjustment. Even in the case of these economies, interest rate, while being administered, can have significant influence on the investment decision in the economy and as a result, can influence the level of aggregate demand and output.

In this model, the role of interest rate is addressed in the context of its impact on the cost of credit and the level of aggregate demand in the economy. The objective is to identify the proximate determinants of interest rate and then establish a link between the borrowing and lending rates of commercial bank. While it can be argued that in the Indian context, until recently, interest rate did not play an equilibriating role in the money market, it is also important to recognise that the policy responses by way of interest rate changes in the past were not completely out of place with developments in the money market and domestic price conditions. Keeping in view the current evolving stage of financial markets in India, it is essential to gather some idea about the determinants of interest rate in order to account for its impact on the investment decisions in the economy. In the developing country context, interest rate determination has been addressed in a variety of ways, keeping in view the underlying structure and characteristics of the financial economy in question and the extent of its integration with the global financial market. Given the fact that for most of the sample period, Indian economy operated under a relatively high degree of capital control, interest rate was mostly determined by the domestic economic conditions. Accordingly, the theoretical framework considered in the model draws on the money market equilibrium conditions and the Fisher's hypothesis of determination of nominal interest rate. The approach set out below has been extensively discussed in Edwards and Khan (1985).

According to the Standard Fisher hypothesis, nominal interest rate (i) is given by,

$$i_t = r_t + \pi^e_t \qquad ...(21)$$

where 'r' is real interest rate and 'π^e' is expected inflation rate. The real interest rate in any period is postulated to evolve as a deviation from its long run equilibrium level, this deviation being brought about by the excess or shortage of money supply over money demand.

$$r = \delta - \mu\ EMS_t + w_t \qquad ...(22)$$

Where 'δ' is long run equilibrium real interest rate, 'EMS' represents excess supply of money and 'w_t' is a white noise residual. The excess supply of money is given by the difference between the actual stock of and the demand for real money balances (m):

$$EMS_t = Ln\ m_t - Ln\ m_t^d \qquad ...(23)$$

As in equation (19), the money demand function is given by,

$$Ln\ m_t^d = \propto_o + \propto_1 Ln\ y_t - \propto_2 (\delta + \pi_t^e) - \propto_3 \pi_t^e \qquad ...(24)$$

which has two opportunity cost variables in $(\delta + \pi_t^e)$ and π_t^e. Assuming a stock adjustment process for real money stock we get:

$$Ln\ m_t = \beta(Ln\ m_t^d - Ln\ m_{t-1}) \qquad ...(25)$$

Where $\Delta Ln\ m_t = Ln\ m_t - Ln\ m_{t-1}$ and β is the coefficient of adjustment such that, $0 \leq \beta \leq 1$. Equation (25) can be simplified as:

$$Ln\ m_t = \beta Ln\ m_t^d + (1-\beta)\ Ln\ m_{t-1} \qquad ...(26)$$

Combining (23) and (26) we get:

$$EMS_t = (1-\beta)\ (Ln\ m_{t-1} - Ln\ m_t^d) \qquad ...(27)$$

which together with (21), (22) and (24) yield the following estimatable version of the reduced form equation for nominal interest rate:

$$i_t = \Phi_o + \Phi_1 Ln\ y_t + \Phi_2 Ln\ m_{t-1} + \Phi_3\ \pi_t^e + w_t \qquad ...(28)$$

Where,

$$\Phi_o = \delta + \mu\ (1-\beta)\ (\propto_0 - \propto_2 \delta)$$

$$\Phi_1 = \mu\ (1-\beta) \propto_1$$

$$\Phi_2 = -\mu\ (1-\beta)$$

$$\Phi_0 = [1 - \mu\ (1-\beta)\ (\propto_2 + \propto_3)]$$

Interest rate in the empirical model was represented by the one-to-three year deposit rate of banks (IB) and the variable of expected inflation was substituted by actual inflation. The estimated parameters of equation (28) are presented below:

$$IB = -\ \underset{(-2.592)}{42.909} + \underset{(2.546)}{10.902}\ Ln\ y \qquad ...(28a)$$

$$-\ \underset{(-1.863)}{4.332}\ Ln\ m_{3(-1)} + \underset{(2.116)}{0.068}\ [(P - P_{(-1)})/P_{(-1)}] \times 100$$

$\bar{R}^2 = 0.65$, DW = 1.77, SEE = 0.70, Mean = 8.89

The above equation implies that lagged real money supply exerts a downward influence on the nominal interest rate while real income tends to increase it. Inflation and interest rate are seen to be positively related though not in a very significant way. Given the estimates of deposit rate from equation (28a), the lending rate of commercial banks is estimated by adding to the deposit rate the intermediating cost, which for simplicity is assumed exogenous in the model and is given by the observed difference between the one-to-three year deposit rate and the weighted average lending rate of commercial banks.[3]

WLR = IB + OPC

Where WLR is weighted average lending rate of commercial banks and OPC is intermediating or operating cost of commercial banks.

Money Supply Determination

The determination of money supply is a process of determination of the sources of variation in reserve money and the money multiplier. Among the various sources affecting reserve money, the major component, *viz.*, the Reserve Bank credit to the Government is determined within the model. The objective here is to bring out the nexus between money supply and fiscal deficit as the primary channel of monetary expansion. As mentioned earlier, Reserve Bank credit to the Government is endogenously determined in the model from the financing side of deficit. Historically, this was the major source of growth of reserve money during much of the sample period under study. The supply of broad money (M_3) is related to reserve money by the following equation, which gives an estimated parameter for the money multiplier.

$$M_3 = \underset{(-2.715)}{-47.278} + \underset{(100.985)}{3.192}\ RM \qquad \ldots(29)$$

$\bar{R}^2 = 0.99$, DW = 1.61, SEE = 56.93, Mean = 1239.48

The estimated money multiplier is placed at 3.19 for the sample period 1971-72 to 1993-94. Ideally, the money multiplier should be functionally related to behavioural factors, such as ratio of currency to deposits, and a policy variable, i.e., the Cash Reserve Ratio. It has also been contended that money multiplier will depend on demand for credit and, hence, on output, since the degree at which a given

quantum of reserve money will translate into money supply will depend on the credit demand in the economy at that point of time. While this position is theoretically valid, it is to be noted that in the Indian context, with an administered structure of interest rate until recently and varying rates of interest for different activities, demand for credit was not a binding constraint. Interest rates charged on some activities were below the market rate and demand for credit at those rates of interest was highly elastic. In fact, the Indian commercial banks do not voluntarily hold any excess reserves and whatever excess reserves they may be holding are involuntary due to inadequate facilities for quick transmission of funds from far flung branches (Rangarajan and Arif, 1990). Further, for a proper estimation of the relationship between money supply and reserve money, at the minimum, it is necessary to adjust the series on reserve money for changes in the Cash Reserve Ratio. In fact, such an adjusted series is found to give a better explanation of changes in money stock, particularly when quarterly data are used (Rangarajan and Singh, 1984). However, since we are dealing with annual time series, adjustments have not been made for changes in Cash Reserve Ratio.

Private Sector Behaviour

Central to the argument of fiscal dimension of the balance of payments problem is the relation between the fiscal deficit and private spending behaviour. Both in the theoretical and empirical literature, there has been a considerable degree of disagreement on modelling the private sector's response to changes in fiscal deficit and its financing composition. In the conventional Keynesian framework, an increase in government deficit, whether caused by a cut in taxes or by increased expenditure, will boost private spending by increasing disposable income. Since consumers are assumed to be myopic and liquidity constrained, the forward looking behaviour goes out of the Keynesian analysis and what become relevant are the current income and current consumption and thus, current taxation and deficit. The finite horizon models in the typical tradition of life cycle hypothesis state that temporary deficits will have minimum effects on private spending, while deficits brought about by permanent tax cuts, will significantly stimulate consumer spending. Both these theories are contradicted by Ricardian equivalence hypothesis, which under the assumptions of infinite

planning horizon and perfect capital markets holds that government deficit will be fully neutralised by opposing economic behaviour of the private sector (Barro, 1974). In other words, government deficit, by increasing the probability of a future tax rise, will result in equivalent reduction of private consumption. Consequently, deficit does not reduce national saving and has no implications for external current account balance.

The mainstream models on fiscal approach to balance of payments follow the Keynesian tradition in modelling private sector response to public deficits, wherein private consumption and investment are lumped together in a single private expenditure function with disposable income as the main explanatory variable (for example, Cambridge Economic Policy Group model, 1976). There are, however, two major limitations of this approach. First, it does not make a distinction between consumption and investment demands of the private sector. These two parts of private absorption may exhibit different behavioural relations with changes in economic activity. Secondly, this approach assumes full exogeneity of private sector in the determination of the current account balance, hence, changes in the latter are explained by changes in the public sector financial balances. In reality, however, private consumption apart from being determined by disposable income can be directly influenced by fiscal policy changes, which brings the 'crowding out' phenomenon into the picture.

Private Consumption

In the light of the above discussion, the private absorption function considered here draws a distinction between the consumption and investment demand. Private real consumption is a function of its real disposable income. While the Ricardian position with regard to government deficit may not seem to be providing a plausible explanation for the intertemporal consumption behaviour of the private sector in developing countries, it has been, however, argued that government consumption may have direct implications for private consumption [Easterly and Schmidt-Hebbel (1993) and Mohanty (1992)]. In order to account for the possible 'crowding out/in' impact, the private consumption function considered here, is augmented with government consumption as an argument. The effect

of inflation on consumption has received considerable attention in developing countries. It is expected that in a low income country, inflation may lead to reduction in saving levels because of the low resistance of poor consumers to cuts in real consumption. Inflation can also depress savings by encouraging flight from currency and bank deposits to consumer durables (under financial repression). Anticipated inflation is expected to stimulate present consumption, while surprise or unanticipated inflation may not have a strong impact on consumption. The empirical evidence in the context of developing countries including India show that real consumption tends to increase with rise in prices, whether anticipated or not (Lahari, 1989). The following equation provides the empirical estimates of various influences on private real consumption expenditure:

$$\underset{}{\text{Ln pc}} = \underset{(3.468)}{1.686} + \underset{(5.416)}{0.615} \text{ Ln pyd} + \underset{(1.855)}{0.107} \text{ Ln con}$$

$$+ \underset{(1.546)}{0.072} \text{ Ln P} \qquad \ldots(30)$$

$\bar{R}^2 = 0.99$, DW = 1.85, SEE = 0.02, Mean = 7.03

The elasticity of private consumption with respect to disposable income is estimated at 0.62. The coefficient of government consumption is positive though small, indicating that private consumption tends to increase with government consumption. This is probably because government consumption expenditure in certain areas may be crowding in private consumption due to their complementary nature. Price level has a positive impact on the real consumption, although the effect works out to be small.

Private Investment

Private investment behaviour is modelled in two equations relating to agriculture and non-agriculture investment. The following equation specifies the private real agricultural investment function:

$$\text{Ln piag} = \underset{(-4.133)}{-3.053} + \underset{(8.261)}{0.956} \text{ Ln yar}_{(-1)} + \underset{(2.109)}{0.210} \text{ Ln pcfag}$$

$$- \underset{(-2.603)}{0.167} \text{ dpiag1} + \underset{(2.714)}{0.165} \text{ dpiag2} \qquad \ldots(31)$$

$\bar{R}^2 = 0.80$, DW = 1.03, SEE = 0.09, Mean = 3.43

Where 'piag' is private gross agricultural investment in real terms, 'yar' is real GDP originating from agriculture, 'pcfag' is real gross public investment in agriculture and 'dpiag1' and 'dpiag2' are two dummies to account for large fluctuations in investment in some years. Private agricultural investment is found to be significantly influenced by the lagged agricultural income, with an elasticity of near unity. Government investment in agriculture has a positive impact on private agricultural investment which reinforces the contention expressed in several studies in this regard [for example, Rath (1989), Shetty (1990), and Krishnamurty *et al* (1997)]. This should be expected as Government provides major infrastructural inputs such as irrigation and research and development in agriculture, which form the critical base for private capital formation.

Real private investment function for the non-agricultural sector is specified through the accelerator framework, where investment is related to the expected increase in demand for output. Following an adaptive expectation framework, the investment equation is expressed in terms of the current year's change in income and the investment level of past one period. In the developing countries, public investment constitutes a key determinant of the private investment. Public investment, especially in infrastructure, increases the long run marginal productivity of private capital and thereby helps promote investment in private sector (Aschauer, 1989). Further, there could be an output linkage, where public capital stock raises the demand for private output. On the other hand, public investment may displace private investment in some sectors by depriving the private sector of scarce physical and financial resources. This phenomenon of what is called 'financial crowding out' is generally believed to be strong in developing countries, where the public sector enjoys preferential borrowing treatment over the private sector. Under this situation, the actual level of private investment may fall short of its desired level on account of the binding borrowing constraint in the domestic and external credit markets. In the developing country context, including India, several models have recognised this dual and conflicting role of public investment in promoting aggregate capital stock [see Sunderarajan and Thakur (1980), Krishnamurty *et al* (1985), Blejer and Khan (1984) and Pradhan *et al* (1988)]. In most of the models, in the Indian context, crowding-out phenomenon has emerged stronger than the complementarity effect.

The present model tests for the competitive impact of public investment on private investment in industry and tertiary sector, by including a financial variable in the private non-agricultural investment function, represented by banking sector's credit to commercial sector and net capital inflow from abroad.

$$\underset{}{pinag} = \underset{(1.936)}{30.801} + \underset{(2.621)}{0.253\ \Delta y} + \underset{(1.692)}{0.372\ (\Delta bcp + capb)}$$

$$- \underset{(-2.168)}{1.420\ wlr} + \underset{(2.107)}{0.486\ pinag_{(-1)}} \qquad \ldots(32)$$

$\bar{R}^2 = 0.83$, $h = -1.035$, $SEE = 22.03$, $Mean = 146.57$

Where 'pinag' is real investment of private sector in the non-agriculture sector, 'bcp' is real bank credit to private sector, 'capb' is the capital account balance (representing the real capital inflow from abroad) in the balance of payments accounts deflated by Wholesale Price Index and 'wlr' is weighted average real lending rate of commercial banks.[4]

The OLS test statistics show that the equation has good explanatory power and is free from autocorrelation problem. The impact of marginal change in current year's output on private non-agricultural investment is estimated at 0.25 in the short run and 0.49 in the long run. An increase in bank credit to the Government for financing its investment is expected to partly 'crowd out' private investment in the same year, the long run impact works out to 0.72. The negative impact of cost of capital on private investment is also confirmed by the coefficient of 'wlr'.

Real Output

The output function is specified in two equations, *viz.*, agricultural and non-agricultural output in order to bring out the sectoral characteristics of output generation in the economy. Agricultural output is related to rainfall index (RAIN), gross cropped area (AREA) and real net capital stock in agriculture (KAGR).

$$Ln\ yar = \underset{(-3.968)}{-7.132} + \underset{(2.139)}{0.169\ Ln\ RAIN} + \underset{(3.425)}{0.989\ Ln\ AREA}$$

$$+ \underset{(6.421)}{1.231\ Ln\ KAGR_{(-1)}} \qquad \ldots(33)$$

$\bar{R}^2 = 0.77$, $DW = 1.80$, $SEE = 0.04$, $Mean = 6.25$

Agriculture output is significantly influenced by the initial level of real net capital stock in agriculture. The elasticity of output to capital stock is estimated at 1.25. Output originating from non-agriculture sector is estimated by a production function, featuring an aggregate demand variable (add), real net capital stock in this sector (knagr) and real money stock (m_3). In the short run, output is expected to respond to demand conditions as firms will use up their stock of inventories and utilise their existing capacity more intensively. This impact is intended to be captured by a demand variable, represented by aggregate demand for domestically produced goods (add) and is defined to include government expenditure, private absorption, exports and imports. This variable brings out the interaction between the non-agriculture sector with the rest of the sectors such as agriculture and trade sector. An increase in agricultural output will generate demand for non-agricultural output as also facilitate the supply of essential raw materials for industry [Rangarajan (1982)]. While exports will have a positive impact on the demand for industrial output, raising its production, imports will act as a leakage for the domestic output. Non-agricultural output function also includes the stock of real money balance as an explanatory variable to proxy bank credit to real sector.

$$\begin{aligned} \text{Ln ynar} = & \underset{(-12.232)}{-2.098} + \underset{(7.936)}{0.488} \text{ Ln add} + \underset{(12.534)}{0.627} \text{ Ln knagr}_{(-1)} \\ & + \underset{(2.058)}{0.045} \text{ Ln } m_3 \qquad \ldots(34) \end{aligned}$$

$\bar{R}^2 = 0.99$, DW = 1.93, SEE = 0.001, Mean = 6.82

All variables included in the equation emerged statistically significant. The elasticity of non-agricultural output to demand is estimated at 0.49 and that with respect to lagged capital stock at 0.63. The stock of real money balance has a positive influence on output. This reinforces the credit view argument of money supply in a developing economy.

External Sector

External sector in the model is divided into three major blocks, *viz.*, export and import of goods and services, interest receipts and payments and net international transfers including non-interest

investment income. Determination of exports and imports in the model is guided by the consideration that fiscal deficit affects the domestic demand and price conditions, leading to changes in the relative prices in the external sector. Demand for real export of goods and services is postulated as a function of world income and exports price relative to world price. Real exports are positively related to world income and negatively to export price relative to world price. Implicit in this specification is the assumption that as world price of exports goes up, world demand would shift in favour of India's exports given her export price. The export demand equation estimated through a partial adjustment process with one dummy to account for unexplained variation in services, which are less price sensitive, is as under:

$$\text{Ln expt\$} = \underset{(-1.469)}{-1.263} + \underset{(2.417)}{0.574}\ \text{Ln wyr} - \underset{(-3.343)}{0.319}\ (\text{pexp\$/wpexp})$$

$$+ \underset{(4.568)}{0.569}\ \text{Ln expt\$}_{(-1)} + \underset{(5.541)}{0.102}\ \text{dexpt\$} \qquad \text{...(35)}$$

$\bar{R}^2 = 0.99$, $h = -0.87$, $SEE = 0.04$, $Mean = 2.413$

Where 'expt$' is export of goods and services at constant dollar price (dollar value of merchandise and services exports deflated by dollar price of exports), 'wyr' is index of world real income, 'pexp$' is index of India's export price (expressed as unit value index of exports (UVIX) deflated by an index of exchange rate) and 'wpexp' is the world export price (unit value index of world exports). The elasticity of export of goods and services to world income is estimated at 0.57 in the short run and 1.33 in the long run and with respect to relative export prices, at 0.32 in the short run and 0.74 in the long run.

The unit value index of exports (UVIX) is specified as an inverted export supply function. Theoretically, export supply is related to domestic economic activity proxied by real income, and export price relative to domestic price to measure the impact of relative profitability of export business *vis-à-vis* domestic sales. Therefore, the export supply function is:

$$\text{Ln expt}^s = \theta_1 + \theta_2\ \text{Ln y} + \theta_3\ \text{Ln (UVIX/P)} \qquad \text{...(36)}$$

Equation (35) can be written in terms of export price as:

$$\text{Ln UVIX} = \Psi_1 + \Psi_2 \text{ Ln y} + \Psi_3 \text{ Ln expt}^s + \Psi_4 \text{ Ln P} \quad \text{...(37)}$$

where $\Psi_1 = (-\theta_1/\theta_3)$, $\Psi_2 = (-\theta_2/\theta_3)$

$\Psi_3 = (1/\theta_3)$ and $\Psi_4 = 1$

Equation (37) was estimated in a partial adjustment framework, dropping exports to avoid its strong correlation with income. The empirical equation which also included a dummy variable to account for sharp fluctuation in export prices in some years is presented below:

$$\underset{}{\text{Ln UVIX}} = \underset{(-3.131)}{-3.467} + \underset{(1.319)}{0.158} \text{ Ln P} + \underset{(2.992)}{0.728} \text{ Ln y}$$

$$+ \underset{(4.958)}{0.482} \text{ Ln UVIX}_{(-1)} + \underset{(6.532)}{0.127} \text{ DUVIX} \quad \text{...(38)}$$

$\bar{R}^2 = 0.99$ h = -1.09, SEE = 0.038, Mean = 4.929

The index of export price is given by pexp\$ = (UVIX/IE), where 'IE' is an index of nominal exchange rate (Rupee to US\$). Exchange rate in this framework plays the passive role of transforming the rupee price of exports into dollar. An exchange rate depreciation, *ceteris paribus,* will bring down the export price and stimulate export demand, depending on the value of price elasticity of exports. Therefore, as in the case of pass through framework, the price elasticity of exports in the model determines the degree with which the trade volumes adjust to a change in the exchange rate (Patra and Pattanaik, 1994). Following equation provides the estimates of exchange rate which is related to domestic price level, current account balance (*minus* indicating deficit) and the change in Reserve Banks' Foreign Assets (ΔRBFA):

$$\text{EXR} = \underset{(10.242)}{5.929} + \underset{(3.898)}{0.029} \text{ P} - \underset{(-4.655)}{0.033} \text{ CAB} + \underset{(11.336)}{0.060} \Delta\text{RBFA}$$

$$+ \underset{(14.050)}{10.936} \text{ DEXR1} + \underset{(5.596)}{4.691} \text{ DEXR2} \quad \text{...(39)}$$

$\bar{R}^2 = 0.99$, DW = 2.13, SEE = 0.639, Mean = 12.84

The signs of the coefficients in the equation are consistent with the theoretical expectation about the influence of various economic forces on the exchange rate. An increase in domestic price level and current account deficit causes the exchange rate to depreciate. In the similar manner, an increase in RBI's absorption of foreign currency

will tend to depreciate the rupee. The marginal increase in exchange rate (depreciation) due to an increase in Wholesale Price Index and current account deficit in the model are placed at 0.013 and 0.033, respectively. These coefficient values reveal the weak influence of domestic price and current account balance on exchange rate. This goes to explain the relative insulation of exchange rate determination from the economic forces during much of the sample period. The equation includes two dummies (DEXR1 and DEXR2) to represent the readjustment of the value of the rupee in 1991-92 and the sharp depreciation in 1992-93, respectively.

Equations 35, 38 and 39 provide the basic building block for the export sector in the model and underline the two-way influence of a domestic price change on export price. Domestic price exerts simultaneous impact on unit value index of exports and exchange rate. The unit value index of exports essentially reflects the prevailing domestic cost conditions. Therefore, an increase in domestic price is expected to harden the rupee price of exports and negatively affect the demand for exports. This is true for an economy with passive and fixed exchange rate system. In India, the system of managed float remained in force for a long time, eventually replaced in stages by a market determined exchange rate system. Even within the system of managed float, exchange rate had been responding to domestic price changes, *albeit* at a slow pace. The empirical estimates of price coefficient in the exchange rate equation also reveal the slow rate of adjustment between nominal exchange rate and price. Allowing for this impact, an increase in domestic price is expected to cause a depreciation in nominal exchange rate and partially neutralise the increase in the supply price of exports.

The demand for real imports of goods and services (impt) is posited as a function of the level of economic activity and import prices (PIMP) relative to domestic price. Unlike the conventional specifications that make import demand a function of real income, the specification considered here relates imports to an aggregate demand variable (ad), which is defined as the sum of private sector absorption, government expenditure and exports, all in real terms. Each of these sectors generate demand for imports, so that the actual import reflects a certain portion of the planned import. The equation includes two dummies, representing the import restriction measures

put in place during the stabilisation programmes in 1991-92 and the sharp decline in services imports in certain years.

$$\text{Ln impt} = \underset{(-2.858)}{-2.115} + \underset{(4.206)}{0.641}\ \text{Ln ad} - \underset{(-10.778)}{0.462}\ \text{Ln PIMP}$$

$$+ \underset{(8.888)}{0.967}\ \text{Ln P} - \underset{(-2.411)}{0.111}\ \text{DIMPT1} - \underset{(-8.060)}{0.182}\ \text{DIMPT2} \qquad \text{...(40)}$$

$\bar{R}^2 = 0.99$, DW = 1.95, SEE = 0.04, Mean = 5.04

The elasticity of real imports of goods and services with respect to the aggregate real demand is estimated at 0.64 and with respect to import prices at 0.46. The elasticity of imports to domestic price level is placed at 0.97.

Interest Income and Payments

A large part of the interest income from external sources accrues by way of income from investment of foreign assets held by RBI. Therefore, the external interest income in rupee value (XII) is related to RBI's foreign assets and the world interest rate, proxied by one year LIBOR.

$$\text{XII} = \underset{(0.485)}{0.678} + \underset{(5.526)}{0.037}\ \text{RBFA}_{(-1)} + \underset{(1.785)}{0.177}\ \text{LBR} \qquad \text{...(41)}$$

$\bar{R}^2 = 0.87$, DW = 1.62, SEE = 0.91, Mean = 1.116

External interest payment (XIP) has two components, interest payment on government external debt, which is determined in the fiscal sector and that on private external debt. Interest payment on private external debt is related to the average interest rate on private debt (I^p_x) and the beginning of the year outstanding private debt ($XDBT^p_{(-1)}$). Hence,

$$IPX = IPX^g + IPX^p \qquad \text{...(42)}$$

$$IPX^p = I^p_x \times XDBT^p_{(-1)} \qquad \text{...(43)}$$

$$XDBT = \Delta XDBT + XDBT_{(-1)} \qquad \text{...(44)}$$

The stock of private external debt is expressed as:

$$XDBT^p = XDBT - XDBT^g \qquad \text{...(45)}$$

The incremental external debt (ΔXDBT) is a function of the current account deficit in the balance of payments and the change in RBI's foreign assets.

$$\Delta XDBT = \underset{(1.304)}{8.575} - \underset{(-13.669)}{1.354}\ CAB + \underset{(7.585)}{0.610}\ \Delta RBFA + \underset{(27.992)}{677.359}\ DXDBT \quad ...(46)$$

$\bar{R}^2 = 0.98$, DW = 2.35, SEE = 22.54, Mean = 106.91

Where 'DXDBT' is a dummy representing the break in the data series in 1991-92 arising out of the change in the classification of external debt since that year. Short term debts have been excluded from the analysis in order to obtain a comparable data series for the sample period. Ideally, the incremental external debt should equal the current account deficit *minus* the drawals from reserves. Reserves could also be accumulated by borrowing from abroad, in which case it would add to the external debt. The signs of the coefficient of current account balance and the change in RBI's foreign assets show a positive association of both these components with the incremental external debt.

IV. THE MODEL AND ITS SIMULATION PERFORMANCE

The complete model is specified in terms of 26 behavioural equations and 33 identities. There are 49 exogenous variables and 17 lagged endogeneous variables in the model. Applying the order condition, it may be seen that the individual equations do not suffer from the over-identification problem. Thus specified, this medium size model attempts to integrate all the major sectors of the economy, with the primary objective to study the monetary growth and balance of payments implications of the fiscal policy. All the parameter estimates of the individual behavioural equations, barring a few, satisfy the criteria of goodness of fit and have *a priori* signs and magnitudes. The complete structure of the model including the identities and definition of variables are reported in Table 1.

The model has been solved by running deterministic simulation in both static and dynamic framework for the period 1975-76 to 1993-94. Based on the comparison of predicted and actual values, Table 2 reports three types of simulation error statistics e.g., the Mean Absolute Percentage Error (MAPE), Root Mean Square Percentage Error (RMSPE) and Theil's 'U' statistic for some key endogenous variables. For most of the variables, MAPE and RMSPE, both under

static and dynamic simulations, stayed within a reasonable range. For example, in the case of some key variables such as government revenue (TR), government expenditure (GXP), money supply (M_3), wholesale price (P), capital stock (kagr and knagr), real output (y), exports (expt$) and imports (impt), the RMSPEs under dynamic simulation are within the range of one to seven per cent. The RMSPE for fiscal deficit is placed at 13.7 per cent under dynamic simulation while for current account balance it is placed at 74.2 per cent. Since these two variables represent the closing identities of the fiscal and external sectors, respectively, the relatively large RMSPE in these two identities reflect the accumulated errors stemming from the individual equation components in these two sectors.

Theil's 'U' coefficient, as a measure of robustness of the model, shows the extent of inequality between the actual and simulated values. If 'U' is 0, there is perfect agreement between the actual and the simulated series. In our case, the 'U' for most of the key endogenous variables is less than 0.1.

Graphs '1 to 4' show the comparison of actual and simulated (reference) values of the key endogenous variables in the dynamic simulation. For most of the variables, the turning points are captured by the simulation. For example, in the case of fiscal deficit and current account balance – the two key endogenous variables in the model – the graphs show the close convergence of simulated series with the actual series. This is also true of the variables like money supply, prices and real income. With the limited available data points, the model has captured reasonably well the structural changes in the Indian economy since 1991-92.

On the whole, the model performs well in terms of tracking the historical path of the majority of variables. While according to the actual data, the average annual rate of inflation and output growth are placed at 8.14 per cent and 4.66 per cent, respectively, during the period 1976-77 to 1993-94, the predicted values of the same variables from the dynamic simulation are placed at 7.90 per cent and 4.64 per cent, respectively. Similarly, the annual average ratios of fiscal deficit to GDP (market price) and current account balance to GDP (market price) are predicted by the simulation at 6.62 per cent and -1.26 per cent, respectively, for 1975-76 to 1990-91 as against the actual ratios of 6.85 per cent and -1.24 per cent.

Table 1

Complete Model Structure

		Behavioural Equations	$\bar{R}^2$	*DW*	*h*	*SEE*	*Mean*
1. Ln DT	=	$-2.17137 + 0.316483 \text{ Ln ynar} + 0.305434 \text{ Ln P}$ (-1.444) (1.042) (2.549) $+ 0.660085 \text{ Ln DT}_{(-1)} + 0.153704 \overline{\text{DDT}}$ (4.749) (5.602)	0.994	—	0.121	0.064	3.987
2. Ln DIT	=	$-2.49598 + 0.346666 \text{ Ln y} + 0.369602 \text{ Ln P}$ (-2.427) (2.073) (2.974) $+ 0.681725 \text{ Ln DIT}_{(-1)} - 0.065361 \overline{\text{DDIT}}$ (6.469) (-4.08)	0.999	—	-1.334	0.025	5.265
3. NTX	=	$-1.43496 + 0.016150 \text{ YM} - 19.0084 \overline{\text{DNTX}}$ (-0.679) (26.4495) (-4.109)	0.971	1.441	—	6.172	40.724
4. Ln con	=	$-2.28749 + 0.753424 \text{ Ln ym} + 0.488608 \text{ Ln con}_{(-1)}$ (-3.984) (4.016) (3.642)	0.985	—	3.876	0.054	5.169
5. Ln ΔTDBT	=	$-0.175347 + 1.07725 \text{ Ln FD} - 1.54867 \overline{\text{DDBT}}$ (-0.603) (18.649) (-4.169)	0.967	2.237	—	0.355	6.882
6. Ln ΔBCG	=	$-3.30739 + 1.33101 \text{ Ln } \Delta\text{DEP} + 0.385007 \overline{\Delta\text{WSLR}}$ (-6.516) (13.924) (2.287) $+ 1.07537 \overline{\text{DBCG}}$ (4.131)	0.930	2.089	—	0.354	3.065

(Contd...)

(...Contd...)

		Behavioural Equations	$\bar{R}^2$	DW	h	SEE	Mean
7. Ln DNB	=	$-7.15106 + 1.44915 \text{ Ln } Y - 0.498085 \overline{DDNB}$ (-14.144) (20.438) (8.8603)	0.972	0.53	—	0.209	3.662
8. Ln P	=	$2.40682 - 0.386965 \text{ Ln } y + 0.253435 \text{ Ln } M_3$ (2.185) (-1.877) (3.524)	0.997	—	-0.93	0.030	4.74
		$+ 0.737810 \text{ Ln } P_{(-1)} + 0.072752 \overline{DP1} + 0.15342 \overline{DP2}$ (7.797) (2.185) (5.892)					
9. PGDP	=	$-10.5967 + 1.16519 P$ (-2.611) (49.526)	0.998	1.617	—	2.538	141.039
10. PGKE	=	$-18.3350 + 1.30327 P - 15.9699 \overline{DPGKE}$ (-7.880) (76.324) (-4.080)	0.997	1.834	—	5.068	143.939
11. ΔDEP	=	$-1.11842 + 0.813803 \Delta M_3 + 8.2263 \overline{DDEP}$ (-0.591) (111.228) (1.689)	0.998	2.12	—	9.325	252.569
12. M_3	=	$-47.2778 + 3.19291 RM$ (-2.715) (100.985)	0.998	1.605	—	56.93	1239.48
13. IB	=	$-42.9098 + 10.9017 \text{ Ln } y - 4.3318 \text{ Ln } m3_{(-1)}$ (-2.592) (2.546) (-1.863)	0.648	1.77	—	0.70	8.886
		$+ 0.0681 [(P - P_{(-1)}) / P_{(-1)}] \times 100$ (2.116)					

(Contd...)

(...Contd...)

		Behavioural Equations	$\bar{R}^2$	*DW*	*h*	*SEE*	*Mean*
14. Ln pc	=	$\underset{(3.468)}{1.68639} + \underset{(5.416)}{0.615267} \text{ Ln pyd} + \underset{(1.855)}{0.106510} \text{ Ln con}$	0.996	1.851	—	0.015	7.03
		$+ \underset{(1.546)}{0.072079} \text{ Ln P}$					
15. Ln piag	=	$\underset{(-4.133)}{-3.05392} + \underset{(8.261)}{0.955718} \text{ Ln yar}_{(-1)} + \underset{(2.109)}{0.210001} \text{ Ln } \overline{\text{pcfag}}$	0.799	1.031	—	0.095	3.439
		$\underset{(-2.603)}{-0.167205} \overline{\text{dpiag1}} + \underset{(2.714)}{0.165432} \overline{\text{dpiag2}}$					
16. pinag	=	$\underset{(1.936)}{30.8012} + \underset{(2.62106)}{0.253447} \Delta y + \underset{(1.692)}{0.372083} (\Delta \text{bcp} + \overline{\text{capb}})$	0.832	—	-1.035	22.034	146.573
		$- \underset{(-2.168)}{1.42006} \text{ wlr} - \underset{(2.107)}{0.485949} \text{ pinag}_{(-1)}$					
17. Ln yar	=	$\underset{(-3.968)}{-7.13205} + \underset{(2.139)}{0.168682} \text{ Ln } \overline{\text{RAIN}} + \underset{(3.425)}{0.988747} \text{ Ln } \overline{\text{AREA}}$	0.772	1.799	—	0.036	6.252
		$+ \underset{(6.421)}{1.23067} \text{ Ln kagr}_{(-1)}$					
18. Ln ynar	=	$\underset{(-12.232)}{-2.09781} + \underset{(7.93597)}{0.487659} \text{ Ln add}$	0.999	1.930	—	0.001	6.819
		$+ \underset{(12.534)}{0.627139} \text{ Ln knagr}_{(-1)} + \underset{(2.058)}{0.04530} \text{ Ln m3}_{(-1)}$					

(Contd...)

(...Contd...)

		Behavioural Equations	$\bar{R}^2$	DW	h	SEE	Mean
19. depag	=	-2.72953 + 0.050066 $kagr_{(-1)}$ (0.380) (4.728)	0.52	1.983	—	4.64	28.64
20. depnag	=	-40.1607 + 0.050198 $knagr_{(-1)}$ (-13.711) (58.510)	0.994	2.05	—	4.18	134.203
21. Ln expt$	=	-1.26315 + 0.573835 Ln wyr (-1.469) (2.417)	0.990	—	-0.869	0.039	2.413
		-0.319581 (PEXP$/WPEXP) + 0.569621 Ln $expt\$_{(-1)}$ (-3.343) (4.568)					
		+ 0.101755 $\overline{dexpt\$}$ (5.541)					
22. Ln UVIX	=	-346657 + 0.158920 Ln P + 0.728536 Ln y (-3.131) (1.319) (2.992)	0.996	—	-1.09	0.038	4.929
		+ 0.482021 Ln $UVIX_{(-1)}$ + 0.126679 $\overline{DUVIX}$ (4.95811) (6.5315)					
23. Ln impt	=	-2.11530 + 0.641406 Ln ad - 0.462192 Ln $\overline{PIMP}$ (-2.858) (4.206) (-10.778)	0.994	1.959	—	0.036	5.038
		+ 0.967421 Ln P - 0.110920 $\overline{dimpt1}$ - 0.182483 $\overline{dimpt2}$ (8.888) (-2.411) (-8.060)					

(Contd...)

(...Contd...)

		Behavioural Equations	$\bar{R}^2$	DW	h	SEE	Mean
24. EXR	=	5.92924 + 0.029026 P - 0.033261 CAB (10.242) (3.897) (-4.655)	0.991	2.126	—	0.639	12.843
		+ 0.059980 $\overline{\Delta RBFA}$ + 10.9361 $\overline{DEXR1}$ + 4.69085 $\overline{DEXR2}$ (11.336) (14.050) (5.596)					
25. XII	=	0.678411 + 0.037683 $\overline{RBFA}_{(-1)}$ + 0.176886 $\overline{LBR}$ (0.489) (5.526) (1.785)	0.870	1.62	—	0.968	4.692
26. ΔXDBT	=	8.57517 - 1.35405 CAB + 0.610279 $\overline{\Delta RBFA}$ (1.304) (-13.669) (7.585)	0.982	2.351	—	22.537	106.908
		+ 677.359 $\overline{DXDBT}$ (27.992)					

Note: 1. Exogenous variables are indicated by a line on top of the variable.
2. Figures in brackets are 't' statistics.

(Contd...)

Table 1

Complete Model Structure (...Contd...)

IDENTITIES

27. $\mathrm{TR} = \mathrm{DT} + \mathrm{DIT} + \mathrm{TM} + \mathrm{NTX} + \overline{\mathrm{SE}}$

28. $\mathrm{TM} = \overline{\mathrm{MR}} \times [(\mathrm{impt} \times \overline{\mathrm{PIMP}}) / 100]$

29. $\mathrm{GXP} = [(\mathrm{con} \times \mathrm{P})/100] + \mathrm{TRP} + [(\overline{\mathrm{pcfag}} + \overline{\mathrm{pcfnag}}) \times \mathrm{PGKE}] \times 100$

30. $\mathrm{TRP} = \mathrm{IP} + \overline{\mathrm{SUBS}} + \overline{\mathrm{OCTR}}$

31. $\mathrm{IP} = \mathrm{IPI} + \mathrm{IPX}^g$

32. $\mathrm{FD} = \mathrm{GXP} - \mathrm{TR}$

33. $\mathrm{IPI} = \bar{I}_d \times \mathrm{IDBT}_{(-1)}$

34. $\mathrm{IDBT} = \mathrm{TDBT} - \mathrm{XDBT}^g$

35. $\mathrm{IPX}^g = \bar{I}^g_x \times \mathrm{XDBT}^g_{(-1)}$

36. $\mathrm{XDBT}^g = \mathrm{XDBT}^g_{(-1)} + \mathrm{EB}^g + \overline{\mathrm{VLC}}$

37. $\mathrm{TDBT} = \mathrm{TDBT}_{(-1)} + \Delta\mathrm{TDBT}$

38. $\mathrm{RCG} = \mathrm{FD} - \Delta\mathrm{BCG} - \overline{\Delta\mathrm{FICG}} - \mathrm{DNB} - \mathrm{EB}^g - \overline{\mathrm{MISCR}} + \mathrm{RCG}_{(-1)}$

39. $\mathrm{EB}^g = \bar{\mathrm{E}} \times \Delta\mathrm{TDBT}$

40. $\mathrm{BCG} = \Delta\mathrm{BCG} + \mathrm{BCG}_{(-1)}$

41. $\mathrm{RM} = \mathrm{RCG} + \overline{\mathrm{RBCS}} + \overline{\mathrm{RBFA}} + \overline{\mathrm{GCL}} - \overline{\mathrm{RNML}}$

42. $\mathrm{BCP} = \mathrm{M}_3 - \mathrm{RCG} - \mathrm{BCG} - \overline{\mathrm{RBFA}} - \overline{\mathrm{OBFA}} - \overline{\mathrm{GCL}} + \overline{\mathrm{BNML}}$

(Contd...)

(...Contd...)

43. wlr = $(IB + \overline{OPC}) - [(P - P_{(-1)})/P_{(-1)}] \times 100$

44. absp = $pc + piag + pinag$

45. add = $absp + con + \overline{pcfag} + \overline{pcfnag} + (expt\$ \times 7.91) - impt$

46. ad = $add + impt$

47. y = $yar + ynar$

48. Y = $(y \times PGDP) / 100$

49. YM = $Y + DIT + TM - \overline{SUBS}$

50. ym = $(YM / PGDP) \times 100$

51. pyd = $ym - [(TR /P) \times 100] + [(TRP / P) \times 100]$

52. PEXP\$ = $(UVIX \times 7.91) / EXR$

53. CAB = $[(expt\$ \times UVIX \times 7.91) / 100] - [(impt \times PIMP) / 100]$
$+ (XII - XIP) + NR$

54. IPX = $IPX^g + IPX^p$

55. IPX^p = $I^p_x \times XDBT^p_{(-1)}$

56. XDBT = $\Delta XDBT + XDBT_{(-1)}$

57. $XDBT^p$ = $XDBT - XDBT^g$

58. kagr = $\overline{pcfag} + piag - depag + kagr_{(-1)}$

59. knagr = $\overline{pcfnag} + pinag + \overline{erom} - depnag + knagr_{(-1)}$

Note: Exogenous variables are indicated by a line on the top of the variable.

Table 2

Simulation Error Statistics of Some Key Endogenous Variables in the Model

Endogenous Variables	*Static Simulation*			*Dynamic Simulation*		
	MAPE	*RMSPE*	*Theil's 'U'*	*MAPE*	*RMSPE*	*Theil's 'U'*
(1)	(2)	(3)	(4)	(5)	(6)	(7)
Fiscal Sector						
TR	1.39	2.60	0.01	4.12	5.77	0.04
GXP	1.16	1.99	0.01	2.09	4.18	0.02
FD	4.99	12.34	0.06	7.41	13.70	0.07
RCG	2.04	4.71	0.02	4.36	7.90	0.05
Real Sector						
pc	1.17	1.67	0.01	1.35	1.71	0.02
piag	7.77	8.76	0.09	10.14	11.54	0.12
pinag	10.46	12.11	0.13	12.28	15.39	0.15
yar	2.43	3.34	0.03	4.05	4.65	0.04
ynar	0.93	1.12	0.01	1.81	1.98	0.02
y	1.00	1.61	0.01	1.62	2.08	0.02
kagr	0.48	0.59	0.01	0.81	0.97	0.01
Kngar	0.47	0.58	0.01	1.43	1.51	0.02
Monetary Sector						
RM	1.87	3.70	0.02	3.93	6.51	0.05
M_3	2.48	2.92	0.03	4.57	6.56	0.05
P	2.14	2.82	0.02	4.68	5.35	0.05
IB	6.21	6.84	0.07	6.29	6.76	0.08
External Sector						
EXR	3.23	4.61	0.04	3.87	6.10	0.05
expt$	0.40	3.36	0.04	0.51	4.41	0.05
PEXP$	2.70	3.66	0.03	4.00	5.21	0.04
impt	2.74	3.48	0.03	3.87	4.77	0.05
CAB	-23.55	116.02	0.23	-19.89	74.23	0.22
XDBT	3.53	5.85	0.03	4.51	9.79	0.05

Note: MAPE = Mean Absolute Percentage Error.
RMSPE = Root Mean Square Percentage Error.

Graph 1

Money Supply

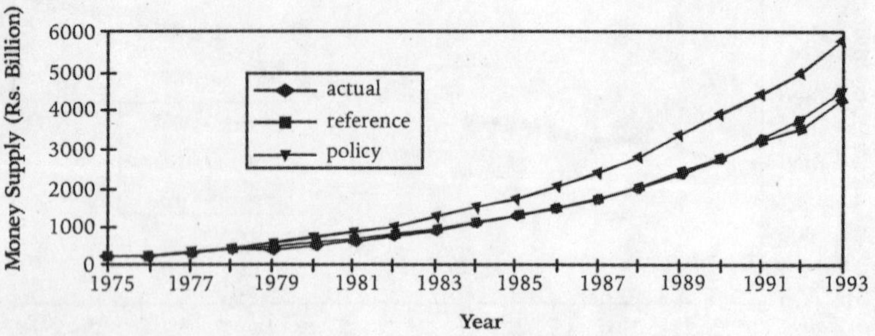

Graph 2

Price Level

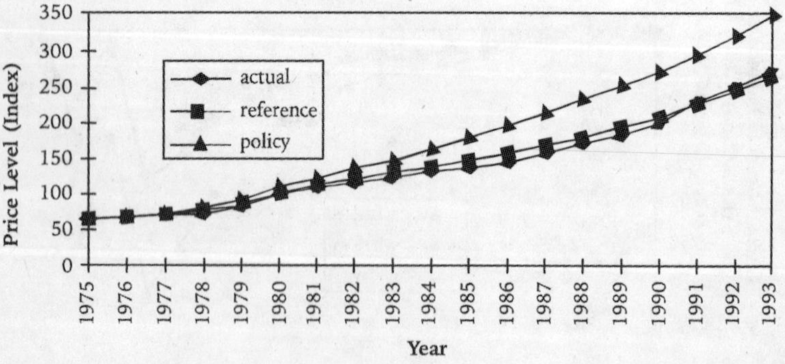

Graph 3

Real Income

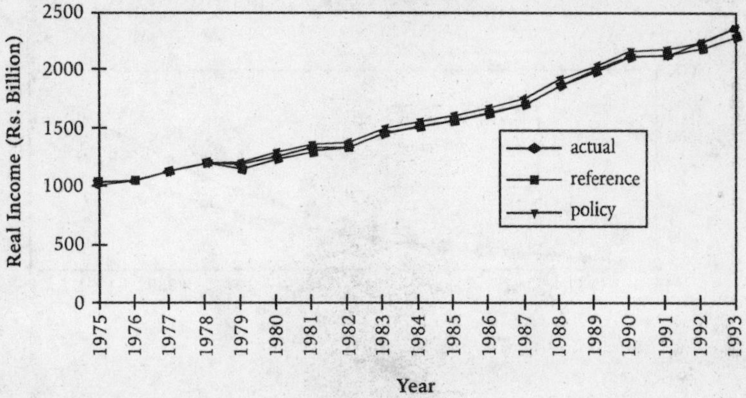

Graph 4

Current Account Balance

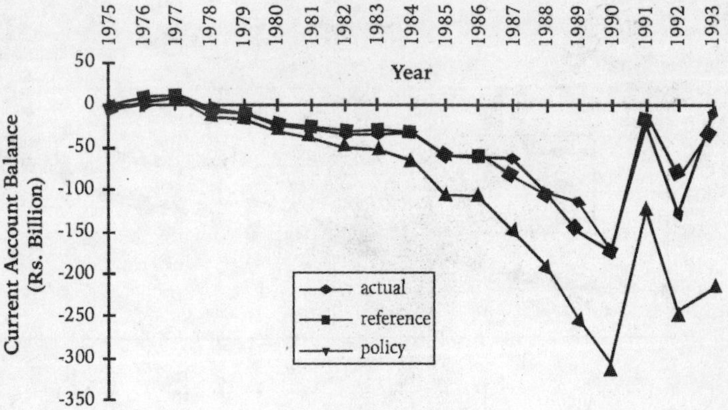

V. POLICY SIMULATION

A basic objective of the empirical model presented is to study the economy-wide ramifications of fiscal impulses which could stem from a policy induced change in one of the exogenous fiscal variables. Fiscal deficits pose various trade-offs for the economy. Such trade-offs involve securing growth and price stability, on the one hand, and maintaining internal and external balances, on the other. Fiscal deficit, as a means to promote growth, has been well recognised in the literature. Its efficacy to do so, however, depends on what happens to various intermediate variables such as prices, interest rate, credit, investment and external leakages such as imports, which are influenced by the fiscal deficit. When deficit is financed by money creation, the trade-off becomes sharper in terms of higher inflation. Apart from the adverse price impact, fiscal deficit implies higher level of domestic absorption which can trigger an increase in imports and widening of current account deficit in the balance of payments. To be sure, the exact nature of the impact of an increase in fiscal deficit on domestic prices and external deficit would depend on various factors, such as the nature of linkages established in the model, the estimated values of the impact coefficients and the lags in the model which provide feed back effects to the system.

The policy simulation exercise conducted in this section is intended to study four types of macroeconomic outcomes stemming from changes in the policy variables. In the first exercise, public real non-agricultural investment is raised by small magnitudes over its historical values during the sample period (1975-76 to 1993-94) in order to study the implications of this policy change for growth, prices, and balance of payments under the alternative financing scenarios. These financing scenarios fall under three major heads: (a) financing by money creation; (b) financing partly by a rise in public sector saving and partly by money creation; and (c) financing by an increase in commercial bank credit to the government sector. In the second exercise, we study the implications of an increase in government current expenditure, financed by bank credit for the price level, output and balance of payments. In the third exercise, the model is given a pure monetary shock in the form of an increase in the RBI's foreign assets. The impact of this policy change is studied

by analysing the changes in paths of the endogenous variables such as money supply, prices, output, exchange rate and the external current account balance. The fourth experiment relates to an increase in world income and its possible implications for exports and the current account deficit in the balance of payments.

In order to evaluate the comparative outcomes, the model is first solved on its dynamic mode by holding all exogenous variables to their historical levels. The simulated path of the variables, therefore, provide the model generated solutions of the endogenous variables during the sample period. In order to allow for policy induced change to be transmitted throughout the system, a particular exogenous variable is chosen for altering its temporal path during the sample period. The repeated shock arising out of this policy change is allowed to work through the system alongwith the feedback effects to provide the policy solutions for the endogenous variables. The policy solutions are compared with the reference solutions with a view to evaluating the impact of the policy change on some key endogenous variables.

Increased Public Investment

Public investment which is an exogenous variable in the model is divided into two broad categories, *viz.*, agriculture and non-agricultural investment. Public investment has a two-fold role in the model. It directly adds to the capital stock and generates output with a lag. In the non-agricultural sector, public capital also competes with private capital to the extent that it crowds out the private sector in the credit market.

In the simulation experiment, real public investment in the non-agricultural sector is raised by 10 per cent over its historical level in each year of the simulation period. There are three key endogenous variables to which this policy change may be addressed: output, prices and current account deficit in the balance of payment. The impacts of this policy under three different financing scenarios are discussed below:

Implications Under the Monetary Financing Scenario

The increased investment expenditure will have an immediate expansionary effect on fiscal deficit, raising the need for net RBI

credit to the Government. As a result, the reserve money will grow passively with the feedback from RBI credit, leading to expansion in money supply and consequent increase in prices. The ensuing output effect is, however, expected to moderate the price rise to some extent. The initial deterioration in the budget balance will feed itself back into the system to the extent that the interest payments will grow in the next period to service the higher level of public debt.[5] The budget balance will also depend on the degree and speed with which government revenues and expenditures adjust to the changes in price and output. On the other hand, the output effect on the budget balance is expected to be favourable, given the built-in-elasticity of tax system. On the financing side, while government borrowing from household is structurally related to nominal output, borrowing from banks is related to growth in bank deposits and in turn to money supply. Consequently, domestic non-monetary borrowing of the Government will rise to partly finance the deterioration in the budget balance in the subsequent period. The need for monetary financing will, however, grow until the budget deficit returns to a stable equilibrium value. The repeated shock, by way of continuous increases in public investment, will set in motion a cycle of adjustment involving money, prices, output and budget deficit, until all endogenous variables in the model reach to their new long run equilibrium values.

Another dimension of the higher public investment expenditure relates to its impact on the balance of payments. The output and price effects of public investment outlay are expected to be accompanied by a deterioration in the current account deficit in the balance of payments. This happens as a part of the increase in domestic absorption stemming from the higher government expenditure spills over to the external current account through a rise in imports. Apart from this income effect, the current account deficit will also be influenced by the changes in relative prices in the wake of a change in domestic price. There are two routes in the model through which the domestic price affects the relative price: the direct effect, where the unit value index of exports is positively related to domestic price and the indirect effect, where the dollar price of exports is negatively related to exchange rate. An increase in domestic price will increase the supply price of exports, resulting in a rise in unit value index of exports. The rise in rupee price of exports will be counteracted, to some extent, by the depreciation in nominal exchange rate.

Consequently, the net impact of the domestic price change on the dollar price of exports, and hence, on the export volume, will depend on the relative strength of both the factors. Since imports are positively related to domestic price, an increase in the latter will also cause the former to rise. The domestic price implications of higher public investment spending, therefore, turns out to be a crucial factor for the current account deficit in the balance of payment.

The quantitative impacts of the above policy simulation on key endogenous variables are presented in Table 3. The impact change refers to the immediate change (within the same year) in the endogenous variables in response to a change in the policy variable, the change is worked out as the percentage deviation in the variable over the base line or reference simulation.

$$d = \frac{1}{n} \sum_{i=1}^{n} \frac{(y^s - y^p)}{y^s}$$

Where 'd' is the annual average percentage deviation from the base line simulation, 'n' is number of years in the simulation period, 'y^s' is the value in the reference simulation (dynamic), and 'y^p' is value in the policy simulation. The short run impact refers to the annual average percentage deviation from the base line simulation during the first two years while the long run impact relates to the annual average percentage change during the entire sample period.

The immediate impact of the policy change is a rise in fiscal deficit and money supply by 16.98 per cent and 3.51 per cent, respectively, over their respective reference solutions in the same year of the increase in public investment. The initial price effect is placed at 0.69 per cent. Real net capital stock in non-agriculture sector and real income are higher by 0.60 per cent and 0.47 per cent, respectively, in the first year. Given the one-period lag between capital stock and output, the initial output effect stems from two sources, *viz.*, the higher level of credit flow to the production sectors, which has come about by the higher level of real money stock and the short run adjustment of output to domestic demand conditions. The increase in domestic absorption creates an instantaneous demand for real imports, which rises by 1.58 per cent in the first year while exports in constant dollar fall marginally by 0.01 per cent, a result that follows from the change in the relative prices against exports.

Consequently, the current account deficit in the balance of payment shows a deterioration of 17.04 per cent in the first year of the policy change. In terms of ratio to GDP, current account deficit registers an increase of 0.08 percentage point from the reference simulation.

Table 3

Policy Simulation 1(a): Impact of Sustained 10 per cent increase in Real Public Investment in Non-agriculture Sector Financed by Money Creation

Endogenous Variables	*Annual Average Percentage Deviation from the Base-Line Simulation*		
	Impact (first year)	*Short Run (first two years' average)*	*Long Run (sample period average, 1975-76 to 1993-94)*
Fiscal Deficit	16.98	18.13	41.50
Government Revenue	0.60	1.08	16.10
Government Expenditure	4.78	5.46	21.92
Money Supply	3.51	5.34	29.31
Prices	0.69	1.30	18.13
Real Capital Stock in Non-Agriculture Sector	0.60	0.97	4.44
Real Income	0.47	0.72	2.66
Real Exports (US $)	-0.01	-0.06	3.97
Real Imports (Rs.)	1.58	2.39	20.66
Exchange Rate*	0.43	0.68	15.62
Current Account Deficit (Rs.)**	17.04	24.97	161.65
(as % of GDP)	(0.08)	(0.13)	(0.67)
External Debt	0.80	1.42	32.54
Interest Payment on External Debt	0.00	0.001	34.14

Note: * (+) Implies depreciation and (-) appreciation.
** (+) Implies increase in deficit and (-) decrease.

In the short to medium run, the adverse price and balance of payment effects continue to dominate the output effect. While during the first two years, the price level rises by an average rate of 1.3 per cent, the growth in output is placed at 0.72 per cent and current account deficit deteriorates by 24.97 per cent (0.13 per cent of GDP).

The short run scenario, in other words, shows a faster rate of deterioration in the internal and external balances than what was witnessed in the immediate horizon.

In the long run, the price and balance of payments situation continue to show sharp deterioration. As the gap between revenue and expenditure increases steadily with inflation and rising stock of public debt, the fiscal deficit rises by an annual average rate of 41.50 per cent, leading to a money supply growth of 29.31 per cent. Prices on an average rise by 18.13 per cent, while real income goes up by an annual average rate of 2.66 per cent. External payments situation records a sharp deterioration with the real import growth averaging 20.66 per cent, and real export in US dollars showing only a small growth of 3.97 per cent, which is primarily caused by the exchange rate depreciation brought about by the combined influence of domestic price increase and the spurt in the current account deficit. The deficit in the current account rises by an average of 161.65 per cent or 0.67 per cent of GDP in the long run. In terms of magnitude, the current account deficit would have increased to 2.08 per cent of GDP in 1993-94, compared to the reference value of 0.36 per cent. Graphs 1 to 4 provides the plots of actual, reference simulation and policy outcomes of major endogenous variables.

As may be seen from the graphs, while the real output growth in the long run starts to taper off, inflation and balance of payment deficits increase to an unsustainable position, reflecting the relative inefficacy of the policy to achieve sustained output growth through monetary expansion.

Financing Implications Under Increased Public Saving and Money Financing

In this scenario, the additional public investment is assumed to be financed partly by an increase in savings of public enterprises while the savings of government administration evolves endogenously with the government revenue and expenditure growth. Historically, the proportion of nominal saving of public enterprises to public investment in the non-agricultural sector varied between 15 to 85 per cent during the sample period 1975-76 to 1993-94. It would seem reasonable to expect that the gross saving of public enterprises rise along with the public investment at a pace which would maintain the

above ratios unaltered during the sample period. Implicit in this is the assumption that gap between the incremental investment and saving in each year is financed by money creation.

The quantitative changes recorded in the key endogenous variables under this financing scenario are summarised in Table 4.

Table 4

Policy Simulation 1(b): Impact of Sustained 10 per cent increase in Public Real Investment in Non-Agriculture Sector Financed by Increased Public Saving and Money Creation

Endogenous Variables	*Annual Average Percentage Deviation from the Base-Line Simulation*		
	Impact (first year)	*Short Run (first two years' average)*	*Long Run (sample period average, 1975-76 to 1993-94)*
Fiscal Deficit	14.31	14.84	25.13
Government Revenue	1.34	1.86	12.40
Government Expenditure	4.66	5.20	15.34
Money Supply	2.98	4.41	18.71
Prices	0.58	1.07	11.37
Real Capital Stock in Non-Agriculture Sector	0.57	0.91	3.88
Real Income	0.43	0.64	2.29
Real Exports (US$)	-0.01	-0.07	2.11
Real Imports (Rs.)	1.38	2.02	13.24
Exchange Rate*	0.37	0.56	9.74
Current Account Deficit (Rs.)**	14.89	21.05	96.35
(as % of GDP)	(0.07)	(0.07)	(0.46)
External Debt	0.70	1.22	21.88
Interest Payment on External Debt	0.00	0.02	23.22

Note: * (+) Implies depreciation and (-) appreciation.
** (+) Implies increase in deficit and (-) decrease.

The long run impacts on prices and balance of payments under this financing scenario are significantly different from the pure monetary financing scenario. In the long run, the annual average increase in fiscal deficit works out to 25.13 per cent, giving a money

supply growth of 18.71 per cent over the reference simulation. The price level shows an annual average increase of 11.37 per cent in the long run. It may be noted that the substantial moderation in the price rise, compared to the pure monetary financing scenario, has come about through a small loss in output growth. The annual average growth in real output over the reference solution is placed at 2.29 per cent under this scenario compared to 2.66 per cent in the pure monetary financing scenario. The ratio of current account deficit to GDP goes up by an annual average rate of 0.46 per cent in the long run. Under this policy exercise, or what may be referred to as restrained monetary expansion scenario, the price and balance of payments impacts remain adverse suggesting that a policy favouring growth in public investment, inconsistent with the saving effort, would likely affect the long term prospects of maintaining a sustainable price and balance of payment situation.

Financing Implications Under Increased Bank Credit to Government

Borrowing from market, mainly commercial banks constitutes an alternative source of financing the additional public investment. Under the bond financing scenario, the macroeconomic impact of fiscal deficit would depend on several factors such as the impact on interest rate, availability of credit to the private sector and the growth of absorption relative to growth in output. Theoretically, operating under a non-accommodating monetary policy environment, an increase in supply of government bonds is expected to increase the interest rate and adversely affect the economic activity elsewhere. Another consequence of the policy is that the increased flow of bank credit to Government could imply reduction of credit for private sector capital formation. These adverse outcomes would have to be evaluated against the monetary stability of the policy which is likely to follow in absence of automatic growth in money supply on account of increase in fiscal deficit.

The policy simulation of above experiment required some change in the framework of the model. Bank credit to Government, which was behaviourally determined in the model, had to be expressed as an identity while the Reserve Bank credit to Government, an endogenous variable, earlier, had to be made exogenous. Under this policy experiment, commercial bank credit to Government is treated as the

residual capital receipt to fill the gap between the fiscal deficit and borrowing from all other sources, including the Reserve Bank credit to Government. The results of this policy outcome are presented in Table 5.

Table 5

Policy Simulation 1(c): Impact of Sustained 10 per cent increase in Public Real Investment in Non-Agriculture Sector financed by Increase in Commercial Bank Credit to the Government

Endogenous Variables	*Annual Average Percentage Deviation from the Base-Line Simulation*		
	Impact (first year)	*Short Run (first two years' average)*	*Long Run (sample period average, 1975-76 to 1993-94)*
Fiscal Deficit	15.39	15.11	17.88
Government Revenue	0.10	0.12	-0.12
Government Expenditure	3.93	3.90	4.04
Money Supply	—	—	—
Prices	-0.09	-0.16	-0.74
Commercial Bank Lending Rate	0.84	1.28	0.76
Real Private Investment in Non-Agriculture Sector	-2.55	-2.90	-8.27
Real Capital Stock in Non-Agriculture Sector	0.36	0.51	0.82
Real Income	0.24	0.32	0.57
Real Exports (US $)	-0.04	-0.10	-0.80
Real Imports (Rs.)	0.42	0.37	-6.37
Exchange Rate*	0.05	-0.01	-0.49
Current Account Deficit (Rs.)**	6.15	3.87	-4.79
(as % of GDP)	(0.03)	(0.02)	(-0.03)
External Debt	0.21	0.24	-0.97
Interest Payment on External Debt	—	-0.37	-3.47

Note: * (+) Implies depreciation and (-) appreciation.
** (+) Implies increase in deficit and (-) decrease.

The outcomes under this policy are perceptibly different from the two other scenarios discussed above. An immediate impact of the policy is that while fiscal deficit rises by about 15.39 per cent in the same year of the increase in public investment, the ensuing output

growth (0.24 per cent) and the unchanged level of money stock bring about a marginal decline in prices. Higher credit flow to Government crowds out private investment in the non-agriculture sector by 2.55 per cent, although the aggregate capital stock in non-agricultural sector rises by 0.36 per cent. This is reminiscent of partial crowding out situation, implying that a part of the loss of bank credit to private sector is made good by the enterprises through other sources. This method of financing government investment also raises the commercial banks' lending rate by 0.84 per cent and affects private investment. The current account deficit witnesses a deterioration of the order of 6.5 per cent (0.03 percentage points in terms of ratio of GDP) mainly brought out by the growth of 0.42 per cent in real imports and a decline of 0.04 per cent in exports. In the short to medium run, fiscal deficit grows by 15.11 per cent per annum, while the impact on other variables are broadly on the lines of those witnessed in the immediate horizon.

In the long run, real capital stock in non-agricultural sector and output growth are placed at 0.82 per cent and 0.57 per cent, respectively, while private real investment declines at a faster rate of 8.27 per cent, resulting in the loss of much of the potential output. The resource gap of the Government shows an annual average increase of 17.88 per cent. As the decline in the price level strengthens in the long run, the real money stock and aggregate demand level falls, and the relative price changes in favour of domestic goods, causing a decline in the real import. This shows up in the perverse effect of some improvement in current account balance. The relative price changes, therefore, have a powerful impact on the current account deficit in the balance of payments.

Increased Current Expenditure Financed by Bank Credit

A policy induced increase in government current expenditure, financed by borrowing from the credit market is associated with both adverse price and income effects, as well as, a deterioration in the balance of payment situation. In this policy simulation, government nominal current transfers (excluding interest payments), which is an exogenous variable in the model was increased by 10 per cent over its actual value in each year of the sample period. The quantitative outcomes of this policy are presented in Table 6.

Table 6

Policy Simulation 2: Impact of Sustained 10 per cent increase in Government Current Transfers Financed by Bank Credit

Endogenous Variables	*Annual Average Percentage Deviation from the Base-Line Simulation*		
	Impact (first two year)	*Short Run (first two years' average)*	*Long Run (sample period average, 1975-76 to 1993-94)*
Fiscal Deficit	3.34	3.50	5.82
Money Supply	—	—	—
Real Income	0.02	0.01	-0.34
Prices	-0.01	-0.01	0.35
Real Exports (US$)	-0.003	-0.004	0.36
Real Imports (Rs.)	0.03	0.03	0.19
Exchange Rate*	neg.	neg.	0.23
Current Account Deficit (Rs.)**	0.45	0.29	3.42
(as % of GDP)	neg.	neg.	0.01
External Debt	0.02	0.02	0.28

Note: * (+) Implies depreciation and (-) appreciation.
** (+) Implies increase in deficit and (-) decrease.
Neg.: Negligible.

It is evident that higher levels of current expenditure imply long run adverse macroeconomic outcomes for the economy which stems from reduction in output level, increased pressure on prices and a deterioration in the current account deficit. This is in contrast to the policy outcomes of financing a higher level of public investment through credit from the market. Public investment, despite its adverse 'crowding out' impact on private investment, raises the output level in the economy and may not imply severe long run balance of payments effects – if not financed by money creation. Efforts to reduce government expenditure should be, therefore, targeted at current expenditures, which have potential adverse macroeconomic consequences for the economy.

Increased Reserve Bank's Foreign Assets

A pure monetary shock to the model by way of an increase in Reserve Bank's Foreign Assets (RBFA) is expected to work through the system in two ways. First, RBFA constitutes a part of the reserve money, hence, there will be an immediate expansionary impact on money supply and prices. Higher real money balances would also go to enhance the credit flow to real sector, leading to some increase in output. The relative prices in the trade sector will, however, undergo a change with implications for trade flows. Secondly, RBFA has a direct implication for exchange rate, which would tend to depreciate with higher absorption of foreign exchange by RBI from the market. This constitutes a second channel of impact on the external balance. The quantitative dimension of this policy change on the key endogenous variables are reported in Table 7.

Table 7

Policy Simulation 3: Impact of Sustained 10 per cent Increase in Reserve Bank Foreign Assets

Endogenous Variables	*Annual Average Percentage Deviation from the Reference Simulation*		
	Impact (first year)	*Short Run (first two years' average)*	*Long Run (sample period average, 1975-76 to 1993-94)*
Money Supply	0.73	1.44	1.75
Prices	0.17	0.40	1.41
Fiscal Deficit	0.36	0.80	1.54
Real Income	0.04	0.08	0.02
Real Exports (US$)	0.25	0.36	0.46
Real Imports (Rs.)	0.22	0.50	1.44
Exchange Rate*	0.70	0.92	1.26
Interest Income on External Investment	—	29.28	40.33
Current Account Deficit (Rs.)**	-0.34	-4.63	1.36
External Debt	0.47	0.66	1.37

Note: * (+) Implies depreciation and (-) appreciation.

** (+) Implies increase in deficit and (-) decrease.

In the first year of the increase in RBFA, money supply increases by 0.73 per cent and price level by 0.17 per cent. The price rise sets in motion an adjustment in government revenues and expenditure and fiscal deficit expands by 0.36 per cent, leading to borrowing from Reserve Bank in the second stage of impact. Real income is higher by 0.04 per cent in the first year. Exchange rate witnesses a depreciation of 0.70 per cent under the combined impact of domestic inflation and Reserve Bank's absorption of foreign exchange from the market. This produces an export growth in dollar terms of 0.25 per cent, while imports in real terms rise by 0.22 per cent. The current account deficit improves by 0.34 per cent over the reference simulation.

In the short to medium run, money supply rises at an annual average rate of 1.44 per cent, leading to a price rise of 0.4 per cent. The annual increase in output averages 0.08 per cent. In the long run, the balance of payment records a deterioration, as the adverse price effects cause imports to rise at a faster rate, despite an increased rate of depreciation in exchange rate. This shows that containing domestic inflation through other policy measures such as sterilisation has to play a critical role, if the depreciation in exchange rate should have an enduring favourable impact on the current account balance.

Growth in World Income

Growth in world income is expected to increase exports of goods and services and improve the current account balance. The economy-wide implications of this change can be studied by solving the model with the repeated favourable shocks during the sample period. The policy experiment conducted in this section is, therefore, intended to capture the temporal changes in key endogenous variables following one per cent increase in world real income (index) over the observed levels in each year of the sample period. This favourable shock to the external sector is expected to work through the model in the following way.

An increase in world income will have an immediate favourable impact on the current account balance. The decline in current account deficit will reduce the stock of external debt and interest payment, leading to further improvement in external balance. However, some of the gains accruing from this favourable shock will be neutralised by

higher imports stemming from the increase in domestic absorption and appreciation of exchange rate, following the reduction in current account deficit.

The quantitative dimension of the policy change is given in Table 8.

Table 8

Policy Simulation 4: Effects of Sustained One per cent Increase in World Income (index) Over the Actual Level

Endogenous Variables	*Annual Average Percentage Deviation from the Base Line Simulation*		
	Impact (first year)	*Short Run (first two years' average)*	*Long Run (sample period average, 1975-76 to 1993-94)*
Real Exports (US $)	0.53	0.67	0.82
Real Imports (Rs.)	0.02	0.02	-0.06
Exchange Rate*	-0.09	-0.13	-0.59
Current Account Deficit (Rs.)**	-5.90	-8.69	-8.86
(as % of GDP)	(-0.03)	(-0.04)	(-0.08)
External Debt	-0.28	0.50	-2.60
External Interest Payments	—	-0.21	-3.18
Fiscal Deficit	-0.02	-0.03	-0.12
Money Supply	-0.004	-0.01	-0.09
Prices	0.005	-0.01	-0.09
Real Income	0.01	0.02	0.02

Note: * (+) Implies depreciation and (-) appreciation.
** (+) Implies increase in deficit and (-) decrease.

The immediate impact is an increase in dollar value of real exports of goods and services by 0.53 per cent over the reference simulation. Imports also rise by 0.02 per cent because of the higher level of domestic absorption. The current account deficit declines by 5.90 per cent in the first year, implying an improvement of 0.03 percentage point in relation to GDP, which brings down the stock of external debt by 0.28 per cent. The improvement in current account balance and consequent reduction in external debt, although brings

down the external interest payment in the subsequent years, this also creates the conditions for exchange rate appreciation. In the long run, the annual average rate of decline in the current account deficit is placed at 0.08 percentage point of GDP, over the base-year scenario. The domestic impact of the favourable world output shock is an increase in real income which leads to an improvement in government resource gap and a decline in money supply and price level in the economy.

VI. CONCLUDING OBSERVATIONS

The major objective of this paper has been to analyse the various interrelationships among fiscal deficit, prices, output and balance of payments and in this context, to evaluate different policy options for maintaining sustainable internal and external balances in the economy. High levels of fiscal deficit pose various problems for the economy, inflation and adverse balance of payments consequences are considered to be the serious concerns of these deficits.

The macroeconometric model presented above, provides an integrated framework to study the external sector dimension of the fiscal deficit alongwith its monetary and real sector implications. The policy simulation results presented in the paper revealed that fiscal deficit, in general, results in widening of current account deficit, although this outcome critically depends on how the deficit is financed. In the case of monetary financing scenario, the price and income effects reinforce each other, leading to a rapid deterioration of external balance in the short run as well as in the long run. The external impacts of deficit are, however, less severe when deficit is financed by increased domestic savings. Thus, in any effort to maintain a sustainable balance of payments situation, domestic economic policy, aimed at maintaining absorption and price at appropriate levels has an important role to play. This underlines the need for an externally consistent budgetary policy, keeping in view a medium term target of current account deficit in relation to GDP.

It is also important to observe that deficit financing to promote public investment and growth involves costs in terms of loss of control in inflation. The policy simulation results presented in the study show that a sustained increase in fiscal deficit, financed by

borrowing from the Reserve Bank leads to a spiral impact on prices in the long run, although in the short run the adverse impact may look quite moderate. Even when the deficit is financed by borrowing from market, a prudent limit for such borrowing becomes essential. In a system of market-determined interest rates, the financing requirement of Government from the market should be consistent with the growth in national savings.

The policy simulation results also show that while growth in world income improves the external payments situation, some of the improvements may be lost due to the exchange rate appreciation. While a viable balance of payments strategy would have to be based on the supportive domestic policies to keep absorption and prices at appropriate levels, any temporary disequilibrium in the balance of payments due to adverse relative price movements may necessitate some adjustment of exchange rate.

Notes

1. Fiscal deficit of the public sector in this analysis is taken as the saving and investment gap of public sector as measured in the National Accounts Statistics following the principles based on the System of National Accounts (SNA). This measure of fiscal deficit will not agree with the comprehensive public sector deficit computed from budget documents because of several accounting differences, such as the cash based accounting in budget *versus* accrual accounting in SNA, the difference in the consolidation of transactions and classification differences mainly arising from the treatment of acquisition of financial assets by the government (IMF, 1986).
2. This impact will not be strong if there are supply constraints or the economy is operating at near full capacity level.
3. The weighted average lending rate refers to the mean lending rates of commercial banks for various ranges of outstanding advances, weighted by the share of the respective outstanding advances to the total.
4. The net capital account transaction in the balance of payments is taken as a proxy for the private capital flows.
5. The increase in interest payment may be, to some extent, offset by higher profit transfers from RBI due to the rising share of RBI's claim on Government in the total debt.

References

Aschauer, David A. (1989): 'Does Public Capital Crowd Out Private Capital?', *Journal of Monetary Economics,* Vol. (24).

Bagchi, Amaresh and Pulin B. Nayak (1994): 'Public Finance and Planning Process, The Indian Experience: A Survey', in Amaresh Bagchi and Nicholas Stern (eds.) *Tax Policy Planning in Developing Countries,* Oxford University Press.

Barro, Robert J. (1974): 'Are Government Bonds Net Wealth?', *Journal of Political Economy,* Vol. 82, No. 6 (November-December).

———. (1989): 'The Ricardian Approach to Budget Deficits', *Journal of Economic Perspectives,* Vol.3, No.2 (Spring).

Bartoli, Gloria (1989): 'Fiscal Expansion and External Current Account Imbalances', in Mario I. Blejer and Chu Keyoung (eds.) *Fiscal Policy, Stabilisation and Growth in Developing countries,* International Monetary Fund.

Bernheim, Douglas B (1989): 'A Neoclassical Perspective on Budget Deficits', *Journal of Economic Perspectives,* Vol.3, No.2 (Spring).

Bhattacharya B.B., R.B. Burman and A.K. Nag (1994): 'Stabilisation Policy Options' A Macroeconometric Analysis', *Development Research Group Study No.8,* Reserve Bank of India (April).

Blejer, Mario I and Adrienne Cheasty (1991): 'Measurement of Fiscal Deficits: Analytical and Methodological Issues', *Journal of Economic Literature,* Vol. XXIX, No.4 (December).

Blejer, Mario I and Mohsin S. Khan (1984): 'Government Policy and Private Investment in Developing Countries', *IMF Staff Papers,* Vol. 31.

Crips, Francis and Wynne Godley (1976): 'A Formal Analysis of the Cambridge Economic Policy Group Model', *Economica,* Vol. 43, No.172 (November).

Easterly, William and Klaus Schmidt - Hebbel (1993): 'Fiscal Deficits and Macroeconomic Performance in Developing Countries', *The World Bank Research Observer,* Vol. 8, No.2 (July).

Edwards, Sebastian and Mohsin S. Khan (1985): 'Interest Rate Determination in Developing Countries : A Conceptual Framework', *IMF Staff Paper,* 32.

Frenkel, Jacob A and Assaf Razin (1987): 'The Mundell-Fleming Model A Quarter Century Later: A Unified Exposition', *IMF Staff Papers,* International Monetary Fund, Vol. 34, No. 2 (December).

Haque, Nadeem U, Kajal Lahiri and Peter J. Montiel (1990): 'A Macro-econometric Model for Developing Countries', *IMF Staff Papers,* Vol. 37, No.3 (September).

Khan, Mohasin S. and Malcolm D. Knight (1981): 'Stabilisation Programs in Developing Countries: A Formal Framework', *IMF Staff Papers,*Vol. 28, No. 1 (March).

Krishnamurty, K. and V. Pandit (1997): 'Exchange Rate, Tariff and Trade Flows: Alternative Policy Scenaries for India', *Indian Economic Review,* Vol. XXXI, No. 1.

Krishnamurty, K., V. Pandit, T. Palanivel and P. Saibaba (1997): 'An Econometric Model for India, 1971-95', (IEG-DSE Research Team), Institute of Economic Growth.

Krishnamurty, K. P. Saibaba and N.A. Kazmi (1985): 'Inflation and Growth: A Model for India' in K. Krishnamurty and V. Pandit (eds), *Macro-econometric Modeling of the Indian Economy: Studies on Inflation and Growth,* Hindustan Publishing Corporation.

Lahari, Ashok K. (1989): 'Dynamics of Asian Savings: The Role of Growth and Age Structure', *IMF Staff Papers,* Vol.36, No. 1 (March).

Mansur, H.A. (1989): 'Effects of a Budget Deficit on the Current Account Balances: The Case of Philippines', in Mario I. Blejer and Chu Keyoung (eds.), *Fiscal Policy, Stabilisation and Growth in Developing Countries,* International Monetary Fund.

Mohanty, M.S. and Himanshu Joshi (1992): 'The Dynamic Interrelationship Between Fiscal and Trade Deficits in India: 1970-71 to 1990-91', *Reserve Bank of India Occasional Papers,*Vol. 13, No.3 (September).

Mohanty, M.S. (1996): 'Budget Deficits and Private Saving in India: Evidence on Ricardian Equivalence', *Reserve Bank of India Occasional* Papers, Vol. 16, No. 1 (March).

———. (1997): 'Macro-Economic Stability, Growth and Fiscal Reform - The Indian Perspective', *Economic and Political Weekly,* Vol. XXXII, No. 6, February 8.

Patra, Michael D. and Sitikantha Pattanaik (1994): 'Exchange Rate, Pass Through and the Trade Balance: The Indian Experience', *Reserve Bank of India Occasional Papers,*Vol. 15, No. 4 (December).

Pradhan, B.K., D.K. Ratha and Atul Sharma (1988): 'Complementarity Between Public and Private Investment in India', *Journal of Development Economics,* Vol. 23.

Polak, J.J. (1957): 'Monetary Analysis of Income Formation and Payments Problems', *IMF Staff Papers,* No.4.

Rakshit, Mihir (1991): 'The Macroeconomic Adjustment Programme, A Critique', *Economic and Political Weekly,* Vol. XVII, No. 34 (August 24).

Rao, M.J.M. and Balwant Singh (1995): 'Analytical Foundations of Financial Programming and Growth Oriented Adjustment', *Development Research Group Study* No. 10, Reserve Bank of India (January).

Rangarajan, C. (1982): 'Agricultural Growth and Industrial Performance in India', International Food Policy Research Institute, Research Report, 33 (October).

———. (1994): 'India's Balance of Payments : The Emerging Dimensions', *Sixteenth G.B. Pant Memorial Lecture* (New Delhi).

Rangarajan, C. and Anoop Singh (1984): 'Reserve Money: Concepts and Policy Implications for India', *Reserve Bank of India Occasional Papers,* June.

Rangarajan, C. and Anupam Basu and Narendra Jadhav (1989): 'Dynamics of Interaction Between Government Deficit and Domestic Debt in India', *Reserve Bank of India Occasional Papers,* Vol.10, No.3 (September).

Rangarajan, C. and R.R. Arif (1990): 'Money, Output and Prices: A Macro-econometric Model', *Economic and Political Weekly,* Vol.XXV, No.16 (April 21).

Rath, Nilkantha (1989): 'Agricultural Growth and Investment in India', *Journal of Indian School of Political Economy,* (January-June).

Sau, Ranjit (1992): 'Making of a Payments Crisis: India 1991', *Economic and Political Weekly,* Vol. XXVII, No. 33 (August).

Shetty, S.L. (1990): 'Investment in Agriculture: Brief Review of Recent Trends', *Economic and Political Weekly,* February 17.

Sundararajan, V. and Subhash Thakur (1980): 'Public Investment, Crowding Out, and Growth: A Dynamic Model Applied to India and Korea', *IMF Staff Papers,* Vol. 27 (December).

Tanzi, Vito (1977): 'Inflation, Lags in Collection, and the Real Value of Tax Revenue', *IMF Staff Papers,* Vol.XXIV, No.1 (March).

Appendix 1

Definition of Variables

Endogenous

DT	=	Nominal direct tax revenue of Government.
DIT	=	Nominal indirect tax revenue of Government.
NTX	=	Nominal non-tax revenue of government administrative departments (includes income from property and entrepreneurship and miscellaneous current receipts).
con	=	Real government consumption expenditure.
ΔTDBT	=	Incremental debt of the Government.
ΔBCG	=	Change in commercial bank credit to Government (March 31).
DNB	=	Government domestic non-bank borrowing, *viz.*, small savings, provident funds and special deposits etc.
P	=	Wholesale Price Index (1980-81 = 100).
PGDP	=	GDP deflator (1980-81 = 100).
PGKE	=	Implicit capital formation deflator in public sector (1980-81 = 100).
ΔDEP	=	Change in aggregate deposit of commercial banks, including co-operative banks (March 31).
M_3	=	Broad money stock (March 31).
IB	=	Interest rate for one to three year bank deposits.
pc	=	Real private consumption expenditure.
piag	=	Real gross private investment in agriculture sector.
pinag	=	Real gross private investment in non-agriculture sector.
yar	=	Output originating from agriculture (1980-81 prices).
ynar	=	Output originating from non-agricultural sector (1980-81).
depag	=	Depreciation in agricultural sector in real term.
depnag	=	Depreciation in non-agriculture sector in real term.
expt$	=	Exports of goods and services in constant US dollar (includes merchandise and invisible exports, excluding transfers, investment income and miscellaneous current receipts).
UVIX	=	Unit value index of exports (1980-81 = 100).
impt	=	Real imports of goods and services in Rupees (includes merchandise and invisible imports, excluding transfers, investment income and miscellaneous current payments).
EXR	=	Nominal exchange rate (rupee to US dollar).
XII	=	External interest income in nominal term.

(Contd...)

(...Contd...)

ΔXDBT	=	Change in external debt.
TR	=	Nominal current revenue of Government.
TM	=	Nominal import tax revenue.
GXP	=	Nominal government expenditure.
TRP	=	Nominal transfer payments of government administration.
IP	=	Total interest payment of Government.
FD	=	Public sector fiscal deficit.
IPI	=	Interest payment on internal debt of the Government.
IDBT	=	Outstanding internal public debt.
IPX^g	=	Interest payment on external debt of the Government.
$XDBT^g$	=	Outstanding external debt of the Government.
TDBT	=	Total outstanding public debt of the Government.
RCG	=	Outstanding Reserve Bank credit to the Government (March 31).
EB^g	=	External borrowing of the Government.
BCG	=	Outstanding bank credit to the Government (March 31).
RM	=	Outstanding reserve money (March 31).
BCP	=	Outstanding bank credit to private sector (March 31).
wlr	=	Weighted average real lending rate of banks.
absp	=	Real private absorption.
add	=	Real demand for domestically produced goods and services.
ad	=	Real aggregate absorption.
y	=	Real GDP at factor cost.
Y	=	Nominal GDP at factor cost.
YM	=	Nominal GDP at market prices.
ym	=	Real GDP at market prices.
pyd	=	Real private disposable income.
PEXP$	=	Index of dollar price of exports.
CAB	=	Current account balance.
IPX	=	Interest payment on external debt.
IPX^p	=	Interest payment on private external debt.
XDBT	=	Outstanding external debt.
$XDBT^p$	=	Outstanding private external debt.
kagr	=	Real net capital stock in agriculture sector.
knagr	=	Real net capital stock in non-agriculture sector.

(Contd...)

(...Contd...)

Exogenous		
DDT	=	Dummy for 1991-92 for the change in the structure of direct taxes.
DDIT	=	Dummy for 1992-93 and 1993-94 for the sharp change in the indirect tax rates.
DNTX	=	Dummy for sharp fluctuations in non-tax revenue in some years.
DDBT	=	Dummy for sharp fluctuation in outstanding debt in 1974-75.
ΔWSLR	=	Weighted average Statutory Liquidity Ratio (SLR weighted by the number of days the ratio was in force).
DBCG	=	Dummy for unusual increase in bank credit to Government in 1977-78.
DDNB	=	Dummy for the sharp decline in government non-bank domestic borrowing in 1974-75.
DPI	=	Dummy representing high inflation years in 1973-74 and 1974-75 due to first oil shock.
DP2	=	Dummy for the second oil shock in 1979-80.
DPGKE	=	Dummy for the sharp decline in implicit government capital formation deflator in 1980-81.
DDEP	=	Dummy for large variation in bank deposits in 1985-86 and 1986-87.
pcfag	=	Public sector gross investment in agriculture in real term.
dpiag1	=	Dummy for the sharp decline in public investment in agriculture in certain years.
dpiag2	=	Dummy for sharp increase in public investment in agriculture in certain years.
pcfnag	=	Public sector gross investment in non-agriculture sector in real term.
capb	=	Net capital account in the balance of payments account deflated by Wholesale Price Index.
OPC	=	Intermediating cost of banks.
RAIN	=	Rain fall index (1970-71 = 100).
AREA	=	Index of gross cropped area (1970-71 = 100).
wyr	=	Index of world output (1980-81 = 100).
WPEXP	=	World price of exports (1980-81 = 100).
dexpt$	=	Dummy for unusual large variation in exports of goods and services in some years.
DUVIX	=	Dummy for unusual decline in unit value index of exports in some years.

(Contd...)

(...Contd...)

PIMP	=	Unit value index of imports (1980-81 = 100).
dimpt1	=	Dummy for a large fall in imports following the stabilisation programme in 1991-92.
dimpt2	=	Dummy for sharp variation in imports in certain years.
RBFA	=	Stock of Reserve Bank's foreign asset (March 31).
DEXR1	=	Dummy representing the readjustment of exchange rate of Rupee in 1991-92.
DEXR2	=	Dummy representing a large depreciation of exchange rate of Rupee in 1992-93.
LBR	=	One year London Inter-Bank Offer Rate.
DXDBT	=	Dummy for change in classification of external debt from 1991-92 onwards.
SE	=	Gross savings of departmental and non-departmental enterprises of the Government.
MR	=	Average import duty rate.
SUBS	=	Subsidies in nominal term.
OCTR	=	Other current transfers of the government administration representing pension, etc.
I_d	=	Average interest rate on government domestic debt.
I_x^g	=	Average interest rate on government external debt.
VLC	=	Valuation change in government external debt.
FICG	=	Financial institutions' investment in government securities (outstanding).
E	=	Proportion of external borrowing in the total borrowing of the Government.
MISCR	=	Miscellaneous capital receipts of Government.
RBCS	=	Outstanding Reserve Bank credit to commercial sector (March 31).
GCL	=	Outstanding government currency liability (March 31).
RNML	=	Outstanding Reserve Bank's net non-monetary liability (March 31).
OBFA	=	Outstanding level of other banks' foreign assets.
BNML	=	Banking sectors' net non-monetary liability.
NR	=	Net external transfers in balance of payments including non-interest investment income and other miscellaneous current receipts.
I_x^p	=	Average interest rate on private external debt.
EROM	=	Errors and omissions in gross capital formation data.

3

Taxation as a Tool of Redistribution in Developing Economies

Reducing inequalities in income is regarded by most developing economies as one of the objectives of economic policy. For example, the Indian First Five-Year Plan states, "It is no longer possible to think of development as a process merely of increasing the available supplies of material goods. It is necessary to ensure that simultaneously a steady advance is made towards realisation of wider objectives such as full employment and the removal of economic inequalities".[1] The same viewpoint is reiterated in the second and third plans. One of the tools available for achieving this objective is fiscal policy which can accomplish this task both through public expenditure and taxation.[2] In this note, an attempt is made to look at some of the problems that might arise if taxation is used as a means to reduce inequalities.

One of the standard ways of measuring the impact of taxation on redistribution is to compare the distribution of income before tax and the distribution after tax. Of course, such a method assumes that taxes have only a distribution effect and not an output effect.[3] The extent to which concentration in income is reduced by direct taxes will depend upon the progressivity of direct taxes. Indirect taxes can bring about a reduction, if, as a group they are designed to fall more heavily on higher income groups than lower income groups.[4] The major difficulty faced in studying the impact of taxation on income distribution in developing economies is the absence of reliable data on income distribution. The only consistent set of data relates to income tax assessees. But as the Committee on Distribution of Income and Levels of Living in India pointed out, the proportion of

---

Economic Development and Cultural Change, Vol. 19, No. 2, January 1971; University of Chicago, U.S.A.

income recipients in the tax paying group was less than one per cent of the total number of income recipients. The National Sample Survey for India gives the distribution of consumption expenditure, and we shall use these data to study what might happen if taxation is used as a tool to reduce inequalities in the distribution of consumption expenditure.[5]

The Method

Studies based on National Sample Survey data have shown that households, according to per capita consumption expenditure are log-normally distributed[6] and that the concentration ratio for number of years was 0.33. Personal income in India in 1965-66 was estimated to be Rs. 21,210 crores, and the planning authorities at that time expected this income to grow to Rs. 39,380 crores in 1975-76.[7] This will mean an increase of 6.3 per cent per annum. Personal consumption expenditure in 1965-66 was estimated to be Rs. 19,310 crores, and consistency with other plan targets required that consumption could grow only to Rs. 32,560 crores in 1975-76. This would imply a growth rate of 5.5 per cent per annum over this period. It was also estimated that given the personal income of Rs. 39.380 crores in 1975-76, personal consumption expenditure in the normal course would likely be Rs. 33.860 crores. Thus, there would arise a need to restrict personal consumption expenditure by appıoximately Rs. 1,300 crores, and this was fixed as the quantum of additional tax revenue to be collected in 1975-76. One can pose this question: if Rs. 1,300 crore are to be collected in the form of additional taxes, how should this tax burden be distributed if an attempt is also made at the same time to reduce the concentration ratio in consumption expenditure by a few points?

The following method is adopted to study what different deciles of population should bear under such a condition: it is assumed that, in the absence of any specific measures, the concentration ratio in personal consumption expenditure in 1975-76 will continue to be 0.33 and that households accord to per capita expenditure would continue to be log-normally distributed. On this basis, personal consumption expenditure of Rs. 33,860 crores was distributed in different deciles. Also, calculated for different deciles was the amount of personal consumption expenditure, given a total of Rs. 32,560 crores

and a concentration ratio of 0.30. The differences between the two figures for each decile (Table 1, col. [6]) would indicate the tax burden to be borne. The relevant calculations are given in Table 1.

Table 1

Consumption Expenditure by Population Deciles

(Rs. in crores)

Population Deciles	*1965-66 (L=0.33)*	*1975-76 (L=0.33)*	*1975-76 (L=0.33)*	*1975-76 (L=0.30)*	*Tax to be Levied: (3) - (5)*	*Rate of Growth Per Annum of (5) over (2)*
(1)	(2)	(3)	(4)	(5)	(6)	(7)
Lowest 10%	569.3	1,008.0	970.3	1,103.1	-95.1	6.8
10-20	852.6	1,509.6	1,452.2	1,592.2	-82.6	6.5
20-30	1,062.1	1,880.5	1,807.1	1,942.9	-62.4	6.2
30-40	1,265.4	2,240.0	2,152.2	2,275.9	-35.9	6.1
40-50	1,479.4	2,619.8	2,520.1	2,622.1	-2.3	5.9
50-60	1,722.7	3,050.0	2,933.6	3,007.9	42.1	5.7
60-70	2,016.3	3,569.0	3,431.8	3,468.3	100.7	5.6
70-80	2,402.7	4,254.1	4,089.6	4,064.5	189.6	5.4
80-90	3,003.4	5,317.6	5,111.9	4,971.8	345.8	5.2
Top 10%	4,755.8	8,420.0	8,091.7	7,511.3	908.7	4.7
Total*	**19,129.7**	**33,868.6**	**32,566.5**	**32,560.0**	....	....

Note: L = Concentration Level.

*: Due to rounding off at various points, the totals differ slightly from the aggregate figures quoted earlier.

Results of the Study

The following results have been obtained from this study:

1. The most striking thing that emerges is that if an attempt is made to reduce the concentration ratio from 0.33 to 0.30 with a tax target of Rs. 1,300 crores, it can be achieved only by collecting Rs. 1,500 crores from the top half of the

population and distributing Rs. 200 crores in subsidies (negative taxes) to the bottom half. If no subsidies are to be given, a reduction of this order in inequality can be achieved only by imposing a far heavier burden on the upper deciles of the population. It may be noted that the per capita income per annum of the top five deciles in 1965-66 was Rs. 966, Rs. 613, Rs. 488, Rs. 409 and Rs. 350, respectively. If it is felt that only the top most decile has an income level that can really bear tax burden, it is easy to see from our calculations, that it would almost be impossible to make any change in inequality with a total burden of Rs. 1,300 crores.

2. Let us assume that the top half of the population can bear the tax burden indicated by our calculations. Even in this situation, it is seen that all deciles of population experience an increase in consumption standards. The topmost decile experiences a growth rate of 4.7 per cent per annum compared with the growth rate of 6.8 per cent enjoyed by the bottom most decile. If no attempt were made to reduce the concentration ratio, each decile would experience the same growth rate of 5.5 per cent. On the contrary, if an attempt were made to push the concentration ratio below 0.30, the difference between the growth rate experienced by the bottom and top deciles would widen. If the tax burden required to bring down the inequality is borne entirely by the top decile, the consumption standards of these people can very well go down.

3. The practical difficulties involved in evolving a tax structure that would impose a specific amount of money burden on different deciles are almost insuperable. Direct taxes, at present, are confined only to the top one per cent of the population and therefore, any widening of this instrument will be very limited. Reliance on indirect tax would imply that the authorities can choose the rates and commodities for taxation in such a way that different deciles would pay specific amounts of tax. As the bottom half does not pay any taxes, commodities consumed by this section would have to be exempted from tax. (Alternatively, if taxes are imposed on commodities used by this section, they will have to be refunded to them).

Conclusion

The possibility of taxation making any dent in income or consumption expenditure distribution of developing economies appears to be very limited. This does not mean that tax policies should not take this objective into account. It must, however, be realised that taxation by itself would not be of much help.

Notes

1. Government of India. *The First Five-Year Plan*, p.3
2. Some empirical studies relating to advanced economies have shown that expenditure policy is more effective than tax policy in reducing inequalities. For example, Merrett and Monk found that in the U.K., Gini coefficient for income before tax was 0.35, while the coefficient for income after all taxes (direct and indirect) was 0.33, and that for income after all taxes and allotted benefits was 0.246 (A.J Merrett and D.A.G Monk, "Structure of U.K. Taxation, 1962-63," *Bulletin of the Oxford University Institute of Economics and Statistics* [August 1966], p. 159).
3. For an elaboration of this point, see Karl W. Roskamp, "The Budget and Interpersonal Distribution: Comments on the Papers of Bela Csikos-Nagy and Alan R. Prest," *Public Finance* 23 (1968): p. 101.
4. The study by Merrett and Monk referred to above finds that indirect taxes increase rather than reduce the inequalities. They found that the Gini coefficient for income before taxes was 0.35, while for income after indirect taxes it was 0.37. On the other hand, a study of incidence of indirect taxation in India finds that the distribution of money burden of indirect taxes among different expenditure groups was progressive (see Government of India, Ministry of Finance, *Incidence of Indirect Taxation 1958-59*, p. 10).
5. We are confining our attention here to the impact of taxation alone without bringing in the effect of public expenditure. Needless to add, in order to find out the net redistribution effect, we must combine both.
6. N.S. Iyengar, "A Method of Computing Engel Elasticities from Concentration Curves", *Econometrica* 28 (1960) : p. 890.
7. These estimates are being revised downward. But these revisions will not affect the nature of the problem highlighted here. It may, however, be pointed out that, with lower growth rates, the task of reducing the concentration ratio becomes more difficult as the tax amount available for redistribution becomes less.

4

Government Securities Market in a Mixed Economy

A Study of India

Financial institutions have come to be regarded as an integral part of the infrastructure needed for the development of an economy. They play a role in the development process by helping to increase the level of savings and investment. The mixed pattern of Indian economy, where the Government has come to play a dominant role, has influenced the growth of the capital market in ways somewhat dissimilar to those found in the developed economies. Also, apart from taking the initiative in setting up a large number of long-term credit institutions, the official policy has been to bring most of the financial institutions under State ownership. This is based on the theory of 'commanding heights' which requires that the State control, through ownership, those sectors of economy which influence the development of other sectors. Direct participation of State in investment activity and State ownership of financial institutions have had two effects on the capital market. One, the government securities market has become an important segment of the capital market and two, the role of the secondary market has been considerably reduced.

The importance of the government securities market stems directly from the major role played by the Government in investment activity. Under the successive Five-Year Plans, the proportions of government investment in India has been steadily increasing. The proportion which was 46 per cent under the First Five-Year Plan rose to 54 per cent under the Second and to 60 per cent under the Third. If we look at the investment in the industrial sector alone, the

Economic and Political Weekly, Vol. VI, No. 11, March 13, 1971.

proportion of government investment to the total was 20 per cent, 54 per cent and 59 per cent, respectively, in the three plans. The importance of the government securities market also depends on the extent to which Government relies on market borrowing as a source of finance. Market loans as percentage of total resources have varied between 10 per cent and 15 per cent under the three Plans (Table 1). In order to assess the relative importance of the government securities market in the capital market, a year to year comparison of the market absorption of government securities by public and the new issues of non-government public limited companies (Table 2) was made. It can be seen that government securities market has absorbed the greater proportion of funds flowing through the market.

Table 1

Financing of Plan Outlays in the Public Sector

(Rs. in crores)

	Actuals I	*Actuals II*	*Anticipated Actuals III*
A. Mainly through Own Resources (i.e., balance from current revenue surplus of public enterprises, railways etc.)	752 (38.4)	1230 (26.3)	2885 (33.4)
B. Mainly through Domestic Borrowings	1019 (52.0)	2393 (51.2)	2390 (38.1)
(1) Market Loans (net)	204 (10.4)	756 (16.4)*	915 (10.6)
(2) Small Savings (net)	243	422	585
(3) Annuity Deposits & Compulsory Deposits	–	–	115
(4) Unfunded Debt	92	175	340
(5) Steel Equalisation Fund (net)	–	40	35
(6) Miscellaneous Capital Receipts (net)	147	46	150
(7) Deficit Financing	333	954	1150
C. Total Domestic Resources (A+B)	1771 (90.4)	3623 (77.5)	6175 (71.5)
D. External Assistance	189	1049	2455 (28.5)
E. Total Resources (C+D)	1960 (100.0)	4672 (100.0)	8630 (100.0)

*: Includes investments by the State Bank of India out of PL 480 funds.

Note: Figures in brackets are percentages to total.

Table 2

Capital Issues by Non-Government Public Limited Companies and Net-Absorption of Government Securities by the Public

(Rs. in crores)

Year	*Total of Ordinary and Preference Shares and Debentures Raised by Non-Government Public Limited Companies*	*Net Absorption of Government Securities by the Public*
1951	7.9	- 9.6
1952	4.7	+ 33.4
1953	12.5	+ 80.5
1954	33.2	+ 92.5
1955	26.2	+ 93.1
1956	45.1	+ 70.6
1957	24.1	+ 113.3
1958	25.9	+ 194.6
1959	43.2	+ 193.1
1960	35.00	- 63.7
1961	35.04	+ 35.6
1962	65.42	+ 99.1
1963	32.97	+ 100.7
1964	60.48	+ 172.8
1965	60.67	+ 137.5
1966	60.00	+ 169.1
1967	81.6	+ 145.1

Source: *Reserve Bank of India Bulletin*, June 1964, March 1967, June 1967 and March 1969.

I. VOLUME, GROWTH AND YIELD OF MARKETABLE DEBT

The internal debt of Government of India rose from Rs. 24 billion in 1951 to Rs. 96 billion in 1968. Internal debt comprises marketable rupee loans, small savings and Treasury bills which are almost entirely held by the Reserve Bank of India. The marketable debt of Government of India and the state governments rose from Rs. 29 billion as at the end of March 1961 to Rs. 44 billion in 1968. This implies a compound rate of growth of approximately seven per cent per annum.

The ownership pattern of debt (Table 3) throws interesting light on the 'market' for government securities. As at the end of March 1967, 38 per cent of the total debt was held by the Reserve

Bank of India and the various departments of the Government. Commercial banks, insurance and provident funds held 50 per cent of the debt. Individuals held 1.2 per cent and joint stock companies 0.3 per cent. The proportion of total debt held by individuals which is very small has declined over the years. Of the debt held by the public, 85 per cent is held by banks, insurance, and provident funds, which are either State-owned or under a statutory obligation to invest a proportion of their assets in government securities.

The rate of interest offered on government securities has been increasing in keeping with the changes in bank rate (Table 4). The bank rate which stood at four per cent in 1960-61 was raised to 4½ per cent in early 1963, to five per cent in September 1964 and to six per cent in February 1965. It was lowered to five per cent in March 1968. The redemption yields at issue prices for bonds maturing in six years for the five successive years beginning 1961-62 were 3.71, 4.10, 4.21 and 4.60, respectively. The five year bond issued in 1966-67 and 1967-68 carried interest at 4.50 per cent. The interest rate offered on state government securities has always been a little higher over that offered on Government of India Securities of similar maturities. The Government has also been attempting to widen the difference between the rate offered on short dated and long dated securities in recent years. In 1964-65 the difference in interest rates between six year and 25 year bonds was 0.54 per cent, whereas, since then the difference has been kept around one per cent.

II. STRUCTURE OF THE SECURITIES MARKET

Constituents of the Market

A broad market requires three conditions to be met: one, the number of buyers and sellers must be large; two, there should be dealers in the market willing to operate on their own and three, there should be a wide spectrum of owners so that there can be a matching of buyers and sellers.[1] Financial instruments are liquid because they are marketable and marketability depends, among other things, on the organisational structure of the market. The three characteristics associated with a broad market are to a large extent absent in the Indian situation. As pointed out earlier, 85 per cent of

Table 3

Ownership Pattern of Central and State Government Securities

	1951	*1956*	*1961*	*1967*
(1) Governments	125.85 (8.4)	168.82 (8.9)	267.57 (9.6)	336.4 (8.1)
(2) Reserve Bank of India	339.93 (22.7)	268.85 (15.2)	707.08 (25.4)	1262.4 (30.2)
(3) Commercial and Co-operative Banks	391.60 (26.2)	438.46 (24.7)	601.07 (21.6)	956.0 (22.19)
(4) Insurance	112.74 (7.5)	167.88 (9.5)	286.02 (13.9)	576.2 (13.8)
(a) Life Insurance Corporation				551.4 (13.2)
(b) General Insurance Companies				9.9 (0.2)
(c) Employees State Insurance				14.9 (0.4)
(5) Provident Funds	–	–	217.55 (7.8)	626.4 (15.0)
(6) Industrial Finance and State Financial Corporation	–	–	4.81 (0.2)	3.7 (0.1)
(7) Reserve Bank of India held on account of others	66.50 (4.4)	107.25 (6.0)	41.19 (1.6)	31.5 (0.9)
(8) Non-residents	59.96 (4.0)	40.89 (2.3)	34.54 (1.3)	15.2 (0.4)
(9) Others (Residual)	399.95 (26.7)	591.00 (33.3)	531.70 (20.6)	361.8 (8.6)
(a) Joint Stock Companies	–	–	38.27 (1.5)	11.4 (0.3)
(b) Local Authorities	–	–	56.67 (2.2)	39.4 (0.9)
(c) Trusts (both public and private)	–	–	171.00 (6.6)	60.0 (1.4)
(d) Individual	–	–	79.33 (3.1)	51.5 (1.4)

Note: Figures in brackets indicates the percentage share of each category of investor to the total debt.

Source: "Report on Currency and Finance, RBI (various issues)."

Table 4

Interest Offered on New Loans Floated by Government of India

Year	*Maturity*	*Coupon Rate (per cent)*	*Redemption* Yield at Issue Price*	*Bank Rate*
1961-62	6 years	3½	3.71	
	8 years	3½	3.74	4%
	20 years	4	4.11	
1962-63	6 years	3¾	3.91	Since Jan 1963 4½%
	10 years	4	4.10	
	23 years	4½	4.50	
1963-64	6 years	4	4.10	4½%
	23 years	4½	4.50	
	10 years	4¼	4.25	
1964-65	6 years	4	4.21	Since Sep 1964 5%
	25 years	4¾	4.75	Since Feb 1965 6%
1965-66	6 years	4½	4.60	
	25 years	5½	5.50	6%
	3 years	4¼	4.25	
	7 years	4¾	4.75	
1966-67	5 years		4.50	6%
	25 years		5.50	
1967-68	5 years	4½	4.50	Since Mar 1968 5%
	15 years	5	5.00	
	25 years	5½	5.50	
1968-69	7 years	4¼	4.25	5%
	27 years	5½	5.50	
1969-70	7 years	4¼	4.25	5%
	30 years	5½	5.50	
1970-71	7 years	4½	4.50	5%
	30 years	5½	5.50	

*: This figure has been calculated because in many cases the issue price has been below face value.

the debt held by the public is in the hands of commercial banks, Life Insurance Corporation and Provident Funds. Life Insurance Corporation is a single State-owned institution in charge of the entire business relating to life insurance. The State Bank and other 14 commercial banks which have been taken over by the Government recently, control almost the entire banking system. The investment policy of the Provident Fund is governed by statutory regulations.

The Life Insurance Corporation (LIC) is interested primarily in long term securities. Of its total holdings of government securities, only about 13 per cent consists of securities with a maturity of five years and less. It is said that LIC comes to the secondary market only to sell long term securities which are approaching the data of maturity. These securities can perhaps be taken by the commercial banks. But they cannot sell long term securities that are needed by LIC, since 75 per cent of the securities held by commercial banks is with maturities of less than five years. Also, situations arise when commercial banks want to sell short term securities while the LIC requires medium or long dated ones. In such cases, to some extent 'switch' operations are possible with the help of the Reserve Bank. The broker who is not able to match the selling order of a bank with the buying order of LIC, can do both the transactions in the form of switch with the Reserve Bank. However, these 'switch' operations have been of a negligible magnitude in recent years. Provident Funds are interested only in long term securities and they rarely enter the secondary market.

It is difficult to estimate the magnitude of transactions that occur among the different constituents in the market. One is led to believe that it is not high. In fact, the nationalisation of the Life Insurance Companies in 1956 and the consolidation of these 200 companies into one corporation led to a considerable shrinkage in the activities of the market. Data on this are not available. But data on 'switch' operations given by the Reserve Bank show the virtual disappearance of 'insurance' from 'switch' transaction since 1956 (Table 5). This may indicate that the other transactions might have also been reduced to a considerable extent. Brokers in the three primary stock exchanges at Bombay, Calcutta and Madras do transact some business as between banks. Here again, the magnitude of transactions is reported to be small. Some brokers point out that the profit margin on buying and selling securities is so small and the cost of borrowings from banks so high, it does not pay to act as dealers. So they are content to match the buying order of one bank with the selling order of another.

It follows that, if government securities possess 'liquidity', it comes not so much from 'marketability' as between constituents of the market, but from the actions of the Reserve Bank.

Table 5

Switch Operations

(Year ended March; Rs. in crores)

	1949	*1950*	*1951*	*1952*	*1953*	*1954*	*1955*	*1956*	*1957*	*1958*	*1959*	*1960*	*1961*	*1962*	*1963*
Insurance	—	—	3.6	1.4	0.2	1.7	5.2	—	1.1	—	0.6	—	—	—	—
Banking	4.7	4.4	29.1	12.6	4.2	6.6	10.6	4.8	2.3	0.6	18.0	0.9	1.2	2.9	0.4
Others	7.5	8.9	29.5	15.3	4.1	6.3	11.1	13.6	12.4	2.7	2.2	1.9	1.6	4.3	2.9
Total	12.2	13.3	62.2	29.3	8.5	14.6	26.9	18.4	15.8	3.3	20.8	2.8	2.8	7.2	3.3

Source: Reserve Bank of India Bulletin, 1964.

Role of Reserve Bank of India

The Reserve Bank of India plays an important role in the gilt-edged market. The open market operations have rarely been used in India as an instrument of credit control. An article describing the operations of the Reserve Bank of India clearly stated: "In general, the open market operations have been used in India more to assist the Government in its borrowing operations and to maintain orderly conditions in the government securities market than for influencing the availability and cost of credit."[2] The Reserve Bank has tried to influence the gilt-edged market in the two ways. First, at the time of most new issues, it has contributed liberally, acting thereby as an underwriter. The justification for this has been that the Reserve Bank performs the role of a wholesaler in the securities market. It buys the new issues in bulk and unloads them in the market as and when it can absorb. Second, the Reserve Bank has given active price support to the securities, the objective being one of building up an orderly market and widening the investor appeal. That such a policy might interfere with its functions as a controller of credit, was well recognised, as exemplified by the following statement: "An essential promotional function of a central bank in the development context is the nurturing of such a broad-based securities market; the limitations to open market policy stem in a situation such as in India more from the structural need to build up an active bond market and the more immediate requirements of assisting the Government in its borrowing operations and these militate against a reliance on these operations for credit control purposes."[3]

That the Reserve Bank contributes to the new issues floated by the Government is an important factor that must be taken into account while assessing the impact of open market operations. The Reserve Bank publishes detailed data on the net absorption of government securities by the public (Table 6). Net absorption refers to the increase in holdings of securities of holders other than the Reserve Bank of India and the Central and state governments. Separate figures are provided on the net market borrowings by the Central and state governments and net cash receipts from the public. The difference between the two gives an indication of the amount subscribed by the Reserve Bank of India at the time of the issue of loans.[4] This figure has varied between Rs. 700 million and

Rs. 1 billion in the last six years. It is against this context that the effect of open market operations must be interpreted. Net sales by Reserve Bank in a year does not imply a restrictive policy unless we know what the Reserve Bank has put in at the time of the new issue of loans. It is, therefore, not correct to claim the preponderance of net sales during the decade of 1951-61 as a sign of the growing maturity of the gilt-edged market. As far as the impact of the economy is concerned, the amount that is relevant is the Reserve Bank's subscription to the new issues plus (or minus) open market purchases (or sales). The effect will be expansionary if the subscription to the new issues is greater than the sales. Such a support to long term securities is a form of deficit financing and must be recognised as such.

Reserve Bank's price support is an important factor contributing to the "liquidity" of government securities. As pointed out earlier, the market activity as such is limited and it is the Reserve Bank's role as "buyer of last resort" (as described by a spokesman of the Reserve Bank of India) that makes it liquid. For many years, the Reserve Bank's purchases consisted of the maturing ones and the sales that of the new issues. Acquiring securities nearing maturity was part of the policy of "grooming" the market for new floatations. Some purchases (or sales) of a grooming nature were also undertaken in the case of loans of corresponding maturities, in order to bring their yields in line with those of the new ones. But in the last few years, the operations have been conducted over a wide range of maturities so that a structure of yields might emerge where the short is lower than the long. All this only goes to show that the market is what the Reserve Bank makes it to be. If the government securities in the last six years have not suffered a serious decline in values, which has been the fate of the industrial securities, it is because of the actions of the Reserve Bank rather than due to the inherent attractiveness of these securities to investors. Differences in the yields of different state government securities of same maturity persist because, by and large, the Reserve Bank does not deal in state government securities.

Table 6

Net Absorption of Government Securities By Public Since 1951-52

(Rs. in crores)

	Net Market Borrowings by the Central and State Governments			*Cash Receipts (net) from the Public**	*Open Market Purchases (-) from/ Sales (+) to the Public #*	*Net Absorption (+) by the Public** (4+5)*
	Cash Receipts	*Cash Payments*	*Net Receipts (1-2)*			
	1	2	3	4	5	6
First Plan						
1951-52	24.3	49.2	- 24.9	+ 1.7	- 11.3	- 9.6
1952-53	15.8	2.9	+ 12.9	+ 12.9	+ 20.5	+ 33.4
1953-54	60.4	63.9	- 3.5	+ 46.3	+ 34.2	+ 80.5
1954-55	160.7	50.9	- 110.7	+ 67.2	+ 25.3	+ 92.5
1955-56	98.6	16.6	+ 82.0	+ 64.2	+ 28.9	+ 93.1
Total	**359.8**	**182.6**	**+177.2**	**+192.3**	**+ 97.6**	**+289.9**
Second Plan						
1956-57	143.7	3.0	+140.7	+ 89.7	- 19.1	+ 70.6
1957-58	99.7	29.0	+ 70.7	+ 28.1	+ 82.2	+113.3
1958-59	241.6	14.8	+226.8	+105.6	+ 89.0	+194.6
1959-60	208.3	33.6	+174.7	+ 82.5	+ 60.6	+143.1
1960-61	179.4	45.4	+134.0	+ 61.4	- 125.1	- 63.7
Total	**872.7**	**125.8**	**+746.9**	**+367.3**	**+ 90.6**	**+457.9**
Third Plan						
1961-62	187.2	50.4	+136.8	+ 72.6	- 37.0	+ 35.6
1962-63	221.2	41.2	+180.0	+119.8	- 24.1	+ 95.7
1963-64	208.8	64.0	+144.8	+ 50.8	+ 44.7	+ 95.5
1964-65	253.5	68.4	+185.1	+ 98.2	+ 74.6	+172.8
1965-66	258.5	27.5	+231.0	+136.4	- 2.2	+134.2
Total	**1,129.2**	**251.5**	**+877.7**	**+477.8**	**+ 56.0**	**+533.8**

(Contd...)

(...Contd...)

Annual Plans						
1966-67	224.9	48.2	+176.7	+106.2	+ 62.9	+169.1
1967-68	243.2	81.3	+161.9	+ 94.7	+ 50.4	+145.1
1968-69##	255.5	103.8	+151.7	+ 98.1	+ 96.0	+194.1
Total	**723.6**	**233.3**	**+490.3**	**+299.0**	**+209.3**	**+508.3**

Note: Figures from 1956-57 onwards are inclusive of investments of PL 480 funds. Figures for 1962-63 and 1963-64 include subscriptions to the 4¼ per cent National Defence Bonds, 1972. Those from 1960-61 onwards are not strictly comparable with the figures for the earlier years consequent on the change in the arrangements in regard to PL 480 funds from May 12, 1960. Figures exclude the Prize Bonds and Gold Bonds.

*: Excluding the Reserve Bank of India and Central and state governments.

#: On the Reserve Bank's Investment Account and Central Government's Cash Investment Account.

**: Figures do not take into account transactions on State Governments' Cash Balance Investment Account, Bank's operations in State Government loans and repayment of State loans held by State Governments.

##: Provisional

The sector-wise distribution of purchases and sales by the Reserve Bank also goes to emphasise that investment in government securities is essentially for "keeps". Insurance and Provident Funds used to figure prominently on the sales side of the bank's account. Since 1960, however, insurance has disappeared from the picture. This fact can only be taken to mean that their investment demands for gilt-edged are met by purchases of new loans than of existing securities. Only banks appear both in the purchase and sales sides of the bank's operations. This is because banks try to meet part of their seasonal requirements by shifting securities to the Reserve Bank.

To sum up, the three major holders of government securities are State-owned commercial banks, Life Insurance Corporation and the Provident Fund. Together they account for 85 per cent of the securities held by the public. Most of these institutions invest in securities only to hold them till maturity. The Reserve Bank of India plays an important part in the market – both at the time of new issues and subsequently. The open market operations of the Reserve Bank have to be interpreted carefully because of the bank's policy of acting as an underwriter at the time of new issues. The total volume of transactions among the constituents of the market is very limited. The

Reserve Bank of India does not stand ready to take the government securities at a given price. It allows the price to fluctuate with changes in interest rate. However, it does support securities at prices decided upon by it. In fact, it is this readiness that imports liquidity to the government securities in India. Marketability in the Indian context implies transferability to the Reserve Bank.

III. PERFORMANCE OF THE MARKET

The total marketable debt of both the Central and state governments rose at a compound rate of 6.7 per cent during the 15 years covering the first three plans. During the same period, debt held by the public rose 5.8 per cent per annum so that the ratio of total debt held by the Reserve Bank and government departments increased from 31.1 per cent in 1951 to 39.7 per cent in 1966. The rate of growth has not been uniform under the three plans. During the First Plan, while total debt rose by 3.5 per cent, debt held by public rose by 5.3 per cent, implying a transfer of debt from the Reserve Bank and Government to non-government public. During the Second Plan, while the total marketable debt rose by 9.4 per cent per annum, debt held by public rose by 6.3 per cent. In fact, the performance of market borrowing during the Second Plan was not so strong as the figures indicate since debt held by public includes investments in government securities by the State Bank out of PL 480 counterpart funds. The marketable debt and debt held by public rose by 7.3 per cent and 5.8 per cent, respectively during the Third Plan. The response to the government borrowing programme does not seem to be related to the growth in income. Debt held by public rose by the same percentage during the Second and Third Plans, whereas, income rose by 22 per cent under the Second and by 13 per cent during the Third. What seems to determine the growth in the debt is the increase in the assets of the institutions holdings debt and government policy relating to them.

A 'Captive' Market

The government securities market has been described by some as a 'captive' market. The implication is that the three main groups of institutions holding government securities are either State-owned or State-controlled, so that government policy can virtually decide the amount to be held.

Insurance companies, even prior to nationalisation, were subject to certain statutory restrictions regarding the investments of the funds. The Insurance Act had laid down that 25 per cent of the funds were to be invested in government securities and another 30 per cent in approved securities. These provisions were incorporated in the Act nationalising the insurance companies. In fact, the proportion of total assets invested in government securities by the LIC has been increasing over the last eleven years. The increase cannot be attributed to 'attractive' rates of interest. The LIC earns a much higher return on such assets as mortgage loans. In fact, the Chairman of the LIC is reported to have observed that the indirect compulsion to invest a high proportion in government securities is reducing the profitability. It may be interesting to note that while in the US the proportion of total assets invested in government securities by insurance companies is only five per cent, in India it is as high as 40 per cent.

The commercial banks are required under the Banking Companies Act to invest a specified proportion of deposits in the form of vault cash, excess reserves, gold and approved securities. This is in addition to the requirement to hold reserves with the Reserve Bank. The secondary reserve requirement which stood at 20 per cent was increased to 25 per cent in 1964.

The increase in the liquidity ratio was intended by the Reserve Bank as a step towards strengthening banks' liquidity and thereby the soundness of the banking system. As it has been pointed out, even with respect to primary reserves, these statutory requirements do not really go to meet the liquidity needs arising out of deposit fluctuations as these funds are really frozen. They increase the liquidity only by preventing an increase in the more illiquid assets such as loans. The imposition of a secondary reserve requirement has meaning only if the ratio imposed is higher than what it would otherwise have been. In 1964 when the ratio was increased to 25 per cent, investments as a percentage of deposits was higher at 31 per cent. But what disturbed the Reserve Bank was the steady decline in the ratio from year to year. The ratio stood at 40.6 per cent in 1956-60. Whatever the historical origin of the ratio, banks now seem to feel that in the absence of statutory requirements, they would not be investing this proportion in government securities. We shall examine this statement in the next section.

Provident Funds consist of contributions made by employers and employees to serve as a form of retirement benefit. Such a scheme is compulsory as far as industrial workers are concerned. But most establishments and educational institutions have such a scheme for all employees. But the disposition and management of such funds are regulated by statute. Till 1967-68, the rule was that all investments should exclusively be made in Central government securities. Since then, some flexibility has been introduced by permitting them to hold a part of their funds in state government securities and in fixed deposits with banks. With the growth in the industrial sector, Provident Funds have tended to grow, so that their share in the total investment of government securities has increased from 5.5 per cent in 1957 to 16.5 in 1967. The original restriction that all investments should be in Central government securities was made to prevent the diversion of funds by the employers for their own benefit. However, lately both employees and employers have been feeling such a restriction as unjust, as these are long term funds and a difference of even one per cent in the return over a period of 30 years makes a considerable difference. The rules have been slightly relaxed as mentioned earlier.

Originally, the restrictions introduced in the various statutes regarding the use of funds were intended to ensure the safety of funds. However, recently the justification is made on public grounds. In her report on economic policy which finally culminated in the nationalisation of banks, the Prime Minister indicated that the liquidity ratio of banks might be increased from 25 per cent to 30 per cent primarily for diverting more funds into the hands of the Government. If one could assume that public investment has a higher 'social benefit' than private investment, such a diversion can be justified. In the case of banks, since Government owns them, a higher or lower return on gilt-edged does not affect the return to the Government as a whole. In the case of LIC, a lower return affects the bonus of policy holders and in the case of Provident Funds, the employees.

To what extent is it justifiable to describe the market as 'captive'? The charge of being 'captive' can hold only if it can be proven that the rate of interest offered on gilt-edged are so unattractive that in the absence of statutory restrictions, these institutions would hold less of these securities.

Let us analyse the problem from the point of view of commercial banks. Table 7 gives for the years since 1950-51, the ratio of investment to total deposits of commercial banks. For many years, banks have maintained a high ratio of investment to deposits even at the peak of the busy season. The high ratio in all these years can only be due to a lack of demand for credit or at least the type of credit that banks were willing to lend. The statutory requirement was way below the level held by banks. It is only since 1961-62 that the ratio has tended to come close to the statutory minimum.

Table 7

Investments to Total Deposits in Scheduled Banks

(percentages)

1950-51	—
1951-52	34.3
1952-53	35.8
1953-54	37.6
1954-55	37.2
1955-56	36.9
1956-57	32.8
1957-58	29.2
1958-59	36.5
1959-60	40.6
1960-61	35.9
1961-62	32.34
1962-63	31.45
1963-64	31.49
1964-65	29.68
1965-66	28.84
1966-67	29.85
1967-68	28.03

Source: Reserve Bank of India Bulletin, July 1969.

It is interesting to note that in the US, even though there is no secondary reserve requirement, banks have maintained between 25 and 30 per cent of their deposits in US government and other state government securities. The requirements of liquidity have compelled banks to hold these securities, even though the return on

governments is less than that on loans. The difference between the return on loans and interest on government securities has not however exceeded 2.25 per cent in the last ten years. In India, however, the difference has been much wider (Table 8). But, on the other hand, the primary reserve requirements in India is only three per cent of total deposits, whereas, in the US on the average it would have been around 15 to 18 per cent of the deposits. The capital deposit ratio is half of what it is in US (Table 9). Taking all these factors together, one is led to believe that if government securities in India did possess the kind of liquidity which they command in the US, banks here too in the normal course would maintain anywhere between 25 to 30 per cent of the deposits in government securities. However, it does raise the other question of how to estimate the liquidity of an asset which forms part of a legal requirement. When assets are frozen, can one legitimately claim that there is still liquidity? But by the same token the question can be asked as to why banks in the US, for example, maintain more than 25 per cent of deposits in government securities while the average level of fluctuation in deposits level is not likely to be of this order at all. In fact, what banks are insuring against is the maximum probable decline in deposits during any given period.[5] In this sense, banks are an extreme type of risk averters. It is partly to compensate for the secondary reserve requirement that the Reserve Bank is more generous in its lending to commercial banks than the Federal Reserve System. There have been months when the borrowings of scheduled banks from the Reserve Bank have amounted to six per cent of the deposits. Such a high level of borrowings is unknown in the American banking system.

Banks have liquidity problem because of the fluctuations in deposits level and loan demand. When there is an active and broad market, this liquidity is provided by government securities. In the Indian context, because of the limited number of holders, Reserve Bank's policies, both with respect to price support of securities and lending to commercial banks, give the necessary liquidity needs. The statutory minimum of two per cent cannot, therefore, be regarded as harsh.[6]

Table 8

Rate of Return on Loans and Investments

(percentages)

	India		*USA*	
	Investments	*Loans*	*Investments*	*Loans*
1950	2.4	4.6	—	—
1955	2.7	4.8	—	—
1960	3.2	5.33	3.14	5.92
1961	2.9	6.1	3.05	5.84
1962	2.9	6.45	3.22	5.93
1963	3.00	6.58	3.38	5.87
1964	3.22	6.67	3.63	5.88
1965	3.21	7.77	3.69	5.85
1966	3.61	8.1	4.02	6.24
1967	3.76	8.3	4.48	6.39

Source: "Statistical Tables Relating to Banks", 1964-1967. *Federal Reserve Bulletin*, 1963-1967.

Table 9

Paid-Up Capital to Total Deposits

(percentages)

	India	*USA*
1960	3.96	9.60
1961	3.94	9.32
1962	3.98	9.23
1963	3.79	9.35
1964	3.52	9.03
1965	3.31	9.26
1966	2.90	9.26
1967	2.72	8.86

Source: "Statistical Tables Relating to Banks", 1964-67, *Federal Reserve Bulletin*, 1963-67.

The statutory restriction applies only to the overall amount of approved securities. Banks are free to determine the composition of the security portfolio since the approved securities include Central and state government securities as also semi-government securities. Banks, however, prefer to hold the bulk of the securities in central government securities even though the return is low. This is probably due to the fact that RBI gives greater price support to Central government securities than to others.

Table 10

Distribution of Assets of Life Insurance Companies in UK, USA and India (1960)

(As percentage of total assets)

	UK	*USA*	*India*
Government Securities	18.5	9.2	51.91
Industrial Bonds	18.8	22.4	6.99
Stocks and Ordinary Shares	21.2	4.2	7.42
Mortgages and Policy Loans	13.6	39.3	8.46

Source: LIÇ Annual, 1960. George Claton WT Osborn, "Insurance Company Investment: Principles and Policy", pp 254 and 257.

Since the demand for current liquidity is much less in the case of LIC and Provident Fund, perhaps, in the absence of statutory restrictions, these institutions might have invested less in government securities. A comparison of the distribution of assets of life insurance companies in USA, UK and India (Table 10) brings out vividly the difference in the policies. While the percentage of total assets invested in industrial stocks and bonds is 40 per cent in UK, and 27 per cent in the US, it is only 14 per cent in India.

Yield on Government and Other Financial Assets

The interest offered on Governments has been increasing. The rate of interest offered on five year bonds rose from 3.5 per cent in 1961-62 to 4.5 per cent in 1967-68. However, the yield on other financial assets such as debentures, fixed deposits in banks and long

term postal savings certificates have also been rising. The interest offered on debentures is between seven and eight per cent and many stock brokers feel that debentures are more easily sold in the market than even government securities. The rate of interest offered has also to be examined in relation to changes in the price level. The Wholesale Price Index rose from 100 in 1952-53 to 212 in 1967-68, thus registering an increase of 5.25 per cent per annum. Of course, the increase in price was not uniform. In 1955-56 the index stood at 92.5. It is since 1960-61 that the price level has been increasing. In some years the increase has been of the order of 20 per cent. The steadily increasing price level makes investments in real assets much more attractive. Non-financial institutions like textile mills which invite deposits have also been paying higher interest rates.

It is the performance of variable dividend industrial securities in the last five years that has caused some concern about functioning of the capital market in India. The index of security prices, which stood at 86.1 in 1964-65, fell to 76.7 in 1967-68. This steady decline in equity prices had made the rate of return negligible. The average annual return to the individual shareholder, computed by taking into account both the change in the price index and the dividend yield on equities, amounted to only one per cent in 1964-65 and 1965-66. Compared to the industrial securities, the price of government securities ruled rather steady. The index of prices relating to government and semi-government securities stood at 95.5 in 1967-68 compared to 98.2 in 1964-65. In 1968-69 the price of both government securities and industrial securities rose. Thus, the return on Government is more attractive than most industrial securities, though not as compared to investments in real assets or certain other financial assets. The point has already been made that the main reason for the price of government securities not suffering a serious decline in price was due to the support policies pursued by the Reserve Bank.

In the last few years, the rate of interest offered on governments has shown a rise. A problem that has not however received sufficient attention is the differential between the short and the long. Given the present yield of 4.25 per cent on seven year bonds and 5.5 per cent on 30 year bonds, expectation of a rise in the interest rate even by 0.5 per cent on both types in the next few years would make invest-

ment today in the long dated bonds unattractive. The differential between the short and the long that exists now does not provide enough cushion for the long dated ones to absorb any capital loss that may be sustained by an increase in interest rate. Thus, from the point of view of rational investor, the long dated bonds are by no means attractive unless no changes in interest rate are expected.

Impact on Other Sectors of Capital Market

To what extent has the growth in the government securities market affected other segments of the capital market, particularly the new issues market and the stock market? It is pointed out, since the major institutions channelling savings are State-owned and since Government diverts a greater part of these resources for its own purposes, the private sector is "starved" of the necessary funds. This is even cited as one of the factors that has contributed to the recent decline in the share prices.

A mixed economy like that of India will have to evolve a scheme by which the available savings can be shared between the public and private sectors. The Government has so far made no change in the statutory requirements relating to the disposition of funds of any of the financial institutions. Since the bulk of the funds of these institutions has always gone to the Government, with rapid growth of these institutions, the Government has been able to meet its requirements much more easily than the private sector. However, the long term credit institutions are primarily intended to help the private sector. These institutions, as has been rightly pointed out, are intermediaries between Government which is the main source of funds and the investors in the private sector.

The recent decline in share prices can be traced to several causes. The private sector has been insisting that it is the high rate of corporate taxation leading to low dividend yield that has been primarily responsible for the setback. It is true that the corporate tax in India is higher than in many other countries. But many industries in India have been enjoying a high priced sheltered home market because of the policy of import substitution. Thus, government policy cuts both ways. As between shares of different companies, there are considerable variations in price fluctuations, leading one to believe that there are many other reasons for the decline in share

prices. Nervousness on the part of the investors seems to have played an important part. The sharp decline in prices occurred after the Chinese attack and the Indo-Pakistani conflict. 'Climate' thus appears to be a significant factor. The decline in the prices of shares in 1966-67 and 1967-68 is due to the recession that hit the industry. The share prices have started rising with the improvement in the economy.

A recent study has pointed out the fact that there is a decrease in the reliance on equity capital as a means of financing new projects and that the proportion of equity capital raised from the general public is falling. An active stock market can come into existence only if companies make a bid to attract enough investors. This would make shares 'marketable' and therefore, 'liquid'.

IV. FUTURE DEVELOPMENT

With regard to the future of the government securities market two questions seem to be relevant. One, should the market for government securities be widened; and two, can the market be widened? If the answer to the first question is negative, the second question does not arise. It is nevertheless useful to analyse the implications of these two questions.

Parties Interested in Widening the Market

There are three parties who may be interested in the widening of the market. They are (1) holders of securities (2) Government and (3) central bank of the country, i.e., Reserve Bank of India. The motivations of the parties may be different but they nevertheless reinforce each other.

Holders are interested because marketability ensures liquidity. Like holders of all obligations, holders of government securities would welcome an active secondary market. Of course, as our preceding analysis has shown, market is not the only means to ensure liquidity. If the central bank of the country stands ready to buy or sell at prices which are not considered unreasonable, 'marketability' can still be ensured.

The Government, like all issuers of obligations, would normally be interested in widening the market because marketability by itself is an attribute which investors desire. A widening of the market

leads to increased marketability and this might facilitate the Government in issuing a larger volume of debt. However, this raises the other issue whether the Government is willing to offer that rate of interest which will make these securities readily marketable. If the Government is not willing to do that, then widening of the market along these lines might become impossible. Government might be content to have a restricted 'captive' market if the subscription to government loans will not increase considerably by the offer of higher rates of interest.

The central bank of a country would normally be interested in a broad and active securities market because this enables the bank to conduct open market operations easily. It has been pointed out that if the market is narrow, sale of even a small volume of securities by the central bank may lead to disorderly conditions in the market. So, a central bank, concerned with the use of open market operations as an instrument of control, may take active steps to widen the market. However, there is the contrary view[7] that in the early stages of the development of capital market, the central bank's efforts to widen the government securities market must be through ensuring stability in bond prices and therefore, open market operations as a means of control may not have a role to play.

If a genuine attempt is to be made to widen the market, a necessary condition is that the rate offered on the securities must be competitive. In the absence of a really competitive rate, the base can be broadened only by the enlargement of the 'captive market'.

Implications of Low Bond Rate

A policy of maintaining low bond yields has important consequences (a) to the Reserve Bank of India; (b) to the Government; and (c) to the institutions holding government securities.

In analysing the securities market in Pakistan, Porter had contended that low bond yields had come in the way of effective implementation of monetary controls. It is true if the central bank, in the first instance, forces banks to hold more than they would otherwise do and then stands ready to convert securities into reserves when desired by commercial banks, monetary controls cease to become operative. Porter for example writes: "Although the State Bank (of Pakistan) is not legally obligated to lend unlimited reserves

to the commercial banks on government security collateral, the banks seemed to have accepted the quota policy on the understanding, that unwanted securities would always serve as collateral. Thus, the quantity of scheduled banks borrowing from the State Bank is determined not by the State Bank, but by the demands of the scheduled banks on their holdings of government securities."[8] He refers to the fact that net free reserves of banks in Pakistan had often become negative, sometimes even to the extent of 20 per cent of the deposits. This, however, is not necessarily a concomitant of a policy of low bond yields. Though the rates offered on securities are not "competitive", the Reserve Bank of India has not been that liberal in regard to its lending policy. The net free reserves of banks had been negative but had never exceeded five per cent of deposits. Thus, the central bank of the country need not necessarily lose control over regulating credit because of low bond yields. The Reserve Bank of India has been following a two-fold policy of fixing maximum interest rates on commercial bank advances and applying a progressively rising rate on the borrowings from the Reserve Bank. These compulsions to hold government securities, far from weakening controls, serve as secondary reserve requirement and apply a brake on expansion of loans. There is, however, a limit to the extent to which banks may be compelled to lend to Government at rates that are not "competitive" because a point will be reached when these rates might make banks unviable as profit making institutions.

The Government, as pointed out earlier, has a choice between raising the interest rate and thereby, widening the market and keeping the interest rate low and be content with a restrictive market. The policy of being content with a restrictive or 'captive' market is not necessarily bad. The 'captive' market in India consists of three major institutions and with the rise in income and the consequent growth of these institutions, the total volume of funds that can be funnelled into government securities can be sizeable. It would pay the Government to turn its energies towards helping these institutions to grow rapidly and thereby increase the subscription to government securities than to attempt at widening the market by offering higher rates of interest.

The low bond yields affects directly the profitability of the institutions holding these securities. It was pointed out in an earlier

section, that given certain assumptions regarding the liquidity of assets, even on the present pattern of yields of Governments and loans, banks would hold 25 per cent of the deposits in government securities. Until recently there was a ceiling on the rate of interest that could be charged by banks on their loans and advances. This is what has partly made the yields on governments competitive at least from the point of view of banks. However, there is a limit to the extent to which Government can insulate the rates on bonds from the other rates in the market. With banks being compelled to offer increasing rates of interest on their time deposits, unless the secondary reserve requirement is fixed at a reasonable level, profitability of banks might be seriously eroded. With the nationalisation of banks, one could argue that even if a higher rate of interest is offered on bonds, the Government would not stand to lose because what it gives with one hand, it takes with another. This may, however, not be the case with respect to investments of Life Insurance Corporation and Provident Funds. A low bond yield affects indirectly the insurance policy holders and the employees in the case of Provident Funds. Even now in the case of Provident Funds, there is a growing feeling that they should have greater freedom than what they have now in allocating their funds.

So long as the Government is able to retain the captive market, the case for raising the interest rate to make it competitive does not arise. If the statutory restrictions are withdrawn, then the Government has no choice but to make the rates competitive. But given the situation as it exists now, there does not seem to be any reason for the Government to drastically change the yield on bonds. However, as market rates rise, it may become necessary for the Government to readjust rates on bonds, so as not to impair the financial viability of institutions such as banks. Nevertheless, within limits, the rate can be kept below the purely 'competitive' rate. The financial institutions themselves may not be concerned with the lack of an active secondary market so long as the Reserve Bank is willing to play the role of 'buyer of last resort'. Just as the function of 'lender of last resort' does not imply the abdication of the function of "controller of credit". Reserve Bank's role as 'buyer of last resort' need not weaken monetary controls so long as the privilege of borrowing on the collateral of bonds is not made automatic.

There are, however, other problems that are bound to rise in the absence of a market as it is normally understood. The present rules regarding investments in approved securities leave it to the discretion of the banks and LIC, the actual composition of the securities portfolio. These institutions have put in most of their funds in central government securities, as the Reserve Bank operates more in these securities than in state government securities. With the nationalisation of banks, there has been an insistent claim on the part of state governments that a larger share of the bank funds must go to states. With no market to differentiate between government security of one state and another, allocation of funds among the various state government securities could become part of a problem of allocation of resources between the Central and state governments. The possibility of allocation of funds along the lines of sharing income tax cannot be completely discounted.

Possibilities of Widening the Market

It was pointed out earlier that, if a genuine market is to be built, a necessary condition is to make the interest offered on government securities competitive. An appropriate increase in the interest rate would have the effect of making the financial institutions hold government securities at the present level, even if the statutory restrictions are withdrawn. However, for a broad market what is required is a wide spectrum of owners, so that at any given time there will be a large number of buyers and sellers. Unless the increase in the interest rate has the effect of widening the base, an active market cannot be built up. It is true that the share of individuals and corporations in the total government securities has not only decreased relatively but has even gone down in absolute amount. A more attractive rate of interest on government securities might, perhaps, induce these sections of the public to hold securities. However, a real widening of the market can come about only with the growth of a large variety of Financial Institutions. Thus, while an increase in the interest rates is necessary for widening the market, that by itself would not be sufficient unless a greater diversification is brought about in the financial structure.

V. SUMMARY

The government securities market in India reflects the mixed character of the Indian economy. The two features of the Indian economy that have shaped the nature of the market as it exists now are (a) the direct and dominant role of the Government in the total investment outlays of the economy, and (b) Government ownership of the major financial institutions. The commercial banks, Life Insurance Corporation and Provident Funds own between them, 85 per cent of the government debt held by the public and all these are either State-owned or under statutory control regarding their investment policy. The investment policy of these institutions becomes part of the allocation of resources between the public (Government) and private sectors. Viewed from this angle, the statutory restrictions imposed on these institutions on their investments takes on a new character.

The rate offered on bonds is not strictly competitive. However, with the increase in the resources of the major financial institutions, the public debt has been growing at the rate of seven per cent per annum. A genuine secondary market is possible only if the rate offered is competitive. There is no active secondary market in India and even in relation to the limited transactions, the Reserve Bank of India plays an important role by supporting bond prices. Perhaps, in the Indian context, even the need for an active secondary market may be questioned. With the major subscribers of government securities under direct control of the State, it is possible for the Government to keep the bond yield below "competitive" level. There is, however, a limit to which the Government can insulate the rates on bonds from other rates in the market without seriously eroding the profitability of the financial institutions. In the absence of a market, the financial institutions may face a problem regarding the allocation of funds between different state government securities. Here again, the problem becomes a part of the general question of allocation of resources between Central and state governments, rather than being purely the investment policy of a financial institution.

Notes

1. For an analysis along these lines, see Richard C. Porter, "Narrow Security Markets and Monetary Policy: Lessons from Pakistan" *Economic Development and Cultural Change,* Vol XIV, October 1965, p. 48.
2. "Open Market Operations of the Reserve Bank of India", *Reserve Bank of India Bulletin,* June 1960, p. 799.
3. V.G. Pendharkar and M. Narasimham, "Recent Evolution of Monetary Policy in India", *Reserve Bank of India Bulletin,* April 1966, p. 350.
4. Part of this difference is accounted for by the subscription of the government departments. But that is negligible.
5. Richard Porter in his model on bank portfolio selection emphasises this point. He writes: "One aspect of the shape of each of these possible paths (of deposits) is of such a great importance to the bank that it is here assumed the only aspect considered by the banks – namely, the lowest point to which deposits fall in each other paths. For it is on this "deposits-low" of the period that the bank is forced to make the most radical adjustment of its assets portfolio in order to meet the demands of its depositors." Richard C. Porter, "A Model on Bank Portfolio Selection", *Yale Economic Essays,* Vol 1, No 2, Fall 1961.
6. Given the returns on various assets and assuming certain liquidity co-efficients relating to assets and liabilities, the linear programming technique was used to derive the optimal portfolio of banks. The model is similar to the one used by Chambers and Charnes for determining the optimum portfolio in American Banks. The model postulates that banks seek to maximize their profits subject to certain liquidity constraints. The liquidity constraints take into account the statutory requirements, capital adequacy as well as canons of prudent banking. The profitability co-efficients of assets were derived from the data on earning and expenses of commercial banks. Liquidity co-efficients relating to assets used in this model were the same as those used by Chambers and Charnes. Such a model shows that banks would maintain a little more than 25 per cent of the deposits in government securities. For detailed description see, C. Rangarajan and J.K. Satia, "Bank portfolio Management – A Linear Programming Approach" (Mimeo).
7. For such a view, see M. Narasimham, "Narrow Security Markets and Monetary Policy – Lessons from Pakistan : A Comment", *Economic Development and Cultural Change,* July 1967, pp. 469-471.
8. Porter, *op cit,* p 52.

5

Government Expenditure and Money Supply Multipliers under Alternative Conditions

Introduction

In the text book discussions of fiscal and monetary policies based on the standard Keynesian model, the stock of physical capital is assumed to be constant. This is a valid assumption if one was to deal only with very short run effects of various policies. But an analysis of dynamic effects are called for when one deals with the various dynamic extensions of the Keynesian model. For example, the introduction of government budget constraint or the explicit allowance for various leads and lags in the behavioural relations makes the model dynamic. Further, when wealth effects are present in the consumption function or in the demand for money equation, it is not logical to assume that the capital stock is constant. One must allow for the changes in wealth due to changes in capital stock. Hence, we consider the following modifications of the standard Keynesian model. First we introduce the government budget constraint which specifies that the total government expenditures equals tax revenue plus the changes in money supply plus the changes in bond supply. Second, wealth which is defined to be the sum of the stocks of capital, money and bonds, is introduced as an additional independent variable, both in the consumption function and in the demand function for money. Third, we introduce the impact of changes in investment on capital stock. In this fairly general model, we analyse the government expenditure multipliers and money supply multipliers under alternative conditions. In the case of

---

Co-author: **V. Sundararajan.**
The Indian Economic Journal, Vol. 30, No.1, July-September 1982.

government expenditure multipliers, we examine the implications under two conditions: one, when the increase in government expenditures are financed by money creation and two, when such increases are financed by bond creation. We analyse the money supply multipliers under two alternative condition: (a) when changes in money supply are brought about by open market operations alone and (b) when such changes in money supply are accompanied by changes in government expenditures alone. While the impact of increase in government expenditures under alternative conditions of financing has received some attention in literature[1], there has not been enough consideration given to money supply multipliers under different policies causing increases in money supply. Also, the earlier studies have not taken into full account the impact of changes in capital stock on wealth[2]. We attempt to give in this paper, a more comprehensive consideration of both types of multipliers. Some of the earlier studies, notably those of Silber (1970) and Blinder and Solow (1974) indicated the possibility that the modified Keynesian model which includes government budget constraint and wealth effects on consumption and demand for money might be unstable under conditions of bond financing of government expenditures. This paper demonstrates rigorously that the model is quite stable when the effects of changes in capital stock on wealth are taken into account.

Our model remains within the framework of Hicks-Keynes IS-LM analysis and discusses how the conclusions of IS-LM analysis and some of its extensions will be modified when some of the restrictive assumptions are removed. Thus, our analysis should be viewed as an exercise in short run dynamics, rather than as a long run analysis. For a truly long run analysis, one might resort to the framework of growth models and the basic framework of IS-LM analysis must be abandoned.[3]

Relationship to Other Studies

Many economists have emphasized the importance of including a government budget constraint in standard macroeconomic analysis of fiscal and monetary policy.[4] They have all argued that traditional macroanalysis has not treated the bond finance and money finance cases of government deficit appropriately and this has led to

erroneous conclusions about the multiplier effects of government purchases. Except for Bent Hansen (1973), who emphasized the importance of including a government budget constraint to highlight the interdependency of fiscal and monetary policies, the other authors have emphasized multiplier effects of government spending when such a constraint is included in a macro model.

Carl Christ (1968) argued that if the government budget constraint is omitted in models of income determination, the multiplier effects of government spending are improperly defined and the multiplier depends upon the method of financing the government purchases. He showed that in a simple macroeconomic model of aggregate demand with a rigid price level, if the government's budget constraint is omitted, the money financed government spending multiplier is underestimated and the effect of tax financed government expenditures is overestimated. Arthur Benavie (1973) extended Christ's model by including an equation for determining price level, allowing for institutional details to differentiate the behaviour of the treasury from that of FED, specifying separate equations for determining demand for bonds and incorporating effects of wealth on demand for goods and assets. He analyzed only the impact multiplier of government purchases and came to the same conclusions as Christ (1968) regarding the effects of omitting the government's budget constraint. He also showed that short-run multiplier effect of government purchases, when the deficit is financed by new money issues, exceeds the multiplier effects, when the deficit is financed by new debt issues. This conclusion was also reached by Silber (1970), who dealt, however, with a much simpler model. Silber (1970) extended the traditional IS-LM framework by including the effects of wealth, defined as the sum of stocks of capital, money and bonds, on consumption and demand for money and adding the government's budget constraint. Unlike Benavie and Christ, he assumed constant tax revenues so that marginal tax rate was zero. With this model he proved:

1. Starting from a period of balanced budget, an increase in government expenditures financed period after period by an increase in money supply will lead to income expanding continuously.

2. If the entire increase in government expenditures is financed by an increase in bonds, the effect on income in the short run will be less than in the case of money finance and after a sufficiently long period, incomes will keep on expanding or contracting continuously depending upon whether the net effect of wealth is expansionary or contractionary. Thus, Silber's model is unstable, mainly as a consequence of a zero marginal rate of taxation. The expanding income is not generating additional taxes which would close the gap to be financed by bonds or money.

Alan Blinder and Robert Solow (1973, 1974) generalized the government's budget constraint, along thc lines discussed by Benl Hansen (1973), to include interest payments on outstanding government bonds. With this simple modification, they are able to show that the long run multiplier for money financed deficit spending is smaller than that for bond financed deficit spending. This striking result is contrary to monetarist's position and is also at variant with conclusion reached by Ott and Ott (1965) and Christ (1968), that in the long run, irrespective of nature of financing the government's deficit, the government expenditure multiplier is simply the inverse of the marginal tax rate. However, Blinder and Solow pointed out that their conclusion is a statement about long-run equilibrium and that the economy described by their model could be unstable. They showed, like Silber, that if wealth effects on consumption is small relative to wealth effects on demand for money (so that net wealth effect is negative) then bond financing is cumulatively contractionary and the economy is unstable. However, in the money financed case the economy is stable, because an expansion in income generates tax revenues which will successively reduce the gap and thus reduce the extent of reliance on money finance in successive periods.

All the works mentioned so far, with the exception of Blinder and Solow (1974), basically ignore the fact that changes in capital stock may alter wealth and this may turn out to have important consequences in a model with significant wealth effects. In fact, in many of these models, capital stock is explicitly included in the definition of wealth but is assumed fixed in subsequent analysis. Blinder and Solow (1974) question the logic of treating short run as a period where capital stock is fixed, and go on to take account in an heuris-

tic manner, the possible consequences of explicitly allowing for variations in capital stocks in their short-run macro model. They argue that if capital effects are brought in the likelihood of stability under bond finance is enhanced in the case of expansionary bond finance. They suggest some sufficient conditions that might ensure stability. But the possibility of contractionary bond finance, when the incomes contract continuously without limit is still possible, according to Blinder and Solow, even with capital stock effects included in the model.

Our paper demonstrates that at least in the case of constant tax revenues, the bond financing of government expenditure is not contractionary in the long run when the effects of changes in capital stock on wealth is taken into account. The long run multiplier effects of government purchases with deficits entirely financed by bond issues is positive and depends crucially on the effects of wealth. Thus, if the marginal rate of taxation is assumed positive, the model will still remain stable in the bond financed case, since the increasing income will raise tax revenues and close the extent of gap that has to be financed by bonds in successive periods. While basic conclusion reached by Silber and others that the government expenditure multiplier when financed by money creation is higher than in the case of bond financing, holds true even if changes in capital stock due to changes in investment are taken into account, the capital stock is likely to rise in the case of money finance leading to larger multipliers. The major conclusion of our paper, however, is that one can rule out contractionary effects of bond financing even in the case when net wealth effects is negative.

The models discussed so far are simply extensions of traditional IS-LM framework. The criticisms of this framework by monetarists have been formalized in a model developed by Karl Brunner and Alan Meltzer (1970, 1972, 1973), who also take explicit account of government's budget constraint. Their model, however, is significantly different, in structure and emphasis, from the traditional IS-LM framework and its extensions. In their model, effect of wealth on real expenditure and money is not direct as in the IS-LM framework, but indirect through their effects on price of real capital and interest rate. Even though they use capital stock as one of the variables in the relationship determining the price of output, they continue the traditional practice of assuming fixed real stock of capital in their

analysis. Since their model determines only the aggregate real expenditure, not its division between real consumption and real investment, variations in capital stock cannot be analyzed. Further, a significant role is assigned to producer's anticipation and purchaser's anticipation of future prices in any adjustment to new equilibrium in their model. Brunner and Meltzer (1970, 1973), compare some of the implications of their model with the implications of standard IS-LM analysis or its variants. A rigorous dynamic analysis of their model is not available, but a graphical analysis presented by Brunner and Meltzer (1973) indicates that even their model does have a stable solution in the case when government expenditure is financed by issuing bond and the tax rates are proportional. In the case of progressive taxes, however, their model seems to be stable.

Description of the Model

The model used for the derivation of the multipliers is as follows:

(1)	$Y = C + I + G$	(Commodity Market Equilibrium)
(2)	$C = a + b\,(Y-T) + uW$	(Consumption Function)
(3)	$I = d - er$	(Investment Function)
(4)	$G = \overline{G}$	(Government Spending)
(5)	$T = \overline{T}$	(Tax Function)
(6)	$M^d = hW + fy - qr$	(Demand for Money)
(7)	$M^s = \overline{M}$	(Supply of Money)
(8)	$M^d = M^s$	(Money Market Equilibrium)
(9)	$W = K + M + B$	(Definition of Wealth)
(10)	$G - T = \Delta M + \Delta B$	(Government's Budget Constraint)
(11)	$K_t = I_t + K_{t-1}$	(Capital Stock Function)

Where,

Y = GNP	r = Interest Rate
I = Private Investment	C = Consumption
G = Government Spending	T = Taxes
M = Money	W = Wealth
K = Physical Capital	B = Government Bonds

The basic assumptions of the model are (a) all the equations are assumed to be linear, (b) prices are held constant, and (c) there is no banking system. In spite of the simplifying assumptions, it is interesting to study the impact of government expenditures and money supply under different conditions. The equations are self explanatory. The model incorporates the modifications listed earlier.

It may be stressed that in this model, wealth has both an expansionary and a contractionary effect on income. The expansionary effect comes via consumption function where wealth has a positive impact. The contractionary effect comes via the rise in interest rate and the fall in investment. The net effect on income of wealth would depend on the values of the parameters involved.[5]

The Derivation of the Multipliers

In this section we describe the procedure adopted for deriving the various government expenditure and money supply multipliers. In an equation system, where lagged variables are involved, we need to evaluate not only the impact multipliers, i.e., the immediate effect of the exogenous on endogenous variables but also the interim multipliers, that is, the impact in the subsequent periods. The total multipliers can then be obtained by adding the impact and interim multipliers.

Such an addition would give the impact of a continuous injection of one unit of the exogenous variable on the endogenous variable. In order to derive the impact and interim multipliers in our model, we rewrite the set of equations presented earlier, in the following way:

(I) $Y_t = a_0 - b_0T + g_0G_t + u_0K_t + (u_0+e_0)M_t + u_0B_t$

(II) $K_t = d_1 + a_1 K_{t-1} + m_1M_t - b_1B_t - y_1Y_t$

(III) (a) $M_t = G_t - T_t + M_{t-1} - B_t + B_{t-1}$

(III) (b) $B_t = G_t - T_t - M_t + M_{t-1} + B_{t-1}$

(III′) (a) $G_t = M_t - M_{t-1} + T_t + B_t - B_{t-1}$

(III′) (b) $B_t = B_{t-1} + G_t - T_t - (M_t - M_{t-1})$

Where,

$$b_0 = \frac{b}{1-b+ef/q}; \quad g_0 = \frac{1}{1-b+ef/q}; \quad u_0 = \frac{u-eh/q}{1-b+ef/q}$$

$$e_0 = \frac{e/q}{1\text{-}b + ef/q}; \quad a_1 = \frac{1}{1 + eh/q}; \quad d_1 = \frac{d}{1 + eh/q}$$

$$m_1 = \frac{e(1\text{-}h)/q}{1 + eh/q}; \quad b_1 = \frac{eh/q}{1 + eh/q}; \quad y_1 = \frac{eh/q}{1 + ef/q}$$

Equation III (a) alongwith equation (I) and (II) would be used to derive government expenditure multiplier under conditions of money creation while III (b) would be used to derive government expenditure multipliers under conditions of bond financing. Equation III (a) alongwith the first two equations would be used for studying the impact of change in money when accompanied by changes in government expenditures. Equation III′ (b) will be used to study the case when money supply increases due to open market operations.

The above equation system is of the form:

$$Y_t = AY_t + BY_{t\text{-}1} + CX_t + DX_{t\text{-}1}$$

where Y is a vector of endogenous variables and X is a vector of exogenous variables. Rearranging we get,

$$Y_t = (1\text{-}A)^{-1}BY_{t\text{-}1} + (1\text{-}A)^{-1}CX_t + (1\text{-}A)^{-1}DX_{t\text{-}1}$$

or

$$= MY_{t\text{-}1} + HX_t + EX_{t\text{-}1}$$

and it follows:

$$\frac{\partial Y_t}{\partial X_t} = H; \quad \frac{\partial Y_{t+1}}{\partial X_t} \; MH + E; \qquad \frac{\partial Y_{t+\theta}}{\partial X_t} = M^{\theta}H + M^{\theta-1}E, \; \theta > 1$$

where $\frac{\partial Y_{t+\theta}}{\partial X_t}$ denotes the matrix of partial derivatives where its ij^{th} element represents the derivative of the ith endogeneous variable with respect to j^{th} exogeneous variable.

Government Expenditure Multipliers

Case 1: We examine first the case when the increase in government expenditures is financed by the increase in money supply. The impact multiplier in this situation is:

$$\frac{\partial Y_t}{\partial G_t} = \frac{(1+u)\left(1+\frac{e}{q}\right)}{1-b+\frac{ef}{q}+\frac{e}{q}[h(1-b)+fu]}$$

The first interim multiplier is given by:

$$\frac{\partial Y_{t+1}}{\partial G_t} = \alpha_0^2 a_1 u_0 \,[m_1 y_1 (u_0+e_0+g_0)] + \alpha_0 [u_1 m_1 + u_0 + e_0]$$

$$\text{where } \alpha_0 = \frac{1}{1+u_0 y_1}$$

It is also seen that a one shot injection converges to a positive figure.

$$\lim_{\grave{e}\to\infty} \frac{\partial Y_{t+\grave{e}}}{\partial G_t} = \frac{u}{h(b-1)+fu}$$

Thus, the total multiplier, which is the sum of the impact and interim multipliers keeps increasing as the time periods increase. An increase in government expenditures financed by an increase in money supply period after period will result in income expanding continuously.

We derived from our model, the impact on capital stock of an increase in government expenditures. It is found that:

$$\lim_{\grave{e}\to\infty} \frac{\partial k_{t+\grave{e}}}{\partial G_t} = \frac{1-b}{h(b-1)+fu} - 1$$

This expression can be positive only if,

$(1-b) > h\ (1-b) + fu$

which can be restated as (1-b) (1-h) - fu > 0. This is quite likely to be the normal situation, though it doesn't have to hold necessarily. The impact on capital stock in this model comes through changes in interest rate. When money supply increases as a result of increases in government expenditure, this has the effect of reducing interest rate. But when by the same token wealth increases, it has the effect of increasing the interest rate. In a two-dimensional diagram relating interest rate and money, we can visualize this as the simultaneous

shifting of both the demand for money curve and the money supply curve. If the money supply impact is stronger than the wealth effect, interest rate will keep falling and as a consequence, capital stock will keep increasing.

Case 2: We examine next the case when the increase in government expenditures is financed by an increase in bonds. In this model the impact multiplier is:

$$\frac{\partial Y_t}{\partial G_t} = \frac{1+u}{1-b+\frac{ef}{q}+\frac{e}{q}[h(1-b)+fu)]}$$

Unlike the case of government expenditures financed by money creation, the effect of the one shot injection in the present case converges to zero. Also, the total multiplier converges to a positive figure. A continuous injection of government expenditures matched by an increase in bonds will result as number of periods gets large in an increase in income of :

$$\frac{u}{\frac{e}{q}[h(1-b)+fu]}$$

Thus, in the bond financed case, the total multiplier is finite unlike the continuous expansion in income noted in the previous case.

As in the previous case, we can derive the impact on capital stock. It is seen that:

$$\lim_{\grave{e}\to\infty} \frac{\partial K_{t+\grave{e}}}{\partial G_t} = -1$$

which means that as number of periods increases, every unit increase in government expenditures (and therefore bonds) results in a unit decrease in capital stock. As pointed out previously, the impact on capital stock in this model occurs through changes in interest rate. In the bond financed case, quite clearly interest rate can only increase as there is only the wealth effect operating. In the money creation case, there is in addition the direct effect of a fall in interest rate due to changes in money supply which is absent here.

It is also interesting to note that if we had not taken into account the changes in wealth due to changes in capital stock, (i.e., if we had

omitted eq. 11), there is a possibility that in the bond financed case, income could be continuously decreasing. In such a model, Silber showed that when the net effect of wealth is negative, income would be decreasing continuously. But the introduction of variations in capital stock completely alters the picture. When the net effect of wealth is negative, the reduction in capital stock offsets the decrease in income, which would otherwise be occurring so that the multiplier does not become negative.

Thus, when the government budget constraint and the effect of wealth are introduced in the typical Keynesian model, we see that when government expenditure is financed by increased money creation, income expands continuously. On the other hand, when it is financed by increasing bonds, the multiplier becomes finite and positive. There is no possibility even in this case of income decreasing.

Money Supply Multipliers

Case 1: We examine first the impact of changes in money supply brought about through open market operations. This is the situation when an increase in money supply is exactly matched by a decrease in the government bonds held by the public. The impact multiplier is given by:

$$\frac{\partial Y_t}{\partial M_t} = \frac{(1+u)\frac{e}{q}}{(1-b)+\frac{ef}{q}+\frac{e}{q}(h-bh+fu)}$$

The interim multipliers are given by:

$$\frac{\partial Y_{t+1}}{\partial M_t} = \frac{\frac{e}{q}(1-b)\left(u-\frac{eh}{b}\right)}{\left[1-b+\frac{et}{q}+\frac{e}{q}(h-bh+fu)\right]}$$

$$\frac{\partial Y_{t+\grave{e}}}{\partial M_t} = \frac{\partial Y_{t+1}}{\partial M_t}\,.\,\ddot{a}^{\grave{e}-1} \quad \text{where,}$$

$$\ddot{a} = \frac{1-b+\frac{ef}{q}}{\left[1-b+\frac{ef}{q}(h-bh+fu)\right]}$$

$$\therefore \quad \frac{\partial Y_{t+\grave{e}}}{\partial M_t} \to 0 \text{ as } \grave{e} \to \infty$$

Further, one can verify that the long run multiplier or the total multiplier is given by:

$$\frac{(\partial Y)}{\partial M_T} = \sum_{\grave{e}=0}^{\infty} \frac{\partial Y_{t-\grave{e}}}{\partial M_t} = \frac{u}{h(1-b)+uf}$$

Thus, the immediate effect of an unit increase in the stock of money matched by bond purchase is positive. The interim multipliers must be interpreted carefully. Since money is a stock variable, when it increases by one unit in any given period, the stock of money is higher by one unit in all the succeeding periods. Therefore, $\partial Y_{t+\theta}/\partial M_t$ is the effect of income θ periods from now, when the money supply is raised by one unit now, but the stock of money is brought back to its original level in all the succeeding periods (i.e. money supply is reduced by one unit in the next period). But the total multiplier is the effect on income in the long run, when money supply is raised by one unit in a given period (no offsetting changes in M taking place in the next period). As we see from the formula for the total multiplier, the long run effect of an increase in money supply is positive. The next question is, is the long run effect bigger or smaller than the immediate effect? To answer this question, we note that the interim multipliers will be positive if $u>(eh/q)$ and negative if $u<(eh/q)$. Since the long run multiplier is obtained by adding the impact and the interim multipliers, we can conclude that the long run effect of an increase in money supply will be larger than the immediate effect in case of $u>(eh/b)$.

The reverse is true if $u<(eh/q)$. Thus, when the net wealth effect is positive, the long run effect on income of an increase in money supply is larger than the short run effect. The opposite is true when the net wealth effect is negative. We can examine what happens to capital stock as a result of increases in money supply. The impact multiplier for capital stock is:

$$\frac{\partial K_t}{\partial M_t} = \frac{\frac{e}{b}\,(1-b)}{1-b+\frac{ef}{q}+\frac{e}{q}\{h(1-b)+fu\}}$$

It can be verified that:

$$\frac{\partial K_{t+\theta}}{\partial M_t} = \frac{\partial K_t}{\partial M_t}\,\delta\theta$$

Therefore,

$$\frac{\partial K_{t+\grave{e}}}{\partial M_t} \rightarrow 0 \text{ as } \grave{e} \rightarrow \infty$$

Further, the long run effect on capital stock is given by:

$$\left(\frac{\partial K}{\partial M}\right)_T = \sum_{\grave{e}=0}^{\infty} \frac{\partial K_{t+\grave{e}}}{\partial M_t} = \frac{1-b}{h(1-b)+fu} > 0$$

Thus, the capital stock increases when money supply is increased through open market operations, both in the long run and in the short run. Also, the long run effect is higher than the short run effect.

Case 2: Next we consider the situation when money supply is increased accompanied by offsetting changes in government expenditures. In this situation, the impact multiplier for income is given by:

$$\frac{\partial Y_t}{\partial M_t} = \frac{(1+u)+\frac{e}{q}(1+u)}{1-b+\frac{ef}{q}+\frac{e}{q}\{h(1-b)+fu\}} > 0$$

It can be verified that:

$$\frac{\partial Y_{t+\grave{e}}}{\partial M_t} \rightarrow 0 \text{ as } \grave{e} \rightarrow \infty$$

and the long run multiplier is given by:

$$\sum_{\grave{e}=0}^{\infty} \frac{\partial Y_{t+\grave{e}}}{\partial M_t} = \frac{u}{h(1-b)+fu}$$

Thus, when money supply increases, accompanied by increases in government expenditures, the immediate effect on income is larger than in the case of open market operations. But the long run effects are identical in both cases. It is quite possible for the effects on income to be very different in the intervening periods.

In the present case, the long run effects can be either smaller or larger than the short run effect, depending upon whether $(1+u)\,(h[1\text{-}b]+fu)+(1\text{-}b)\left(\frac{eh}{q}-u\right)$ is positive or negative. If the wealth effect is negative $\left(u<\frac{eh}{q}\right)$, the expression will be positive and long run effect will be smaller than the short run effect. But even when the net wealth effect is positive, it is possible to have smaller long run effects. Compared to the case of open market operations, in the present case it takes a much stronger positive wealth effect to produce a long run multiplier that is larger than the short run multiplier.

The effects on capital stock in the case of money supply increases, matched by increases in government expenditures is very different compared to the case of open market operations. The impact multiplier for capital stock is:

$$\frac{\partial K_t}{\partial M_t}=\frac{\frac{e}{q}\left[(1-b)\,(1-h)-f\,(1+u)\right]}{1-b+\frac{ef}{q}+\frac{e}{q}\left\{h(1-b)+fu\right\}}$$

The interim multipliers converge to zero and the long run multiplier is given by:

$$\sum_{\grave{e}=0}^{\infty}\frac{\partial K_{t+\grave{e}}}{\partial M_t}=\frac{(1\text{-}b)\,(1-h)-fu}{h\,(1-b)+fu}$$

From the expressions for the multipliers it is seen that the capital stock may decrease as a result of an increase in money supply, unlike in the case of open market operations when capital stock always increased when money supply increased. In fact, we can establish the following conditions. As money supply increases, if (1-b) (1-h) < fu then the capital stock will decrease both in the long run and in the short run. If (I-b) (1-h) > f (1+u), then capital stock will increase both in the long run and in the short run. If fu < (1-b) (1-h) < f (1+u), then the capital stock will decline in the short run, but will increase in the long run.

We have examined in this section the impact of increases in money supply (*a*) when it is caused by purely open market operations and (*b*) when it is caused by increases in government expenditures. We find that in the latter case, the immediate impact of changes in money on income is greater than in the former. But the long run effect on income is the same in both cases. The impact on capital stock is different both in the short run and in the long run.

Conclusions

The addition of government budget constraint, the introduction of wealth variable in the consumption function and in the demand function for money and the explicit introduction of capital stock as a component of wealth in the typical Keynesian model throws new light on the government expenditure multipliers and money supply multipliers. The addition of government budget constraint enables us to study the impact on income under alternative conditions of financing of government expenditures or bringing about an increase in money supply. The long run multipliers studied are on the basis of continuous injection of government expenditure or money. The major conclusions that emerge from this study are: (a) when government expenditures are financed by money creation, income expands continuously. The capital stock may increase or decrease while the former is likely to be the normal situation; (b) when the increased government expenditures are financed by bond creation, the multiplier becomes finite and positive. There is no possibility of income multipliers becoming negative. The capital stock declines; (c) when increases in money supply are brought about purely through open market operations, the multiplier converges to positive figure and both in the short run and in the long run capital stock increases; (d) when money supply is brought about by an increase in government expenditures, the immediate impact of change in money on income is greater than in the case of open market operations. But the long run effect is the same as in the open market operations case. The capital stock may be increasing or decreasing depending on certain conditions.

Limitations of the Model

While the model serves to highlight some of the dynamic implications of policy shocks in a Keynesian model that incorporates adjustments in capital stock, both the long run and short run implications of the model are, however, limited by the assumption of completely sticky prices and the assumed absence of a balance of payments constraint. While the sticky price assumption may be justified for short run analysis in some circumstances, a long run analysis clearly requires that account be taken of the impact of money growth on inflation, inflation expectation, nominal interest rates, and exchange rates. In such an extension of the analysis, the distinctions between anticipated and unanticipated components of monetary impulses, and between real and nominal interest rates would play a crucial role in the policy transmission mechanism, in addition, the gap between actual and potential output (based on capital stock under its full utilization) would also influence inflation prospects. In particular, real interest rates will not respond to changes in money growth alone in the long run, with long run changes in nominal interest rates mainly reflecting changes in inflation and inflation expectations, and hence, any short run expansionary impulse on real output, following a monetary shock-owing to larger investment and capital stock-would be short lived. Some or most of the adjustments to monetary shocks would occur also through adjustments in inflation and balance of payments. A comprehensive analysis along these lines would call for extensions of the model to endogenize inflation, account for expectation formation, and incorporate balance of payments effects.

Notes

1. Carl Christ (1968) introduced a government budget constraint in the simple Keynesian model and discussed fiscal and monetary policies. Silber (1970) introduced wealth effects on consumption and demand for money, in addition to government budget constraint and discussed the fiscal policies in such a model. Others who have emphasized the importance of including a government budget constraint in standard macroeconomic analysis of fiscal and monetary policy are: Musgrave (1959), David Ott and Alliot Ott (1965), Carl Christ (1967 and 1969) Roger Spencer and William Yohe (1970), Bent Hansen (1973), Arthur Benavie (1973), and Alan Blinder and Robert Solow (1973, and 1974). Monetarists have generally insisted that there arc important differences between deficits financed by issuing money and deficits financed by issuing bonds. See Karl Brunner and Alan Meltzer (1973) for a monetarist model that explicitly incorporates the government budget constraint.
2. Foley and Sidrauski (1971) take full account of the impact of changes in capital stock on wealth and production functions within the framework of a two sector growth model on which prices and markets for various assets and commodities arc superimposed. Blinder and Solow (1974) provide some conjectures on the likely consequences of including the changes in capital stock in the IS-LM analysis with government budget constraint and wealth effects.
3. See Foley and Sidrauski (1971) for a discussion of fiscal and monetary policy in the framework of a two sector growth model. In their analysis prices and markets for consumption goods, investment goods, bonds and money are explicitly introduced and all the markets are assumed to be in equilibrium at full employment level. Dale Henderson and Thomas Sargent (1973) use the Foley. Sidrauski model, but assume fixed capital stock (so that output variations occur through changes in labor only) and go on to discuss fiscal and monetary policies.
4. See footnote 1 for a list of writings that employ government budget constraint.
5. Silber (1970, Pp. 469-70) has shown that the positive impact of increases in wealth on consumption spending is u and the negative impact of wealth on investment spending [via the positive impact of wealth on the rate of interest] in eh/q. Thus the net effect on income of wealth is positive if $u > eh/q$ and negative to case $u < eh/q$.

References

Blinder, Alan S. and Robert M. Solow, "Does Fiscal Policy Matter?" *Journal of Public Economics*, Vol. 2 (November 1973).

Blinder Alan S. and Robert M. Solow, "Analytical Foundations of Fiscal Policy." *in The Economics of Public Finance* edited by Alan S. Blinder and others (The Brookings Institution. Washington, 1974), pp. 3-115. especially pp. 45-57.

Brunner, K. and A. H. Meltzer, "A Monetarist Framework for Aggregative Analysis" *in Kredit and Kapital*, Heft 1, Proceedings of the First Konstanzer' Seminar on Monetary Theory and Monetary Policy, (ed by Karl Brunner) University of Konstanz 1970.

Brunner, K. and A.H. Meltzer, "Money Debt and Economic Activity" *Journal of Political Economy*, Vol. 80 (1972), pp. 951-977.

Brunner, K. and A. H. Meltzer, "Mr. Hicks and the Monetarists" *Economica*, Vol. XL, No.157, (February 1973), pp. 44-59.

Christ, Carl F, "A Short-Run Aggregate – Demand Model of the Interdependence and Effects of Monetary and Fiscal Policies with Keynesian and Classical Interest Elasticities," *American Economic Review*, Vol. 57 (May 1967). pp. 434-443.

"A Simple Macroeconomic Model with a Government Budget Restraint," *Journal of Political Economy*, Vol. 76 (January/February 1968) pp. 53-67.

"A Model of Monetary and Fiscal Policy Effects on the Money Stock, Price Level and Real Output," *Journal of Money Credit and Banking*, Vol.1 (November 1969), pp. 683-705.

Foley, Duncan K. and Miguel Sidrauski, *Monetary and Fiscal Policy In a Growing Economy*. The MacMillan Company, Collier-MacMillan Limited, London.

Hansen, Bent. "On the Effects of Fiscal and Monetary Policy: A Taxonomic Discussion," *American Economic Review*, Vol. 63 (September 1973), pp. 546-571.

Henderson, Dale and Sargent Thomas, "Monetary and Fiscal Policy in a two Sector Aggregative Model," *American Economic Review*, Vol.63, No.3 (June 1973), pp. 345-365.

Musgrave, Richard A, *The Theory of Public Finance* (New York 1959) pp. 526-555.

Ott, David, J., and Alliot F. Ott, "Budget Balance and Equilibrium Income," *Journal of finance*, Vol. 20 (March 1965), pp. 71-77.

Silber, William L., "Fiscal Policy in IS-LM Analysis: A correction," *Journal of Money Credit and Banking*, Vol, 2 (November 1970) pp. 461-473.

Spencer, R. W. and W. P. Yohe, "The Crowding Out of Private Expenditure by Fiscal Policy Actions", Federal Reserve Bank of St. Louis, *Review*, Vol. 52 (October 1970), pp. 12-24.

Part IV

External Sector

6

Impact of Export Fluctuations on Income

A Cross-Country Analysis

Introduction

The degree of export fluctuation and its impact on income have been the subject of a number of investigations. A major bone of contention has been whether developing countries experience a greater degree of fluctuation in exports than developed countries and whether such fluctuations affect the growth rate of developing countries. In this paper we address ourselves to the second issue – the impact of export fluctuations, particularly on the income of the developing countries. For this purpose we construct comparable econometric models for a number of countries — mostly developing but some developed — and derive from these models the export-income multiplier that can throw light on the question of which countries are affected more by export fluctuations. We find that the procedure of using cross-country regressions adopted by a number of writers for studying this issue is defective. In section I we outline the theoretical model employed and develop the method used for bringing out the impact on income of changes in exports. In section II we present the econometric models estimated and the findings that emerge from them. Section III gives our conclusions.

I. METHODOLOGY OF INVESTIGATION

Country Models *versus* Cross-Country Regressions

Most of the previous studies (Macbean, 1968; Maizels, 1968; Massell *et al.*, 1972; Cohen, 1968) of the impact of export fluctuations

---

Co-author: **V. Sundarajan.**

The Review of Economics and Statistics, Aug. 1976, Vol. LVI, No.3.

on income have used cross-country regressions to investigate the relationship between exports and income. Some of these studies can be criticised for reaching the conclusions they did even within the framework adopted by them. But the central issue in trying to understand the relationship between exports and income is the proper methodology for investigating the problem. As Maizels (1968) in a review of Macbean's book pointed out, a cross section study implies, there is a single relationship between export earnings and income, so that all observed points fall on a single curve. Given the considerable differences in the way in which the different economies are organized, it would be surprising if such a single relationship existed between income and exports for all countries. If the impact of exports on income varies from country to country, a cross-country regression may show no relationship in spite of the fact that a strong relationship exists when each country is considered separately. Thus, the conclusions reached on the basis of cross-country regressions must be deemed to be suspect. Also, relating the instability index in income with the instability index in exports throws no light on whether export fluctuations leads to fluctuations in income. Fluctuations in income are caused by a wide variety of factors, and fluctuations in exports is only one and in some countries, a relatively minor one among them. For a correct understanding of the problem, one must isolate from the total fluctuations in income, those due to exports alone and then compare them with expert variations.

With this in mind, we proceed to study the problem in the following way. We construct for each of the countries that is being studied an econometric model. From this model we derive the export-income and export-investment multipliers. Since lagged variables are involved, we need to derive the dynamic multipliers. These multipliers show how serious export fluctuations are for each country. Taking the past changes in export proceeds as given, we simulate for each country the impact of these changes on income. Next we assume that exports have been growing at a steady rate for each country and derive what the income would have been in such a situation. We then compare these two derived income series to find out the effect of export fluctuations. A comparison of the growth rates of these two simulated incomes will show the impact of export fluctuations on growth. The econometric model employed for the computation of multipliers and for the purposes of simulation is described below:

The Model Specification

The model which we use makes explicit three important ways in which exports might influence Gross National Product and investment. By being a part of aggregate demand, exports will have the usual Keynesian type multiplier effect. By contributing to the availability of foreign exchange reserves, it facilitates imports and the import of capital goods will contribute to increased investment. Exports might affect aggregate demand through their effects on money supply, since trade surplus and capital inflow lead to an increase in money supply, broadly defined.

The model consists of an import function, a consumption function, an investment function, and three-definitional identities including the national income identity.

$$C = c_1 Y + c_2 C_{-1} + c_0 \quad \text{...(1)}$$

$$M = m_1 Y + m_2 E + m_3 KI + m_4 EA_{-1} + m_5(PE/PM) + m_6 M_{-1} + m_7 \quad \text{...(2)}$$

$$I = b_1 M + b_2 Y - Y_{-1} + b_3 MS + b_4 I_{-1} + b_0 \quad \text{...(3)}$$

$$MS = MS_{-1} + E - M + KI + DD \quad \text{...(4)}$$

$$EA = EA_{-1} + E - M + KI \quad \text{...(5)}$$

$$Y = C + I + G + E - M \quad \text{...(6)}$$

The variables used are:

Y = Gross National Product.
C = Private Consumption.
I = Gross Fixed Investment.
M = Imports.
MS = Money Supply at the end of the period.
EA = Stock of Foreign Assets at the end of the period.
G = Total Government Expenditure.
E = Exports.
KI = Net Foreign Capital Inflow of the Non-banking Sector.
DD = Change in the total Credit of the Banking System.
PE = Unit Value of Exports.
PM = Unit Value of Imports.

The variables C, I, M, MS, EA and Y are the endogenous variables. The other variables are treated as exogenous. The values of the variables with a one year lag are denoted by Y_{-1}, C_{-1}, EA_{-1}, etc. In equation (1) the total personal consumption expenditures are treated as a function of GNP. Equation (2) states that the volume of imports in any given period is influenced by income, stock of foreign exchange at the beginning of the period, and importing capacity currently made available, determined in turn by volume of exports, foreign capital inflow and terms-of-trade. Using exports as an explanatory variable in the import function also takes into account the requirements of imports in the manufacture of exportable products. Equation (3) is an investment function where gross investment is treated as a function of imports, money supply and change in GNP.

Equations (4) to (6) are definitional identities. Equation (4) is the money supply identity, which states that the change in money supply is equal to the change in total domestic credit of the banking system, trade surplus and net capital inflows of the non-banking sector. Equation (5) is the balance of payments identity, which states that the change in the stock of foreign assets (capital outflow) is the sum of trade surplus and capital inflows. Equation (6) is the national income identity.

The model, however, does not have a separate export supply function and thus, may fail to incorporate several other interactions between income and exports. For example, certain domestic disturbances, such as export crop failures, will affect exports while affecting income at the same time.

II. EMPIRICAL FINDINGS

Estimation of Equations

The system of equations presented in Section I provided the basic framework of the models estimated. The total number of countries for which models were estimated were 13, of which 11 were developing countries and two developed countries. For the various countries, the data on the required variables in current currency units were taken from the *International Financial Statistics*. All the relevant variables of a specific country were deflated by its Gross Domestic

Product (GDP) deflator. The data on GDP in current currency units, as well as in real terms, were obtained from *United Nations Year Book on National Income Accounts*. The deflated series were used in estimating the regression equations. The equations were estimated by ordinary least countries. For each behavioural relation, the set of independent variables that led to the highest adjusted R^2 was selected. The choice of variables in an equation was also guided by whether or not the resulting equation system led to a convergent sequence of dynamic multipliers. Some of the estimated coefficients are presented in Table 1.

Table 1

Some Estimated Parameters

Country	m_2	m_3	m_4	$\frac{c_1}{1-c_2}$	$\frac{b_1}{1-b_4}$
Argentina	0.6871	0.6871	0.7099	0.6730	0.6115
Australia	—	0.5674	0.5971	0.5760	1.0100
Brazil	0.9097	0.9883	0.1880	0.8287	0.8430
Ceylon	0.6854	0.6854	0.6427	0.7720	1.090
Chile	0.5099	0.5099	0.1610	0.6386	1.0010
Colombia	0.8296	0.6448	0.6740	0.7730	0.8920
Ghana	0.3996	0.3996	0.4557	0.7080	0.8760
India	0.6312	1.1614	0.3217	0.6780	0.8348
Malaysia	0.6175	0.3809	—	0.4900	1.1400
Mexico	0.5801	0.5329	0.4302	0.7450	1.0462
Philippines	0.8895	0.8220	0.7635	0.6580	1.0430

Note: The complete set of estimated equations can be obtained from the authors.

The estimated coefficients along with the three identities were used to derive the impact multiplier of exports ($\partial Y_t/\partial E_t$ or $\partial I_t/\partial E_t$) as well as the interim multipliers ($\partial Y_{t+n}/\partial E_t$ or $\partial I_{t+n}/\partial E_t$, n=1, 2,...). The dynamic multipliers for exports thus derived are summarized in Table 2.

Table 2

Impact and Total Multipliers

Country	$\partial Y / \partial E$			$\partial I / \partial E$		
	Impact Multiplier	3-year Multiplier[a]	Long-Run Multiplier	Impact Multiplier	3-year Multiplier[a]	Long-Run Multiplier
Argentina	2.3003	1.6975	1.8764	0.4393	0.7084	0.6137
Australia	4.1399	1.7335	2.3926	1.1599	0.5706	1.0141
Brazil	1.7537	2.2460	2.2750	0.5603	0.7743	0.8333
Ceylon	2.6118	3.3673	3.4228	1.4458	1.0013	0.7806
Chile	1.6423	2.1916	2.7336	0.3039	0.6489	0.9817
Colombia	0.8898	1.9513	3.6606	0.3826	0.7749	0.8877
Ghana	5.3278	2.4780	2.9985	0.9483	0.5434	0.8742
India	2.0306	2.5861	2.6117	0.618	1.0051	0.8353
Malaysia	0.5149	0.8394	1.6302	0.1107	0.3023	0.7815
Mexico	2.9474	4.5734	5.2382	0.7985	1.2029	1.3593
Philippines	0.8236	1.9567	3.7499	0.4235	0.9447	1.3407
Britain[b]	3.3322	2.5992	2.1109	0.9004	0.7312	0.3292
Canada[b]	1.8557	2.0971	1.9279	0.8454	0.7905	0.2635
United States[c]	1.9900	2.0800	2.1300	0.2000	0.3400	0.2800

Note: Given the linear model, $X_t = AX_t + BX_{t-1} + FZ_t$ where X = vector of endogenous variables, Z = vector of exogenous variables, and A, B, and F are matrices containing estimated parameters, the impact and interim multipliers can be computed using the formulate

$$\frac{\partial X_t}{\partial Z_t} = (I-A)^{-1}F \; ; \qquad \frac{\partial X_t + n}{\partial Z_t} = [(I-A)^{-1}B]^n \, (I - A)^{-1}F\delta \qquad n = 1, 2....$$

a. 3-year multiplier represents the change in the endogenous variable in any given year due to an increase in exports of one unit per annum during the current year and in the two previous years (assuming that exports do not change in other periods).

b. Based on equations estimated by the authors, which can be obtained upon request.

c. Derived from estimates provided by Evans and Klein (1969).

In order to isolate the impact on income due to changes in export proceeds alone (all other exogenous influences being held constant), first the change in income was calculated with the help of equation (7), assuming that the magnitude of changes in real exports was that actually observed.

$$Y_t - Y_{t-1} = \sum_{n=0}^{\infty} \frac{\partial Y_{t+n}}{\partial E_t} (E_{t-n} - E_{t-n-1}). \qquad \ldots(7)$$

The equation simply states that the change in income today is a distributed lag function of changes in exports (when all other exogenous variables are assumed constant). The lag coefficients are simply the various dynamic multipliers, already computed. A formula similar to equation (7) was used to obtain changes in income that are due to changes in terms-of-trade alone, assuming that the magnitude of changes in terms-of-trade was that actually observed. By summing these two changes in income, one obtains the change in income that can be interpreted as due to change in export proceeds alone. The change in income thus obtained, was added to the known level of income in an initial year to derive a simulated income series. Along the same lines, simulated incomes were computed assuming that real exports grew at a constant rate per annum. For this calculation, the assumed rate of growth of real exports was the actual average annual rate of growth of real exports obtained by regressing the logarithm of real exports on time.

Average annual rates of growth of the two types of simulated incomes, as well as those of other relevant variables, are presented in Table 3. All the rates of growth were computed by regressing the logarithm of the variables on time. Indices of instability were computed for the relevant series and are presented in Table 4. The index of instability used was the one suggested by Coppock (1962).

Analysis of Equations

An examination of the estimated equations relating to the developing countries reveals the following. The import functions show that in all countries except Malaysia, stock of foreign exchange at the beginning of the period has a significant effect on imports. In most of the countries, the immediate impact of exports and of capital inflows on imports are identical; in Colombia, however, exports have a larger effect, while in India and Australia, capital inflows have a greater impact. In only five of the countries do terms of trade have the expected sign in the import function. In all the countries examined, imports have a strong effect on investment, as seen from column 5 of Table 1. In five countries, money supply has a significant impact

on investment. The long run propensity to consume out of GNP varies from 50 per cent to 78 per cent, as seen from column 4 of Table 1.

Table 3

Rates of Growth

(percentage per annum)

Country	*Real GNP*	*Simulated GNP 1*[a]	*Simulated GNP 2*[b]	*Real Exports*	*Export Proceeds*
Argentina	3.1297	0.6433	0.9340	4.1747	34.994
Australia	4.8459	1.9873	1.2354	4.5286	7.3483
Brazil	5.4918	1.3849	0.9225	6.5594	45.5180
Ceylon	4.3855	0.7777	-0.2110	-0.9755	0.7299
Chile	2.8531	2.9908	3.0062	7.6715	38.3097
Colombia	4.4554	1.4670	1.8950	1.6755	13.6795
Ghana	1.1427	0.5928	-3.8949	-4.3740	4.7211
India	3.9031	0.3235	0.2874	1.9323	5.7584
Malaysia	6.3564	2.2710	2.4792	4.7180	6.4282
Mexico	6.0034	1.2448	1.8451	1.5059	5.7270
Philippines	4.8950	3.7172	3.4651	8.6875	13.6728

Note: a. Simulated income with actual changes in real exports and terms-of-trade.
b. Simulated income with steady growth in real exports and actual changes in terms-of-trade.

Export Multipliers

As can be seen from Table 2, the long run income export multipliers for the developed countries are in the region of 2 whereas for most of the developing countries (9 out of 11), the multipliers are much higher than 2. The long run investment-export multipliers are always higher in developing countries than in developed countries. In most of the developing countries, the long run multipliers or the three year multipliers of exports are higher than the impact multipliers.

Table 4

Index of Instability

Country	*Real GNP*	*Simulated GNP 1*	*Simulated GNP 2*	*Real Exports*	*Export Proceeds*
Argentina	1.0466	1.0559	1.0014	1.2548	3.4415
Australia	1.0214	1.0960	1.0063	1.0969	1.2502
Brazil	1.0215	1.0415	1.0010	1.2837	4.0311
Ceylon	1.0293	1.0456	1.0035	1.0648	1.0632
Chile	1.0790	1.0258	1.0064	1.0996	2.9241
Colombia	1.0163	1.0189	1.0021	1.0991	1.6406
Ghana	1.0089	1.2383	1.0011	1.3086	1.2566
India	1.0384	1.0132	1.0012	1.0883	1.3088
Malaysia	1.0148	1.0326	1.0034	1.1366	1.1867
Mexico	1.0191	1.0274	1.0005	1.0535	1.2470
Philippines	1.0467	1.0218	1.0054	1.0950	1.7192

Note: Given the series X_t, the index of instability is computed by the formula

$$\text{antilog} \sqrt{\frac{\Sigma[\log(X_t/X_{t-1}) - \log(X_t/X_{t-1})]^2}{n-1}}$$

where 'n' is the number of observations, and $\log(X_t/X_{t-1}) = (1/n\text{-}1)\ S\log(X_t/X_{t-1})$.

Export Fluctuations and Economic Growth

The impact of export fluctuations on economic growth can be analysed by comparing the two simulated income series, one based on the actual changes in the export proceeds and the other based on a steady percentage increase in real exports. The simulated income series computed under the assumption of steady growth in real exports corresponds to the situation where there is a lower amount of instability in export proceeds than in the actual situation. It is seen from Table 4 that in all countries the simulated income due to the actual changes in export proceeds alone exhibits a greater degree of instability than the simulated income due to export changes at a constant percentage rate per annum. Thus, it is fair to conclude that a reduction in the instability of exports leads to a reduction in the instability of income.

An examination of the rates of growth of simulated incomes presented in Table 3 shows that in five of the countries examined, the rate of growth in simulated incomes, when exports grow steadily, is greater than the rate of growth in simulated incomes when exports fluctuate, as in the sample period. In Australia, Brazil, Ceylon, Ghana, India and the Philippines, a steady change in exports leads to a reduction in the average growth rate of income. In Ghana and Ceylon, there is a decline in income when exports move steadily. This is due to the fact that in these countries real exports declined over the sample period and a steady decline is far less preferable than a decline with fluctuations. In the latter case, occasional increases in real exports have a positive effect on income that might offset the negative effects due to decreases in exports. In India, the difference in the growth rates between the two income series is negligible. Australia and Brazil are really the exceptions where one observes a clear reduction in the rate of growth in income when there is a lessening of the instability in exports.

III. CONCLUSIONS

This study is an attempt to understand the relationship between income growth and export fluctuations. To avoid the pitfalls of cross country regressions, separate econometric models were estimated for 11 developing countries. From these models the export-income multipliers and the export-investment multipliers were derived for all the countries. It was found that the long run multipliers relating to both income and investment were generally larger for developing countries than for developed countries. In addition, for each country, the dynamic multipliers were used to derive the income path which is attributable to the changes in exports as they actually occurred. Also, the income path was derived assuming that real exports grew at a constant rate each year. A comparison of these two simulated income series definitely shows that for each country, an increase in the instability of exports leads to an increase in the instability of income. However, the impact of instability in exports on income growth rate is not in the same direction in all countries. In the case of only two countries, there is a decline in growth rate when there is an increase in instability of exports. The policy implication is that the usefulness of international schemes for stabilizing primary product prices or the export earnings of less developed countries has to be examined for each country separately on the basis of an analysis of its economic structure.

* The authors acknowledge the financial support from a National Science foundation Institutional grant to New York University. They are grateful to the referees for valuable suggestions in improving the paper.

References

Cohen, B., "Relative Effects of Foreign Capital and Larger Exports on Economic Development", this REVIEW 50 (May 1968), pp 281-284.

Coppock, J.D., *International Economic Instability* (New York: McGraw-Hill Book Co., Inc.,1962).

Evans, M.K., and L.R. Klein, "Experiment with Econometric Analysis of the U.S. Konjunktur Position", in M.Bronfenbrenner (ed.) *Is the Business Cycle Obsolete?* (New York: John Wiley & Sons, 1969).

Mac Bean, A.I., *Export Instability and Economic Growth* (Cambridge, Mass: Harvard University Press, 1968).

Maizels, A., "*A Review of Export Instability and Economic Growth,*" *American Economic Review* (June 1968), pp 575-580.

Massell, B.F., S.R. Pearson, and J.B. Fitch, "Foreign Exchange and Economic Development: An Empirical Study of Selected Latin American Countries," this REVIEW 54 (1972), pp 208-212.

7

India's Balance of Payments

The Emerging Dimensions

No other issue has dominated economic policy making in the last few years as much as the problems arising from India's balance of payments. The situation by the end of 1990 had become so critical that the country was almost on the brink of default. Foreign exchange reserves of the country were barely adequate to finance three weeks imports. Since then, however, the turnaround has been dramatic. Even as we survey the emerging dimensions of India's balance of payments, it is useful to look back and trace briefly the developments in India's external sector since the Seventies.

Trade Policy: An Overview

As we embarked on a period of planning, during the Fifties, import substitution came to constitute a major element of India's trade and industrial policies. Planners more or less chose to ignore the option of foreign trade as an engine of India's economic growth. This was primarily due to the highly pessimistic view taken on the potential for export earnings. A further impetus to the inward orientation was provided by the existence of a vast domestic market. In retrospect, it is now abundantly clear that the policy makers not only under-estimated the export possibilities but also the import intensity of the import substitution process itself. It has been as a consequence that India's share of total world exports declined from 1.91 per cent in 1950 to about 0.53 per cent in 1992.

The inward looking industrialisation process did result in high rates of industrial growth between 1956 and 1966. However, several weaknesses of such a process of industrialisation soon

---

Sixteenth Govind Ballabh Pant Memorial Lecture (January 18, 1994).

became evident, as inefficiencies crept into the system and the economy turned into an increasingly 'high-cost' one. Over a period of time, this led to a 'technological lag' and also resulted in poor export performance.

In the meantime, some change in the attitude towards exports became perceptible. Several export promotion measures were put in place from the early 1960s. The 1966 devaluation, while not resulting in the expected improvement in trade deficit due to a combination of circumstances, brought out the problems stemming from an overvalued exchange rate. Nevertheless, it will be correct to say that until the end of the 1970s, exports were primarily regarded as a source of foreign exchange rather than as an efficient means of allocating resources. Import substitution over a wide area remained the basic premise of the development strategy.

Foreign trade policy issues became the subject of intensive discussion in early Eighties. It came to be realised that a scheme of import licensing under which imports were permitted only to the extent that domestic production fell short of domestic demand, irrespective of difference in cost and prices, could only lead to inefficiency. The view gained ground that a more liberal policy of imports of capital goods and technology would enable India to reap the benefits of international division of labour. The attempt, therefore, was to move away from import substitution *per se* towards efficient import substitution, so that considerations relating to cost and efficiency were incorporated in the overall policy framework. It also became increasingly clear that production for export could not be isolated from production for the home market and that trade policy had to be integrated with the policy for domestic industrialisation.

While the signs of liberalised trade policy became visible in the latter half of Eighties, it was only in 1991 that the country embarked on a truly liberalised trade policy with a short negative list of exports and imports and with quantitative controls over imports withdrawn for all, except consumer goods. It was recognised that trade, exchange rate and industrial policies must form part of an integrated policy framework, if the aim was to improve the productivity and efficiency of the economic system.

A Decade of Comfort: Balance of Payments in the Seventies

India's balance of payments remained comfortable during the Seventies. The adjustment to the first oil shock of 1973-74 was rendered smooth by a happy combination of buoyant exports, spurt in private transfer receipts and increased inflow of aid. Exports, benefited by the expansion in global trade, rose at an annual rate of 6.8 per cent in volume terms and by 15.6 per cent in US dollar terms during the decade. An effective depreciation of the rupee occurred due to the link with Pound Sterling until 1973 and later, because of the lower growth in prices in India relative to other countries. Private transfers rose seven-fold from $ 296 million in 1974-75 to $ 2175 million in 1979-80 and in fact, in the post first oil shock period, financed roughly 80 per cent of the trade deficit. Within two years of the shock, the current account balance turned into surplus and it was only in 1978-79 that a deficit of about 0.2 per cent of GDP appeared. The utilisation of aid was significant and was substantially higher than the financing requirement for the decade, allowing for a build up of reserves. At the close of the decade the foreign exchange reserves stood at $ 7361 million providing cover for over seven months of imports.

The Period of Difficulties: Balance of Payments upto 1981-82

During the Eighties, issues relating to the balance of payments came to occupy the centre stage in terms of India's macroeconomic management. The impact of the second oil shock of 1979, the full effects of which spilled over into the Eighties, was more severe than of the event of 1973-74. Between 1978-79 and 1981-82, imports almost doubled. The increase in POL imports accounted for a little over half the increase in the overall imports. This was followed by the second-round effects on non-POL imports. Export performance was depressed by the severe international recession of 1980-83 and recorded a volume growth of just a little over three per cent. Net invisible receipts continued to provide support to the balance of payments, largely in the form of earnings from tourism and the sustained buoyancy of private transfers. However, the sharp widening in the merchandise trade deficit resulted in a turnaround in the current account balance from a surplus in 1977-78 to a deficit in

1981-82 of the order of US $ 3,166 million or 1.8 per cent of GDP. Adjustment efforts consisted essentially of an Extended Fund Facility (EFF) negotiated with the IMF, although there were also intensified efforts to improve domestic production of crude petroleum.

Easing of Pressure: Balance of Payments during 1982-83 to 1984-85

A reprieve came during the period 1982-83 to 1984-85, with the easing of pressure on the balance of payments mainly due to a decline in the volume growth of imports from an average rate of 11.0 per cent during 1978-82 to a little over two per cent. Net oil imports (net of crude oil exports which commenced in 1981-82 after the discovery of crude oil in Bombay High), declined substantially as domestic production spurted to 29.0 million tonnes by 1984-85. This, indeed, was the main cause of the easing of the balance of payments. Non-POL imports rose at an average rate of 3.6 per cent in dollar terms. Exports, however, grew only at an average rate of 3.2 per cent, in volume terms, due to a combination of adverse internal and external conditions. The invisibles account deteriorated as the interest payments to service external borrowing acquired a steady rising trend. Private transfers stagnated with the arrest in the labour migration boom. As a result, invisibles including private transfers and other surpluses, which had financed 89 per cent of the trade deficit in 1978-79 could meet only 57 per cent of the trade deficit in 1984-85. The current account deficit fell to US $ 2,416 million or 1.2 per cent of GDP in 1984-85 and reserves, which were US $ 5,952 million at the end of the year, stood to cover a little over four months of imports. 29 per cent of the financing requirement of the first half of the Eighties was met by the EFF. Commercial borrowings and non-resident deposits emerged as important sources of finance, meeting 21 per cent and 15 per cent, respectively, of the financing need. However, external assistance remained the major source of foreign capital inflows, accounting for 39 per cent of the financing requirement.

The Build up to the Crisis: Balance of Payments during 1985-90

The second half of the Eighties witnessed the building up of strains on the balance of payments. Current account deficits acquired

a structural character, remaining at high levels throughout. Large trade deficits occurred year after year despite a robust growth in exports. Recovering from the stagnation in 1985-86, the volume growth of exports in the succeeding four years ranged between 10 to 12 per cent per annum on an average. The share of manufactured exports rose from 56 per cent in 1980-81 to 75 per cent in 1989-90. Imports in US dollar terms rose in every year of the period. The volume of net POL imports increased from 12.4 million tonnes in 1984-85 to 23.5 million tonnes in 1989-90. However, the fall in crude oil prices during the period helped to contain the oil import bill. On the other hand, non-oil imports rose sharply by an average of 13.4 per cent in US dollar terms partly due to large imports of foodgrains in 1988-89. Imports of capital goods rose by an average of 16.2 per cent during the period. Export-related imports as well as other miscellaneous imports also rose significantly. The category of non-DGCIS imports, comprising defence imports and imports of ships and aircrafts etc., also rose significantly from about US $ 1.2 billion in 1985-86 to US $ 3.1 billion by 1989-90. The support from invisible receipts fell in the face of steadily growing interest payments and the outgo on account of profits, dividends, royalty, technical fees and professional fees. The current account deficit averaged $ 5.8 billion or 2.4 per cent of GDP during the period as against the Planning Commission's estimate of 1.6 per cent. The period also marked a deterioration in fiscal imbalances as the ratio of gross fiscal deficit to GDP rose from 6.3 per cent in the first half of the Eighties to 8.2 per cent during 1985-90. Repurchases from the IMF under the EFF exacerbated the deterioration in the balance of payments. External assistance, commercial borrowing and non-resident deposits shared equiproportionally in the financing need. The result was a doubling of external debt and a rise in the debt service ratio from 13.6 per cent in 1984-85 to 30.9 per cent in 1989-90.

The Crisis: 1990-92

Even though the events of the recent years are fresh in our mind, it may be of interest to recall the sequence of events. The Gulf crisis of 1990 led to an unprecedented crisis in the balance of payments. The immediate impact was the rise in the oil import bill. It also resulted in a decline in workers' remittances as well as additional burden on repatriating and rehabilitating non-resident Indians from

the affected zones in West Asia. As a consequence of the increase in the price of oil as well as certain other oil related imports, the trade deficit for the year 1990-91 deteriorated by around US $ 2 billion. Since, there was a deterioration in the invisible account also, the overall current account deficit in 1990-91 at US $ 9.7 billion was US $ 2.8 billion higher than in the previous year.

The major problem faced in 1990-91 was, how to finance the current account deficit? With the deficit rising, the only way it could be met was by drawing down the reserves. As at the end of December 1990, the foreign currency assets of the Reserve Bank of India stood at US $ 1.2 billion. This was despite the drawal of our reserve tranche in IMF of SDR 487 million. The low level of reserves in its turn triggered a number of consequences. India's recourse to the commercial borrowing totally dried up as the credit rating agencies down graded India. Simultaneously, there began an outflow of non-resident Indian deposits. In addition, there were serious difficulties in the rolling over of short-term credit, which was roughly of the order of US $ 5 billion. While current account deficit of the order of $ 8 billion was easily financed in 1988-89, a deficit to $ 9.7 billion in 1990-91 became almost impossible to finance. The task before the Government, therefore, was to explore means to finance the deficit. It was under these circumstances that India approached the IMF for an accommodation under the CCFF and first credit tranche.

The year 1991-92 began badly with a further draw down to reserves. The tasks before the Government were, on the one hand, to take steps to bring about a sharp compression in imports and on the other, to find sources of 'exceptional financing' to meet the current account deficit. A tight monetary policy was, therefore, put in place. Severe import compression measures which were adopted earlier continued to operate. For raising the needed reserves to meet the current account deficit, unorthodox steps were taken, including the pledging of gold. In the meanwhile, a stand-by arrangement with IMF was negotiated. Steps were also taken to obtain fast disbursing assistance from the World Bank, Asian Development Bank and some bilateral donors. Adjustment in the exchange rate, along with structural reforms in trade, industrial and foreign investment policies were simultaneously initiated. The loss of reserves was stemmed and from October 1991 onwards there was a steady build up. With the

sharp decline in the absolute level of imports, 1991-92 ended with a current account deficit of less than one per cent of GDP.

Recent Developments

During 1992-93, overall export performance remained subdued with a growth rate of 3.1 per cent in US dollar terms over the year. Exports to the General Currency Area, however, exhibited resilience in the face of recession in industrial countries and social disturbances, which affected transportation activity in Bombay. These exports rose by 10.4 per cent during 1992-93. Exports to the Rupee Payment Area, mainly to the erstwhile USSR, fell by 62 per cent in dollar terms and acted as a drag on the overall exports. The invisible account recorded a deterioration as travel receipts continued to suffer from the decline in tourist arrivals. Private transfers remained broadly stable. On the other hand, there was a rise in the outgo on interest payments, royalties, technical fees and miscellaneous payments. As a result, the current account deficit which had shrunk to $ 2.1 billion in 1991-92 rose to $ 4.9 billion or 2.1 per cent of GDP in 1992-93.

During 1993-94, a distinct improvement in the balance of payments has occurred. A strong export growth of over 19 per cent in US dollar terms, fall in international prices of crude oil and the continuing slack in non-POL imports have resulted in a sharp contraction in the merchandise trade deficit. During April-November 1993, it was US $ 532 million as against US $ 3,097 million in the same period of 1992. The decline in international interest rates has also provided a measure of saving in the invisibles account. Strong growth in remittances in response to the introduction of the market determined exchange rate has helped to counteract the deceleration in earnings from tourism. Despite some slackening in export growth in recent months, by current reckoning, the year could well end with a current account deficit of significantly less than one per cent of GDP.

At the same time, significant developments in the capital account have taken place. There is clearly a perceptible shift in the financing pattern in favour of non-debt creating flows, which by present trends, could amount to about US $ 3 billion by the end of the year. This would be accompanied by a reduction in the dependence on traditional capital flows such as aid and commercial borrowings. There

are also policy efforts to reduce dependence on the FCNRA Scheme and to offer in its place, attractive deposit avenues to non-residents, which however do not carry exchange guarantees from the RBI.

The Management of Balance of Payments: Some Issues

Linkages Between Fiscal and External Policies

Imbalances in the external sector reflect the fundamental fact that aggregate absorption in the economy is in excess of the domestically produced goods and services. Measures to reduce excess demand in the economy, therefore, constitute an important policy ingredient of the adjustment towards creating a sustainable balance of payments environment. Excess absorption can originate either from the private or the public sector or from both. In reality, however, it is the fiscal deficit of the public sector that is found to be associated with excess demand and the consequent deterioration of the current account balance. The link between the fiscal deficit and the current account balance can be derived from the following economy-wide financial balance identity:

Current Account Deficit = Income – (Consumption + Investment + Government Expenditure) = (Fiscal Deficit) + (Private Saving – Investment Gap).

Or, in the usual notation:

$$(X - M) = Y - (C + I + G) = (T - G) + (Sp - Ip)$$

This relationship between the internal and external sectors is merely an ex post identity and it does not bring out the dynamics that takes the economy from the initial balance to a new one. The identity, nevertheless, underlines an important policy issue. An improvement in the current account balance can be achieved either by an improvement in the combined balances of the private and public sectors or by an increase in national income relative to domestic absorption. There is, of course, one exception to this generalisation, which stems from the Ricardian equivalence proposition, which assumes that government fiscal plans will be fully neutralised by opposing economic behaviour of the private sector. Ignoring the debt neutrality proposition, the absorption approach recognises fiscal dimension to the current account improvement.

The dynamics of the inter-relationship between domestic absorption and external balance works both through income effect and price effect and, therefore, the speed with which a given domestic policy change can bring about external adjustment depends on the relevant elasticities and marginal propensities out of income. In a situation of crisis, the identity implies that serious policy measures aimed at curtailing domestic absorption will be a necessary pre-requisite for improving the external situation. However, over the medium term, what the identity means is that a sustainable level of current account deficit is related to the relative rates of growth of income and absorption. Thus, in any effort to maintain a reasonably comfortable level of current account deficit, domestic economic policy aimed at maintaining absorption at an appropriate level has an important role to play.

Developments since 1985 clearly show how precariously balanced is our balance of payments. Any external shock such as a rise in oil prices can put the economy in a serious situation at least in the short run. A tight balance of payments situation is, however, endemic for developing countries. Literature on development economics used to emphasise the two gaps that countries in the process of development were likely to face, namely, the domestic savings and investment gap and the external gap between imports and exports. To be comfortable, the current account deficit must be kept at a level that can be financed by normal capital flows. When the total stock of external debt is low, it becomes possible to finance a fairly large level of current account deficit because the lenders are prone to be less demanding at that time. Therefore, the ease with which the deficit can be financed should not become the criterion for incurring debt. Taking several factors into account, our country should move towards reaching a level of current account deficit which is no more than one per cent of the GDP.

The Merchandise Trade Balance – What Lies Ahead?

The viability of India's balance of payments, over the next several years will crucially hinge upon a vigorous export drive with exports growing by at least 15 per cent per annum in US dollar terms. The ability to achieve this rate of growth, however, would necessarily depend upon the international trading environment, which has recently

been witnessing rapid structural and policy changes. East-Asian economies stand out as outstanding examples of how a strong growth of export can contribute significantly to a sharp increase in income. By establishing a pro-export regime supported by various forms of State intervention, these countries achieved rapid increases in productivity. But a relevant question which arises in this context is, whether the export-push strategies that succeeded in the golden age of world trade growth between 1950 and 1973 can still be successful in today's environment. Despite misgivings on several aspects of the recently concluded agreement, at least from the trade angle, the successful completion of Uruguay Round should provide greater opportunities for exports from developing countries, including India. The tariff reduction offers from developed countries cover US $ 464 billion of the industrial imports. The share of duty free merchandise imports to the developed countries from developing countries, are expected to rise from 22 per cent to 45 per cent. The progressive dismantling of the Multi-Fibre Agreement should strengthen India's exports in areas where it has a strong comparative advantage. India's share in the enhanced market access through tariff reduction has been tentatively estimated between US $ 1.5 billion to US $ 2 billion per annum. However, the emergence of regional trading blocs is a matter of concern. Whether these trading blocs turn out to be fortresses or friendly coalitions, is something that the future alone can tell. However, India needs to develop an appropriate strategy to confront the emerging situation. Today, India's share in the world exports stands at 0.5 per cent. If the global exports increase by five per cent annually, even with an annual growth rate of 20 per cent in US dollar terms. India's share in world export would still be below one per cent after a five year period. Thus, it will not be the international trading environment which will constrain India's ability to sustain an export growth rate of 15 per cent per annum in US dollar terms, as much as its ability to build the necessary infrastructure to support such an export drive and create necessary domestic surpluses.

During the current year, import growth has been sluggish. As of now, the level of imports are lower than the previous year. While the slow growth in industrial production is one of the reasons, there are also certain fundamental factors which are operating to slow down import growth. With greater confidence in the stability of import policy, imports for inventory purposes have come down. The

stability of the exchange rate has also reduced imports in anticipation of need. Besides, the market determined exchange rate has also reduced imports in anticipation of need. Besides, the market determined exchange rate has encouraged larger sourcing of domestic supplies. The income elasticity of imports, which used to be around 1.5, has already shown a decline. With real output growing at an annual rate of 5 to 6 per cent and some rise in import prices, as recovery sets in among developed economies, imports can be expected to grow at a rate of 9 to 10 per cent in the coming years. During the recent period, the category of non-DGCIS imports has been subdued, mainly reflecting the deceleration in defence expenditure and the lack of access to international financial markets, which in turn has prevented the acquisition of ships and aircrafts. In the medium-term, a pick-up in these imports can be expected for maintenance reasons. POL imports presently account for roughly a quarter of total imports. The demand for POL in the economy has been growing and shortfalls in domestic production have added to the underlying growth in import requirements. The import bill has not shown any sharp increase because of the low price for oil, now prevailing in the international markets. In any future projections for imports, one needs to be conscious of the fact that oil prices can at any time rise again. A potential area of threat to the viability of our balance of payments, therefore, lies in oil imports. Better conservation and augmenting the domestic sources of energy must constitute an integral part of the balance of payments management strategy. However, as a short-term measure when oil prices are low, we should build our inventories or enter into some futures contracts. With an export growth of 15 per cent per annum and import growth of 9 to 10 per cent per annum, the future scenario may turn out to be manageable. However, there can be slippages on both counts and we need to guard ourselves against these. Even when the current account deficit comes down, the balance of payments will still need watching, as financing requirements will be large because of the repayments of old debts that will fall due.

Issues in Exchange Rate Management

Exchange rate management plays a role complementary to trade policy. With the abandonment of the Bretton Woods exchange rate rules, exchange rates of most countries have been floating. In the first decade of the floating exchange rate regime, serious concerns were

expressed on the volatility and mis-alignment of currencies. However, in the more recent period, there has been a general acceptance of the floating exchange rate regime, with all its shortcomings. In fact, many developing countries, including India, have opted for a market determined exchange rate system.

Influencing the exchange rate movement is one of the instruments available for correcting the imbalances in the current account. Obviously, besides exchange rates, there are a host of other factors, such as, world demand, quality of products, marketing skills and supply availabilities which have a bearing on export growth, particularly of developing countries. Nevertheless, many studies including those on India have shown, that real effective exchange rate is an important explanatory factor of export growth. Considerable attention, therefore, has to be given to the behaviour of the real exchange rate.

The foreign exchange market in India today arouses considerably more interest than ever before. Over the past two years, significant changes have been brought to bear on the exchange rate regime as part of the overall strategy to improve the functioning of the financial system. It is towards this goal that a correction for over-valuation through two step downward adjustment of the rupee was undertaken in July 1991. Simultaneously, the EXIM Scrip Scheme was introduced under which certain imports were permitted only against export entitlement. The merit of the scheme was, that besides providing additional incentives to exporters through premium on the scrips, it tried to establish a quantitative link between imports and exports. This was followed by a dual exchange rate arrangement, which entailed the surrender of 40 per cent of the exchange earnings at the official rate facilitating import of certain commodities at the official exchange rate. During the period of the Liberalised Exchange Rate Management System (LERMS), the market performed remarkably well, equilibrating 60 per cent of current receipts which were realised at the market exchange rate with a large section of imports, which had to be financed by foreign exchange obtained from the market. The market exchange rate itself remained stable; the spread between official and market rates moved in a relatively limited range around 17 per cent. The overall stability in market conditions witnessed during this period, in

fact, enabled the unification of exchange rates later. The new exchange rate system came to be market-determined and almost all foreign exchange transactions began to be put through the market from March 1, 1993 onwards.

The market response has so far been heartening. In the initial months, exchange rate rapidly came down from the February 1992 level and has remained more or less steady at the level of Rs. 31.37 per dollar. There has been no similar period in recent history when the rate has remained so stable for such a period of time. In fact, the period has been marked by fairly substantial purchase of foreign exchange by the Reserve Bank of India. Between April 1993 and December 1993, the Reserve Bank bought US $ 8 billion, while it sold US $ 1.4 billion. The net purchase, thus, amounted to around US $ 6.6 billion. This enabled the Reserve Bank to improve the quality of reserves by eliminating the volatile elements. The large inflow of resources has come because of the substantial improvement in the current account deficit as well as capital flows in the form of portfolio investment by foreign financial institutions and the raising of resources by corporate entities in the foreign markets.

The large purchases made by the Reserve Bank of India have prevented the appreciation of the rupee. While capital inflows do play an important part in the transformation process and may, to some extent, reduce the adjustment cost, its impact on the real exchange rate has also to be kept in mind. Capital inflows which result in a real exchange rate appreciation can have adverse consequences for export promotion. Besides, one has to take a view on the sustainability of such flows over the long period.

There has been considerable discussion in recent days about the convertibility of the Indian rupee. Perhaps, this was a subject which would not have merited discussion a few years ago. It is the unification of the exchange rate and more so, the strength shown by the rupee in the last several months which have brought to the fore the issue of convertibility. In fact, the question of convertibility does not arise when the exchange rate is over-valued. Convertibility essentially means the ability of residents and non-residents to exchange domestic currency for foreign currency, without limit, whatever be the purpose of the transactions. A distinction, however, is made between current account convertibility and capital account convertibility. In

relation to current account convertibility, there is a clear definition which is embedded in Article VIII of the International Monetary Fund Articles of Agreement. The clause reads "no member shall, without the approval of the Fund, impose restrictions on the making of payments and transfers for current international transactions." This implies that anyone, whether domestic importers or foreign exporters, should be able to exchange domestic money for foreign currency to settle any transactions involving the purchase of goods and services from abroad. With the significant changes that have occurred in India's exchange rate system, as well as the foreign trade regime, we have very nearly achieved convertibility on current account transactions. However, there still are restrictions relating to some of the invisible transactions, such as travel. To conform to Article VIII of the IMF, we will have to remove or considerably relax controls on these items.

On capital account transactions, convertibility implies the movement of funds in and out of the country without restrictions. While such a regime may stimulate greater flow of investment, there are risks attached to it. The major risk is the possibility of capital flight. Another risk is the possibility of macroeconomic instability arising from the movement of short-term capital movements, very often described as 'hot money'. A free movement of funds will lead to integration of financial markets and, therefore, an efficient domestic financial system free from administrative restrictions is a pre-requisite for the introduction of capital account convertibility.

In relation to convertibility on capital account transactions, it must be noted that there already are some elements of the capital accounts transactions which enjoy that status. For instance, in the case of both direct and portfolio investments, foreign investors have the freedom to bring in funds and take them back. However, as far as resident Indians are concerned, they are subject to control as regards their external borrowings. It should be possible to introduce convertibility on capital transactions in stages, giving greater freedom regarding short-term and long-term borrowings. A further strengthening of the reserve position will help in this regard. Its structural strengthening will help to even out any volatility in the flow of funds. The international capital markets will also have to open up for our borrowers which can occur in a bigger way only when the credit

rating of the country improves. This again should be possible as the macroeconomy stabilises further and we are able to further build up our foreign exchange reserves.

Elements in the Capital Account

Over the last two decades, there have been significant compositional shifts in the pattern of external financing. External assistance played a dominant role in financing current account deficits during the Seventies. This even enabled building up of the reserves. However, during the first half of the Eighties, the share of external assistance fell to 38 per cent. Drawals under the EFF contributed 29 per cent while commercial borrowings accounted for 21 per cent. NRI deposits provided 15 per cent of the financing need. During the second half of the Eighties, the share of commercial borrowings and non-resident deposits rose, each meeting 23 to 24 per cent of the financing need. External assistance declined to 29 per cent, reflecting poor utilisation of concessional loans, while the reserves met 12 per cent of the financing and the rest came by way of other capital flows. In relation to capital account, there are three elements on which some observations may be appropriate.

Commercial Borrowings

Recourse to external commercial borrowings in the form of loans from international banks, bond placements, trade-related credits and institutional lines was essentially a phenomenon of the Eighties. In the face of a deterioration in the utilisation of external assistance and persistent large deficits in the current account, commercial borrowings emerged as an effective source of external finance. During 1985-90, commercial borrowings provided 24 per cent of the financing need, almost equal in importance to external assistance. During the late Eighties, the cost of commercial borrowings was on favourable terms to the country with average maturity of seven years. Gross disbursements of commercial borrowings averaged $ 2.0 billion per annum over the second half of the Eighties, rising to a peak of $ 2.8 billion in 1988-89. In 1989-90, the year immediately preceding the payments crisis of 1990-92, gross disbursements of commercial borrowings amounted to $ 2.5 billion, comprising, mainly trade-related credits and syndicated bank loans. Borrowing in the form of

securitised instruments, especially in the Japanese bond market also entered the portfolio of India's commercial exposure.

Bank loans and bond placements virtually stopped during the years of the payment crisis, as India's credit rating was downgraded. Export credits supported by official export credit agencies emerged as the single source of commercial borrowing. Net of repayments, commercial borrowing yielded an outflow of $ 0.5 billion in 1992-93.

In the current year 1993-94, even though credit rating continues to be low, preventing access to international financial markets, there are encouraging developments. While trade related credits continue to be the major source of disbursements, there has been a modest increase in access to bank loans. Borrowings in the form of loans, including trade credits, presently account for 50 per cent of disbursements. Placements of convertible bonds in the Euro market have emerged as an important source of commercial borrowing and could well account for a third of gross disbursements during the year. There could also be modest disbursements through other securitised instruments. Aggregate disbursements could be in the range of $ 2.5 billion to $ 3.0 billion during 1993-94.

In the years to come, disbursements of commercial borrowings could be even higher than the levels reached in the late Eighties reflecting the international perception of strengthening of the fundamentals of the economy. Access to syndicated loans and securitised borrowings could return to the levels of pre-crisis years. Euro issues would remain an important avenue of accessing commercial markets. Thus, even though amortisation of commercial borrowings would be in the range of $ 2 to 3 billion per annum over the next few years, with a peak of $ 5 billion in 1996-97, as the India Development Bonds mature, in net terms, commercial borrowings could well yield inflows of $ 1 billion per annum over the medium term.

NRI Deposits

During 1985-90, non-resident deposits accounted for 23 per cent of the financing need. In a large measure, the inflow of funds under these deposits was a response to conscious policy incentives in the form of attractive interest rate differentials, exchange risk guarantees to banks and fiscal concessions. However, the experience of the crisis of 1991-1992 clearly revealed that excessive dependence on non-

resident deposits must be avoided. Mobilisation of deposits under the FCNRA was also not cost effective, especially when the hidden costs in terms of exchange guarantees are taken into account. In pursuance of the recommendations of the High Level Committee on Balance of Payments, a restructuring of the FCNRA Scheme was effected during 1993-94. Deposit maturities up to two years have been discontinued and interest rate differentials narrowed. Simultaneously, two new schemes, *viz.*, the Foreign Currency Non Resident (Banks) Scheme and the Non-Resident (Non Repatriable) Rupee Deposit Scheme have been introduced. While carrying all the features of the FCNRA Scheme, exchange guarantees are no longer borne by the RBI under these schemes. Thus, for the depositor, the incentives for depositing in India continue to be available. Incentives have also been offered to banks to encourage them to mobilise deposits. To compensate for the withdrawal of exchange guarantees and yet encourage banks to mobilise funds, these deposits have been made free of reserve requirements. Under the NR(NR)RD Scheme, banks are even free to fix interest rates corresponding to various maturities.

The response to these policy initiatives has been encouraging so far. Outflows from the FCNRA Scheme have been more than compensated for by inflows under the new schemes. Indeed, if all the deposit schemes are taken together, there has been a net inflow of $ 180 million upto November 1993. This healthy trend is expected to continue but it is necessary to ensure that these deposits come out of the genuine savings of non-resident Indians.

Short-term Debt

Short-term debt, which constituted 10 per cent of total debt at the end of March 1990, has been reduced sharply, as efforts have gone into liquidating the overhang accumulated in the period up to 1991. The level of short-term debt as a percentage of imports or as a percentage of total debt is less than that of other comparable countries. As has happened in many countries, recourse to short-term credit to bridge the balance of payment deficit can land the country in serious problems. When the situation turns bad, short-term credit can be easily withdrawn by not being rolled over. Short-term credit must, therefore, be restricted to the level required to finance purely trade.

The current policy in regard to the management of short-term debt aims at ensuring that it is permitted only for trade-related purposes and under normal terms.

External Debt

A country's external indebtedness is a mirror image of the behaviour of the current account in the balance of payments. In this sense, the outstanding volume of India's external debts represents the accumulation of deficits in the current account over the past years. Based on the data now available, India's external debt – as at the end of March 1993 amounted to US $ 85.4 billion. Bulk of this debt was accumulated in the Eighties. Although India is the fourth largest debtor, in terms of nominal value of debt (according to World Bank, World Debt Tables: 1993-94), the volume of debt comes down when measured in terms of 'present value method'. The share of concessional loans at around 35 per cent is quite high as compared with other developing countries.

India's external debt, as proportion of GNP, was less than 12 per cent in 1980. In 1985 the Debt-GNP ratio at 19.3 per cent was still one of the lowest. In 1992, the Debt-GNP ratio jumped to 32.3 per cent. It has marginally exceeded the ratio for Brazil though it is lower by three percentage points than that of Mexico. India's debt ratio remains lower than that of Pakistan (48 per cent), Indonesia (67 per cent) and Thailand (36 per cent). However, the debt service ratio in 1992-93 at 30.4 per cent was higher than that of Brazil though significantly lower than that of Mexico. This is explained by the fact that the external sector is a small part of the GDP in India.

Debt owed to multilateral institutions constitutes the largest component of external debt with its share rising from 25.6 per cent at the end of March 1990 to 29 per cent at the end of March 1993. Multilateral debt is for the major part, concessional, although the concessional element declined from 66 per cent to 62 per cent over the reference dates. Bilateral debt, the next largest category in India's debt stock, has remained virtually unchanged in terms of its share between the end of fiscal 1990 and 1993 at around 18 per cent. Bilateral debt is largely concessional in character.

The level of external debt, however, should be such that debt service payments over a period of time are within reasonable limits.

While there is no precise way of determining what this ratio should be, the general view is that debt service payments as a proportion of exports of goods and services should not normally exceed 30 per cent. When exports of goods and services tend to grow faster, then the burden comes down.

In terms of debt management, the initial efforts have been to hold down and phase out the volatile and costlier components. There are ceilings on the levels of publicly guaranteed commercial borrowings and short-term debt. Policy measures have also been instituted to reduce the dependence on FCNRA and to have in its place alternative schemes, which are cost-effective in terms of the absence of exchange guarantees from the monetary authority. The non-repatriable deposits will reduce the external debt. The sweeping changes brought in under foreign investment, technology and industrial policies have also ushered in a compositional change in the pattern of capital flows which lends strength to the debt management strategy. Even as debt is being consolidated, the gaps in external financing have been filled by an inflow of non-debt creating flows in the form of direct and portfolio investment from abroad. The inflow of foreign investment during 1993-94 is large by the standard of our past record. As the process of reform gathers momentum, these flows of foreign investment can be expected to be maintained and even increased. An enduring strategy of sustainable debt management essentially is a function of the behaviour of the current account. With the decline in current account deficit to around one per cent of GDP and the compositional changes in the flows to finance the deficit, it may be possible to bring down the stock of external debt and the debt service ratio.

Foreign Currency Reserves and Reserve Management Strategy

The payments crisis of 1990-92 clearly underscored the acute problems of liquidity and international confidence that arise when reserves are depleted to finance overall deficits in the balance of payments. The High Level Committee on Balance of Payments recommended a reserve management policy which envisages a moving target range of foreign currency reserves fixed from time to time taking into account factors such as the need to instil confidence in

the international financial community, the capacity to meet debt service obligations, the need to smoothen the seasonal flux in foreign exchange transactions and the ability to counter speculative attacks on the currency.

The institution of the market determined exchange rate system has led to a massive inflow of foreign exchange into the country. In the absence of demand for foreign exchange in the market, these surplus inflows have been purchased by the RBI to build up the reserves. The accretion to the reserves has been accompanied by a healthy reorganisation of the components thereof. It has enabled the ebbing away of costly and volatile elements such as swaps, FCBOD, FCNRA and the overhang of short-term liabilities. The foreign currency reserves at US $ 9.9 billion provide cover for about 5.4 months of imports. While this is a healthy development, it is by no means high as compared to other developing countries such as Argentina (7.1 months of imports), Brazil (10.4 months of imports), Singapore (6.3 months of imports) and Thailand (6.7 months of imports). However, the cover that reserves provide should be interpreted to include debt service payments, as recommended by the High Level Committee. By this criterion, our foreign currency reserves presently stand cover for 3.7 months of imports and debt servicing which can be taken as a core level of reserves to be maintained at any point of time. It must be recognised that there will always be some transitory elements in the composition of reserves.

Conclusion

We have come a long way from the crisis years of 1990-91 and 1991-92. The period of nightmare is now over. But the lessons of the period should not be forgotten. The ease with which financing requirements can be met from different sources, should not become the basis for incurring current account deficits. This is very often deceptive. In fact, international capital flows are fair weather friends. They begin to reverse and flow back the moment trouble spots appear. We, therefore, must aim at a level of current account deficit which can be sustained by normal capital flows.

The key to the maintenance of a viable balance of payments, lies in stepping up exports. Our level of imports is one of the lowest even when compared with many of the developing countries. If

exports grow at an annual rate of 15 per cent in dollar terms and with a modest current account deficit, we should be able to meet adequately our import requirements. It is sometimes asked whether a liberalised trade regime can land us back in the problems we faced a few years back. The discipline of the market determined exchange rate should steer us towards a near equilibrium situation. The market may also provide some advance warning signals. However, some elements of our merchandise trade balance, such as energy imports, will require special attention if we are to protect ourselves from external shocks. With an annual growth in exports of 15 per cent, which is a must, and with the change in the composition of the financial flows, we can look forward with cautious optimism to less traumatic years in relation to balance of payments.

8

The Exchange Rate System

Some Issues

It is now more than a decade since the world abandoned the system of fixed but adjustable exchange rates which was the centre-piece of the old Bretton Woods system. That system collapsed in 1973 with no official agreement on what was to replace it, and the major currencies were set afloat in world currency markets. These arrangements, which at first had no official international sanction, were later legitimised by the Second Amendment to the Article of Agreement of the IMF in 1978 which allowed members to adopt exchange rate arrangements of their choice.

The new system, which some have called a "non-system", is characterised by a mix of exchange rate arrangements. Major currencies float relatively freely in world currency markets. The countries forming the European Monetary System, float as a group against other major currencies and maintain a form of managed floating within adjustable margins against each other, with well defined rules of intervention backed by currency swap arrangements. The developing countries have not resorted to independent floating but have either pegged their currencies to one of their major currencies or, increasingly to a basket of currencies. Whatever the exchange rate arrangements adopted, all countries face a world in which exchange rates vary considerably and often unpredictably. In the ten years and more that the new system has been in operation, considerable experience has been gained and a degree of consensus has emerged on the functioning of the system and its shortcomings. The object of this

---

Co-author: **Montek S. Ahluwalia**

Presented at a Round Table organised by the Indian Council for Research on International Economic Relations (1984).

paper is to review the main elements of this consensus and to identify the outstanding issues in this area which remain on the agenda of international monetary reform.

The Experience with Floating Rates

In evaluating the experience with floating rates we must avoid the temptation to lay entirely the blame for the dismal state of the world economy in recent years on the exchange rate system. It is clear that world production and world trade grew much more rapidly under the old Bretton Woods system than they have during the period of floating rates. It is also true that developing countries, on the whole, have experienced much greater difficulty in almost all dimensions under the new regime. This does not however establish that the exchange rate arrangements were the prime cause of the difference in performance. There is a multitude of factors which affect world trade and production growth, and within that, the prospects and performance of the developing countries. The exchange rate system is an important part of the totality of influences on the functioning of the world economy, but it is not 'the only' influence, and we certainly cannot assume that the world would have been a better place, *ceteris paribus*, if only the old fixed rate system had remained in place. On the contrary, one of the elements on which there is a wide consensus is the view that structural developments in the international economy in the two decades after Bretton Woods had made the fixed rate system unworkable. It is important to understand the reason why the fixed rate system became infeasible, since any recommendation regarding exchange rate arrangements in the future must deal with these structural developments as given.

Infeasibility of Fixed Rates

The proximate cause of the breakdown of the Bretton Woods system was the inability to maintain the fixed dollar price for gold. The United States did not take effective corrective action when the dollar came under increasing pressure in the late Sixties, by when the 'dollar shortage' of the Fifties had been converted into a "dollar glut". This in turn has been attributed to the fundamental asymmetry in the Bretton Woods institutional arrangements in which there

were no effective disciplinary instruments that could be used for surplus countries and the key reserve currency country.

The basic problem arises because the maintenance of external equilibrium with a set of fixed normal exchange rates requires that the major trading countries accept the fixed nominal exchange rates as parametric, and adjust their domestic economic policies to ensure external account viability at these rates. This requires a substantial sacrifice of domestic policy objectives to the requirements of external equilibrium. Assuming that the initial exchange rate structure corresponds to a set of equilibrium real exchange rates, for sustaining real exchange rate structure through stable nominal rates requires that the rates of inflation in different countries should not diverge. Since differences in economic performance and in the importance attached to different domestic economic objectives, typically reflect themselves in different rates of inflation, the requirement that inflation rates should not diverge imposes an important restriction on domestic economic management. It is a restriction that may prove extremely cumbersome under certain circumstances.

It is in these circumstances that the alternative of delinking domestic economic management from the maintenance of exchange rate stability gained in intellectual acceptability. Floating rates enable countries to pursue independent domestic economic policies, making their own choices about the relative importance to be given to conflicting domestic objectives such as employment and price stability, while the requirements of external equilibrium are met by allowing nominal exchange rates to adjust to achieve the required real exchange rate configurations. In its extreme form, the delinking argument could be stretched to assert that co-ordination of policies was simply not necessary. Paul Samuelson, participating in a seminar in late 1978 put it as follows: "I have heard people say that we have to have coordinated policies under floating exchange rates. That is what we don't have to have. Germany can fight inflation if it wants to, that is its own business under a properly running floating exchange rate. If the Germans and the Swiss wish to regard us as banana republics, if our political system insists upon making compromises, which it does not insist upon making it is precisely floating exchange rates-not the automatic gold standard, not the Bretton Woods standard — that makes this possible".

Floating Rates in Practice: Volatility, Overshooting and Misalignments

The actual experience under floating rates has belied expectations-that the new system would provide an easy way of insulating domestic policy from external balance considerations. Countries have in fact followed uncoordinated macroeconomic policies, but floating has not ensured a reconciliation of these policies with a satisfactory external equilibrium. There is a widespread feeling that currency swings have been excessive, that exchange rates have tended to overshoot and that there have been persistent currency misalignments. In short, there is widespread agreement that the external balance achieved under floating rates does not constitute an "equilibrium" or at any rate not a "satisfactory equilibrium".

The Annual Report of the IMF for 1984 makes this distinction as follows:

"In a narrow sense one can even say that, in the absence of intervention by the authorities in foreign exchange markets, exchange rates are always at equilibrium levels, since they are simply a reflection of the preferences and expectations of market participants engaged in free and open trading based on information available to them. But that observation does not imply that serious misalignments cannot occur in terms of the relative prices at which international trade takes place. Whenever stable domestic economic and financial conditions are absent, developments in financial markets can lead to swings in exchange rates, that while reflecting the free play of forces in the foreign exchange market, may not be consistent with the proper functioning of the adjustment process in the goods markets."[1]

On this view, Paul Samuelson – as quoted above is thinking of what the IMF calls equilibrium in the narrow sense, which can be achieved by floating rates whatever the stance of macro-policy in different countries. However, equilibrium in the wider sense, according to the IMF, must be understood in terms of the proper functioning of the adjustment process in the goods market. The IMF does not define what exactly constitutes proper functioning but one can discern two alternative definitions in the discussions on this subject. One is to define equilibrium in terms of bringing the current deficits in line with sustainable levels based on some notion of underlying or long term capital flows. This is in effect what Williamson,

in the nostalgic jargon of Bretton Woods, calls "fundamental equilibrium".[2] A second and more ambitious definition of "proper" functioning would impose normative considerations on the basic stance of macroeconomic policy adopted in the industrialised countries. Much of the discussion on the functioning of the international adjustment process does indeed follow these lines and have focussed on the need for macroeconomic coordination among the major industrialised countries as a necessary condition for a satisfactory functioning of the world economy.

Ignoring for a moment the broader case for macroeconomic coordination, it is worth considering to what extent floating exchange rates can at least generate "fundamental equilibrium" in Williamson's sense. In other words, given the adoption of particular macroeconomic stances by major industrialised countries, can we assume that a system of floating rates would be conducive to achieving fundamental equilibrium without persistent currency misalignments? And would the resulting exchange rates be stable?

At the outset, it is important to recognise that exchange rate stability under floating rates can at best be understood in terms of stability in the real (price adjusted) exchange rates. Once an equilibrium real exchange rate structure, consistent with the basic stance of macroeconomic policy is achieved, we can expect that nominal exchange rates will change in response to inflation differentials to maintain the equilibrium real exchange rate. There can be no presumption of stability in nominal exchange rates as long as inflation rates are not the same and they are surely not likely to be the same if the switch to floating rates has been necessitated precisely because macroeconomic policy could not be effectively coordinated.

Even the achievement of equilibrium real rates in Williamson's sense in a floating rate system may not be easy. For one thing it is simply not true that as long as the exchange rate is allowed to vary, the current account can be brought in line with equilibrium requirements – whatever the stance of macroeconomic policy. It has long been known that exchange rate variations can generate equilibrium only if accompanied by an appropriate mix of domestic policy. Where the domestic policy stance is not supportive to adjustment – and this has often been the case – mere flexibility in the exchange rate will not suffice to bring about external balance.[3]

There are also several reasons why a regime of floating rates may generate unnecessary volatility and misalignment. For one thing, the fact that exchange markets adjust rapidly to current account changes, while goods markets adjust slowly to exchange rate changes means that exchange rate adjustments are likely to lead to "overshooting". An exchange rate depreciation induced by a current account imbalance may lead in the short run to a further worsening in the current account imbalance because of the well known "J curve effect", and this in turn could lead to further exchange rate depreciation. Such "overshooting" would be particularly large if the spot exchange rate is heavily influenced by perceptions regarding short term movements in the current account.

Another extremely important factor that militates against the achievement of 'equilibrium' Real Effective Exchange Rates in the traditional sense discussed above, is the increased importance – if not dominance of capital account transactions in the determination of exchange rates. The removal of capital movement restrictions combined with the enormous expansion in the volume of offshore funds held in world financial markets, has meant that capital account transactions among currencies arising from portfolio switches, can dwarf the size of current account transactions and exert a dominant influence on exchange rate movements. The factors which determine these asset choice decisions include the overall macroeconomic policies and prospects of different countries, and expectations of changes in these policies. Expectations are necessarily subject to considerable uncertainty. The possibility of random destabilising movements is further increased because information available on a day to day basis is often of a tenuous kind, yet it can have a substantial effect in terms of the volume of funds moved in the market.

All these factors making for volatility, overshooting and misalignment are exacerbated by certain institutional characteristics of the foreign exchange markets. The argument that speculation in the forward market will stabilise exchange rates under a floating rate regime, which was an important argument in the armouring of the early advocates of floating, especially Miton Friedman, simply does not square with institutional realities. Banks and multinational corporations which are the main institutions involved in making portfolio choices among foreign currency assets, are typically risk averse and

tend to avoid "weak currencies" or currencies "under pressure". This contributes to cumulative crises facing individual countries which can contribute to serious overshooting of the exchange rate.

Having established that the operation of a floating rate system is likely to lead to exchange rate instability and overshooting, it is necessary to consider whether these phenomena are quantitatively important, and if so, what costs they entail. It is useful in this context to distinguish between volatility and misalignment. Volatility refers simply to fluctuations either from period to period or around some trend level and these fluctuations may be measured either in terms of nominal or real exchange rates. Misalignment refers to divergence of the exchange rate from some notional equilibrium level. Volatility does not necessarily imply misalignment, since the exchange rate may be volatile; because the equilibrium rate is volatile in which case there is no misalignment as such (although this is unlikely to occur in practice). Misalignment also does not necessarily imply volatility since exchange rates may be relatively stable but persistently misaligned in terms of their equilibrium levels.

The evidence on volatility can be summarised as follows. There is clear evidence that whether we take nominal or real effective exchange rates, volatility was greater after 1973 than before.[4] The weighted average of monthly changes in nominal effective exchange rates of seven major industrial countries was 0.2 per cent during 1961-70. This rose to almost 1.2 per cent over the period 1974-83 which is a six-fold increase. There is also evidence that the extent of volatility has increased over time in the period of floating rates. This may be seen in Table 1 which compares the average daily volatility in spot dollar rates for three major countries in the period 1973-79 with the average for subsequent years. There is a significant increase in day to day volatility. Volatility, as measured by the Real Effective Exchange Rate, has also shown a rise according to the IMF study cited above. Volatility in Real Effective Exchange Rates of the seven major industrial countries was 0.38 per cent in 1961-70 and increased to 1.22 per cent in 1974-83, a three-fold increase compared with the six-fold increase when measured in nominal terms.

This brings us to the question: does volatility matter? The existence of volatility in the sense of random fluctuations adds to uncertainty in foreign trade transactions. The uncertainty can be reduced

by hedging in forward markets but this does not solve the problem. In the first place, hedging involves costs and these costs may be measured by the bid-offer spreads in the forward markets. It is interesting to note that these spreads have risen sharply since 1979 itself – a reflection of the increase in uncertainty in world exchange markets. Secondly – and this is very important – hedging is possible only over a relatively short period, typically six months and at most a year. While this is adequate for trade payments lags, it is not adequate for longer period contractual payments obligations as for example on debt servicing. At present, no effective mechanisms exist to hedge against exchange rate movements over longer periods, as many countries may wish to do especially in so far as debt obligations are concerned. Finally, developing countries typically do not find it easy to engage in forward market activity so that the effective scope for hedging available to economic agents in developing countries are relatively limited.

Table 1

*Daily Volatility of Selected Spot Dollar Exchange Rates**

Years of Quarters	*Deutsche Mark*	*Japanese Yen*	*Pound Sterling*
1973 - 79 average	0.40 (0.36)	0.29 (0.25)	0.30 (0.27)
1980 "	0.47 (0.42)	0.52 (0.45)	0.37 (0.35)
1981 "	0.73 (0.67)	0.55 (0.52)	0.65 (0.57)
1982 "	0.55 (0.53)	0.64 (0.61)	0.46 (0.40)
1982 - 1st quarter	0.51 (0.40)	0.65 (0.45)	0.45 (0.33)
2nd quarter	0.57 (0.54)	0.61 (0.56)	0.44 (0.40)
3rd quarter	0.63 (0.59)	0.61 (0.53)	0.52 (0.47)
4th quarter	0.49 (0.39)	0.68 (0.46)	0.45 (0.38)
1983 - 1st quarter	0.62 (0.59)	0.62 (0.59)	0.46 (0.32)

Source: *Annual Report* 1982-83, Bank for International Settlements, p. 142.

*: Volatility is measured by the average absolute value of day-to-day percentage changes. Figures in brackets are adjusted for the trend factor during the period and thus indicate the degree of "excessive" movements.

Thus, volatility has a cost and the cost has increased as the extent of volatility has increased. The cost is larger for developing countries than for developed countries. For the developed countries the consensus of opinion, thus, far seems to be that the costs of volatility are on the whole not large enough to have disrupted the level and pattern of trade. For developing countries there is some evidence that volatility in real exchange rates has had adverse effects (Coes 1981 on Brazil and Diaz-Alejandro 1976 on Colombia) but it appears that in these cases, the real exchange rate uncertainty arises from erratic pegging practices and not the erratic market movements of a floating rate.[5] This has relevance for the question of how developing countries should manage their exchange rates in a world of floating rates — a point we return to later in this paper.

These are very large magnitudes and it is interesting to note that the misalignments have continued over a fairly prolonged period. There can be no doubt that they would have a quantitatively significant impact on both the level and pattern of world trade. The costs of misalignment are many and varied. They give the wrong price signals leading to misallocation of resources. Because of adjustment costs, they involve loss of potential production and employment for the economy since resources cannot, in fact, move as much as required by misaligned exchange rate. Most dangerous of all, they give intellectual respectability to protectionist pressures especially since the industries affected are not only those that should naturally be phased out but also those suffering purely from exchange rate misalignment. Williamson makes the important point that while protectionist pressures increase in countries where the currency is overvalued, this is not likely to be offset by comparable pressures to liberalise where the currency is undervalued. On the contrary, there may be over investment, in export or import competing industries on the strength of the undervaluation of the exchange rate which, when the misalignment is removed, will have to be abandoned. In short, sequences of overvaluation and undervaluation may ratchet up the degree of protectionism with clear economic costs.

Some Policy Issues

The above review of the functioning of the floating rate system indicates that the system has not functioned as smoothly as its

proponents had expected. Floating rates have certainly not made the world immune from the adverse consequences of uncoordinated macroeconomic policies. On the contrary, inappropriate microeconomic policies and often at the root of the serious misalignments that have emerged under the system. These difficulties focus attention on a number of policy issues that are relevant in designing a better exchange the system. In this section we comment briefly on each of these.

Target Zones

Since fixed exchange rates are infeasible and floating rates have not solved the problems, there has been our understandable search for intermediate solutions and one of these is the concept of "target zones". The term is extensively used but is not always precisely defined. The basic idea seems to be that national authority, instead of taking the view that the exchange rate can settle where it will, should instead declare some sort of commitment of managing the exchange rate so that it stays at or near an equilibrium real effective rate. Instead of the narrow band of permissible variation allowed under the old Bretton Woods system, the intention seems to be to allow wider variation and also to have soft margins.[6] Since the target zone is in terms of real effective rates, the nominal exchange rate band is expected to be continually adjusted to take account of inflation differentials. The target zone should be published and it should be understood that monetary policy and sterilised intervention would be used to keep the exchange rate within the target zone as far as possible.

It is difficult to be confident about how a system of target zones would work in practice. On the one hand, the proposed width of the zone and the existence of the soft margins suggests that a significant degree of instability and misalignment would still arise. However, the implicit commitment to manage the exchange rate by using monetary policy and sterilised intervention can be expected to dampen these tendencies. In effect the "target zone" approach could provide mechanical signals from the exchange markets to domestic policy management to counter any excessive departure of exchange rates from fundamental equilibrium. The knowledge that such contracting policy would be triggered would also help to stabilise expectations in currency markets.

An important qualification on the effectiveness of the target zoning is that it is likely to be most effective only when target zones for the major currencies are determined in a mutually consistent manner. The target Real Effective Exchange Rates to be pursued by the major countries must be consistent with the patterns of current surpluses and deficits envisaged and there must be confidence that intervention will be symmetrically followed by countries at either end of the band. All this implies a high order of macroeconomic co-ordination to which we revert later in this paper.

The Need for Reserves

An important issue arising out of the adoption of floating rates is what it does to the need for reserves. The two dominant characteristics associated with the floating rate system are its equilibrating and insulating properties. As a result of the operation of both these properties, it was argued that the demand for international reserves would go down and that countries could manage with a lower order of reserves than under fixed exchange rate system. At a theoretical level, the arguments in support of insularity as mentioned previously, were at fault because they did not take into explicit account, capital account transactions. The actual experience of floating rates has also belied the anticipation that demand for reserve would go down. Frenkel has estimated[7] the demand function for reserves using cross section data for all the years from 1963 onwards and tested whether there was a shift, after floating, in the values of the co-efficients of the independent variables such as variability of international receipts and payments, the level of GNP and the average propensity to import. The equations showed that the demand for reserves has not been affected by the shift to floating rates. The fact that the demand equations remained unaffected implies that countries still feel the need for holding owned reserves inspite of the increased access to the capital markets and bank borrowings. Indeed, the demand for reserves may have been underestimated to the extent that the actual holding of reserves by developing countries in the second period may have been less than the desired holding.

Large scale official intervention in exchange markets also shows the continued need for holding reserves. It is estimated that official intervention under floating rates might have been even greater than under fixed rate. According to the annual report of the Deutsche

Bundesbank, interventions in the market were of the order of DM 18 billion in 1980, DM 21 billion in 1981 and DM 7 billion in 1982. Further data in this regard have been provided in a recent IMF study.[8]

The Working Group on Exchange Market Intervention has opined that such interventions had occurred not only for the purpose of ironing out temporary fluctuations but also for the purpose of 'resisting rate movements which bear no relation to the fundamentals'. Except for the U.S., the other central banks in recent years have chosen to intervene whenever they feel there has been a misalignment in the exchange rate. Thus, the equilibrating property has not necessarily been ensured by the floating rate system. Consequently, the need for reserves has not diminished.

Under floating rate system, it is true countries acquire an extra degree of freedom in policy formulation and implementation because they do not have an exchange rate to defend.

However, as stressed earlier, this does not free completely domestic economic policy from external factors. This is particularly when the framework has to take into account the inter-dependence which comes from both the capital market side and the international currency side. The recent experience with the U.S. dollar provides a telling example of the situation. A high interest rate arising from unusually large budget deficits has led to large scale attraction of the capital inflows into U.S. which in turn have tended to maintain a strong dollar. The other countries which have experienced capital outflows are not in a position to pursue independent monetary policies and let their interest rates to be determined solely by domestic considerations. Even under a fixed exchange rate system, a high interest rate will attract capital inflows. But once the exchange rate has reached the top of the band, further capital inflow will be held back, even if rates of interest are raised because there is always some risk of a fall in the exchange rate. However, with the floating rate, capital inflow can be accelerated by the prospect of a further appreciation of the currency. In short, a country may not have much more freedom in its monetary policy with floating exchange rate system than under fixed exchange rate system. In any case, the adoption of target zones would require monetary policy to be supplemented by intervention as discussed earlier. Consequently, the

need for reserves to prevent the domestic economy from having to adjust too frequently to external shocks remains large.

A continued need for reserves under the floating exchange rate system needs to be emphasised because there has been a persistent opposition to the creation of new international liquidity in the form of SDRs, on the ground that additional reserves are not needed. From the way floating rate system has been functioning, neither from the point of view of the developed countries nor from that of the developing countries, can it be argued that additional reserves are not needed.

Implications for Developing Countries

Much of the discussion about exchange rate systems focusses on exchange rate options in the industrialised world. The issue of exchange rate options for the developing world have, in general, received much less attention. Developing countries clearly have a deep interest in the efficient functions of the international exchange rate system even among industrialised countries and any modifications in this area, which improves the functioning of the world economy and world trade, would contain significant advantages to the developing countries. Apart from this aspect, however, there are exchange rate options that individual developing countries must necessarily face.

Most developing countries have chosen to peg rather than float for a variety of reasons. The merits of this decision are not examined here; to do so would take us well beyond the scope of this paper. But it is relevant to ask, how should developing countries peg their exchange rates? Increasingly, developing countries have pegged to a blanket of currencies. In some cases the basket is tailor-made, taking account of trade directions for example, and in other cases the basket is simply ready-made in the form of the SDR.

There is extensive theoretical work on what is the optional basket and how basket weights should be determined, all of which is designed to ensure a change of basket which stabilises the nominal effective exchange rate at some desired level. However, stabilisation of the nominal effective exchange rate is important only in circumstances in which domestic inflation rates closely follow inflation rates in trading partners. This is not likely to be the situation in most developing countries, so that stabilisation of the Nominal Effective

Exchange Rate will, in general, not stabilise the Real Effective Exchange Rate at a desired level, which is what matters.

This suggests that it is less important to worry about the design of the currency basket, which determines the extent of nominal exchange rate stabilisation, than to ensure that exchange rate policy is sufficiently activist to ensure that real effective exchange rates move in a desired fashion. It may not be possible to design a basket that ensures that this objective is automatically achieved, which in turn means that whatever the basket is adopted, realignments of the basket may be necessary so that real effective rates remain on target.

A second issue which is extremely relevant in a world of floating rates in which large exchange rate variations are likely over the medium-term is the currency composition of external debt. Since it is not possible to hedge over long periods developing countries must ensure that the composition of their foreign assets and liabilities is such as to minimise risk. In general, this calls for much greater diversification in the currency composition of debt with due allowance to interest rate differentials.

Coordination of Macroeconomic Policy

Whether the exchange rate system is floating, fixed or a combination of the two, there is no way that a country can insulate itself from external factors. It is an illusion to think that the floating rate system provides an escape route. This lack of insulation enforces interdependence. The more dominant an economy, the more wide spread is the impact of its domestic economic policy on other countries. Therefore, a satisfactory exchange rate system can emerge only if macroeconomic policies of the major industrial countries are stable, mutually consistent and conducive to satisfactory performance of the world economy. In fact, the 1978 amendment to the IMF Articles recognises this and enjoins the member countries to endeavour to direct its economic and financial policies towards the objective of fostering orderly economic growth with reasonable price stability. On paper, the amended articles imply a more active role for the Fund in its surveillance over exchange rate policies. The practice, of course, has been woefully inadequate.

In the light of the experience of the last few years, there is an increasing near universal emphasis on the need for coordination of

domestic economic policies. This raises a critical institutional question. How is such coordination to be achieved and who is to participate in it? Coordination would, indeed, be partial if the synchronisation of policies is confined to industrial countries aimed at minimising the imbalances among them. The international monetary system must remain 'international'. The goal that is sought to be achieved must be one of the optimal global welfare.

The equilibrium that results from any given set of macropolicies in industrialised countries affects the whole world often in powerful ways. The persistence of a system which compels the flow of savings from developing countries to developed countries – as is currently happening – is surely inherently inequitable and in the long run also, inefficient in the strict sense. On the contrary, the system should facilitate the flow of resources from the developed to the developing. The surveillance of the exchange rate policy of member countries has no meaning unless it seeks, as Article 1 of the IMF Agreement asserted 'to contribute to the promotion and maintenance of high levels of employment and real income and to the development of the productive resources of all members as primary objective of the economic policy'.

Notes and References

1. IMF, *Annual Report* 1984, p. 35.
2. Williamson. J., *The Exchange Rate System.*
3. See for example Artus, Jaques R. and Young, John H., "Fixed and Flexible Exchanged Rates: A Renewal of the Debate", *IMF Staff Papers,* Vol. 26, 1979.
4. "Exchange Rate Volatility and World Trade". *Occasional Paper No.28,* International Monetary Fund, p. 12.
5. See Williamson *op. cit.* Donald V. Coes, "The Crewling Peg and Exchange Rate Uncertainty" in *Exchange Rate Rules* (ed.) John Williamson and Carlos Diaz-Alejandro, "Foreign Trade Regimes and Economic Development: Colombia" New York: NBER.
6. Williamson (1983), for example, suggests a band of 10 per cent width on each side.
7. J.A. Frenkel, "International Budgetary and Monetary Control", paper presented at the conference on International Money, Credit and the Role of the SDR.
8. Exchange Rate System: Lessons of the past and options for the future, *Occasional Paper No. 30,* International Monetary Fund.

9

Exchange Rate Adjustments

Causes and Consequences

In early July 1991 (July 1 and July 3), the RBI effected exchange rate adjustments in which the value of the rupee declined by about 18 to 19 per cent against major currencies. These adjustments have to be viewed in the context of developments in the balance of payments and the foreign exchange reserves position and I would, therefore, like to first give you the broad contours of the problem.

The Seventh Plan saw a widening of India's current account deficit. The ratio of current amount deficit to GDP averaged 2.2 per cent during the period 1985-90 which was far above the figure of 1.6 per cent projected for this period in the Seventh Plan document. In absolute terms, the current account deficit averaged Rs. 7,771 crore (US $ 5.5 billion) as against that of Rs. 2,277 crore (US $ 2.3 billion) during the Sixth Plan period. During 1990-91, the balance of payments position, which was already under severe pressure, worsened considerably. The current account deficit increased sharply by about US $ 1.1 billion from that in the preceding year, reaching an estimated US $ 7.3 billion, equivalent to about 2.5 per cent of GDP.

The current account faced pressure simultaneously on several counts. There was a sharp deceleration in the growth of exports (down from the average annual 10 per cent volume growth of the preceding four years), a steep increase in POL imports (of US $ 2.2 billion) and a decline in net receipts from invisibles. The adverse shocks arising from the Gulf crisis contributed in no small measure

---

Speech delivered at the Seminar on "Devaluation: Its Impact on Foreign Trade" organised by Bombay Management Association in Bombay on August 2,1991. Reserve Bank of India Bulletin, Sept. 1991.

to this deterioration, with the hike in oil prices, partial loss of export markets and reduced remittances.

Exacerbating the deterioration in the current account was a drastic fall in the usual modes of financing, particularly commercial borrowings. Also, the net inflow of non-resident deposits decelerated. The extent of shrinkage of external financing implied that even current account deficits of the order of those prevailing in 1988-89 or 1989-90 could not be financed.

The combination of developments on the current and capital accounts necessitated a massive draw down of reserves, as well as, recourse to IMF resources. During 1990-91, foreign currency assets declined by US $ 1.2 billion despite the draw down of India's Reserve Tranche position of SDR 487.26 million ($ 666.50 million) and a drawal of US $ 1.8 billion from the IMF. The severe pressures on the external position have persisted during the current financial year (1991-92), with a further fall in foreign currency assets of US $ 1.1 billion during April. Thereafter, the fall in reserves has been contained and the reserves stand today at around US $ 1.3 billion.

Several measures were taken to improve export realisation, to cut imports and thus, shore up reserves. These included raising the cost of imports by applying steep cash margins and also raising the cost of credit. Apart from the approach to the IMF, additional support was sought from other international institutions and bilateral sources. Gold transactions also provided bridge finance.

The Exchange Rate Adjustments: Rationale, Timing and Magnitude

The response to the balance of payments difficulties has to be at two levels. First, in the short-run, there is an immediate need to stem the drain on foreign exchange reserves and to meet the liquidity and financing problem. Second, the fundamental imbalance on the trade and current account has to be corrected. As I mentioned, the balance of payments position had been weakening over the past several years. This reflected the growing internal imbalance, in macroeconomic terms, of spending more than we were producing. Over and above this, we face increasing cost of financing. An adjustment to more sustainable levels of capital flows has become imperative.

Downward adjustment of the exchange rate of the rupee is one of the instruments among others, for resolving these problems. A situation of continuing depletion of foreign exchange reserves generates destabilising market expectations. In the immediate short run, the exchange rate adjustment helps to reverse market expectations and thereby, stems the outflow of capital in the first instance and later encourages its inflow. Over the short and medium-term, the downward adjustment becomes an instrument to improve the country's international competitiveness and to correct the imbalance in the trade and current account deficit. It raises the relative price of traded goods (by increasing the domestic price of foreign currency) to non-traded (or home) goods, thereby encouraging production of tradables while discouraging their consumption.

The Real Exchange Rate (RER) of a currency which is the nominal exchange rate adjusted for the relative change in prices in the respective countries is a proxy for a country's degree of competitiveness in world markets. A Real Exchange Rate appreciation reflects a deterioration in the country's international competitiveness, while an RER depreciation reflects the converse.

Between October 1990 and March 1991, the Real Effective Exchange Rate (REER) of the rupee appreciated by about two per cent as a result of widening inflation differentials between India and the major industrialised countries[1]. And the REER increase was despite continuing, albeit slower, nominal depreciation (2.4 per cent against five currencies, over the same period). Further, in the five-month period between February 1991 and June 1991, the Nominal Effective Exchange Rate decreased only by 2.5 per cent while the inflation differentials continued to widen. All this had resulted in an erosion of India's international competitiveness.

In fact, with respect to twenty of our trade competitors, the REER of the rupee appreciated for a long time — by over 20 per cent — between 1979 and 1986. It is only from 1987 that the rupee has been depreciating in real terms compared with these countries and by 1989 we were only back to roughly the same Real Exchange Rate as prevailed in 1979.

Indeed, many of our trade competitors have made substantial exchange rate adjustments over the past few years. China and Indonesia for instance, have depreciated their currency against the US dollar

more than India has despite lower inflation; over the period end-December 1980 to end-December 1989 (the latest available), China depreciated by 68 per cent and Indonesia by 65 per cent while India depreciated by only 53 per cent against the US dollar, whereas the increase in consumer prices in China and Indonesia were lower (at 100 per cent and 111 per cent, respectively) against India's 114 per cent over the same period.

To restore the competitiveness of our exports and in general, to bring about a reduction in the trade and current account deficits, it had become imperative to make a downward adjustment of the rupee. In determining the extent of adjustment, it is necessary to bear in mind four relevant factors; (1) differentials in the price levels between India and the major industrialised countries, (2) extent of real depreciation of the currencies of the countries competing with India, (3) the degree of correction required in our balance of payments and (4) market expectations. Taking all these factors into account, the depreciation of the rupee value by 18 to 19 per cent seems appropriate.

A question that has been raised in this context is: why such a large exchange rate adjustment over a short span of time? Couldn't we continue to make small changes in the exchange rate as we had been doing? The answer lies in the role of expectations. In certain circumstances, it is better to make a significant adjustment and dampen anticipations, so as to attract remittances and capital inflows. Even in these days of fluctuating exchange rates, many countries have effected large, discrete devaluations in the recent past. Countries which made discrete changes of over 20 per cent in the Eighties include Indonesia, China, Bangladesh and Philippines. Such changes also help to make certain other adjustments more easily – such as the removal of export subsidies.

Yet another question that has been raised is that why the adjustment was made in two stages than in one. Basically the first adjustment enable us to test the reaction, so to say. After a second adjustment, it has been made clear that there will be no further change. In a regime of fluctuating exchange rates, it is impossible to stay fixed in relation to all currencies. The rupee is staying more or less steady in relation to the dollar and consequently, the rupee-sterling rate fluctuates according to the relative length or weakness of the pound-sterling in relation to dollar.

Impact on the Trade Balance

For the depreciation of a currency to become effective, the relative price change should bring forth the requisite change in production and consumption patterns. Exchange rate depreciation could lead to an improvement of current account only if export volumes rise and/or import volumes fall sufficiently to outweigh the price effect. Various formulae have been derived to indicate the conditions under which the trade balance would improve. The basic condition (known as the Marshall-Lerner condition) is that if the sum of the price elasticities of the demand for exports and imports exceeds unity, a Real Exchange Rate (RER) depreciation should improve the trade balance (if initially the trade balance is not in deficit and there are no supply bottlenecks). There have been subsequent modifications to this formula, relaxing its assumptions.

It is claimed that the price elasticities of demand for Indian exports and our imports are intrinsically low and, therefore, exchange rate depreciation would not help in improving the trade balance. It has also been argued that production patterns are not sufficiently flexible to respond to exchange rate changes. Some have pointed to the experience of the past few years where, despite Real Exchange Rate depreciation, the trade deficit has not improved.

To answer these criticisms, we need to know:

1. Is the RER relevant in determining exports? and
2. Is the RER a relevant factor in containing imports?

First, the RER has been an important factor in determining our export growth. From 1986-87 to 1989-90, export volume growth was running at a strong 10 per cent average annual rate. This period coincides with a sharp real exchange rate depreciation; the real effective exchange rate depreciated about 25 per cent between 1985 and 1989. Similarly, the period 1975-76 to 1978-79, when the REER depreciated almost 20 per cent, also witnessed strong export volume growth (an average annual 6.8 per cent) led by manufactured exports (a volume growth of over 13 per cent per annum on average). Between 1979 and 1985, the REER appreciated and export volume growth was stagnant.

It would be wrong to relate export volume growth to one factor alone such as the Real Effective Exchange Rate. There are a host of

other factors such as world demand, quality of products, marketing abilities and supply availabilities. Nevertheless, many studies have shown that the REER is an important explanatory factor of export growth.

Econometric estimation shows that the elasticity of exports with respect to the REER is -0.66, i.e., for a one percentage point depreciation of the REER, export volume would increase by 0.66 of one per cent.[2] Exports of manufactured goods are even more price-sensitive. In this context, we need to note that the composition of India's exports has undergone significant changes, since the mid-Sixties. Manufactured exports today constitute over 70 per cent of total exports.

How does the exchange rate play a role in export promotion? Exchange rate depreciation increases the domestic currency proceeds from exports. The exporter may pass this benefit on, by reducing the foreign currency price of his exports, in which case, export demand should respond positively. Or, if the exporter does not pass through the benefit by lowering his export price, then he would realise a higher profitability and should have an incentive to increase his supply and improve quality. Depending on the commodity, therefore, either one of the mechanisms may be predominantly operative.

In answer to the second question, I would like to state that despite notions to the contrary, our imports are also sensitive to relative price changes. A study done by us recently shows that the price elasticities are greater than one for manufactured goods and machinery and transport equipment, which amounted to an estimated 50 per cent of total imports in 1989-90.[3] This does not mean that consumer demand for other imports is not responsive to prices. In many cases higher import prices are not passed through to consumers because of administered prices. If imports, as a whole, are not that price sensitive, it is because a proportion of our imports – such as defence imports and bulk imports – are insulated from price factors. Consequently, the impact of the change in the value of currency is not fully reflected in imports.

I would also like to add that the exchange rate is important not only for the trade balance but also for private transfers. In fact, financial flows respond to price signals more quickly than do the flows of goods, which are typically slower to adjust. And invisibles are an

important part of our current account transactions. Gross receipts from invisibles is almost as large as the trade deficit. Therefore, exchange rate depreciation should have a positive effect on the current account balance too.

In talking of the impact of the exchange rate changes, one must reckon with lags in the response to exchange rate changes. There is the well known "J curve effect" of the improvements in balance of payments occurring after an initial deterioration. However, in the present context, when imports are subject to various monetary restrictions, one should expect to find the impact on the trade balance sooner.

For the depreciation of the currency to become truly effective, it is necessary to ensure that domestic prices do not rise to wipe out the price advantage provided by such a depreciation. It is quite true that depreciation, through an increase in the price of imported goods, will exert an upward pressure on prices. However, in the Indian situation imports still constitute only about eight per cent of the GDP. An analysis done using the input-output table of 1983-84 indicates that the maximum upward pressure on prices due to the downward adjustment in the value of rupee may be around three per cent. This assumes that there is a complete pass-through of the price effect on all commodities. However, we need to take into account the effect of other policy measures that have been simultaneously undertaken. A tight monetary policy has been in place for several months. By bringing down the budget deficit from 2.1 per cent of the GDP in 1990-91 to 1.3 per cent of the GDP in the current year, the pressure on prices arising from aggregate demand would be reduced. This should counter-balance to some extent the inflationary pressures.

As economists are fond of saying, the depreciation of the rupee is a necessary but not a sufficient condition for export growth and for an improvement in the balance of payments. A complementary set of policies needs to be put in place which will facilitate expansion of output, particularly for exports and curb aggregate demand to keep prices under check. This is precisely what has been done. In the immediate short run, exchange rate adjustment should facilitate the realisation of outstanding export receipts and accelerate, in general, the inflow of remittances by quelling the destabilising market expectations. With some time lag, it should improve the balance of trade

by stimulating the growth in exports and curbing the increase in imports. The tight monetary policy, however irksome it may be, has to be continued till such time as the balance of payments shows a significant improvement. In conjunction with the fiscal adjustments during the current financial year, the various measures that have been taken should make the difficult balance of payments situation manageable.

Notes

1. The Nominal Effective Exchange Rate (NEER) is a weighted average of the bilateral nominal exchange rates of the rupee against the foreign currencies. The Real Effective Exchange Rate (REER) is NEER adjusted for price differentials.
2. The estimated export demand function for India for the period 1977-90 is given below:

$$\ln EXQ = \underset{(3.73)}{4.28} + \underset{(5.38)}{0.71} \ln WGDP - \underset{(5.26)}{0.66} \ln (REER)_{-1}$$

$$\bar{R}^2 = 0.94 \quad DW = 1.7 \quad F = 104.90$$

t-statistics are given in parentheses.

EXQ: Export Volume Index, India; WGDP: Index of World Domestic Product. The REER as defined earlier is used with a one-period lag.

3. The import functions estimated for India's imports of manufactures, and machinery and transport equipment are:

$$\ln MGQ = \underset{(0.33)}{0.59} + \underset{(9.77)}{2.09} \ln GDPFC - \underset{(4.80)}{1.27} \ln RPMG$$

$$\bar{R}^2 = 0.91 \quad D.W. = 0.95 \quad F = 88.10$$

and

$$\ln MTEQ = \underset{(0.17)}{0.11} + \underset{(6.62)}{2.10} \ln GDPFC - \underset{(6.99)}{1.04} \ln RPMTE$$

$$\bar{R}^2 = 0.94 \quad D.W. = 1.84 \quad F = 59.84$$

MGQ and MTEQ are volumes of India's imports of manufactures, and machinery and transport equipment, respectively RPMG and RPMTE are the ratios of their import prices to their respective domestic prices, and GDPFC is India's gross domestic product at factor cost (1980-81 prices). For a more detailed analysis of export and import functions see (1) Kannan, R., *"Nominal and Real Effective Exchange Rate of Rupee", 1975-90*, (Mimeo), RBI, June 1991, and (2) Patra, M.D., and Rajiv Ranjan, *The Structure of India's Imports, 1970-89*, (Mimeo), RBI, April 1991.

10

Report of High Level Committee on Balance of Payments

April, 1993

EXECUTIVE SUMMARY

Introduction

A High Level Committee on Balance of Payments was constituted by the Government under the Chairmanship of Dr. C. Rangarajan, with Secretary, Deptt. of Economic Affairs (DEA), Secretary, Department of Industrial Development, Secretary, Ministry of Commerce, Secretary and Chief Consultant, DEA, and a nominee of Governor, RBI, as Members and Joint Secretary (External Commercial Borrowing), DEA, as Member Secretary, (vide G.O. No.1(24)/91-BP dated November 19, 1991).

Lessons of Recent Experience

The Committee reviewed the developments in the external sector during the Seventh Plan. The highlights of these developments were:

(i) There was a rise in the debt-service ratio from 13.6 per cent to 21.0 per cent.

(ii) Use of reserves was minimised mainly on account of capital flows and also as a result of recourse to short-term debt to finance imports of canalised commodities.

(iii) Exports achieved a very high growth rate except in the first year of the Plan. The share of manufactured exports increased but import-intensity also rose sharply. The growth rate in imports was broadly in line with the GDP growth.

(iv) Although non-oil imports (in US Dollars) rose on an average annual rate of 4.12 per cent, the total import bill did not rise because of relatively lower oil prices despite the volume of import of Petroleum, Oil and Lubricants (POL) increasing significantly. and

(v) Invisible account, which had given considerable support to balance of payments in the past, showed a sharp deterioration.

The Committee identified the following as the most important lessons learnt from the management of balance of payments in the Seventh Plan.

(i) No country can live beyond its means for long without running into difficulties. Budgetary deficit, revenue deficit and fiscal deficit all have implications for the drafting of resources from the household and other sectors. Combined with inadequate returns on investments made out of borrowings, they contribute to a situation wherein the environment was not conducive to a healthy balance of payments situation.

(ii) The current account deficit must be limited to a level that can be sustained by normal capital flows. The overhang of continuous current account deficit can be corrected only in the medium-term.

(iii) Export possibilities of India have been grossly under-estimated and the import-intensity of a strategy of import substitution not understood adequately.

(iv) There was an under-estimation of the impact of unrealistic exchange rate on the diversion of foreign exchange inflows from official to private channels.

(v) The composition of capital flows is even more important than their size in as much as they affect the future liabilities on both capital and current account.

(vi) While the opportunities available through foreign investments were not exploited, there was reliance on high-cost NRI deposits and external commercial borrowings which, though relatively inexpensive at that time, tended to result in bunched repayments.

(vii) An appropriate Real Effective Exchange Rate would constitute a necessary, though not sufficient, condition for export growth.

(viii) The level of foreign currency reserves and their management should be such as to provide assurance to international financial and trading community about the country's ability to service its obligations.

Review of Recent Developments

The Committee submitted an Interim Report which outlined the Liberalised Exchange Rate Management System (LERMS) in February 1992. The LERMS was introduced with effect from March 1, 1992 as a first step towards the full convetibility of the rupee on current account. The new system attempted to combine the advantages of a relatively stable managed float and the balancing properties of a freely floating rate of exchange by creating two exchange rate channels.

With the downward adjustment of the external value of the rupee in 1991 and the introduction of LERMS in March 1992, the rupee cost of the imports have gone up considerably and consequently, the basis on which custom duty has been levied had grown larger. Accordingly, the tariff levels can be reduced without adversely affecting the quantum of revenue accruing to the exchequer from this source. If this is not done, high tariff rates combined with higher import values would push up the cost of imports to a considerable extent. The Committee was of the view that from the point of view of improving export competitiveness it is necessary to ensure that custom tariff levels are comparable to those prevailing in competitor countries, many of which have reduced their rates substantially. The process of such a reform should, however, be structured and well thought out giving adequate notice to the domestic industry, both in order to cushion the impact on revenues and to ensure that there is a reasonable opportunity to Indian industry to become internationally competitive.

The Committee noted with satisfaction that the changes in the area of Foreign Exchange Budget provided the necessary preconditions for a gradual movement towards fuller convertibility of the rupee on current account. It, therefore, recommended that the

mechanism of allocation of foreign exchange should be dispensed with from 1993-94. The Committee expected the financial advisers in the Ministries to exercise appropriate control over foreign exchange expenditure just as they were expected to exercise control over rupee expenditure.

The Committee noted that the freedom granted to users in sourcing foreign exchange for their requirements had resulted in not only ease of operations but also relatively lower cost at which external commercial debt had been made available to Indian entities. It was found that the drawal of foreign currency loans had been less than in the previous years, but the overall availability of foreign exchange for import of capital goods had matched the demand.

Broad Policy Considerations

The Committee noted the need for redefining self-reliance in the light of the following statement of the Finance Minister: "Our vision of a self-reliant economy should be an economy which can meet all its import requirements through exports, without undue dependence on artificial external props such as foreign aid". Over the medium-term, therefore, the Committee considers that an atmosphere of liberal trade regime with a self-correcting exchange rate and a gradual movement towards international competitiveness would have to be the basic objectives.

The Committee felt that there should be a distinct shift in the policy framework in favour of equity as against debt in the matter of capital receipts from abroad. It recognised that Foreign Direct Investment (FDI) would contain both equity and debt, and the system of approvals would be applicable to all external debt. Hence, as an operational guideline, the Committee recommended that the approval of debt (excluding aid from bilateral and multilateral sources) linked to equity be limited to a ratio of 2:1.

The Committee felt that considerations of prudent debt management would imply restricting growth in the stock of NRI deposits, containing net addition to other external commercial borrowings outstanding and a cautious recourse to instruments such as India Development Bonds. Recourse to external debt for balance of payments support would have to be discouraged unless it is on concessional terms or with a very long maturity. Recourse to

exceptional financing, including IMF credit would be inevitable, but the objective would be to phase out such needs by the terminal year of the Eighth Plan.

Exchange Rate Policy

The Committee recommended that consideration be given to (i) a realistic exchange rate, (ii) avoiding use of exchange mechanisms for subsidisation, (iii) maintaining adequate level of reserves to take care of short-term fluctuations, (iv) continuing the process of liberalisation on current account, and (v) reinforcing effective control over capital transactions. The key to the maintenance of a realistic and a stable exchange rate is containing inflation through macroeconomic policies and ensuring net capital receipts of the scale assumed in BoP projections.

The Committee made the following observations on the working of LERMS:

(i) After the introduction of LERMS the rupee exchange rate was quite stable and there were very few volatile fluctuations in the market.

(ii) One major expectation from LERMS, was that the gap between the hawala rate and the market rate would be brought down and hawala transactions would be eliminated. Though the hawala market still exists, the gap between the hawala rate and the market rate appears to have narrowed down considerably and the turnover in hawala transactions was also reported to have come down substantially.

(iii) Exim Scrips were not applicable to beneficiaries of inward remittances under the earlier regime but under LERMS, 60 per cent of inward remittances were also converted at market rate. This was expected to improve remittances through official channel. However, the procedural delays for remittances through the banking system and the incomplete reforms under FERA appeared to have constrained the realisation of full benefits of LERMS.

(iv) Exporters justifiably felt that since 40 per cent of their export proceeds were being converted at the official rate of exchange, LERMS actually carried a tax on exports.

(v) The general belief that LERMS was only an interim measure and that full convertibility of the rupee on current account might be introduced at any time in the near future, appeared to have resulted in a postponement of foreign investment decisions.

(vi) In terms of magnitudes of flows, the expectation that 40 per cent of current account receipts would finance special imports, appeared to have been fully realised.

The Committee, in the light of experience gained under LERMS, considered two options in moving towards convertibility on current account: change the proportions to reduce transactions at official rate as an intermediate step or to bring about a unified market without any intermediate step.

The Committee noted that while the intermediate step would have the advantage of moderation in inflationary pressures and fiscal deficits, the earlier disadvantages such as the implicit tax, albeit to a lesser extent, on exports and inward remittances etc. would continue to exist.

The unified rate system, under which the exchange rate for all foreign exchange transactions would be determined by the market forces, would have the advantages of the elimination of the tax on exports and inward remittances, removal of the contradictions in respect of ACU transactions, transactions with the erstwhile USSR and the remittances and payments through NRE accounts and an end to uncertainties and the related anticipatory actions. As against this, some risks and disadvantages such as inflation on account of higher prices for essential commodities, strains on containing the fiscal deficit because of the higher budgetary provision needed for the debt servicing and the import needs of defence, higher cost of importing fertilizers, affecting both prices for farmers and the amount of subsidy needed, etc., were noted.

In weighing the advantages and the disadvantages, the Committee took into account, factors such as the relative stability of the market rate of exchange of the rupee leading to the expectation that the unified rate will be in alignment with the market rate established in the past few months, the measures taken to transmit changes in exchange rate to the domestic prices of POL and the favourable

macroeconomic indicators such as the lower rate of inflation, the anticipated growth rate and the sustainable fiscal deficits inspiring confidence to effect changes.

The Committee, after weighing the advantages and the disadvantages of the two options, recommended that a decision be taken to unify the exchange rate, as an important step towards full convertibility.

Foreign Currency Reserves

The Committee made a general recommendation that a reserve target range should be fixed from time to time and the foreign currency reserves should always be within the range and not allowed to fall below the floor. It has traditionally been the practice to view the level of desirable reserves as to percentage of the annual imports, e.g. reserves, enough to meet three months' imports or four months' imports. However, this approach would be inadequate when a large number of transactions and payment liabilities, other than those relating to import of commodities arise. Thus, liabilities may arise either for discharging short term debt obligations or servicing of medium term debt, both interest and principal. Hence, the Committee recommended that while determining the target level of reserves due attention should be paid to the payment obligations in addition to the level of imports.

The Committee recommended that the option of RBI converting gold into foreign currency reserves should be constantly reviewed, though an immediate case for exercising such an option is not established. Additionally, the Committee recommended that a part of gold reserves, say 30 per cent, should be available for conversion at short notice into currency resources to meet contingencies.

External Assistance

Considering the vital role that can be played by timely utilisation of external assistance in placing the country's balance of payments position on a sound footing, the Committee recommended that immediate action be considered in the following areas:

(i) A review of the existing projects with a view to identifying those where the progress is slow, those that need redefining of project scope or coverage and where cancellation

would be better than continuing to pay commitment fees and keeping them in our books.

(ii) As recommended by the National Development Council, 100 per cent of external assistance may be passed on to the states for all sectors.

(iii) Additional Central assistance may be released to the states on a monthly basis. The advances at any point of time may be limited to around eight per cent of the accepted reimbursement during the year.

(iv) Since availability of rupee resources is one of the major constraints, priority may be accorded to externally-aided projects in making plan allocations and corresponding budget provisions. However, overall resource availability has to be increased to ensure adequate and timely absorption of external aid without sacrificing the larger segment of projects other than those externally aided.

(v) The contracting procedures will have to be streamlined and decentralised so that reference to Government would become unnecessary. General guidelines on evaluation procedures should suffice.

With a view to eliminate certain ambiguities in the administration of external assistance, the Committee recommended that the Department of Economic Affairs may continue to play the role of a nodal agency in terms of developing pipeline (to specifically address the issue of resource availability, commitment of user-unit and issues of direct lending/on-lending/additionality), negotiating external assistance and monitoring implementation. However, the issue of direct lending *vs* on-lending should recognise the need for disintermediation by Government. Consequently, a framework is recommended indicating the different uses, users and methods to be adopted for different categories of external assistance.

The rupee debt of the country is of three categories, *viz.*, NRI deposits denominated in rupees but repayable in foreign currency, NRI deposits denominated and repayable in rupees, and bilateral arrangements, especially with the former Soviet Union, where the debt is expected to be discharged by exporting goods and services to non-residents but liabilities are expressed in rupee terms as per

agreed rates. The Committee noted that India and Russia have reached a new agreement on the mechanism for determining the rupee value of the Rouble denominated debt.

Commercial Borrowings

The Committee noted that, on the whole, in terms of cost, maturity, currency composition, markets, liability management and exercise of control over individual transactions, the performance in regard to external commercial borrowings was satisfactory. However, the events following the Gulf crisis led to a drastic change in India's commercial borrowing prospects and policies. The flow of funds virtually stopped when the Credit Rating Agencies announced a downgrading of the rating for India and Indian entities in 1990.

With this background the Committee identified the major issues that have to be addressed in the context of external commercial borrowings. The Committee recommended the following approach:

(i) Considering the maturity profiles and the fact that a large part of external commercial debt is through institutional sources, the amounts that can be subjected to refinance would be just about US $ 500 million per year for the next two years. As long as there is a possibility of raising commercial borrowings with longer maturity to sustain the overall balance, there is no advantage in giving signals of distortion for such small amounts by taking recourse to debt refinance mechanism.

(ii) There is a danger that recourse to debt-equity swaps would reinforce sentiments that would equate India with some of the countries that have defaulted in honouring their debt obligations. The Committee, therefore, concluded that debt-equity conversion was not a desirable option for debt management in India.

(iii) There is a need to keep the option of sovereign borrowing in external commercial markets open, but it should be exercised when the need and cost-advantage are established.

(iv) The Committee felt that (a) caution should be exercised in creating permanent institutions or corporate bodies for mobilising gold; (b) gold bonds may be launched

immediately as an experiment; and (c) a review be made of the economics of such a scheme in 1993-94.

(v) The practices of liability management should be encouraged.

(vi) On an average, the disbursements of external commercial borrowings should not exceed US$ 2.5 billion per year during the Eighth Five-Year Plan.

(vii) No approval should be accorded for any commercial borrowing with a maturity of less than five years.

(viii) The Committee recommended a cautious approach to guarantee for external borrowings.

NRI Deposits

The Committee recommended that there was a need for a deliberate policy shift with regard to FCNR deposits with a view to reducing volatility and the cost and to make it attract the genuine savings of NRIs. To this end, the Committee suggested that the NRI deposit scheme be modified on the following terms:

(a) FCNR deposits should have a minimum maturity of one year; and

(b) The differential between international interest rates and FCNR rates should be progressively reduced to ensure that the scheme benefits only the genuine savers.

The Committee was also of the opinion that a market for NRI Bonds should be developed to satisfy the investor appetite among NRIs for some form of medium term investments in India with facility for secondary trading.

Short Term Debt

The Committee noted that serious concerns had been expressed about the level of short term debt and its contribution to the crisis situation in the recent past.

In the light of past experience, the Committee recommended that the policy of the Government and the RBI in regard to the management of short term debt should be on the following lines:

(i) Short term debt should be permitted only for trade-related purposes and under normal terms;

(ii) Recourse to short term debt should not be taken as an instrument for protecting the reserves;

(iii) No roll-over beyond six months should be resorted to in regard to any short-term facilities without careful consideration of the implications;

(iv) Any short-term debt not governed by the above considerations should be specifically approved by RBI after satisfying itself that recourse to such debt was trade-related or on genuine cost considerations; and

(v) RBI should set up a monitoring system for short term debt so that it is possible to ascertain with a reasonable amount of accuracy the extent of such debt that may be outstanding at any point of time.

Structure of External Debt

The Committee noted with satisfaction, the Reports of the Policy Group and Task Force on External Debt Statistics of India and its adoption by the Government and the Reserve Bank of India. The Committee also noted that a Standing High Level Committee on Debt Management had been constituted by the Government. They would facilitate improvements in the structure and management of external debt.

In regard to the future directions in the structure of debt, the Committee recommended necessary policy and procedural changes to bring about the following: quick disbursement of concessional and semi-concessional flows; disintermediation of Government to the maximum extent in aid and flows; absorption of aid only when it is consistent with the requirements of the enterprise concerned or department/State concerned; and continuation of NRI deposits at a level that would ensure no net outflow but with longer maturities profile; insistence on a minimum maturity of five years for commercial borrowings except for purposes of consolidation of short-term debt; recourse to commercial sources of financing, essentially to meet foreign currency expenditures, particularly for non-tradeable goods, priority sectors like oil and fertilizer, export oriented units, etc., or

borrowings linked with inflow of equity; and a prudent policy of extending guarantees by sovereign or public sector financial and banking institutions.

Foreign Investment

The Committee felt that the steps already taken would go a long way in promoting the confidence of foreign investors for investing in India. The Committee noted the important parameters of a global nature that would determine the scope and limits for foreign investments in the immediate future and examined the concerns of foreign investors.

Having recognised the concerns of the foreign investors, the Committee, recommended that a National Investment Law be seriously considered codifying the existing policy and practices relating to dividend repatriation, disinvestment, non-discrimination subject to conditions that may be specified, employment of foreign nationals, non-expropriation, and sanction and servicing of external commercial borrowings. Such a law could also provide for policy procedures and institutional framework for approval of investments under the non-automatic route, according pioneer status or domestic-investor status, new instruments of private commercial flows and applicability of local or international laws. Such an Investment Law need not, in any way, exclude consideration of bilateral investment treaties.

The Committee noted with satisfaction the most recent liberalisation measures in FERA and recommended that an appropriate framework be evolved to promote Indian investment abroad in desired directions, countries and sectors in addition to liberalising procedures.

Exports

To achieve the targets set forth in the Eighth Plan and reflected in the balance of payments projections in this Report, the Committee recommended measures for export promotion including,

(i) Movement towards fuller convertibility of the rupee since partial convertibility imposes a tax on exports;

(ii) Reforms in interest rates on export credit to ensure reasonable costs to exporter;

(iii) Stability of existing export incentives, i.e., an assurance that the incentives would continue;

(iv) Encouraging deemed exports by measures such as freedom for Indian bidders to bid in foreign currency when they bid under ICB procedures; (since implemented)

(v) Simplification of Export-Import Policy especially replacing quantitative curbs on exports with duties.

BoP Projections for Medium Term

In making the balance of payments projections, the Committee kept in view (a) the macroeconomic parameters as envisaged in the Eighth Plan, (b) likely impact of the policy changes, (c) outlook and prospects of international trade, and (d) updated estimates for 1991-92 and the latest available estimates for 1992-93.

An average annual growth in exports of at least 15 per cent in dollar terms over the medium term is considered necessary as well as feasible. The Committee strongly recommended that trade policy and exchange rate regime be managed not only in a stable manner but also oriented towards export promotion.

The Committee believed that the import growth rate might be marginally higher than what had been estimated on the basis of import elasticity to GDP at 1.5.

Net inflows in the 'invisibles' component of the current account are estimated to contribute almost a negligible share, even though there would be a turn around from a net outflow within a year or two.

The Committee felt that the order of current account deficit envisaged, *viz.*, 1.6 per cent of GDP, can be met through a sustainable level of net capital receipts.

Exceptional financing arrangements of the order of $ 3 billion per year on a gross basis would be necessary during the medium term. However, these could be reduced somewhat through better export performance, better 'Invisibles' receipts and higher investment inflows, all of which is not impossible.

Balance of Payments – Statistical Issues

The Committee recommended certain changes in the compilation and presentation of balance of payments statistics. Having identified

the major factors contributing towards a difference between DGCI&S data and BoP data in respect of imports, the Committee recommended that:

(i) All Defence debt may be formally registered as commercial debt as per the normal practice.

(ii) Debt in respect of Rupee Payment Area (RPA) may be reflected separately in the capital account consistent with recently concluded Rupee-Rouble Agreement.

(iii) In respect of Defence debt to general currency area (GCA), principal repayment is to be reflected in the capital account and interest payment under 'Invisibles'.

(iv) Where imports do not pass through customs declaration, concerned agencies may be requested to report in a consolidated form, the value of imports on a routine basis for purposes of incorporation into the customs data, and

(v) Information system may be established through Ministry of Shipping and Ministry of Petroleum to obtain information on payments made but not reflected in customs data.

The Committee recommended that a Technical Group be appointed by RBI with representatives from the Ministry of Finance and the Ministry of Commerce similar to the Policy Group on External Debt Statistics, to review in detail, timeliness compilation methods and suitability of reporting systems for purposes of management of balance of payments.

I. INTRODUCTION

1.1 A High Level Committee on Balance of Payments was constituted by the Government under the Chairmanship of Dr. C. Rangarajan, with Secretary, Department of Economic Affairs (DEA), Secretary, Department of Industrial Development, Secretary, Ministry of Commerce, Secretary and Chief Consultant, DEA, a nominee of Governor RBI, as Member and Joint Secretary (External Commercial Borrowing), DEA, as member-Secretary (Vide G.O. No. 1(24)/91-BP dated 19.11.1991). The following are the terms of reference:

(a) To make projections of the various elements in balance of payments over the next five years and estimate the financing gap taking into account the repayment obligations.

(b) To study the appropriate mix of capital flows and to suggest measures to bring about the desired changes.

(c) To examine and suggest ways of changing the existing structure of debt.

(d) To examine the possibility of converting certain types of existing debt into equity, to suggest ways to enhance the flows of invisible earnings, including private remittances through the banking system, and

(e) To examine the functioning of the existing exchange rate regime in the context of the move to Exim-Scrip and to consider the implications of a shift to convertibility on current transactions in the near future.

1.2 In order to tackle the severe BoP crisis faced by the country during 1990-91 and 1991-92, the Government took several emergency measures such as the raising of foreign currency resources using gold, the downward adjustment of the external value of the rupee, drastic curtailment of imports, etc., to pull the economy back from the brink of default in debt service. Simultaneously, with a view to finding a long-term solution to the problem, the Government undertook policy initiatives such as a macroeconomic stabilisation programme through a planned reduction in fiscal deficit and, a trade policy reform to create an environment which would give an impetus to increase India's share in world trade, in general, and growth in the country's exports, in particular. The package included Industrial Policy Reforms to promote a more efficient and competitive industrial economy and reforms to improve and streamline the working of the public enterprises. It was in this context that the need for making medium term projections of the country's BoP scenario and for evolving appropriate measures to bring down the current account deficits to sustainable levels was felt. The formulation of the Eighth Five-Year Plan warranted that these policy initiatives be integrated with a medium term strategy for the management of the external sector.

1.3 The Committee was required to give its report by March 1, 1992. However, it submitted an interim report and sought extension of time which was granted by the Government. In the context of the all-encompassing and complex nature of the tasks entrusted to the

Committee, the members have been holding continuous and extensive discussions among themselves and with the other officials. Various background papers prepared in RBI, GoI and the Planning Commission on several aspects of BoP management and policy were made use of by the Committee in its work.

II. LESSONS OF RECENT EXPERIENCE

2.1 The Committee noted the following developments during the Seventh Plan.

(a) There was a widening of current account deficit, the ratio of such deficit to GDP averaging 2.4 per cent as against the projection of 1.6 per cent.

(b) Current account deficit was financed by external assistance, commercial borrowings and deposits by non-resident Indians increasing the debt-service ratio from 13.6 per cent to 21 per cent by the end of the Plan.

(c) Use of reserves was minimised mainly on account of capital flows and partly due to recourse to short term debt to finance imports of canalised commodities.

(d) Exports achieved a very high growth rate except in the first year of the Plan.

(e) The share of manufactured exports increased but their import-intensity also rose sharply.

(f) The growth rate in imports was broadly in line with GDP growth.

(g) The non-DGCIS imports mostly accounted for by defence, increased substantially (the other factors being procedural variations in exchange rate adopted and difference in timing of payments *vis-à-vis* commodity movement).

(h) Non-oil imports (in US dollars) rose at an average annual rate of over 12 per cent but total import bill did not rise because of the fortuitous circumstances of relatively lower oil prices, though volume of import of POL increased significantly, and

(i) The invisible account which had given considerable support to the balance of payments in the past showed a sharp deterioration with stagnant earnings from tourism, a modest increase in private transfers and mounting interest burden.

2.2 Thus, the positive developments on the export front were overshadowed by the structural problems in external sector. With the onset of the Gulf crisis and political uncertainties, such a fragile situation resulted in a crisis situation of such magnitude that economic policy making had to be almost totally devoted to the management of balance of payments during 1991-92. The Gulf crisis had an immediate effect on India's oil import bill. It could, however, have been managed with appropriate restraints on imports but for the liquidity crisis caused by the rapid withdrawal of NRI deposits and denial of normal access to external commercial borrowings as a result of the downgrading of India's credit rating. The liquidity crisis expressed itself in terms of a total denial of short term facilities and difficulties in honouring letters of credit. Such a situation required harsh measures of import restriction, access to exceptional financing through IMF, World Bank, ADB and bilateral channels and temporary utilisation of gold available with Government and RBI for raising foreign currency resources to meet contractual commitments.

2.3 The Committee noted that, with the onset of relative political stability and initiation of a package of economic reforms, there had been some restoration of international confidence. Even so, the sustainability of balance of payments required not only substantial support from multilateral and bilateral agencies but also recourse to two somewhat extraordinary measures, namely, an Amnesty Scheme by which private remittances were encouraged and the India Development Bonds at a relatively high cost.

2.4 The Committee, after a careful review of experience, identified the following as the most important lessons of experience in the management of balance of payments:

(a) No country can live beyond its means for long without creating adverse consequences. Thus, budgetary deficit, which has implications for money supply; revenue deficit, which has implications for the resources available out of

current revenues for developmental expenditures, and fiscal deficit; which has implications for the amount of resources drafted from the household and other sectors combined with inadequate returns on investments made out of borrowings, all contributed to a situation where the macroeconomic environment was not exactly conducive to a stable balance of payments situation.

(b) Current account deficit must be limited to a level that can be sustained by normal capital flows. What is normal cannot be defined but it could be reasonably assessed. While current account deficit in any particular year, for reasons such as drought or volatility in POL prices may be inevitable, persistent deficits financed by relatively expensive capital flows are bound to adversely affect the sustainability of balance of payments.

(c) Overhang of persistent current account deficits can be corrected only in the medium-term. In other words, while a sustainable balance of payments position may be defined as a level of current account deficit that can be met by normal capital flows; to achieve such a goal of sustainability, there would be need for exceptional financing during the transition to a stable situation.

(d) In respect of exports, it is clear that the exports possibilities of India have been grossly underestimated and the import intensity of a strategy of import substitution not understood adequately. Export acceleration on a sustained basis would require across-the-board improvements in infrastructure, labour productivity efficiency of industry and in the macroeconomic environment.

(e) Management of imports requires a focused attention on a few commodities or users of importance rather than an attempt to control a large number of small and individual transactions. Thus, the three important areas which would ensure substantial import substitution are POL products, fertilizers and imports on account of defence. As a medium term strategy, there is need to concentrate on reducing the dependence on imports in respect of these products.

(f) In regard to the invisible account, the impact of an unrealistic exchange rate on the diversion of foreign exchange inflows from official to private channels was underestimated. The impact of interest burden on invisibles was not fully recognized. The potential of tourism in providing balance of payments support is yet to be fully exploited.

(g) While current account transactions can be subjected to short term restrictions, the liabilities created out of debt will have to be discharged and hence, a medium-term framework requires considerations of debt liabilities that have already been incurred as also the sustainable level and composition of external debt that can be incurred afresh.

(h) The normal capital flows have a quantitative relation to the financing of current account deficit in a particular year, but the composition of such capital flows is more important in as much as it affects the future liabilities on both capital and current accounts. Further, the use to which the capital flows are directly applied will determine the capability to service liabilities.

(i) At a time when the aid flows were getting constrained and their concessionality flows gradually eroded, reliance was placed on high-cost NRI deposits which proved to be volatile. External commercial borrowings, which were relatively inexpensive have, however, tended to result in bunched repayments. The window of opportunities available through encouraging foreign investments has not been exploited, though other countries have accessed this source on a large scale. The volatility of flows in capital account and the link of such flows with BoP performance require greater attention in future.

(j) While a number of factors such as world demand, quality of products, marketing skills and supply availabilities have a bearing on export growth in the medium-term, an appropriate Real Effective Exchange Rate would constitute a necessary though not sufficient condition for export growth.

(k) The level of foreign currency reserves and the management of such reserves should be such as to provide the much

needed assurance to the international financial and trading community about the country's ability to service its obligations. Hence, a targeted level of reserves as a proportion of imports, would be required to convince the international community about the determination to manage the external sector on a sustainable basis.

III. REVIEW OF RECENT DEVELOPMENTS

3.1 The Committee submitted an interim report on the Partial Convertibility of Rupee (PCR) in February, 1992. (The Report may be seen at appendix). The Liberalized Exchange Rate Management System (LERMS) was introduced with effect from March 1, 1992 as a first step towards full convertibility of the rupee on current account. The main objectives behind the introduction of LERMS were the fulfillment of the need for a market-oriented and flexible exchange rate mechanism as a means to achieve self-reliance through improved export performance and a reduction in the scope for illegal transactions in foreign exchange so that the flow of inward remittances into the country can be increased substantially. With the introduction of PCR, except for a few essential commodities, the task of allocating scarce foreign currency resources to various uses has been shifted from GoI/RBI to the market and price acts as the vehicle for such allocation. The PCR system attempts to combine the advantages of a relatively stable managed float and the BoP balancing properties of a freely floating rate of exchange, by creating two exchange rate channels. In the market channel, the exchange rate is determined by the demand for and supply of foreign exchange, where access is free for all foreign exchange transactions (with a few exceptions). In the official channel, the exchange rate continues to be determined by the RBI but access is restricted.

3.2 Since under the new trade policy, all goods may be freely imported except those included in a short Negative List, Government has indeed ceased to control the quantum of imports into the country and through that the demand for foreign exchange. This function, as mentioned earlier, is now being determined by the price ruling in the market. Thus, under the new strategy for managing BoP, the market, through its pricing mechanism would regulate to a large extent the quantum of permissible (trade account), authorised

(invisible account) and approved (capital account) transactions that would be put through by the public. If the relaxation of import trade controls were to result in an increasing demand for foreign exchange, the consequent rise in its price would provide an incentive for export growth.

3.3 Having assigned a crucial role for the market forces of demand and supply in the determination of the external value of the rupee, it has become imperative to have an efficient institutional arrangement in place that would monitor the functioning of the system closely, reduce acute imbalances between demand and supply and the consequent volatility in exchange rates and review the official exchange rate with reference to the market rate on a regular basis. The Committee noted that such systems have been put in place in the form of a Standing Group on the forecasting of Foreign Exchange Reserves (RBI), the Balance of Payments Monitoring Group (Ministry of Finance) and the Committee on Transitional Arrangements (RBI/MOF/MOC).

3.4 With the liberalisation measures being introduced to revitalise the economy and the goal of self-reliance having been redefined in a more positive sense, the role of customs duty in the country's fiscal structure has had to be re-oriented. It has been recognized that a growing economy needs to import a larger volume of fuel and other important industrial inputs and also capital goods signifying technological upgradation and that such imports should be financed by its own exports and not through external support like foreign aid. Further, it has been noted that for boosting exports to the required extent, the prime requisite would be to make Indian industry internationally competitive. With the downward adjustment of the external value of the rupee in 1991 and the introduction of LERMS in March, 1992, the rupee cost of imports has gone up considerably and consequently, the base on which customs duty is levied has grown larger. Accordingly, the tariff levels can be reduced without adversely affecting the quantum of revenue accruing to the exchequer from this source. If this is not done, high tariff rates combined with higher import values, would push up the cost of imports to a considerable extent, thereby affecting the competitiveness of Indian Industry and possibly causing cost-push inflation. Therefore, the Committee is of the view that from the point

of view of improving export competitiveness, it is necessary to ensure that customs tariff levels are comparable to those prevailing in our competitor countries, many of whom have reduced their customs duty rates substantially. The process of such a reform should, however, be structured, and well thought out giving adequate notice to the domestic industry – both in order to cushion the impact on revenue and to ensure that there is a reasonable opportunity for Indian industry to become internationally competitive.

3.5 The highlights of the new Exim-Policy are: i) External trade is free, subject only to a negative list of imports and a negative list of exports; ii) Negative list of imports is the smallest ever; iii) Negative list of exports has been pruned; iv) Negative lists would be administered, as far as possible, by general schemes. Case-by-case licensing would be minimised. Actual user conditions have been eliminated except in a few special cases; v) Import of capital goods has been liberalised. They are no longer in the negative list of imports. Imports of second-hand capital goods have been allowed, in some sectors without licence and in others under licence; vi) Raw material imports have been liberalised. Barring a few items, they are no longer in the negative list of imports; vii) Value-based Advance Licences have been introduced with self-certification, they being made available for Export Houses, Trading Houses and Star Trading Houses; viii) The EOU and the EPZ schemes have been liberalised. These schemes have been extended also to agriculture, horticulture, aquaculture, poultry and animal husbandry. EOU/EPZ units may now export through Export Houses, Trading Houses and Star Trading Houses; ix) The definition of Deemed Exports has been streamlined; x) The crucial roles of EPZs, Export Houses, Trading Houses and Star Trading Houses have been recognised; and xi) A national campaign for quality awareness is proposed to be launched. The Committee noted that there had been an orderly transition from import compression to import of required commodities and that imports had proved to be price elastic. There appears to be a distinct reduction in inventory levels because of the assured supply of imported commodities and the high cost of holding inventory. There is also judgmental evidence to show that some amount of import substitution is taking place in the economy.

3.6 Exports, however, have not picked up rapidly, largely because of the climate of recession prevailing in the industrialised countries, the disruption in rupee trade with the former USSR and also the time-lag between reforms and results. There is, however, clear evidence of acceleration in the rate of growth of exports to general currency areas, especially in the very recent past. The Committee concluded that it would, therefore, be premature now to evaluate fully the export performance of the industry on the basis of the reforms introduced, though the trends are distinctly encouraging.

3.7 The foreign exchange budget of Government of India traditionally covered almost the entire requirements of foreign exchange of the public sector. However, the coverage has been drastically reviewed for 1992-93. Firstly, canalisation is itself restricted to a few commodities as part of the EXIM policy. Even here, the foreign exchange budget is restricted to foreign exchange made available at official rate and therefore, to select POL products and fertilizers. Allocations, however, are made for import of food grains from the foreign exchange budget. In regard to some other essential commodities which are canalised, such as edible oils, access to market rate is permitted and hence, they do not form part of the foreign exchange budget. This approach helps in passing on international prices to the domestic market moderated by appropriate fiscal policies. Thus, immunising the management of external sector from domestic policies in respect of prices of individual commodities has added some stability to the management of the external sector. Secondly, even with regard to the Departments during 1992-93 a number of public sector undertakings which were originally part of the foreign exchange budget were removed therefrom. This gave them greater autonomy. Even public sector undertakings of Defence have been removed from the foreign exchange budget. Thirdly, even in regard to foreign exchange requirements for the Departments, the foreign exchange budget was made applicable only for acquisition of goods for which foreign exchange was made available at official rates. Fourthly, the Departments as well as the canalising agencies are permitted to access foreign exchange at the market rate if their requirements exceed what has been provided for in the foreign exchange budget. This gave freedom and maneuverability to the various agencies to promptly meet the domestic demands without being constrained by foreign exchange budget allocations. Fifthly, in order

to ensure proper management of foreign exchange reserves, the outflow of foreign exchange at the official rate through the foreign exchange budget is subjected to management in cash terms by imposing monthly ceilings on drawl of such foreign exchange. Finally, the practice of utilising the canalising agencies as instruments of protecting the foreign exchange reserves by encouraging them to import commodities under short term credit arrangements has been discouraged with a view to eliminating such a procedure altogether, as soon as possible. The Committee noted that all these measures tended to impart the necessary freedom to the various agencies within the public sector in managing their foreign exchange needs and give incentives for saving on foreign exchange. Inventory management has also been made easier. The incentive to export and earn foreign exchange has been provided for the public sector undertakings. The Committee noted with satisfaction that these measures in the area of Foreign Exchange Budget, impart necessary pre-conditions for a gradual movement towards fuller convertibility of the rupee on current account. It, therefore, recommends that with the objective of moving towards full convertibility, the mechanism of allocating foreign exchange should be dispensed with from 1993-94. The Committee expects the financial advisers in the ministries to exercise appropriate control over foreign exchange expenditure, just as they are expected to exercise control over rupee expenditure.

3.8 The import of raw material components was, till recently, facilitated by the availability of foreign exchange, partly through normal channels and for some time being linked with Exim Scrips. Such a differentiated and administered approach has been replaced by the general arrangement of access through market rate and for select commodities access through foreign exchange at the official rate. Further, the insistence on utilising short term credits to protect reserves was dispensed with, once the crisis situation was overcome. On the whole, therefore, the import of raw materials and components is now governed by a free access to foreign exchange without the constraints of specific user-wise allocative mechanisms. In regard to capital goods, the traditional approach has been to indicate the sources of foreign exchange including, in particular, linkage with foreign currency loans, either through the Development Financial Institutions or by insistence on direct external commercial borrowings. In some cases there was a linkage with utilisation of bilateral

credits. This system which required a number of clearances within the Government and by various financial agencies – domestic as well as international – has now been replaced by freedom to the individual entrepreneurs to decide on the source of funding for import of capital goods. The users are now at liberty to choose the means of financing, depending on their own requirements and market conditions. The mix would be debt, equity or foreign exchange from the market. Thus, both the providers of foreign capital and the users of foreign capital in India are at liberty to negotiate and utilise the sources depending on their requirements. This procedure has imparted greater freedom and competitiveness in transactions relating to external borrowings. The Committee noted that the freedom granted to users in sourcing foreign exchange for their requirements has resulted in not only ease of operations but also relatively lower cost at which external commercial debt was made available to Indian entities. It was noted that the withdrawal of foreign currency loans had been less than in previous years, but the overall availability of foreign exchange for import of capital goods had matched the demand.

3.9 The Committee noted the following parameters of the new Industrial Policy and steps taken by the Government to attract foreign investment:

(a) Majority foreign ownership, even up to 100 per cent in certain sectors, is allowed.

(b) Foreign equity proposals need not necessarily be accompanied by foreign technology agreement.

(c) Automatic approval is given by the Reserve Bank of India for Foreign Direct Investment up to 51 per cent foreign equity in 34 high priority industries if foreign equity covers the capital requirements of imported capital goods which must comprise plant and machinery which are new and not second-hand.

(d) Automatic approval by Reserve Bank of India for majority foreign equity holding up to 51 per cent in trading companies primarily engaged in export activities subject to the condition of dividend balancing for a period of seven years.

(e) Proposals outside the criteria in (c) & (d) are to be considered by the Secretariat of Industrial Approvals/Foreign Investment Promotion Board/Project Approval Board.

(f) Automatic approval for raising foreign equity up to 51 per cent in the existing companies also allowed by the RBI provided the proposed activities are in the high priority area.

(g) For foreign technology agreements in high priority industries, automatic approval allowed, subject to the condition that the lump sum payment does not exceed Rs. 1 crore and royalty does not exceed five per cent on domestic sales and eight per cent on exports.

(h) Payment of dividends only in the case of consumer goods industries would be monitored by the RBI to ensure that outflows on account of dividend payments are balanced by export earnings. The general condition of dividend balancing has been withdrawn for items other than consumer goods.

(i) All payments flowing from the approval of foreign technology agreements are to be met through foreign exchange purchased at the market rate.

(j) Phased manufacturing programme is no longer applicable.

(k) Disinvestment of equity by foreign investors can take place at the market rates on the stock exchanges.

(l) India signed the Multilateral Investment Guarantee Agency Protocol on 13.4.1992.

(m) General permission is now granted to companies with more than 40 per cent non-resident interests to accept appointment as an agent or technical or management adviser of any company in India in any activity of a trading/commercial or industrial nature.

(n) Companies with more than 40 per cent foreign interest may now borrow money and accept deposits in India for which the Reserve Bank of India will accord general permission.

(o) Companies with more than 40 per cent foreign equity are granted general permission to deal in immovable property in India.

(p) Foreign companies have also been permitted by RBI to open liaison offices and branches in India on receipt of applications from them.

(q) Foreign companies are now free to use their trade marks for domestic sales.

IV. BROAD POLICY CONSIDERATIONS.

4.1 The committee deliberated on major policy considerations relevant to management of balance of payments, *viz.*, redefinition of self-reliance in trade policy, convertibility of the rupee, the approaches to medium term development, emphasis on foreign equity flows, optimum utilisation of debt, role of tariffs, management of external sector and need for transparency.

Redefinition of Self-reliance and Trade Policy.

4.2 The first step, in our long term strategy to tackle the country's BoP problems, it was felt, would be to re-examine our earlier understanding of one of the key objectives we had set for ourselves, namely, self-reliance. In this respect, it would be apt to quote from the speech made by the Honourable Finance Minister, while presenting the Budget for 1992-93.

"Self-reliance in today's world of integrated global markets cannot be achieved merely by reducing import dependence and insulating the economy from the world. Following that path will only lead to more import controls and promote inefficiency and corruption. It will perpetuate an environment in which Indian entrepreneurs will not have the flexibility they need to compete with other developing countries in world markets. The resulting inability to export will actually make us more, rather than less, dependent on the outside world. Our vision of a self-reliant economy should be of an economy which can meet all its import requirements through exports, without undue dependence on artificial external props such as foreign aid."

4.3 In this background, the approach to self reliance has been set by the Committee in the following terms.

(a) Improve export earnings and receipts on invisible account especially on account of tourism and remittances.

(b) Ensure that essential imports take place and generally imports are restricted to the available receipts on current account supplemented by a sustainable level of net capital receipts.

(c) Aim at a sustainable level of net capital receipts by gradual reduction in exceptional financing (such as IMF facilities and fast disbursing flows from multilateral/bilateral agencies) and debt servicing burden.

(d) Add to the foreign exchange reserves to avoid a contingency of "liquidity crisis", and

(e) Eliminate dependence on short-term debt for BoP support by restricting the use of short term facilities up to a six-month period for trade-related purposes, under normal terms, on a voluntary basis by importing agencies concerned.

Convertibility and Trade Policy Changes

4.4 While announcing the new trade policy last year, the Government mentioned its intentions to move towards full convertibility of the rupee on the trade account. The PCR has been introduced to provide a boost to exports as well as to efficient import substitution, to reduce the scope for bureaucratic controls and to reduce the incentives for illegal transactions in foreign exchange.

4.5 The strategy of managing trade followed till recently was to partly subsidise exporters to make up for negative protection implicit in the domestic policy and contain imports through canalisation, physical controls and restricted regime of imports in general. Such an administered system led to current account deficits well beyond what was sustainable, resulting in increased recourse to commercial borrowings and volatile NRI deposits; short term debt of less than one year was rolled over and reserves were drawn down. The trade policy changes are now redirected to ensure that exporters have non-discriminatory and inbuilt attractiveness

through exchange rate and other fiscal and monetary measures rather than being eligible for case-by-case disbursements of compensatory payments. The importers would also have a generalised access to imports moderated by tariffs to protect indigenous industry, ban on imports of consumer goods, and a very small list of items subject to quantitative restrictions as an interim measure.

4.6 Over the medium term, therefore, the Committee considers that an atmosphere of liberal trade regime with self-correcting mechanism of exchange rate and a gradual movement towards international competitiveness would have to be the basic objectives.

The Planning Commission's Approach

4.7 The Eighth Five-Year Plan estimates the sustainable level of current account deficit for the next five years at 1.6 per cent of the GDP. This has to be treated as a ceiling rather than as a target. Secondly, exports are expected by the commission to grow at a rate of 13.6 per cent in volume terms. However, the initial conditions of world recession, uncertainties in trade in rupee payment areas and the extent of impact of reform measures will have to be reckoned with. Thirdly, the import elasticity of GDP growth has been estimated by the Planning Commission at 1.5. However, given the low level of imports at the beginning of the Five-Year Plan, due to the import compression measures warranted by the limited access to capital receipts, the average growth rate in imports may be higher than what is indicated by import elasticity. Finally, consistent with the Planning Commission's approach both in terms of access and sustainability, debt should be restricted, the composition of the capital account should show a distinct bias in favour of equity, and there should be continued reliance on external assistance and a decline in the recourse to commercial sources and NRI deposits.

4.8 The Committee thus adopted the basic parameters of the Eighth Five-Year Plan, which are in a sense normative, and took note of subsequent domestic and international developments to make recommendations with immediate operational significance.

Composition of Capital Receipts

4.9 Financing of current account deficits, even at the levels projected by the Planning Commission, is likely to present difficulties,

unless the perception of India as a country risk changes favourably in the international credit markets. It would, therefore, be appropriate to encourage equity investments with a view to increasing forex inflows into the country as well as to promote industrial growth consistent with the Plan targets. Foreign Direct Investment is also expected to increase competition in the Indian industry and improve manufacturing efficiency leading to higher exports. As has been mentioned, growth in exports to the projected levels, is a pre-requisite for achieving the key objectives of self-reliance and restriction of current account deficit to 1.6 per cent of GDP. In emphasizing equity flows, qualitative aspects in terms of the priority sectors (such as power and telecommunications), technology imports (in sunrise industries like electronics, computer software and biotechnology), and the size of industry (such as the medium-sized, preferably in collaboration with existing medium-sized Indian industry) have to be kept in view.

4.10 Considering all this and also the fact that the servicing of debt has an immediate adverse implication for forex outflows from the country unlike in the case of servicing equity, the Committee felt that there has to be a distinct shift in the policy framework in favour of equity from debt in the matter of capital receipts from abroad. Further, the Committee feels that it is not only the quantum of equity but also the areas of application of Foreign Direct Investment that is important. Moreover, the Committee cautions against extending concessions or facilities to foreign investors which are more favourable than what are offered to domestic investors and also against enhancing external debt to supplement equity. In fact, efforts should be made to replace debt flows with equity flows. However, the Committee recognises that Foreign Direct Investment will contain both equity and debt, and the system of approvals is applicable to all external debt. Hence, as an operational guideline, the Committee recommends that the approval of debt (excluding aid from bilateral and multilateral sources) linked to equity, be limited to a ratio of 1:2.

4.11 With the limited availability of external debt, it becomes imperative that it is put to optimum use. The primary concern should be to ensure that priority sectors such as the nontradeables, mainly power sectors and telecommunications, oil industry, fertilizers, the export sector, etc., are not starved of the much needed

foreign currency resources. Care also should be taken to see that external debt is not contracted for meeting requirements of rupee resources. With a view to lessening volatility, efforts should also be made to bring about an appropriate maturity pattern of the country's external debt. Since short-term debt is considerably more volatile, the endeavour should be to tilt the maturity profile of external borrowings in favour of the long-term. Such longer maturities are helpful in reducing immediate pressures on BoP in the form of debt service obligations, providing the much needed breathing space to stimulate exports from the country.

4.12 In operational terms, the Committee felt that considerations of prudent debt management would imply restricting growth in the stock of NRI Deposits, containing net addition to other external commercial borrowings outstanding and cautious recourse to instruments such as India Development Bonds as part of commercial sources. Recourse to external debt for balance of payments support would have to be discouraged unless it is on concessional terms or with very long maturity. In terms of magnitudes also, the Committee felt that recourse to external debt should be continuously monitored over the Eighth Plan Period to ensure sustainability, cost-effectiveness and use-efficiency. However, recourse to exceptional financing including IMF credit would be inevitable but the objective would be to phase out the exceptional financing needs by the terminal year of the Eighth Plan.

Transparency

4.13 A healthy public debate on the BoP position of the country, the targets for sustainable levels of current account deficit and external debt and the strategies proposed to be adopted to achieve the planned objectives would result in building up a viable concensus in favour of the proposed plan of action. This would go a long way in the timely achievement of the objectives. It is, therefore, worth pursuing increased transparency as a goal in itself, both at the stage of formulating the long term policy framework for BoP management as well as at the stage of operationalising the policy framework. Transparency is important to enable economic agents to take well informed decisions.

4.14 The Committee, therefore, concluded that greater transparency in operational terms would involve the following.

(i) Making public, update statistics on balance of payments as in the case of trade statistics by DGCIS.

(ii) The guidelines on external commercial borrowings including prioritisation are made available to the public as general guidelines.

(iii) The conditions under which foreign exchange financing for imports is permissible are not only non-discriminatory but also made known to public as general guidelines.

(iv) The regulations governing commercial flows, especially foreign investment, should be positive and explicit in terms of automaticity rather than as an exception to general rule of restriction, and

(v) The control mechanism in regard to capital transactions should be well laid down, systematic and subject to monitoring and reviewed from time to time.

V. EXCHANGE RATE POLICY

5.1 The Exchange Rate Policy during the Eighth Five-Year Plan and beyond will have to clearly reflect technological developments, the world of integrated global markets and the consequent redefinition of self-reliance. Firstly, it is necessary to recognise that an appropriate exchange rate policy is a prerequisite, though not a sufficient condition for a sustainable balance of payments position. Secondly, there is a need for a constant review of the differentials in price levels between India and other countries and the extent of movement of values of currencies of the countries competing with India with a view to making necessary corrections required in the exchange rate. Thirdly, a transparent and stable policy towards exchange rate minimizes distortions through market expectations. Fourthly, the exchange rate should, as far as possible, not be an instrument of cross subsidisation as between commodities either for import or export. The appropriate instrument will have to be fiscal or even monetary but not the exchange rate. In any case, the whole package should be transparent and non-discriminatory. Fifthly, while efforts should be

made at all times to maintain an appropriate Real Effective Exchange Rate, there are bound to be both transitional problems and strains on the system due to seasonal factors, protectionist tendencies in the world, etc. They will still have to be tackled more by a combination of fiscal and sector-specific methods rather than through multiple exchange rates or cross-subsidisation in terms of differential prices of foreign currency. Sixthly, recent experience in regard to introduction of partial convertibility and exchange rate adjustment shows that it is possible to have a stable exchange rate through emphasis on a realistic exchange rate and a dominant role for the market. However, it should be recognised that a stable exchange rate was possible only because of some amount of restrictions on trade and invisibles, apart from very close control over capital transactions that create future liabilities. Hence, it is necessary to ensure that both a realistic exchange rate and a gradual relaxation of restrictions on current account transactions have to go hand in hand. In the medium term, care has to be taken to ensure that there is no capital flight through liberalised windows of transactions under invisibles. Finally, also in the medium term there is no escape from a very close control over all capital transactions so that future liabilities are kept under control.

5.2 The Committee, therefore, recommends that consideration be given to a realistic exchange rate, avoiding use of exchange mechanisms for subsidisation, maintaining adequate level of reserves to take care of short term fluctuations, continuing the process of liberalisation on current account and reinforcing effective control over capital transactions. Further, the key to the maintenance of a realistic and a stable exchange rate should, in the view of the Committee, be possible by containing inflation through macro-economic policies and ensuring net capital receipts of the scale assumed in BoP projections.

In its interim report (copy enclosed as Appendix), the Committee recommended the adoption of partial convertibility on current account. It noted with satisfaction that the PCR system implemented so far conformed to the dual system (the ratio of 60:40 in the allocation of foreign exchange receipts between the free market and official channels) and supplementary policy changes in trade and tariff regimes were adopted. Minor variations were warranted in respect of the treatment of grants, aid-receipts, import of drugs etc.

Transitional Problems

5.3 While recommending the adoption of partial convertibility on current account, the Committee had envisaged certain transitional problems, particularly, the overhang of Exim Scrips, non-applicability of LERMS for Asian Clearing Union arrangement and likely disadvantages to capital intensive service industries such as international shipping and airlines which are akin to 100 per cent EOUs in several respects. The Committee has noted with a great satisfaction that most of those transitional problems envisaged in its interim report were solved smoothly through a 'Transitional Arrangements Committee on LERMS'. Also, contrary to fears expressed in some quarters that thc rupee may undergo a steep depreciation, there has been remarkable stability in the official exchange rate as well as in the spread between the official and market rate of exchange. Rarely did the spread exceed 20 per cent and mostly it remained around 17 per cent.

Review of Performance

5.4 The Committee noted the following important features of performance of partial convertibility:

(a) One of the fundamental fears expressed at the time of introduction of LERMS was that there would be a steep fall in the external value of the rupee. Consequently, inflationary pressures on the economy were expected. Actual experience, however, was more in conformity with official expectations. While the official (middle) rate continued to be Rs. 25.89 per dollar till December 3, 1992, the market rate ranged between Rs. 30 to Rs. 31.50 per dollar. The rupee exchange rate has been quite stable and there have been very few volatile fluctuations in the market.

(b) One major expectation from LERMS was that the gap between the hawala rate and the market rate would be brought down and hawala transactions would be eliminated. Though hawala market still persists, the gap between the hawala rate and the market rate appears to have narrowed down considerably and the turnover in hawala transactions is reported to have come down substantially.

(c) LERMS has provided an additional incentive to a large body of exporters who were entitled to receive Exim Scrips to the extent of 30 per cent of their exports. (Exporters who were entitled to receive Exim Scrips to the extent of 40 per cent of their exports may have, however, suffered marginal losses with the introduction of LERMS.) The major advantage of LERMS over Exim Scrips, namely, that it is simpler, straightforward and promotes general efficiency, has been appreciated by various industrial and exporters' associations.

(d) Exim Scrips were not applicable to beneficiaries of inward remittances under the earlier regime but under LERMS, 60 per cent of inward remittances are also converted at the market rate of exchange. This was expected to improve remittances especially through official channel. However, the procedural delays for remittances through banking system and incomplete reforms under FERA appear to have constrained realisation of full benefits of LERMS.

(e) Exporters justifiably feel that since 40 per cent of their export proceeds are being converted at the official rate of exchange, PCR actually carries a tax on exports.

(f) The general belief is that PCR is only an interim measure and that full convertibility of the rupee on current account may be introduced at any time in the near future. There is definitely an element of uncertainty in this regard and expectations that full convertibility will be introduced shortly appear to be resulting in a postponement of foreign investment decisions.

(g) In terms of magnitudes of flows, the expectation that 40 per cent of current account receipts would finance special imports appears to have been fully realised. The system, in brief is poised for further progress.

Future Actions

5.5 The Interim Report of the Committee clearly listed the steps beyond partial convertibility. Broadly speaking, the steps contemplated were:

(a) Minor adjustments in the system in the first few months by keeping a close watch.

(b) Measures to transmit exchange rate to domestic prices (in regard to special etc.).

(c) Impose a proportion between access to foreign exchange at official rate and at market rate even in respect of special category transactions so that, over a period, the portion at market rate is increased.

(d) Bring in a unified market as the difference between official rate and market rate narrows.

(e) Step-by-step movement towards full convertibility on current account.

The Committee, in the light of experience gained under LERMS, considered two options in moving towards convertibility on current account, change the proportions to reduce transactions at official rate as an intermediate step or to bring about unified market without any intermediate step.

Intermediate Step

5.6 The intermediate step consists of changing the proportions to reduce official transactions, whereby, the number of items and amounts available for official rate transactions would be reduced and percentage of surrenders of foreign exchange receipts at official rate gets correspondingly reduced to say, 15 to 20 from 40. The advantages of the intermediate step are:

(a) Allocations at official rate to POL would continue to be made, though at a far lower level.

(b) Some fertilizers can continue to be imported at official rate, thereby making available fertilizers at reduced prices and moderating impact on fertilizer subsidies.

(c) Budgetary allocations for import as well as debt-servicing of Defence Department would continue to be computed at official exchange rate.

(d) Life saving drugs would continue to be available at the official exchange rate, and

(e) Risks of inflationary effect of POL prices, fertilizers prices, and fiscal deficits continue to be moderated.

As against these advantages, the disadvantages are as follows:

(i) Implicit tax on export earnings though on a reduced scale, compared to the present system, would continue to operate, thus, undermining the policy of export-thrust.

(ii) Similarly, NRI remittances would pay an implicit tax to subsidise imports of POL, fertilizers, departmental payments for imports etc.

(iii) The contradictions inherent in the dual exchange system in so far as they relate to ACU transactions and trade with erstwhile USSR will continue.

(iv) As long as a dual exchange rate system operates, there would be pressure to expand access to foreign exchange at official rate, and

(v) In view of the uncertainties, and expectations anticipatory actions such as withholding of foreign investment decisions or even remittance of export-earnings may continue.

Unified Rate

5.7 The option of unified rate implies that exporters and other earners of foreign exchange will convert all their earnings at market rate and all imports will, correspondingly, take place at one market rate. The exchange rate for all transactions would thus be determined by market forces. Foreign exchange would, however, continue to be available only for purposes approved or authorised by Reserve Bank of India. The RBI would continue to have the option at its discretion of buying or selling foreign currency from the authorised dealers (who will continue to be subjected to FERA discipline). The advantages of such a system are:

(a) The justifiable demand of exporters that they should have the benefit of market rate (and not subject to a tax) can be met.

(b) The cumbersome procedures of claiming a part of import needs at official rate through Advance Licence mechanism can be eliminated to help exporters.

(c) The large number of workers who make remittances to India would have the full benefit of market rate.

(d) The existing contradictions in rates applicable to remittances and payments through NREA account would be removed.

(e) Similarly, contradictions between dual exchange rate system and transactions in respect of ACU and erstwhile USSR will also be removed.

(f) There will be an end to uncertainties and anticipatory actions on this account.

(g) A clear signal would be emitted to inspire the confidence of the international community, and

(h) There could be a distinct psychological impact on our people which should help reverse capital flight and further reduce hawala transactions.

As against these advantages, there are some risks and disadvantages that should be assessed. These are:

(a) If the international prices of POL harden during the course of the year, some of the anticipated surplus on "OCC account" may not come about, if all and not a part of imports are paid for at unified rate. Thus, there is need to monitor the developments and consider review of POL prices during later part of the year.

(b) There would be additional cost of importing fertilizers, affecting both prices for farmers and amount of subsidy needed.

(c) Additional budgetary provisions would be needed, depending on where unified exchange rate settles, for debt servicing and import needs of defence.

(d) Import of life saving drugs would be more expensive than at official rate.

(e) There are possible risks of inflation on account of prices of essential commodities and, strains on containing fiscal deficit. But these would be off set by possible liberalised imports that would be afforded.

Assessment

5.8 In weighing the advantages and disadvantages, the Committee took into account the following factors:

(a) Under LERMS, market rate has proved to be reasonably stable and within the range of anticipated levels. Hence, the unified rate, in the normal course, should be in alignment with the market rate established in the past few months. Technically, unified rate should settle between the ruling official and market rates.

(b) Measures have already been taken to transmit changes in the exchange rate to domestic prices in respect of POL.

(c) The macroeconomic environment in terms of rate of inflation, anticipated growth rate and sustainable fiscal deficit inspires confidence to effect changes.

5.9 The Committee, after weighing advantages and disadvantages of the options, as described above, recommends that a decision be taken to unify the exchange rate, as an important step towards full convertibility.

VI. FOREIGN CURRENCY RESERVES

6.1 The Committee is of the view that the crisis in balance of payments in the recent past was essentially a crisis of confidence and a liquidity crisis. Such a liquidity crisis could have been managed without resorting to fire-fighting operations, if adequate levels of foreign currency reserves were at all times maintained. No doubt, there is a trade-off between accumulating the reserves and permitting imports to take place. However, allowing the reserve drawdown for what could have otherwise been regular and recurring imports (without replenishments of such reserves on an assured basis in a foreseeable future) implies serious erosion of the maneuverability in the management of balance of payments.

6.2 The Committee, therefore, makes a general recommendation that a reserve target range should be fixed from time to time and the foreign currency reserves should always be permitted to operate within the range and in any case under no circumstances below the floor.

6.3 It has traditionally been the practice to view the level of desirable reserves as a percentage of the annual imports – say reserves to meet three months imports or four months imports. However, this approach would be inadequate when a large number of transactions and payment liabilities arise in areas other than import of commodities. Thus, liabilities may arise either for discharging short-term debt obligations or servicing of medium-term debt, both interest and principal. Hence, the Committee recommends that while determining the target level of reserves, due attention should be paid to the payment obligations in addition to the level of imports. The Committee recommends that the foreign exchange reserves targets be fixed in such a way that they are generally in a position to accommodate imports of three months.

6.4 In the view of the Committee, the factors that are to be taken into consideration in determining the desirable level of reserves are: the need to ensure a reasonable level of confidence in the international financial and trading communities about the capacity of the country to honour its obligations and maintain trade and financial flows; the need to take care of the seasonal factors in any balance of payments transaction with reference to the possible uncertainties in the monsoon conditions of India; the amount of foreign currency reserves required to counter speculative tendencies or anticipatory actions amongst players in the foreign exchange market; and the capacity to maintain the reserves, so that the cost of carrying liquidity is minimal.

6.5 The Committee also noted that the Reserve Bank of India maintains a stock of gold of about 351 tonnes in addition to the foreign currency reserves. While the currency reserves provide the necessary liquidity, the gold reserves are expected to provide comfort. Often, it is argued that financial circles are aware of the comfort of gold and hence, conversion into currency is merely a change in the form of asset. However, there is reason to believe that this approach resulted in some adverse consequences. Firstly, the price of gold which was ruling at $ 460 per oz. on an average in 1981, has come down to a level of a little over $ 380 in 1989-90 and dropped to $ 360 in 1991. In other words, if the gold had been converted into foreign currency, this loss could have been avoided. Secondly, if the gold had been leased, a return of 0.25 per cent to one per cent

would have been obtained and the value of gold per oz., today after crediting the lease value would be a little over $ 400 per oz. Thirdly, if gold had been converted into foreign currency and invested, the foreign currency resources would have been enhanced even further. Fourthly, at a time when the reserves were falling, in view of the fact that the RBI Act does not effectively permit utilisation of gold beyond 15 per cent of its holdings in the Issue Department, the international community started withdrawing support to India and even insisting that the Letters of Credit established by Indian banks should be reconfirmed by a foreign bank. Fifthly, when the problem did arise, it became inevitable for the country to sell a part of its gold. The Committee recommends that the option of RBI converting gold into foreign currency resources should be constantly reviewed, though immediate case for exercising such an option is not established. Additionally, the Committee recommends that a part of gold reserves, say 30 per cent, should be available for conversion at short notice, into currency resources to meet contingencies.

VII. EXTERNAL ASSISTANCE

7.1 External debt has been an important source of financing the current account deficit. India's external debt may be classified for purposes of convenience into (a) multilateral (b) bilateral (c) commercial (d) non-resident Indian deposits (e) short-term loans and (f) rupee-debt. Each one of these forms of debt has its own characteristics and they will have to be considered before taking a total view of debt management and outlook for external debt in the medium term. Multilateral and bilateral sources are generally treated as "external assistance".

7.2 Multilateral assistance, particularly from the World Bank group, has been the single most important source of support to India's balance of payments. There has, however, been a gradual reduction in net transfers on account of multilateral assistance for a number of reasons, such as reduction in the overall aid flows in the world, entry of larger claimants (especially China) and the repayment obligations that have come about over a period. The Committee considers that the amount of resources available on concessional terms has been somewhat static even in nominal terms in the recent past.

7.3 The Committee noted that the most serious problem in regard to multilateral flows is the large amount of committed but undisbursed aid. Such amounts have been rising progressively in the last decades. Thus, any significant improvement in the power sector would substantially improve the overall utilisation of external assistance. The following are some of the major reasons or constraints in aid utilisation:

(a) The nature of the projects themselves are such that they take on average about five years to be implemented.

(b) Delays involved in project approvals and tender finalisation.

(c) Paucity of rupee resources (both in the case of Central Ministries and state governments) reflecting inadequate preparedness, budgetary constraints and non-convergence of the project interests and Plan priorities.

(d) Non-adherence to financial and other covenants agreed to at the time of negotiation. Property Tax Reforms, Water Tax Revision, Electricity Tariff Revision. etc., are some of the examples.

(e) Absence of cost-related tariff structure in the power sector adversely affects the finances of the State Electricity Boards (SEBs). SEBs are thus unable to provide adequate funds for the power projects resulting in the delayed utilisation of external assistance.

(f) Problems caused by delays in land acquisition and rehabilitation and resettlement of displaced persons.

(g) Sometimes major changes are sought to be made even after the finalisation of the projects, resulting in delayed utilisation of external assistance.

7.4 In respect of bilateral assistance also, there has been a problem of utilisation. Experience gained in this regard shows that some of the projects are taken up merely because foreign exchange is available only through bilateral credit. Secondly, bilateral approach, where credit is often made available on a tied basis, has resulted in high-cost imports. Often the concessionalities are absorbed by the Government and the project authorities are compelled to procure

equipment at higher than market price simply because bilateral aid is available. In such a situation, to the extent concessionalities are absorbed by the Government, the project authorities have little incentive to ensure quick absorption of bilateral aid.

7.5 The Committee noted the major suggestions made by 9th Finance Commission in its Report for 1990-95 regarding the utilisation of external assistance. These were: (a) The entire aid should be passed on to the states for externally-assisted projects; (b) For projects under IBRD, Government of India should recover loans from state governments over the same period as provided by IBRD; and (c) for the projects under IDA, the maturity period for the loans to the states should be increased to 30 years and the loans should carry an interest rate of six per cent.

7.6 The Committee also noted that the National Development Council (NDC) made the following suggestions in this regard at its 42nd Meeting on October 11, 1990. (a) The entire aid meant for the externally-assisted projects should be passed on to the States; (b) Advances may be given by the Government of India against the likely additionality; (c) Weaker states may be assisted to formulate projects which would be entitled for external aid; and (d) Any formal and informal ban on such projects in Special Category States should be removed.

7.7 The undesirable consequences of large unutilised aid are well recognised. Firstly, it reflects adversely on the absorptive capacity of the economy and the management of projects and may reduce the possible continued support from the multilateral agencies. Secondly, delayed implementations of the projects involves locking up of resources without productive results. Thirdly, there are instances where committed amounts of aid had to be cancelled as a result of such delays. Fourthly, over a longer period, there are distortions in implementation both on account of cost escalations and the changes in the rupee value – the latter adversely affecting the amount of foreign currency resources that should be available against rupee expenditure. Fifthly, commitment charges are paid on unutilised aid.

7.8 Considering the vital role that can be played by timely utilisation of external assistance in placing the country's balance of payments position on a sound footing, the Committee recommends that immediate action be considered in the following areas:

a) A review of the existing projects with a view to identifying those where the progress is slow, those that need redefining of project scope or coverage and where cancellation would be better than continuing to pay commitment fees and keeping them in our books.

b) As recommended by the NDC, 100 per cent external assistance may be passed on to the states for all sectors.

c) Additional Central assistance may be released to the states on a monthly basis. The advances at any point of time may be limited to around eight per cent of the accepted reimbursement during the year.

d) Since availability of rupee resources is one of the major constraints, priority may be accorded to externally-aided projects in making Plan allocations for both Five Year and Annual Plans and corresponding budget provisions. However, overall resource availability has to be increased to ensure adequate and timely absorption of external aid without sacrificing the larger segment of non-externally aided projects.

e) The contracting procedures will have to be streamlined and decentralised so that reference of Government would become unnecessary. General guidelines on evaluation procedures should suffice, since, with the introduction of LERMS, foreign exchange allocation by sources and uses is more or less dispensed with. In order to ensure that the domestic industry is encouraged to bid, the bidding procedures should be such as to give adequate opportunity to the domestic industry for competing for such contracts. (The Committee noted with satisfaction that the Government has already taken measures to allow Indian bidders to bid in foreign currency in respect of multilateral and bilaterally-assisted projects.)

f) The approval procedures and monitoring mechanisms will have to be reviewed to ensure adequate preparedness and timely actions.

7.9 In a review of the existing practices with regard to administering the external assistance, the Committee found certain

ambiguities, more particularly in the backdrop of the recent reform measures in the external sector of the economy. These, related to the lack of plan provisions for externally aided projects executed by the government departments, terms and conditions of the assistance passed on to PSUs and states, absorption of concessionality in assistance by the Government and use of concessional flows for commercial purposes. The Committee, therefore, recommends the following broad approach to reorient the administering of external assistance:

(a) Department of Economic Affairs may have to continue to play the role of a nodal agency, in terms of developing pipeline, negotiating external assistance and monitoring implementation. With relief in work on individual cases after LERMS, there is scope to focus on adequate planning for externally aided projects. In particular, there is need for a medium term framework of project pipeline which will specifically address issue of resource availability, commitment of user-unit and issues of direct lending/on-lending/ additionality.

(b) The issue of direct lending *vs* on-lending should recognise the need for disintermediation by Government. The suggested framework needs to be worked out on the following lines:

	Terms	Use	User	Method
1.	Bilateral & Multilateral (Other than Soft Loans)	Commercial Activities	PSUs (Centre and States)	Direct (not through Central or State Budgets)
2.	Soft Loans (esp. IDA)	Social Sectors	Departments in Centre or State or Autonomous Agencies specially set up	Through Budget
3.	Grants	Social Sectors	NGOs or Government	Umbrella Agreements for NGOs and Budget for Government as Grants to State Govt. also.

Rupee Debt

7.10 External debt denominated in rupees has different dimensions. First, there are NRI deposits which are denominated in rupees but require to be discharged in foreign currency at the option of the depositor. Clearly, this is not a rupee debt even though it is rupee denominated. Second, there are NRI deposits which are non-repatriable which implies that the debt has to be discharged in rupees and as per present arrangements, there need be no outflow of goods and services to non-residents. Third, there are bilateral arrangements, especially with the former Soviet Union, where debt is expected to be discharged by exporting goods and services to non-residents but liabilities are expressed in rupee terms as per agreed rates.

7.11 The former USSR extended to the Government of India a number of State credits for both defence and a civilian sector projects in India. The credits were denominated in Roubles but repayments by India were to be made in rupees by means of export of Indian goods. The rate of exchange between the rupee and Rouble for determining the repayment schedule was established by the Protocol of November 1978 between the two countries. The formula provided for changes in the value of rupee in relation to a 16-currency basket (the old SDR basket) but assumed that the value of Rouble to be invariant. As per this formula, the Rouble appreciated from Rouble 1 = Rs. 10 to Rouble 1.00 = Rs. 31.7874 when the exchange rate was last notified on 17.11.1991. The principal debt outstanding as on 31.3.1992 was Rouble 9871 million which at the last announced protocol exchange rate, amounted to Rs. 31,377 crores.

7.12 The Committee noted with satisfaction that India and Russia have reached a new agreement on the mechanism for determining the Rupee value of the Rouble denominated debt. The agreement provides for the principal amount of the debt as on 1.4.1992 being converted from Roubles to Rupees using the exchange rate on 1.1.1990 as determined by the Protocol. The amount of the principal debt as on 1.4.1992 would also be converted from Roubles to Rupees using the exchange rate on 1.4.1992 as determined by the 1978 Protocol. The difference in the two amounts, as calculated above, would be fixed in Rupees and would be rescheduled and repaid in annual instalments over a period of 45 years. This reschedule portion would carry no interest. It will also have no protection against

any fluctuation in the value of the Rupee for a period of five years. Thereafter, it will be indexed to the SDR if the average annual depreciation of the rupee exceeds three per cent over this five years period. Similar reviews will be conducted at the end of every five year period. This means that this portion of the debt will not be indexed if the rupee depreciation is three per cent or less per year on the average.

7.13 As per the agreement with Russia, Rs. 19,660 crores will be repaid with interest over the next 10-12 years in accordance with the schedule laid down in the credit agreements. The balance amount of Rs. 11,682 crores will be paid without interest over the next 45 years.

7.14 In accordance with the above agreement, the likely debt service payments to the former USSR over the next five years would be on average about Rs. 2,400 crores per annum. These amounts will be paid in rupees against which Russia will buy Indian goods and services for export to Russia.

7.15 Simultaneously, the new trading arrangements with Russia provide for trade in freely convertible currencies. Such trade could also provide for dollar denominated counter trade deals through ESCROW accounts opened in India. However, such counter-trade deals would have to be negotiated on a case-by-case basis and no definite guidelines have been laid down. It is expected that a portion of defence imports would be done on the basis of counter trade deals.

VIII. COMMERCIAL BORROWINGS

8.1 External commercial borrowings are defined to include debt owed to international banks, borrowings in bond markets, suppliers' credits, export credits supported by official export credit agencies and loans provided on commercial terms by specialised multilateral or bilateral institutions like IFC(W), Commonwealth Development Corporation, DEG of Germany etc. (Definition has since been changed).

8.2 Recourse to external commercial borrowings (defined as those with a maturity of more than one year) was essentially a phenomenon of Eighties. The instruments of the supplier/buyer credits and the syndicated bank loan market were mainly used. An entry was also made in the securitized instrument market and the public bond

market in Japan emerged as an important source since 1989. Recourse was also taken to offshore leasing as a cost effective arrangement and a diversified source of funds. In terms of maturities, it was possible to obtain commercial credits on an average maturity of seven years. The cost of funds was extremely favourable to India. While Japan emerged as an important source, the markets, by and large, continued to be diversified. Over 80 per cent of such commercial borrowings were by public sector-both financial and non-financial ones. During late Eighties, a large inflow was on account of the development financial institutions which were encouraged to borrow well in advance of their requirements of disbursements under foreign currency loans. There were also instances when ECB was approved to finance imports of raw materials and components by Public Sector Undertakings. Thus, recourse was taken to external borrowings virtually for balance of payments support in the recent past. The Committee noted that on the whole, in terms of cost, maturity, currency composition, markets, liability management and exercise of control over individual transactions, the performance in regard to obtaining external commercial borrowings was satisfactory.

8.3 However, the events following the Gulf war led to a sea change in India's commercial borrowing prospects and policies. The flow of funds from international commercial banks and bond markets virtually stopped when the Credit Rating Agencies announced a downgrading of the rating for India and Indian entities in 1990, taking into account both the BoP situation and the political uncertainties. There was no scope to access the bond market with such a rating. Under the circumstances, as part of crisis management, importers were required to resort to external borrowings for a minimum period of one year for raw materials and components and for at least two years for capital goods imports. There was also a freeze on the foreign currency resources parked by the development financial institutions with the RBI. Export credits supported by official export credit agencies emerged as the single important source of external funds. Soon, even the export credits were reaching the exposure limits and the premia for individual borrowers increased. The problem turned out to be essentially one of access rather than cost. The picture, however, changed slightly for the better after the initiation of the reform package in 1991. There was an improvement in the exposure limits by the institutional sources and premium has been gradually reduced.

Till now, the availability of untied funds in the form of bank loans and bond market issues continues to be uncertain.

8.4 In this background, the Committee identified the major issues that have to be addressed in the context of external commercial borrowings. These are: (a) The desirability and the scope for debt refinancing. (b) The scope and limits for debt equity swaps. (c) The desirability of incurring sovereign debt. (d) Use of gold bonds for raising debt. (e) Further scope for liability management. (f) Appropriate timing and magnitudes for re-entry into commercial borrowings through bond market. (g) Determining the levels of sustainable commercial debt. (h) Prioritising the utilisation of commercial debt. (i) A view on the maturities and instruments and (j) A view on extending Sovereign guarantees.

8.5 On consideration of the experience gained so far, the practices and procedures of international financial markets and the policy parameters for managing balance of payments in general and external debt in particular, the Committee recommends the following approach in regard to each one of the issues mentioned above:

(a) India has demonstrated its determination to honour all contractual obligations. At no point of time the option of debt rescheduling was considered. There is no need, therefore, to pursue this option. However, proposals have been received from some of the international bankers suggesting debt refinance, i.e., borrowing to specifically repay loans due. Considering the maturity profiles and the fact that a large part of external commercial debt is through institutional sources, the amounts that can be subjected to refinance would be about 500 million dollars per year for the next two years. As long as there is a possibility of raising commercial borrowings with longer maturity to sustain the overall balance, there is no advantage in giving signals of distress for such small amounts by taking recourse to debt refinance mechanism. The Committee considers that it would not be advisable to consider the option of debt refinance.

(b) Debt-equity conversions refer to an arrangement, whereby, an external lender converts the foreign currency loan to a borrower into an equity stake in the same country on

mutually negotiated terms. The converted equity could be acquired by the original lender or sold by him to investors. In theory, debt conversions have certain immediate advantages for all participants. The process helps the lender to realign his exposure portfolio according to his risk preference and business objectives. From the borrower's point of view, the debt burden is removed and from the country's point of view, the servicing of debt is replaced by payment of dividends linked to performance. No doubt, debt equity conversions have been important options of debt reduction for several highly indebted countries. However, the position of India is different from any of these countries. First, debt-equity swaps have taken place in many countries as part of rescheduling programmes. Second, debt equity conversion has taken place at a time when the country is in default and its external debt is quoted at a substantial discount in secondary market trading abroad. In the case of India, none of these circumstances exist. The concept, therefore, does not essentially apply to India which has a flawless debt service payment record. In the circumstances, there is a danger that recourse to debt equity swaps would reinforce sentiments that equate India with some of the countries that have defaulted in honouring their debt obligations. The Committee, therefore, concludes that debt equity conversion is not a desirable option for debt management in India.

(c) Suggestions have been received that India should borrow in the international financial markets as a sovereign in addition to the present practice of accessing external commercial borrowings essentially through public sector enterprises and to some extent through private enterprises. Such a sovereign borrowing could be accessed by the Government itself or by creating a separate designated entity. The main arguments in favour of sovereign borrowing seem to be that a centralised approach may provide access in terms of larger quantities; that there could be better execution; that economies of scale can be captured and that it will clearly give signals of Government being in direct command over commercial borrowings. In the recent

past, given the credit rating of India, many lenders are advocating sovereign borrowing as a desirable option and indicated that to the extent sovereign guarantee is being insisted upon for many enterprises, there is no great advantage in accessing commercial markets though entities rather than by the Government directly. The Committee examined this issue in the light of the following considerations, namely, (i) consistency with structural reform; (ii) quantum of commercial borrowings; (iii) cost of commercial borrowings; (iv) control and management; and (v) signals to the international financial community. Firstly, as part of structural reform, there is greater emphasis on autonomy to public enterprises and participation of private enterprises even in core sectors like power. Further, as part of such reform and reduction in the fiscal deficit, a policy of disintermediation of the Government is being encouraged. Secondly, as regards the quantum, the approach is to keep a cap and restrict the quantum of borrowings on commercial terms. Moreover, it is necessary to introduce mechanisms by which the use for commercial borrowings is linked to the borrowing itself to avoid recourse to such borrowings for balance of payments support. Under the circumstances, recourse to sovereign borrowing would be warranted only if it is established that the enterprises are unable or unwilling to raise requisite amount of commercial borrowings to sustain the balance of payments. Thirdly, as regards the cost, experience so far shows that leading players in the market have been able to get reasonable terms. With the diversification of ownership of some of the leading entities, the cost would be slightly more than the cost for sovereign borrowing. Fourthly, the major issue in regard to control and management relates to the approval procedures and proper monitoring of decentralised, enterprise-oriented borrowing. The systems that have been in place have worked satisfactorily so far. Fifthly, in terms of signals, recourse to sovereign borrowing may give an impression to the international financial community that India wants to be active in raising external commercial debt, while in reality, the attempt should be to

try and curtail such borrowings. But, most importantly, sovereign borrowings could demonstrate the strengths of presence of larger player on a more continuing basis. Under the circumstances, the Committee recommends that there is need to keep the option of sovereign borrowing in external commercial markets open, but exercise it when the need and cost-advantage are established.

(d) Suggestions have been received that the gold available in the country should be mobilised and such gold should be used for purposes of raising foreign currency loans. Implicit in the proposal is the assumption that gold is used as a collateral for raising foreign currency resources. Firstly, some assessment has to be made as regards the quantum of gold that can be raised from the public in India – either by the Government or by RBI for purposes of raising foreign currency loans. Given the not so satisfactory experience of gold mobilisation in the past, even during periods of war, when patriotic fervour was expected to contribute to the success of the scheme, it is doubtful whether substantial quantities can be mobilised now. Secondly, provision of gold as a collateral may or may not provide additional access to commercial borrowings. In fact, if the general approach is to contain the commercial borrowings, there is no reason to devise mechanisms for additional access. Therefore, providing gold as a collateral may give an indication that India is not in a position to raise loans on commercial terms without the collateral of gold. Thirdly, purely as a financial proposition, it may be difficult to sustain the operation of using gold as collateral unless the cost of commercial borrowings without collateral is significantly higher than what is currently indicated in the markets. Fourthly, the gold already available with the RBI itself can be used in the first instance for raising foreign currency resources before taking recourse to raising of gold from the market. Finally, at a time when import of gold is being liberally permitted through the NRI mechanisms, the special status of gold ceases to exist. The Committee, however, noted that there is a substantial body of opinion in favour of mobilising gold not only for the large quantities expected but also for changing attitudes

of people to gold. Hence, the Committee recommends that (a) caution be exercised in creating permanent institutions or corporate bodies for mobilising gold; (b) gold bonds may be launched immediately as an experiment by Government as part of public debt; and (c) a review be made of the economics of such a scheme in 1993-94.

(e) Liability management is an important area. Given the globalisation of the financial markets, liability management has acquired significance, since it is possible to take recourse to currency swaps, etc., which are mutually beneficial to the parties involved. Some progress has already been made in regard to liability management and in particular, these have been decentralised to some of the experienced and leading players. The Committee recommends that the practices of liability management be encouraged.

(f) Entry into bond markets and loan markets is technically possible even now by Indian entities in selected markets. However, the Committee feels that unless the balance of payments situation requires an urgent entry, effort should be made to encourage the enterprises to make an entry into these markets only when the circumstances are favourable to establish a good effective market. Mere enthusiasm of lenders and excess liquidity in international markets or cash compulsions of a borrowing entity should not be the major considerations in approving re-entry into these markets. The Committee thus recommends adequate preparation and assessment before permitting re-entry of large players.

(g) The level of external commercial borrowings is an important consideration. It is necessary to ensure that the total amount of commercial borrowings is fixed in advance and every effort made to restrict commercial borrowings to that level. Adopting such an approach and making that approach fairly transparent would ensure greater confidence in international markets about the management of external debt apart from ensuring controlled and sustainable balance of payments transactions. The Committee, therefore, recommends that on an average, the disbursements of

external commercial borrowings should not exceed US $ 2.5 billion per year during the Eighth Five-Year Plan.

(h) In addition to the quantum, the Committee recommends a deliberate policy or prioritising the use to which external debt is to be put. Priority for non-tradables such as power, core sectors like oil and fertilizers, and liberal access to units with export obligation is called for. In particular, the Committee recommends that commercial borrowings be prohibited for balance of payments support, unless it is for very long maturities and funds are obtained for special purposes or under somewhat concessional terms.

(i) As regards maturities, given the current repayment obligations, whereby over half of the outstanding debt on account of commercial borrowings will have to be discharged in the next four years, the Committee recommends that no approval be accorded for any commercial borrowing with a maturity of less than five years for the present; and every effort be made to seek borrowings with an average maturity of at least five years. Exceptions could, however, be made in regard to the consolidation and conversion of short-term debt into medium term debt.

(j) The question of guarantees in respect of borrowings has to be examined in terms of the policy of extending sovereign guarantee, charging guarantee fee, offering counter guarantee and guarantee by public sector Development Financial Institutions or Banks. In the past, sovereign guarantee was extended to public sector institutions only, though an exception was made for a World Bank lending to the private sector. However, wherever possible, Public Sector Institutions were encouraged to obtain borrowings without guarantee. There was no uniform policy of levying guarantee fee to public sector, inviting a comment from Comptroller and Auditor General that this meant a hefty subsidy. More recently, in respect of Public Enterprises, which are being restructured and privatised, lender's consent was made conditional on extending sovereign guarantees, even when originally there was no such guarantee. In the recent past, public sector banks/ DFI's are

seeking counter guarantee from Government so that their capital adequacy norms, which are now being insisted upon, could be fulfilled more easily. In any case, some of the lenders were content in the past with DFIs/Public Sector Banks guarantees since they were wholly owned by Government/RBI. However, with the proposed reform, lenders' attitude to such guarantees is uncertain. Overall, given the recent downgrading of credit worthiness and uncertainties due to reforms, lenders may be inclined to insist on guarantees in the near term. Borrowers would tend to seek such guarantee not only to ensure access but also to gain on cost even if access is available without such a guarantee. Yet another aspect of reform is encouraging private foreign investment in the power sector. In view of the difficulties of ensuring payments by SEB's for power supplied, lenders are seeking repayment guarantee, though there are no doubts about transformation of rupees into foreign currency for servicing debt or equity. On a careful consideration of all these factors, the Committee recommends the following approach to guarantee for external borrowings: (i) Sovereign guarantee should continue to be available only to public enterprises and in exceptional cases to private sector limited to the financing by multilateral agencies like World Bank/ADB – as in the past; (ii) PEs should continue to be encouraged to approach the market without guarantee, though in the very near term it may be difficult due to credit worthiness criteria; (iii) to enable reform, where lender's consent requires continuing or extending guarantees in respect of existing loans to PE's, such guarantees should be available; (iv) to encourage disintermediation in administration of external assistance, guarantees may be extended to PEs to replace direct intermediation; (v) in all cases of guarantees, guarantee fee should be levied broadly aligned with market practices (i.e. about 2.75 per cent) and exceptions should be made only for specified reasons; (vi) Government should refuse counter guarantee for any guarantee by DFIs/public sector banks; (vii) public sector financial institutions should explicitly recognise the importance of capital adequacy

norms and additional capital needs before entering into large scale commitments on guarantees; (viii) In regard to power sector, suggestions are made that sovereign guarantee should be extended in respect of private sector also. No such guarantees should be considered since issues of adequate control over management/performance and discrimination between domestic and foreign companies will arise. However, firm arrangements to ensure payment for power supplied by all power generating companies (domestic or foreign, public or private) have to be devised. These may include opening of escrow accounts in a mutually agreed bank and pledging receivables of select area.

IX. NRI DEPOSITS

9.1 The policy during the Eighth Five-Year Plan and beyond in respect of NRI deposits will have to be clearly drawn from the past experience of excessive reliance on them to finance external funding requirements with adverse consequences. Three important approaches were adopted to attract NRI deposits in the past: (a) Maintaining a liberal interest rate differential over the prevailing international interest rates for dollar and other currencies with a view to providing an incentive; (b) RBI assuming full exchange risk on FCNR deposits in all maturity brackets; and (c) extending fiscal concessions to the NRI transactions. The combined effect of the policies has been that a substantial inflow of NRI deposits has been in FCNR account. The large interest differential between international interest rate levels and FCNR rates has, over the years, provided a built-in incentive to banks to arbitrage the funds, so that the original objective of NRI deposits mobilising the genuine savings of the working Indian population abroad has receded to the background. Since the funds were attracted by interest differential and prompted by temporary opportunities, as soon as the first sign of difficulties appeared in the economy, there was a reverse flow. During April-December, 1991, there was a net outflow of US $ 1.5 billion under FCNR account alone, besides about $ 30 million under the NR(E)R deposits, as against an inflow of about $ 397 million under FCNR Account and outflow of $ 31 million under NR(E)R Account, in the corresponding period of the preceding year. The total

outstanding balance under FCNR account dropped sharply from \$ 10.6 billion at end-March, 1991 to \$ 8.5 billion at end December, 1991.

9.2 The Committee, therefore, recommends that there is need for a deliberate policy shift with regard to FCNR deposits with a view to reducing the volatility and the cost and to make it attract the genuine savings of NRIs. To this end, the Committee suggests that the NRI deposit scheme be modified on the following terms:

(a) FCNR deposits should have a minimum maturity of one year; and

(b) The differential between international interest rates and FCNR rates should be progressively reduced to ensure that the scheme benefits only the genuine savers.

9.5 The Committee noted that the RBI introduced in April 1992 a new scheme for attracting non-repatriable deposits where there is complete freedom of banks from the CRR and SLR requirements, which at present stand at 15 per cent and 30 per cent, respectively on the funds mobilised. There are no priority sector financing obligations also. The Committee noted that there is need to accelerate this trend and broadbase the instruments for tapping the NRI funds.

9.6 The Committee also noted an important aspect of FCNR deposits whereby the foreign exchange risk is presently borne exclusively by the RBI. There are no precise estimates available on the impact of the exchange risk on the RBI over the last several years. It is necessary that this practice yields place to a system whereby banks are encouraged to mobilise deposits based on competitive rates and their credit standing and the funds are retained by them for onlending in foreign currency for the clients' needs.

9.7 The Committee is also of the opinion that a market for NRI Bonds should be developed to satisfy the investor appetite among NRIs for some form of medium term investments in India with facility for secondary trading. A series of NRI Bonds issued over a period of time would also provide the much needed stability in the quantum of NRI resources available to the country. With necessary approvals from the regulatory authorities in various countries, the bonds could also be issued as general bonds targeted at both NRIs as well as foreigners. The Committee, however, feels that NRIs

should be treated as a separate and distinct investor segment because (i) the concerns and aspirations of NRIs are quite different; (ii) the fiscal concessions in India provided in the NRI bond schemes would not be of interest to the foreigners; and (iii) the interest that we pay on NRI bonds – even if it is marginally higher than normal – will not become a benchmark for the general borrowings of Indian entities in the international financial/capital markets. Besides, Indian entities like ONGC, IDBI, SBI, etc. could always access the international capital markets with bond issues targeted at all investors (such as Yankee Bonds, Samurai Bonds, Euro Bonds, etc.) whenever specific needs arise.

X. SHORT TERM DEBT

10.1 The Committee noted that serious concerns have been expressed about the level of short term debt and its contribution to the crisis situation. However, in the view of the Committee, the problem was not so much the magnitude of short term debt since its level, as a percentage of imports or as a percentage of total debt, is less than that of other comparable countries. The problem, however, arose due to the fact that short term debt was used not for purely trade financing purposes, but as a means of protecting the reserves. Secondly, short-term debt which was normally incurred for a period of six months was rolled over more than once because of the inability of the country to release foreign exchange reserves for discharging such debt. Thirdly, most of the short term debt was incurred by a single canalising agency, *viz.*, the Indian Oil Corporation and the bulk of the burden was borne by one bank, *viz.*, State Bank of India. Finally, there was a mismatch in terms of receipt of rupee resources by the canalising agency and corresponding discharge of its liabilities with the result that there were substantial rupee resources available with the canalising agencies which were placed in the short term money markets. These agencies had, of course, to bear the burden of exchange risk fluctuations.

10.2 In the light of past experience, the Committee recommends that the policy of the Government and the Reserve Bank of India in regard to the management of short term debt should be: (a) short term debt should be permitted only for trade-related purposes and under normal terms. Normal terms may be defined as trade-related debt permissible through routine procedures of authorised dealers

under the Exchange Control Regulations; (b) recourse to short-term debt should not be taken as an instrument for protecting the reserves; (c) no rollover beyond six months should be agreed in regard to any short term facilities without careful consideration of the implications; (d) any short term debt not governed by the above considerations should be specifically approved by RBI after satisfying itself that recourse to such debt was on genuine cost considerations or trade-related considerations; (e) Reserve Bank of India should set up a monitoring system for short-term debt, so that it is possible to ascertain with a reasonable amount of accuracy, the extent of such debt that may be outstanding at any point of time.

XI. STRUCTURE OF EXTERNAL DEBT

11.1 The broad characteristics of structure of external debt of India can be summarised as follows:

(a) Debt outstanding as a percentage of GDP may appear relatively large, but a substantial part of it is on concessional terms and, therefore, the burden of such debt is in reality less than what is apparent.

(b) The average maturity of external debt and, in particular of external commercial borrowings is longer than in regard to many of the developing countries.

(c) However, external debt on account of Non-Resident Indians, which so far has not been treated as part of external debt, has a maturity of three years and below.

(d) The NRI sources which account for a significant part of debt on commercial terms is characterised by volatility and relatively high cost.

(e) Since commercial borrowings commenced in the late Eighties and some of them have bullet maturity, about half of the total external commercial borrowings outstanding are due for repayment during the Eighth Five-Year Plan itself. In addition, India Development Bonds amounting to 1.6 billion dollars along with most of the interest is due to be repaid in the terminal year of the Plan. Further, repayments on account of IMF are bunched in the last two years of the Eighth Plan.

(f) In addition to the treatment of non-resident deposits as part of external debt, there is a special liability of external debt owed to the erstwhile USSR.

(g) The total debt servicing needs, viewed as a percentage of exports, is still moderate compared with most developing countries. In fact, since the dividend liability is still at very low levels, the total liabilities to service debt and equity for India would be far less than those for most other developing countries.

(h) While strict control has been kept on the approval of individual loans, in terms of cost, maturity and instruments, the policy frame available for ensuring the productive use of such external debt has proved to be inadequate. In other words, the large receipts on account of NRI deposits and a part of external commercial borrowings have turned out to be more in the nature of balance of payments support than addition to the productive capacity of the country.

11.2 The Committee noted with satisfaction the Reports of the Policy Group and Task Force on External Debt Statistics of India and its adoption by the Government and the Reserve Bank of India. The Committee also noted that a Standing High Level Committee on external debt has been constituted by the Government. These would facilitate improvements in the structure and management of external debt.

11.3 In regard to the future directions on the structure of debt, the Committee recommends necessary policy and procedural changes to bring about the following: (i) Quick disbursement of concessional and semi-concessional flows; (ii) disintermediation of Government to the maximum extent in aid flows; (iii) absorption of aid only when it is consistent with the requirements of the enterprise concerned or department/state concerned; (iv) continuation of NRI deposits at a level that would ensure no net outflow but with longer maturities profile; insistence on a minimum maturity of five years, for commercial borrowings except for purposes of consolidation of short-term debt; (v) recourse to commercial sources of financing essentially to meet foreign currency expenditures, particularly for non-tradeable goods, priority sectors like oil and fertilizer export oriented units etc. or borrowings linked with inflow of equity; and (vi) a prudent policy

of extending guarantees by sovereign or public sector financial and banking institutions.

XII. FOREIGN INVESTMENT

12.1 Foreign investment has played a very limited role in the Indian economy so far. Total Foreign Direct Investment approvals during the years 1986 to 1990 amounted barely to Rs.180 crores per annum on an average when other comparable developing countries managed to register foreign investment of enormous magnitudes. Thailand had an average foreign investment flows of US $ 1.6 billion during the last three years, while China registered an inflow of US $ 3 billion in 1990-91. Other countries like Indonesia and Malaysia have also been receiving foreign investment of substantial amounts.

12.2 The Committee noted the major changes in the government's policies towards attracting foreign investments, which have been put in place since July, 1991, to create a favourable climate. The new foreign investment policy has, apart from addressing the irritants in the old regime, brought about a new impetus towards upgradation of technology levels, integrating Indian industry into global economy, and, more importantly, bringing in non-debt resources (as a favoured option compared with debt flows).

12.3 The Committee felt that the following steps already taken would go a long way in promoting the confidence of foreign investors for investing in India.

(a) Signing of the MIGA convention by India.

(b) Allowing foreign brand names to be used in India.

(c) Removal of the condition of dividend balancing (for all except industries in the consumer goods sector).

(d) Removal of licensing of industrial capacities.

(e) Simplification of import-export procedures.

(f) Relaxation of exchange controls and removal of the rigours of FERA, specially regarding hiring of foreign technicians, and purchase of immovable property in India.

(g) Opening up of Indian stock markets for the foreign institutional investors.

(h) Partial convertibility of the rupee.

(i) Emergence of SEBI as an effective watchdog institution.

12.4 In considering our approach to attract foreign investment, the Committee felt that we have to draw lessons from the experience of other countries. Briefly stated, these are:

(a) Government has played a crucial role in attracting foreign investment to desired sectors and was not simply liberalising in a passive way.

(b) Foreign investment policies were used as instruments of technological upgradation. For example, a 'pioneer status' in Singapore was accorded to foreign investment units linked to high technology. In particular, technologies in which the country was either backward or technologies which were considered essential in a strategic way were encouraged.

(c) There has been a link between multi-national companies' activities and foreign trade. To this extent, MNCs play an important role. However, the tax-regime had to be so arranged to ensure that there was no negative flow through transfer pricing.

(d) In the recent past, there is a rapidly expanding role for smaller and medium enterprises. Further, the growth of investment in service sector is far higher than investment in manufacturing sector.

(e) A modern financial sector, combining efficiency and proper regulation is increasingly perceived as an important element of encouraging investment flows.

12.5 The Committee further noted the following important parameters of a global nature that would determine the scope and limits for foreign investments in the immediate future.

First, since several developed countries are facing recession, the immediate scope for investment flows into the Indian Economy may be constrained; Second, even if such flows occur, there may be a tendency for West Europe concentrating in East Europe (and Russia); North America concentrating on South Asia and China; Third, while Indian liberalisation is impressive with reference to the past, relative to other countries, the status of liberalisation and social commitment

to liberalisation in future are inadequate; Fourth, the inherent competitive strengths; policy framework such as existing infrastructure (Power, Telecommunications) are still far from adequate to interest foreign investors; Fifth, the "story" that existing foreign investors have to tell about Indian regulatory framework has to turn positive.

12.6 The Committee gathered that the current concerns of foreign investors are:

(a) The dividend repatriation is governed by FERA. While the investors appreciate our impeccable record of automatically permitting repatriation of dividends, once the conditions are satisfied, they have a feeling of discomfort because this is in the nature of relaxation of a regulation rather than a right available under law. They are also concerned about complex reporting needs and long-winding procedures because this is governed by exemption from regulation.

(b) As regards disinvestment, they appreciate the progress made from the earlier CCI guidelines. However, even though the liberalised framework has been incorporated under FERA, as amended on 8.1.1993, the disinvestment guidelines are still in the form of an administrative decision, and a press release. They have no doubt about transformation into foreign currency once the procedures are followed. However, a transparent formalised policy through law, incorporating the existing status, would be preferred.

(c) While, because of the constitutional and legal provisions in the country, no discrimination is made between an Indian company and a foreign company, unless specified as part of the condition of clearance of such foreign equity, the foreign investors would prefer non-discriminatory element to be codified. No doubt, social conditions can be prescribed under such a code.

(d) The restrictions of FERA on employment of foreign nationals have been liberalised on 8.1.1993. It would be easier to transact business if such permissions are codified into a formal law rather than making them permissible by non-restriction.

(e) The policy framework and institutional set up currently in vogue for clearing foreign investment under non-automatic route are in the nature of administrative arrangements. A clear-cut idea about priorities, preferences and procedures would be essential. Hence, institutional arrangements for non-automatic route can be formalised and made transparent through a law.

(f) While it is generally appreciated that India does not indulge in nationalisation unless it is in public interest and that too with adequate compensation, a formal incorporation of that provision into a law or treaty would provide the necessary assurances to shareholders of the investing companies.

(g) Certain institutions such as IFC (Washington) have sought and obtained domestic investor status. Instead of passing separate legislation for according such status, this could be incorporated into an investment law, enabling according such status by gazette notifications.

(h) While there are discussions about new instruments of flow of foreign investments such as BOT (Build, Operate and Transfer), there is no clear-cut legal framework governing such operations.

(i) In regard to commercial borrowings, it is appreciated by the informed investors that Government of India's approval is required for every borrowing of a duration of more than one year. This is a requirement under FERA. After such an approval, registration with Reserve Bank of India is enough to provide the right to the borrower to pay interest and principal on schedule as per the agreement straightway through the authorised dealer. However, there is no formal statement of such rights automatically accruing, though this is the current practice. A formal provision would enable the foreign investors to be convinced about the superfluity of seeking guarantees against transformation or assurance of preferred credit status.

(j) The applicability of laws and the arrangements are governed by individual agreements which are cleared by RBI or filed with RBI. There is no recognised policy and procedural framework so far.

(k) There is no provision for special treatment for foreign investors bringing in high technology. In other words, there is no provision in the existing legal framework which could determine the parameters for according formally a 'pioneer status', and benefits that could flow.

(l) There are concerns about high rate of taxes, especially capital gains. These should be comparable with other developing countries.

(m) There are, above all, doubts as to whether India can provide reliable infrastructure (given persistent shortages) and skilled labour force (not simply skilled professionals),

(n) Finally, there are, what are described as 'hassle factors', *viz.*, cumbersome procedures for entry operations and exit.

12.7 In the light of the above, the Committee recommends the following approach to foreign investments:

(a) There is a need to have a strategy for attracting investments by country, sources, technologies, size of companies and sectors.

(b) Our growth process is substantially determined by domestic savings and investment; foreign investment plays quantitatively very small but qualitatively a significant part (in terms of foreign trade technology competition inducements). The strategy, policy and procedures should reinforce the qualitative aspects.

(c) Government policy towards Foreign Direct Investments has to be discriminating. An open-door policy is not likely to produce optimum results unless supported by checks and balances.

(d) Competitive granting of concessions by way of tax or subsidies is neither necessary nor adequate. Government should maximise the benefits from the technology brought in by foreign investors. This can be done by identifying the thrust areas/sectors for foreign investments and working out the linkages so that technology gets absorbed at the earliest.

(e) It may be advisable to de-emphasize cheap labour availability alone as an incentive for foreign investments — what we

should emphasize is skilled and semi-skilled labour, information services, etc. which have better chance of being competitively provided by our economy. This implies focus on services sector.

(f) Our policy of attracting foreign investment into India should be matched by a well worked out policy of encouraging Indian companies to invest in joint collaboration/ takeovers and promote companies in other countries especially in trading blocks like EEC. However, given the balance of payments implications efforts should be made to emphasize less capital intensive skill or service oriented activities for Indian investments abroad.

(g) Government policy for foreign investments is perhaps best set in the context of a stable macroeconomic policy with manageable fiscal deficit, moderate rate of inflation, realistic exchange rate and above all, a system of accountability in which the basic economic and legal framework of the country is reliable and adequate. The foreign investors expect the system to guarantee enforcement of contracts and the flexibility to shift investment with the minimum of difficulty. The importance of simple and unified legal framework, limited but effective contact institutions in India and transparent (rather than case by case) approaches should be recognised.

(h) Evolve necessary legal and institutional framework to meet the concerns of foreign investors, in particular, a positive statement of our policies and practices rather than through exceptions.

12.8 The Committee, having recognised the concerns of the foreign investors, recommends that a National Investment Law be seriously considered, codifying the existing policy and practices relating to dividend repatriation, disinvestment, non-discrimination subject to conditions that may be specified, employment of foreign nationals, non-expropriation, and sanction and servicing of external commercial borrowings. Such a law could also provide for enabling policy procedures and institutional framework for approval of investments under non-automatic route, according pioneer status or

domestic-investor status, new instruments of private commercial flows and applicability of local or international laws etc. Such an Investment Law need not in any way exclude consideration of bilateral investment treaties.

Indian Investments Abroad

12.9 Till recently, the effort was to link clearance of Indian equity abroad with export of Indian equipment. Further, we had proceeded under the assumption that capital-flight can occur if we liberalised Indian investments abroad. However, a few months ago there was a relaxation. According to the relaxation, all cash remittances upto US $ 500,000 were approved on automatic basis. The scheme was administered by the inter-Ministerial Committee in Commerce Department. Individual cases in the past and cases other than automatic route in the recent past required approval of Finance Minister and Commerce Minister. FERA was the legal instrument through which this policy and procedure was implemented. The Committee emphasises need to review this policy due to a number of developments. Firstly, when we are liberalising Foreign Direct Investment, we should encourage Indian joint ventures abroad. Secondly, with partial convertibility of rupee, the idea that capital flight has to be controlled through regulatory administration may have to be given up. Thirdly, with increasing opportunities for services sector and skills in India, it should be possible to encourage Indian investments of a less capital-intensive and more skill intensive nature abroad. Fourthly, strategic presence may be needed because of emerging trade blocks such as EEC. Finally, globalisation would involve close interaction between Indian and foreign companies on a global scale. The Committee noted with satisfaction the most recent liberalisation measures in FERA and recommends that an appropriate framework be evolved to promote Indian investment abroad in desired directions, countries and sectors in addition to liberalising procedures.

XIII. EXPORTS

13.1 The viability of the balance of payments and the economic reform programme rests on a robust export performance in the coming years. The macroeconomic balance in the Eighth Plan suggests an export growth of 13.6 per cent per annum in volume terms

which translates into about 15 to 16 per cent in dollar terms at 1991-92 exchange rate and prices. The achievement of this target is beset with several problems. The world economy is yet to recover from the recession experienced in the past two years. The Indian exporters are still adjusting to the collapse of the erstwhile Soviet Union, which was a major market for their products. The domestic industrial production scene is not encouraging. The Indian industry which has been protected far too long is yet to acquire export culture. Infrastructural and other constraints still plague exporters. Procedural complexities, having their origins in an environment where import prevention was of higher priority than export achievement, continue to bedevil the aggressive push that is needed on the export front.

13.2 Nevertheless, the export targets set forth in the Plan are achievable, provided a package of export incentives is appropriately designed. There has to be full recognition that till the end of the Eighth Plan period, at least, export incentives should not only remain, but would need to be reinforced. In fact, the export incentive package should form an integral part of the economic reform programme.

13.3 The experience of successful exporting countries including the East Asian economies shows export incentives are required to complement exchange rate and import liberalisation policies to enable exporters to compete effectively with foreign competitors in world markets on an equal footing. This is also necessary to make exports as profitable as domestic sales. Hence, there is a case to provide incentives to the export sector to neutralise the effects of high tariffs, high interest rates, inflation and high infrastructural costs.

13.4 It is, however, recognised that direct export incentives are temporary arrangements and, over the medium to long-run, the export environment must be stimulated by exchange rate policy; rationalised tariff system where protection is based only on tariffs and not quantitative restrictions; product specific and market specific promotion and marketing strategies; and macroeconomic stability.

13.5 To achieve the targets set forth in the Eighth Plan and reflected in the balance of payments projections in this Reports, the Committee recommends the following:

(a) Movements towards fuller convertibility of the rupee since partial convertibility imposes a tax on exports.

(b) Reforms in interest rates on export credit to ensure reasonable costs to exporter.

(c) Stability of existing export incentives, i.e., an assurance that the incentives would continue.

(d) Encouraging deemed exports by measures such as freedom for Indian bidders to bid in foreign currency when they bid under ICB procedures (since implemented).

(e) Simplification of Export-Import Policy especially replacing quantitative curbs on exports with duties, and

(f) Procedural Reforms; including removal of the procedural complexities that still exist in our customs, banks, ports, import licensing in DGFT's organisation, and various departments/agencies of the Central and state governments to align them with the practices prevailing in the rest of the world.

13.6 Given such an export environment, the targets set forth in the Five Year Plan and reflected in the Reports, though formidable, is well within our reach. This is so since the share of Indian exports in total world exports is abysmally low at 0.5 per cent and major items of our export form a small proportion of the imports of these goods by our trading partners (0.2 per cent). Moreover, the share of exports to GDP at around 6 to 7 per cent is not fully compatible with the capabilities of the country.

XIV. BoP PROJECTIONS FOR MEDIUM TERM

14.1 In line with the considerations and proposed approach on the different elements in the balance of payments, projections have been made for the medium term time frame coinciding with the Eighth Plan period.

14.2 In making the balance of payments projections, the Committee has kept in view (a) the macroeconomic parameters as envisaged in the Eighth Plan; (b) likely impact of the policy changes; (c) outlook and prospects of international trade; and (d) updated estimates for 1991-92 and the latest available estimates for 1992-93.

14.3 The BoP projections for the period 1992-93 to 1996-97 mainly suggest that, to sustain the level of foreign exchange reserves

considered necessary minimum by the Committee over the medium term, to maintain on average a current account ratio not exceeding 1.6 and to control the external debt level, the different components of the BoP will have to be targeted and realised in a manner consistent with the medium-term projections estimated by the Committee.

Exports

14.4 An average annual growth in exports of at least 15 per cent in dollar terms over the medium term is considered necessary as well as feasible. The Committee considers the export component as the most crucial one to meet the sustainable level of CAD. In projecting the 15 per cent growth rate for export, the Committee has assumed recovery in international trade from 1993-94 onwards on the basis of the latest available indications from the growth prospects as well as trade outlook for the developed countries, the envisaged growth in industrial sector during the Eighth Five-Year Plan, impact of changes in trade policy and exchange rate policy and likely influence of Foreign Direct Investments particularly in the export- oriented sectors. The Committee, therefore, strongly recommends that the trade policy and exchange rate regime be managed not only in a stable manner but also induced towards export orientation.

Imports

14.5 Growth in imports during the medium term is estimated to be higher than what the Plan estimates assume because of the large decline in the base. Thus, in dollar terms the imports are estimated to grow by about 12 per cent per annum compared with a volume growth of 8.4 per cent assumed in the Eighth Plan estimates. Reducing the scope and control on imports through the Foreign Exchange Budget mechanism with an objective to finally eliminate the FEB mechanism, free access to foreign exchange to PSUs, measures to decontrol the imports through trade policy changes, increase in export-related imports, and a likely slow recovery in domestic output of crude and petroleum products at least in the next one or two years lead the Committee to believe that the imports growth rate may be marginally higher than what has been estimated on the basis of import elasticity to GDP at 1.5 for the past.

Invisibles

14.6 Net inflows in the 'Invisibles' component of the current account are estimated to contribute almost a negligible share, even though there would be a turnaround from a net outflow within a year or two. Travel receipts can contribute to a limited extent only in increasing net receipts in the 'invisibles' account. A 10 per cent growth in dollar terms through travel receipts on a recovered base for 1992-93 should be possible, once the policy changes in tourism sector are implemented. However, there are reasons to believe that travel payments may also increase by about nine per cent per annum as a result of liberalisation in exchange controls, abolition of travel tax and other related policy measures. Net receipts on transportation account based on export related transactions for inflows and the time trend for outflows do not suggest any significant contribution. Another major component under invisibles account, *viz.*, interest payments has been estimated on the basis of projections of debt servicing on the loans outstanding as at end-March 1991, transactions with IMF as included in the capital account and estimated borrowings during the medium term as incorporated in these projections. As for private transfer receipts, a 10 per cent growth in dollar values has been assumed, considering that reconstruction activities in the Gulf region would lead to increased emigration, the proportion of skilled and professional labour force emigrating would increase and remitting money through this channel would continue to remain attractive consequent upon the exchange rate policy changes.

Current Account Balance

14.7 The projections for different components in the current account would result in a declining Current Account Deficit (CAD)/ GDP ratio from estimated 2.9 per cent in 1992-93 to 0.5 per cent in 1996-97 and an average of 1.6 per cent during the five year period. The Committee feels that this order of current account deficit, *viz.*, 1.6 per cent of GDP can be net through a sustainable level of net capital receipts.

Capital Account

14.8 Medium term projections for the different components in the capital account are mainly based on the considerations and recommendations made by this Committee in respective chapters.

14.9 Based on the estimates for current account and capital account components over the medium term, it is clear to the Committee that the need for exceptional financing arrangements of the order of $ 3 billion per year on gross basis would be necessary during the medium term. However, this would be reduced somewhat through better export performance, better 'invisible' receipts and higher investment inflows – all of which is not impossible.

XV. BALANCE OF PAYMENTS – STATISTICAL ISSUES

15.1 A reference was made by the Government to the Committee to give its recommendations on the discrepancies between the value of imports as reported by the DGCIS and those reported by the Reserve Bank of India. The Committee had the benefit of preliminary notes and discussions held by a separate Committee appointed by RBI for the purpose sometime ago. The Committee had the benefit of the Report of the Policy Group on External Debt Statistics constituted by the Reserve Bank of India.

15.2 In the light of these, it has been possible to identify the reasons for the discrepancies:

(a) The single largest item accounting for the difference appears to be the payments on account of defence. Some of the imports by the Ministry of Defence and the Defence public sector undertakings pass through customs and they are incorporated in the data accordingly. However, other purchases on account of defence are paid through deferred payment arrangement. These are not formally recorded as debt in the Ministry of Finance, Government of India, and these are also not recorded as external commercial borrowings by the Reserve Bank of India. Under the circumstances, all payments made towards discharging the past obligations by the Defence Department, both to rupee payment area and general currency area, get reflected in the difference between the DGCIS statistics and the balance of payment data.

(b) In addition, some imports made by Defence and other security organisations claim exemption from customs declaration and as such do not get reflected in the DGCIS statistics.

(c) There are differences in the valuation methods of foreign currencies between the Reserve Bank of India and Customs.

(d) There are leads and lags in physical imports and payments. They distort the picture in particular years when there are large transactions.

(e) Some cases, where payments are made by ONGC for acquiring material for its overseas operations, may not be reported to Customs. Similarly, acquisition of ships, civilian aircraft and other assets offshore by shipping companies and airlines may not get reflected in the customs data.

15.3 Having identified, the major reasons, the Committee recommends the following changes in the compilation and presentation of the balance of payment statistics.

(a) All defence debt may be formally registered as commercial debt whenever it is for more than one year, and trade-related debt whenever it is for one year or less as is the normal practice.

(b) Debt in respect of rupee payment area may be reflected separately in the capital account without making a distinction between principal and interest, consistent with recently concluded Rupee-Rouble agreement.

(c) In respect of defence debt to general currency area, differentiation may be made between principal and interest according to loan agreements. All such agreements may be treated on par with other commercial borrowings in regard to procedures of registration with the Ministry of Finance and the Reserve Bank of India. Consequent changes in presentation of balance of payments statistics to show interest under invisibles and principal under capital account will have to be made.

(d) Where imports do not pass through Customs declarations, concerned agencies may be requested to report in a consolidated form, the value of imports on a routine basis for purposes of incorporation into the customs data.

(e) Information system may be established through Ministry of Shipping and Ministry of Petroleum to obtain information

on payments made but not reflected in Customs in respect of shipping companies and ONGC, since goods do not enter the country.

15.4 The Committee further recommends that a Technical Group be appointed by Reserve Bank of India with representatives from the Ministry of Finance and the Ministry of Commerce similar to the Policy Group on External Debt Statistics, to review in detail the timeliness, the compilation methods and the suitability of reporting systems for purposes of management of balance of payments.

INTERIM REPORT OF THE COMMITTEE ON BALANCE OF PAYMENTS

February 1992

Exchange Rate Management

The Government of India have constituted a High Level Committee on Balance of Payments to make medium term projections and evolve appropriate measures to bring down the Current Account deficit to sustainable levels vide Ministry of Finance, Department of Economic Affairs Order No. F.No.1(24)/91-BP dated the 19th November 1991. (Copy enclosed)

> One of the terms of reference of the Committee [para 3(v)] reads as follows: "to examine the functioning of the existing exchange rate regime in the context of the move to Exim-Scrips and to consider the implications of a shift to convertibility on current transactions in the near future."

The Committee was also required to consider submission of interim reports on particular aspects which required urgent consideration (vide para 4). During the deliberations, a consensus developed in the Committee towards urgent consideration of issues relating to the management of the exchange rate system in the light of the introduction of Exim Scrips in July 1991. Accordingly, the Committee is submitting this Interim Report on this subject. In submitting its recommendations in this Interim Report, the Committee emphasises that the actions suggested do not in any way pre-empt the recommendations of the Committee on the other terms of reference.

Introduction

The current year and the past year have been two extremely difficult years in the post Independence history of our country. These difficulties have risen mainly due to the problems in our balance of payments. Even as we have tided over the immediate problems, it is necessary to move towards a situation when the balance of payments becomes sustainable on an enduring basis. The Eighth Plan Directional Paper has indicated that the sustainable level of current account deficit for the next five years will be 1.4 per cent of the GDP. This will amount to approximately $ 4 billion per annum at current prices in US dollars. Assuming an overall growth rate of 5.6 per cent per annum in the economy and an import elasticity 1.5, it has been estimated that this order of current account deficit will require that exports in volume terms grow at 13.6 per cent per annum in the next five years. This is indeed a daunting task. Under these circumstances, it is necessary that the overall policy stance and more particularly, the exchange rate regime is such as to positively favour export growth. In this part of the report, the Committee is addressing the issue of exchange rate regime in the light of the experience with Exim Scrip Scheme.

Exim Scrip Scheme

2. EXIM Scrip was introduced in August 1991 as an important reform in the trade policy replacing a complicated system of incentives including a system of REP licences which were given to exporters at different rates for different commodities. The Exim Scrip Scheme helped to put in place a generalised incentive structure for all exports with a wider commodity coverage, a higher average entitlement and less dispersion in rates than in the REP system. It also reduced the need for budget subsidies to exports. By all accounts, the scheme has been well received by the exporting community and has operated well. There are demands for expanding the coverage of Exim Scrip beyond areas of goods trade and professional services to cover other foreign exchange inflows. A number of suggestions have been made to simplify the procedures, and to identify mechanisms of avoiding malpractices and operating the Exim Scrip directly through the banking system.

3. The Committee considered the existing Exim Scrip system with a view to:

(a) Correcting inadequacies and drawbacks in its operations.

(b) Expanding the coverage of such mechanisms. and

(c) Improving upon the nature of the system so that it could provide a base for the changes in the future.

Options

4. In examining the Exim Scrip Scheme and possible alternatives, the Committee was governed by some important considerations. These are:

(a) Containing current account deficit at a sustainable level.

(b) Strengthening the balancing properties in the scheme and thereby ensuring an equilibrium within a larger subset of transactions.

(c) Imparting the necessary degree of flexibility in the exchange rate system.

(d) Ensuring that the cost of the essential imports does not rise abruptly.

(e) Keeping capital outflows under close control and monitoring. and

(f) Replacing unnecessary burdensome case-by-case, regulatory mechanisms of exchange control with simpler, more efficient and transparent system-to enhance productive efficiency and ease of transactions.

5. The Committee considered a number of options to bring about improvements in the system. In this task, suggestions received from industrial and trade organisations, informal consultations with professionals, the background technical papers prepared in the Ministries of Commerce, Finance, Planning Commission and Reserve Bank of India as well as interactions with these institutions and the Ministry of Industry have been the major inputs.

6. The options considered in regard to coverage of Exim Scrip Scheme were:

(a) Expanding the Exim Scrip entitlement and correspondingly, usage to cover imports of all trade transactions except banned items, canalised commodities, and government departmental requirements.

(b) Expanding Exim Scrip entitlements to services, remittances including the hotel industry, tourism, etc. and corresponding usage to all authorised service payments, and

(c) Expanding the use of the instrument to all transactions, including those on capital account.

7. In terms of achieving the basic objectives stated earlier, the options considered were:

(a) Re-defining the eligibility of Exim Scrip on a uniform basis but based on net rather than on gross export earnings.

(b) Replacing the Exim Scrip instrument with suitable arrangements within the banking system.

(c) Issuing of foreign exchange certificates by banks which could be freely traded to replace the existing Exim Scrips.

(d) Identifying a separate category of rupees called "convertible" rupee which will be basically operated through the banking system applicable to a class of export-import transactions with the necessary premium determined in the market, and

(e) Introducing a Partially Convertible Rupee system (PCR) involving two channels. These are: the official channel which will be used for meeting priority requirements at official exchange rate, and the market channel for rest of the transactions where the exchange rate will be determined by the market forces, replacing existing Exim Scrip.

Proposed System

8. The proposed system of exchange rate arrangement has been evolved by detailed examination of all options mentioned above through a series of mutual consultations. The Committee had the benefit of analysing quantitative implications as well as procedural aspects in regard to all the above options.

9. The Exim Scrip Scheme, as it operates now, is limited in scope. It will have to be extended to cover a larger set of export and import

transactions if the equilibrating properties of the Scheme are to be enhanced. The Scheme, besides covering trade transactions, must also include invisible transactions in order to establish equality of treatment between service earnings and trade earnings. However, it is feared that with the extension of the Exim Scrip Scheme, the number of transactions will become large and the system may become cumbersome and difficult to operate. Besides, the entitlements are based upon actual export earnings for which certificates have to be obtained from the banking system. Already, there are instances of forgeries of such certificates. Inclusion of service earnings and remittances will require that the system operate through the banking system, since it would be difficult for the office of the DGFT to handle such claims. The Committee, therefore, felt that the new scheme, while retaining the essential element of the link between exports and imports, should be one that is operated through the banking system and eliminates the need for issue of licences. The basic elements of the new system should be:

(a) Ensuring the equilibrium between demand and supply in respect of a fairly large sub-set of external transactions given the capital flows.

(b) Confining such market operations to authorised and approved transactions and thus, operating within the framework of import regulatory regime as may be prescribed, and

(c) Establishing an orderly market mechanism with a built-in provision to intervene in the market.

10. The Committee felt that the most suitable alternative to the present exchange rate system supplemented by EXIM Scrip Scheme will be a dual exchange market system with transactions in one market being settled at the official exchange rate and another market in which the transactions will be settled at a market determined rate. Even in the second market, all transactions that can be put through will be authorised and approved transactions. Nevertheless, the second market will play an important role in equilibrating demand and supply through changes in the rate in the immediate short run and over a period, through appropriate shifts in exports and imports.

11. The features of the system recommended by the Committee are as follows:

(a) All receipts under current transactions, – both merchandies exports and invisible receipts – will continue to be required to be surrendered to authorised dealers.

(b) Except for 40 per cent of the proceeds which would be credited in rupees at the Reserve Bank official rate, the rate of exchange for the balance of the 60 per cent of the earnings will be at the free market rate quoted by the authorised dealers. These proportions have been based on the expected export earnings through goods and services and private remittances and the value of essential imports.

(c) The Reserve Bank of India will thus buy 40 per cent of the current account receipts at the official rate of exchange.

(d) The authorised dealers would be free to retain the remaining 60 per cent of foreign exchange and sell it at the market rate for all authorised and approved transactions.

(e) The foreign exchange received by the Reserve Bank of India at official exchange rate is meant exclusively to cover government departmental needs and to import four essential commodities, namely, crude oil, diesel, kerosene and fertilisers as authorised by the Government of India through its Foreign Exchange Budget. In addition, foreign exchange at official rate will be made available to meet 40 per cent of the value of advance licences and special imprest licences issued by the Ministry of Commerce. The Reserve Bank of India would sell foreign exchange to the authorised dealers at its official rate for meeting the above authorised requirements. RBI will continue to announce the official buying rate against select currencies as is being done at present.

(f) As regards to all other import transactions, they will have to be met out of the foreign exchange available in the free market. Indicative free market exchange rates may, however, be announced by Foreign Exchange Dealers' Associations of India, every working day in consultation with a group of banks.

(g) Receipts and payments on capital account will continue to be subject to control. The exchange rates for these transactions will, however, be at the free market rate.

Mechanics

12. The mechanics of the proposed system are fairly simple.

(i) Of the total export earnings, 60 per cent would be settled at market rate and 40 per cent at official rate. All import transactions, including those which require authorisation and excepting two categories mentioned below, would be settled at market determined exchange rates. Imports of specific government departments and imports of such critical commodities as mentioned earlier, will be at official exchange rate. Further, exporters would continue to obtain their import requirements under advance licences, special imprest licences, etc. to the tune of 40 per cent of the value of such licences at official exchange rate. This is intended to ensure that the average rate on imports is the same as the average rate on export earnings.

(ii) In respect of services also, all recipients would be eligible to obtain rupees at market rate to the tune of 60 per cent of their earnings/remittances. All payments in the invisibles account of balance of payments will have to be met by obtaining foreign exchange at market rate.

(iii) In respect of capital account, all inflows and outflows including the government requirements will be at market rate.

(iv) However, the official grants received by the Government will be accounted for at official rate and inflows as well as outflows under IMF will also be at official rate.

Transitional Arrangements

13. There is need to make some transitional arrangements to implement the system. These include:

(a) Making available foreign exchange at the official exchange rate by RBI for imports related to the outstanding Exim Scrip and for RBI to honour all outstanding forward commitments and swap liabilities.

(b) Continuing with the current practice in respect of ACU and RPA (Asian Clearing Union and Rupee Payment Area under bilateral agreements) transactions, pending discussions to

bring such arrangements in alignment with the liberalised exchange rate arrangement.

Likely Benefits

14. (a) The advantages of the proposed system in respect of various categories of people are fairly obvious. Firstly, the incentive to exporters will be higher since the entitlement ratio will be increased from a level of 30 per cent for Exim Scrip to a level of 60 per cent of foreign exchange earnings. In other words, as long as the premium in the free market rate works out to be more than half the current premium on EXIM scrip, the exporters will be better off. This calculation needs to be modified to the extent that all imported inputs will have to be obtained at the market rate whereas at present a premium needs to be paid only for those imports which are on Exim Scrips. In general, however, exports which have a relatively low import intensity or where imports presently are not on OGL will be benefited. To protect exports where import intensity is high, provision should be made to ensure that imports against advance licences, special import licences, etc., can be made against release of foreign exchange at official rate upto 40 per cent of their licence value. This will ensure neutrality between the exchange rate on imports and the exchange rate on export earnings.

(b) Secondly, with the uniform entitlements for free market transactions, agricultural products and other products with less import intensity will find exports attractive.

(c) Thirdly, the large number of workers who have been remitting money and who have been denied any of the advantages of exporters so far, would immediately gain, since they would also be eligible for market rates to the tune of 60 per cent of the remittances.

(d) Fourthly, with the liberalisation in transactions relating to travel, advertisement, development/promotion, etc., for industry, trade and business, it would be far easier to conduct their operations. Further, all payments that are required from time to time – such as technology payment can be automatically made by access to foreign exchange at market rates. In fact, industry can freely access foreign exchange at market rate for their permissible import requirements, irrespective of whether they are capital goods, raw materials or components.

Precautionary Steps

15. It is necessary to recognise that there are certain inherent risks which will have to be attended to while formulating procedures. The effective premium may get increased or reduced for various reasons, thus, increasing uncertainties to the exporters and importers. With the expected level of export earnings and capital flows on one side and the import demand on the other, the premiums can be kept within reasonable limits. There is also a possibility of fluctuations through market manipulations by large players which may require constant monitoring and, if necessary, intervention on the part of the Reserve Bank of India. There may be an element of seasonality which could create pressures and make the premium volatile and this may have to be countered by RBI. If total inflows happen to be less than assumed, the total amount available for Government and priority sectors would automatically come down, unless the Reserve Bank draws down its reserves or converts foreign exchange from the market into foreign exchange at official rate.

Policy-linkages and Procedural Changes Needed

16. The implementation of the proposed system would necessarily have an impact on policy and procedures in fiscal policy, trade policy, industrial policy, public enterprise operations, exchange control mechanisms, reserve management etc. The major elements of relevance in this regard are summarised below:

(a) In the fiscal area, the customs revenue is likely to be higher, other things being the same, to the extent the valuation of imports would be based on the market exchange rate. It is, however, necessary to ensure that the tariff rates, together with higher import values, do not result in a sharp increase in import costs. Mechanisms will have to be put in place to ensure that the notification by the Ministry of Finance on the monthly valuation, reflects the market rate. It may also be necessary to review whether these rates should be applicable for one month or for a lesser period, say, 15 days. Secondly, debt servicing obligation by the Government will be higher in rupee terms. The inflow of resources in foreign currency on account of rupee expenditure, reimbursed by multilateral agencies, may be less

than what the inflow would be at official rate. Since, overall, there are net receipts under capital account to the Government, the adoption of market exchange rate should augment the receipts side of the budget. Thirdly, abolition of travel tax may be necessary to give appropriate signals to discourage hawala transactions and this may imply a marginal reduction in the revenue, but could be compensated by withdrawal of tax exempt status for transactions in foreign currency (bills paid to hotels, withholding tax on external borrowings). Fourthly, and most importantly, replacement of quantitative restrictions with tariffs would need careful targeting and fine tuning of tariff rates in respect of specific goods.

(b) In regard to trade policy, a variety of lists will have to be replaced by a simple banned/negative list. Secondly, some of the incentive mechanisms, currently in operation to provide a premium on earnings in foreign exchange, will become superfluous. Thirdly, it will be necessary to concentrate efforts on proper evaluation and administration in issue of automatic licences, special imprest licences etc. for exporters.

(c) In regard to industrial policy, the instrumentalities of OGL and Exim Scrip for preferential treatment would not be available any longer. Arrangements for technology payments and clearances for import of capital goods will have to be modified accordingly.

(d) The liability of public enterprises in terms of debt servicing is likely to increase, in so far as they have contracted foreign currency loans directly without the intermediation of the Government. A preliminary analysis shows that major public enterprises such as DFIs, Air India and Shipping Corporation of India are in some way or the other protected or compensated by their own operational parameters. If there are any individual cases requiring financial restructuring to meet these obligations without serious disruption, the Department of Public Enterprises may have to examine them on a case-by-case basis.

(e) Comprehensive arrangements will have to be put in place in the area of exchange control by the RBI. Firstly, the banks/ authorised dealers would have to be governed by the prudential guidelines to be communicated by the Reserve Bank, keeping in view the more important elements of the trade policy. Secondly, reporting mechanisms will have to be developed from all authorised dealers in a way that parallel information is generated for official channel and market transactions of exchange transactions. Thirdly, liberalisation and detailed guidelines on appropriate authorisation for service payments will have to be worked out. This is an essential requirement to avoid capital flight through the route of services. Fourthly, various NRI related accounts will have to be subjected to changes in the procedures so that the NRIs will also have an advantage of market mechanism. For instance, NREA may have to be valued at market rates only. Fifthly, special arrangements entered into with the Asian Clearing Union and the bilateral dealing with the former USSR will have to be renegotiated to bring them in alignment with the new policy.

(f) In regard to reserve management, RBI may have to take action on four fronts. Firstly, it has to ensure that the level of reserves is adequate to meet the requirements of a smooth transition and also to be able to intervene in the market effectively. Secondly, in addition to reserves at official exchange rate RBI may have to maintain a mechanism whereby the authorised dealers can park their foreign currency resources with the RBI and earn interest thereon. This may require some legislative changes. Thirdly, RBI should, wherever warranted, enter the market to the extent possible to influence the premium to avoid speculation and cartellisation. Finally, RBI may have to maintain a separate internal record of capital receipts and debt service payments on government account. In a way, these operations can also provide a vehicle for RBI being a large player in the market.

Steps Beyond Partial Convertibility

17. In order to achieve the full benefits of integrating the Indian economy with the world economic system, we need to move step by step towards full convertibility of current account transactions, keeping in view the developments in the macroeconomic situation and the world trading environment. Thus, further measures beyond what has been proposed must be taken as soon as internal and external conditions permit. Currency convertibility, as a financial concept, simply means the ability of the residents and non-residents to exchange domestic currency for foreign currency without limit at market rates. Currency convertibility implies the absence of restrictions on foreign exchange transactions and not necessarily on international trade or capital flows. However, to free one without the other will effectively limit the use of a given currency. Thus, in the final analysis, convertibility as a financial concept should be accompanied by liberalisation of trade so that there is both "financial" and "commodity" convertibility. The scheme that has been suggested in this report, which at this stage can be described as partial currency convertibility, should pave the way towards a system of full convertibility. However, the timing and the pace will have to be determined taking into account the macroeconomic stability achieved within the country and the international trading and capital market environment

18. In the scheme outlined in this report, the larger the set of special imports, the higher is the proportion that must be retained by the Reserve Bank of India at the official rate. However, the larger the gap between the average rate received by the exporters and other earners of foreign exchange and the market rate, the stronger will be the temptation to continue using illegal channels for remittance. In moving towards a more unified system, any transaction unconnected with public good or cost-push reasons should be removed from the set of special transactions importable at the official exchange rate as quickly as possible. The shifting of public good and other items from the list of special transactions can be done in two stages. The first stage can be to reduce the official allocation of foreign exchange to these imports and to increase the proportion of exchange they have to buy from the market. This can be accompanied by a simultaneous reduction in the RBI retention ratio so that the inflows in the market channels are correspondingly increased.

At a later stage when the difference between the official rate and market rate narrows special category transactions can be eliminated altogether with a unified market coming into place. The movement towards such a system is possible only if the importers of goods such as POL and fertiliser are in a position to transmit the changes in exchange rate to domestic prices.

19. On balance, the Committee recommends an immediate introduction of the new exchange rate management system described above. Simultaneously, close watch should be kept on the system, as it operates in the first few months to take care of minor adjustments which may be necessary.

C. RANGARAJAN
MONTEK S. AHLUWALIA
A.V. GANESAN
ASHOK DESAI
S.S. TARAPORE
Y.V. REDDY

F.No.1(24)/91-BP

Ministry of Finance

Department of Economic Affairs

B.P. Section

New Delhi, the 19 November, 1991

ORDER

It has been decided to constitute a High Level Committee on Balance of Payments to make medium term projections and evolve appropriate measures to bring down the Current Account deficit to sustainable levels. The Committee will be composed as follows:-

i.	Dr. C. Rangarajan, Member, Planning Commission	Chairman
ii.	Secretary, Department of Economic Affairs	Member
iii.	Secretary, Department of Industrial Development	Member
iv.	Secretary, Ministry of Commerce	Member
v.	Secretary and Chief Economic Adviser, Department of Economic Affairs	Member
vi.	A nominee of Governor, Reserve Bank of India	Member
vii.	Joint Secretary (ECB), Department of Economic Affairs	Member-Secretary

2. Additional Members may be co-opted or experts called as special invitees by the Chairman as and when required.

3. The following are the terms of reference:-

i. to make projections of the various elements in the balance of payments over the next five years and estimate the financing gap, taking into account the repayment obligaitons;

ii. to study the appropriate mix of capital flows and to suggest measures to bring about the desired changes;

iii. to examine and suggest ways of changing the existing structure of debt;

iv. to examine the possibility of converting certain types of existing debts into equity; to suggest ways to enhance the flows of invisible earnings, including private remittances through the banking system; and

v. to examine the functioning of the existing exchange rate regime in the context of the move to Exim-scrips and to consider the implications of a shift to convertibility on current transactions in the near future.

4. The Committee will submit a final report by 1st March, 1992. It may submit interim reports on particular aspects which require urgent consideration.

(K.B.L. Mathur)

Director (FEB)

TECHNICAL APPENDIX

PARTIAL RUPEE CONVERTIBILITY (PCR SYSTEM): IMPLICATIONS FOR EXPORTERS

Prepared by: Arvind Virmani, Ministry of Finance

1. IMPORTS FOR EXPORTERS

Exchange neutrality for exporters requires that the exchange rate applicable to their imports be the same as that received for exports. Thus, exporters must be given the facility to buy 40 per cent of their FE requirement for purchase of imported inputs at the official rate, with the rest purchased at the market rate. The foreign exchange applicable to their imports would then be identical to that applicable to their exports. This has two very beneficial consequences: (i) Any remaining incentive to increase the import intensity of export production (e.g. for engineering goods and chemicals) is eliminated; (ii) The system is neutral with respect to value added, in that an exporter is not discouraged from undertaking assembly, processing, packaging, service activities and even entre-port trade.

This system for providing imports to exporters requires only minor changes in the Advance and Special Imprest licences so that the same licence could be used to get 40 per cent of the exchange at the official rate. Similarly, suitable changes can be made in the procedures for imports by EOUs and EPZs.

2. INCENTIVES TO EXPORTERS

The system, as defined above, can be compared directly with the EXIM scrip system for exporters who import inputs under the advance licence, as well as EOUs and EPZs. Such imports get EXIM scrips to the value of 30 per cent of their Net Foreign Exchange (NFE basis) earnings, i.e., after deducting imported inputs into production. With a 60 per cent market and 40 per cent official ratio for PCR, exporters using this system will get the same total incentive if the market premium is half that of EXIM scrips. They will be better off, regardless of import intensity, as long as the market premium is more than half the EXIM scrip[1]. Table 1 illustrates two cases in which

EXIM premium is 20 per cent and 25 per cent, and the PCR market premium is 12 per cent and 15 per cent respectively. Thus, all exporters using the Advance licence (AL- NFE) route will gain from the switch to the PCR system if the market premium is more than half the EXIM premium.

There is also a set of exporters who use the duty drawback system for imports. Such importers get a 30 per cent export entitlement on the basis of their gross export earnings, and use part of their EXIM scrips for importing required imports. A little algebra shows that an exporter would not use this system if the ratio of EXIM imports to total (non-special) imports was greater than 0.3[2]. In such cases, the explicit benefits from using the Advance Licence cum EXIM scrip on Net Foreign Exchange basis (AL-NFE route) are greater than for the Gross EXIM route for all import intensities (Table 2). An exporter would, therefore, use this system if and only if the administrative costs of dealing with the licensing authorities exceeds the nominal benefits of using the Advance Licence system. This nominal difference as given in Table 2, therefore, provides us with an estimate of the administrative costs to the exporter (who does not switch to AL-NFE route), of dealing with the import licensing authorities. Only exporters with low imports against EXIM scrip and high costs of dealing with licensing authorities would find it profitable to get EXIM scrips on gross basis.

Table 3 shows the gains to exporters from using the EXIM scrip route, from changing over to the PCR system under two conditions:

i) The exporter continues not to use the advance licence option. There are two sub-cases : If the ratio of EXIM scrips imports to total imports is more than 50 per cent, all exporters, irrespective of total import intensity, gain from the change over (1A and 2A). When the ratio of EXIM scrip import to total (market) imports is 40 per cent, the exporters with import intensity less than 30 per cent gain, while those with import intensity greater than 30 per cent lose [row titled NET GAIN (Gross basis) under 1B and 2B].[3]

ii) The exporter starts using the Advance Licence system after the PCR system is introduced. As noted above, the values

in table 2 provide an estimate of administrative costs to such exporters of dealing with licensing authorities. Using these values, the row marked GAIN (switch to AL) shows the net gain to such exporters from switch over to the advance licence system. Thus, even exporters with import intensity above 30 per cent will have a net gain if they start using the AL system.[4]

The overall conclusion is, therefore, that exporters will have a greater incentive to export than they had under the EXIM scrip system, as long as the PCR market premium is more than half of the EXIM scrip premium.

Notes

1. $0.6p(I-M) \geq 0.3\ P(I-M)$ if $p \geq 0.3P/0.6 = 0.5\ P$. 'M' is the import intensity (excluding special goods) of exports. P the premium on EXIM scrips, and 'p' the premium in the market channel over the official rate.
2. $(0.3 - xM)\ P < 0.3P\ (I-M)$ if $x < 0.3$.
3. $(0.6 - M)\ p \geq (0.3 - xM)P$ iff $p/P \geq (0.3 - xM)\ /\ (0.6 - M)$.
4. To the extent that some highly import intensive exports have administrative costs which are even higher than estimated, they will lose from the change to PCR.

Table 1

AVG Gain to Exporters using Advance Licence (Exim on NFE Basis) [(in Switch from EXIM to PCR System (as % of export value)]

	Ratio	Premium (P or p)	Import Intensity (M)						
			10%	20%	30%	40%	50%	60%	70%
CASE 1									
EXIM	0.3	20%	5.4%	4.8%	4.2%	3.6%	3.0%	2.4%	1.8%
PCR	0.6	12%	6.5%	5.8%	5.0%	4.3%	3.6%	2.9%	2.2%
NET GAIN	=		**1.1%**	**1.0%**	**0.8%**	**0.7%**	**0.6%**	**0.5%**	**0.4%**
CASE 2									
EXIM	0.3	25%	6.8%	6.0%	5.3%	4.5%	3.8%	3.0%	2.3%
PCR	0.6	15%	8.1%	7.2%	6.3%	5.4%	4.5%	3.6%	2.7%
NET GAIN	=		**1.3%**	**1.2%**	**1.1%**	**0.9%**	**0.8%**	**0.6%**	**0.5%**

Notes:
1. EXIM = 0.3*P(1-M) as % of export value.
2. PCR = 0.6p(1-M) as % of export value.
3. GAIN = 0.6p (1-M) – 0.3P(1-M) = (0.6p-0.3P)*(1-M)>0 if p>P/2
4. GAIN = (0.6p-0.3P) as % of NFE earning (Independent of Import intensity)

Table 2

Advantage to Advance Licence User Over EXIM-Gross Receiver: Administrative Cost of Dealing with Import Licensing Authority (est)

Cases	*Premium (EXIM PCR), (P,p)*	*Total (X)*	*EXIM imports as % of*	*Import Intensity (M)*						
				10%	*20%*	*30%*	*40%*	*50%*	*60%*	*70%*
CASE 1										
1A	20%	12%	55%	0.5%	1.0%	1.5%	2.0%	2.5%	3.0%	3.5%
1B	20%	12%	40%	0.2%	0.4%	0.6%	0.8%	1.0%	1.2%	1.4%
CASE 2										
2A	25%	15%	55%	0.6%	1.3%	1.9%	2.5%	3.1%	3.8%	4.4%
2B	25%	15%	40%	0.2%	0.5%	0.8%	1.0%	1.3%	1.5%	1.8%

Notes:

1. NFE BASIS:- EXIM = 0.3*P(1-M); PCR =0.6*p(1-M).
2. GROSS BASIS:- EXIM =(0.3-xM)P; PCR = (0.6-M)p.
3. IMPLICIT COST OF DEALING WITH LICENCING AUTHORITIES >0.3P(1-M)–(0.3xM)P=(X-0.3)MP- Administrative cost of using AL–NFE Route for those who get EXIM on gross basis.

Table 3

AVG Gain to Exporters Using Duty Drawbacks (EXIM on Gross Basis)
[(in Switch from EXIM to PCR System (as % of export value)]

	Ratio	Premium	Import Intensity (M)						
		(P or p)	10%	20%	30%	40%	50%	60%	70%
CASE 1									
1A. [EXIM Import (X)			55%]						
EXIM	0.3	20%	4.9%	3.8%	2.7%	1.6%	0.5%	-0.6%	-1.7%
PCR	0.6	12%	6.0%	4.8%	3.6%	2.4%	1.2%	0.0%	-1.2%
NET GAIN (Gross basis)=			1.1%	1.0%	0.9%	0.8%	0.7%	0.6%	0.5%
1B [EXIM Import (X)=			40%]						
EXIM	0.3	20%	5.2%	4.4%	3.6%	2.8%	2.0%	1.2%	0.4%
PCR	0.6	12%	6.0%	4.8%	3.6%	2.4%	1.2%	0.0%	-1.2%
NET GAIN (Gross basis)=			0.8%	0.4%	0.0%	-0.4%	-0.8%	-1.2%	-1.6%
GAIN (Switch to AL)=			1.1%	1.0%	0.8%	0.7%	0.6%	0.5%	0.4%
CASE 2									
2A [EXIM Import (X) =			55%]						
EXIM	0.3	25%	6.1%	4.8%	3.4%	2.0%	0.6%	-0.8%	-2.1%
PCR	0.6	15%	7.5%	6.0%	4.5%	3.0%	1.5%	0.0%	1.5%
NET GAIN (Gross basis)=			1.4%	1.2%	1.1%	1.0%	0.9%	0.8%	0.6%
2B [EXIM Import (X)=			40%]						
EXIM	0.3	25%	6.5%	5.5%	4.5%	3.5%	2.5%	1.5%	0.5%
PCR	0.6	15%	7.5%	6.0%	4.5%	3.0%	1.5%	0.0%	-1.5%
NET GAIN (Gross basis)=			1.0%	0.5%	0.0%	-0.5%	-1.0%	-1.5%	-2.0%
GAIN (Switch to AL)=			1.3%	1.2%	1.1%	0.9%	0.8%	0.6%	0.5%

Notes:
1. GROSS BASIS:- EXIM = (0.3-xM) P; PCR = (0.6-M) p.
2. NET GAIN (Gross basis) = (0.6-M) P – (0.3-XM)p = (0.6p-0.3P) + (xP-p) M.
3. NFE PCR = 0.6p (1-M).
4. GAIN (switch to AL) = 0.6p(1-M) – (0.3-xM) P – Admin cost (table 2) = 0.6p(1-M) – 0.3P + xMP – (x-0.3) MP = (0.6p-0.3P)*(1-M) > 0 if p>P/2.